Field Research in Political Science

Field research – leaving one's home institution in order to acquire data, information, or insights that significantly inform one's research – remains indispensable, even in a digitally networked era. This book, the first of its kind in political science, reconsiders the design and execution of field research and explores its role in producing knowledge. First, it offers an empirical overview of fieldwork in the discipline based on a large-scale survey and extensive interviews. Good fieldwork takes diverse forms yet follows a set of common practices and principles. Second, the book demonstrates the analytic benefits of fieldwork, showing how it contributes to our understanding of politics. Finally, it provides intellectual and practical guidance, with chapters on preparing for field research, operating in the field and making analytic progress while collecting data, and on data-collection techniques including archival research, interviewing, ethnography and participant observation, surveys, and field experiments.

Diana Kapiszewski is Assistant Professor in the Department of Government at Georgetown University.

Lauren M. MacLean is Associate Professor in the Department of Political Science at Indiana University.

Benjamin L. Read is Associate Professor in the Politics Department at the University of California, Santa Cruz.

Strategies for Social Inquiry

Field Research in Political Science: Practices and Principles

Editors

Colin Elman, *Maxwell School of Syracuse University*
John Gerring, *Boston University*
James Mahoney, *Northwestern University*

Editorial Board

Bear Braumoeller, David Collier, Francesco Guala, Peter Hedström, Theodore Hopf, Uskali Maki, Rose McDermott, Charles Ragin, Theda Skocpol, Peter Spiegler, David Waldner, Lisa Wedeen, Christopher Winship

This new book series presents texts on a wide range of issues bearing upon the practice of social inquiry. Strategies are construed broadly to embrace the full spectrum of approaches to analysis, as well as relevant issues in philosophy of social science.

Published titles

John Gerring, *Social Science Methodology: A Unified Framework, 2nd edition*
Michael Coppedge, *Democratization and Research Methods*
Thad Dunning, *Natural Experiments in the Social Sciences: A Design-Based Approach*
Carsten Q. Schneider and Claudius Wagemann, *Set-Theoretic Methods for the Social Sciences: A Guide to Qualitative Comparative Analysis*
Nicholas Weller and Jeb Barnes, *Finding Pathways: Mixed-Method Research for Studying Causal Mechanisms*
Andrew Bennett and Jeffrey T. Checkel, *Process Tracing: From Metaphor to Analytic Tool*

Forthcoming titles

Jason Seawright, *Multi-Method Social Science: Combining Qualitative and Quantitative Tools*
Peter Spiegler, *A Constructive Critique of Economic Modeling*

Field Research in Political Science

Practices and Principles

Diana Kapiszewski
Georgetown University

Lauren M. MacLean
Indiana University

Benjamin L. Read
University of California, Santa Cruz

CAMBRIDGE
UNIVERSITY PRESS

University Printing House, Cambridge CB2 8BS, United Kingdom

Cambridge University Press is part of the University of Cambridge.

It furthers the University's mission by disseminating knowledge in the pursuit of education, learning and research at the highest international levels of excellence.

www.cambridge.org
Information on this title: www.cambridge.org/9780521184830

© Diana Kapiszewski, Lauren M. MacLean and Benjamin L. Read 2015

First published 2015

Printed in the United Kingdom by TJ International Ltd. Padstow Cornwall

A catalogue record for this publication is available from the British Library

Library of Congress Cataloguing in Publication data
Kapiszewski, Diana.
Field research in political science : practices and principles / Diana Kapiszewski, Lauren M. MacLean, Benjamin L. Read.
    pages   cm – (Strategies for social inquiry)
ISBN 978-1-107-00603-4 (Hardback) – ISBN 978-0-521-18483-0 (Paperback)   1. Political science–
Fieldwork.   2. Political science–Research.   3. Political science–Research–Methodology.   I. MacLean,
Lauren M.   II. Read, Benjamin Lelan.   III. Title.
JA86.K37 2015
320.072′3–dc23   2014025961

ISBN 978-1-107-00603-4 Hardback
ISBN 978-0-521-18483-0 Paperback

Contents

Figures

Tables

Preface

This book emerges from a trend toward new thinking, teaching, and writing about fieldwork in the discipline of political science since the early 2000s. We see at least four interacting dynamics prompting these scholarly discussions. First, political scientists of all epistemological, methodological, and substantive persuasions have paid increasing attention to the critical links among theory, research design, and analysis. This focus has opened the door to conversations about the fundamental role that the systematic collection and careful consideration of data play in the development and success of each.

A second factor that has led political scientists to more actively and critically assess the processes and challenges of collecting data in context is the ongoing development, institutionalization, and systematization of qualitative and interpretive methods. The effective use of these methods often relies heavily on data collected through interpersonal interactions, encouraging scholars to consider the conduct and meaning of those exchanges.

A related development is the evolving dialogue about pluralism in the discipline, and emerging debates and innovations in multi-method research. Even as scholars who are passionate about their particular approach to research are writing and organizing amongst themselves in subgroups, discussions have emerged across the discipline about the intellectual benefits of using multiple approaches to analyze data. A logical next step is to consider the strengths and weaknesses of the multiple approaches available to collect, scrutinize, process, and combine them.

An additional factor encouraging a steadier focus on fieldwork is the increasing emphasis on reflexivity and transparency in political science. Both at the level of the discipline's flagship association as well as among many individual political scientists, greater attention is being paid to transparency with regard to how research is designed, how data are collected and analyzed, and how conclusions are drawn.

These dynamics together have encouraged and inspired political scientists to begin to think more carefully about how to plan and execute field research.

That, in turn, has fostered consideration of how we can share and benefit from the immense amount of collective knowledge accumulated by the generations of political scientists who have ventured out from their home campuses to explore field sites near and far. Every scholar who has conducted fieldwork has learned invaluable lessons about how to do so effectively. Yet, while practically every scholar has also passed some knowledge on to others, this informal and piecemeal transmission is inefficient and inevitably incomplete. In short, to date political scientists have not fully capitalized on the significant yet scattered stock of knowledge about conducting field research in the discipline.

In combination, we submit, these dynamics and realities have produced a growing trend toward thinking and writing about field research in political science – scholarship that draws on and complements the wealth of literature about fieldwork in cognate disciplines, but also stands apart, reflecting disciplinary differences. This trend has had its most visible instantiation in the various short courses on field research and archival methods taught annually during the American Political Science Association (APSA) meetings since 2001, and the modules on fieldwork, ethnography, historiography, and archival research taught at the Institute for Qualitative and Multi-Method Research (IQMR) each year since 2002. As a result of these courses, hundreds of graduate students have received training in field methods.

These courses also serve as the most direct origins of this project. Through teaching these courses, which all three co-authors have done, and through additional presentations on field research we have offered around the United States as well as in intensive workshops in a variety of international settings from Romania to Botswana, we have been repeatedly struck by how hungry many colleagues, and particularly graduate students, are for guidance on how to plan and carry out field research. That hunger, we believe, has two main sources, which bring our discussion full circle. It springs in part from gaps in the methods curricula of many political science graduate programs, as methods courses tend to focus heavily on the analysis, rather than the collection, of data. It is also rooted in the absence of a disciplinary consensus on, and (the increasing amount of scholarship notwithstanding) the lack of an established corpus of texts about, field research in political science – what it is, what constitutes *good* field research, and what value it adds to scholarship.

This book is our response to these evolving dynamics, pressures, and needs. It has several ambitions. First, it offers an empirical overview of political scientists' field research practices and how they have evolved, based on a large-scale survey of political science faculty and an extensive series of in-depth interviews. Second, it elucidates the analytic benefits of field research, showing how it contributes to our knowledge about politics. We demonstrate the creative ways in which scholars use many types of data-collection techniques, and how they iterate among data gathering, data analysis, and research design. All these processes enhance conceptualization, measurement, the formulation of descriptive and causal claims, the identification of causal mechanisms – and thus theory building. Third, the book provides intellectual and practical guidance for those embarking on fieldwork. Indeed, one of our central themes is that field research in political science takes very diverse forms, yet is bound together by common concepts, logics, and practices. These fundamental similarities and synergies allow us to offer this guidance – and to identify a set of principles that underpin good field research. In short, the book aims not merely to serve as a primer on field research, but also to fill gaps in the discipline's growing methods literature.

We anticipate that the book will be of interest – and hope it will be of assistance – to those who are preparing to strike out on field research for the first time or embarking on new kinds of fieldwork, be they undergraduates, master's students, Ph.D. candidates, or faculty. Yet we also believe it will be useful to other constituencies: to faculty who advise graduate students; to scholars considering the tradeoffs among different data-collection techniques and forms of data for the research they plan to do; to all political scientists who are reading, reviewing, or otherwise evaluating scholarship based on field research; and to anyone who teaches methods courses at any level. We also expect that the book will be of use to those working in the policy world, and to non-governmental organization and donor groups that want to evaluate programs and initiatives they have put in place.

In addressing all of these groups, we are reaching across what may seem like stark dividing lines, speaking to scholars in different subfields, who employ different analytic methods, and who have contrasting epistemological philosophies. Our eclecticism is intentional. We strongly believe that fieldwork is a common disciplinary good, one in which all political scientists can productively engage, and one from which all can learn. As such, while we acknowledge disciplinary divides and realize that scholars hailing from different traditions think about the processes and products of field research differently, we hope that our guidance, examples, and arguments will resonate with all political scientists, and that all types of scholars can adapt what we are saying to their own intellectual predilections and sensibilities.

To be clear, this book is hardly the first or the last word on the conduct of field research in political science. Rather, we see our contribution as advancing an ongoing, vital, vibrant, and extraordinarily fruitful conversation about fieldwork in the discipline. Indeed, as part of our effort to foment that debate and dialogue – in political science and cognate disciplines as well – we have created a companion web site for this volume (www.psfieldresearch. org). The purpose of the site is to disseminate information and lessons about field research in a comprehensive and dynamically updated fashion. Ultimately, we envision the site including interactive features that will allow those who conduct fieldwork to share their knowledge and experiences more easily, quickly, and effectively.

In this spirit, and as a real-life demonstration of the ongoing discussion of field research in the discipline, we wish to acknowledge the many people to whom we owe a debt of gratitude for inspiring, encouraging, and making possible the writing of this book. First we would like to give very special credit to Evan Lieberman, Julia Lynch, and Marc Morjé Howard, who taught the first version of the APSA short course in 2001. Their vision and pioneering spirit provided the foundational inspiration for this project, and they deserve credit for some of the ideas on the process of field research that are developed here in Chapters 3, 4, and 10 (Lieberman, Howard, and Lynch 2004). We also acknowledge the other scholars who have co-taught the APSA short courses or IQMR modules on conducting field research, including Melani Cammett, Naomi Levy, and Sara Watson. We are indebted to the editors of the Cambridge University Press Strategies for Social Inquiry series – Colin Elman, John Gerring, and James Mahoney – for proposing the idea for this volume, for patiently fielding our many questions and requests, and for offering guidance and insights on the project. And we are grateful for the support and assistance of our editors, John Haslam and Carrie Parkinson, and the rest of the team at Cambridge.

We would like to thank the many political scientists who so helpfully discussed draft chapters of the book at several Midwest Political Science Association and APSA conferences; those who read a draft of the book (and helped us refine our survey) as part of the weekend Research Group during IQMR in June 2010; all who took part in the manuscript review session at Indiana University in December 2011; those intrepid individuals who "test drove" the draft manuscript in their graduate seminars and whose students gave us extraordinary feedback (in particular, Jaimie Bleck at the University of Notre Dame, Jennifer Brass of Indiana University, David Siddhartha Patel at Cornell University, and Hillel Soifer at Temple University); the dozens of colleagues who pre-tested our survey on field research practices in the discipline; the survey methodologists at UC Berkeley, Northwestern University, and Indiana University who helped us design a better instrument; the 1,142 political scientists who took the survey; and the 62 scholars who were kind enough to grant us interviews, spending hours revealing the "scaffolding" and evolution of their projects and offering their thoughts on the underpinnings, conduct, and future of field research in the discipline. We thank APSA's administrative committee for helpfully allowing us to sample from the organization's list of US-based political scientists for our survey, and we thank Sean Twombly for facilitating this. We are also grateful to all those involved in the several institutions whose existence and influence have been supportive as we developed the ideas in this book, including the Consortium for Qualitative and Multi-Method Research and APSA's Qualitative and Multi-Methods Research section and Interpretive Methodologies and Methods group. Finally, we are thankful to our graduate students, Neil Chaturvedi (UC Irvine) and Katie Scofield (Indiana University) for their research assistance at various points in the writing of the book.

We also owe a huge debt to the people from whom we learned about field research, and those who demonstrated so clearly to us its importance and value. Diana thanks the justices, clerks, government officials, academics, and so many others in Buenos Aires, Argentina, and Brasília, Rio de Janeiro, and São Paulo, Brazil, who gave selflessly of their time to help her understand their country. Lauren extends thanks to the many people and communities in Côte d'Ivoire, Ghana, Kenya, and the United States who have shared their time and insights about politics and life. Ben thanks the many people in Beijing, Taipei, and elsewhere who sat for in-person interviews, filled out questionnaires, or responded to phone surveys; he is especially grateful to the neighborhood leaders who put up with his presence and questions during his "site-intensive" loitering.

Finally, we each owe immense thanks to those who have supported us personally through the process of writing this book. Diana's unending thanks and love go to her husband Kapi, who kept her company on Skype during many long days in the field, and whose love, patience, and kindness are perpetual sources of strength. Lauren could not do any of this without the tremendous support and happy distractions of her husband, Jason, three children, Jasper, Skylar, and Benjamin, and the entire "village" of extended family and friends who help keep them going. Ben gives heartfelt thanks to his wife Yingwei, whose hard work, multi-disciplinary learning, and buoyant spunk provide inspiration every day.

1 Field research in political science: practices and principles

"Fieldwork continues to be the most productive and exciting part of what we do."
Philippe Schmitter (quoted in Munck and Snyder 2007, 337)

Fieldwork is "one of the more disagreeable activities that humanity has fashioned for itself."
William Shaffir and Robert A. Stebbins (1991, 1)

Field research – leaving one's home institution in order to acquire data, information, or insights that significantly inform one's research – has been a critical form of inquiry in political science since at least the 1950s. Countless books and articles produced by scholars from all subfields of the discipline, including many milestone works, have drawn on fieldwork to illuminate and answer fundamental questions about the political world. Scholars who have set out to talk to policy makers, survey citizens, and comb through archives have amassed new knowledge that has enriched our understanding of politics in the United States and around the globe.

Yet what constitutes field research in political science, how we do it, and its status in the discipline have remained curiously underspecified and under-examined. Until the early 2000s, very few political scientists had written or taught about field methodology. The term "field research," its definition, and many of the techniques political scientists employ in the field were borrowed from other disciplines, notably anthropology, sociology, history, and even economics. In fact, an extensive survey of the literature suggests that scholars from other disciplines continue to dominate intellectual output on the topic, in particular those from anthropology (e.g., Gupta and Ferguson 1997a; Amit 2000; Wolcott 2005; Bernard 2006; Borneman and Hammoudi 2009) and sociology (Burgess 1994, 1995; Emerson 2001a; Bailey 2006; Schutt 2009).[1]

---

[1] In the early 1990s, more anthropologists and sociologists conducted field research than scholars in any other social science discipline (Shaffir and Stebbins 1991).

Indeed, our research turned up only a handful of books on fieldwork written by political scientists (Ward 1964b; Feldman, Bell, and Berger 2003; Heimer and Thøgersen 2006; Carlson *et al.* 2010) – although several books target the social sciences generally (e.g., Robson 2002; Perecman and Curran 2006). Perhaps not surprisingly, anthropologists and sociologists writing about field research rarely address or incorporate political science and its special concerns.[2] Thus not only is the vast majority of the existing literature on fieldwork not designed *by* political scientists – it is not designed *for* them. Of course, perspectives from other fields have much to offer. Yet the topics about which political scientists conduct research and write, our theoretical frameworks, and our methodological concerns only partially overlap with those of other social scientists, rendering certain fieldwork practices and norms from other disciplines less relevant.

In addition to lacking authoritative and comprehensive accounts of and guidance on conducting field research, the discipline has also wanted for systematic assessments of its principles, processes and practices. Political scientists often summarize how they went about collecting data in the field when writing up their research (some more systematically than others), but relatively few have composed stand-alone pieces *about* the conduct or analytic value of field research. Most political science methods texts, like most methods courses, focus on conceptualization and measurement, research design, *analyzing* and deriving inferences from data, and making arguments and building theory. They dedicate far less time to addressing the challenges and imperatives entailed in *collecting* data – to conceptualizing, planning, and conducting fieldwork.

Because there has never been anything like a unified template for field research – a set of accepted patterns specifying in general terms what political scientists *should* do or *actually* do in the field – we remain unclear as a discipline about the nature and value of field research. Some political scientists retain the stylized image of a year-long trip as the hallmark of field research in the discipline. Others hold stereotypical notions that field research necessarily involves either deep ethnographic observation or qualitative interviewing of elites. Even among those who engage in field research, deep divisions exist concerning how to understand the enterprise, how to carry it out, and how to think about the information they gather. Views about

---

[2] Few of the anthropologists or sociologists writing on field research even acknowledge that political scientists conduct fieldwork: political scientists were rarely mentioned as belonging to the "intended audience" of these books.

the value of fieldwork likewise vary significantly, in part because we have no standards to evaluate it. For some political scientists, field research is essential – almost a rite of passage – for establishing credibility as experts on the phenomena they study. Others have overtly questioned the utility and necessity of fieldwork, challenging its potential to contribute to theory building, and suggesting that graduate students in particular are more likely to achieve professional success by mastering cutting-edge analytic techniques and applying them to existing data (e.g., Stevenson 2005). Still others locate themselves in a pragmatic middle ground, focused on acquiring the data they need to answer their questions, and open, but not committed, to gaining that information through field research.

The traditional lack of scholarly focus on and debate about fieldwork in the context of (tacit) disciplinary disagreement on its practices, principles, and utility has generated a number of problems. First, it has impeded the development of common frameworks for thinking and teaching about field research in political science. There is no vigorous discussion around or evolving disciplinary understanding of how to generate data in the field, how to assess the evidentiary value of information collected through field-work, or how that information can be put to work to tackle crucial analytic tasks and address significant social science questions. As a result, scholars often lack the training they need to meet the diverse challenges (financial, emotional, ethical, and analytical) that field research involves – let alone to carry out the tasks they carefully described in their prospectus or project plan (Mertus 2009, 1–7). Of course, tips and ideas about doing field research are passed from scholar to scholar in an ad hoc manner. Yet ultimately the many missteps and obstacles that fieldwork inevitably involves – as well as the inventive solutions that field researchers devise – remain buried in scholars' memories, or perhaps in the boxed-up notes in their attics. Political scientists thus often reinvent the wheel when planning and executing fieldwork. The lack of focus on field research also has negative ramifications for fieldwork's image and reputation, for our ability to assess its merits objectively, and for the quality of scholarship based on field research.

Encouraging signs of change have emerged, however. In disparate conference papers, journal symposia, and book chapters, political scientists have begun to write more about field research procedures, issues, challenges and debates (see, e.g., Lieberman, Howard, and Lynch 2004; Loaeza, Stevenson, and Moehler 2005; Carapico et al. 2006; Read, MacLean, and Cammett 2006; Wood 2007). Further, graduate students now have a few more opportunities to learn about field research: more departments are offering pertinent methods courses, and other intensive training opportunities have become available.[3] The emerging literature and teaching on field research in the discipline suggest that political scientists are increasingly eager to debate the practices and value of fieldwork. Still, space constraints on articles and time constraints on courses often conspire against in-depth, nuanced treatment of field research's challenges, strategies, and analytic benefits.

The time is thus ripe for a reconsideration of, and a sustained disciplinary debate on, the conduct and value of field research in political science. As the previous discussion highlights, the literature on political science methodology has a significant gap that needs to be filled. Yet it is not *solely* that gap that necessitates a broad disciplinary discussion about field research and, we would argue, a book on field research in the discipline. An additional – and even more fundamental – motivation is the indisputable fact that without properly generated data there is no social science. Sustained, intense debate about the data generation and interpretation processes that fieldwork entails will help us to think more critically and creatively about, be more truthful and transparent about, and ultimately improve, fieldwork *methodology*. It will help us do better political science. And it will help us demonstrate the strength of field research as a mode of inquiry, as well as the contribution fieldwork makes to the generation of knowledge about politics.

We capitalize on these imperatives and trends to write the first full-length methods text on the design and execution of field research in political science.[4] We draw on multiple types of expertise and new empirical evidence gathered through an online survey, more than sixty interviews, and a review of published scholarship about, and based on, field research. Our survey of political scientists based at colleges and universities in the United States provides data on multiple parameters of fieldwork as employed in actual research projects, as well as short narratives about challenges faced and

---

[3] For instance: the two short courses on doing fieldwork offered annually at the APSA conference; several modules on field research offered at the IQMR held each June at Syracuse University; the summer institute on survey research techniques at the University of Michigan (under the Institute for Social Research program); the workshop on Designing, Conducting, and Analyzing Field Experiments, co-sponsored by the Institution for Social and Policy Studies at Yale University and the Inter-University Consortium for Political and Social Relations; the Summer Institute on Conducting Archival Research at George Washington University; and workshops sponsored by the National Science Foundation, such as one on Interpretive Methodologies in Political Science, held in August 2009 at the University of Toronto.

[4] To be clear, while other books on field research in the discipline exist, they mainly focus more narrowly on the challenges of doing fieldwork in a particular region of the world, such as China (e.g., Carlson *et al.* 2010), or on a particular technique, such as interview research (e.g., Mosley 2013a) or field experiments (e.g., Gerber and Green 2012).

strategies adopted in the field.[5] In addition, we interviewed a diverse group of political scientists who have conducted fieldwork for a wide variety of projects.[6] We interviewed scholars from every subfield in political science, ranging in rank from doctoral students to full professors with distinguished chairs, working at top-tier research universities and smaller liberal arts colleges alike. We guaranteed anonymity in these interviews in order to elicit respondents' unguarded perspectives and reflections on their experiences conducting fieldwork and lessons learned. Finally, we carefully analyzed books and articles based on fieldwork. Our frequent failure to find, in that work, clear descriptions of the data-collection techniques scholars used or justifications for their choices reinforces our call for a disciplinary dialogue on the expectations for good field research.

Finally, we draw on our own experiences as field researchers – both our mistakes and our successes. Together, the co-authors have conducted research in a wide range of field sites, from some of the wealthiest cities of the advanced industrialized world to some of the more remote villages of the Global South. In addition to their level of development and infrastructure, these field contexts vary in the extent and quality of democracy at the level of the regime, and with regard to the nature and conduct of everyday local politics. Correspondingly, we faced diverse conditions on the ground, producing contrasting challenges, obstacles, and opportunities. We have also employed diverse methodological approaches and data-collection techniques. Advising graduate students has also helped expand our knowledge of fieldwork experiences and contexts. Except for some research conducted in the United States, we have largely experienced fieldwork as non-natives, although our graduate students have recounted to us the complexities of conducting research in their hometown or "native" land.

Our goals: depicting and demystifying fieldwork and demonstrating its contributions

The book has three central goals. First, we offer an original, empirical study of the variety of field research practices used by US-based political

---

[5] See the Appendix for an explanation of the survey methodology.
[6] See the Appendix for detailed information on the number of scholars interviewed by gender, rank, and subfield.

scientists and how they have changed over time. Grounded in that inquiry, which clearly demonstrates that there is no single "correct" model of fieldwork, we advance an understanding of fieldwork that captures its heterogeneity. High-quality fieldwork takes a variety of forms in terms of length of stay; frequency of visits; number of field sites; and number, type, and combination of data-collection techniques employed. Furthermore, rigorous fieldwork is undertaken by scholars with different epistemological leanings, reflects a variety of methodological approaches, and occurs at different points in the research cycle and in a scholar's life and career trajectory. Our inquiry also reveals how multiple factors – for instance gender, career stage, and the ranking of a scholar's institution – shape fieldwork practices.

Second, we aim to demonstrate how field research has contributed to the production of knowledge about politics – and continues to do so, even in the face of evolving disciplinary pressures and the increasing availability of datasets from many corners of the globe. Through analyzing published political science scholarship as well as responses to our survey and interview questions, we assess the benefits and value of field research for theory development in the discipline. Moreover, we identify the multiple practices and processes through which fieldwork generates that value, leading us to reconceptualize field research as entailing both the generation *and analysis* of data, with a great deal of iteration between the two.

Given this goal, it bears noting that we operate with a specific – although encompassing – definition of data. We draw a distinction between the raw information a researcher hears, reads, senses, and collects in the field as well as the diffuse observations she makes, on the one hand, and data on the other. For us, data are materials and observations that have been processed by the researcher – considered in relation to the context from which they were drawn and assigned some analytic significance – such that they can be employed in her analysis. A researcher's impression of an interviewee's credibility (an observation) becomes a datum if and when the researcher uses it to evaluate the evidentiary value of the information that respondent provided. A researcher's sense of the power dynamics in a room (an observation) becomes a datum when it is used as an indicator of (i.e., to measure or evaluate) the authority structure in a certain context. Sometimes such materials are organized into a systematic, standardized, row/column format, but they need not be. Sometimes they are considered "causal process observations" (Collier, Brady, and Seawright 2010), but again, this is not necessary for something to be considered data. Our conceptualization of data is agnostic to form, and appreciative of the fact that data can play many different roles in quantitative, qualitative, and interpretive analysis.[7]

Third, we hope to demystify fieldwork and provide guidance for how to do it better. We highlight the operational, intellectual, and interpersonal challenges that arise when conducting field research, and offer a wealth of practical strategies and advice – based largely on the real-life experiences of a wide range of field researchers – to help political scientists evaluate their skills, decide what kind of field research to do, and conduct fieldwork efficiently and effectively. The book should thus be helpful to a broad audience. Advanced undergraduates conducting field research during a volunteer, internship, or study-abroad program;[8] graduate students heading into the field for the first time; as well as faculty planning their first fieldwork trip, contemplating new types of field research in unfamiliar contexts, or considering how to make field research more effective and enjoyable – as well as faculty who teach methods classes or advise graduate students – should all find it useful.[9]

Given this intent, some of what we say may seem commonsensical and perhaps even obvious. Yet simply because something is mundane or commonplace does not mean it is unimportant or impossible to overlook. This is particularly true when one is operating in a context in which much is unfamiliar, juggling multiple tasks, and facing many new challenges simultaneously, as field researchers do. Moreover, time and money are precious when conducting field research, and scholars often have just one opportunity – or at most a few – to collect data in context for any particular project. Accordingly, small missteps can have enormous consequences, potentially putting months of research in jeopardy. It is also true that what may seem like an obvious point, or an obviously superior practice, is in fact only one of multiple ways of looking at or going about things. We thus err on the side of inclusivity with our advice.

Even if some of our guidance is aimed at those who are new to field research, we believe that much of what we offer will be useful to all political

---

[7] This definition notwithstanding, throughout the book we deploy the commonly used term "data-collection techniques" to refer to the processes scholars employ to gather information and materials in the field.

[8] Barrett and Cason (2010) highlight a large increase in undergraduate experiences abroad, growing 143 percent from 1997 to 2006/7. They also note a shift to non-European contexts.

[9] Even though much of the book's evidence emerges from interviews with US-based scholars or English-language books and articles (as discussed below), many of the arguments are relevant for scholars working at institutions around the world.

scientists, regardless of their level of experience. To be clear, we do not provide A-to-Z instruction on the use of particular data-collection techniques – although we supply (and urge readers to consult) an extensive bibliography of specialized work addressing the fundamentals of interviewing, survey research, ethnography, archival research, field experiments, and other such techniques. Rather, we seek to *contextualize* these techniques, providing high-yield pointers on their application in the field, considering how scholars' position and the context in which they are working affect their use, and suggesting how field researchers can objectively evaluate alternative techniques against analytic goals and theoretical motivations to develop an optimal field research design.

In accomplishing these goals, the book converses with several bodies of literature. First, it engages with the published literature on fieldwork in other disciplines (i.e., anthropology, sociology, history, economics, geography, and psychology) as well as the relatively new and emerging literature in political science. Second, it draws on more specialized work on particular data-collection techniques. Third, the book connects with the discussions and debates in the methodological literature in political science focused on research design, concepts, and causal mechanisms from quantitative, qualitative, and interpretivist perspectives.

Contemporary political science debates around field research

This book's three major goals relate to the explicit and implicit debates within political science concerning field research. We discuss a series of these contested issues below. We begin with debates among believers over what constitutes field research. We then turn to the debates between believers and skeptics over whether field research has value. Finally, we consider broader debates in the discipline about the possibility and desirability of shared standards for social science research, acknowledging how they might shape the practices and evaluation of field research.

Debates among believers over the definition and nature of field research

Even scholars who believe field research is valuable differ over its definition and nature. As noted at the outset, we understand field research to refer to leaving one's home institution in order to acquire data, information, or insights that significantly inform one's research. This definition diverges from others offered in the literature in important ways.[10] Wood (2007, 123), for instance, defines field research as "research based on personal interaction with research subjects in their own setting." In the foreword to Perecman and Curran's edited volume, Featherman (2006, xviii) suggests field research involves "taking social science questions or hypothetical propositions constructed about one societal or cultural setting into another." And Shaffir and Stebbins (1991, 5) assert that "fieldwork is carried out by immersing oneself in a collective way of life for the purpose of gaining firsthand knowledge about a major facet of it."[11]

Our definition is more encompassing and more inclusive than these and others. For us, field research can be done in one's own neighborhood – it does not necessarily entail going to a foreign context. Further, we hold that field research need not involve extensive interpersonal interaction. Hence, our understanding includes such techniques as archival research and passive observation. For us, as soon as a scholar enters and engages in a context beyond her home institution in order to learn about her research topic (even if this simply entails requesting documents from an archivist or collecting maps of the region from a government agency), she has begun to do field research. Our definition does leave out certain data-collection techniques, such as online surveys, downloading survey data collected by others,[12] and phone or Skype interviews from one's office. While these practices indubitably represent useful data-gathering techniques, by our definition and understanding they do not constitute *field* research. A key aspect of our definition is that the scholar is gathering evidence *in context* – within the settings where the political decisions, events, and dynamics of interest took place or are recorded.

Finally, our definition highlights the fact that field research entails more than simply collecting data. While doing so is unquestionably a crucial part of fieldwork, scholars who conduct field research simultaneously engage in a varied set of analytic tasks. These range from informal "back of the brain" cogitating (rethinking an interviewee's responses, or comparing what one read in a newspaper with what one heard in a focus group), to organizing and processing data, to carrying out process tracing or employing other methods

---

[10] It bears noting that field research is not explicitly defined in most political science work that is written about it or that references it.

[11] There are other definitions. Emerson (1983) and Schatz (2009b), for instance, both offer even more ethnographic and anthropological conceptualizations. See also Wedeen (2010).

[12] Note, however, that if one were to travel to Zimbabwe to acquire the same dataset, we *would* categorize that as field research.

in an effort to evaluate their hypotheses, and everything in between. As we will argue more forcefully later, it is precisely the informed iteration between data generation and data analysis that lends field research much of its power as a mode of inquiry.

If believers in field research differ in relatively nuanced ways as to the definition of the term, they sometimes disagree to a greater degree on how to conduct field research. Of course, scholars working in urban versus rural settings, and democratic versus authoritarian regimes, or peacetime versus conflict zones (Lee-Treweek and Linkogle 2000, Sriram *et al.* 2009) may use radically different techniques in the field.[13] Yet the deeper divergences about how to approach fieldwork spring from scholars' contrasting epistemological and ontological views. More positivist quantitative and qualitative scholars on the one hand, and interpretivist researchers on the other, are often understood to ask different questions, design their research differently, engage with their field sites differently (looking for different things using different techniques), think of themselves as researchers differently (holding differing views of reflexivity, for instance), consider power relationships between themselves and those they study differently, have different views on the possibility and desirability of objectivity, and have different standards for rigor – to name just a few distinctions. One symbolic marker of this divide is seen in the discrete and uncoordinated short courses on field research these two "camps" now offer at the American Political Science Association meetings.

The multi-faceted nature of this debate – and the fact that all participants value the field research enterprise – militate against our discussing each "side's" viewpoint on each aspect of the debate. Presumably, the central dividing line has to do with the possibility of objectivity in, and of identifying truth through, field research and social science research more generally, and the utility of delving into the meanings political action has for political actors. We return to these issues below.

Debates between believers and skeptics about the value of field research

Far-reaching though the above differences of perspective are, debates between believers and skeptics go much deeper, centering on the intrinsic value of field research and scholarship produced based on data gathered

---

[13] Mertus (2009, 168) suggests that new communication and transportation technologies have made it easier for a wide range of researchers to travel to the heart of conflicts. She notes that during the Vietnam War only a handful of journalists went to the battlefields, while during the Balkan wars of the 1990s, journalists and academics flooded into the region.

in the field. Most obviously, skeptics suggest that field research is unsystematic, entailing repeated ad hoc decisions and changes on the fly that undermine the promise of the scientific method. Our research on the fieldwork practices of political scientists suggests that this is a misperception. We challenge the characterization and the conclusion below. Two related but more fundamental critiques are more difficult to evaluate and dismiss.

Some skeptics argue that fieldwork inevitably produces biased and thus questionably valid data, and thus biased and questionably valid research. On the one hand, the mere presence of the researcher in the context being studied (let alone his or her interventions) changes that context, biasing the data collected therefrom. Shaffir and Stebbins (1991, 15) express this point, suggesting that "the undisciplined procedures of fieldwork enable researchers, to a greater degree than practitioners of other methodologies, to influence the very situations they are studying, thereby flagrantly violating the canons of scientific objectivity." On the other hand, some allege that the immersion of the researcher in the field context can cause a loss of objectivity that leads to biased data generation and research. Barrington Moore indicted "poor fieldwork" as having "inconsistencies, obvious bias and lovie dovie" (Munck and Snyder 2007, 106).

Becker (1970, 43–44), however, makes a cogent counter-argument, suggesting that data gained via fieldwork are *less* likely to be biased, for two reasons. First, people are constrained to act more honestly by the very fact of being in a social situation (rather than in a laboratory); second, a fieldworker's more continuous presence in the context he is studying allows him to gather more data and test his hypotheses more thoroughly. In a similar vein, Juan Linz insisted that a greater amount of time in the field would not have undermined his analytic perspective but rather would have allowed him to document his argument more powerfully (Munck and Snyder 2007, 188). Indeed, some hold that fieldwork teaches us so much that it is used as an evaluative marker: it forms part of the process through which graduate students and others prove their ability as independent scholars and establish credibility as experts on the places they study. As a senior Asia scholar once commented to a beginning graduate student: "You need to go over there and have your ticket punched."[14] Interpretive scholars might offer a different response to the allegation of bias: guilty as charged. Such scholars believe that the knowledge produced through interpersonal interaction is inescapably "biased" if that means that the researcher ineluctably places her imprint on it.

---

[14] Personal communication with Read, *c.* 1996.

Another argument put forth by skeptics is that scholars who collect data via fieldwork are by definition limited in terms of their ability to generalize the conclusions they draw on the basis of those data.[15] To begin with, perhaps on the assumption that it must always be ethnographic or small-n in nature, field research is often associated with idiographic (or case-centered) approaches and is criticized by scholars who take a nomothetic approach. More broadly, some wonder how much research based on deep immersion in particular cases (a few parts) can tell us about the larger whole more generally. The late Samuel P. Huntington was essentially making this point when, asked his opinion of fieldwork, he responded, "I don't believe in it!" He went on to clarify that he was being facetious, but added that fieldwork can render the scholar "a prisoner of a particular experience," so that any positive benefits are outweighed by how difficult it becomes to make empirical generalizations (Munck and Snyder 2007, 223).[16]

Yet field researchers can and do adopt both idiographic and nomothetic approaches. In fact, as our survey data suggest and a review of published scholarship shows, many scholars combine them (Tashakkori and Teddlie 2003; Lieberman 2005; Fearon and Laitin 2008). Indeed, political scientists carrying out small-n comparative work have long been encouraged to replace proper names with relevant variables (*à la* Przeworski and Teune 1970) in part to make it easier for them to generate a causal story that will apply to a broad set of cases. Moreover, political scientists often undertake field research with the aim of developing broad theories or testing widely applicable hypotheses; indeed, some would insist that the generation of well-grounded understandings of particular cases is a prerequisite for any grand theorizing.

Broader methodological debates about standards for political science research

A third and broader set of methodological debates, while not focused explicitly on the nature or value of field research, has clear reflections in the other two discussions and implications for how field research is perceived and judged. We refer to debates among quantitative, qualitative, and interpretive scholars concerning how we draw valid descriptive and causal inferences about the political world and, more broadly, what constitutes rigorous

---

[15] We will leave aside our views on the inherent value of fully understanding a particular context, what went on there, and why, and the question of whether producing generalizable theory must be the goal of all social scientific inquiry, and consider the critique on its own terms.

[16] When asked whether scholars can do fieldwork and be broadly comparative theoreticians, Barrington Moore replied skeptically: "I don't think you can swing it" (Munck and Snyder 2007, 107).

research. In their ground-breaking book – sufficiently prominent to be universally recognized in the discipline as "KKV" – King, Keohane, and Verba (1994) argue that a single logic of inference underlies (good) political science scholarship. Brady and Collier's edited volume (2010) challenges the appropriateness of applying the KKV model of research to all social science questions, arguing that different methodologies with dissimilar epistemological underpinnings can co-exist and complement each other. Yet the Brady and Collier volume does not fundamentally disagree with the premise that there can be "shared standards" for evaluating social science research. Gerring (2012) likewise argues for a unified framework for social science research.

In contrast, Goertz and Mahoney (2012) argue that quantitative and qualitative research are the products of two distinct "cultures," implying that it would be difficult to develop one set of standards against which both types of scholarship could be judged. Yanow and Schwartz-Shea (2008) raise an even more fundamental epistemological challenge, delineating a sharp boundary between positivist and interpretive views and objectives of research.[17] They articulate an interpretive mode of research more focused on understanding how meaning is constituted by people, and would likely consider inappropriate the evaluation of their work against standards derived from a supposed "single logic of inference."

All of these debates relate in key ways to the conduct of field research (i.e., the generation and analysis of data in the field), the evaluation of field research, and the production of scholarship based on data gained through field research. Each invokes fundamental epistemological differences and cleavages. And at the heart of each are questions about how to design and conduct rigorous social science research, and whether social scientists can (and should) identify standards for inference and for "good" research more generally. What those standards might consist of and how widely shared they could be across heterogeneous methodological terrain remain open questions, of course. Yet any consensus political scientists ultimately reach will have critical implications for fieldwork in the discipline.

As such, readers might expect us to take a clear stand on these debates. Yet we have intentionally taken no epistemological position, and have sought to make this book ecumenical. We have strived *not* to assume (let alone judge) readers' epistemological predilections or trespass on their methodological

---

[17] We offer here a very small window on these debates for illustrative purposes; for instance, we leave out extensions of these debates with those who advocate a formal analytic or experimental approach.

choices. We simply aim to help them to conduct fieldwork as effectively as they can given those preferences and priors. Put somewhat differently, rather than beginning from a particular epistemological stance, we developed the book largely on the basis of what our research on fieldwork – and field-workers – in the discipline taught us about the principles and practices that underlie good field research. That is, as scholars conducting research in the "field" of political science, we proceeded inductively rather than deductively.

What became clear to us is that the Manichean positions reviewed above are a poor guide to actual practice. Our survey and interview data indicate that many (if not most) field researchers occupy a middle position on the epistemological spectrum, calling into question the various efforts to delineate boundaries between these groups. Indeed, we found that scholars who enter the field with a positivist bent sometimes confront realities that make them question that model and adopt a more interpretivist posture, eventually ending up somewhere in the middle. These findings suggest, and we firmly believe, that there is a considerable gray area – an encompassing methodological middle – in which positivists and interpretivists can product-ively discuss the practices and merits of fieldwork, and the considerable amount that they share. The existence of this gray zone implies that it may in fact be possible and productive to identify adaptable fundamentals that underlie much field research in the discipline. We have sought to do so.

Our stance, then, is that the practice of field research "belongs to" no one – and belongs to everyone. The more scholars who engage in debates about its conduct, the richer the discussion, and the stronger fieldwork methodology will become. In sum, we seek to speak in a unified way to a diverse discipline in an effort to provide all political scientists with strategies that will motivate them to carry out, and help them excel at – and enjoy – field research.

Our arguments: the nature, practices, and principles of political science field research

In this section, we advance the book's three key arguments, which speak directly to the concerns discussed above. First, while the shape and nature of fieldwork differ dramatically across the discipline, field research has a common center – shared challenges, opportunities, and inclinations that cut across significant geographical and epistemological divides. Second, while fieldwork practices in the discipline are varied, most scholars employ a multi-dimensional approach: they use several data-collection techniques, apply them to multiple analytic tasks in a given project, and iteratively update elements of their research design, theory, and concepts as they learn and analyze in the field. Third, many field researchers follow a set of core principles (if sometimes only implicitly) – engagement with context, flexible discipline, triangulation, critical reflection, ethical commitment, and transparency – that help them to maximize the potential that fieldwork's practices hold. We draw on these arguments to show – and forcefully argue – that fieldwork is vital for collecting new data, stimulating innovative ideas and perspectives, and producing rigorous and path-breaking social science scholarship no matter what one's research paradigm.

The nature of field research: commonality within diversity

Data from our original survey and interviews testify to the many different forms that political scientists' fieldwork has taken over the past several decades, and to the variation across subfields, departments, and individual scholars that continues to mark the enterprise today. Yet despite significant diversity in form and function, we argue that some central and uniting commonalities characterize much fieldwork in the discipline. We share below just a few findings that underpin this argument, which are further developed in Chapter 2.

While most political scientists conduct fieldwork in the United States and Western Europe, our respondents reported field sites in 150 countries. Likewise, far from the stereotypical notions that field research either involves deep ethnographic observation or qualitative interviewing of elites, significant heterogeneity exists in terms of what political scientists actually do in the field. As we discuss in more detail in the next subsection, scholars often employ a variety of data-collection techniques, including archival research, surveys, and field experiments, and engage in a range of analytic tasks. Accordingly, the length of time political scientists spend in the field also varies widely, from a few weeks to over two years.

The degree to which research projects rely upon fieldwork also differs considerably across the discipline. For some scholars, field research involves immersing themselves for a year or two at a site overseas, and writing a study that draws entirely or mainly from information gathered at this locale. For others, field research entails weekend trips to other states or provinces, a month spent at a national archive, or a series of short visits to cities in multiple countries over the course of several years. For these scholars, field research may not be the primary vehicle for collecting data but a supplement, preceding or following the quantitative component of a multi-method inquiry, for instance. Political scientists who conduct field research also do so in pursuit of different goals. For instance, some seek to adjudicate among rival hypotheses while others strive to interpret lived experiences. And field research projects also differ widely in both levels and types of grant support.

In short, what constitutes "fieldwork" for political science varies considerably – and will likely continue to diversify due to changing family structures, evolving disciplinary standards, and major shifts in geopolitical tensions and even nation-state boundaries. Moreover, an ongoing revolution in information and communication technologies is reshaping field research week by week. These changes have made it both much simpler to access troves of information without ever leaving one's office, *and* far easier to travel to, and work and live in the field. These realities challenge already tenuous notions about what it means to do fieldwork in our discipline and what value doing so adds. They simultaneously create an environment rich with possibilities for innovation, triangulation, and syncretism (i.e., blending data collected via fieldwork and through other means). The diversity our inquiry uncovered buttresses our contention that no single template or stereotype can be applied to political science field research.

Yet despite this diversity – and the fact that scholars from every political science subfield are conducting field research, including political theory and public administration – field research in the discipline is marked by certain central tendencies. To begin with, fieldworkers often face similar types of challenges. A first set is logistical, including where to live, how to travel, and how to recruit and effectively manage people on a research team. Graduate students who are required to take a sequence of methods courses and simultaneously experience countervailing pressures to compress the time spent in getting their degree face additional challenges when seeking to conduct fieldwork. And securing funding for field research can be difficult even for seasoned faculty well-versed in grantsmanship. Yet some of fieldwork's most significant challenges are emotional, ethical, and analytic.

Field research for most scholars is emotionally stressful. Adapting to different cultures and managing security concerns in new contexts, as some field researchers are called upon to do, can take a toll (Mertus 2009). Indeed, many researchers reported experiencing hardship conditions in the field – for instance, political repression or a lack of infrastructure. Moreover, field-workers must deal with the frustration that obtaining entrée, satisfying gatekeepers, and negotiating roadblocks of innumerable kinds can often entail. They also confront loneliness, or the equally daunting challenge of *never* being alone. And they face the constant strain of performing a role and negotiating their personal identity, deciding who they want to be as a researcher, who they want to be when "off-duty," and what correspondence to maintain between the two (Punch 1986, 17; Brown 2009).

Concerning moral and ethical challenges, while field researchers are obligated to be honest in their work, they sometimes have to consider whether, when, and how much to keep their interests and purposes under wraps. They need to manage risks to respondents when interacting with them and when writing up their research, and devise ways to maintain anonymity and confidentiality while still developing persuasive descriptive and explanatory accounts (Sriram 2009). The fact that fieldworkers often have to deal with these challenges "situationally and spontaneously," under less-than-ideal circumstances, and without the benefit of reflection or the ability to seek advice from trusted colleagues or advisors makes them even more difficult to address (Punch 1986, 13).

Field research also entails a set of widely shared analytic challenges. "Field research design" – developing a practical plan for implementing a research design in the field – begins well before scholars leave for their field sites and continues after they arrive. Indeed, while in the field, scholars often need to select cases and engage in sampling (sometimes at multiple levels), operationalize (and, sometimes, re-operationalize) concepts so that on-the-ground measurement is valid and reliable, and evaluate the evidentiary value and analytic usefulness of the data collected. And they must carry out all of these tasks with an eye to the methods they will use to analyze the data. These tasks are difficult to get right on the first try (which is sometimes the only "try" scholars have), and doing them all simultaneously is tough under the best of circumstances. In short, while no single archetypical model of field research predominates in political science today, scholars often need to surmount similar sorts of obstacles while seeking to accomplish similar types of analytic tasks in the field.

Yet the multiple versions of fieldwork in which political scientists engage have much more than challenges in common. There are identifiable commonalities in the overall contours of field research in the discipline as well. For instance, our survey data reveal that most investigators use more than one data-collection technique in the field, and this has been the case for decades. Furthermore, scholars often combine multiple analytic approaches: many projects use some combination of quantitative, qualitative, and/or interpretive methodologies, frequently contemporaneously. Indeed, the vast majority of field research projects have a qualitative dimension, including those that are primarily oriented toward obtaining quantitative data. These findings suggest that a good number of field researchers may lack a hard and fixed epistemological commitment to a single methodological tradition. Their failure to fall neatly into the categories the discipline has sought to establish presents an opportunity for dialogue and information sharing about the processes political scientists employ to analyze and understand the political world. And, finally, we contend that scholars produce intellectual value in all types of fieldwork – in part due to the multiple tasks they accomplish simultaneously in the field, and the way in which they iterate among them, to which we turn next.

Fieldwork practices: variety and iteration

Most scholars go into the field to obtain data or source material of some kind. Yet, as we suggested earlier, our research reveals that fieldwork helps political scientists to advance many aspects of a research project – not only data collection, but also research design, data analysis, and ultimately theory development. Moreover, we found that scholars cycle repeatedly among the range of practices connected to these phases of research during their time in the field – that is, they iterate. We argue that this *iteration* (the updating of elements of research design as information acquired in the field is analyzed) is critically important to the way in which field research contributes to the generation of political knowledge and development of theory.

Research design

Political scientists have generated an extensive body of prescriptive literature focusing on research design (e.g., King, Keohane, and Verba 1994; Van Evera 1997; Geddes 2003; Collier and Gerring 2009; Brady and Collier 2010) as well as particular design aspects such as case selection (Collier 1995; Collier and Mahoney 1996; Box-Steffensmeier, Brady, and Collier 2008), and the comparative method and case studies (e.g., Collier 1993; Locke and Thelen 1995; George and Bennett 2004; Mahoney and Goertz 2004; Lynch 2005; Gerring 2007). Yet this work tends not to discuss explicitly how field research contributes to design decisions such as case selection, or how key methodological decisions and debates intersect and interact with the choices and exigencies of data collection or field research more generally. This may be because the subtle ways in which fieldwork often informs the creation of knowledge are not always boldly announced in the final published work. We believe that they should be.

Most broadly, field research puts scholars in a position to encounter the unexpected and unexplored, and thus to benefit from serendipity. This can take the form of stumbling upon a new – and thus unstudied – political issue or movement. It might present itself in the form of lunch-break conversations with scholars from other institutions and disciplines who introduce new ideas. Or it might mean noticing documents or statements that contradict received wisdom in the discipline, suggesting anomalies or new puzzles. In all of these important, yet frequently unheralded ways, fieldwork shapes and informs our research choices and sets the stage for innovation.

Once a scholar has decided upon a research topic, particularly at the early stages, field research can help her to sharpen her vision of what the project is about, and aid her in formulating or re-formulating significant research questions. Preliminary research trips, or early stages of longer trips, often provide critical information for case selection as well, making it possible to identify cases that are likely to yield the greatest theoretical payoff while avoiding ones that would prove unworkable or irrelevant.

Political science concepts – "rule of law," "democratic consolidation," "power" – are often complex and highly abstract, complicating our ability to develop them. Field research is indispensable for helping scholars nail down what the key concepts in their work actually mean. It puts researchers in vantage points from which to observe gaps between concepts and reality and nuances that facilitate conceptual precision. Unfortunately, the wealth of political science scholarship on the issue of concept formation (e.g., Collier and Mahoney 1993; Collier and Adcock 1999; Adcock and Collier 2001; Goertz 2006) infrequently discusses fieldwork's contributions to this crucial research goal. The many real-life examples from scholars' research that we include in this book show the important ways in which field research facilitates conceptualization.

Field research is likewise important for measurement – and for testing the validity and reliability of measures. Measurement error is a ubiquitous problem that political scientists have developed a range of strategies to address (see e.g., Adcock and Collier 2001). Being in the field offers scholars opportunities to assess the face validity of their measures (through consultation with other experts and scholars) and perhaps even to have others code some of their cases on key parameters, subsequently checking inter-coder consensus. Careful fieldwork can also help illuminate whether context-specific indicators might capture concepts better than uniform measures (see, e.g., Locke and Thelen 1995).

Data collection

Field research is obviously critical for collecting data. Even in today's digitally interconnected world where instant communication across vast distances and immediate access to immense amounts of information are commonplace, it remains true that much data can only be obtained through personally engaging with individuals and institutions, and up-close, on-the-ground study. To give just a few examples, the opinions of migrant farm workers in a distant rural area, historic records buried deep in government archives, and the complex internal processes of a particular social movement can only be accessed by being there.[18] As we have noted and Chapter 2 demonstrates in more detail, political scientists employ diverse data-collection techniques in the field, and most scholars use multiple techniques, thoughtfully and creatively combining them to gather, triangulate among, and verify the data they are gathering.

Collecting data in the field enhances our comprehension of the context of the political dynamics we study. Regardless of the kind of data with which one is working (even archival data), seeing them in context rather than in isolation can lead to more, and more accurate, insights. For instance, understanding the environment in which a survey was conducted – and getting the "back-story" and details about the trials and tribulations of administration from those who fielded it – helps one interpret the resulting data. Moreover, by generating their own data in context, researchers are freed from relying on the (possibly implicit or unknown) data-collection decisions and practices of other researchers or institutions.

Analysis for inference and interpretation

Conventional wisdom might hold that fieldworkers focus hungrily (if not frantically) and single-mindedly on gathering data, squirreling information away onto hard-drives and into boxes for later perusal and parsing. Our research shows that this is far from the case. Rather, political scientists who conduct field research are *constantly* examining, considering, and processing

---

[18] Wood (2007, 126) outlines four scenarios in which discovering the "preferences and beliefs of political actors" might require engaging with them: (1) when the political actor is at a permanent disadvantage as a result of repression, domination, or lack of education; (2) when scholars seek to disaggregate an organization or movement into factions or individuals whose beliefs and preferences may differ from the official line available in publications; (3) when scholars seek to understand internal processes of a group, which may become available only through participant observation or interviews; (4) when actors have reasons to hide or obscure preferences and beliefs from public view – i.e., engage in strategic interactions with others.

the data they are generating, deploying a diverse array of analytic techniques to develop and refine their questions and their answers. Of course, because political scientists undertake field research at different stages of their projects and employ diverse analytic methods, they engage in distinct combinations of analytic tasks and do so in many ways. Moreover, the degree to which scholars engage in analysis in the field appears to be correlated with how long they spend there. Nonetheless, most scholars engage in some sort of analysis while carrying out fieldwork. They do so to several ends.

First, the immersion and engagement with context that fieldwork often entails encourage analysis aiming to produce descriptive inference. We believe that the descriptive aspects of research projects are far more significant than the general sense of opprobrium that lingers around the word "description" would suggest. Particularly in understudied contexts, such as those emerging from conflict or authoritarian rule – but actually just about everywhere – documentation and analytic description are crucial to the social science enterprise. Put simply, by offering investigators the opportunity to observe myriad on-the-ground dynamics, fieldwork helps them to generate clear, detailed accounts and to "get the story right."[19]

Beyond being important in its own right, accurate description is obviously a fundamental foundation for explanation: if one's descriptive assumptions or understandings are off, one is unlikely to develop a valid causal story.[20] As such, field research also helps scholars get the *causal* story right by allowing them to better understand causal processes and mechanisms, and to evaluate how well their hypothesized account, and alternatives, accord with local dynamics. It can also offer political scientists the opportunity to observe causal processes at work,[21] thus facilitating process tracing (see, e.g., Bennett 2010). As Wood (2007, 125) asserts, analyzing contingent events, critical junctures, and path dependence often depends on process tracing that is impossible without field research.[22] Observing first-hand meetings where decisions are being made, collecting oral histories, and talking face-to-face with eyewitnesses and participants can all provide persuasive evidence of causal processes. In particular, field research can help scholars identify causal

---

[19] Of course, it is important to guard against getting caught up in some romanticized view of reality sold to us in the field. As we discuss below, triangulation in particular helps scholars to do so.

[20] King, Keohane, and Verba are among those who endorse this point (1994, 34).

[21] To put this another way, fieldwork allows scholars to gather causal process observations (CPOs) that would otherwise remain elusive at best (Brady and Collier 2010; Collier 2010).

[22] On contingency, critical junctures, and path dependence, see Mahoney (2000), Pierson (2000), Lieberman (2001), Bennett and Elman (2006), and Barnes and Weller (2012).

mechanisms (see Mahoney 2003, 363–365; George and Bennett 2004, 132–149), and to evaluate them by assessing their observable implications.

Likewise, fieldwork reveals causal complexity and conjunctural causation (Ragin 1987, 2000; Mahoney and Goertz 2006). Scholars who engage in field research obtain a first-hand view of complicated political dynamics, affording them an appreciation of how unusual it is for a single cause to determine any outcome. They develop intuitions and collect evidence that make it possible for them to weigh the relative effects of multiple causes and assess how they interact with each other to produce the outcome of interest. Scholarship based on fieldwork can thus faithfully reflect the intricacies of empirical reality, offering perhaps more complete, if more complex, causal stories.

Field research also facilitates the testing and sharpening of scholars' arguments. Political scientists who have conducted interviews are familiar with the experience of indirectly posing one or more hypotheses to an interlocutor in order to gauge her response. Texts or records can also be read with an eye to whether they square with or challenge one's key propositions – or suggest another account altogether. Accessing multiple data sources in the field offers countless opportunities to identify facts or views that run counter to one's hypotheses. Naturally, the subjective perspectives of interested parties should not be taken as the gospel truth – yet field researchers often feel that they are better off obtaining such reactions than remaining ignorant of them. Literature on hypothesis testing and theory generation (Fearon 1991; Tilly 1997; Mahoney 2000) sometimes overlooks fieldwork's contributions in this regard.

Iteration

The previous subsections demonstrated that political scientists engage in an extensive set of research tasks while in the field, revealing fieldwork to be a fundamentally *analytic* undertaking. We conclude our description of fieldwork practices by arguing that *iteration* among those tasks is a ubiquitous aspect of field research, and one that is essential to the critical role fieldwork plays in producing knowledge about politics. As scholars observe and learn in the field, they commonly pivot multiple times, shifting from collecting data to analyzing them; from analysis back to research design; and from research design on to data collection, and on to analysis again. What guides and propels this iteration are scholars' ongoing efforts to make sense of and structure the information they are gathering, what they are learning about their subjects and cases, and what it all means for their project, their questions, and their answers. The simple reality is that, as scholars critically reflect on what they are learning about the field context, their ideas change, and those changes can necessitate renegotiation of certain aspects of their project.

As scholars iterate, they review and revise their research design – reformulating their research question, refining concepts, developing new hypotheses, identifying more appropriate cases, developing and enhancing research instruments (e.g., interview protocols and survey questionnaires), and so on. These design revisions, in turn, often lead them to collect more or different data, or to modify their analysis in some way, in the search for valid answers to their research questions. While veteran researchers intuitively appreciate the benefits of iteration, the way in which iteration occurs is rarely openly discussed, and its benefits (and costs) are infrequently explicitly acknowledged, in the published scholarship based on field research.[23]

In fact, the notion of iteration in political science research has already been recognized as legitimate by scholars from diverse methodological traditions.[24] Scholars with more interpretive epistemological leanings strongly resist imposing pre-established concepts and categories at the outset of a research project: iteration has long been a central and essential element of their approach to social inquiry. Schwartz-Shea and Yanow write that, according to the "abductive reasoning" logic of interpretive research, inquiry begins with a puzzle or a tension, then undertakes a search for insight and understanding in which "the researcher tacks continually, constantly, back and forth in an iterative-recursive fashion between what is puzzling and possible explanations for it" (2012, 27, also 32, 55–56). In the mid-1980s, Ragin wrote eloquently about what he called the dialogue of ideas and evidence in social research, explaining that "most hypotheses and concepts are refined, often reformulated, after the data have been collected and analyzed" (1987, 164). George and Bennett (2004, 73) hold that "some

---

[23] The multiple tasks scholars carry out in the field highlight a related – but distinct – aspect of research based on fieldwork: it is not linear but rather *dynamic*. While the pre-fieldwork, fieldwork, and post-fieldwork phases of the research process might have particular *emphases* (research design in the first, data collection in the second, and data analysis in the third), none of the three phases is fully delimited or self-contained, and in none of the three do scholars focus on (or complete) just one task.

[24] Moreover, political scientists are hardly the only ones to identify the utility of iteration. For instance, in technology design, a software company might release a web-based product in an unfinished state, then enhance and rework it incrementally based on responses from users. One discussion of the etymology of the term "iteration," including its applications in technology and mathematics, can be found in a *New York Times* language column: www.nytimes.com/2010/06/13/magazine/13FOB-onlanguage-t.html.

iteration is often necessary" among the design, execution, and assessment phases of case study research.[25]

Collier, Seawright, and Munck, drawing on Ragin (2004), Munck (2004), and Tarrow (2004), note that "the refinement of theory and hypotheses through the iterated analysis of a given set of data is an essential research tool, and researchers lose other aspects of analytic leverage by not employing it" (2010, 62). Indeed, iteration is clearly foundational to a Bayesian view of probability in which a scholar's beliefs about the likelihood of hypotheses constituting valid explanations ("priors") are updated as new data are discovered. Even King, Keohane, and Verba, while arguing that theories should not be modified in a way that narrows their scope after data have been collected, allow that "the need for creativity sometimes mandates that the textbook be discarded!" (King, Keohane, and Verba 1994, 21–22).[26]

Despite some disciplinary consensus on the value of iteration, by drawing attention to and arguing for the importance of iteration to fieldwork, and thus highlighting its profoundly inductive nature, we are spotlighting and reinforcing precisely the aspects of field research that many of its detractors find most objectionable. Methodological texts often portray (and thus implicitly advocate for) a strictly linear research process, rather than one marked by feedback loops and reformulation (e.g., McNabb 2010, 29–39). For some, iteration might sound very akin to unguided intellectual wandering. Fieldwork's inductive nature flies in the face of the increasing emphasis in some corners of political science on the primacy of deductive reasoning. And some field research skeptics might consider iteration to be the qualitative analogue of "curve fitting" in quantitative work – repeatedly re-specifying a statistical model, swapping variables in and out, until something "interesting" is found; most methodologists would agree that this is not good practice (as would we).[27]

We seek to counter these negative views on iteration. We argue that fieldwork's iterative nature and the mid-course adjustments it allows are essential to the ways in which field research contributes to the production of knowledge about politics. Fieldwork often involves exploring what is poorly understood and confronting new, complex empirical realities; as such,

---

[25] They also discuss iterative processes in case study research elsewhere in the book: pp. 84, 112, etc.

[26] Van Evera (1997, 105) and Mahoney (2010, 134, 141–142) also highlight the value of iterative processes.

[27] The statistical issue concerns parameter estimation: engaging in curve fitting will eventually result in finding something with certainty, but leaves one open to capitalizing on chance to discover spurious relationships.

induction and iteration are unavoidable if valid inferences are to be drawn and interpretations developed. Indeed, the repeated discovery that fieldwork entails is one of its strengths as a research technique. Engaging in iteration allows scholars to integrate their growing knowledge and new ideas into their projects, and to respond directly to relevant changes in research conditions. As a result, they can develop and test well-grounded hypotheses and explore the most appropriate research questions and cases – which are not always the same propositions, questions, and cases that seemed promising when the project was being designed, based on existing theory, from the comfort of the home institution. Quite obviously, continuing to pursue explanations, questions, and cases that are clearly dead-ends does not advance research but rather impedes the generation of valid findings and strong arguments.

Moreover, and to emphasize, the iteration in which field researchers engage is intensely analytic, rather than unguided or ad hoc. It is a constant process of correction and refinement driven by their ongoing consideration of the evidence gathered and their continual mapping of evidence to theory in a directed attempt to find valid answers to their questions. To say that fieldwork is inductive and iterative in no way implies that it lacks rigor or is haphazard and unsystematic; it simply connotes that it is neither linear nor purely deductive.

Of course, iteration is not costless and we do not mean to suggest that it is; we are not positing that the skeptics' points are completely wrong all of the time. There are tradeoffs associated with most changes scholars make to their projects based on new discoveries in the field. Revising one's ideas and assumptions, and carefully considering and then introducing even small modifications can be distracting and can delay a project, for instance. The costs, downsides, and inferential implications of iteration should be carefully considered, articulated, and evaluated – *and this is precisely our point*. Acknowledging the multiple analytic processes in which political scientists who undertake field research engage, recognizing how they iterate among them and between them and data collection, and evaluating the costs and benefits of doing so, will produce multiple benefits.

Recognizing and validating fieldwork's iterative nature will encourage field researchers to be more forthcoming and transparent about the fieldwork enterprise – and about its complicated and synthetic nature. We imagine and hope this will be liberating as it will allow researchers, as a group, to counter the misleading "immaculate conception" narrative of fieldwork – that scholars design the perfect project before heading into the field, and execute that research design to a "T." Allowing for more open discussion and creative thinking about fieldwork, in turn, will encourage scholars who wish to engage in field research but may be daunted by the (misguided) idea that they need a valid and fully executable plan prior to departing. More discussion of iteration and fieldwork practices more generally will also help us to improve those practices – to identify the potential pitfalls associated with fieldwork's inevitably iterative nature and develop strategies to avoid or address them. Doing so, in other words, will help researchers prepare for the circuitous path down which their inquiry will likely take them. Being more forthcoming about the field research process will also facilitate evaluation of fieldwork and scholarship based upon it. Accordingly, we call on all field researchers, regardless of their position on the epistemological spectrum, to acknowledge, discuss, and even spotlight the special role of iteration in field research projects – to give voice to what they have learned and will learn through experience.

In short, because field research involves the collection of data using multiple techniques and the analysis of data at multiple levels – and due to its iterative nature – it contributes mightily to the production of knowledge and the building of theory in political science. Yet we hasten to add that the experience of field research is not just a scientific one of gathering data and triangulating and developing internally valid descriptions and explanations of political dynamics. It often entails a set of *human* interactions that helps to spur passion about the normative issues that underlie the research questions that drive our scholarly inquiry.[28] We invite and encourage those who engage in field research to consider the many less concrete but still critical ways in which they benefit from engaging productively with the people whose behavior and institutions they strive to understand. These, we submit, are also important aspects of fieldwork's value added.

The principles of field research

The above discussion of the multi-purpose and iterative nature of field research leads naturally to our third argument: that a shared set of principles underlies political scientists' diverse fieldwork practices. We discuss six core principles – engagement with context, flexible discipline, triangulation,

---

[28] Robert Dahl made this point when discussing his best students: "Passion, absolutely. That's a quality of all the best students . . . [they] have some connection with the real world and real people in it. Their interest in the study of politics is more than library- or mathematics-driven. There is some understanding, almost at the gut level, of what the world outside is" (Munck and Snyder 2007, 144).

critical reflection, ethical commitment, and transparency – that we identified inductively through our analysis of the experiences of a wide range of scholars of different ranks, genders, and ages, employing different analytic approaches, in diverse subfields. To be sure, no single individual mentioned all six, nor did our respondents use precisely the same terms. But, collectively, they repeatedly described and seemed to agree intuitively on the significance of the same set of principles. Despite the fact that these principles already seem to guide the fieldwork of many scholars, they are rarely articulated consciously or publicly. Indeed, as of this writing, even the APSA Organized Section on Comparative Democratization has no explicit criteria for its award for the "Best Field Work" prize for dissertation students.[29]

We argue – and seek to demonstrate throughout this book – that these principles undergird good political science field research, and help fieldwork to contribute to knowledge accumulation and theory generation. In so doing, we hope to encourage scholars to adopt these principles, and to open a dialogue about their utility as criteria for evaluating field research. Explicit articulation and tailored application of these principles, we hold, will enable scholars to do better fieldwork, which will contribute to more powerful analysis, compelling writing, and an expansion of what we know about politics. We hope that these principles can provide guidance to faculty and graduate students who are unsure what to do when facing particular situations in the field. And we believe that operating according to the principles can help scholars with limited funds supporting their research to maximize the intellectual potential of their field forays. Moreover, these principles offer a common vocabulary for discussing field research – a lexicon that will help scholars to articulate the strength and value of what they have accomplished in the field, and aid those who seek to evaluate others' fieldwork.

Before discussing the six principles, we offer a few clarifications. First, these principles can serve as guidelines for conducting fieldwork and evaluating its practices and processes, but not for assessing the *products* of fieldwork. That is, they neither reiterate nor supplant established standards by which political science research of all kinds is evaluated.[30] Second, we intentionally use the term "principles" rather than "standards" to resist the

---

[29] The prize description emphasizes that the fieldwork should be "innovative" and "difficult" but those terms are left unspecified.

[30] Indeed, the quality of one's fieldwork *practices* and *processes*, and the quality of the *product* one generates on the basis of fieldwork, are not perfectly correlated: it is possible to conduct highly effective fieldwork and yet create unsatisfactory publications on the basis of it (although the inverse is probably far less likely).

notion of a rigid, top-down designation, or one uniform set of expectations. We also avoid the term "best practices" as this also seems to imply an effort to identify a single, specific template. We argue throughout the book that one size does not fit all when it comes to field research. Yet we believe that most scholars can customize and apply these core principles.

Finally, given that the six principles were more often implied by our respondents than articulated self-consciously, and because some were emphasized more than others, the six vary in terms of the degree to which they are empirically descriptive – i.e., the extent to which they faithfully reflect the way political scientists actually *do* carry out fieldwork. Yet the principles are normatively prescriptive: informed by multiple perspectives, we believe they represent guidelines for how most scholars *should* conduct field research. Of course, due in part to the synergies and the tensions among the principles (which we discuss in more detail in Chapter 11, the book's conclusion), each is best conceptualized as a continuum: different scholars will contemplate, and different contexts necessitate, a different weighting of each principle vis-à-vis the others.

Engagement with context

Engagement with context gets to the essence of field research. According to our definition, inserting oneself into the context where the political dynamics of interest occurred, or are recorded, is a defining feature of field research, and one of the reasons it is such a rich source of knowledge. What engaging with context means and how political scientists do so, however, vary considerably across locations, researchers, projects, and time. Engagement might include incorporating local scholarship and sources into one's study; having a host institution or an NGO connection; or partaking in discussions or collaborating with local scholars. It may mean intense, direct conversations and social interchange with people in one's field sites – or it may not. Moreover, engagement with context is neither synonymous with, nor necessarily proportional to, cumulative time in the field: it concerns the nature or even the *spirit* of a scholar's connection to the field site. Likewise, we are not suggesting that all field researchers need to actively engage with context at every single moment in the field. How much time scholars need in order to meaningfully engage with context can vary considerably, in particular with a researcher's previous knowledge of that context. Developing a deep knowledge of the language, history, and culture of a place prior to visiting can help scholars with scarce resources to engage more fully and quickly despite their inability to spend long weeks or months in the field.

Flexible discipline

A creative tension lies at the core of the second principle of field research. By flexible discipline, we mean carefully preparing for, planning, and organizing fieldwork – considering its goals, anticipating possible obstacles, and systematically tracking progress – while simultaneously allowing time, room, and energy for adaptation to inevitable hurdles, unexpected challenges, and unforeseen opportunities. Flexible discipline, then, is part and parcel of the analytically driven iteration discussed previously. Of course, scholars will put more or less emphasis on the different halves of this term. While all field researchers need to keep their eyes on the prize, those who equate being disciplined with being systematic, and flexibility with a lack of rigor, will err toward the noun rather than the adjective. Overall, however, given the inevitable vagaries of most research contexts, and the obstacles *and* opportunities that they can deliver, we think scholars are best served, most of the time, by leavening their discipline with a healthy, thoughtful dose of flexibility.

Triangulation

By triangulation, we mean collecting data – to measure a certain concept or to demonstrate that a particular relationship exists, for instance – from multiple sources. More loosely, we also use the term to refer to gathering diverse perspectives and viewpoints and voices. Sometimes utilizing a variety of data-collection techniques can facilitate access to the relevant range of viewpoints, but triangulation does not require doing so. Likewise, the idea is not to gather *as many* data points as possible, but rather to gather data and sources that comprehensively represent the empirical reality under study, and provide the most opportunities to identify facts or views that run counter to one's hypotheses. Triangulating strengthens faith in a study's inferences and conclusions, although naturally scholars should be cautious in drawing both even when distinct sources seem to point in the same direction.

Critical reflection

Another principle underlying good field research – one that is again closely tied to its iterative nature – is critical reflection. Scholars should be actively thinking about and evaluating their practices, the data they are collecting, and what they are learning throughout the fieldwork process. Put differently, outstanding field researchers reserve mental space to critically process, and make connections among, data and ideas – and they do so as they carry out their daily work. Adopting this cognitive habit allows them to advance intellectually in the field, to catch problems early on, to remain aware of what they have accomplished and what still lies before them, and to take advantage of opportunities to sharpen their projects. While the value of engaging in such self-scrutiny might seem obvious, it is easy to develop tunnel vision in the field and plod onward, engrossed in the challenges of setting up interviews or the logistics of survey administration. Such behavior can lead vital questions to go unasked, or data to be incorrigibly tainted. Rather than shrugging off and dismissing their micro-epiphanies and the small, nagging doubts that seep into their consciousness, field researchers should nurture and attend to them, repeatedly asking themselves, "What does that tell me?"; "What am I doing wrong here that I will later regret?"; "What could I be doing better?" This recurrent and self-conscious consideration of options and choices, and their short- and long-term implications, lays the foundation for the principles of ethical commitment and transparency discussed below.

Ethical commitment

Another core principle of good field research is ethical commitment to the individuals whom researchers involve in their projects, and to those in the field site more broadly. The downsides of acting *un*ethically – for one's research, the research community, and researchers who wish to work in one's field site in the future – seem clear. Yet how researchers think about acting ethically varies widely, and scholars make different choices depending on the sensitivities of their project and the peculiarities of the fieldwork context, among other factors. Indeed, we can envision a spectrum of ethical commitment: scholars on one end might have a "do no harm" conception of ethics, or a commitment to minimizing potential risks to study participants and the field-site communities during the study period. Those on the other end may emphasize a more ambitious notion of beneficence or feel an obligation to ensure that their research has some positive impact. Those at the former end may see it as ethically sufficient to submit their projects to all relevant Institutional Review Boards (IRBs), and follow the strictures those boards dictate. Yet for many, acting ethically is more than being legally compliant, and we encourage researchers to consider holding themselves to a higher standard.[31] At bottom, self-conscious consideration of where one

---

[31] See also Scheyvens and Storey (2003, 233–237).

sits on the ethical spectrum, and self-regulating and active commitment to that position, underpin all good field research.

Transparency

Finally, the best field researchers are transparent about their practices and processes. Building on the principles of critical reflection and ethical commitment, operating transparently involves openly describing one's relationship with the field setting and its inhabitants; tracking, documenting, and justifying the choices one made, strategies one employed, and iteration in which one engaged while generating data; detailing how the reliability and validity of those data were evaluated; and clearly articulating how one began to analyze and interpret data in the field (for instance, indicating what evidence was used to develop hypotheses and how they evolved). This principle in particular is being introduced on a more prescriptive than descriptive basis. Books and articles based on data gathered in the field, if they address fieldwork practices at all, generally contain brief summaries of data collection, analysis and interpretation, or the iterative updating of research designs. Being more candid and forthright will help scholars to demonstrate the power of their work, and help readers to evaluate it better, facilitating the accumulation of knowledge (Punch 1986, 15).[32]

Summing up our arguments, then: field research in political science is heterogeneous, yet is marked by a common, uniting center. Scholars employ a variety of data-collection techniques and engage in an equally diverse range of analytic tasks while in the field, and do so in iterative, mutually reinforcing ways. Finally, six principles underlie the best of political science field research, and their tailored application can strengthen fieldwork in the discipline. These arguments make clear why fieldwork is able to make such important contributions to political science and to our understanding of politics at home and around the world. Field research stimulates innovative ideas and perspectives, encourages scholars to ask and answer significant questions, and helps us to produce knowledge and develop theories about politics, policy, and power – the core issues that animate all political science research. In the chapters that follow, we develop these arguments further with the goals of fomenting a spirited dialogue about, and improving the conduct of, political science field research.

---

[32] We understand that publication word-limits, given the space that being transparent about qualitative research requires, may dampen enthusiasm for transparency. We discuss this challenge in Chapter 11.

The road ahead

The rest of the book proceeds in several parts. Chapter 2 surveys the varied currents that have shaped the development of field research in post-World War II political science. It also draws on our survey of fieldwork in the discipline to paint a nuanced picture of its practices, underlining both their heterogeneity and commonalities. Chapters 3 and 4 examine how fieldwork's intellectual and operational aspects intersect. Chapter 3 considers the logistical and analytic preparations that precede field research, and Chapter 4 offers practical advice for managing data, research, and people in the field. Both discuss how scholars can effectively (and simultaneously) serve as Principal Investigator and Project Manager of their research ventures.

Chapters 5 through 9 form the basis of a data-collection tool chest, examining the main data-collection techniques that political scientists employ in the field: collecting pre-existing materials (including but going well beyond archival techniques); conducting interviews, oral histories, and focus groups; employing site-intensive methods (i.e., participant observation and ethnography); engaging in survey research; and conducting field experiments. To emphasize, our goal is not to offer detailed instruction on using these techniques, but rather to contextualize them – to discuss how employing them *in the field* affects their deployment and the information thereby gathered. The chapters address the benefits and downsides of each technique, comparing and contrasting their employment and function and discussing how they can be combined. They also consider how to evaluate the evidentiary value of the data collected through using these techniques, and illustrate how those data can contribute to theory building in political science. Finally, the chapters highlight some challenges researchers face when using the techniques in the field and offer strategies for addressing them. Naturally, we aim for each chapter to be useful for scholars who already use the technique in question. Yet we believe that scholars who do not use a particular technique can also learn by reading about it, considering the inferential leverage they could gain from employing it or gaining insights that will be valuable while using other data-collection techniques. We also hope reading the chapters will help political scientists to become better consumers of scholarship based on field research, and better teachers of its practices.

Chapter 10 returns to thinking about the research endeavor as a whole. It emphasizes the inevitability and importance of engaging in analysis – beginning to process and make sense of data – while still in the field, and offers practical advice on how to do so. The chapter also discusses how to manage the transition away from the field and return back to one's home institution. Finally, Chapter 11 summarizes the book's key arguments; explores how changes in world politics, technology, funding levels, ethical norms, and disciplinary standards for research transparency will shape the practice and teaching of field research in political science in the future; and offers a call to arms to improve the process, and realize the promise, of fieldwork in the discipline.

2 A historical and empirical overview of field research in the discipline

The August 1943 issue of the *American Political Science Review* included an unusual item, a short polemic titled "A challenge to political scientists." Its author was a young scholar, William Foote Whyte, who in the same year published *Street Corner Society*, a study of Italian gangs based on years of immersive research in Boston's North End. He alleged that with few exceptions, political scientists failed to understand and illuminate the workings of actual politics. This he attributed to excessive concern with the normative aspects of politics and an unwillingness to probe beneath the surface of democratic institutions into the relationships, class structures, and ethnic hierarchies that underlie them. He audaciously instructed political scientists to become "participant observers in the field of practical politics":

The complexities of the [political] organization can be understood only by one who is in a position to talk intimately with a number of men of various ranks *and*, at the same time, to observe their behavior through the course of political activity. It takes time to establish such a position and to gain such information ... Furthermore, it requires a skill in personal relations, a flexibility in adapting oneself to different sorts of people. This does not flourish in the academic realms of political science. It develops only through intensive field experience. (Whyte 1943, 696–697)

Whyte's challenge provoked rejoinders, but these focused on his call to "leave ethics to the philosophers," not on his criticism of the empirical weakness of political science research (Hallowell 1944, 1946; Dexter 1946). Gabriel A. Almond mildly agreed that "a greater stress on field research in practical politics" would benefit the discipline (1946, 284).

It is no accident that this critique came when it did, and from a University of Chicago sociology Ph.D. It was the "Chicago School" that, in the 1920s, led the adoption within sociology of the study of local communities and subcultures through prolonged in-person field research. Major figures of this program, notably Robert Park and his associates and students, including

Robert Redfield and W. Lloyd Warner, championed the value of participant observation for understanding urban life (Bulmer 1984; Whyte 1994; Fine 1995; Platt 1996).

The Chicago School, in turn, took inspiration from the field methods that anthropologists pioneered in this period and in prior decades. Early versions of the methods used by cultural anthropologists emerged in the late nineteenth century in the work of observers like Charles Booth, Beatrice Webb, and Sidney Webb, which included first-hand observation in working-class homes. Researchers such as Alfred Haddon and Franz Boas initiated the study of non-Western societies through expeditions to places such as the Torres Strait and the Northwest coast of the United States. Bronislaw Malinowski's extended stay "right among the natives" (Malinowski 1961, 6) on several New Guinea islands during World War I is often cited as a foundational influence on anthropology's expectations for field research, centering on observation of and interaction with the subject population over years. Malinowski's influence remains undeniably powerful, even though his work later raised profound questions about his racial beliefs and his power relationship with his subjects.[1]

It is not the case, of course, that, prior to an epiphany in the mid twentieth century, political scientists eschewed everything that this book defines as field research. Whyte himself acknowledged that political scientists sometimes conducted interviews, and he singled out for praise the dissertation of David Harold Kurtzman, who studied vote-buying in Philadelphia intensively over a period of four years.[2] Still, it is fair to say that our discipline took many cues from sociologists and anthropologists when it finally began to adopt field methods more wholeheartedly, starting in the 1950s. Moreover, as Chapter 1 observed, political scientists have, until very recently, been disinclined to reflect on and write about field research methods in formats other than the abbreviated methods sections of their empirical work.

This chapter begins by considering the expansion of field research in the US political science profession after World War II, identifying several forces that drove that development. Of course, the discipline does not generally catalogue its scholarly products in terms of whether or how they draw on

---

[1] See Burgess (1982), Shaffir and Stebbins (1991), Gupta and Ferguson (1997b, 6), Wedeen (2009), and in particular the detailed description and critique of Malinowski's fieldwork in Emerson (2001b). On the partially related Chicago School of Political Science, see Heaney and Hansen (2006).

[2] As Whyte notes, this 1935 dissertation, "Methods of controlling votes in Philadelphia," was apparently never published, though its author went on to a prominent career.

source material gathered through fieldwork.[3] Moreover, it is hardly possible to do justice to all the books and articles that fieldwork has enabled and enriched over the course of nearly seven decades. Thus, this section of the chapter focuses on the evolution of major research programs and key debates. It illustrates the fact that scholars of all subfields of the discipline have undertaken field research and used it to generate influential work. It observes that field research in political science has been syncretic – drawing on multiple distinct traditions, often ones pioneered by other disciplines. And it demonstrates that field research has been uneven in its coverage, focusing heavily on certain places and less on others.

The second part of the chapter draws on our survey of US-based political scientists, as well as our interviews, to paint a vivid portrait of field research in the discipline. It starts with a descriptive overview, presenting information on our survey respondents and the hundreds of projects they reported: where they went, challenges they faced, funding they obtained, languages they used, how much time they spent in the field and so forth. From there, we turn to data that amplify and provide evidence for the arguments introduced in Chapter 1 concerning the nature of field research in the discipline and the kinds of practices it employs. Survey and interview data alike convey the heterogeneity of research practices but also common themes among them: the ways in which researchers in the field tend to draw on multiple streams of data, employ more than one mode of analysis, engage in many kinds of analytic processes, and rethink and redesign their projects iteratively on the basis of what they learn in the field.

The post-war expansion of field research

A range of forces and institutions helped drive the expansion and development of field research in political science after the mid twentieth century. Evolving paradigms in the discipline put a premium on the collection of data, often fine-grained data on individual political beliefs and behavior. And in the post-war period the US academy created institutions that facilitated new forms of research at home and abroad. The federal government, in some

---

[3] Thus, for example, "state of the discipline" overviews, review essays, methodological texts and debates, manifestos laying out this or that theoretical concept or paradigm, and other meta-writings are rarely organized around or even address field research as a category. Asked to name important or classic works in their subfields that drew centrally on field research, some of our interviewees had difficulty coming up with a clear-cut list.

cases motivated by the geopolitical competition of the Cold War, financed and encouraged many of these institutions. At the same time, it would be misleading to reduce every innovation to a simple outcome of such high-level processes. The imperative of understanding new problems and generating new answers, often motivated by particular debates within their subfields and by dialogues with other disciplines, have been just as important in encouraging scholars to conduct field research.

To begin with, the behavioral revolution, which began after World War II, pushed scholars to extend their inquiries beyond elites and the formal workings of institutions to examine public opinion and political processes. In American politics, the behavioral revolution is associated with the rise of nationwide survey projects such as the early post-war election projects, conducted by the University of Michigan, which eventually became the American National Election Studies.[4] But it also is reflected in publications such as Robert Dahl's *Who Governs?* (1961), which involved substantial data-gathering in New Haven, Connecticut. Dahl's book, which responded to work by sociologists – Floyd Hunter's field-based study of Atlanta (1953) and C. Wright Mills's *The Power Elite* (1956) – sparked critical reactions and led to an ongoing debate over "community power." This debate drove political scientists as well as sociologists to investigate cities and other localities in an intensive fashion, aiming to lay bare the sinews of power relations within them (Agger, Goldrich, and Swanson 1964; Wolfinger 1971, 1973; Domhoff 1978; Gaventa 1980; Polsby 1980; Stone 1988, 1993; Gendron and Domhoff 2009).

Post-war Americanists benefitted from previously unavailable sources of data and opportunities for up-close study of politics. The National Archives were established in 1934, and expanded rapidly in the decades that followed. Franklin D. Roosevelt founded the first Presidential Library in Hyde Park, New York, in 1939. In 1955, this pattern was institutionalized by the Presidential Libraries Act as a means through which to preserve for study the documents of all administrations from Herbert Hoover on – resulting in what are now fifteen libraries and museums around the country. In 1953, APSA began its Congressional Fellowship program, which by 2011 had provided some 2,400 scholars, journalists, and other professionals a chance to observe the workings of Congress from the vantage point of 10-month staff positions on Capitol Hill.[5]

---

[4] www.electionstudies.org/overview/origins.htm, accessed October 3, 2012.
[5] www.apsanet.org/content_4162.cfm, accessed August 23, 2012. Biggs (2003) chronicles the Congressional Fellowship program.

Fieldwork in the discipline's subfields

Over the course of decades, field research in American politics has resulted in influential publications in all major domains of inquiry. At the national level, notable works address policy-making processes (Bauer, Pool, and Dexter 1963; Kingdon 1984; Light 1995); bureaucracies and regulation (Carpenter 2001, 2010); congressional representatives (Fenno 1978; Swain 1993; Miler 2010), the presidency (Beckmann 2010), the Supreme Court (Segal and Spaeth 1993), and interest groups and think tanks (Kollman 1998; Rich 2004; Teles 2008; Baumgartner *et al.* 2009). Studies of social policy have been informed by up-close research on people who participate in or are subject to government programs, from welfare recipients to veterans to prisoners (Lin 2000; Soss 2000; Campbell 2003; Mettler 2005; Allard 2009; Lerman 2013). At the local level, fieldwork has informed research on ideology (Lane 1962), regional politics (Key 1949), race (Cohen 1999; Kim 2000; Miller 2008), immigrants (Wong 2006), urban politics (Katznelson 1982; Berry, Portney, and Thomson 1993), policing (Brown 1981; Ostrom 2010, 7–11), state legislatures (Barber 1965), political participation (Huckfeldt and Sprague 1995; Gerber and Green 2000; Walsh 2004; Han 2009a; Redlawsk, Tolbert, and Donovan 2011; García Bedolla and Michelson 2012), and social movements (Blee 2002; Frymer 2008; Skocpol and Williamson 2012). Needless to say, this is merely a sampling of relevant work, and further examples can be found elsewhere in the book, particularly in the five chapters on particular data-collection techniques. Our point is simply that field research informs the study of a wide range of topics within American politics.[6]

Even more dramatic transitions took place in the post-war period with regard to analyzing politics beyond the borders of the United States. Political scientists rapidly began to conduct field research in a great variety of contexts, including smaller European polities and less-developed countries (LDCs) in Latin America and, as colonial rule waned, in Africa and Asia. Underlying and encouraging intellectual shifts in the subfield of comparative politics at this time was the Social Science Research Council (SSRC). This body was founded in 1923 at the initiative of Chicago political scientist Charles E. Merriam in collaboration with leaders of the national professional associations for economics, sociology, and statistics, who were eventually

---

[6] In compiling this selection of field research-based work in American politics, and the subsequent discussions of work in other subfields, we have drawn on our interviews, email exchanges with fifteen other scholars, and other sources. We have not attempted to provide a fully representative sample of work published in each subfield, let alone an exhaustive treatment.

joined by the leaders of the national associations for anthropology, history, and psychology (Worcester 2001, 20). By the early 1950s, the SSRC was actively promoting area studies research and administering a wide range of committees and funding sources. Its Committee on Comparative Politics (chaired by Gabriel Almond from 1954 to 1963) was influential in setting the agenda of this subfield at least into the late 1960s.

The US government's role in fueling the expansion of international field research, motivated in no small part by geostrategic concerns, can hardly be overstated. The exchange program and grants brought into existence by the Fulbright Act of 1946 have supported research by many social scientists, among other purposes of the program. The National Defense Education Act of 1958 established Title VI federal funding, supporting programs that remain powerful influences on teaching and research to this day, notably Foreign Language and Area Studies Fellowships and what are now called National Resource Centers promoting area-specific training and study. The programs opened many research opportunities, but also led political scientists to concentrate their attention on the parts of the world they targeted, to the neglect of others. It was during the post-war period that national area studies associations began to form in the United States, as well.[7] Finally, some foreign governments have also established programs that fund field research, such as the German Academic Exchange Service.

This pattern of funding and institutional development helps explain the special place that field research occupies in the subfield of comparative politics. For comparativists rooted in Title VI centers organized around area specialization, language training, and longstanding multi-disciplinary traditions of scholarship, academic culture encouraged or even demanded deep immersion in the countries under study. Within these communities, a field stay lasting at least a year, and perhaps including advanced language study and cultivating a well-rounded historical and cultural conversancy with the country or region in question, was considered a normal part of doctoral training. Indeed, such norms became embodied in institutions such as the Inter-University Program for Chinese Language Studies (started in Taipei in 1963, later moved to Beijing) and in the firm requirement of some Fulbright and other grants that the recipient remain in-country for a full calendar year.

---

[7] As Munck notes, the Association for Asian Studies, the American Association for the Advancement of Slavic Studies, the African Studies Association, the Latin American Studies Association, and the Middle East Studies Association all were created between 1941 and 1966 (2007, 46n26). Most associations subsequently created area studies journals.

These research subcultures have engendered countless field projects, facilitating unprecedented immersion in overseas locales, but have also drawn criticism on grounds that they isolate area specialists from the ideas and research programs of other parts of the discipline (e.g., Geddes 2002). And, of course, many comparativists pursued cross-national or inter-regional modes of inquiry. Nonetheless, the stamp that these institutions have placed on parts of the comparative politics subfield is unmistakable.

Such institutions were not the only reason why comparativists have been drawn to overseas fieldwork, however. For many, traveling to other parts of the world has an intrinsic appeal. And in contrast to political scientists studying courts, politicians, or voters within the United States, who have had ready and increasing access to research materials from their home institutions, comparativists often have had little choice but to go into the field for their sources. This was especially true before the 1990s, when data frequently did not exist, were not reliable, or were not relevant to many of the pressing questions in developing countries on which scholars were beginning to focus.[8] Indeed, what appears to be the first book on field research in political science was targeted specifically at those setting out for developing areas (Ward 1964b). Even with the changes that the internet and the electronic proliferation of available data have brought, it remains true that many kinds of information require on-the-ground collection.

Starting in the 1930s, America's expanding universities absorbed faculty and graduate students from Europe and elsewhere (Loewenberg 2006). In some cases, these scholars' backgrounds facilitated post-war field research on their home countries or other countries where their native language prevailed.[9] In later decades, an influx of international talent continued from Asia, Latin America and other developing areas as well as Europe, further pluralizing international research. The assumption that the US-based political scientist traveling abroad is necessarily a foreign outsider marked by "the differences of appearance, speech, and living patterns that distinguish the foreigner from the native inhabitant," which may often have been accurate a generation ago, is far from consistently correct today (Ward 1964a, 61).

According to our survey, comparativists have been responsible for about half of all field research projects in the discipline. The topics under

---

[8] For example, regarding public opinion data: the World Values Survey was initiated in 1990, while regional surveys in the developing world were established even later with the Latinobarometro beginning in 1995, the Afrobarometer in 1999, and the Asia Barometer Survey in 2001.

[9] As Munck and Snyder's interviews make clear, Juan Linz and Arend Lijphart are examples (2007, 150–209, 234–272).

exploration have evolved over the years. Earlier work in comparative politics was marked by a tendency toward broad issues such as political development, modernization, and political culture. More recent work has been focused on specific actors, dynamics, and processes, producing a panoply of scholarship on issues such as migration (Ellermann 2009; Adida 2014; Goodman 2014), associations (Haddad 2007; Jamal 2007; Tsai 2007), voter–politician links like networks and clientelism (Wantchekon 2003; Baldwin 2013), public opinion (Baker 2009; Tessler 2011), social movements (Stokes 1995; Perry and Li 1996; Baldez 2002), and much more. Comparativists have delved into topics in Europe and other industrialized settings, from civic culture (Banfield 1958; Putnam 1993) to labor (Thelen 1991) to parties (Kitschelt 1989; Grzymala-Busse 2002) to social policy (Immergut 1992; Pierson 1995; Häusermann 2010; Jacobs 2011). In developing-world settings, they have examined politics at the national level (Liddle 1996; Ames 2001; Slater 2010; Vu 2010) and at the local and micro level (Scott 1985; Kohli 1987; Boone 1992; Schatz 2004; O'Brien and Li 2006; Thun 2006; Fox 2007). Comparativists have also pioneered new approaches for conducting research in repressive, authoritarian political environments (Wedeen 1999; Carlson *et al.* 2010). Comparative researchers have pursued up-close exploration of subjects that once tended to be studied in indirect ways, such as rebellion and insurgency (Reno 1998; Wood 2003; Weinstein 2007) and racial or ethnic identity and conflict (Brass 2003; Chandra 2004; Yashar 2005; Straus 2006; Fujii 2009; Habyarimana *et al.* 2009).[10]

If fieldwork was once unusual in international relations (IR), it has become substantially more common over time.[11] One examination of some 300 studies of international organizations published in the 1960s revealed that only 16 involved what the author considered to be field research techniques, including interviews and observation (Alger 1970, 431–432). Yet, as early as the 1950s and 1960s, a handful of researchers were already studying institutions like the United Nations, the Council of Europe Assembly, and the International Labor Organization through fieldwork (Alger 1963, 1966, Haas 1964; Miles 1970). And today, many IR scholars regularly visit their countries of specialization to exchange ideas with local experts, and

---

[10] As noted in the discussion of American politics, in these subfield overviews we do not strive for a fully representative treatment but merely aim to convey the range of subjects that have been studied through field research. Many further examples follow in later chapters.

[11] In our survey, discussed later in this chapter, projects by scholars identifying IR as their primary or secondary subfield grew over time as a percentage of all field research projects, from 24 percent in the 1960s and 1970s to 37 percent from 2000 on.

some do stints of service in government agencies and multilateral organizations, enriching their understanding of the practice of statecraft (Barnett 1997, 2002; Krasner 2009, 254–274). Field research has contributed to work on traditional topics within this subfield, such as alliances (Pressman 2008), sovereignty (Carlson 2005), decision-making (Saunders 2011), and other aspects of foreign policy. Yet the scope of subjects under study has broadened to include global governance in dozens of issue areas, international legal regimes, tribunals, and courts (Bass 2000; Peskin 2008), epistemic communities (Cross 2011), transnational social movements (Lynch 1999; Khagram 2004; Sikkink 2011; Brysk 2013), civil wars (Lischer 2005, 2011), peacekeeping (Howard 2008; Autesserre 2010), nuclear proliferation (Hymans 2006), and international political economy (Mosley 2003; Newman 2008). The constructivist movement and its insistence on examining norms, ideas, and the creation of identities and interests has clearly been one impetus driving new forms of empirical research.[12] While these phenomena can be studied in multiple ways, many international relations scholars have fruitfully explored them through interviews, archival work, and immersive forms of observation.

While political theorists might not generally be known for their peripatetic ways, the work of influential figures such as Benedict Anderson (1991) – who conducted research in Indonesia in the 1960s prior to being banned by the Suharto regime, and also lived in Thailand – illustrates the crucial contributions field research makes to intellectual progress even in this disciplinary subfield.[13] Many theorists travel to distant libraries and repositories to examine rare texts and archival materials or exchange ideas with local experts (e.g., Kohn 2003; Jenco 2010; Seth 2010; Bajpai 2011; Keating 2011; Thomas 2012). In other cases, theorists have explored questions of political philosophy through interviews with ordinary citizens (Hochschild 1986; Monroe 1996; Jung 2008; Apostolidis 2010). Other work, too, examines empirical processes through field research in ways that are in dialogue with political theory (Bonura 2008; Leebaw 2011; Pachirat 2011; Ciccariello-Maher 2013). The recency of most of these examples may reflect trends in the subfield, such as the influence of postcolonial studies and a broadening of subject material beyond canonical Western texts and topics, that have driven theorists into work that rewards field research. The push for comparative political

---

[12] Finnemore and Sikkink make this argument in their review of constructivism, though they do not make a link between constructivism and field research in particular (2001).

[13] A biography of Anderson at http://postcolonialstudies.emory.edu/benedict-anderson (accessed November 24, 2013) mentions his research in Indonesia and Thailand; see also Cheah (1999).

theory since the late 1990s has helped to spur projects that cut across conventional boundary lines and investigate new terrain; some scholars in this camp have explicitly stated that "political theorists may realize the need to join their comparativist colleagues in language study, historical research, and fieldwork" (Jenco 2007, 753; see also Flikschuh 2014).[14]

In short, while we might tend to associate field research with comparative politics – and while many scholars who identify with this subfield do in fact gather data in the field – field research is a disciplinary, not subfield-based practice. Information gathered through interacting with actors and players in context informs our analysis in an immense range of topics across all subfields[15] and research agendas in the discipline of political science.

Fieldwork's syncretic nature

In all subfields, when it comes to field practices and techniques, political scientists have absorbed influences from a wide array of research traditions, spanning multiple disciplines and even extending outside the academy. The influence of Chicago-style sociology and anthropological ethnography has already been mentioned, but it is worth pointing out that these influences have come in waves over time, with successive generations looking again and again to developments in other disciplines.[16] Over the course of decades, field research practices in anthropology and sociology evolved and were contested in various ways (Tolman and Brydon-Miller 2001; Borneman and Hammoudi 2009). In particular, anthropologists and sociologists interrogated their role in broader structures of power (e.g., of colonialism, the West, the academic institutions) and some questioned the possibility of

---

[14] Jenco cites Cheah, who writes that "what is needed is work of genuine comparative reach; detailed and empirically grounded research on particular regions outside the North Atlantic; and a theoretically sophisticated understanding of the complexity of material culture and social-scientific evidence" (Cheah 1999, 17). In advocating "philosophical fieldwork," Flikschuh writes that she means "a preparedness to step outside one's comfort zone *conceptually* rather than physically," but notes that "I do believe that physical exposure to different contexts can be conducive to appreciating the intelligible distinctiveness of others' moral and philosophical thinking" (2014, 15). On comparative political theory, see Dallmayr (1997, 2004) and Godrej (2009).

[15] Because political science departments in the United States vary in how they self-organize by subfield, we have focused in this section on the four most commonly shared subfields of American politics, comparative politics, international relations, and political theory. As we show, field research is also prevalent and used to investigate a wide range of questions in departments that include a subfield of public administration and public policy.

[16] As shown in Chapter 6, interviewing techniques have been shared among disciplines for many decades, and as Chapter 7 illustrates, political scientists have continually drawn on examples of participant observation and ethnographic research from sociology and anthropology.

scientific objectivity in their field research. These debates have resonated to a certain degree in political science, with some scholars embracing post-modern epistemologies while others remain committed to forms of positivism that shrug off such critiques.[17]

While the work of political scientists who have taken a "historical turn" – whether in American political development, political theory, comparative historical work, or international relations – and who thus grapple with texts and archival material may initially have drawn somewhat on methods used by historians, scholars in the discipline have developed their own (often more selective) archival approaches. The development of survey research methods, discussed in Chapter 8, has featured much interchange with sociologists, economists, and others. As Chapter 9 makes clear, field experiments in politics have been encouraged in part by the work of development economists, and that of laboratory-based experimentalists in psychology, economics, and political science itself. The enterprising efforts of investigative reporters, and journalistic practices and experiences more generally, have inspired some political scientists.[18] In certain cases these templates are explicitly cited, studied, or imitated; in other cases they are merely taken as inspiration. Often the adoption of other research traditions is ad hoc and eclectic.

This *syncretic* aspect of field research in our discipline is a great strength. With no single set of practices enshrined as orthodoxy, political scientists have continually innovated by adopting varied sets of tools in order to obtain data and answer research questions. Yet too often, we believe, scholars have taken up the practices of other disciplines with little reflection. In so doing, they may have neglected possibilities for dialogue with other methodological lineages through which they might learn about the strengths and weaknesses of those borrowed techniques, and how to use them critically and effectively. For example, as Chapter 7 illustrates, scholars in our discipline engaging in what we group together as site-intensive methods often identify with just one tradition within that rubric, either ethnography or participant observation, to the neglect of the other. Moreover, this borrowing facility may have inhibited the emergence of a more unified self-identity among field researchers in

---

[17] For example, Wedeen explores these issues in her discussion of the varied forms of ethnography practiced by political scientists (2010).

[18] One interview respondent (BR-8, August 16, 2012) mentioned, as an example related to his own work, reporter Jonathan Rubinstein's book based on a year in which he joined the Philadelphia police force (1973). Alfred Stepan, among others, notes synergies between his early work as a foreign correspondent in Brazil and his academic research (Munck and Snyder 2007, 399–403, 406–410).

political science, and a common conception of what it is they do. We hope at least partially to fill those gaps with this book.

The uneven geographic coverage of field research

The story of political science field research is not one of monolithic, unchecked expansion to all possible locations and topics. As we will see later in the chapter, while field research does extend to a great many places around the world, it exhibits a pattern of heavy concentration on certain regions and countries. Perhaps unsurprisingly, American academics conduct many field projects in the United States itself; they also visit Europe and particularly Western Europe in great numbers. Latin America, East Asia, and some parts of South Asia also receive sustained attention. Meanwhile, field research in (for instance) Africa, Central Asia, and Southeast Asia is spotty at best.

Multiple causes contribute to this uneven coverage. On the one hand, political dynamics have shaped, and continue to shape, the fieldwork emphases of political scientists. Closed borders, political repression, and military conflict have rendered field research impractical or impossible in certain parts of the world for periods of time. During China's insular Mao era, for example, an entire generation of social scientists grew accustomed to observing events in the mainland from afar, interviewing émigrés in places like Hong Kong and reading between the lines of newspaper reports and broadcast-media transcripts. As Tessler and Jamal observe, for decades, research on political attitudes, values, and behavior in the Middle East was heavily constrained with regard to "the countries where systematic survey research could be conducted, the degree to which representative national samples could be drawn, and the extent to which sensitive questions could be asked" (2006, 433). Indeed, as our survey data attest, researchers studying areas ridden with military conflict, ethnic strife, or violent crime must weigh a complex set of concerns, from personal security to ethics, in assessing whether or not fieldwork is feasible.

Yet restrictions or risk factors that deter research in certain places do not explain all of the waxing and waning in the scholarly attention paid to certain regions and particular countries. As we mentioned before, the priorities of organizations that contribute significantly to funding field research have also played an important role in directing researchers' geographic focus. Likewise, scholars tend to take an interest in countries that loom large in geopolitical significance and that have well-developed area studies institutions training specialists and encouraging research. The poorest countries of the world, conversely, for the most part receive scant or sporadic attention. The precise mix of causes aside, the upshot is that we know far more about the on-the-ground politics of some places than of others. Our hope is that this book might contribute to evening out our knowledge base by helping scholars imagine branching out and pursuing research projects in less-traveled terrain.

The shape of field research in political science

The nature of field research and the general absence of aggregate information about political scientists' fieldwork practices would ordinarily make it difficult to go beyond a broad-brush characterization of trends punctuated by reference to specific examples. The desire for more precise and fine-grained data about field research in the discipline motivated us to conduct a survey of political science faculty, the Field Research in Political Science (FRPS) survey. Here we present some basic findings from this inquiry.

We have several objectives in this discussion. Most generally, we aim to convey key aspects of the nature of field research in our profession and flesh out the preceding discussion of the development of field research over time. In so doing, we also provide support for the arguments that we introduced in Chapter 1. First, while the form and function of fieldwork differ quite significantly from one political scientist to the next, there are also significant commonalities across fieldwork in the discipline. Second, a central commonality is political scientists' eclecticism, both with regard to data-collection techniques and data-analysis techniques: most scholars employ several data-collection techniques and engage in multiple types of analysis in the field, relating to every stage of political science inquiry; moreover, most scholars iterate between data collection and analysis, updating key aspects of their research design as they go. Third, field research is often guided by a set of core principles, which help to account for why it is an irreplaceable way to accumulate knowledge and generate theory about politics.

The survey

As discussed in detail in the Appendix, this survey was administered online from November 2011 to August 2012. In all, 1,142 political scientists with faculty appointments at US academic institutions took the survey.

The questionnaire asked about respondents' overall preparation for and experience with field research, but focused on questions concerning discrete *field research projects*.[19] Each respondent who had conducted field research was asked to complete a battery of questions about her first such project, and then another about her most recent project, if applicable. Respondents were then given the option of completing a third battery of questions if they felt that another project was "most representative of how you approach field research." Collectively, 899 of the respondents reported on 1,468 discrete field research projects.

It is important to point out some of the survey's limitations. Ideally we would have liked information on field research stretching back to the early post-World War II era. But the gradually moving window of living memory as well as other constraints did not allow us to reach quite so far back in time. The earliest field research project reported in the survey commenced in 1955, but only twenty-two projects in the dataset were initiated before 1970. In short, the data prior to the 1970s are sparse. Indeed, the survey generally provided more data on relatively recent projects than on those farther in the past. The median project began in 2001, and only a quarter of all projects in the dataset began in 1992 or earlier.

The sampling frame was derived from a list, provided to us by APSA, intended to include every US-based political science faculty member (not merely APSA members). This list appears to have excluded many emeritus and retired members of the discipline, however. As explained in the Appendix, while our invitation emphasized that we encouraged the participation of all faculty "even if you have never done field research," only 182 respondents (16 percent) had never conducted fieldwork and had no plans to do so.[20] This evident response bias makes it problematic to compare respondents who have done field research and those who have not, or to model propensity to conduct field research. Thus, in this book, we employ data only from

---

[19] Our survey of the discipline presented our definition of field research, which at the time of the survey was, "leaving your home institution to collect data or information that significantly informs your research." After synthesizing what we learned from the survey, and upon further critical reflection, we modified our definition slightly to the one we use for the purposes of this book: "leaving one's home institution in order to acquire data, information, or insights that significantly inform one's research." We are confident that presenting this subsequent definition in the survey rather than the one we advanced would have had no material impact on survey responses.

[20] The respondents who had not done field research, and sixty-one others who reported only being in the planning or early stages of their first field research projects, were asked a short, separate battery of questions. We plan to report results from those questions in a separate article.

those respondents who reported having completed or nearly completed one or more field research projects; we treat this as comprising a random sample of political science faculty with field research experience, mostly excluding those in the discipline who had already retired by 2011, rather than of all political science faculty. Likewise, the data most accurately reflect field research in the discipline since the 1970s.

Profile of field researchers and their projects

Who does field research: gender, ethnicity, and subfield

Who does field research? The data paint a picture of substantial and increasing diversity. The proportion of women among field researchers grew steadily from 21 percent in the 1960s and 1970s to 42 percent in projects from the year 2000 on. The latter figure is significantly larger than the proportion of women in the overall pool of political science faculty in the United States (30.2 percent in Fall 2011, according to APSA's list of US-based political scientists). Scholars who identified as Asian, Black, Latino, Native American, Arab American, or who specified a multi-racial identity constituted just 3 percent of field researchers in the early years covered by our study, but 15 percent in the last decade.[21]

In terms of subfield specialization, as noted earlier in the chapter, political scientists often think of field research as something that mainly comparativists do. Yet the data provide a reminder that this is not necessarily the case. As Figure 2.1 illustrates, Americanists and scholars of international relations made up a significant portion of the respondents who reported having done field research – and members of smaller subfields, from methods to political theory to public policy, also do plenty of field research.[22] In fact, while comparativists constitute an outsized fraction of field researchers, the percentage of fieldworkers in the discipline constituted by scholars from each other subfield is generally proportional to the percentage of the overall discipline that those subfields comprise.

---

[21] For comparison, the 15 percent figure is slightly higher than that found in 2004 for all non-student APSA members identifying as Native American, Asian American, Latino, African American, or "other." See Chart I.A.6: Ethnicity Distribution of Current APSA Members in U.S., www.apsanet.org/imgtest/IA6.pdf.

[22] Figure 2.1 shows all subfield affiliations, not merely primary affiliations. If only primary affiliations are considered, some proportions change noticeably – political scientists whose *primary* subfield is methodology, for instance, make up less than 1 percent of those who have completed a field research project.

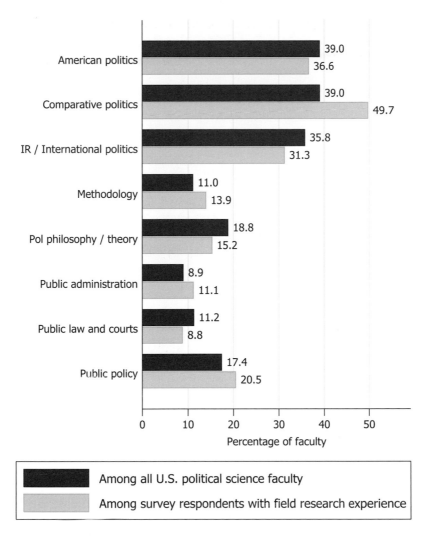

American politics — 39.0 / 36.6
Comparative politics — 39.0 / 49.7
IR / International politics — 35.8 / 31.3
Methodology — 11.0 / 13.9
Pol philosophy / theory — 18.8 / 15.2
Public administration — 8.9 / 11.1
Public law and courts — 11.2 / 8.8
Public policy — 17.4 / 20.5

Percentage of faculty

■ Among all U.S. political science faculty
▨ Among survey respondents with field research experience

Figure 2.1   Subfield affiliations

Note: Faculty in database of US political scientists: 10,558. Survey respondents with at least one field research project: 899. 79.4 percent of faculty in the former and 65.6 percent in the latter indicated more than one subfield affiliation.

Experience with field research

Respondents from all subfields reported a wide range of experience levels with respect to field research. Some had never gone into the field while others had a dozen or more projects under their belts.[23] A histogram

---

[23] It is not always a straightforward matter to determine when a project has been completed, as scholars may draw on data they have collected over a period of years to inform one or more projects, or

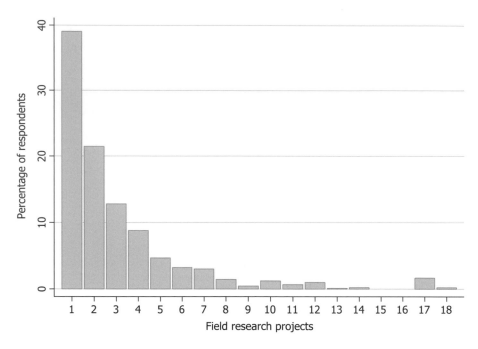

Figure 2.2 Number of completed field research projects
Note: Completed projects include those for which the field research was finished, or close to finished, at the time of the survey. Number of respondents with at least one field research project: 899.

(Figure 2.2) shows this distribution in full. Among respondents with any field research experience, 39 percent had completed just one project, while 27 percent had finished four or more projects. About half (49 percent) of all reported projects were dissertation projects or extensions thereof, while the remainder were projects begun sometime after the dissertation, whether in a non-tenure-track position (4 percent), as an assistant professor (17 percent), an associate professor (15 percent), or a full professor (15 percent).

Preparation for field research

Because of the trepidation that many graduate students express before venturing forth, we sought to determine whether, in general, political

---

may do research for a number of projects during any fieldwork trip. For purposes of the survey, a field research project was considered completed if "most" or "all" of the field research for it had been finished.

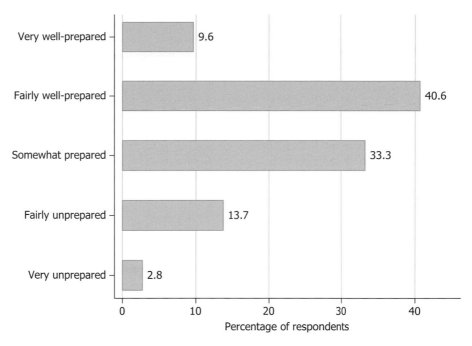

Figure 2.3 Overall preparation for first field research project
Note: Number of respondents: 945.

scientists feel they have adequate training and background when they set out on field research projects. Accordingly, we asked: "In retrospect, how well-prepared were you prior to your *first* field research trip?" Responses to this question were mixed. As Figure 2.3 demonstrates, about half of those who answered this question were "fairly" or "very" well-prepared, while the other half were only "somewhat prepared" or less. One might expect that researchers headed for destinations outside the United States would feel less well acquainted with field sites and thus less well prepared, but among such researchers the proportion feeling at least fairly well prepared was still 48 percent. Of course, for some researchers, field sites are familiar places, whether from their childhood backgrounds, pre-graduate school travel, or coursework. Of respondents who had completed a field research project, 84 percent indicated that graduate courses about the areas of research, study or travel in those locations, or relevant research, work, or volunteer experience had helped them prepare. Being well prepared for fieldwork situates scholars to pursue the kinds of engagement with context and critical reflection that we suggest are central to good field research.

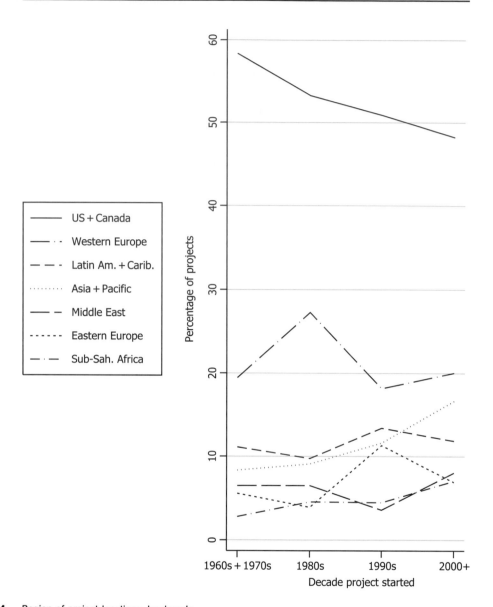

Figure 2.4 Region of project locations, by decade
Note: Total number of projects: 1,307. Some projects include locations in multiple regions.

The geography of field research

The distribution of field research projects by region over time in our sample is shown in Figure 2.4.[24] Most immediately noticeable is the predominance of

---

[24] In general, the World Bank's categories were used to define regions, with some exceptions to keep the data in line with general conventions in political science – such as differentiating Western Europe

projects in the United States and Canada[25] throughout the period under study, though the proportion of field research done in these two countries has declined slightly over time. Fully half (50 percent) of all reported projects included at least one location in the United States, sometimes in addition to other international locations.[26] Conversely, 57 percent of projects involved travel to at least one non-US location: more than a quarter (26 percent) of projects discussed by survey respondents entailed work in Europe, about 14 percent involved work in Asia and the Pacific, 12 percent in Latin America and the Caribbean, 7 percent in the Middle East, and 6 percent in Sub-Saharan Africa.[27] Together, Western and Eastern Europe, and in particular the former, have played host to a large plurality of international field research locations: 45 percent of all international projects included locations in Europe. Projects in Asia and the Pacific, and those in Latin America and the Caribbean, occupy the next tier, with Asian destinations growing notably in prominence over the last four decades. Projects involving the Middle East, Eastern Europe, and Sub-Saharan Africa each constitute 10 to 13 percent of all international projects, with Eastern Europe having experienced a temporary surge in the 1990s, the Middle East growing in popularity since the 1990s, and Africa research expanding slowly but steadily since the 1960s. These trends hint at a broad pattern of fieldwork in the discipline following important changes in macro-political dynamics.

The map in Figure 2.5 presents a visual picture of all field research locations reported in the survey, with the size of each bubble proportional to the number of projects for which the corresponding location served as a research site. Table 2.1 provides more detail on the most common destinations. Again, the overall prominence of locations within the United States is striking, reemphasizing the reality that fieldwork is not just for comparativists. Further, while Washington DC is the most-frequented city among American research destinations, included in 30 percent of domestic projects, most research in the United States happens in places other than the capital;

and Eastern Europe rather than combining them both with Central Asia. The Middle East category includes Turkey and North Africa.

[25] Projects in Canada constituted a small minority within this category; only 17 projects in the dataset included one or more locations in Canada, fewer than for Peru.

[26] Because international projects are similar to those based in the United States in some ways but different in many others, in many of the figures we report survey findings separately for international and domestic research.

[27] Some projects involved locations in multiple regions. Therefore, these figures sum to more than 100 percent.

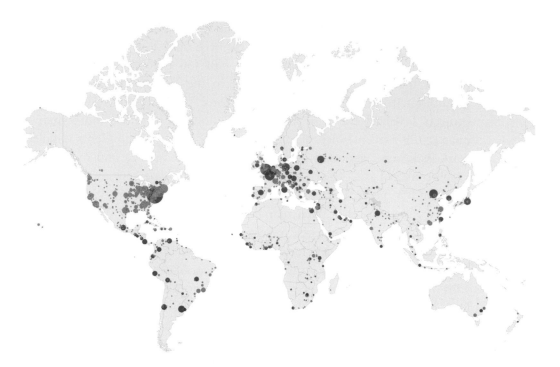

Figure 2.5   Map of field research locations
Note: Capital cities are in dark gray. Circle size is proportional to the number of projects in which the location was reported as a research site. A full-sized version of this map can be found at www.psfieldresearch.org.

85 percent of locations in domestic projects were outside Washington.[28] Apart from major cities like New York and Boston, the locations of major research universities, Presidential Libraries, and national archive facilities are also notably represented, as well as state capitals. A total of 355 unique cities and localities within the United States were reported.

In international research, the cluster of large bubbles in Europe reinforces the fact that this region has received much attention. London is the foreign city most visited by US-based political scientists doing field research, followed by Paris, Beijing, Berlin, and Brussels. Naturally, such locations are sometimes visited in order to learn about other countries, such as former colonies.[29] In terms of other countries and regions that emerge as research

---

[28] To be precise: the unit here is not the location but the project-location. Thus, the 61 instances of New York City as a location in a field research project, the 45 instances of Boston, the 35 instances of Atlanta, etc., together total 85 percent of all project-locations in projects limited to the United States.
[29] For example, of the 97 projects including the United Kingdom, 12 indicated that the purpose of the research was to study the politics and history of countries other than the UK itself, through colonial archives and other sources.

Table 2.1 Top 40 field research locations: domestic and international

US location	Projects	Country	Projects
Washington DC	212	United States	670
New York City NY	61	United Kingdom	97
Boston MA	45	Germany	69
Atlanta GA	35	France	68
Chicago IL	32	China	61
Los Angeles CA	28	Belgium	41
Austin TX	26	Japan	36
Ann Arbor MI	24	Russia	35
College Park MD	20	Italy	32
Abilene KS	18	Argentina	30
Minneapolis MN	17	Mexico	29
Denver CO	17	Brazil	25
Simi Valley CA	15	India	24
Sacramento CA	13	Netherlands	24
Philadelphia PA	13	Switzerland	23
Independence MO	13	Hungary	21
San Francisco CA	13	Poland	21
Detroit MI	12	Spain	20
Columbus OH	12	Turkey	20
Seattle WA	12	Chile	19
Baltimore MD	11	South Korea	18
Palo Alto CA	10	Peru	18
College Station TX	10	Venezuela	17
New Orleans LA	10	Israel	17
Phoenix AZ	9	Canada	17
Jackson MS	8	Costa Rica	17
New Haven CT	8	Bolivia	16
San Diego CA	8	Colombia	15
Hyde Park NY	8	South Africa	15
St. Louis MO	8	Egypt	15
Springfield IL	8	Austria	14
Princeton NJ	8	Taiwan (ROC)	14
Cambridge MA	7	Ukraine	13
Montgomery AL	7	Ireland	12
St Paul MN	7	Denmark	12
Norman OK	6	Hong Kong (UK/China)	12
Richmond VA	6	Kenya	11
Rochester NY	6	Nigeria	11
Raleigh NC	6	Czech Republic	11
Des Moines IA	6	Norway	10

Note: Number of projects involving at least one research location: 1,337.

focal points, China and Japan are the most-visited non-Western countries; and field researchers leave particularly large footprints in South Korea, India, and the major cities of Central and South America. In fact, among all subnational locations outside the United States reported by our respondents, fully 52 percent were national capitals.[30] Southeast Asia, Central Asia, and most parts of Africa have received far less attention than other areas have. We have previously noted some evident reasons why scholars flock to certain field locations and avoid others: trends in the discipline, assumptions on the part of funders about what places most deserve study, issues of security and political accessibility, and the existence of strong area studies institutions for some but not all regions. The data we look at next provide further details and perspective.

Waxing enthusiastic about what seemed to him the ubiquity in the developing world of "young American research scholars bent on field work," Lucian Pye once wrote that: "There is no land too remote, no village too ordinary or too primitive, no governmental process too imposing or too esoteric for this new breed of scholar" (1964, 5). Our data only partially bear out this impression: we find that not only are political scientists often drawn to politically central cities, they also gravitate toward richer countries. Figure 2.6 shows the countries of research locations broken into income categories based on the World Bank's classification system. The high-income category includes Organization for Economic Co-operation and Development (OECD) members as well as other rich countries such as various Gulf states and Singapore. Upper-middle-income countries include, for instance, Iran, Romania, and Malaysia; the lower-middle income bracket includes Indonesia and Senegal; and the poorest category includes Haiti, Kenya, and Nepal, for example. As the figure shows, three-quarters of projects scholars reported on were carried out partially or entirely in high-income countries. Even among international projects alone, only 9 percent included a country in the poorest income bracket. Further, outside of the developed world, attention is concentrated on countries that loom large in size and global prominence. For example, of all projects that included at least one country in the lower-middle income category, fully 38 percent included China or India. Of projects that included any of the 103 countries in the two middle-income

---

[30] Here too, the unit is not the location but the project-location. Thus, the 73 instances of London as a location in a field research project, the 59 instances of Paris, the 41 instances of Beijing, etc., together total 52 percent of all project-locations. If we look only at projects in lower-middle or low-income countries, the proportions are similar: 48 percent of project-locations in such countries are capitals.

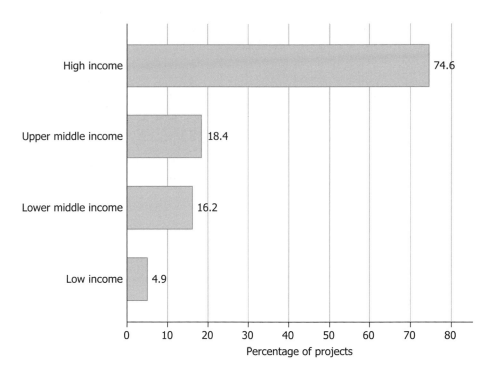

Figure 2.6 Income group of countries visited in project
Note: Total number of projects: 1,468. Income groups are taken from the World Bank's World Development Indicators 2010. Some projects include locations in multiple income groups.

categories, a third involved visits to at least one BRIC.[31] Meanwhile, only eleven projects in the dataset reported Nigeria as a destination (0.8 percent of all projects, 1.4 percent of all international projects); 8 projects included Indonesia; 3 included Pakistan; 3 included Vietnam; 2 included Saudi Arabia; and 1 included Malaysia. A total of 55 countries were studied by no one at all in our sample.[32]

Particular field settings can pose a range of challenges beyond those connected with socioeconomic level, of course – costs, one might say, of engagement with certain kinds of contexts. The survey tried to ascertain the incidence of some of the field-site conditions that can affect the conduct of research, in two main categories. One concerned particular kinds of social conditions that might complicate research: gender inequality; intolerance

---

[31] That is, Brazil, Russia, India, or China.
[32] Many of these countries are tiny and obscure, but other are less so, such as Azerbaijan, Belarus, Cameroon, Central African Republic, Chad, Laos, Libya, Montenegro, and Sudan.

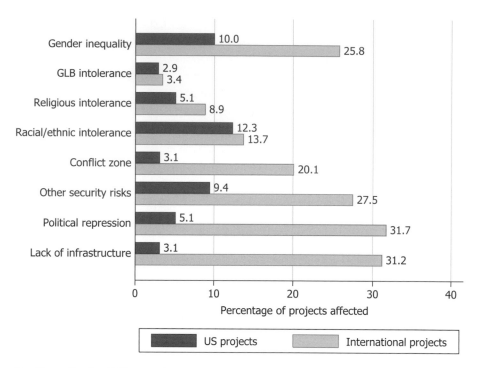

Figure 2.7   Conditions affecting field research, by project location
Note: Number of projects with locations only in the United States: 569. Number of projects with some or all locations outside the United States: 768.

for gays, lesbians, or bisexuals; religious intolerance; and racial or ethnic intolerance. The other concerned, in essence, security and political challenges.[33] Figure 2.7 depicts the frequency of these conditions. All told, in about 24 percent of US-based projects the conduct of research was affected by at least one of these challenges, a figure that rises to 62 percent among projects that extended to international locations. These data remind us that researchers' experiences in the field vary substantially, and advice that applies to one investigator may not apply to another. But they also suggest a commonality: by highlighting the real problems and risks that field research can pose, the data reinforce the importance for all fieldworkers of training, planning, and full-spectrum preparation for the varieties of adverse circumstances that can make field research difficult (see Chapter 3). They also suggest that flexibility and resourcefulness are

[33] Specifically, these were defined as "conflict zone"; "other risks to personal security, e.g., high crime rates"; "repressive political environment"; and "lack of infrastructure, e.g., electricity, potable water, transportation, etc."

indispensable skills that all scholars must develop in order to navigate their way through fieldwork environments.

Number of trips to the field and length of stay

We consider the number of trips made in the course of a project to be an important dimension of research, with significance for advising, funding, and the way we think about fieldwork. As noted previously in this chapter, in one model of fieldwork, absorbed from disciplines like anthropology, researchers travel to and steep themselves in a research site for a year or two, then return to their home institution to write up. Indeed, fellowships for international research sometimes require researchers to spend an uninterrupted year in-country, and this may be part of some advisors' expectations. Yet scholars may find it more productive, or simply necessary, to conduct fieldwork in a series of shorter stints, whether for personal, intellectual, or other reasons. Sometimes scholars may return to their home institution only briefly between trips, for a quick break; at other times they may take longer hiatuses from the field, processing and reflecting on the data they have gathered quite thoroughly before going back for more.

The FRPS faculty survey data show that, while plenty of political scientists engage in long-term, single-trip immersion, it is not the most common form field research in the discipline takes. First, researchers frequently spread their time in the field across multiple separate trips.[34] All told, only one quarter of reported projects (27 percent) involved just a single trip. On average, political scientists made five or six trips (5.6) in the course of a given project. Researchers working in sites that were relatively close to their home institutions tended to shuttle back and forth between the two more often. As Figure 2.8 shows, those conducting US research within the city or state in which they were based made ten or more trips 44 percent of the time, while only 21 percent of those traveling to other states made that many forays. But even those traveling to international locations made nearly four trips on average (the median number of trips in such projects is two). One implication of the above is that field researchers often have more than one chance to get the material they need. Another implication is scholars have opportunities

---

[34] The survey instrument clarified: "By separate trip, we mean leaving your permanent home or home institution, going to one or more of the project locations, then returning." Note that the time between trips could be short (e.g., returning briefly for a conference or vacation) or long (e.g., returning from the field for the academic year, then going back the next summer).

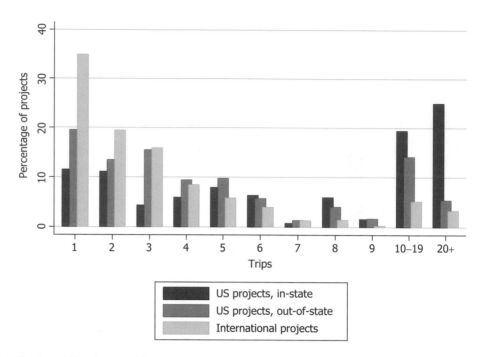

Figure 2.8   Number of trips, by project location
Note: Number of projects with locations only in the United States: 549. Number of projects with some or all locations outside the United States: 756.

to iterate, updating their design and engaging in additional analysis as they travel back and forth to the field.

The practices of political scientists often diverge from the long-term-immersion model in a second way as well: only slightly over one quarter of reported projects involved the researcher spending a total of one year or more in the field. Figure 2.9 shows a significant contrast between domestic projects and international projects in this regard. Scholars researching just in the United States were much less likely to spend 365 days or more in the field (regardless of the number of trips across which those days were spread) than were scholars conducting international research (16 percent of projects and 33 percent of projects respectively). Moreover, in just 18 percent of all international projects, total time-in-field was a month or less – which is true of 45 percent of US-based projects. The variation observed here relates to an important distinction explored in the chapters that follow: between lean-and-mean research trips that focus tightly on a set of well-defined goals, and more expansive sojourns where research can proceed in a more open-ended and broad-spectrum fashion. In either type of project, we have contended,

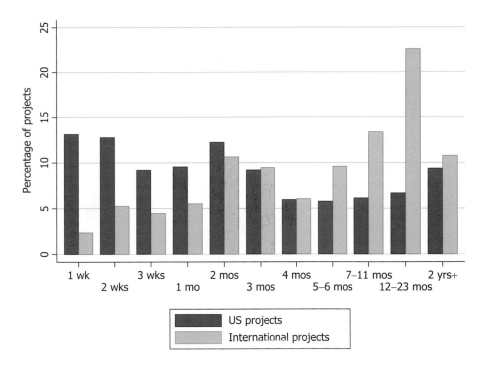

Figure 2.9   Time spent in field, by project location
Note: Number of projects with locations only in the United States: 555. Number of projects with some or all locations outside the United States: 762.

scholars can engage with the context in the consequential ways that make fieldwork a valuable research technique.

The amount of time spent in the field provides insights into the ways in which field research intersects with political scientists' career trajectories and life cycles. It is demonstrably the case that political scientists whose dissertations involved field research tended to take longer to obtain their Ph.D.s compared with those who started field research only later in their careers, or never did field research (8.5 months longer, on average).[35] Anecdotally, it can sometimes seem that political scientists do their most ambitious field research while in graduate school or early stages of their careers, scaling back fieldwork later.[36] The survey evidence on domestic field

---

[35] A two-group mean-comparison t-test placed the mean difference between 5.2 months and 11.8 months at the 95 percent confidence level.

[36] An interviewer (Munck and Snyder 2007, 187) stated to comparativist Juan J. Linz the proposition that: "As we move on in our lives and careers, it often gets harder to do fieldwork because we accumulate personal and professional obligations that make it difficult to spend a lot of time in the field. As a result, the typical pattern is to do fieldwork for the dissertation and first book and then shift

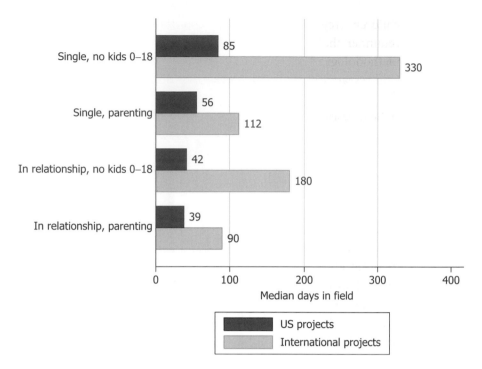

Figure 2.10 Time spent in field, by relationship/parenting status and project location
Note: Number of projects with locations only in the United States: 542. Number of projects with some or all locations outside the United States: 744. Relationship and parenting status were reported as of the start of the project. Relationship was defined as a marriage, domestic partnership, or other committed relationship.

research does not bear this out. But among 245 respondents who reported on two international field research projects, the later project was about 4 months shorter than the first, on average.[37] The survey also provides concrete evidence to support one other proposition that intuitively rings true: researchers' life circumstances affect the kinds of projects they carry out and the ways in which they pursue them. As Figure 2.10 shows, political scientists who were single and were not parents of children under the age of 18 tended to spend more time at their field sites than did those in marriages, domestic partnerships, or other committed relationships, and those raising

away from fieldwork in subsequent research." Linz explained that "My experience was actually the opposite of what you describe."
[37] A paired mean-comparison t-test placed the mean difference between 80 days and 164 days at the 95 percent confidence level. Four outlier projects were dropped for this analysis.

children (regardless of relationship status).[38] These patterns serve as a reminder that the forms of research we pursue are not driven entirely by methodological or intellectual considerations; rather, one way or another, field research is often made to fit into our lives.

Funding for field research

Regardless of life circumstances, field research requires money. The amounts involved vary widely, however. Projects reported in our survey ran the gamut from shoestring operations to lavishly financed ventures. Among projects involving research only in the United States, about half had less than $5,000 in total funding, while the top 9 percent of projects drew on $50,000 or more.[39] Among projects that included at least one international location, only about 20 percent scraped by on less than $5,000, while the top 18 percent involved at least $50,000. It stands to reason that overseas research costs more than projects confined to the United States, and indeed, the median international project absorbed $17,276 in funding while the median domestic project used only $4,810. (All funding amounts are in constant 2011 dollars unless otherwise stated.)

With regard to funding sources, about half of the time scholars reach into their own pockets to support part or all of their fieldwork. Personal savings were used in 48 percent of all projects, with the median amount lying just over $2,000 among projects that required any personal funds.[40] Much more commonly, however, political scientists rely on funding from other sources: 73 percent of US-based projects, and 94 percent of international projects, included some non-personal funding. Political scientists commonly obtain support from their own colleges or universities: this was the case for 52 percent of US-based projects and 66 percent of international projects, with median funding amounts of $3,810 and $6,137, respectively. Funding from government granting agencies and other public sources looms particularly large in international research, with a median amount of $23,184 going to the 34 percent of international projects that obtained support from these sources; by contrast, only 15 percent of projects within the United States were

---

[38] The survey's "relationship status" question asked whether respondents were "single" or "married, or in a domestic partnership or other committed relationship" – admittedly not an exhaustive set of possibilities.

[39] Total funds include personal funding provided by the researcher him- or herself as well as funds coming from public and private granting agencies and one's own institution.

[40] A relatively large proportion (56 percent) of US-based projects involved the use of personal savings, but the amounts were relatively smaller (median: $1,380) compared to international projects (43 percent, median: $2,730).

supported by government funds, with $11,595 the median amount among those that were. Private organizations gave financial assistance to 23 percent of domestic projects and 31 percent of overseas projects, in amounts somewhat smaller than those awarded by government sources. These figures showcase the importance of becoming familiar with the range of sources that are available to fund field research, investigating granting agencies' processes and procedures, and learning to write strong, compelling funding proposals as part of preparation for field research.

Figure 2.11 plots trends over time among dissertation projects only, a category that allows for particularly meaningful comparisons across projects on this dimension. This graph illustrates, first, the previously noted funding difference between US and international projects. Second, the graph depicts the difference (for international fieldwork) between projects carried out by doctoral students in top-20 programs and projects by those in other departments:[41] consistently over time, students at elite institutions marshal more funds for field research, particularly for international projects. This resource gap needs to be borne in mind when considering the kinds of field research projects that are feasible for graduate students. Third, Figure 2.11 shows a general decline, in inflation-adjusted dollars, in funding used in field research projects, even as nominal funding levels have by and large increased.[42]

These changes are proceeding in step with other trends. Researchers working in the United States are making fewer trips per project, with the average declining from 11.2 in the 1960s and 1970s to 5.8 in first projects begun since the year 2000.[43] Field researchers are also spending less time in the field per project. Domestic projects shortened from an average of around 200 days from the 1960s through the 1980s to just over 100 days since 2000, and international projects declined from an average of more than 400 days in the 1960s and 1970s to 273 days since 2000.[44] These trends may be the result

---

[41] Top-20 departments were coded on the basis of the National Research Council's 1995 rankings, as recoded by H. Joseph Newton of Texas A&M University. See www.stat.tamu.edu/~jnewton/nrc_rankings/area39.html, accessed August 26, 2012.

[42] This figure may somewhat overstate the decline in purchasing power, as constant 2011 dollars were calculated using standard Consumer Price Index (CPI) values for the United States, whereas some field research inputs (e.g., airline tickets) may have become relatively cheaper due to deregulation, and the value of the dollar in overseas locations, of course, varies. Also, for the relatively sparse 1960s/1970s data, it may be that respondents selectively reported big, costly projects.

[43] These numbers are derived from first projects alone to enhance comparability across projects. The average number of trips in international projects has changed little over time, hovering at just over three trips.

[44] These numbers too are derived from first projects alone.

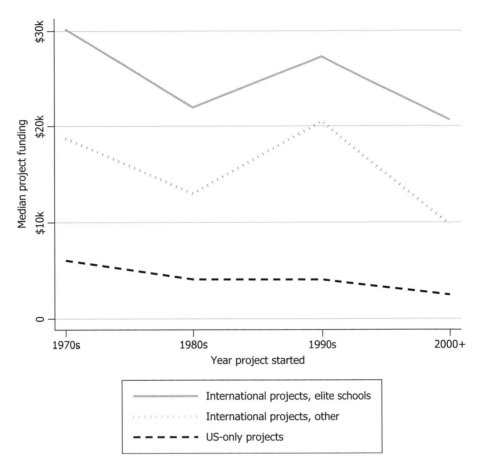

Figure 2.11   Total funds for dissertation field research projects, by decade and project location
Note: Funding is shown in constant 2011 US dollars. Number of dissertation projects with locations only in the United States: 244. Number of dissertation projects with some or all locations outside the United States: 374. Elite departments are PS Ph.D. programs ranked in the top 20 of the 1995 NRC rankings, as recoded by J. Newton (www.stat.tamu.edu/~jnewton).

of funding declines, or, indeed, the cause: on a per-day-in-field basis, median real funding levels have not, in fact, declined over the years. The trends may also stem from the greater availability of digital data, or many other factors. Regardless of their precise origin, they indicate a notable evolution in how field research is conducted. On the one hand, less time spent in the field might mean that scholars are increasingly able to carry out somewhat more streamlined and expeditious projects. On the other hand, some researchers may not have the choice to spend as much time

Table 2.2 Non-English languages used most frequently in field research projects

Language	Number of projects
Spanish	179
French	136
German	82
Russian	64
Chinese (Mandarin)	63
Arabic	42
Portuguese	31
Japanese	29
Turkish	19
Italian	19
Hindi	16
Polish	15
Hebrew	14
Dutch	14
Korean	13
Serbo-Croatian	12
Swahili	8
Czech	6
Hausa	5
Romanian	5

Note: Number of projects in which at least one non-English language was used: 658.

as they would ideally prefer and have to make difficult tradeoffs in terms of the questions they ask and how deeply they engage with the field sites in order to answer them.

Language use and preparation

Conducting overseas research often suggests the need to make a significant investment, with regard to money and time, in language study – another potential cost of field research. Much of the field research reported in the survey was conducted using English, due in large part to the high frequency of domestic projects: 93 percent of projects carried out in the United States (including Puerto Rico) involved no languages other than English. However, only 20 percent of international projects entailed using just English. Table 2.2 lists the most frequently used non-English languages across all the field research projects reported in the survey. Spanish was the single most

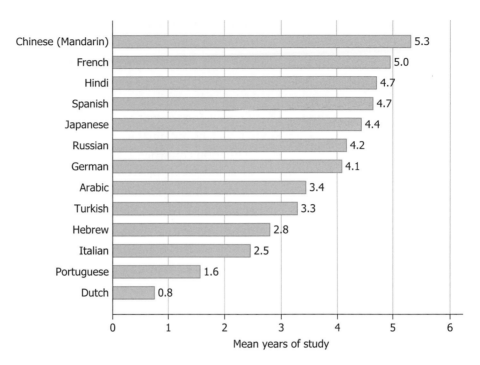

Figure 2.12 Years of language study, by language used in field research
Note: First field research projects only. Native languages not included. Languages used in 10 or more projects reported.

frequently used language, followed by French, German, Russian, and Chinese. All told, 87 distinct non-English languages or variants were reported.[45]

The survey also collected data on researchers' prior training and degree of fluency in the languages they used to conduct fieldwork. Sometimes, field research in non-US locations involved the use of at least one language that was a native tongue for the researcher, whether that be English used by an American in Abuja or Hindi used by an Indian in Uttar Pradesh. In 21 percent of international projects, non-English native languages were employed, testifying to the number of US-based field researchers with upbringings in other countries or in linguistically diverse households. More often, though, political scientists reported using languages that they had acquired through study. The average number of years of study varies by language, as Figure 2.12 makes clear.[46] Some languages were studied in a relatively abbreviated way,

---

[45] Some seven distinct dialects of Arabic were reported, for example.
[46] Survey takers were instructed that "years of study should reflect formal training at the time of this field research project."

perhaps just in advance of fieldwork, while others were cultivated for years. The reasons for this are surely multiple. Foreign Language and Area Studies (FLAS) funding is available for some languages (including Chinese and Russian) and not others; some languages (like French and Spanish) are extensively taught in US high schools. Expectations of advanced fluency – and indeed the *need* for fluency (dependent upon how many of the people with whom the researcher will be interacting are proficient in her native language) – vary across destination countries. It is also possible that, for some languages, there are larger numbers of heritage learners (those with some exposure to a language during their upbringing) requiring relatively little classroom training to become field-ready. The time invested in language training represents an important facet of field research, and, as these data imply, can entail a significant cost, but, again, may be important for the kind of engagement that we suggest is a hallmark of good field research. Current reductions and threats to eliminate the Department of Education's Title VI funding for language education thus have significant implications for the future of field research, as discussed in Chapter 11.

Practices of field researchers

So far we have considered the overall profile of field research projects and the scholars who undertake them. Here we turn to examining data on field researchers' specific practices. What do political scientists do in the course of these projects, and what do their practices suggest about the general nature of fieldwork in the discipline? As Chapter 1 indicated, one core contention of this book – and commonality of fieldwork in the discipline – is that political scientists who engage in field research employ multiple data-collection techniques *and* engage in a diverse mix of practices that extend far beyond data collection. Moreover, most political scientists *iterate* between data collection and data analysis as they carry out field research. That is, for many scholars, the very framing of their project remains productively and necessarily in play while they are in the field. Iterating among the research tasks we discuss below allows them to strengthen and refine their project's design, and ultimately conduct better research.

One important variable with regard to fieldwork practices is how much data for any particular research project scholars who engage in fieldwork collect in their field locations. While an initial hunch might be "the lion's share," projects ranged very widely in this regard. As the histogram in Figure 2.13 shows, less than a quarter of all reported projects involved the

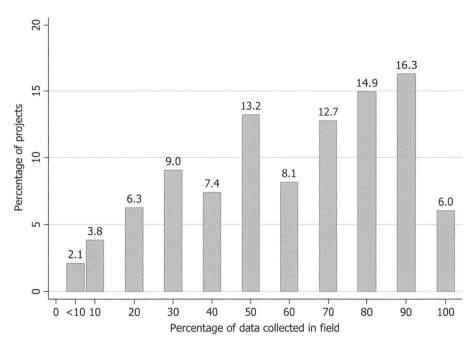

Figure 2.13 Proportion of project data collected in the field
Note: Total number of projects: 1,326.

collection of 90 or 100 percent of the data in the field, and in two-fifths of projects, field research accounted for no more than half of all the data that were collected. Information gathered in context, in other words, is commonly combined with data gathered through other means; fieldwork sometimes provides supplementary data rather than the primary wellspring of source material. This opens the opportunity for triangulation – and highlights the importance of considering strategies for integrating data from different types of sources, and techniques for evaluating the evidentiary value of data with varying provenances in order to assess how heavily to rely on them as one engages in analysis.

As Figure 2.14 shows, the proportion of data underlying particular research projects that is collected in the field has gradually declined over time for both international and US projects. This trend may have many root causes. To name just two, it may be caused by a contraction in funding for field research, or by the rising availability of online data and their increasing use as a complement to data gathered in person. This graph also demonstrates that, overall (considering all non-US locations, developed and developing alike), researchers going abroad tend to obtain a greater fraction

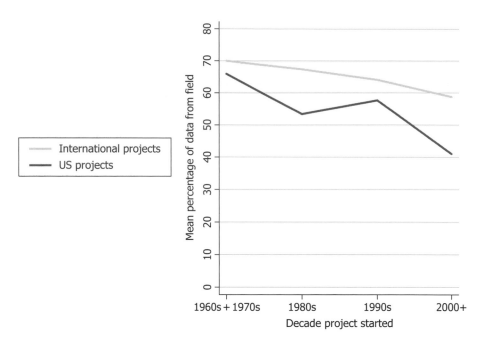

Figure 2.14 Proportion of project data collected in the field, by decade and project location
Note: Dissertation projects only. Number of projects with locations only in the United States: 245.
Number of projects with some or all locations outside the United States: 379.

of their data from the field than do scholars who carry out fieldwork in the United States – perhaps because there are more pre-existing datasets, troves of records and archives, and other non-field sources more readily at hand for research on American politics.

For each field research project, the survey asked researchers to report which of thirteen data-collection techniques they made "significant use of" while in the field.[47] The results show that political scientists use a wide array of strategies to gather data in the field; moreover, they are omnivorous in their appetites, commonly employing a wide range of techniques rather than just one or two. This further establishes the point that field researchers often triangulate: they take advantage of the richness of local contexts to gather and combine multiple forms of information creatively, using results from one

---

[47] To clarify: the fourth category was defined as "Compilation of quantitative data (in ways other than the above)" and the last three were "Collection of articles or data from newspapers, radio, or other media (other than those found in archives)"; "Collection of published books, reports, etc. (other than those found in archives)"; and "Collection of other documents, e.g., maps, brochures, posters, etc. (other than those found in archives)."

type of inquiry to inform and refine another. The single most prevalent technique was interviewing, which figured significantly in about 81 percent of all projects. Rarely, it seems, do scholars pass up opportunities to shed light on their topics by posing questions in face-to-face conversations. Substantial numbers also reported gathering quantitative data (through surveys, field experiments, laboratory experiments, and other means), and collecting media reports, documents and other published material both inside and outside of archives. Smaller numbers conducted oral histories or focus groups.

Figure 2.15 shows the techniques used in projects by researchers in three major subfields (American politics, comparative politics, and international relations).[48] It begins to suggest ways in which the day-to-day work of field research varies in different parts of the discipline, with Americanists (for instance) doing somewhat more collection of survey data and other forms of quantitative data than comparativists and IR scholars, and somewhat less interviewing and collection of media reports and other publications. Notably, a full 45 percent of projects by comparativists employed ethnography or participant observation; members of other subfields also employ these techniques, but not as commonly. While the prevalence of particular techniques does vary among branches of the discipline, the data also caution against associating any one form of data collection exclusively or too closely with a particular subfield.

While we have noted that political scientists tend to employ more than one technique to gather data, even more striking is that, since the 1960s and still today, most political scientists use multiple data-collection techniques in the course of a *single project*. Indeed, a typical project drew on five data-collection techniques, and 31 percent of all projects involved *seven or more* techniques.[49] While the use of multiple techniques is common in all types of projects, this tendency is particularly pronounced in international research. As Figure 2.16 depicts, just considering fieldwork in the United States, 65 percent of projects involved four or more data-collection techniques, while among international projects, the corresponding figure was 81 percent. In US projects, the median number of data-collection techniques was five, as opposed to a median of six for international projects.

Our interviews accorded with this and provided details concerning how political scientists put multiple techniques to work. Our respondents

---

[48] The other five subfields are omitted here, for the sake of simplicity.
[49] The median number of data-collection techniques used is 5, and the mean is 4.9.

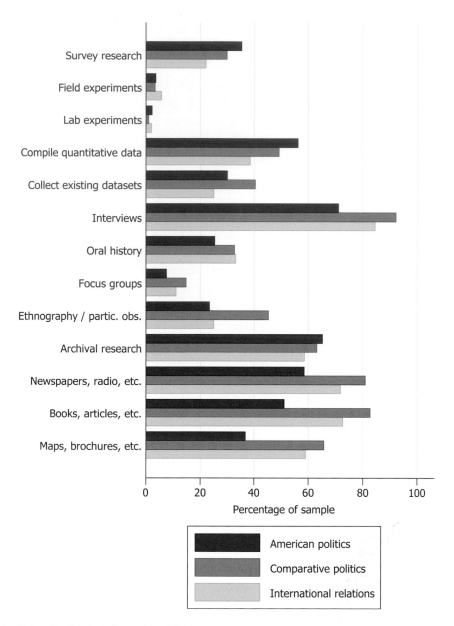

Figure 2.15 Data-collection techniques, by subfield
Note: Number of projects in American politics: 376; comparative politics: 519; international relations: 251.

recounted availing themselves of a wide variety of data-collection techniques, and it was the rare scholar who mentioned using just one strategy to gather data. One scholar of international relations in Europe indicated that he commonly did interviews and archival research, sampled secondary sources,

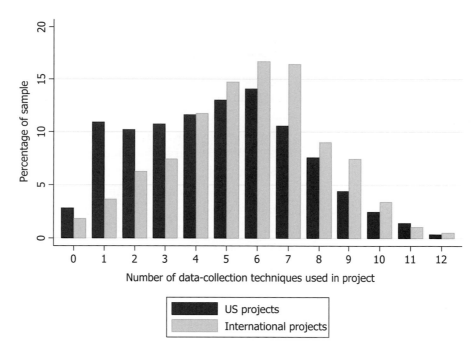

Figure 2.16 Number of data-collection techniques, by project location
Note: Number of projects with locations only in the United States: 569. Number of projects with some or all locations outside the United States: 768.

collected newspaper articles, engaged in participant observation, did ethnography, and collected quantitative data.[50] Moreover, we found that political scientists pair and combine data-collection techniques in perhaps unexpected ways. An investigator examining political economy in Sub-Saharan Africa, for instance, carried out a survey, did open-ended interviews, conducted a survey experiment, and did archival research (all in the same project).[51] Another combined surveys with Geographic Information Systems (GIS) analysis, as well as ethnographic methods.[52] And many others highlighted how "soaking and poking" and open-ended interviews were indispensable for determining how to carry out surveys or experiments in the field.[53]

As Chapters 8 and 9 show, it is in fact common for political scientists to employ multiple techniques in the process of setting up, interpreting, and

---

[50] Interview, DK-6, July 31, 2012.   [51] Interview, LM-13, September 7, 2012.
[52] Interview, LM-8, August 30, 2012.
[53] Interviews, LM-13, September 7, 2012; BR-2, July 30, 2012; BR-6, August 14, 2012. We discuss the meaning of "soaking and poking" in Chapter 7.

following up on surveys and field experiments. In short, the deployment of multiple techniques within a single project – a form of triangulation – is a hallmark of data collection in political science field research.

An overarching argument of this book is that field research can inform many facets of the design and execution of research projects. It might seem obvious that one conducts field research because needed data or source materials are not otherwise available, and thus "gathering data" is the primary task in the field. Yet the survey provides powerful evidence that scholars make progress on multiple aspects of the research process – in addition to accumulating data – while conducting fieldwork, a point that we highlight in the chapters to come.

The questionnaire asked respondents to "indicate the tasks or analytic processes that the research you conducted *in the field* facilitated,"[54] and offered yes/no responses in nine different categories.[55] As Figure 2.17 shows, the overwhelming majority of respondents found their fieldwork to have been important for understanding the context of what they were studying, and for grasping causal processes. Yet substantial majorities also reported that critical elements of research design were also furthered by experiences in the field. These include the core tasks of developing or refining the research question, the hypotheses, and the concepts at issue. All told, in 76 percent of projects on which respondents reported, field research facilitated at least five analytic tasks or processes. In a clear majority of projects, fieldwork facilitated seven or more analytic tasks. In as many as 22 percent of projects, respondents reported that their field activities fed into *all nine* of the analytic tasks about which we inquired. While international projects involved a slightly larger number of analytical tasks than did domestic projects (an average of 6.8 in the former and 6.2 in the latter), the data demonstrate that reshaping or adjusting the major ideas and parameters of an inquiry on the basis of what is learned in the field – i.e., iteratively updating research design – is very common in both international projects and those based in the United States.

All this likely rings true for many readers with field experience, as it did for our interviewees. To briefly preview the many ways in which field research helped our interview respondents to carry out key analytic tasks,[56] many

---

[54] Emphasis in the questionnaire.

[55] As spelled out fully in the questionnaire, these were "Understanding the research context, Developing or refining the research question, Developing hypotheses, Developing concepts, Developing measures or operationalizing concepts, Selecting cases, Gathering previously unavailable data, Testing hypotheses, [and] Understanding causal processes."

[56] Each example is expanded on later in the book.

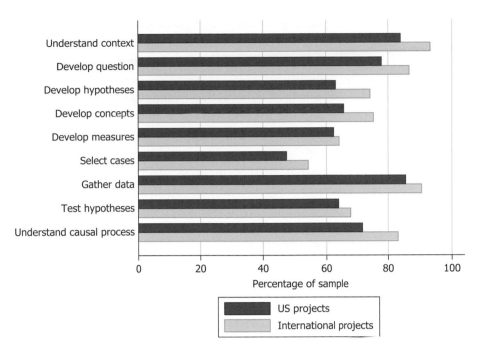

Figure 2.17   Analytical tasks and processes facilitated by field research, by project location
Note: Number of projects with locations only in the United States: 569. Number of projects with some or all locations outside the United States: 768.

(although not all) of our interviewees emphasized how field research – particularly in the early stages of a project – helped them to sharpen their vision of what the project was about, and to formulate, re-formulate, or refine their research question, whether those changes concerned the empirical focus of the project,[57] or its theoretical moorings.[58] Our interviewees also discussed carrying out case selection and sampling in the field, sometimes at multiple levels – for instance, identifying court cases to analyze,[59] communities in which to study grassroots organizations,[60] or individuals to survey.[61] Others suggested that field research was indispensable for refining concepts; developing and testing measures of key concepts – for example, immigration;[62] and challenging standard typologies – for instance, of party systems.[63]

[57] Interview, DK-9, August 2, 2012.
[58] Interview, LM-4, August 27, 2012. To be sure, other interviewees (e.g., BR-4, August 9, 2012; BR-5, August 13, 2012) reported that their research questions did not change in the field.
[59] Interview, DK-9, August 2, 2012.   [60] Interview, DK-13, August 8, 2012.
[61] E.g., interview, BR-14, October 24, 2013.   [62] Interview, BR-6, August 14, 2012.
[63] Interview, DK-7, August 1, 2012.

Many consider inference – and particularly causal inference – to be the central purpose of political science research. While the ways in which fieldwork can contribute to gaining descriptive and causal leverage are generally undervalued, our interview respondents repeatedly emphasized how fieldwork helped them to draw valid descriptive and causal inferences, and develop and test hypotheses. For instance, one scholar emphasized how field research illuminated the causal connections between electoral institutions and campaigning styles.[64] Our interviewees also offered examples of how field research enabled them to observe and thus better understand causal processes and mechanisms, particularly through in-depth process tracing – to understand, for instance, the spread of new nationalist ideologies in mid-twentieth-century Mexico.[65]

The examples briefly recounted above illustrate the many analytic functions that data gathered in the field can perform (that is, they highlight the *versatility* of those data), demonstrate the many ways in which field research helps political scientists build theory, *and* highlight the iterative nature of fieldwork. Indeed, our interview respondents described an extensive set of feedback loops and repeated shifts from research design to data collection to analysis and back again, often leading to significant changes in their projects – from rethinking the puzzle at the heart of a project to redefining key concepts.[66]

If field researchers display a common tendency to draw on multiple data-collection techniques and to update central design elements of their projects dynamically on the basis of incoming information, they also quite commonly employ more than one mode of analysis. FRPS survey respondents were asked to characterize "the approach or approaches that [they] took, overall, when doing the analysis for and writing up" their projects. They checked yes or no to four categories – formal/game theoretic, quantitative, qualitative, and interpretive – selecting all that applied. The questionnaire gave no definitions of these terms, leaving it up to respondents to apply their own understandings of these categories. An overwhelming majority (87 percent) included "qualitative" among their responses, and roughly half of reported projects involved interpretive analysis (54 percent) and/or quantitative analysis (49 percent; 51 percent including game theory). Game theoretic analysis figured in only 6 percent of projects. Figure 2.18 indicates some differences among the subfields of American politics, comparative politics,

---

[64] Interview, DK-7, August 1, 2012.   [65] Interview, DK-2, July 26, 2012.
[66] Interviews, DK-15, August 21, 2012 and BR-9, August 16, 2012, respectively.

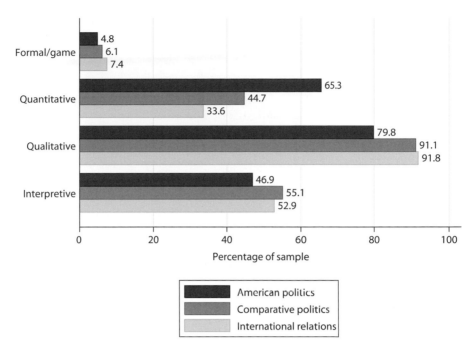

Figure 2.18 Approach to analysis, by subfield
Note: Number of projects in American politics: 376; comparative politics: 519; international relations: 251.

and international relations, such as the substantially larger proportion of projects by Americanists employing a quantitative approach compared to those by comparativists or IR specialists.

While some investigators work exclusively within one methodological tradition, in only 25 percent of projects did researchers report employing just a single mode of analysis. Rather, scholars who engage in field research often consciously adopt multiple analytic approaches, using some combination of quantitative, qualitative, and/or interpretive methodologies.[67] To give just one example, a scholar we interviewed had artfully combined interviews, participant observation, and formal modeling.[68] The Euler diagram in Figure 2.19 illustrates this eclecticism with three overlapping ellipses, each representing the proportion of projects in which a given analytic

---

[67] Not everyone, of course. At least one of our interview respondents specifically argued against methodological pluralism (at least on an individual level), professing a "lack of belief" in multi-method research due to the untenability of combining very different epistemologies. Interview, LM-18, September 14, 2012.
[68] Interview, DK-16, August 21, 2012.

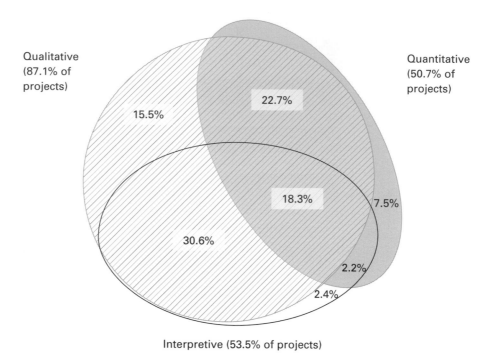

Qualitative
(87.1% of
projects)

Quantitative
(50.7% of
projects)

22.7%

15.5%

18.3%   7.5%

30.6%

2.2%

2.4%

Interpretive (53.5% of projects)

Figure 2.19   Multiple approaches to analysis
Note: Number of projects including at least one approach to analysis: 1,331. Formal / game theoretic approaches were combined with quantitative approaches for this graph.

approach was employed.[69] As it shows, 43 percent of projects used quantitative analysis in conjunction with qualitative and/or interpretive methods. Qualitative and interpretive analytic approaches were also frequently paired (49 percent). Remarkably, in nearly a fifth of projects (18 percent), respondents said they used qualitative, interpretive, *and* quantitative approaches. Moreover, while the terms "mixed method" or "multi-method" have attained wide currency in political science only recently, scholars doing field research have been mixing methods for a long time. For example, while 41 percent of projects started in the year 2000 or later involved both qualitative and quantitative approaches to analysis, the same was true of 36 percent of projects in the 1960s and 1970s. The use of multiple methods does vary by subfield, however. About half of projects by Americanists and public law scholars employed both qualitative and quantitative approaches, but only

[69] The relatively small number of formal/game theoretic approaches was combined with quantitative approaches for this graph.

39 percent of those by comparativists, 27 percent of those by IR specialists, and 15 percent of those by political theorists did so. In short, as we noted earlier, many field researchers are not tightly and exclusively tied to a single epistemological foundation.

Conclusion

Accounts of the history of political science rarely pay much attention to the place of field research in the discipline's trajectory. This chapter has sketched out some of the main forces that drove political scientists to embrace field research in multiple forms and in myriad locations, beginning in the post-World War II period. These forces included intellectual trends and influences such as the behavioral revolution, ethnography, and experimentalism, some of which stem from other disciplines. Political scientists both adopted these trends in syncretic fashion and simultaneously developed field methods in their own ways as well. Major institutions, many of them creations of the US government, have also played roles in encouraging field study. While our survey was unable to capture the entirety of this evolution, limited as it was to the past three or four decades, it provides a broad and objective overview of some of the key dimensions of field research as practiced in our discipline. In our analysis, we have sought not only to include compelling descriptive information, showing the general shape of field research and ways in which our findings confirm or cut against conventional wisdom, but also to highlight important themes that will run throughout this book.

As many of our interviewees agreed, "fieldwork" has often been thought of as something that scholars of comparative politics do, something with less resonance in other subfields. While field research is especially salient among comparativists, we have seen that political scientists from virtually all sub-fields engage in field research – the practice belongs to the entire discipline. Americanists in great numbers have set out for field sites, and these are widely dispersed across the country; the nation's capital is just one of many destinations. International relations scholars have sit-downs with diplomats, bureaucrats, and NGO activists. And plenty of political theorists, scholars of public policy, and others also take to the road in search of sources, ideas, and insights, whether delving into government archives in Manila or watching oral arguments at the US Supreme Court.

Political scientists have journeyed to places far and wide, as the map of research locations testifies. Yet field research has been uneven in its coverage, with the United States itself, Europe, and certain capitals in Latin America and East Asia (as well as India) receiving relatively large numbers of visits, and other areas markedly fewer. Some of the less-studied countries are known for conflict or political restrictions that have surely inhibited field study, but it also appears that poor countries, or those without the benefit of area-studies communities in which political scientists participate, have been relatively neglected. These patterns, and other factors, also shape the languages that political scientists employ overseas, with five or six languages constituting mainstays of competence and presumably further influencing the choice of research locations and topics.

The many different forms and varieties that field research can take belie any single pattern or template. In part this variation stems from particular communities within political science engaging in dialogues with members of other disciplines and borrowing selectively from them. This chapter has also noted multiple ways in which projects inside the United States tend to differ from those that are carried out overseas, such as funding patterns, length of stay, number of trips, and the prevalence of adverse conditions that complicate fieldwork. Our data suggest that the stylized image of a well-funded, long-haul field research *trip* is actually not the norm. To be sure, for some scholars, field research means immersing oneself for a year or two at a site overseas, and writing a study that draws entirely or mainly from information gathered at this locale. But for others, field research means weekend trips to other US states, a month spent at a national archive, or a series of short visits to cities in multiple countries over the course of several years. Others employ field research not as the primary vehicle to collect data but as a brief add-on contributing supplementary information to a multi-method inquiry. We also observed a gap between funding levels for dissertation projects at top doctoral programs and at other institutions, and more generally saw that projects range from self-funded endeavors to those backed by six- or even seven-digit grants. Variation in all of these conditions and circumstances may seem to complicate any effort to specify what, exactly, "field research in political science" is.

Yet in the midst of all this diversity, we find commonalities. For instance, we have identified a tendency toward a kind of eclecticism, a wide-angle perspective on the field setting. Field researchers by and large avail themselves of multiple kinds of information and data-gathering techniques while engaging in the field context. They also tend toward plural and overlapping approaches to analysis; while some are strictly quantitative in orientation and others purely qualitative, many blur those boundaries. Even projects that center around numerical data typically also have a qualitative dimension to them. We have also seen a tendency to use data gathered through field research to shape or reshape fundamentals of the design and conceptualization of research projects, to measure important ideas or variables, to generate and test arguments, and to grasp causal mechanisms. On a practical level, our survey suggests ways in which political scientists pragmatically adapt field research based on their own needs and the constraints and opportunities found in a given piece of research.

The perspective on over-time change provided by the survey suggests that some field research practices in the discipline have evolved over the decades, while others have stayed more constant from the 1960s to the present. In the aggregate, political scientists spent less time in the field on a per-project basis in the past decade than they did in prior decades. This may be either cause, effect, or both of the related reality that recent projects have less overall funding, in real terms, than was once the case. Researchers these days more often combine data gathered from the field with data from other sources than they did in the past. Yet the findings also suggest that some practices that are commonly understood to be emerging are actually old hat for political scientists – such as the use of multiple research techniques or combining qualitative and quantitative work.

A full seventy years after William Foote Whyte delivered his challenge to our discipline, his specific indictment clearly no longer applies; field research practices *do* flourish in the realm of political science. They range far beyond the kind of Chicago-style direct observation and long-term cultivation of informants that Whyte had in mind, extending to techniques such as surveys, archival investigation, and experiments. Yet field researchers today recognize the core truth in his message: up-close study of actors and events, whether in person or through first-hand texts and records, provides insights into politics that otherwise would be missed. In the rest of this book, we offer detailed examinations of the specific processes and techniques that make the acquisition of such insights possible, enjoyable, and analytically productive.

3 Preparing for fieldwork

As Chapter 2 showed, field research practices in the discipline of political science are tremendously diverse.[1] Scholars conduct field research in a wide variety of contexts, stay for varying periods of time, and employ different techniques to collect data that they use for a range of purposes. Despite this heterogeneity, political scientists often face similar intellectual and logistical challenges when preparing for field research. Regardless of whether they are doing initial groundwork for a survey project on agenda-setting by state legislators in the United States, or observing social movement organization for two years in Ecuador, researchers must learn as much as they can about their topic, and carry out multiple research design – and field research design – tasks in advance of departure. They must also determine how many trips to take, for how long, and when to go – plus apply for funding, obtain IRB approvals, connect with other scholars, and make logistical arrangements before starting the actual data collection.

Further complicating preparing for field research is the reality that political scientists have few resources to help them effectively complete these steps. As discussed in more depth in Chapter 1, only a handful of graduate programs offer formal training in field research. Indeed, only 22 percent of respondents to our faculty survey with field research experience had taken a graduate course specifically on field research methods, although 39 percent reported having taken a graduate course that *dealt with* field research. Only 9 percent of respondents indicated that they had participated in one of the APSA short courses or IQMR modules focused on field methods. Hence, while most political science graduate students are required (or strongly encouraged) to take courses in statistical analysis, they get far less training concerning collecting data – for instance, with regard to the challenges of

---

[1] Some of the ideas developed in this chapter originated with Evan Lieberman (2004).

constructing and carrying out an original survey,[2] or deploying any of the other data-collection techniques scholars use in the field.

Due to this lack of formalized training, most political scientists who conduct fieldwork teach themselves how to design it, prepare for it, and carry it out. Doing so entails a significant individual investment of time and energy, however, and is often frustrating given the significant gaps in the existing literature. On the one hand, as we noted in Chapters 1 and 2, while other disciplines – anthropology and sociology in particular – have produced a wealth of provocative and insightful literature on doing field research (e.g., Amit 2000; Emerson 2001a; Bailey 2006; Lofland *et al.* 2006; Perecman and Curran 2006; Borneman and Hammoudi 2009), the questions asked, epistemological perspectives taken, and methods employed in political science may differ from those of these other social science disciplines.

On the other hand, political scientists also find the methodological literature in their own discipline wanting. As noted in Chapter 1, the relatively small subset of this literature that treats data collection, rather than analysis, tends to focus on using one single research method without addressing strategies to prepare for fieldwork as a whole. And even the vital work addressing research design tends to disregard its field dimensions. The existing methodological literature in the discipline of political science, in other words, leaves out important issues involved in designing and preparing to conduct *field* research. Topics such as how the availability of funding and other "real-life" circumstances shape how long scholars can stay in the field and thus the selection of cases, what it means – practically – to execute one's research design in the field, and what kinds of pressures different field contexts put on data collection and project design more generally are not discussed. Consequently, there is often a big gap between political scientists' research design document (the dissertation prospectus, grant proposal, etc.) and what they actually *do*, operationally, in the field.

This chapter aims to fill these gaps. It offers strategies and concrete steps researchers can take to design and prepare for field research. The chapter makes several overarching points. To begin with, designing research and designing *field* research (i.e., developing a practical plan for implementing one's research design) are linked yet distinct processes, equally important for successful empirical research. Also, in order to effectively design a project

---

[2] In recognition of this gap in training, in 2013 an APSA working group on Survey Methods for Developing Countries was organized to facilitate discussion about the challenges of survey implementation in the field.

requiring field research, scholars need to know a good deal about the field context and to build that knowledge into the structure of the project. Given that imperative, we encourage political scientists to think of fieldwork as forming part of a long process that begins months before they leave their home institution: the more thorough scholars' pre-departure work, the more effective they are in the field. Yet, here and throughout the book, we encourage flexible discipline. We urge scholars to have a "Plan B" for many aspects of their project, and perhaps even multiple alternative plans for different types of contingencies. Every scholar encounters unanticipated obstacles, and considering alternative ways to carry out critical research tasks in advance will ease circumnavigation of the inevitable roadblocks.

The chapter proceeds as follows. The next section examines the links between the basic elements of research design and fieldwork design. We show how building knowledge about both the research topic and the potential field site(s) is necessary to design fieldwork effectively. The third section discusses the importance of clearly identifying what information needs to be collected in the field and developing an appropriate data-collection plan. The fourth section considers how to structure fieldwork overall, i.e., deciding how many trips to take, how long to stay in the field on each trip, and when in the research cycle to carry out field research. The fifth section highlights how the field context, as well as researchers' methodological backgrounds and personal preferences and situations, shape the design of fieldwork. With the basic parameters of fieldwork design established by this point in the chapter, the sixth section discusses in more depth the intellectual and logistical aspects of preparing for fieldwork.

The challenges outlined here, and in Chapters 4 and 10, may seem like easy ones to address, and the strategies we suggest may appear straightforward and obvious. Yet scholars conducting research in the field are often seeking to accomplish 100 things at once, struggling to manage their lives, those working with them, and the research project as a whole. As such, it can be difficult to remember all the tasks that need to be done. And when the inevitable dilemmas of fieldwork demand "on the spot" problem-solving, it can be challenging to develop good, justifiable strategies on the fly.[3] Moreover, solutions to the problems faced in the field are not always unequivocal or clear – and even small missteps and oversights when preparing for field research can have expensive, time-consuming, and stressful consequences.[4]

---

[3] Interview, LM-17, September 11, 2012.
[4] We thank Colin Elman for encouraging us to frame our approach in these terms.

As such, we have sought to be comprehensive in our examination of potential pitfalls and suggested solutions. While each field researcher will negotiate the challenges we discuss differently, we hope these chapters provide a starting point for thinking through some of the analytic quandaries and personal predicaments confronted when doing field research.

(Field) research design

Research design and *field* research design go hand-in-hand, continually interacting with, informing, and influencing each other. While we lay out the basic steps of research design and field research design in an ordered, linear sequence for the purpose of logical presentation, we maintain that both processes are fundamentally iterative and frequently jumbled together. As scholars think and learn more about their projects and the context in which they are carrying them out, they skip back and forth between research design and field research design, and among the different stages of each.

Building broad and deep knowledge of the context in which fieldwork will be conducted – coming to understand the relevant history, culture, and political situation of one's field sites – is a necessary prerequisite for effective research design. Knowledge of the field helps scholars to identify a relevant and appropriate research question, to learn how to think about key concepts and relationships among them, and to consider what cases might be used to investigate the question. As one political theorist who conducted archival research in Europe suggested, the value of "do[ing] your homework ahead of time" cannot be overestimated.[5] This remains true even when the field sites are right around the corner. A scholar of international relations who did archival research in the United States and elite interviews in Washington DC reinforced this point, saying, "The better prepared you are, the more you are going to get out of an interview"[6] – and, we would add, field research in general. While this knowledge-building begins in the early preparation stages, it continues throughout the life of the project, and perhaps even after the resulting thesis, book, and/or articles have been published.

How can this knowledge be built? Obviously scholars should delve deeply into existing research on the topic of interest, using electronic databases, archives, and contacts with other scholars to track down relevant books, articles, dissertations, theses, conference papers, substantive blog entries, etc.

[5] Interview, LM-4, August 27, 2012.   [6] Interview, LM-15, September 10, 2012.

Taking detailed notes from these sources (establishing background facts, identifying unanswered questions, hypotheses, empirical gaps, etc.) and developing an extensive bibliography can be very useful. If some of the research is based on concrete data sources or surveys, it might even be possible to call or email the author and request the sources, survey, or any related qualitative data collection or quantitative dataset.

Scholars should also read current and archived editions of local newspapers (which are often available online). As they do so, they might keep running lists, for example, of key people who continually appear in the news – a "who's who" for their field site or research area that can be annotated with relevant information. A senior comparativist described how she spent months in advance of dissertation fieldwork poring over newspaper articles, making a list of elites to help her develop effective interview questions later on.[7] Another option is to build a glossary of specialized terms that the scholar will need to recognize, understand, and produce fluently in conversation. Researchers might also create a timeline of important events to assist in keeping straight key dates,[8] and in particular maintain a running list of significant *current* events and issues. Interviews with elites sometimes begin with a "quiz" during which the respondent seeks to find out how much the researcher knows about what is going on in the field site. "Doing well" on the quiz (i.e., appearing informed) can set the tone for the rest of the interview (Leech 2002a).

All of the above efforts to accumulate knowledge about one's topic and field site(s) help scholars to take the first crucial step in research design: to identify a research question. The research design literature discusses in detail what makes a "good" research question (e.g., Booth, Colomb, and Williams 2003; Shapiro 2004, 2007; Schwartz-Shea and Yanow 2012, 24–43). The notion of unearthing a "puzzle" is often emphasized, in interpretive as well as positivist research; also stressed is the importance of one's question – and its potential answers – having recognizable larger implications, both empirical and theoretical (Grofman 2001; Geddes 2003).[9] As one senior scholar put it, good field research asks questions that have "both breadth and depth," which are well grounded in the context but also "go beyond one little village

---

[7] Interview, LM-8, August 30, 2012.

[8] Chapter 10 discusses this idea in more depth and mentions several types of software to build such timelines.

[9] On beginning with puzzles, surprises, or tensions in interpretive research, see Schwartz-Shea and Yanow (2012, 27).

in Senegal."[10] In short, one should choose compelling questions, the answers to which matter on the ground and in the academy – already a tall order.

Yet characteristics of the potential field context also impinge on this (and other) design decisions. The question needs to be one around which the scholar can build a research design that is realistic and executable in the field sites in which he is considering working. On the one hand, the data needed to answer the question must be available for gathering. For example, for a researcher wishing to illustrate variation in electoral participation across six cities in three Latin American countries in the early part of the twentieth century – hypothesizing a connection between these historical trends and regime stability later in the century – the historical electoral data to measure these trends must be accessible. On the other hand, it must be possible for the *individual scholar who will be conducting the field research* to collect the data. A scholar who is irredeemably uncomfortable in cities, for instance, might be fascinated by dramatic variations in the level and sophistication of community organizing across major urban centers in the United States – but poorly suited to carrying out the fieldwork required to explain them. In a case like this, the research question can be revised to maximize the individual researcher's personal preferences and strengths. This revision is not only legitimate, but essential for success.

Following the identification – and concrete and clear specification – of the research question, scholars begin to develop an intellectual plan for answering that question. This entails drawing on relevant literature to think through the problem, identifying explanatory factors (or independent variables) that might cause the outcome being studied (or variation in that outcome or dependent variable), and developing hypotheses (or perhaps even a theory) about how the causes lead to the outcome, considering what causal mechanisms might underlie those hypotheses, and thinking through what their observable implications might be. Of course, the researcher should also carefully consider potential rival explanations for the same set of outcomes. Likewise, she should begin to think about how she will evaluate her hypotheses once she is in the field – how will she operationalize her independent variables, assess causal mechanisms, and identify observable implications on the ground? A more interpretive researcher might prefer to avoid establishing fixed meanings of concepts and specifications of hypotheses prior to departure, in order to privilege meanings that emerge during field research itself through close interaction with people, communities, or

---

[10] Interview, LM-8, August 30, 2012.

documents under study. Scholars in this tradition would still prepare for field research by exploring bodies of theoretical work that will later be brought into dialogue with bottom-up findings from the field (Schwartz-Shea and Yanow 2012, 45–57).

The formulation of theoretical explanations critically informs the next important step in the research design: selecting cases to study (see Mahoney and Goertz 2004; Box-Steffensmeier, Brady, and Collier 2008; Mahoney 2010; Gerring 2012). Case selection, of course, happens at multiple levels. Scholars must decide on the appropriate cases at the macro level, for example selecting what world region(s), country/ies, branch(es) of government, broad policy area(s), or world event(s) to study. They must also take some meso-level decisions, for example, which sub-national regions or towns, time periods, sectors, political parties, or civil society groups to examine. And, inevitably, they will face a series of micro-level decisions such as which households, individuals, documents, or paragraphs within a document to select for data collection or analysis. As a rule of thumb, the lower the "level" of the decision, the less likely that researchers will have reliable access to fine-grained information about the population of cases in advance of departing for their field sites, and the more likely the decision will need to be deferred until they arrive in the field. Even for case-selection decisions that are postponed, scholars can begin to develop the strategy they will implement to choose cases, or at least start to think through the questions they will need to ask once they reach the field site: what will they need to measure, see, or do, in order to select cases that will offer inferential leverage on the question at hand?

To give an example, in researching informal institutions and citizenship in Africa, MacLean (2010) chose to study Ghana and Côte d'Ivoire (a macro-level decision) because they shared similar levels of economic development, comparable degrees of integration into the global economy, and had both recently managed democratization with the incumbent winning the first two rounds of multi-party elections. These were all explanatory variables of potential theoretical importance for the research question. MacLean then faced the meso-level question of which subregions within each of the countries to compare. She was able to make some of these meso-level decisions from afar but others required a preliminary field trip to confirm. Ultimately, MacLean chose subnational regions in each country that shared similar precolonial ethnic histories (and thus precolonial chieftancy institutions and customary land and inheritance systems), additional key variables for explaining different outcomes. Another meso-level choice, the selection of comparable village communities, was facilitated by discussions with regional and district-level government officials as well as in-person meetings with village chiefs during a predissertation field trip. None of the criteria used to make the choice – estimated population size, distance to a paved road, level of infrastructure,[11] and overall willingness to participate in a research study – was knowable in advance of the preliminary trip to the potential field sites. Finally, all micro-level decisions were made once MacLean and her research team arrived and conducted a census of housing units in order to draw a random sample.

Of course, things might not go as planned – the tentative case-selection strategy a scholar designs from afar may not work on the ground. As with many (field) research design decisions, and in line with the principle of flexible discipline, it is an excellent idea to have a well-developed "Plan B" that can be implemented if one's favored case-selection strategy cannot be used. The foundation for the "Plan B" is the above process of reflecting critically on the theoretical and logistical rationale for case selection at each level, and identifying which cases might be "next best" if studying one's favored cases turns out to be infeasible. This discussion again illustrates the dynamic and iterative nature of field research. While much research design occurs before leaving for the field, initial designs are often repeatedly adapted during fieldwork.

Once these main parameters of research design have been outlined, scholars can continue to develop their more detailed field research design within those bounds. Given the research question and the project being constructed to answer it, exactly what information needs to be collected, how, and when? And at what point or points in the research process should a scholar conduct fieldwork, which field sites should she visit, and how long should she stay in each? We offer suggestions for addressing these questions in the next two sections of the chapter.

Developing a data-collection plan

Designing field research entails identifying what information needs to be gathered in the field, and developing a coordinated set of strategies for

---

[11] Level of infrastructure was a criterion not only because of its theorized effect on the outcomes, but also considering its potential effect on the health and safety of the research team.

gathering it.[12] Scholars should carefully consider exactly what data need to be collected in order to measure central variables, evaluate key hypotheses (a scholar's own, and rivals), illuminate causal processes and mechanisms, and assess observable implications; what techniques will be used to collect those data; and where, how, and in what order they will be deployed. As one scholar advised, "You really need to think ahead of time about what evidence would confirm your hypothesis, and what would disconfirm it. It's very easy not to do the latter. What is really important is that work laying out the project at the beginning."[13] Making these choices entails thinking through whether quantitative, qualitative, interpretive, or some combination of methods will be used to *analyze* the data gathered and to generate claims and conclusions, as one's choices concerning analytic methods inform the form in which data must be collected. Even for researchers who do not think in terms of variables and hypotheses, it is a good idea to consider in advance what information they will collect and how they will collect it, and what they will need to see (or not see) on the ground in order to know they have figured out the answer to their question or arrived at their interpretation.

We advocate developing a data-collection plan, and offer two templates in Figure 3.1 and Table 3.1.[14] As the name suggests, a data-collection plan outlines the data a scholar needs to gather in order to understand and evaluate key concepts, measure variables, test hypotheses (or evaluate the importance of potential explanatory factors), answer the research question, and wrap a convincing, compelling account around that answer. By formulating a data-collection plan, the scholar moves from theorizing abstract concepts to structuring the quest for concrete bits of evidence in the field. A data-collection plan can be usefully thought of as the operational components of a dissertation prospectus, or proposal for grant funding, disaggregated and broken down into bite-sized pieces. One might make such a plan for each separate fieldwork foray or create one master data-collection plan for various closely timed field stays.

---

[12] See Chapter 1 for our definition of data. For us, data may take many different forms (e.g., words, numbers, images, etc.); see also Schwartz-Shea (2006, 92–93) and Weldes (2006, 178).

[13] Interview, LM-15, September 10, 2012.

[14] Our notion of a data-collection plan originated with the idea of a "to-get list," developed by the first trio of scholars to teach the APSA Short Course on "Strategies for Field Research in Comparative and International Politics" from 2001 to 2003: Evan Lieberman, Julia Lynch, and Marc Morjé Howard. See Lieberman, Howard, and Lynch (2004). Our conceptualization of a data-collection plan expands this initial idea by emphasizing the dynamic and iterative updating of the plan as well as its potential adaptation by scholars at various stages of research, employing different research designs, and having diverse epistemologies.

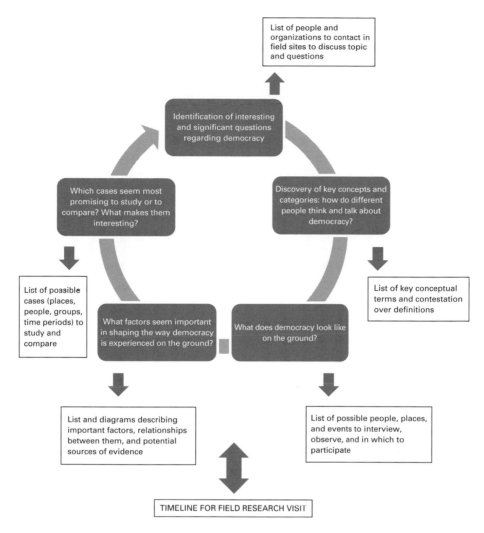

Figure 3.1   Example of an open-ended or exploratory data-collection plan

Table 3.1 displays a more structured and variable-oriented data-collection plan that a scholar with prior knowledge of or strong hunches about the data sources in a field context might adopt. This plan reflects a systematic approach to data collection focused on clarity, planning, and efficiency. Yet this plan embodies both discipline *and* flexibility. We recognize that because it is impossible (and inadvisable to seek) to completely plan fieldwork in advance, most scholars change many aspects of their initial data-collection plans as they conduct fieldwork. By advocating such a system, we in no way

Table 3.1 Example of a structured and variable-oriented data-collection plan

	Concept	RESEARCH DESIGN Sub-dimensions of concept	Operationalization (measures/ indicators)	What Data needed to evaluate/measure	FIELD RESEARCH DESIGN Where and how Location of data and data-collection techniques	When Data-collection sequencing during field stay	How long Time data collection will take
Outcome (DV)	Democracy	Participation	Voting participation (percentage of citizens that registered/voted)	Data on voter registration and participation rates over time	Request from National Electoral Commission	Before departure or upon arrival	2 weeks
				Expert opinion on voting patterns	Interviews with experts	Month 5–6	2 months
			Contacting of local officials	Citizens' contacting behavior	Interviews with citizens	Month 5–6	2 months
		Competition	Number of political parties	Electoral data over time	Request from National Electoral Commission	Before departure or upon arrival	2 months
			Opposition share of state assembly	Electoral/ government data	Request from government offices; download from government web sites	Month 2–3	1 week
			Number of alternations of chief minister	Secondary sources	Access in library	Before departure	1 week

Explanatory factor	Concept	Indicator	Data source	Method of collection	Timing	Duration
Explanatory factor #1 (IV) Education	Literacy	Adults' and children's ability to read	World Bank Development Indicators (adult literacy / primary school enrollment rates over time)	Download from World Bank web site	Before departure	1 day
			Government data	Request from Ministry of Education	Month 1	1 week
	Civic literacy	Knowledge of civic institutions	Citizens' views	Interviews with citizens	Month 3–4	2 months
Explanatory factor #2 (IV) Variation in economic development at regional level	Size of regional economy	GDP	National and state government data	Request from Ministries of Finance	Month 4–5	Several weeks
	Poverty at household level	Number of people living below the poverty line	National and state government data	Request from Ministries of Economy	Month 4–5	Several weeks
Explanatory factor #3 (IV) Class structure	Size of the middle class	Number of people in the 3rd/4th quintile of income	World Bank Development Indicators	Download from World Bank web site	Before departure	2 months
		Number of people who own a television	Expert opinion	Interviews with local economists and sociologists	Month 4–5	3 months

seek to discourage the iteration that is fundamental to good fieldwork, or to deny or diminish the importance of staying open to the creative, framework-changing ideas that fieldwork can generate. Structure and creativity are not necessarily at odds, but rather can easily feed and inform each other synergistically. Indeed, one of the reasons scholars do fieldwork is because it can wholly reshape the way that they think. Expressing a common theme from the interviews for this book, one scholar explained that field research provides "an opportunity to hear something that you hadn't thought about or known about previously."[15] In short, our motivation for offering this data-collection plan is our belief that many scholars will be better able to hit the ground running, and will engage more effectively in and better capitalize on iteration, with an initial version of such a plan in hand.

Interpretive scholars contemplate a much less linear process of research, in which concepts and key pieces of evidence for meaning-making emerge from the context and from respondents' understanding thereof, rather than being imposed a priori (Schwartz-Shea and Yanow 2012). For interpretive scholars, the notion that the fieldwork process could be mapped out in such detail months in advance might seem preposterous and counterproductive. Such scholars might be more comfortable with a relatively open-ended approach, such as the cycle outlined in Figure 3.1. Using this template still involves planning and list-making, but is less constraining and structured, and quite naturally and clearly iterative. Scholars who are at an exploratory stage of their projects might likewise resist a highly specified data-collection plan. Yet even these researchers, we believe, can benefit from thinking through their hunches, or contemplating where they might look for ideas and evidence to emerge.

Of course, these two types of plans are not irreconcilably different. In order to generate each, scholars must think carefully about what precisely they intend to examine, how to conceptualize it (and what sub-dimensions their conceptualization might entail),[16] and how to evaluate it. Moreover, both template plans reflect a movement from broad and abstract reflection to more concrete tasks. Both also allow for iterative updating as scholars gain more knowledge in the field. Moreover, in neither case is the data-collection plan the last word in mapping out fieldwork. Scholars' data-collection plans inevitably spawn associated "to do" lists that include the precise tasks they will need to accomplish in order to fill out their plan and gain the additional information they need to answer their questions. Such lists might include

---

[15] Interview, LM-15, September 10, 2012.   [16] See Goertz (2006) on subdimensions of concepts.

items like "contact professors at the local university," "hire three research assistants," "identify interview respondents in Taipei from various walks of life," "get bids from several survey firms," or "check the data archive at Academia Sinica for relevant existing studies." Developing these accompanying lists can strengthen and bolster one's data-collection plan, no matter what type it is.

In short, regardless of how political scientists position themselves in terms of our discipline's methodological and epistemological debates, we contend that thinking through the range of information they seek to obtain in the field and making a plan for gathering it is an essential step in pre-field preparation. We hope field researchers will amend, reimagine, twist, and augment the data-collection plan templates we offer to accommodate their way of approaching fieldwork, the nature of their questions, the stage of their project, and their epistemological assumptions.[17] These customizations might lead their "output" to look very different from the two examples we discuss next.

Example data-collection plans for a project on democracy

Consider how two scholars might employ different data-collection plans to approach the same broad topic – the tremendous variation in the quality of democracy across states in India. The open-ended data-collection plan in Figure 3.1 reflects more uncertainty about the project, perhaps due to a lack of available preexisting data or published literature, or because of an epistemological commitment to remaining flexible throughout the process of research design. As a consequence, the researcher begins with the broad topic of democracy and then works to identify a puzzle and accompanying research question. Indeed, the formulation or sharpening of a research question may be the primary objective of an exploratory field trip. The circular shape of the sample data-collection plan illustrates how the scholar cycles repeatedly through the exploration of potential concepts, outcomes, explanations, and cases in order to refine the study question and theoretical framework. This scholar will not arrive in the field in search of the data to

---

[17] Modifications to our templates might be minor or quite major. A field experimentalist, for instance, might further tailor the more structured data-collection plan to describe the creation of the experimental treatment as well as the nature of randomization among the population. Other scholars might envision developing something completely different – a mental map, causal diagram, or a more curvilinear or overlapping Venn diagram with different goals and tasks identified in the different circles or rings. See www.psfieldresearch.org for additional types of data-collection plans.

measure democracy according to several predetermined indicators; instead, he goes to the field to discover how the very notion of democracy is discussed and understood by different groups.

The planning for this more open-ended or exploratory field project centers on thinking through the potential range of related concepts and explanatory factors in order to develop preliminary lists of contact people, organizations, places, or political events to investigate in India. Thus, each of the more abstract primary research design tasks (featured in the shaded bubbles on the primary circuit) generates several concrete lists of candidate questions, outcomes, and cases (featured in the rectangular spin-off boxes) to be fleshed out and evaluated continually as the open-ended investigation progresses. Throughout the field stay, the scholar remains conscious of the amount of time remaining for fieldwork in order to prioritize the sequencing and duration of various tasks.

In contrast to the exploratory approach detailed above, the more structured and variable-oriented data-collection plan in Table 3.1 assumes that the scholar has tentatively settled on a research question and arrived at some hypotheses to be tested. This type of plan might include seven parameters. The information in the three left-hand columns emerges from the scholar's research design. A scholar begins with the most general concepts: the outcome to be explained (or the dependent variable [DV]) and the key explanatory factors (or the potential independent variables [IVs]).[18] Moving across the columns of the table, the researcher considers sub-dimensions of these concepts, and next identifies specific measures or indicators for each. In this example, democracy is conceptualized as having two subdimensions, participation and competition. Participation could be operationalized as the percentage of adult citizens that have registered to vote, or that actually showed up at polling stations and cast a ballot in the most recent round of state elections. Or the researcher might investigate non-electoral types of participation, such as the frequency with which citizens contact local officials to express demands or resolve problems. Competition could also be operationalized with multiple indicators or measures, including, for example, the number of political parties, the opposition share of the state assembly, or the number of times a new chief minister has come to power. When these conceptual subdimensions have multiple possible measures, the

---

[18] If a project explores more than one outcome, or includes multiple links of a causal chain, it might be advisable to create several separate data-collection plans.

task is to prioritize the indicators that are most appropriate and most feasible. The alternative indicators then become part of "Plan B."

The scholar's attendant field research design occupies Columns 4 through 7. As noted above, the first task is to identify the data that need to be collected in the field in order to evaluate or measure the project's main outcomes and potential explanatory factors. What pieces of evidence might the scholar need in order to assert that the explanatory factors to which he points caused the variation he seeks to explain? As we discuss in more detail in Chapter 4, prioritization is important: which data are absolutely necessary, and which are helpful but perhaps less critical? In what form should the scholar collect the needed data? The answers to these questions help researchers to identify the locations of the appropriate data and what data-collection technique(s) to employ to gather or generate them.[19] Finally, scholars should think about when during the field stay it would be best to collect different pieces of data, and attempt to estimate approximately how long each data-collection task might take.[20]

To continue with the example, data on registration and voting will no doubt be important for measuring participation in India. Given that triangulation among multiple data sources is a principle underlying good field research, the researcher might also wish to elicit expert opinion concerning patterns in voter registration and turnout. The data-collection strategies implied, then, are accessing electoral data from state electoral commissions and conducting expert interviews with, e.g., polling station organizers, party observers, external election monitors, and so on. Concerning sequencing, the gathering and evaluating of official electoral data should happen relatively early during fieldwork, as understanding how the outcome of interest varies informs the development of possible explanations (and perhaps case selection). Collecting (and interpreting) these data could take a couple of weeks, depending upon how centralized and publicly available they are.

The scholar may have several hypotheses for why certain regions of India are marked by a higher quality of democracy – relating to education, economic development, and class structure. Each of these concepts has

---

[19] The advantages and disadvantages of the main data-collection techniques, and what factors scholars should consider when determining whether or not to use them, are discussed in Chapters 5 through 9.

[20] In estimating time, researchers should keep in mind the likelihood of not working at 100 percent productivity during the entire fieldwork period due to illness or other unplanned contingency, as well as the utility of building in time for analysis and writing, as discussed in Chapters 4 and 10.

subdimensions and could be measured in several ways. For instance, concerning education, the researcher might decide to gather data on both literacy and civic literacy, collecting information from the World Bank, the Indian government, and citizens themselves. The scholar also needs to think through what evidence he will need to show that one (or both) of those factors *actually caused* variation in levels of political participation; while collecting data on causal mechanisms is not explicitly included in this plan, it could easily be added. Finally, the researcher needs to consider what other information he will need to tell his tale, and to evaluate how compelling one hypothesis is compared to alternative explanations. These data are likewise not included in the current plan, but they – and the sequencing and timing of collecting them – also need to be considered. These questions and issues are all important ones for scholars to consider long before they enter the field, and to continue to contemplate once they are there.

The advantages of a data-collection plan

Creating a data-collection plan well in advance of travel to the field has a number of benefits. First, sometimes a subset of the data identified as particularly important can be gathered before leaving one's home institution. Alternatively, it may be possible to evaluate the suitability and accessibility of potential data sources prior to departure. For instance, the scholar carrying out the example project above should be able to find out whether Indian electoral data are available online for the districts and time periods included in the study. Creating a data-collection plan also encourages scholars to consider alternate ways of designing certain aspects of their research and field research – i.e., to develop some "Plan B's" – with regard to case selection, indicators for key concepts, sources, and data-collection methods. Thinking through some alternatives will help them to modify their research design or field research design, as they will almost inevitably have to do as they learn more about the context in which they are conducting research – because new cases emerge as more important or feasible, because needed sources are unavailable or incomplete, or for many other reasons. In short, systematically considering the range of data sources and then collecting multiple types of data for any particular analytic purpose can only strengthen one's analysis.

Creating a data-collection plan pushes scholars to move from general ideas and concepts to specific data targets. Moreover, entering the field with a well-developed plan helps scholars to clarify research tasks and manage objectives. It also helps them to assess how the information they are gathering relates to their inquiry, and whether they are collecting sufficient data for each aspect of the project; in other words, the plan helps scholars to keep data collection and the details of fieldwork linked to the larger project. One of the biggest challenges researchers carrying out fieldwork face is seeing both the forest *and* the trees, and the data-collection plan helps them to do just that. In sum, we believe that the more complete a scholar's data-collection plan – the more clearly he thinks about the timing and sequencing of research tasks, and the more data-related questions he asks and answers prior to leaving for fieldwork – the better prepared he will be to begin to collect data in the field.

Structuring field research

Designing field research also requires scholars to make decisions about when they will conduct fieldwork and how they will structure their time in the field. We consider two key questions: how many fieldwork trips to take and how long to stay in the field on each trip (and if visiting multiple field sites, how long to stay in each).

We distinguish three types of fieldwork trips as seen in Table 3.2: short trips, medium-length trips, and long-haul stays. The key distinguishing features are the overall profile of the trip, its degree of structure, the length of time spent in the field, and the number of field sites visited. Short trips are generally either exploratory or targeted but not both, and are typically either high breadth (and low depth) or high depth (and low breadth). We consider short trips to be those of fewer than 30 days. While the majority of short trips include only one location, our data suggest that perhaps a third to nearly one half of short field visits include more than one location, or perhaps multiple sites that are found in close proximity to one another. Medium-length trips may be exploratory, targeted, or some combination of the two, and allow a moderate level of breadth and depth of data collection. These trips generally run from 1 to 5 months and may involve one or more field sites. Long-haul trips may also be exploratory, targeted, or some combination of the two, and allow the highest levels of breadth and depth of data collection. Such trips are generally of 6 months' duration or longer, and may involve one or more field sites. Of course, there are a range of possibilities between these ideal types.

A scholar's research question and research design heavily influence the number and length of their fieldwork trips. The point or points in the

Table 3.2 Overview of three types of fieldwork stays

Type	Overall profile	Structure	Length of time in field	Number of field sites visited	Analytic tasks	Advantages	Disadvantages
Short	Exploratory	High breadth; low depth	Up to 30 days	Usually one or two	Identify research topic and question Acquire necessary language skills Select cases Conceptualize key variables Generate hypotheses	Forced efficiency Analytic reflection through moving in and out of field site Easier assessment of feasibility of and institutional support for subsequent fieldwork Shortest absence from home	Potential for greater logistical costs Scheduling difficulties Highest chance of missing data Inadequate time to observe and build knowledge of context Highest level of time-imposed stress
	Targeted	Low breadth; high depth			Refine research question Select cases Generate hypotheses Address gaps in data collection	Forced efficiency Analytic reflection through moving in and out of field site Quick identification of variation Shortest absence from home	
Medium-length	Exploratory, targeted or a combination	Moderate breadth; moderate depth	1 to 5 months	One or more	Refine research question Select cases Conceptualize key variables Collect data Develop and test hypotheses	Moderate opportunity to reduce logistical costs Interactions with research subjects can be rescheduled while retaining perception of urgency	Moderate chance of missing data Moderate absence from home Moderate level of time-imposed stress

				Understand causal processes	More in-depth data collection Opportunity to gain moderate knowledge of context	
Long-haul	Exploratory, targeted or a combination	High breadth; high depth	6 months or more	One or more	Refine research question Select cases Conceptualize key variables Collect data Develop and test hypotheses Understand causal processes	Highest opportunity to reduce logistical costs Most opportunities to build extensive networks Most in-depth data collection Opportunity to gain deeper knowledge of context Lowest level of time-imposed stress	Lack of urgency may result in inefficiency by researcher or respondents Prolonged absence from home Potential for data overload Less opportunity for critical reflection away from field site

research cycle at which field research occurs also affects the types of trips, however. In general terms, fieldwork tends to be more structured the later it occurs in the life of a particular project, as the scholar develops more precise ideas about what information she needs. Researchers may take multiple types of trips in the course of a given project. For example, a researcher might take a short exploratory trip early on in a new project, a long-haul trip later, and then a final short targeted trip to obtain a few last pieces of data.

The goals scholars pursue on these different types of trips vary, and thus the data-collection plans they take with them will evolve in length, detail, and specificity. For instance, scholars frequently take a short exploratory trip (in some cases, a pre-dissertation probe) as they develop a study. Among domestic field research projects reported in the FRPS faculty survey, 33 percent included a preliminary, exploratory trip; for international projects, the percentage was 47. Such trips, which often occur during university breaks, serve many purposes: they can help scholars to identify, narrow, or further develop a research topic; to generate more precise research questions; to acquire or improve language skills; to obtain formal research clearance and affiliation; or to assess the feasibility of different sorts of projects, the availability of data, and general field conditions. Put differently, they help scholars to avoid research and fieldwork design mistakes that can result from making decisions purely on the basis of information available from their home institution. Modest amounts of internal or even external funding can often be obtained for preliminary field research, and scholars who have the opportunity to take such trips should seriously consider doing so. As one of our interviewees explained:

None of us knows anything before we go into the field ... We don't know what the relevant questions are; we don't have enough nuance to design a study well. Also, we have no experience doing fieldwork ... We need to spend time learning, and the only way to learn how to do fieldwork is to do it.[21]

Alternatively, a scholar might take a series of short, targeted trips as she carries out research. Or she might take a single short, narrowly focused follow-up trip after the bulk of her research has been completed – perhaps even once she has begun to write – to obtain a few pieces of missing information, explore a concept or sub-question that emerged during the analysis

---

[21] This faculty member even advises graduate students that, if they have to choose between failing their comprehensive exams and doing an exploratory trip, they should fail their exams. Interview, DK-15, August 21, 2012.

and write-up, or follow-up on a dynamic that was just beginning to unfold during a previous visit to the field site. Scholars might also take one or more short targeted trips later in the research cycle to add a case study or shadow case (i.e., an abbreviated case study in which only certain key elements are highlighted for comparative purposes) to a more fully developed quantitative or comparative historical analysis.

There are advantages and disadvantages to taking short trips. One benefit is efficiency: a short time-frame imposes discipline on the researcher, forcing him to focus on gathering the most important information without delay. Taking such brief trips also compels researchers to break out of "data-collection mode," take stock of and analyze the information being collected, and consider what data are still needed to answer their questions. As one scholar noted, "You can go and do some of the fieldwork but then you can stop and reflect, do more legwork, and talk to someone else to reflect on what you've done. It's so intense when you are out there and out of your element and trying to get as much as you can with the time you have."[22] Finally, shorter trips to different field contexts can help – and may compel – researchers to identify relevant comparisons and contrasts more quickly.

Yet short trips also have down-sides.[23] Settling into a new context, even if one plans only the briefest of stays, can be time-consuming. A series of abbreviated visits can also be more costly than one long one: staying in hotels is typically more expensive than renting an apartment, and airfare to visit several research locations can also be expensive (especially if one is traveling with an ever-growing mountain of data). Short trips can also complicate data collection. It can take a long time to get the necessary permissions to visit archives and libraries, and to access other data sources. Short trips can also generate scheduling difficulties. For instance, the individuals a researcher wishes to interview may not be around or available during the period she is in their city or country. Moreover, respondents may be reluctant to invest time in a researcher's project if, by their estimation, the scholar is investing little time learning about their context. More broadly, short trips may not afford researchers enough time to collect the data they need to answer their questions or to understand complicated political phenomena. And short trips offer little time to adjust if (when) things do not go according to plan.

---

[22] Interview, LM-14, September 7, 2012.
[23] Some of these disadvantages may be mitigated when a scholar takes multiple short trips to a single field site.

Medium-length and long-haul trips entail different analytic tasks, and have different attendant advantages and disadvantages. Because the contrasts between these two types of trips are mainly differences of degree, we treat these two types of trips together. Some scholars confess that they feel pressure to take "at least" a medium-length trip, if not engage in long-haul fieldwork. These pressures may emanate from funding sources (some grants stipulate continuous residence in a field site for 9 months to 1 year) or from their advisors who had earlier done extended field stays.[24] These institutional and disciplinary norms may be changing, however, as funding for fieldwork fluctuates and more scholars have working partners and spouses.

Medium-length and long-haul trips have a number of features that recommend them. Such trips afford researchers a better opportunity to experience another setting or culture. Certainly more in-depth research and data gathering are possible during medium-length and long-haul trips; a greater variety of data-collection techniques can be employed, and more triangulation is possible. Further, long-haul trips in particular give researchers the ability to develop an extensive network of local contacts, which can greatly facilitate the employment of a range of data-collection techniques. Trips of longer than a month likewise offer researchers more time to identify additional interesting dynamics and ideas for future projects. Scholars who take such trips also experience less time-imposed stress.

Medium-length and long-haul trips also have their disadvantages, however. Such trips may involve being far from family and friends for a long time, leading some researchers (and their loved ones) to feel as if their personal lives have been placed "on hold." Further, the lack of pressing urgency during long-haul trips in particular can have a number of negative implications. Researchers who feel that they have ample time to carry out data-collection tasks can be more easily distracted and pulled into side projects or initiatives; it can be harder for them to keep their "eyes on the prize," that is, collecting the data they need in order to complete their projects. Additionally, this perceived lack of urgency may rub off on local colleagues and research assistants, and may also affect scholars' interactions with interviewees, gatekeepers, and other people whose cooperation is essential. If the scholar needs permission to access a certain archive, for instance, bureaucrats may feel no urgency to grant it when he has indicated he will be

---

[24] Interview, LM-16, September 11, 2012.

in the country for a year. Likewise, if potential interview respondents know the researcher will be in their country or city for a long period, they can keep putting him off.[25] Finally, researchers who take long-haul trips amass a tremendous amount of data that must be sorted through and organized. This can take a lot of time and may become an excuse for postponing data analysis and writing, either in the field or once back at the home institution.

As we hope readers have gathered, there is no single correct way to structure field research. The optimal structure – i.e., the structure that maximizes the likelihood of collecting the data one needs and generating an answer to one's question – will differ from project to project. In the next section, we discuss several factors that affect researchers' choices in terms of the frequency, length, and sequencing of fieldwork trips.

Factors shaping fieldwork design

For any project, what data to collect and what data-collection techniques to utilize are driven in large part by the research question and the research design – i.e., the hypotheses that a scholar has developed from the relevant theoretical literature about the outcome or variation she wishes to explain and how she has conceptualized and plans to measure key variables (the elements in the three columns under the "Research design" heading in the sample data-collection plan in Table 3.1). To the extent that there is standard advice about fieldwork design, it is that choices about what data to collect, where and how to collect them, when to do so, and how much time to take (i.e., the elements in the four columns under the "Field research design" heading in the sample data-collection plan in Table 3.1), should be driven by similar concerns. We certainly consider this guidance to be sound. We have also noted that the point in the research cycle at which fieldwork occurs affects its contours. Yet contextualizing fieldwork leads us to see that several *additional* factors – the analytic methods a researcher anticipates employing, the particularities of the field sites she will visit, and her personal preferences – also influence how she designs and conducts her field research.

---

[25] A common strategy is simply to respond to inquiries about the length of time one plans to stay in a field site with vague references to "a few months" – estimates that can continually be extended.

Methods

In line with the idea that fieldwork is an iterative enterprise, the methods a researcher intends to use to analyze the data he collects can influence what kinds of data he gathers and in what form. As such, scholars should identify the methods they hope to employ (and achieve some competency in them) before fieldwork begins. For instance, if quantitative techniques are the best choice for answering a scholar's question, then a large number of observations will be needed (perhaps ideally in the form of a random sample), and the data gathered will need to be internally comparable and quantifiable; if the data will be collected from individuals, a large number of structured interviews, a survey, or an experiment is likely called for (see Chapters 6, 8, and 9). To offer another example, researchers hoping to construct an index variable from structured interviews need to be sure to ask questions corresponding to each component of the index in order not to lose data points.[26] Researchers hoping to use content analysis to analyze responses to interview questions may wish to tape and transcribe the interviews in order to capture the precise words respondents employed. Similarly, if the researcher intends to use content analysis on government documents, he should plan to photocopy, scan, or take digital pictures of them, as opposed to taking detailed notes.

The analytic methods a researcher will employ may also influence how he structures fieldwork. For instance, suppose a scholar plans to complement a large-N quantitative analysis with a series of case studies. If both facets of the project require original data, and if the results from the quantitative analysis will be used to select cases for the qualitative aspect of the project, he will likely need to carry out fieldwork in at least two phases. This has implications for when and how much funding he seeks to acquire, how he schedules the academic year in which the data gathering will take place, and more. These examples address just a few of the many possibilities. Our point is that scholars should seek to identify the methods they will use to analyze their data early in the research process, and consider the implications that using those methods has for data collection specifically, and the structure of fieldwork in general.

Field site(s)

The nature of a scholar's field site(s) affects field research in myriad ways – particularly with regard to what data he can collect and what

---

[26] Interview, BR-10, August 21, 2012.

techniques are best for collecting them. Because we discuss these issues in more detail in Chapters 5 through 9, we offer here just a few ideas. To begin with, logistics and infrastructure can often have a very meaningful impact on what is possible in the field. Will there be reliable electricity? What about dependable access to high-speed internet? Will photocopying data sources be simple and inexpensive, or problematic and costly? Arranging interviews may take longer in a field site where cell-phone coverage is poor.

Certain characteristics of a scholar's field sites may also influence how he structures research. For instance, is there anything about the locations a scholar wishes to study – their overall accessibility or distance from each other – that suggests visiting them during a single long trip, or taking multiple trips and having more than one home base? Might something about the intended field sites – cultural, political, or even weather-related cycles, for instance – recommend traveling sooner rather than later, or at a particular time of year? In some country contexts, for instance, roads may be impassable in certain areas during the rainy seasons of the year. To offer another example, a scholar studying cross-party coalition building in Congress will need to schedule field visits to Washington, DC when Congress is in session so that representatives are in the capital rather than visiting constituents.

Finally, attributes of the field site will also affect scholars' more specific choices about data-collection techniques. For instance, the ease with which a scholar can access relevant actors – be they peasants, cabinet members, party leaders, or community council members in an urban slum – might inform whether he chooses interviews as a primary data-collection technique. Similarly, the availability of polling data and accessibility of newspaper articles will influence how scholars are able to evaluate public opinion. Scholars can begin to investigate these data-availability questions prior to embarking on field research.

The answers to these types of questions – which amount to no more than the tip of the iceberg – have serious implications for one's data-collection plans and how one structures field research. Which field-site characteristics are most relevant and consequential will differ from project to project – and of course no scholar knows everything about his field sites prior to leaving his home institution. Nonetheless, learning as much as possible about multiple aspects of each field site prior to arriving, and considering the implications of those characteristics for fieldwork design, will smooth the research process.

Personal attributes

Finally, scholars' personal preferences, personal lives – and personalities – also play a role in how they design and conduct their fieldwork. Many political scientists whom we interviewed described how the structure of field research evolved over their career and lifecycle. Some were unable to replicate the singular and intensive focus that marked dissertation research, as multiple competing demands – such as those from collaborators, teaching, administrative service, marriage, children, personal health issues, and elder care – pulled on them and their subsequent research projects.[27] In response, these scholars relayed that they built later research projects so that they required less extended stays, entailed field sites closer to home, or involved collaborating with bigger research teams or delegating research tasks to research assistants. As Chapter 2 noted, our survey discovered that this tendency for later projects to involve less time in the field than first projects applied to international but not domestic research.

Operationally, as scholars design and structure field research, they should think carefully about how much time they can allocate to being in the field, and who might accompany them. With regard to time, what is the minimum amount of time they need to achieve basic goals comfortably, and what is the maximum amount of time they can spend in case of delays? They should also consider whether there any important events or dynamics in the foreseeable future (for instance, the desire for a family or the ticking of the tenure clock) that recommend a particular timing, length, or sequencing for fieldwork.

In terms of family, in the past, the field researcher was often the sole breadwinner for the household, so it was common for spouses and families to tag along for extended field research stays.[28] Today, given the greater prevalence of two-income families, a field researcher's spouse can find it difficult to arrange time off from work (if he or she cannot continue to do his or her job remotely while in the field). Scholars thus need to consider on which trips (if any) family members might accompany them. If a scholar is taking an extended trip and family members can travel, should they accompany the scholar during his or her whole trip or perhaps just during the

---

[27] In his presentation at the "Field research in Africa in the 21st century" roundtable at the 2013 APSA meeting (August 29), Dennis Galvan suggested that over the career of a political scientist, fieldwork varied along three dimensions: length of field stay, intensity of direct engagement, and nature of collaboration with local scholars.

[28] Interview, DK-15, July 18, 2012.

summer months?[29] Several scholars described the many benefits of bringing children to the field, including "contributing global citizens to the world."[30] Others, however, acknowledged the difficulties of finding appropriate child-care or schools, and the emotional hardships involved, especially for older kids when uprooted from one of their parents, their friends, or routines.[31] The amount of funding scholars have secured can also influence whether dependents may come along, and for how long.

With regard to data collection, what emotional, psychological, and ethical challenges and issues are foreseeable? As we noted before, rather than developing a field research design based on a perceived "ideal type," scholars should design fieldwork that they *personally* can conduct effectively. For scholars who thrive on human interaction, designing fieldwork that requires spending months on end alone in an archive may not be the best choice. Likewise, researchers who have rarely or never "roughed it" (or have not enjoyed doing so) should think twice about carrying out research in a remote village in rural Cameroon. We do not mean to suggest, of course, that fieldwork should not be challenging, and that scholars should not push themselves to do things they are mildly uncomfortable doing. This is almost inevitable. For instance, it is the rare scholar who looks forward, without any trace of anxiety, to picking up the phone to request the first few interviews. Nonetheless, we recommend scholars take their personal situation, limitations, and preferences into account – as one set of factors among many – when designing field research.

Additional preparation for fieldwork

In addition to – and as a complement to – developing their research design and field research design, scholars can and should carry out an extensive series of tasks in preparation for field research. We discuss here a crucial subset of those tasks: applying for funding, soliciting IRB approval (when necessary), developing networks, identifying a research affiliation, preparing documents, and making logistical arrangements.[32]

---

[29] Some of these dilemmas will affect male and female scholars differently. Tripp (2002) examines the challenges women face in doing international field research.

[30] Interview, LM-12, September 6, 2012.

[31] Interviews, LM-2, April 14, 2012; LM-6, August 30, 2012; LM-9, August 30, 2012; LM-12, September 6, 2012.

[32] Barrett and Cason (2010) offers a more detailed discussion of logistical preparations. See also the FRPS website (www.psfieldresearch.org) for further suggestions on logistical preparation.

Applying for funding

Funding is obviously critical to doing field research. And, yet, as noted in Chapter 2, our survey data suggest that inflation-adjusted funding levels – at least for dissertation field research in political science – may have declined somewhat in recent years. We recommend that all scholars begin to apply for funding well over a year before they wish to access it, and that they tap a broad range of funding sources. Outlining a fundraising strategy and identifying key potential funders, in other words, are critical aspects of the field research design process.

There are many sources of information about available grants including email lists, other scholars who study similar topics, and the Graduate Division or Sponsored Programs Office of one's home institution.[33] As such information sources reveal, available grants go well beyond the best-known ones such as the Fulbright grants through the Institute for International Education, the Fulbright-Hays Doctoral Dissertation Research Abroad Grants, the Social Science Research Council's grants, and the National Science Foundation Dissertation Improvement grant. Scholars should seek to identify additional sources – perhaps specific to their substantive interests or geographic area of research. All scholars, particularly those who are not citizens of the country in which they are studying or working, should check grant eligibility criteria closely. They should also ask colleagues about the informal politics associated with different awards. For example, long-standing and often heated discussions continue on many campuses and within professional associations concerning the tradeoffs associated with accepting grant money from the United States Department of Defense or other intelligence and security agencies. Additionally, faculty and graduate students must carefully consider the potential conflicts of interest posed by corporate sponsorship or donor funding of their research.[34] While consultancies sometimes provide generous resources for field research, researchers may find themselves constrained in terms of project design and implementation, data ownership, and voicing interpretations of the results that may be critical of the sponsor organization (Wight 2008; Kayuni and Mohmed 2013).

Scholars should consider applying for more funding than they anticipate they will need. There is no shame in declining grants (and listing grants that were declined on one's CV may even enhance one's professional profile).

---

[33] Often the researcher's home institution holds regular workshops to provide support in the application process.

[34] At most institutions, faculty members are required to sign annual conflict-of-interest disclosure forms.

Moreover, fieldwork is often more expensive than scholars anticipate. Whether or not their funding applications require a budget, scholars should create a detailed accounting of projected fieldwork costs, asking other researchers who have recently worked in the context they hope to visit for guidelines on potential costs.[35] Finally, if researchers are successful with more than one grant, there are often ways that those grants can be combined, even if funders initially suggest that this is impossible.

While applying for funding can be a harrowing process, doing so has potential intellectual as well as pecuniary benefits. Writing effective, compelling funding proposals requires researchers to clearly formulate their core research question, cogently argue why it is important, and persuasively explain how they will answer it, demonstrating the feasibility of conducting the proposed research. Carrying out each of these tasks can help a project to crystallize in the researcher's mind.[36] Since grants are highly competitive, scholars must clearly demonstrate how the proposed study fulfills the funder's objectives (as outlined in the call for applications, and other materials concerning the funder). We recommend that scholars ask colleagues who have successfully applied for the grants they are targeting to share their application experience (and, ideally, their winning proposal). Of course, scholars should make time to solicit advice and feedback from colleagues as they revise and polish their proposals. Grant writing is not something that is accomplished overnight.

Obtaining IRB approvals

While Chapter 4 considers field research ethics in more detail, here we examine one critical aspect of that broader topic, as it intersects with preparing for field research: obtaining the relevant permissions from the Institutional Review Board (IRB) at one's home institution, and possibly elsewhere.[37] IRB approval is required for all US-based scholars conducting research with human subjects. Accordingly, as they design their field research, scholars should investigate whether their project needs to be

---

[35] Budget examples are available at www.psfieldresearch.org.

[36] See the SSRC pamphlet on the art of writing winning grant proposals (Przeworski and Salomon 1988, rev. 1995).

[37] Some organizations and communities, and governments well beyond the United States, have their own independent IRB or research permit approval processes. To give two examples, many American bureaucratic agencies have separate IRBs, and the government of Rwanda has an extensive research permit application process.

reviewed. Many scholars we interviewed were under the impression that IRB processes have become more stringent over time, but they vary dramatically across institutions.[38]

The process of passing one's project through the home institution's IRB can take an extended period of time and may entail more than one application attempt. Moreover, many universities require some type of ethics training, often an online tutorial and exam.[39] Starting as early as possible, then, is advisable. Scholars who will be dealing mainly with elites may be granted an "exemption," meaning their project is excluded from further IRB oversight (although they nonetheless must follow all IRB guidelines and carry out research as they indicated on the forms submitted to the IRB). Human-subjects guidelines were developed in connection with psychological and clinical trials, so the paradigm is one of avoiding harm or discomfort to the subjects (Yanow and Schwartz-Shea 2008; Brooks 2013). Consequently, scholars working with "vulnerable" populations – that is, individuals whose reputations could be compromised, or who could be placed in danger if the researcher's work is made public – may not be able to obtain an exemption. Those scholars may still qualify for an "expedited" review but will often need to file a renewal application annually until they have completed collecting and analyzing data.[40]

Scholars should carefully consider the kind of informed consent they will want to elicit when they interact with research subjects. In contexts (or under conditions) where respondents may balk at having to sign a form indicating that they were apprised of the risks and rewards of interacting with a researcher, obtaining oral consent may be a more feasible option. Scholars might consider giving study participants a one-page handout with project and contact information even if they are only soliciting oral consent, as one scholar who worked with rural populations in refugee areas did.[41] For some highly sensitive topics and contexts, researchers may consider conducting covert or unobtrusive research (Pachirat 2009). Being premised on the research subjects not being informed at all about a study, covert research, without a doubt, raises a host of tough ethical questions and dilemmas. We contend that researchers should reflect carefully and seek to identify

---

[38] Interviews, LM-8, August 30, 2012; LM-12, September 6, 2012; LM-15, September 10, 2012.

[39] Typically all members of the research team must undergo this required training, even research assistants based in the field sites.

[40] Expedited review is usually faster because it is done by the IRB chairperson or one IRB reviewer rather than convening the full Institutional Review Board.

[41] Interview, LM-16, September 11, 2012.

the degree of disclosure about their research objectives that is simultaneously ethical and productive. For this and all other human subjects-related matters, scholars should work closely with their institution's Review Board, as well as trusted colleagues who have knowledge about the specific field sites they plan to visit, beginning as far in advance of their departure date as possible.

Developing networks and obtaining research affiliation

Networking with scholars in related research communities in the United States and (where relevant) in the sites where one anticipates conducting research can help field researchers to build their knowledge of the research topic and cases, and can be professionally rewarding.[42] Researchers might request feedback on their project from such individuals; ask them to identify additional local contacts;[43] or arrange to meet with them at political science, area studies, or thematic conferences. One researcher described how meeting in Chicago with members of the diaspora of the community he would ultimately visit helped him establish critical contacts in the field.[44] Another recounted how her personal activism in the anti-apartheid movement on her university campus in the United States helped her meet important union leaders in Southern Africa.[45] Scholars might also consider getting on email lists regarding their topic or area, which can help to reveal who the "players" in the field are. Another option is to contact NGOs and think-tanks (based in the United States and abroad) where people have done relevant work on the scholar's topic. It may even be possible to set up some introductory interviews via email before traveling to one's field site; in seeking to do so, scholars might attach a one-page summary of their project (discussed later) to help potential respondents understand the nature of the study and why the researcher wishes to speak with them. In short, an enormous amount of networking can be done, and groundwork laid, before scholars leave their home institution.

Scholars should also consider whether having a research affiliation in their field sites might be useful.[46] Having an affiliation can facilitate entrée into the local academic community, and may make a favorable impression on interview subjects. Further, including a letter from the host institution

---

[42] Interviews, LM-4, August 27, 2012; LM-12, September 6, 2012.

[43] Two strategies for identifying relevant local scholars are to search through the web sites of local universities, and identify local journalists with bylines on the topic of interest.

[44] Interview, DK-12, August 8, 2012.   [45] Interview, LM-12, September 6, 2012.

[46] The politics of affiliation are discussed in greater detail in Chapter 4.

with grant applications can be very useful (and is required in some locales, and for some grants).[47] Having a connection with someone at the target institution – perhaps through another scholar who recently conducted fieldwork in one's field site – can make the affiliation easier to obtain. Yet a number of issues need to be kept in mind when choosing a research affiliation. First, the local reputation of the institution matters: how will this institutional affiliation be seen by potential interview respondents, or by those who will decide whether access to archives and other data sources will be offered or denied? Second, if the affiliation costs money, what services or benefits are provided for that fee? Often institutions have a library, computers, databases, or office or meeting space available only to affiliated associates. Scholars should also inquire and agree upon in advance what the institution expects of its affiliates. Some institutions have few requirements, whereas others demand teaching or other time-consuming forms of service that may obstruct progress with fieldwork.

Preparing materials for use in the field

Another important pre-departure task is to draft some of the materials that will be used in the field. First, researchers can devise different ways to present themselves and their research for varying audiences. They may write out several versions of a one-page description of the project (and themselves) to attach to emails requesting interviews or other assistance with data collection. Revealing no analytic hunches and keeping the narrative vague, one goal of these summaries is to illustrate the importance of the project and highlight the researcher's qualifications for carrying it out. If interviewing will be an important data-collection technique, or if the project entails a survey, another helpful idea is to begin to draft the interview protocol or questionnaire, or at least develop the list of topics that will likely be addressed in those interactions (further discussed in Chapters 6 and 8). Draft protocols and questionnaires may be necessary for one's IRB application, and writing them helps scholars to check that their research design and fieldwork design can be translated into action. Finally, scholars might consider drafting letters or emails that they will send to request interviews, access to archives, and so on. Carrying out each of these tasks helps the researcher to clarify her

---

[47] Notably, in some countries, the travel visa is contingent on having a local research affiliation.

thinking about the project, and to arrive at the most positive and productive way to introduce it to others.[48]

Particularly for younger scholars, letters of introduction from a relevant senior scholar can help to open doors in the field. For graduate students, a "gold seal" letter from their department chair indicating that they are in good standing at their university can sometimes facilitate entrée.[49] All scholars might consider asking people who have done fieldwork in the locations where they plan to conduct research, and who have interacted with the types of people with whom they wish to interact, what (if any) documentation appeared to be helpful as they sought to gain access to archives, respondents, and other desired data sources. Several of the scholars interviewed for this book mentioned the importance of having printed business cards to give out.

Making logistical arrangements

Finally, many logistical issues need to be dealt with prior to leaving for the field. To mention just a few, scholars traveling overseas will need to figure out what visa they need and where to obtain it. The visa application process can be lengthy, so researchers should get started well in advance of their planned departure. Further, they should consider what other official documents will need to be taken to the field and which are best left at home (with, perhaps, a copy taken to the field).[50]

Scholars also need to think in advance about what health issues may arise in the field, and prepare to the degree that they can. First, they should find out what (if any) vaccinations are recommended and obtain them.[51] Researchers should also confirm that their health insurance covers them in another state, or overseas, and perhaps inquire about how payment for treatment is reimbursed. Another option (required by some grants) is medical evacuation insurance. It can also be advisable to look on the local

---

[48] Scholars writing in a non-native language may wish to find someone to help revise the initial drafts of these materials. More generally, researchers who will be operating in a non-native language in the field should objectively assess their language skills and potentially consider the options for improving fluency as well as building the relevant specialized vocabulary. Finding a language partner to practice speaking – and perhaps with whom to exchange emails – can be extremely helpful.

[49] These letters can sometimes require several weeks to be produced so planning ahead is essential.

[50] A non-exhaustive list of documents researchers might consider taking to the field would include: passport and copies, prescriptions, driver's license, student or faculty ID, International Student Identity Card, photocopy of social security card, documents required when visa was obtained, etc.

[51] The Centers for Disease Control web site has geographically specific information.

US embassy web site to see whether there is a list of recommended doctors, clinics, or hospitals. Finally, scholars might consider taking with them any medications they need or may need, particularly if their field site is remote.

Money issues should also be considered in advance. Scholars may be dealing in cash more often in the field, particularly in international research, than they are used to doing when they are at home. It is a good idea to think through how that cash will be accessed, and what sorts of fees will be charged (and how to avoid them, if possible). Depending on the length of stay, one option is to open a bank account in a local bank in the field site, although how easy it is to do so varies by location. It may also make sense to determine what credit cards can be used in the locations one will be studying. Often, bank and credit card companies should be notified of the dates and locations of travel and where to contact the scholar in order to verify activity and prevent fraud or theft. It is also worth investigating in advance whether one's credit card company charges a fee for foreign currency transactions.

Scholars should also decide what pieces of technology to take, and which they should purchase at the field site.[52] When preparing for overseas research, the question of whether to take one's regular mobile phone, to rent or buy a local phone, or to go without a phone bears consideration. A related imperative is identifying a workable computer back-up system. Most scholars who have done fieldwork have at least one tale of woe involving a dead hard drive or lost data. The fear of losing part or all of their data while in the field should motivate scholars to back-up regularly.[53] Beyond these ideas, we recommend scholars keep their own running list of items to take to the field.[54] Another good idea is to practice with all of the gadgets prior to leaving for the field to assure that they are all in functioning order, and the scholar is familiar with how to use them (while tech support is perhaps more readily accessible).

Beginning to think about one's living situation in the field is also advisable. Several scholars we interviewed described the uncertainty surrounding living

---

[52] A non-exhaustive list of items to consider would include: laptop, software/installation CDs for various applications, web camera, microphone/headset, USB drive; USB hub (so devices in excess of the number of USB ports one's computer has can be plugged in simultaneously); networking equipment; portable printer and toner; flatbed or handheld scanner, photocopier, fax, digital camera, voice recorder; cell phone; PDA; and cords and cables for all devices.

[53] Back-up systems can take many different forms, including web-based systems such as Dropbox and iCloud; external hard drives; and solid-state USB drives.

[54] For instance, a laptop lock, business/interview attire, electronic signature, university letterhead (actual and electronic), business cards, etc.

arrangements as frightening and stressful.[55] Talking with other scholars who have lived in one's potential field sites can help when considering housing options.[56] For instance, scholars might think through the tradeoffs of renting an apartment versus staying in a residence hotel,[57] and of renting an apartment sight-unseen versus obtaining temporary lodging for a few weeks upon arrival and personally viewing housing options. Sometimes local universities have rooms available for visitors, or offices to help identify housing options. Internet web sites for foreigners can offer some ideas, and local newspapers may also have listings (which may be searchable online). While comfort and cost are two important criteria when identifying and choosing among housing options, the choices scholars make can also have an impact on their intellectual progress, for instance, by making it more or less difficult to establish rapport with potential respondents. Such connections are discussed in more depth in the next chapter. In sum, a great deal of intellectual and logistical preparation can be carried out in advance of field research. While many of the above points may seem unmissable, it is very easy to forget the obvious in the hectic time leading up to field research. As such, there is no time like the present to begin.

Conclusion

There is significant interplay between research design and fieldwork design: the latter is essentially a practical plan for implementing the former. Yet fieldwork design is not simply a straightforward, mechanical derivative of research design. Many factors beyond social science theory and one's variables shape what data are sought, what techniques are used to collect them, and how fieldwork is structured more generally. The point in the research cycle at which scholars venture into the field, the analytic methods they anticipate employing, their personality, and myriad contextual dynamics – many of which are subject to rapid change – can affect how scholars design and conduct field research. As we will emphasize repeatedly throughout this book, researchers should try to think through a "Plan B" for crucial aspects of their project so they can remain nimble and flexible. In short,

---

[55] Interview, LM-16, September 11, 2012.

[56] Likewise, these people may know what documentation is needed to rent an apartment.

[57] Concerning shorter field trips, it bears noting that not all apartments can be rented month-to-month; a one-year lease may be more typical. Talking to others who have held month-to-month leases, or have done roommate swaps, can generate ideas of how to accommodate a shorter-term stay.

designing field research entails an extensive series of tradeoffs and choices, and *doing* field research often requires renegotiating those original choices and implementing next-best options. This does *not* mean scholars should simply throw in the towel and neglect planning in favor of dealing with contingencies only once they are encountered in the field. Carefully planning data collection and structuring fieldwork leaves one well-positioned for those inevitable renegotiations.

These thoughts, in addition to the lengthy list of preparations we have outlined, amount to a *lot* of "do's," "don'ts," and "why haven't you yet?'s." Our goal is obviously not to overwhelm scholars who are planning field research, or reify an ideal preparation process. To restate a point made earlier, just as there is no single correct type of fieldwork, there is no master, magical fieldwork design. Every project is different, and what is useful to one scholar may not be useful for another. Nonetheless, starting the preparation process early and engaging in critical reflection from the start will help all scholars to do better field research.

In closing, we offer some thoughts on identifying the moment at which to leave for the field. The longer the field trip, the higher the stakes, and the more likely the researcher will not feel ready to leave. In general, however, scholars are ready to go before they think they are. One simple criterion scholars can use to evaluate whether they are ready is if they know the first ten people or organizations to contact in the field site. As we have emphasized, there is a tremendous amount that scholars can do, and should do, in preparation for field research. Yet there is also a point of diminishing returns. Researchers who are anxious about leaving for field research might liken doing so to taking off a Band-Aid; once they have spent significant time readying themselves and their materials, there is little point in postponing the inevitable. Moreover, scholars should recall that fieldwork is often a rewarding experience. Whether traveling far or just down the street, for a year or for a week, fieldwork offers scholars the chance to meet interesting people who are directly involved with their research topic, explore other cultures and political/social systems, and, indeed, see their home context from a very different perspective. To those who have thoroughly prepared but still have nagging hesitations we say, *carpe diem*!

4 Managing in the field: logistical, social, operational, and ethical challenges

Despite having done everything conceivable to prepare in advance, most scholars face unexpected opportunities, challenges, and choices while carrying out field research.[1] Moreover, as one scholar warned, "Things will go wrong, in big and small ways!"[2] We hasten to note that these realities should not discourage scholars from preparing for fieldwork. Having carefully prepared in advance helps researchers to think through the unforeseen issues, questions, and tradeoffs – and smoothly handle the unanticipated contingencies, obstacles, and challenges – that they will inevitably face as they carry out their research in the field.

Taking the initiative to engage in advance preparation is all the more important because, as we have noted, political science as a discipline and most social science graduate programs do not do as much as they could to prepare scholars for the intellectual challenges that fieldwork entails. They likewise do little to prepare researchers to be managers of large projects. Yet conducting field research demands that scholars *simultaneously* serve as Principal Investigator (PI), or intellectual leader of their project, *and* Project Manager (PM), or management head. As PI, scholars need to focus on their (potentially evolving) research design, problems of causal inference, and the broader theoretical significance of the inquiry. As PM, however, they must be attuned to the details of logistical, budgetary, and personnel issues, and their overall production timeline. These concurrent roles can pull researchers in competing directions and be very difficult to balance.

This chapter addresses some of the common challenges that political scientists – in their position as both PIs and PMs – confront when conducting fieldwork. The first section briefly examines the multiple types of challenges that field researchers may face as they seek to adjust to their field sites (especially when the contexts are unfamiliar, and/or they are engaging

---

[1] Some of the ideas developed in this chapter originated with Marc Morjé Howard (2004).
[2] Interview, DK-8, August 8, 2012.

in long-haul fieldwork). The next four parts of the chapter discuss four categories of challenges field researchers typically encounter: logistical, social, operational, and ethical. Negotiating each type of challenge can be tough in its own right. But field researchers frequently face multiple problems, coming all at once from unexpected corners, which must be resolved immediately. Furthermore, the way scholars choose to address these challenges can have serious implications for the effectiveness of their field research and the subsequent quality of their research findings.

We highlight two caveats before proceeding. First, as in the previous chapter, some of the insights and strategies offered here might seem intuitive and basic. Indeed, the guidelines we discuss may be of most value to scholars who are about to embark on their first field project. Nonetheless, even the points that seem obvious when read here may not be readily remembered in the heat of the moment in the field, particularly when scholars are making high-stakes choices involving significant tradeoffs. Moreover, even seasoned fieldworkers face new challenges each time they enter the field. We believe it is productive and important for all researchers to think systematically about – to *critically reflect* on – the logic and rationale for decisions they make in the field, and we hope the strategies we suggest here will help them to do so. Second, this chapter's suggestions will need to be adjusted if the researcher is operating in her "native" context. While the distinction is not nearly as simple as "insider" versus "outsider," adjustments upon arrival will obviously be quite different for someone returning home, and for someone arriving in an entirely unfamiliar location. And, of course, the way each of the chapter's points applies to a scholar and his work will depend on his research question and project, the specific context of his field site, and the length of stay. Nonetheless, we hope all scholars will be able to draw adaptable ideas and insights from what we present here.

Adjusting to the field

Conducting field research can be an intense experience, and scholars often share some mixture of excitement and trepidation as they arrive in their field sites. This can be true whether the researcher is flying halfway around the world, driving to a different region of his home country, or walking to a different neighborhood in his hometown: degrees of cultural difference do not necessarily co-vary with geographic distance. Indeed, for scholars working close to home, field research often involves a greater number of short trips, creating many more arrivals, but with less time to adjust. Taking short trips to familiar places may even create the expectation (in a scholar's own mind, or in the minds of his colleagues and/or research subjects) that adjustment should not be necessary. Nonetheless, commencing fieldwork practically always involves some sort of transition, and thus some need for adjustment.

To begin with, many researchers experience – and must accommodate – physical and cultural dislocations in their field sites. MacLean's memory of her first arrival in The Gambia is relived powerfully whenever an airplane door opens, and she is surrounded again by hot, humid, and smoky air. Even with years of language and area studies training, and several previous field-work trips now under her belt, she still feels a visceral wave of panic until she arrives in her first night's lodging. A scholar carrying out a series of short targeted trips in her home country (in this case the United States) also attested to experiencing cultural dislocations as she arrived in field sites in different regions. She noted significant differences across locations, and struggled to figure out why the greetings and informal banter that seemed to produce some acceptance and camaraderie with the middle-class, white, female librarians (who were not that much different from herself) at the archives in Illinois did not achieve the same success in Texas or Montana.[3]

Another sort of adjustment is to the intensity and pressure of fieldwork. Even if life at their home institution was hardly carefree, scholars frequently recounted in interviews how the intense pressure to "get things done quickly" was "exhausting."[4] As we saw in Chapter 3 (see Table 3.2), time-imposed pressure and stress can be greatest for scholars carrying out short trips as compared to long-haul stays. Regardless of the length of stay, many scholars recounted worrying about their productivity in the field or experiencing extreme anxiety as to whether the project would fail. Overall, scholars highlighted the strongly contrasting highs and lows of their personal experience of fieldwork.[5]

Given the ubiquity of these experiences, our aim is to share strategies that can help political scientists adjust more readily to their field sites. First, as we detailed in the previous chapter, we recommend that scholars prepare as much as possible in advance for the multiple hurdles faced in the field. Part of this multi-faceted preparation is readying themselves for fieldwork's repeated adjustment challenges. While "culture shock" can hit scholars immediately and forcefully upon arrival, it may descend at essentially any point during a field stay. Awareness of (and sometimes discomfort with) cultural differences of many types (e.g., the weather, sanitation options, food, social behavior, gender relations, etc.) may persist unabated or strike intermittently during one's time in the field. Likewise, the loneliness that separation from one's home institution, family, and friends may provoke, particularly for those on longer field research trips, can also ebb and flow.[6] Scholars should anticipate these sorts of feelings, and think through how they might reach out when necessary to their support networks, whether local or virtual. One senior scholar emphasized the value of establishing new routines of regular sleep, exercise, and contact with friends, family, and colleagues in the field,[7] and these can also be considered in advance.

Second, even if the possibility of a hard transition seems remote given a scholar's previous knowledge of or experience in a field site, or in view of a compressed timetable for the visit, setting aside time at the beginning of their visit to get set up to live, and get organized to conduct research, benefits most scholars. Doing so can ease the transition, reduce frustrations, and maximize productivity throughout the project. To offer just a few examples, scholars conducting fieldwork overseas might establish an account with a local cell phone and/or internet service,[8] or perhaps purchase equipment such as a laser printer or fax machine in the field site. Of course, scholars need to balance the concerns of local appropriateness with professional presentation. For example, they should consider how having access to the internet in a place where that access is known to be exorbitantly expensive, or appearing in the field location with elaborate gadgetry, might affect the opinions of local people who may ultimately be research subjects, and thus the information scholars will collect from them.

Our third suggestion might be implemented at various points during a field stay, but plans to carry it out can be made before scholars even reach the field. Every researcher needs breaks from their field site during which they worry less about what is locally appropriate and can just be themselves. Many researchers we interviewed mentioned the importance of talking with

---

[6] Interviews, LM-17, September 11, 2012; BR-5, August 13, 2012. More senior scholars note that the experience of fieldwork is much less lonely now with the greater ease and lower cost of keeping in touch via telephone, email, and video chat. Interview, LM-22, October 2, 2012.

[7] Interview, LM-17, September 11, 2012.

[8] Colleagues and neighbors can offer advice about the best phone providers and plans (for instance, whether a contract or pre-paid system is optimal) and input concerning whether different buildings and residential locations are wired differently for the internet.

other scholars while in the field – perhaps meeting for a coffee at a cafe, taking an afternoon walk, or attending a happy hour together. While such discussions of course added to their evolving stock of knowledge about their field sites, they also expanded long-term professional networks and allowed investigators to speak and reconnect in the language and culture of social science. Another scholar highly recommended taking a few short breaks from research to do paid consulting.[9] Of those doing fieldwork overseas, several found occasional visits with non-academic expatriates based in the field-site area, such as Peace Corps volunteers, missionaries, NGO workers, business people, Foreign Service officers, or journalists, to be emotionally supportive and informative.[10] One graduate student talked about how attending his "home church" on Sundays made him feel grounded.[11] And another scholar described how coaching a local basketball team made all the difference to her mental and physical health and productivity.[12]

As we discuss a bit more later in the chapter, for scholars engaged in long-haul trips, more extended breaks to reconnect with friends and family can sometimes be useful as well. Some researchers felt they benefitted from returning home for a visit. Indeed, the powerful conflict that many researchers experience between their "field researcher identity" and their "home identity" is frequently best recognized and worked out when away from the field site. Others may enjoy bringing friends or family members to their field sites – whether they are around the corner or around the world. Since researchers adjust to the field in different ways over the course of their project, these strategies can be used, customized, and combined, often well beyond arrival.

Logistical challenges: managing life as Principal Investigator and Project Manager

Scholars face a wide range of logistical choices and challenges as they arrive in the field and begin to conduct research.[13] Tourist-oriented web sites and guidebooks offering detailed information about their field sites can aid scholars to address some of these challenges. Yet such resources do little to

[9] Interview, LM-16, September 11, 2012.
[10] Interviews, LM-9, August 30, 2012; LM-16, September 11, 2012.
[11] Personal communication, July 29, 2012.   [12] Personal communication, October 3, 2013.
[13] See www.psfieldresearch.org for further discussion of additional logistical challenges faced in the field.

help scholars consider the implications that seemingly straightforward logistical choices may have for their research and their ability to collect data in the field. We use two logistical choices most scholars will face – choosing accommodations and modes of transport – to illustrate how the apparently clear-cut decisions that scholars make in their Project Manager (PM) role may profoundly influence the quality of field research. Our objective is to highlight the importance of *simultaneously* thinking of these decisions from the point of view of Principal Investigator (PI).

When choosing accommodations and forms of transport, for instance, scholars will consider cost, safety, and convenience. Their decisions will also be influenced by whether they are completely new to a field site or familiar with or even at home in the area – as well as by whether part or all of their family has accompanied them to the field. Several mid-career or senior faculty members noted that the logistics of fieldwork had become much harder now that they juggled the needs of working spouses, multiple children, and aging parents.[14] The nature of the field site and the length of the fieldwork stay will, of course, also affect these choices. Thus, a scholar working for a long weekend in suburban Cleveland and one spending six months in Grozny, Chechnya will have very different options and tradeoffs when deciding upon housing and transport.

Yet scholars should also consider how study participants' perceptions of them will be shaped by where they live and the transportation they use. Some towns, neighborhoods, or buildings have strong identities. They might be popularly known to be dominated by a particular ethnic group, to house people of a certain socioeconomic status, to be primarily populated by local migrants or foreign expatriates, or even to be tied to a particular political party. For example, the Bridgeport neighborhood of Chicago is known historically as a white, Irish-American enclave with strong ties to the Democratic Party machine. This may not necessarily pose any problem, but scholars should be aware of the reputation of their new "hometown" area.

Similarly, how researchers get from place to place can also function as a "signal," leading to the opening of some doors or the closing of others. On the one hand, using local transportation may provide opportunities for learning about the field site and/or research topic by observing, interacting, and chatting with people while waiting or riding around town. "Take public transportation, and this gives you the pulse of what's happening around

---

[14] Interviews, BR-2, July 30, 2012; DK-7, August 1, 2012; BR-3, August 6, 2012; LM-6, August 30, 2012; LM-9, August 30, 2012.

you," one of our interviewees advocated.[15] Furthermore, being able to navigate local transportation may boost the researcher's credibility with some individuals and groups in the field site. And, in certain contexts, having a car can make a researcher appear wealthy and may make him more vulnerable to theft and requests for bribes from officials.[16] On the other hand, having access to a private car may save time. For instance, one scholar we interviewed recounted that due to her inability to buy or rent a car, she was constantly scrambling to figure out the options to move her research team to the next remote field site.[17] Moreover, access to private transport can legitimize the scholar in the eyes of some individuals and groups as an established professional with more autonomy and power.[18] Again, however, scholars need to consider what their form of private transport signals about them. One researcher reported that her NGO contacts were "crucial for the success of the project,"[19] but that joining the convoy in which they moved about the field site required her to emphasize to study participants that she was *not* an employee of the NGO.[20]

In sum, many choices that we might think of as purely "logistical" are simultaneously intellectual when made in the context of field research. Choices about where to live and how to travel – as well as about many other things – may change the tone of one's interactions, result in different levels of access to people or materials in the field, and may even lead to respondents censoring what they share with a researcher. Scholars should take these eventualities into account as they make logistical decisions.

Social challenges: managing relations with people in the field

Every scholar also faces challenges in managing social relations while in the field. These range from initial dilemmas about how to gain entrée into the field site, to questions that emerge with more prolonged engagement in a site (for instance, concerning how to navigate friendships in the field), to the critical issues involved in hiring assistants to help conduct the research.

---

[15] Interview, BR-7, August 15, 2012.

[16] Furthermore, where transportation is scarce, having a car may bring local requests for transport, some very difficult to refuse, but all reducing the time available for conducting research.

[17] Interview, LM-13, September 7, 2012.   [18] Personal communication, August 30, 2013.

[19] Interview, LM-16, September 11, 2012.

[20] Interviews, LM-11, August 31, 2012; LM-16, September 11, 2012.

Initial social challenges: gaining entrée

Gaining entrée – to organizations, communities, or networks, for instance – is an immediate challenge for many field researchers. Doing so can be particularly difficult when moving among multiple, disparate field sites in far-flung locations.[21] Critically reflecting on this challenge and addressing it in appropriate ways can help scholars avoid future roadblocks – only some of which may be obvious to them at the start. As Chapter 3 mentioned, scholars can do a great deal as they prepare for fieldwork to help make connections, and many of these initiatives can be continued once they are in the field. As with many other aspects of field research, we recommend that scholars start with the least daunting tasks when it comes to gaining entrée – the low-hanging fruit – and build to the more challenging ones.[22]

One strategy that facilitates gaining entrée is to continue deepening one's knowledge of the research topic by gathering and reading locally produced information – sources that could not have been found at home prior to departure. For example, researchers might dig into smaller newspapers that are not available online, or listen to local radio programs. For one scholar we interviewed, a small, relatively new Islamic newspaper that was only available in hard copy at the field site was very illuminating for her research question.[23] Local research centers or universities may have their own specialized libraries, sometimes with rich troves of unpublished and non-digital working papers, policy reports, local theses, etc. Likewise, it can be useful to spend time in bookstores, museums, or even government agencies that distribute or sell statistical data or maps.[24] Sources collected in these locations can often be scanned and converted into PDFs for easy transport,[25] and should certainly be incorporated into one's running bibliography. Researchers can also continue to flesh out their working list of key actors, timeline of big issues, and/or lexicon of key terms related to their research question.

---

[21] Interview, DK-11, August 7, 2012.

[22] Interview, LM-18, September 14, 2012. Among other reasons, beginning this way allows scholars who are not working in their native tongue to improve their language skills, perhaps by taking classes or contracting a locally based tutor.

[23] Interview, LM-5, August 27, 2012.

[24] Interview, LM-18, September 14, 2012. As mentioned in Chapter 3, it can be helpful to affiliate with a local institution in one's field sites, and the people who work there (or are otherwise associated with it) may be able to facilitate access to the venues (local archives, national libraries, etc.) in which these types of materials can be found.

[25] Researchers should develop an organizational filing system for the electronic files that is consistent – for example, using the date and content (i.e., "2007.05.28.U.S. Supreme Court decision on immigration").

Once in the field, researchers can also follow up in person with the contacts initiated as they prepared for fieldwork, and work to expand their set of contacts more generally. This process can take a significant amount of time at the beginning of a new project; indeed, one of our interview respondents reported spending the first five months establishing these networks.[26] Yet laying this groundwork can pay off handsomely as one's networks continue to grow and deepen with repeat visits to a field site over time.[27] Indeed, one scholar described building his networks of access and expertise in concentric circles, beginning with the most-accessible individuals in the center, adding new layers of contacts and cases as his knowledge and reach grew, and eventually accessing the toughest outer ring of contacts later during the field stay.[28] The first week of fieldwork in Damascus, for example, is most likely *not* the ideal time to attempt to land an interview with the leader of the main opposition group. Of course, many scholars, but particularly more junior ones, will find it difficult and may put off picking up the phone or going to the office to contact even the individuals in the "inner-most rings" for fear of imposing on their time. Yet it is essential to recall that, while researchers are asking for local individuals' time and help, they are also potentially broadening the network of contacts for their interlocutors by introducing themselves and their project.[29] Moreover, the benefits of exchanging ideas can be mutual.

Scholars can begin by reaching out to what might be termed "soft" contacts. For instance, they might exchange introductions with local scholars at institutions where they are affiliated,[30] or get in touch with academics or analysts based in other universities, research institutes, think tanks, NGOs, or policy organizations in the field site. As one senior faculty member we interviewed suggested, local scholars often "know exactly what you want and what you need" and are "usually more than pleased to speak."[31] Another researcher recounted how her primary contact at her host institution not only shared ideas based on his own research and expertise, but also provided her with a list of names and email addresses of people he thought it would be helpful for her to contact.[32] Academics can also suggest the names of graduate students, past and present, who are working on a topic similar to

---

[26] Interview, DK-13, August 8, 2012.
[27] Interviews, DK-12, August 8, 2012; LM-5, August 27, 2012; LM-13, September 7, 2012.
[28] Interview, LM-6, August 30, 2012.   [29] Interview, DK-19, August 27, 2012.
[30] The research affiliation may also be able to provide an official letter of introduction that will be helpful in making other contacts down the road.
[31] Interview, LM-18, September 14, 2012.   [32] Interview, LM-5, August 27, 2012.

the researcher's. They may also be aware of upcoming academic or policy conferences that fieldworkers may wish to attend or, toward the end of fieldwork, at which they might present their work.[33] These conferences can help scholars get the lay of the land, revealing who the experts and key players are with respect to a particular topic, what relationships and synergies exist between individuals and organizations, and what conflicts may be brewing. The staff of local and international NGOs can also share extensive insights about the key actors in the public, private, and non-profit sector.[34] Personnel at US embassies overseas can sometimes provide valuable contacts and insights into local politics and recent events,[35] as can journalists.[36] Depending on the topic, the leaders and staff of religious and community service organizations may also be able to help make introductions.

For certain projects, the researcher may need to move beyond her growing network of soft contacts in order to solicit formal or informal government approval to enter and conduct research in the field site(s). For example, MacLean obtained written and verbal authorizations from national, regional, and district ministry officials as well as village-level chiefs and elders before she began research in villages in Ghana and Côte d'Ivoire. A scholar's earlier discussions with soft contacts can often help him to understand the politics and dynamics of this process.[37] Sometimes government approval of the study is conveyed via a formal document that scholars must present in order to access particular sources. One scholar, emphasizing how vital it was to "use the official channels," spent two weeks in discussions with the headquarters of an organization in the capital city in order to obtain a stamped letter of permission to contact political leaders lower in the hierarchy.[38] In other cases, the approval process is more informal and personalized. In many contexts, multiple individuals, groups, and/or organizations inside and outside of government may need to coordinate in order for approval to be

---

[33] Interviews, DK-8, August 1, 2012; LM-4, August 27, 2012.

[34] Interview, LM-13, September 7, 2012.

[35] Often, Political Officers, Economic Officers, and Consular Officers have extensive knowledge and in-country contacts that they may be willing to share with visiting scholars. Where expatriate Foreign Service Officers do not usually reside in one place for an extended period of time, frequently local embassy staff do have long tenures and can be very well connected.

[36] Interview, LM-9, August 30, 2012.

[37] In some contexts scholars begin by obtaining approval from the lowest unit in the hierarchy and then move up the chain of command securing additional permissions; in others, it is the reverse; and, in still others, it is a combination of the two, where the unofficial consent of the lowest unit stimulates the approval of the highest authority.

[38] Interview, LM-13, September 7, 2012.

granted. Again, extensive preparation and a deep background in the area
can help scholars to understand how key processes work.

In many places, even once approval for a project has been awarded by the
powers-that-be, the appropriate greetings must be exchanged at lower levels
before the actual research can begin. Sometimes this process can be quite
elaborate and time-consuming. Scholars may even feel frustrated, at what
they perceive to be a waste of time, just when they are trying to get their
project up and running. Yet many of our interviewees affirmed that this
initial investment was returned many times over in the respondents' trust
and willingness to participate freely and candidly in their field projects.[39]
In other contexts, the proper greetings may be less prolonged and occur on
a more individual basis – for example, a cordial exchange of business cards
at the beginning of an interview.

As scholars move outward – as their list of contacts grows and, potentially,
becomes more heterogeneous – they may wish to create new versions of
the one-page project description they wrote in advance of embarking on
field research (see Chapter 3), or improve the content and delivery of their
"elevator pitch" about their project. They may even rework their interview
protocols and survey questionnaires.[40]

Of course, gaining entrée is not a discrete task that is "completed" at the
beginning of the field stay. It is an ongoing process that is initiated well
before arriving in the field, and continues throughout (and arguably even
after) one's fieldwork. For example, a scholar whom we interviewed pointed
out that participants in her research project in Palestine initially trusted
her because they knew she had grown up in a neighboring village. Even so,
she had to continue working to build on that trust throughout her time
in the field.[41] Moreover, as our discussion will have suggested, the process
of making inroads differs dramatically by context. Obtaining entrée was a
different experience for a long-time native of shantytowns in Buenos Aires,
Argentina[42] than for a young female graduate student in "somewhat sexist"
Portugal in the 1980s.[43] In the months immediately following the end of
apartheid, another scholar found that being a foreigner in South Africa might
have actually helped to open doors.[44] MacLean noted similar advantages

---

[39] Interviews, LM-5, August 27, 2012; LM-8, August 30, 2012; LM-13, September 7, 2012.
[40] Scholars who wish to amend such materials generally need to file a request to do so with their
IRB – and receive its approval – before beginning to use revised interview protocols or questionnaires
in the field.
[41] Interview, BR-7, August 15, 2012.   [42] Interview, DK-16, August 21, 2012.
[43] Interview, LM-17, September 11, 2012.   [44] Interview, LM-12, September 6, 2012.

of being perceived as an outsider when she interviewed state government officials in Oklahoma City on their role in a locally contentious policy issue. Regardless of the researcher's positionality, many scholars with whom we spoke emphasized that the most important way to gain entrée was to engage with genuine interest and demonstrate polite respect throughout their time in the field.[45]

Emerging social challenges

Beyond the problem of how to get a foot in the door, additional social challenges that can impact the conduct and quality of a scholar's research may emerge more slowly over time as he becomes more engaged with people in the field. Some researchers may not expect to have a personal social life while doing field research, but many ultimately do. As one of our interview respondents noted: "When you haven't done fieldwork before, and you are leaving to go somewhere, you think that you are putting your life on hold. But, you get out there, and you have a life. You have friends and relationships, and you adjust to the changes."[46] Of course, ultimately researchers must make choices about how to conduct themselves socially in the field based on their own individual values and personal needs. Some scholars may enjoy and benefit from a high degree of social interaction throughout their field visit, while others may need more time alone to feel comfortable. Nonetheless, it is quite unusual for scholars conducting fieldwork to have no interaction at all with individuals living in the field site – and, when they do, sometimes interpersonal issues result.

Interpersonal dilemmas unrelated to one's research may at first seem to belong to a separate, private realm. Yet these seemingly private challenges can have a critical impact on one's professional reputation, what one is able to do in the field, and thus on the quality of the field research. Successfully completing most field research projects requires that scholars set professional boundaries, and constantly demonstrate interpersonal respect. This does not preclude developing relationships during fieldwork, and many researchers have developed fruitful and long-lasting friendships and romantic relationships in the field. Nonetheless, such relationships must be handled thoughtfully. Many researchers take trips to the same field site repeatedly

---

[45] Interviews, DK-19, August 27, 2012; LM-12, September 6, 2012; LM-14, September 7, 2012; LM-22, October 2, 2012.

[46] Interview, LM-16, September 11, 2012.

over a long professional career, and other researchers will likewise seek to visit those locales. Thus scholars need to consider not only their own long-term personal reputation, but also that of their local affiliate institution, their home institution, and potentially scholars from their home country more broadly when interacting with people in the field.

Scholars might employ several strategies to navigate what can be complex and delicate issues. Learning about the culture and context of the field site can help scholars begin to understand what is locally permissible behavior for someone of their age, gender, and marital status. For example, in some places, a female scholar who shares a beer with a colleague in a bar may unwittingly signal promiscuity. Even a one-on-one interview in a public plaza between a man and a woman may be interpreted locally in unintended ways. Being familiar with the context will also help scholars understand signals being sent by others' invitations, and know when and how to respond in the negative politely. Sometimes humor can lighten a scholar's rebuff of an unwanted advance by a stranger, close colleague, or neighbor – yet again, the humor must be context-sensitive. Particularly if one is operating in a foreign language, it can be very helpful to actually practice potential responses for imagined future encounters. It is particularly crucial for scholars making short trips to new contexts to critically reflect on their behavior (and that of others) and act with caution, as the lack of background knowledge and experience makes reading social cues more difficult and misunderstanding even more likely.

Of course, it can be just as important to know when and how to say "yes" to personal invitations. While, for some scholars, giving in to personal demands on their time may seem to represent an unwanted distraction from their work, time spent socializing can build rapport and trust in the field-site community and hence improve the subsequent productivity of formal research activities. Visiting socially with neighbors, colleagues, or even study participants can also be an enjoyable way to reciprocate with the field-site community.

A final emergent social question, briefly mentioned earlier in the chapter, concerns how to handle relationships with family and friends at home if one is in the field for an extended period without them. These are intensely personal decisions. Our best advice is for scholars to have candid conversations about how the separation will be navigated *before* leaving for the field. Sharing the experience of the field site by inviting family and friends to visit periodically can be enjoyable and reinvigorating, but scholars should remember that it can be particularly difficult to balance work commitments when family and friends who have traveled from afar are present. Moreover, many scholars find they need to get away from the intense pressure, demands, and social atmosphere of the field site in order to rest, rejuvenate personally and intellectually, and reconnect with their significant others. Clear communication in advance about mutual expectations for the daily routine and the trip as a whole are again crucial in these instances.

Recruiting and managing research assistants

For many scholars, research assistants (RAs) make numerous types of valuable (and, sometimes, indispensable) contributions to their research projects. RAs well-versed in the research topic can offer significant intellectual assistance. Some scholars noted that they were much more efficient when they delegated specific tasks to a research assistant with the appropriate skills.[47] Other scholars argued that recruiting and training a team of RAs, while more work, gave them much more control over the quality of the data collected when compared to subcontracting discrete research duties, such as fielding a survey, to a private firm.[48] Moreover, some scholars recounted feeling safer or more culturally accepted when a research assistant accompanied them in the field site.[49] Research assistants can also offer camaraderie. Of course, a scholar's need to hire an RA depends upon the contours of her project, and her ability to do so relies critically on the availability of funds. But even scholars taking short trips and working with limited budgets frequently find it valuable and possible to hire at least one person to help with some well-defined task.

At the same time, it is important to recognize that recruiting and managing RAs represents a significant commitment. Moreover, finding the appropriate people to hire, training them, and overseeing and guiding them can be challenging, particularly for scholars for whom managing people is completely new. And, depending upon the type of work they are called on to do, hiring RAs can have serious implications for the intellectual quality of one's project.

Before seeking to recruit assistants, scholars should carefully consider which skills – for instance, familiarity with social science methodology,

---

[47] Interviews, LM-2, April 14, 2012; LM-5, August 27, 2012.

[48] Interviews, LM-1, April 13, 2012; LM-8, August 30, 2012; LM-9, August 30, 2012; LM-13, September 7, 2012. See Chapter 8 for a more detailed discussion of the tradeoffs involved with managing versus subcontracting survey research.

[49] Interviews, BR-6, August 14, 2012; BR-7, August 15, 2012; LM-5, August 27, 2012.

or facility in certain languages – they would like their RA(s) to have. They should also think through what social characteristics they would ideally like their assistant(s) to possess. And they should contemplate what type of time commitment they will require from them.[50] They might also seek to anticipate how the desired qualities might change during field research. For instance, one scholar we interviewed described how the skills her RA needed to have changed over the course of the study as her own ability to communicate in Swahili improved.[51] Finally, researchers may wish to prioritize the qualities they desire in case no candidates with the ideal combination of qualities apply.[52]

While skills and availability seem like straightforward criteria for choosing RAs, how their gender, ethnicity, age, social class, and membership in other social categories might affect their participation in a research project may be less clear. Accordingly, we offer some examples. In field contexts with patriarchal cultural norms and strictly segregated public and private spaces for men and women, RAs' gender will play a significant role in the research. One male scholar found it nearly impossible to interview women in urban centers of North Africa until he hired a female RA who worked independently.[53] Yet recruiting qualified female RAs can be difficult in countries where very few women have the opportunity to complete secondary school or pursue a university education.

Fujii (2009, 32) discusses in detail the multiple criteria she considered when she selected an interpreter to assist her in conducting interviews in post-genocide Rwanda. She chose an interpreter who would not be quickly stereotyped as belonging to a particular ethnic category based on physical characteristics, hoping that doing so would make both Hutu and Tutsi respondents feel more comfortable sharing their views. In her study on sectarian parties in Lebanon, Cammett (2013) employed the opposite strategy, choosing assistants who *were* obviously associated with a particular group and matching them with their "peer" respondent groups. In a slightly different vein, MacLean found that better-educated, urban-based RAs had difficulty according the power of informed consent (and most importantly, refusal) to potential respondents who were "just villagers." Meanwhile, the village residents perceived the RAs as "strangers" from a foreign region of their nation. In later rounds of fieldwork, MacLean chose RAs with less

---

[50] Interview, LM-5, August 27, 2012.   [51] Interview, LM-16, September 11, 2012.
[52] Interviews, LM-11, August 31, 2012; LM-13, September 7, 2012.
[53] Personal communication, March 2, 2012.

education who were born in the region and recognized as belonging to "local" ethnic groups, but who had no immediate familial connections in the sampled village (MacLean 2010, 247).

Researchers who anticipate using RAs should begin to think through, and consult with trusted colleagues about, how they will recruit appropriate assistant(s), and address the challenges of doing so, early in their field stay.[54] One strategy that can be useful is to draw on local contacts to advertise the RA position, and then interview a subset of the applicants.[55] Researchers noted that this competitive vetting process allowed them to leverage local colleagues' knowledge of local talent, while simultaneously preventing those colleagues from imposing a candidate who was not genuinely suited for the position.[56] Some scholars emphasized the importance of having RAs complete a brief trial period of work to evaluate whether they were a good match for the position.[57]

Part of ensuring that the match is a good one is clearly communicating responsibilities, and developing a structure of compensation that fairly rewards RAs for their role in one's project.[58] Scholars should ask local colleagues about what rate and periodicity of remuneration to offer and, if applicable, which benefits to provide (i.e., meals, accommodation, health care or sick leave / vacation days).[59] Both parties should sign a written document or informal contract,[60] clearly laying out the expectations and rewards for both the PI and the RA. Several researchers preferred to pay RAs for the work they completed during a set time period (e.g., a month) rather than piece rates (e.g., for completing a certain number of questionnaires), suggesting that RAs did better work when they were paid a daily, weekly, or monthly salary for their overall contribution to the project rather than rushing to hit their target.[61] Another strategy is to provide additional

---

[54] Many people can provide translation and other kinds of help, even if they are not formally hired and paid as RAs (interview, LM-13, September 7, 2012); of course, it is incumbent upon the researcher to show appropriate respect and recognition for the contributions of individuals hired under such less-formal arrangements.

[55] Interviews, BR-14, October 24, 2013; LM-5, August 27, 2012; LM-8, August 30, 2012; LM-13, September 7, 2012. Some scholars prefer to cast a wider net by distributing flyers announcing the available position; for examples, see www.psfieldresearch.com.

[56] Interview, LM-8, August 30, 2012.

[57] Interviews, LM-10, September 18, 2012; LM-13, September 7, 2012.

[58] For several examples of RA contracts, see www.psfieldresearch.com.

[59] In some very poor contexts, it can be important for the researcher to ensure that all project members have adequate food and safe drinking water so they can remain healthy and productive. Directly providing meals rather than offering a per diem, for example, will prevent RAs from saving the latter for other expenditures.

[60] Interview, LM-5, August 27, 2012.   [61] Interview, LM-13, September 7, 2012.

incentives, such as rewarding the completion of the full duration of the contract or the delivery of high-quality work. Scholars should consider what types of rewards would be particularly meaningful and beneficial to their assistants. For instance, Kapiszewski periodically invited one of her RAs to accompany her when she interviewed high-profile respondents,[62] thus making a professional connection for the RA that it would otherwise have been very difficult for him/her to make. Lastly, researchers should consider what professional supplies and equipment – pens, notebooks, digital recorders, cell phones (or airtime or call credit) – they should provide in order to help their RAs be successful in the field.[63]

The next step is to train the RA(s).[64] Depending on the number of RAs and the range of assignments, the training can last a few days, a few weeks, or a few months. Researchers should provide guidance on the specifics of *what* is to be done and *how* it is to be done, and also convey the underlying logic of *why* the tasks are to be carried out in a certain way. RA training should begin with a discussion of the overall purpose of the field project as a whole. The principles and practices of ethical research should be explained carefully. Then, researchers can explain the objectives and methodology,[65] and detail the day-to-day duties expected of the RAs; here the way in which RAs' social characteristics might affect their work could be openly addressed. One way to apply the concepts discussed during the training sessions is to pre-test the survey questionnaire or interview protocol (or other relevant research tool), and then facilitate a focus group discussion among the RAs about what did and did not work well.

Even after extensive training, RAs require ongoing management and supervision in order to reinforce the training and achieve success. Cell phones, the internet, and GPS technology have revolutionized the management and supervision of RAs in the field: today, scholars can agree upon certain times to talk or text daily with their assistants, allowing them to monitor their assistants' progress and troubleshoot problems as they arise.[66] Still, many researchers emphasized the importance of regular, face-to-face

---

[62] Scholars adopting this practice should think carefully about how having the RA present will affect the interview, the respondent's comfort level, and the type and quality of the data they collect.

[63] Interviews, LM-8, August, 30, 2012; LM-13, September 7, 2012.

[64] For an example of an RA training manual, see www.psfieldresearch.com.

[65] While scholars might anticipate that these tasks could be tedious, or that they might experience some resistance from assistants who might not see the value of their particular way of doing things, Kapiszewski found that her RAs were extremely appreciative of the social science methodology that she taught them implicitly and, once she recognized their interest, explicitly.

[66] Interview, LM-13, September 7, 2012.

interaction with their RAs. Depending on the size of the team and whether the researcher will remain in the field as they work, it can be valuable to hire a local field supervisor to coordinate and manage the RAs. While everyone "has to find their own management style,"[67] many scholars emphasized the importance of communicating with RAs frequently, openly, and respectfully.[68] Kapiszewski sought to motivate the RAs she hired in Argentina and Brazil by creating a sense of team spirit among them, highlighting their contributions during regular meetings, and celebrating milestones in the project.

Thoughtfully recruiting and thoroughly training RAs, and continually supervising, guiding, and motivating them once they are hired, take an enormous amount of time, effort, and patience. However, doing so has tremendous payoffs if done well, and huge costs if not done at all.[69] We recommend that, very early in their fieldwork stint, scholars begin to carefully consider the benefits and challenges of hiring people to work with them. And we encourage them to award these individuals appropriate credit for their contributions throughout their time in the field, and as they are writing up their research.

Operational challenges: managing data collection and staying organized

Having considered some of the logistical and social challenges field researchers often encounter, we now turn to the multiple operational challenges scholars who conduct field research face. While more experience doing fieldwork does not make such operational hurdles disappear, it can make them easier to scale.[70] This section offers a range of strategies – many shared with us by the diverse set of scholars whom we interviewed in connection with this book – that we hope will help scholars confront such challenges. We examine how to: (1) implement a data-collection plan; (2) capitalize on technology in the field; and (3) stay organized.

Implementing a data-collection plan

Regardless of how carefully scholars formulate their data-collection strategy, most face unexpected problems as they seek to implement that strategy on

---

[67] Interview, LM-13, September 7, 2012.

[68] Interviews, LM-8, August 30, 2012; LM-11, August 31, 2012.

[69] Some of the potential costs include having to replace an RA who quits mid-way through the project or to redo survey interviews when the RA did not follow the sampling methodology.

[70] Interviews, LM-6, August 30, 2012; LM-8, August 30, 2012.

the ground, and many need to adapt their plan to the contingencies of the field context. One basic problem scholars often confront upon arrival is that of quickly becoming overwhelmed by the volume of information available in the field, and losing sight of their project's big-picture objectives. We suggest scholars regularly take inventory of the progress they are making toward completing the tasks outlined in their data-collection plan. This plan can serve as an important touchstone, helping scholars to keep their study's overarching questions and goals in mind, and determine how much they have accomplished toward achieving those objectives.

As a scholar begins to make headway in collecting data, priorities often have to be reconsidered and revised. Researchers may find that more data are available than originally anticipated. While at first blush data abundance hardly seems to be a problem, when this occurs, they may need to critically assess and prioritize those data. Keeping data collection tied to the data-collection plan can help a researcher exercise discipline in the field and not become overloaded with information that may never be used. Alternatively, scholars may discover that key data sources are too biased to be useful. Or researchers may encounter obstacles even accessing the data sources listed in their original data-collection plan. A particular census map may be missing for a local government office, or a certain archival box may be frustratingly unobtainable. A seemingly phantom respondent may never return phone calls, or the field site may become so dangerous that respondents on whom a scholar has been counting suddenly disappear or go silent.

When facing these latter types of challenges, scholars must carefully consider the costs of continuing to hunt down elusive data sources. Rarely is any single source so intrinsically valuable that the whole project would stall in its absence. Consulting their data-collection plan helps researchers to think beyond the particular obstacle they are facing and consider how to explore their research question, or measure a variable of interest, from other angles, using alternative sources. That is, such obstacles encourage and reinforce the importance of triangulation – gathering data from various sources and multiple perspectives in order to corroborate a particular account, check facts, enhance measurement, or illuminate how concepts are constituted and contested. Collecting data in several separate ways at once allows scholars to maintain momentum and continue progress even when encountering obstacles on a particular data-collection front. Circumnavigating such obstacles may lead scholars to re-prioritize data sources or even revise the sequence or timing of data collection. Again, the data-collection plan a scholar brings with her to the field is simply a draft framework that is often revisited and reformulated during her time in the field.

This brief discussion of some strategies scholars can use to address data-collection obstacles simply offers a general orientation. We discuss problems of access and bias more specifically in Chapters 5 through 9, which address particular data-collection techniques. And, in Chapter 10, we consider strategies for identifying whether the problems scholars are encountering are just the inevitable obstacles of field research, or something more serious. Overall, and to repeat, routinely checking their evolving data-collection plan can help scholars to reorient themselves with the big theoretical picture, and allow that big-picture vision to guide the prioritizing (and re-prioritizing) and sequencing (and re-sequencing) of data-collection tasks.

Technology in the field

The many kinds of portable electronic devices that can now be brought into the field, and, more generally, emergent forms of technology that enable or augment field research processes, can significantly ease data collection and create the potential for innovation. These technologies and the data-collection strategies they facilitate are important to discuss because of their potential to change the face of field research in political science, *and* because of the innovative ways scholars have begun to combine them since the mid-1990s with the more traditional data-collection techniques on which this book focuses.

To begin with the most basic, the ever-increasing amount of information available on the internet and the continued growth of cellular networks both geographically (to remote corners of the world) and demographically (to nearly every socioeconomic and age group) have transformed how scholars collect data in the field. With this increase in information available on the web, it has become simpler for scholars to find contact and background information for some respondents and organizations. Further, cell phones allow for quicker and easier meeting scheduling (even in advance of arrival to the field site). One scholar described his frustration in the 1990s when "you would wait sometimes three hours before they would come out and tell you to come back in a week; and then you would have wasted a whole day for one interview."[71] Cell phones also significantly facilitate communication within research teams. Mid-career and senior scholars we interviewed remarked how their efficiency in the field has

---

[71] Interview, LM-22, October 2, 2012.

increased exponentially now that almost everyone uses cell phones, making shorter and more targeted trips more feasible than in the past.[72]

Further, some field researchers are employing laptops or small tablet computers to enter interview data directly in electronic form, thereby avoiding the use of notebooks or paper questionnaires. One scholar claimed that this technology had "revolutionized" the way she worked in the field.[73] The ability to compile data digitally in real time is particularly helpful when doing a large number of interviews, as in some survey projects.[74] In addition to efficiency considerations, this technology can also help field researchers protect the human participants in their study: interview data can be uploaded to and encrypted on a remote server immediately, thereby making respondents' identifying information relatively inaccessible. Of course, laptops and tablets can also be used to enter many other types of data – for instance, information garnered via archival research (depending upon archival rules regarding tool use; see Chapter 5).

The use of MP3 players to record interviews is likewise expanding. Scholars exploring highly sensitive and controversial topics have also used MP3 players in more creative ways – for example, giving respondents headphones and playing digital recordings of the most difficult questions. In this way, study participants are given more privacy and discretion in responding with intentionally innocuous pre-coded answers,[75] as no one else can overhear the questions.

While cell phones and laptops have become commonplace and, for many, indispensable technological tools in the field, the use of other types of technology is less typical, but growing. One example is technologies that track and analyze spatial relationships. Space-based Global Positioning System (GPS) technology allows researchers to use hand-held receivers (either a dedicated device or sometimes integrated in a cell phone) to map and record the precise geographic location of respondents or other items of interest. Then, scholars can use Geographic Information Systems (GIS) to link these data to other variables such as the incidence of crime or the location of schools, police stations, or polling places, presenting them in a spatial format that can make them easier to visualize, interpret, and analyze.[76] For example, Cammett and

---

[72] Interview, LM-9, August 30, 2012.   [73] Interview, LM-8, August 30, 2012.
[74] Interview, LM-10, September 18, 2012.   [75] Interview, LM-1, April 13, 2012.
[76] Anthropologists, demographers, geographers, historians, and sociologists have done more to integrate spatial variables into their analyses than have political scientists (Tarrow 2006); see Sinton and Lund (2007) for a basic introduction to GIS and Kocher and Laitin (2006) for an excellent discussion of potential applications of GIS in political science.

Issar (2010) used information on the spatial locations of the Sunni Muslim Future Movement and Shiite Muslim Hezbollah welfare programs in Lebanon to investigate under what conditions they served out-group members. GIS has also been used to trace the evolution of nation-state boundaries in studies that assess the legacies of colonialism (see Abramson and Blair 2011). Geographic information technologies can also help scholars develop sampling frames, particularly in sites where few (if any) maps exist, such as the uncharted and exploding slum neighborhoods in many developing countries.[77]

A related technology that is emerging as useful in field research – in particular in tandem with "on-the-ground" data-collection techniques – is remotely sensed or satellite imagery. Satellite imagery can provide critical pieces of data that are not reliably available from other sources. For example, Lyall (2009) sought to analyze the relationship between government bombing of Chechnya between 2000 and 2005 and subsequent insurgent activity, but was unable to get information from the Russian government about what locations they had bombed. Instead, he used satellite images to identify which villages had been targeted by Russian authorities. Lyall was then able to draw on evidence from prior field research and existing datasets to analyze differences with regard to insurgency between matched treatment and control villages. Another researcher described how his original plans to use remotely sensed images changed when he discovered that government officials had been employing such images to verify land claims. Worried that the intention of his project would be misunderstood, this scholar switched to using a handheld GPS instrument to achieve approximately the same goals, but with the added advantage of spurring insightful discussions with the residents on the ground about who has the authority to measure land and with what consequences.[78]

Another set of potentially useful technologies are the interactive social media sites of Web 2.0. Moving beyond traditional media's more passive dissemination of news and public information, social media sites have become public arenas for political interaction, discussion, contestation, and even mobilization. These sites have thus stimulated new sets of questions for political scientists and provided new kinds of tools for analyzing politics. For example, scholars have examined how social networking sites facilitated

---

[77] Personal communication with Jeff Paller, July 2012; see also Landry and Shen (2005) and Vigneswaran and Quirk (2013), as well as Chapter 8.
[78] Interview LM-3, November 16, 2013.

coordination efforts among demonstrators during the Arab Spring uprisings in the late 2000s and early 2010s, gathering Twitter feeds and data from sites like Facebook and YouTube.[79] These sites are also a tremendous resource for background information, facilitating preparation for interviews in the field.[80] On a different note, researchers might use their own social media sites to obtain potential contacts from their networks and post preliminary analysis and findings from the field.

Of course, new technological devices are not an unalloyed good. For instance, taking notes on a laptop during an interview may increase the physical, material, or psychological distance between researchers and study participants, particularly in more rural, remote, or impoverished field sites. Moreover, some researchers might question what will be missed or lost if scholars are less immersed in the field due to technology use, or if the more-compressed field stays that technology has the potential to facilitate become the norm.[81] Others might worry that an increasing emphasis on technology will direct research activities to locations where the desired technologies are available, meaning that particular questions or locations might systematically be under-studied.

Yet as surely as technology will continue to evolve and develop, so will views on and solutions to these challenges. For instance, some researchers concerned about the negative effect laptops might have on rapport have found that the smaller size of tablets, combined with the nearly ubiquitous use of cell phones all around the world, makes these devices less foreign and more acceptable.[82] Other scholars suggested that research assistants may be highly motivated when they are given such new technology-based tools to carry and use in the field, and possibly keep at the end of the project.[83] As with many fieldwork choices, assessing the tradeoffs involved in using these technologies – weighing the logistical imperatives one worries about as PM and the intellectual concerns one has as PI – becomes easier as scholars become more familiar with their field sites.

---

[79] See Howard *et al.* (2011) for an example of this sort of analysis drawn from the discipline of Communication. See also the analysis of censorship of social media posts in China by King, Pan, and Roberts (2013).

[80] Interview, LM-22, October 2, 2012. Parakh Hoon made a related point during his presentation at the roundtable discussion on "Field research in Africa in the 21st century" at the APSA Annual Meeting, August 29, 2013.

[81] Parakh Hoon made a similar point during his presentation at the roundtable discussion on "Field research in Africa in the 21st century" at the APSA Annual Meeting, August 29, 2013. See also Jeff Paller (2013).

[82] Interview, LM-8, August 30, 2012.   [83] Interview, LM-1, April 13, 2012.

Systematic organization of the project

A fundamental operational challenge of fieldwork is developing systems to organize the tremendous quantity of data one is collecting, the contacts one is making with individuals and organizations, and one's synthetic thoughts and analytic progress. Each scholar's personal preferences will dictate a different optimal system. Our overarching suggestion is that scholars make their systems simple enough to be navigated easily and expanded over time. They should have organizational logics or rationales that are easy to recall, rather than being overly complex and labyrinthine such that documents, contacts, and thoughts disappear without a trace.

Organizing data

An organizational system may sound intuitively like an excellent idea, but keeping the data one is gathering well organized from the start and through-out the study is critical for at least two reasons. First, remaining organized allows a scholar to be more *effective* – better able to see what facets of the project have already been covered, and where more evidence is needed. Again, the idea behind fieldwork is not to collect as *much* data as possible, but rather to collect the data that are *necessary* to build a compelling argument. Second, the more organized a researcher is, the more *efficient* she is. Fieldworkers are often strongly tempted to photocopy and stash in big undifferentiated boxes labeled "field research" countless documents that look potentially important to read later. However, confronting a mountain of disorganized data upon returning to one's home institution can induce procrastination and stall the analysis and writing process.[84] Scholars who have organized their data as they collected them can jump into (or, ideally, continue) the writing process much more readily once they and their materials have returned to the home institution.

It is wise to begin developing a system for organizing data even prior to arriving in the field. Since scholars usually collect and generate data in both electronic and hard-copy form, it can make sense to have parallel filing systems for organizing electronic and physical materials.[85] Of course, no particular filing system will work in all cases since the best way to organize data will depend on the data-collection techniques being utilized and the type

---

[84] Such boxes can also be extremely expensive to ship back from the field.
[85] A related question is how much data collected in physical form to digitize while in the field; digitizing can save on space and shipping costs.

of data being collected, as well as scholars' own predilections and logics.[86] Further, scholars will likely refine their systems as they employ them. We recommend developing systems that are simple to remember and to maintain conscientiously.[87]

Finally, it is worth re-emphasizing a point forcefully made in Chapter 3: all information collected and generated in digital format – data, contacts, and thoughts – should be backed up regularly (and truly as often as possible). Many universities have free space available on their servers, and commercial services such as Dropbox can also be utilized. Scholars needing to encrypt sensitive data should investigate which systems can accommodate this step. Practically everyone who has conducted field research has horror stories of data lost or nearly lost in the field. Hard drives die. Computers or papers get wet, lost, or stolen – or may even get confiscated in some contexts. The clear lesson from all of these experiences is to back up early and often.

Organizing contacts

Developing a system to organize and manage research contacts likewise facilitates efficient operation in the field. Whether or not their project relies primarily on interviews, most scholars will interact with a variety of people and organizations while in the field. Field research requires a higher degree of organization and greater specificity of contact information than most scholars use for their personal contacts in their everyday life. For example, in addition to the usual phone numbers and email addresses, it is often valuable for researchers to keep track of how they made a particular contact (for example, who referred them to the contact or where they located the name), when the contact was called or met, what follow-up is necessary, etc. Beyond these logistical notes, which supplemental details are important will differ by project. For example, in some projects, data related to people's ancestry, ethnicity, age, job history, political affiliation, property holdings, or associational memberships may be relevant.

While the system one adopts is a personal choice,[88] we again emphasize that it must be easy to use, scrupulously maintained, and frequently backed up. Scholars might construct a dedicated contacts-management system for each research project – one that is not integrated with their personal

---

[86] Issues particular to specific data-collection techniques are covered in more depth in the book's later chapters.
[87] See an example of a filing system: www.psfieldresearch.org.
[88] See an example of a contacts database template: www.psfieldresearch.org.

contacts. They could employ database software,[89] or simply make clear and well-organized lists using Word or Excel. Keeping contacts well-organized makes it easy to eventually produce lists of interviewees or tables of cases for use in publications based on field research.

Organizing thoughts about the project

As they carry out field research, scholars continually sort through and reflect critically on the information they are gathering, what it is teaching them, and what it means for their project. Indeed, it is through these ponderings that scholars iteratively alter, update, and refine their projects, as we emphasize throughout the book. Depending on their approach to research, during their time in the field, scholars may reconcile their research design with the empirical situation they are observing on the ground; challenge their previous understandings of how categories are constituted; revise measurement schemes; modify the way they are thinking about outcomes and variables; puzzle through causal processes and seek to identify causal mechanisms – or engage in a broad range of other analytic tasks. They will make countless observations and arrive at myriad insights, ranging from minor intuitions to big "a-Ha!" moments along the way. The multiple observations and analytic connections scholars make every day in the field can provide a rich context for understanding the other data they are collecting. Indeed, as Chapter 7 notes, such everyday observations are important data in their own right, even in projects that are not explicitly ethnographic.

Despite their importance, scholars may be reluctant to record these observations and insights. On the one hand, they may believe they could not possibly forget such great intuitions. Yet even intensely vivid insights can become fuzzy memories all too rapidly, particularly once the researcher leaves the field site. On the other hand, they may feel that conducting more interviews, collecting more data, and gathering more evidence are better uses of their time in the field.[90] Yet these insights can be critical to the formulation (or reformulation) of scholars' data-collection logics and strategies.

As we discuss in more detail in Chapter 10, we urge scholars to systematically document this buzz of intellectual activity. They might organize their daily or weekly schedules to create and protect time for this documentation of thoughts. Scholars might begin by organizing and reading through the

---

[89] For example, Microsoft Access; Microsoft Outlook or Gmail Contacts can also be tailored for this purpose.
[90] Interview, LM-22, October 2, 2012.

notes from the interviews they conducted that week, the documents they collected, or the government data accessed, jotting down thoughts that occur to them as they do so. Those synthetic thoughts might be centralized in a field notes journal (either physical or digital). Another possibility is to create dedicated documents – for instance, one that summarizes thoughts on the outcomes or dependent variables being studied, and another that includes thoughts on how well the data being gathered appear to support the main hypotheses being tested in the study. It can also be helpful to have a document for ideas for future projects. Cataloguing amazing new ideas for later consideration can help scholars to resist the urge to run off in a wholly new direction while in the field. Some scholars find that the best way to organize their thoughts is to actually begin to draft an article or book chapter. Again, specific organizational styles will vary. The key is to track one's thoughts and organize them so that they can be rediscovered and refined over the course of the field study.

Ethical challenges: managing power, positionality, and expectations

A commitment to ethical practices is one of the six core principles we identify as underlying good field research. Indeed, we have reserved discussion of ethical questions to the end of this chapter on managing challenges in the field *not* because they are unimportant, but rather because ethical issues and concerns shape and undergird all of the challenges and strategies presented in this chapter (and, indeed, throughout the book). As we began to discuss in Chapter 3, managing ethical issues is a difficult, ongoing challenge for scholars conducting fieldwork – "a constant," as one scholar put it.[91] Negotiating such issues involves more than simply securing IRB approval from one's home campus or obtaining consent at the beginning of an interview.[92] Moreover, field researchers often have to figure out the most appropriate responses to ethical challenges – responses that draw on their knowledge of the field context and affirm their own values – quickly, and under circumstances that do not facilitate critical reflection.

Our interviews revealed that while political scientists generally shared an abstract commitment to ethical practices in the field, they conceptualized and operationalized that commitment in different ways. Drawing on their views, we can identify a continuum of ethical practice (see Table 4.1), with points

---

[91] Interview, DK-16, August 21, 2012.   [92] Interviews, DK-5, July 31, 2012; DK-11, August 7, 2012.

Table 4.1 Continuum of ethical practice

	Minimalist ethical practice		Maximalist ethical practice
Goal	Do no harm		Provide benefit
Time horizon	Immediate, short-term		Extended, long-term
Guidelines for action	IRB document		Multiple including Belmont principles, project participants, etc.

along the continuum reflecting scholars' positions on three key dimensions: goals; time horizon; and sources of guidance for their actions.

At one end of the continuum, scholars have a more procedural and minimalist conception of ethics, involving adhering to campus IRB requirements to protect human subjects from harm (negative consequences from the study) in the short term. Scholars toward the middle of the continuum might go beyond the one-shot application of specific IRB rules, drawing continually on "common sense"[93] to navigate broader ethical questions throughout their research projects. At the other end of the continuum, several scholars suggested that the standard for ethical field research should be higher than "to do no harm."[94] They proposed that scholars draw on sources such as the Belmont principles of respect, justice, and beneficence, and/or input from project participants, to do research that "demonstrates respect for [the] experience [of those we involve in it],"[95] that is "salient,"[96] and that has a "positive impact."[97] Scholars at this end of the continuum also contemplate a longer time horizon of responsibility, considering for instance how ongoing political processes could eventually adversely affect those known to have participated in the study.[98] To be clear, we are not advocating that scholars situate themselves at any particular point along this continuum: there is no single normatively ideal position for all researchers and projects. We do, however, urge scholars to frequently reflect critically on their values, where they stand on the ethical issues that can arise in the course of field research, and why they adopt the positions that they do.

In addition to their position on this abstract continuum, the field context significantly shapes how scholars negotiate ethical issues. For example,

[93] Interview, DK-12, August 8, 2012.
[94] Interviews, BR-19, December 4, 2013; LM-13, September 7, 2012; DK-19, August 27, 2012.
[95] Interview, DK-19, August 27, 2012.   [96] Interview, LM-16, September 11, 2012.
[97] Interview, LM-13, September 7, 2012.   [98] Interview, LM-17, September 11, 2012.

ethical questions may be particularly salient and urgent for those who work in conflict zones or in countries with highly authoritarian regimes. In these field contexts in particular, scholars have the responsibility to learn what questions are too sensitive or dangerous to investigate.[99] Furthermore, they may need to be willing to put their research projects on hold and even leave the field site (at least temporarily) if told by the relevant authorities that it is unwise to continue.[100]

Yet it is not only in high-risk and dangerous settings that thorny ethical issues arise. Subtle yet critical ethical issues can arise in practically any context, in relation to virtually any project. For example, questions of differential power and positionality are ubiquitous, and play out in different ways across field contexts (MacLean 2013). While the dynamics of positionality have been thoroughly debated in other disciplines,[101] they are rarely discussed in political science despite significant variation in viewpoints within our discipline. Some scholars assume that researchers can obtain objective information more or less unproblematically (Steinmetz 2005). Others insist that positionality cannot be eliminated, and emphasize the importance of considering how a scholar's identity and that of his study participants may shape data collection.[102] For example, one scholar noted that her status as "just a student" facilitated the cooperation and support of the field-site communities.[103] Others described how their rising academic rank over the years facilitated access to certain government and industry elites.[104] Yet it can be difficult to understand how scholars' identities are perceived by individuals in the field context, how those perceptions might shift over the period of field research, and how they might influence the data that study participants are willing to point out or provide. For instance, when an (American) faculty member shared her sense that her status and that of illiterate, elder women in a rural African community were essentially equal given the latters' level of wisdom and indigenous knowledge, a local colleague quickly challenged her "delusions of power relations," reminding her that the women saw her as a "powerful professor from America with a car."[105]

---

[99] Interviews, DK-18, August 24, 2012; LM-8, August 30, 2012.

[100] Interview, LM-8, August 30, 2012.

[101] Anthropologists, for example, have suggested that one's positionality cannot be erased even by studying "up," i.e., studying those who are more powerful than the researcher, or by conducting autoethnography with one's peers (McCorkel and Myers 2003).

[102] Interview, LM-18, September 14, 2012.   [103] Interview, LM-16, September 11, 2012.

[104] Interviews, LM-6, August 30, 2012; LM-15, September 10, 2012.

[105] Interview, LM-8, August 30, 2012.

What can scholars concerned with issues of positionality do? First, they might take careful notes – in a field notebook, or together with the notes they took when administering the survey, doing the interview, or interacting with the archivist in question – on how they believe their interpersonal interactions shaped data collection. Alternatively, they might adopt a more participatory and collaborative approach to field research, soliciting ongoing critical feedback on their relative position and its effects on information exchange from study participants themselves (McCorkel and Myers 2003; Nagar, Ali, and Collective 2003; Chacko 2004; Khan 2005). Of course, as Norton (2004, 84) points out, this narrowing of the distance between investigators and research participants entails tradeoffs: "Familiarity, experience and affection limit what one sees, but they also open what might remain concealed or unnoticed."

A related ethical dilemma that scholars should consider and discuss in advance of fieldwork is compensation for study participants.[106] Participating in a field research project can involve considerable time and effort for research subjects, raising the question of how to show thanks and reciprocate appropriately. Scholars resolve this conundrum in a variety of ways, with the field context significantly influencing their choices. Indeed, some researchers acknowledged that, even though they do not consider it to be "morally appropriate" to give small gifts to study participants, it was nevertheless culturally expected in their field sites.[107] Scholars concurred that there is no universally acceptable gift, and that it can be useful to solicit local advice and give relatively small, in-kind gifts that will be valued by the recipients.[108]

In many advanced industrialized countries, research subjects are routinely given cash payments as a reward for their participation in a survey or experimental study. Several researchers working in developing countries noted that, due to the practices of academics, donors, government agencies, and NGOs who had worked in their field contexts in the past, their study participants increasingly expected some sort of payment, allowance, or per diem.[109] While some researchers reported paying a small cash amount to participants in survey and experimental projects, for instance, others declared that they "*never* paid anyone" for an interview.[110] Offering benefits for project participation puts upstream pressure on, and raises questions of equity and fairness in relation to, participant selection. Some scholars resolved

---

[106] Interviews, LM-13, September 7, 2012; LM-16, September 11, 2012.
[107] Interview, LM-13, September 7, 2012.
[108] Interviews, LM-8, August 30, 2012; LM-13, September 7, 2012; LM-16, September 11, 2012.
[109] Interviews, BR-2, July 30, 2012; LM-16, September 11, 2012.
[110] Interview, LM-6, August 30, 2012.

this dilemma by compensating organizations or communities instead of individuals, by organizing local archives, providing electronic and hard copies of the data they collected, or sending brief reports giving the analytic highlights relevant to a particular group.[111] Others used a highly transparent process of randomization to select study participants, including a public lottery (Chapter 9 discusses how this technique is employed in some field experiments).

Ethical dilemmas do not end when researchers return home. Some scholars have observed or heard about illegal activities,[112] or have collected significant information that could cause serious harm if published or otherwise made public. In very rare circumstances, researchers have faced demands for their data from corporations, national governments, or even international bodies such as the International Criminal Court.[113] Other scholars felt ethical pressure emanating from the opposite direction: they wished to publish their results rapidly and widely, particularly in non-academic outlets in hopes of facilitating policy dialogue and intervention with regard to the problems they had studied in-depth.[114] Finally, several researchers acknowledged the ethical problems that local displeasure about their analysis and writing can raise. One researcher operating in a more democratic setting recalled how study participants' initial anger with the portrayal of political events or dynamics gave way to a discussion focused on whether the analysis was fair and well supported.[115] In more authoritarian settings, however, both researchers and study participants have experienced more serious consequences for the publication or presentation of unwanted perspectives, such as the destruction of project data, refusal for future visa reentry or exit, or even physical intimidation and prison.[116] Scholars, in particular those working in less free settings, should try to anticipate such issues and discuss how to respond to them with their core network of trusted colleagues so they are better prepared in the unlikely event that they should arise.

Conclusion

Engaging in field research stimulates a wide range of emotions. Some scholars recall their initial fieldwork experiences warmly as "honeymoon"

---

[111] Interviews, LM-13, September 7, 2012; LM-22, October 2, 2012.

[112] Interview, DK-16, August 21, 2012.   [113] Interview, DK-12, August 8, 2012. See also Reno (2013).

[114] Interview, LM-6, August 30, 2012.   [115] Interview, LM-15, September 10, 2012.

[116] Interview, LM-22, October 2, 2012 on becoming a *persona non grata* and being denied a return visa. See also Subotic (2010).

periods, during which their discovery of every new intimate detail about their research topic and field sites caused them to fall more deeply in love with each. Others recount the constant anxiety of living in a new and difficult place, compounded by the mortal fear of failing to accomplish their intellectual and professional goals while there. Our interviews suggest that most scholars' experiences lie somewhere between these two poles – or oscillated between the two depending on the hour or day.

This bouncing from jubilation to stress, we believe, is related to the ongoing logistical, social, operational, and ethical challenges of engaging in field research: while scholars quickly learn that they will face all of these difficulties at some point, they can rarely predict when they will face any particular one. Field research, in other words, entails a great deal of uncertainty. The emotional roller-coaster probably also relates to the broader challenge of serving as both PI and PM for one's project, which requires continual refocusing from the big picture to the smaller details. Because successes on the big-picture and small-details fronts are not necessarily correlated, exuberance due to progress on the first can co-exist with frustration relating to a potentially significant roadblock connected with the second.

The strategies outlined here should be useful for navigating some of the challenges fieldwork entails, no matter where a scholar is conducting research or what data-collection techniques she is employing. Details of their implementation, however, will depend on a scholar's question, the field site in which she is working, and the scholar herself. In the following chapters, we offer extensive discussions of the main data-collection techniques political scientists use and the issues that arise when employing them in the field.

5 Thinking outside the (archive) box: discovering data in the field

The previous two chapters explored the broad challenges researchers face when preparing for fieldwork and operating in the field. This chapter and the next four focus more specifically on data-collection techniques that political scientists use while conducting field research. As we have emphasized, fieldwork entails much more than collecting information. Nonetheless, data generation is unarguably a central component of field research.[1] Our objective in Chapters 5 through 9 is to contextualize these data-collection techniques, considering what challenges their deployment in the field entails and offering strategies to address them. More broadly, the chapters discuss the techniques' advantages and disadvantages, consider how they can be combined, and address how to evaluate the evidentiary value of the data they generate. Most critically, the chapters demonstrate how collecting data using each technique contributes to the accumulation of knowledge and development of theory in political science.

We begin with perhaps the least well-specified data-collection technique employed by political scientists who conduct field research: gathering pre-existing materials. This mode of collecting information is fundamentally different from the more interactive techniques covered in the next four chapters – interviews, site-intensive methods, surveys, and experiments. Of course, collecting pre-existing materials often involves *some* interaction with people – in order to gain access to them (speaking with an archivist, asking to peruse a private collection, or asking permission to take a photograph), to sample them, or to capture them. As with all interactions in the field, scholars should critically reflect on these more fleeting exchanges and their implications for the information being collected. The basic difference between searching for, identifying, discovering,

---

[1] Our definition of "data," introduced in Chapter 1, bears rearticulating here: for us, data are materials (information or observations) that have been collected and processed by a researcher – considered in context and assigned some analytic significance – such that they can be employed in his analysis.

and gathering pre-existing materials in the field and the other modes of data collection we discuss in this book is that gathering pre-existing materials does not entail *generating* sources or information in the way that conducting interviews or experiments does.

Some might equate collecting pre-existing materials with archival research (e.g., gathering government documents, other historical matter, or newspaper articles from a defined location). However, as our chapter title suggests, pre-existing materials of use to a scholar's project may reside in many locations beyond archives. Indeed, a central contribution of this chapter is to encourage scholars to think creatively about *other* data sources they can exploit in the field. Statistical datasets, maps, NGO advocacy papers, political party platforms, photos, posters, pamphlets, brochures – even bumper stickers and graffiti (to name just a few), can all be important sources of data that can help researchers build their arguments. Some of these diverse data sources can be found in specialized locations, and their discovery can be purposive and directed; others surround researchers in the world they experience every day, and their discovery is often more accidental or serendipitous.

Despite this potential richness, if collecting pre-existing materials is mentioned at all when fieldwork is taught in graduate methods courses, short courses at the APSA annual meeting, or the IQMR, generally only archival research is discussed.[2] This gap may result from the generalized impression that pre-existing materials found outside of archives cannot yield usable data, or that the process of collecting them is either straightforward (and thus does not need to be taught) or chaotic (and thus cannot be taught). The lacuna may also spring from a view that few political scientists carry out research projects based *exclusively* on pre-existing materials. Alternatively, the lack of attention to collecting such materials may be due to a belief that appropriate archival methods differ so much across research questions and field sites that none is broadly applicable – or because the literature addressing archival methodology (even in the discipline of history) is somewhat limited.[3]

Regardless of its origins, the gap is unfortunate given the important role such materials often play in political science inquiry. Most scholars collect

---

[2] Dedicated workshops on archival research, such as the annual Summer Institute on Conducting Archival Research (SICAR) associated with the Program on Conducting Archival Research (POCAR) at George Washington University, also exist.

[3] Personal communication with three senior historians, March 14, 2011; July 23, 2012; July 24, 2012. The consensus among these scholars was that, while archival research is often discussed, and history graduate students explore texts grounded in archival research through their coursework, ultimately they learn archival work "by encounter."

pre-existing materials at some point in their fieldwork. The results of our survey of US political science faculty bear out this assertion: 70 percent of field research projects in our sample drew on various sorts of media sources when collecting data, 68 percent involved the collection of books and articles, 64 percent included archival research. In terms of numerical sources, 49 percent entailed compiling quantitative data through means other than surveys and experiments,[4] and 32 percent involved collecting existing datasets. These sorts of pre-existing materials, which political scientists so often instinctively pick up, can significantly shape how they think about their question and their topic. Depending on the project, not being more systematic about collecting and considering such materials, and more reflective about how they influence our thinking, can mean lost opportunities. Indeed, perhaps due to a generalized impression that many of these types of sources (perhaps with the exception of archival documents) do not constitute "real data," they are infrequently cited in analyses, and the role they play in knowledge generation is rarely acknowledged in scholars' publications. This omission represents a threat to research transparency, leaving the empirical base of researchers' analyses underspecified.

Our goal in this chapter, then, is to offer a provocative primer on identifying and collecting pre-existing materials, with a particular emphasis on archival research. The chapter proceeds as follows. In the next section, we encourage scholars to think creatively about the many sources and types of pre-existing data that may be useful for their work, arguing that "thinking outside the (archive) box" can pay big analytic dividends. We also consider the differences between collecting pre-existing materials and engaging in the more interactive data-collection techniques discussed later in the book, and show how the two modes of data collection can be productively combined. We then demonstrate how pre-existing materials collected in the field can contribute to theory building in political science. Next we consider some of the challenges inherent in collecting pre-existing materials – identifying and sampling sources, addressing missing information, and evaluating and identifying bias – and suggest some strategies to address them; this section also raises some ethical considerations. The chapter's last substantive section briefly discusses preparing for and engaging in archival research, highlighting some unique aspects of archival settings.

---

[4] In some of these projects, scholars may have been building collections of new data rather than collecting pre-existing data.

Collecting pre-existing materials, and comparing and combining their collection with more interactive data collection

Pre-existing sources of innumerable types can be found in practically any field site. Indeed, no matter what the substantive or temporal focus of their projects, most researchers will at some point gather artifacts of popular culture, government documents, maps, public opinion data, political party brochures, newspaper articles, or other types of pre-existing materials. Table 5.1 outlines a suggestive range of such sources, noting some of the locations in which they might be found.[5]

As the table suggests, pre-existing materials come in many forms. We hesitate to make much of the conventional distinction between primary and secondary sources, as many pre-existing materials might qualify as both.[6] A report by an NGO might contain both raw facts of a political issue and analysis of it, for example. Distinctions can sometimes be drawn, however, with regard to how "official" or "formal" pre-existing materials are. For instance, a statistical dataset acquired from a government ministry may be more official, a garment reprinted with a political leader's photograph happened upon in a bazaar may be less official, and a set of position papers found scattered about various NGOs may be somewhere in between. Nonetheless, all can be useful to political scientists.

Pre-existing data sources can also vary greatly in terms of accessibility. Sometimes restrictions are in place, and other times protective gatekeepers (political actors or researchers) stand between data and researchers. Moreover, pre-existing materials can reflect particular agendas, contain varied biases, or intentionally emphasize (and deemphasize) particular aspects or dynamics of the phenomenon of interest. All of this can affect their deployment as evidence in scholars' analyses. For example, public records may stress administrative considerations and downplay political pressures on officials, while the press and officials' correspondence or memories may do the opposite (Tosh 2000, 59).

Broadly speaking, scholars may identify pre-existing materials of potential relevance to their work in two sets of ways. On the one hand, sometimes

---

[5] Tosh (2000, 27–47) outlines and discusses, from a historian's viewpoint, the main categories of documentary material.

[6] By "primary" sources, we mean "raw" or "original" sources contemporary to the event or dynamic to which they relate; by "secondary" sources, we mean written interpretations of the past – an analytical product that may draw on primary sources (Thies 2002, 356). Tosh (2000, 29–31) discusses the blurry line, and relationship, between the two, and emphasizes historians' preference for primary sources.

Table 5.1 Examples of pre-existing source materials and where to find them

Source materials	Locations
• Posters, postcards, bumper stickers, graffiti, invitations, flyers, popular-culture visual or audio materials (printed cloth, art, songs, etc.), and other informal/unofficial materials	The broad research setting
• Maps, satellite imagery, geographic data • Official documents, files, reports (diplomatic, public policy, propaganda, etc.) • Government statistics (e.g., on population, sewage systems, roads, GDP, budgets, immigration, trade, poverty) • Correspondence, memoranda, communiqués, queries, complaints • Parliamentary proceedings • Minutes from intra-governmental and inter-governmental meetings • Testimony in public hearings • Speeches, press conferences • Military records • Court records • Legal documents (charts, wills, contracts) • Chronicles, autobiographies, memoirs, travel logs, diaries	Archives (national or local, government or private) Government agencies/entities (e.g., congressional offices, ministries, etc., at various levels)
• Private papers • Brochures, posters, flyers • Press releases, newsletters, annual reports • Records, papers, directories • Internal memos, reports, meeting minutes • Position or advocacy papers, mission statements • Party platforms	Individuals or organizations (e.g., political parties, unions, businesses, hospitals, schools, religious entities, interest groups, universities, NGOs, etc.)
• Radio broadcasts (transcripts) • TV programs (transcripts) • Magazines, newspapers • Electronic media	Media
• Published collections of documents, gazetteers, yearbooks, etc. • Private papers • Books, articles, dissertations, working papers	Libraries (university, national, local)

the fieldwork setting serendipitously *produces* such materials, or offers cues and clues that point to sources scholars might not have anticipated gathering. For instance, a scholar might be handed a flyer at a demonstration, or glimpse a telling bumper sticker on a passing car or revealing graffiti on a wall. One researcher studying informal workers in Peru befriended a street vendor who began to lend her documents from a large archive he had created over the previous decade on the legal and social evolution of street vending in his district of Lima; ultimately, she photocopied 850 pages that served as a "data goldmine" for her project.[7] Here the identification and collection of pre-existing materials are by nature unsystematic, unplanned, and accidental; scholars are generally not following pre-determined rules about what to collect (and often have little choice).[8] In order to benefit from these opportunities scholars need do little more than remain alert and engaged, actively monitoring the world around them – and, of course, reflect critically on why they may have happened upon, or been provided, certain materials.

On the other hand, pre-existing materials can be collected more purposively. Scholars often set their sights on certain types of sources – e.g., archival documents, court records, legislative minutes, newspaper articles, datasets, press releases, or secondary sources (historical accounts, for instance) – and go about acquiring them in a much more directed way.[9] They might do so by requesting them from the entity that produced or stores them; downloading them from the relevant organization's web site; or obtaining them from a library or electronic academic journal. For instance, one comparativist captured the entire population of television advertisements run by the main presidential candidates in several recent elections in three countries, and also acquired videos containing every television spot from several previous presidential elections in each country.[10] More specifically, archives, newspapers, and other types of sources themselves can be searched and selected systematically.

Even in view of this heterogeneity, the processes of collecting pre-existing materials (and the materials themselves) have certain similarities that set them apart from more interactive data-collection techniques (and the

---

[7] Interview, DK-1, July 20, 2012.

[8] To be clear, we are not suggesting that these events are fully random; using flyers as an example, their distributors may choose to give them to some people and not to others on the basis of factors over which the researcher has little control, and of which he may often remain ignorant.

[9] The distinction is not iron-clad; scholars may happen upon particularly useful documents when they are searching for others, for instance.

[10] Interview, DK-3, July 27, 2012.

information gathered through employing them). Pre-existing materials tend to be inanimate objects (maps, newspaper articles, documents, statistics). Accordingly, as noted earlier, while identifying, selecting, and capturing pre-existing sources may involve human interaction, extracting information and observations from them does not. Relatedly, while people or groups can be affected in many ways by a scholar interacting with them to obtain information, pre-existing materials cannot: documents do not react to being gathered and read in the way that interview respondents react to being prodded for answers to questions.[11] At a minimum then, the bias inherent in a pre-existing source notwithstanding, it becomes no *less* valid through the collection process.

These sources' pre-existing nature and non-reactivity can have downsides, however. A researcher cannot ask a dataset to produce another column containing the type of information he was hoping to find, or ask a piece of graffiti to tell him more. There are more potential silences when extracting information from pre-existing materials, and it may be more difficult for the researcher to understand sources with which he cannot interact.[12] Relatedly, such sources' pre-existing nature means that they are remnants and artifacts that reflect the choices and interests of *other* scholars or actors – influences that often remain unknown to a researcher who pulls them from an archive box decades or centuries later.[13] Further, many long days, weeks, and months in an archive may fail to yield the precise information a scholar needs and could access if he could just *talk* to the relevant actors. There is also more likely to be an intermediary between the researcher and pre-existing materials – a clerk in an archive, the individual who assembled a relevant dataset, or the person who took the meeting minutes of interest – lengthening the distance between him and the actual information source. All of these properties of pre-existing sources must be taken into account as scholars seek to assess their evidentiary value and deploy them to underpin their analyses.

As technology advances, more pre-existing materials are continually becoming available and scholars' relationships with their sources are evolving. The web can be thought of as an electronic archive – or an archive

---

[11] Of course, scholars *do* react to data sources, and may even see the same data in a different light over time.

[12] See Hill (1993, 68) for an evocative description of the difference between interactive and archival research; interview, LM-7, September 20, 2012.

[13] The coding of documents and interpretation of artifacts, etc., are active processes with plenty of latitude for choice.

of archives (for more on this notion, see Sentilles 2005). Online worlds, Facebook, YouTube, blogs, and other types of social media can be rich sources of information relevant to political science analyses.[14] And pre-existing data increasingly come paired with locational coordinates or other geographic information. The future will likely see more applications of these and other techniques for collecting information and generating data that do not centrally involve interaction with people. These techniques, of course, test the boundaries of our definition of fieldwork, the central component of which is "being there." Optimizing understanding, we would argue, requires developing creative ways to combine such digital materials with on-the-ground investigation or other means of engaging with the contexts from which they hail.

More generally, combining pre-existing materials with information collected using more interactive techniques – which can help scholars to engage in triangulation, one of our six principles of good field research – allows the strengths of the data gathered using one mode of collection to offset the weaknesses of those gathered using another, yielding rich intellectual payoffs. For instance, there is great potential for productive overlap and synergies between the site-intensive methods (SIM) discussed in Chapter 7 and the techniques discussed here. That chapter adopts an encompassing view of observation, discussing and encouraging both the sustained, focused kind of observation involved in ethnography and participant observation, *and* the less focused, less planned, and less sustained observation of context in which political scientists engage constantly while in the field. The observations about individuals and interactions made by scholars engaging in SIM, sometimes fleeting and always lacking in physical permanence, offer critical context for the concrete pre-existing materials scholars collect (often simultaneously), helping them to understand and interpret those sources.

Engaging in interviewing in tandem with collecting pre-existing materials can also be extremely productive. For scholars carrying out research on recent political events, the names of potential interview subjects – political figures, journalists who were present at important events, secretaries, note-takers, translators – may appear in newspaper or magazine articles. Other pre-existing sources, such as memoirs and archival documents, can also help scholars to identify people or groups whose involvement in the processes under study remained invisible, and whose voices had been absent from

---

[14] Chapter 4 offers examples, and Chapter 11 discusses how new technologies are shaping the future of field research.

conventional political narratives. Collecting and analyzing pre-existing materials can also help scholars prepare, and better capitalize on opportunities, for in-depth interviewing. For instance, the researcher who collected videos of presidential candidates' advertisement spots also conducted interviews with those candidates and others about their campaign strategies, and his familiarity with the videos allowed him to formulate more specific and better questions.[15] Another scholar with whom we spoke interviewed civic association leaders in South Africa about a membership recruitment flyer she had obtained at one of the association's other branches. The respondents' lack of awareness of the flyer revealed weaknesses in the association's overall organizational structure as well as political cross-pressures between the association and the ruling political party.[16]

Likewise, interview respondents can point researchers to archival sources they had not previously identified (or reveal that they have collections themselves!), or raise relevant questions that scholars can subsequently investigate through archival sources. For instance, in carrying out his project on city politics in Taipei, Read delved into almanacs of election records housed in Taiwan's national library to find supplementary information and verify facts that shaped or conditioned his findings from interviews with people involved in those elections. For another scholar who was coding newspapers for "taboo content" and identifying articles concerning political activism, interviews helped her to refine her coding strategy and categories, get a better sense of the history of and motivations for activism, and more fully understand the relationship between journalists and activists.[17] Information drawn from pre-existing materials can also help researchers better understand, cross-check, clarify, or fill in gaps in what they previously learned through interviews.[18] Finally and most specifically, interviewing archive gate-keepers and archivists can sometimes facilitate archival access by defusing tensions (drawing in those who could create obstacles for one's project) – as well as providing additional insight on the documents being gathered. Interviewing such individuals can also help scholars to understand where the organization whose archives they are accessing fits in the political scene, to fill in narrative holes and make sense of documents, and to test out hunches developed on the basis of those documents.

---

[15] Interview, DK-3, July 27, 2012.   [16] Interview, LM-25, October 21, 2013.
[17] Interview, DK-5, July 31, 2012.   [18] Interview, DK-1, July 31, 2012.

Pre-existing materials, then, come in many shapes and sizes, can be collected more or less purposively, and share several qualities that distinguish them from data collected via more interactive techniques. It can often be quite productive to combine the collection of pre-existing sources with more interactive modes of data gathering as such materials – particularly those happened upon serendipitously – often represent fragments of information whose analytic importance is only revealed through their combination with other observations. Even when combining is not possible (as occurs, for instance, when studies focus on dynamics that happened so far in the past that oral narratives about the event cannot be produced), scholars can still cross-check information by triangulating among different types of pre-existing materials.

Using pre-existing materials to build theory

Despite the broad citing of archival sources in political science scholarship, some researchers may be skeptical about the evidentiary value of the information that can be drawn from pre-existing sources and the contribution it can make to political science inquiry. Some may even hold that the kinds of sources on which this chapter focuses (and archival sources in particular) *inhibit* broad theory building because the minutiae and descriptive detail they contain can lead scholars to tell a story that is either too partial or too nuanced. Our own experiences, and our empirical study of field research in the discipline and scholarship produced on the basis of fieldwork, suggest otherwise. Drawing on pre-existing materials of the types discussed here can add empirical depth to a research project and demonstrate strong knowledge of on-the-ground dynamics. Moreover, such materials can make a significant contribution to every stage of research – formulating research questions, selecting cases, conceptualizing and measuring key variables, generating potential explanations, and illuminating causal processes and mechanisms – and, thus, to theory building.

Developing research questions

Information drawn from pre-existing materials concerning the details or dynamics of political events may help scholars to identify, refine, or more precisely formulate a research question; to confirm that a chosen question has merit (or does not); or to discover an entirely new question, problem, or issue to be studied. For example, seeing a Communist party poster on a wall alerted a scholar of international relations in South Asia to how big an issue corruption in government was at the time of his research, and led him to focus on the issue in a sustained way. Doing so enriched his work considerably and enhanced its relevance, as corruption ultimately brought down the sitting administration.[19] To offer another example, Soifer (2006) initiated his study of various types of state power in Chile and Peru by skimming a small sample of archival documents. This initial research enabled him to identify patterns worthy of exploration, pin down the time period over which divergences in state power emerged, and determine what questions to ask when considering a larger sample of documents.[20]

Case selection

Information drawn from pre-existing materials – a census, or the full complement of documents surrounding a particular diplomatic crisis, for example – can also help scholars to identify the universe of cases for a particular phenomenon, and can inform case selection at the macro, meso, and micro levels. Skocpol and her coauthors (Skocpol, Marshall, and Munson 2000; Skocpol 2003), in their examination of the nineteenth-century origins of associationalism in the United States, sifted through records from multiple organizations with the goal of building a relatively complete dataset of associations that had enrolled as members 1 percent or more of the American population since the 1830s. In another instance, a scholar studying Supreme Court decisions in India used mentions of particular rulings in newspapers and the secondary literature to create a list of decisions that were "politically important" to the central government. He subsequently vetted that list through a series of interviews with experts, and then returned to print media, reading four newspapers to verify that the cases were indeed politically important in the way he had defined the term in his project.[21] Scholars can also use statistical data they collect in the field to make case-selection decisions. A comparativist studying identity formation in the Balkans sought a sample of schools that varied with regard to the ethnic division of the town in which they were located and by their curriculum. Data on

---

[19] Example mentioned by a participant in a workshop for this book manuscript held at Indiana University, December 2, 2011.

[20] Personal communication, November, 26, 2010.   [21] Interview, DK-8, August 1, 2012.

population demographics and documents on school organization gathered from various governmental, non-governmental, and international organizations helped her make selection decisions.[22]

Conceptualization and measurement

Pre-existing materials can also help scholars to define their key concepts (or refine their "pre-field" definitions), and develop contextually valid measurement strategies. Cardona's (2008) analysis of how the institutional design of the Colombian security forces affected the type of armed challenge the government tended to face during the 1946–1954 civil war known as *La Violencia* is a good example. Cardona operationalized and measured institutional design using information drawn from internal documents from the ministries of defense and the interior, press reports from the late nineteenth and early twentieth century, and correspondence from national political figures involved in designing the security forces. Further, he used police personnel records, governors' correspondence, and documents found in archives in the state of Antioquia to operationalize and measure types of armed challenge to the regime.[23] In order to research the effect of exposure to French repression of a 1947 revolt in Madagascar on current self-reported levels of freedom of expression there, Garcia Ponce and Wantchekon (2011) used recent individual-level survey data, as well as maps and information drawn from archives, to trace insurgency movements and the French reoccupation of the territory.

To offer two additional examples, in her study of opposition to authoritarianism in Syria, Wedeen used such materials as political cartoons and politically oriented television programs – the "forms taken by everyday political contests in Syria" (1999, 87) – to sketch (i.e., to measure) both the contours of resistance and the regime's attempts to limit and direct the opposition (by selectively tolerating critiques and expressions of resistance in such materials). In another example, Zuern (2011) used cartoons, associational flyers, and social movement posters to examine the evolution of community organizing and the meaning of democracy in South Africa. One cartoon, for instance, vividly depicted the transformation in how local associations conceived of their rights, shifting from portraying smaller figures on the sidelines of a frame submissively asking for a few "breadcrumbs"

---

[22] Interview, DK-9, August 1, 2012.   [23] Personal correspondence, January 30, 2011.

of local material rights, to a tall figure at the center, triumphantly holding over his head the "whole loaf" of "full political rights" (Zuern 2011, 49).

Hypothesis testing and generation

Political scientists have also used many types of pre-existing materials to test their hypotheses, refute rival claims, and generate new causal propositions. For instance, in *Useful adversaries* (1996), Christensen advances the argument that the United States and China clashed in the 1950s (in the Korean War and the 1958 Taiwan Straits crisis) because conflict allowed leaders on both sides to mobilize domestic constituencies for larger strategic purposes. He illustrates those mobilization efforts and shows how conflict facilitated them – and refutes competing claims about the roots of the conflict – using information drawn from decades of academic studies of the period in question, opinion polls, memoirs, a range of primary documents from archives and published collections, speeches and telegram communications, and even political cartoons from American and Chinese newspapers. In another example, Jacobs used detailed information concerning decision makers and decision-making processes drawn from documents found in fifteen archives in the United States, Canada, Germany, and Britain to test hypotheses about the considerations that informed policymakers' and interest groups' choices during particular historical episodes. Doing so allowed him to show how these individuals' high-level conceptualization of choices correlated with the kinds of considerations on which they focused (Jacobs 2011).

Illuminating causal processes and mechanisms

Finally, information drawn from pre-existing materials can help scholars to understand causal mechanisms and processes better – to get at *why* political phenomena are related in a certain way. Archival documents addressing the nitty-gritty of particular political dynamics can be extraordinarily valuable sources for process tracing, for instance. In his book on variation in regime type across five Central American countries in the early twentieth century, Mahoney (2001) showed how critical junctures are choice points, using information drawn from myriad documents (i.e., internal memoranda, laws, decrees, etc.) from multiple presidential administrations to emphasize agency, thus fortifying his path-dependent explanation. More specifically, he used pre-existing materials to identify the dilemmas and strategic choices that Central American leaders faced during the period of liberal reform in the nineteenth century, and to demonstrate how their choices and strategies led to regime variation the following century.[24] Another scholar sought to demonstrate that state elites adopted new nationalist ideologies in mid-twentieth-century Mexico through the "cooptation of cultural producers" – the integration of intellectuals, artists, and activists formerly associated with the Communist party into the state apparatus and, in particular, onto textbook commissions. He did so by examining meeting documents from those commissions, identifying attendees, and tracing their histories back to the Communist party.[25]

In sum, as these examples demonstrate, pre-existing materials can aid scholars in achieving analytic goals at every stage of research – and thus can contribute to theory building. Of course, as with all data-collection techniques, scholars must reflect critically as they gather pre-existing sources. For instance, as noted previously and discussed further in the next section, information collected from fragmentary pre-existing materials often gains meaning through its combination with information drawn from other sources. Moreover, researchers should consider the implications of allowing pre-existing materials to shape their research questions, the way they conceptualize key phenomena, etc. Choosing questions in this way may make perfect sense when a researcher is focusing on deeply historical topics – particularly if choosing other questions would mean a dearth of data.[26] Yet doing so may lead to the systematic under-study of particular topics, or areas, or groups of people, and thus to skewed and uneven knowledge generation.[27] Scholars can mitigate these concerns by discussing in their published work other questions they *considered* asking and how data-availability put those questions out of bounds. Even with these caveats, we strongly disagree with the contention that collecting pre-existing materials draws scholars into an intellectual vortex that prevents them from seeing the big picture and taking steps toward developing theory to explain crucial political dynamics.

---

[24] Personal communication, James Mahoney, March 23, 2011.   [25] Interview, DK-2, July 26, 2012.

[26] Indeed, the more accessible data sources are, the easier and more transparent (and thus more replicable) data collection is, and the more easily data sources can be verified by other researchers.

[27] For example, governments in the developing world and elsewhere often lack systematic and reliable statistics on the informal economy, landlessness, illegal money transactions, the role of vulnerable social groups, and illegal migration flows – yet these are topics that are crucial to study (Sadiq 2005, 189).

Collecting pre-existing materials: challenges and strategies

Field sites hold vast seas of potentially relevant pre-existing materials. This situation presents researchers with a series of challenges: making decisions quickly (and under pressure) about what is important for their project and what is not; finding and collecting the information necessary to answer their questions; and evaluating its evidentiary value. Many of these challenges result from two signature qualities of pre-existing materials: they were generated by someone else for another purpose, and they cannot "talk back." As one international relations scholar warned, "The archives were not organized to fit your project!"[28] In this section, we offer some strategies to assist scholars with these challenges.

Before doing so, however, we emphasize the importance of beginning to collect pre-existing materials *early* in one's field stay. There are many reasons to do so. Sometimes these materials are "low-hanging fruit" – publicly available and located in places (e.g., archives and libraries) that are familiar and comfortable for academics. These qualities can make gathering such materials relatively easy, and make doing so a good way for researchers to ease into fieldwork and immediately make progress. Collecting them may be less challenging physically or emotionally than interviewing or beginning to set up an experiment, for instance. Conversely, pre-existing materials that appeared (from one's home institution) to be relatively safe and easy to collect can turn out to be challenging to gather once one is in the field. Materials that seemed to be publicly available may have an elaborate permission process that can take months to complete. Scholars who postpone collecting supposedly easily accessible information until the end of their research trips may be unpleasantly surprised to discover they have run out of time.

Further, even after scholars verify that data are readily available and easily collectable, the situation can change. Archives can close (or flood, or burn down), and archive staff can go on strike. In what was undoubtedly an unusual run of bad luck, a week after one scholar initiated dissertation research in an archive in Rio de Janeiro, she received a note on her desk indicating that library workers were going on strike; a month later, when they came back to work, the archive closed for inventory; and a few weeks after that, library workers went back on strike.[29] Government ministries, or any

---

[28] Interview, LM-15, September 10, 2012.   [29] Interview, DK-5, July 31, 2012.

type of organization, can move, entailing a months-long packing up of all documents. And staff can curtail access to certain materials, or remove information they had made available online, without warning. Contacts who have promised access to certain types of information can get fired or become reluctant to provide that access.

Finally, scholars' assumptions about the existence or contents of data sources they postpone collecting can be inaccurate. For instance, Mazzuca and Robinson (2009) planned to develop a new theory of proportional representation in Latin America based on data gathered from historical accounts of electoral reform in the region. When they discovered that no in-depth historical studies existed, however, they had to "become historians" themselves, carrying out archival research and eventually producing two papers: a historical account of power-sharing in late nineteenth- and early twentieth-century Colombia (the "secondary literature" they had originally sought), and an additional piece (drawing on the first) summarizing the cases in light of the theory.[30] The lesson is clear: scholars should identify and determine the accessibility of crucial pre-existing materials early in their field stay, and collect them as soon as they can.

Identifying and selecting sources

While scholars whose data-collection repertoire includes gathering pre-existing materials will want to cast a wide net (Trachtenberg 2006, 162), they will inevitably have to make choices about what to collect.[31] That is, they will need a selection or sampling strategy – a plan for choosing a subset of the available materials.[32] Scholars' choices will generally be guided both by pragmatic considerations based on field conditions, and by the analytic purpose for which they envision using the materials in question. When working in archives, or faced with a library of NGO documents or multiple datasets, scholars should ask themselves: what questions do I want to ask this archive, library, or dataset? To which aspect of my project will the information I gather contribute, and how? How will it help me answer my research question?

---

[30] Personal communication, November 20, 2010.

[31] While our overall advice is for scholars to focus their searches, series or collections that seem only tangentially related to their topic can contain valuable treasures, and so may be worth a quick skim.

[32] If sources are scattered about various locations, selection choices may need to be made at various levels – location, archive, collection, and materials, for instance.

Beyond these general questions, however, how can scholars decide which pre-existing materials to collect? Trachtenberg describes a theory-guided selection strategy in which scholars start by gathering and analyzing the sources that are the easiest to access, iteratively acquiring a sense of the "architecture" of historical problems, and from there develop an appropriate research strategy and set of questions to ask (2006, 30–50, 140–146, 163–168).[33] One of our interviewees noted that political scientists may have to approach archives in ways that are somewhat different from those of historians:

The historian is often interested in something close to a blow-by-blow account, ordering a series of events or processes chronologically and without gaps, whereas the political scientist is (especially if going in with theoretical hunches) interested in something close to collecting those data relevant to the observable implications of theory. Often the political scientist is having to do the archival work for numerous cases. He or she can't afford to make the same per-case investment. It can be overwhelming to the extent one starts to think too much like a historian about the extensiveness of data you need to collect.[34]

In a similar vein, and particularly in connection with selecting archival materials, Saunders recommends scholars apply what she refers to as a "theoretical filter" in order to identify particular substantive, temporal, or geographic cut-off points.[35] Researchers should be sure not to apply such a filter in a way that would amount to "cherry picking," however, focusing too much on finding evidence for their reconstruction of an event or their favored hypotheses, and failing to pursue and examine information that would disconfirm their explanation or substantiate rival accounts of the phenomenon of interest.

It bears mentioning that it may sometimes be appropriate, given a scholar's analytic goals, to assume a position at either extreme of the sampling spectrum. On the one hand, researchers who use pre-existing materials very selectively in their studies – simply to fill in blanks or missing information – may search archives just for particular documents, and thus not need a specific selection strategy at all.[36] On the other hand, even though most scholars will select sources purposively, random sampling from a wider

---

[33] Trachtenberg's Appendix II (2006, 217–255) identifies an extensive range of published, semi-published, online, archival, and open sources relevant to international history.

[34] Interview, BR-4, August 9, 2012.

[35] Elizabeth Saunders, 2010, "Archival methods of research," IQMR, Syracuse University, Syracuse, NY.

[36] Interviews, DK-2, July 26, 2012; DK-7, July 24, 2012.

population of letters, or minutes, or newspaper articles may be possible, and can help scholars resist the "temptation to focus on the strange, the exotic, and the unusual" (see Prior 2003, 150–154, on sampling).

Of course, all sampling decisions are project-specific. Historically oriented social scientists might use various strategies to evaluate secondary sources and select historical accounts as the empirical referents for their studies, for instance.[37] In an archival context, whether to select documents from certain years, related to or written by certain people, or produced in certain contexts, for example, depends on document accessibility, the researcher's particular intellectual and theoretical goals and how the documents chosen will advance them, and the analytic methods the scholar is employing. The selection choices of a scholar who plans to use information drawn from newspaper articles in her analysis will likewise depend on factors such as the availability of the newspapers (and the form in which they are available, which impacts their searchability), the scholar's research goals, the techniques she will use to analyze the articles, and the methods she will employ to draw inferences in her overall project.[38]

Two concrete examples are illustrative. When Mahoney was researching Central American political regimes (2001), rather than examining documents from the entire liberal-oligarchic era (approximately forty years from the late nineteenth through the early twentieth century), he focused on the single presidential administration in each country during which the main liberal reforms were passed. And he engaged in "targeted primary source research," examining the documents on which historians had drawn already, identified by reading the published secondary historical literature on Latin America's liberal-oligarchic era. This sampling strategy was appropriate because his goal was not to unearth new facts or create new data points, but rather to bring new theoretical principles and a different methodological approach to bear on documents that historians had perused before him, comparing them in a new way to see if he could replicate historians' inferences while building a broader theory.[39] Another scholar doing archival research on early Latin America who wished to paint a holistic picture of state development chose to examine only government ministries' annual

---

[37] For a series of competing strategies, see Goldthorpe (1991, 219–225), Lustick (1996, 615–616), Thies (2002, 362–364), Curthoys (2005, 357–363), and Isacoff (2005); Trachtenberg (2006, 51–78, 199–216) offers a survey of sources of bibliographic information.

[38] See Stockmann (2010, 113–116) on drawing samples from media sources.

[39] Interview, James Mahoney, March 23, 2011.

reports (including statistical data) rather than delving into a plethora of fine-grained documents from multiple ministries.[40]

Scholars are likewise focusing – and placing parameters on – their data collection when they make decisions (or when decisions are made for them) about how to *capture* data.[41] To briefly reiterate our discussion from Chapter 4, scholars might take notes, take digital pictures,[42] photocopy,[43] scan, print from micro-fiche, read (particularly critical) documents into a voice recorder, or some combination of these. Some archives might make their documents available electronically.[44] The important point is that data-capture decisions have analytic implications. Reproducing a source or parts thereof (e.g., scanning or photographing) can often be done comparatively quickly, but will entail less filtering, reduction, and processing. By contrast, when scholars take handwritten notes, they gather information more slowly, but are initiating filtering, reduction, and processing in the act of capture. These tradeoffs are important to consider when scholars face data-capture decisions.

No matter which sampling and data-capturing strategies scholars adopt, they can evaluate the value for their project of any particular source by mapping it back to their data-collection plan. Doing so reveals how pertinent to the project's overall goals the source is, and can help researchers resist what may be a strong temptation to overload. Returning to the principle of flexible discipline, the data-collection plan can help scholars to assess the relevance of information they were searching for and found, *and*

---

[40] Personal communication, junior comparativist, November 26, 2010.

[41] Not all of the options discussed here will always be available; some archives may not allow cameras, may disallow flash, or may place heavy restrictions on quoting from or copying materials (Hill 1993, 24).

[42] It is not necessary to purchase a fancy digital camera in order to take pictures of documents or newspaper articles; a 10-megapixel camera is sufficient. It can be helpful if the camera has an LCD screen that flips out (so what is being photographed is visible to the seated photographer), and if its battery can be removed. Scholars are advised to buy multiple batteries, as well as a tripod with long extendable legs. They should also determine early on what type of software they will use to organize their pictures. Scholars should practice with all of their equipment and technology at home prior to entering the field to avoid technical difficulties on site.

[43] See Hill (1993, 53) for a compelling set of advantages to photocopies.

[44] Accessing digital editions of newspapers can help scholars to find specific articles, or engage in systematic searches for articles on particular topics using carefully chosen key words. They should consider the reliability of the newspaper's search engine or the external search engine (e.g., Factiva) they are using, and remain mindful of the biases that may be built into search engines developed by for-profit companies. They should also keep in mind that if they search some subset of the sample of newspapers relevant to their study online and another subset manually, their selection technique will differ across the sample, potentially compromising their ability to compare the number or types of articles appearing (which may or may not matter depending upon the contours of their analysis).

of "unanticipated information" that they did not seek or expect to encounter. Moreover, as we have emphasized, scholars should clearly and systematically document and justify all of their decisions concerning data collection. Why were certain documents or articles examined but not others, why were some documents collected while others were not, why were particular documents captured one way and others a different way – and what implications did those choices have for the analysis? Clearly documenting their strategies can help researchers to think clearly about those choices, potentially improving their analysis, and can make it easier for them to solicit advice on the matter. Doing so also makes it easier for scholars working in more than one field site to adapt the sampling, collection, and capture strategies used in one context to another. Keeping track of one's selection choices and their justifications also facilitates their communication in final written products, thus facilitating transparency.

Dealing with missing and elusive information

Many researchers will face the opposite challenge: not *limiting* their search, but dealing with missing and elusive information. For instance, state records are often incomplete, especially for distant times or marginal populations, and particular archival documents or whole collections may be unavailable.[45] Relevant data may be scattered across many locations. At the document level, sources a scholar is able to access may not yield critical information – a particular person's name, or the day on which something occurred – making the researcher want to shake the recalcitrant newspaper or document and demand, "Why can't you tell me *this*?!" Meeting minutes might leave out important comments, and other sources may only be available in "sanitized" or redacted form (Trachtenberg 2006, 157). Indeed, as discussed in the next subsection, the challenge is even greater when one considers that sources may be absent (and existing sources may lack information) that scholars are not even aware they are missing. Such known and unknown silences can be as analytically consequential as they are frustrating.

---

[45] If the root of the problem seems to be disorganization, one way to "give back" to an archive is to help with organization. One scholar did so at the library at the Museo General de la Policía in Bogotá, an archive managed by one of the institutions he was studying. Parts of the archive were in complete disarray, and one room in particular was full of enormous (approximately 4 feet x 18 inch) ledgers of police personnel records from the 1890s to the 1940s stacked in disorganized piles. This scholar lugged them around, organized them, and catalogued them, leaving the catalog with the archive staff (personal correspondence, January 30, 2011).

Beyond changing their research design, what strategies can scholars use to deal with missing information?[46] First, we suggest that they carefully consider *why* certain sources or bits of information might be missing. The reasons for their absence may imply something of substantive relevance to the project. Moreover, determining why they cannot be located can help in identifying and correcting for any resulting biases, a point to which we return in the next subsection (Trachtenberg 2006, 159). Scholars may also try to determine whether the sources in question are randomly or systematically missing. For example, governments are often legally authorized to impound records for some period of time after they are produced, and place extra controls on or withhold indefinitely particularly sensitive information (Tosh 2000, 43–44). Further, archival collections can be destroyed (unintentionally or intentionally). Under apartheid, the South African state archives methodically destroyed documentary records that could harm the image of the state; today, tattered brown manila envelopes that appear to have once housed large stacks of documents contain nothing more than a slip of paper that says "*Vernietig* / Destroyed" (see Tosh 2000, 42; Pohlandt-McCormick 2005, 299, for more examples). In addition, individuals or organizations may intentionally withhold information from archives so that it is *not* destroyed. Again in the context of apartheid South Africa, activists self-censored, avoiding committing certain types of information to paper or destroying records pre-emptively so they would not fall into the hands of police or security; further, the African National Congress often hid its documents or took them abroad (Pohlandt-McCormick 2005, 300).

Second, it is important to calmly and carefully assess how crucial the missing source or elusive information is for what scholars are trying to measure or evaluate, or the argument they seek to develop. Is it a smoking gun? Can they carry out the analytic task at hand without it? Third, thinking creatively about what substitutions might be valid and whether there is another way to access the information sought is advisable.[47] If the National Archives are not open, or do not seem to contain the relevant documents, might they be found in archives in state or regional capitals? Could important documents concerning ex-colonies be held in archives of former colonial capitals? Maybe other scholars or organizations have reproduced and

---

[46] For more general discussion of having a "Plan B" for multiple facets of one's project, see Chapter 3; for guidance on changing analytic strategies or significant aspects of one's project while in the field, see Chapter 10.

[47] Indeed, where official documents are housed can itself be a revealing piece of data (Polillo 2008, 7).

assembled some or all of the sources for which a researcher is searching. He can also seek to determine whether a related local organization has a clipping service that identified and preserved just the types of newspaper articles he seeks to find. (Scholars who find such a goldmine will need to inquire about the goals that organization was pursuing when selecting articles, and the methodology they employed.) Or perhaps the sources of interest have already been published or made available online.

One scholar of international relations in Europe, upon discovering that a major historical political figure's documents were impounded, turned to the published writings of his press spokesman, who had attended all cabinet meetings and one-on-one sessions in which the figure participated, taking verbatim notes.[48] When another IR scholar could not locate articles on the Indian government's decision-making concerning nuclear weapons, he drew information from diplomatic records found in archives in the United States and the United Kingdom.[49] Of course, even if scholars can obtain *all* the pre-existing materials they seek, they should continually consider how they might triangulate – pairing those materials with information garnered via other data-collection techniques.

Identifying bias in and evaluating the evidentiary value of pre-existing materials

Information drawn from certain types of pre-existing sources may seem more objective than data gathered using more interactive data-collection techniques – perhaps because it is quantitative, for instance, or officially produced. Yet pre-existing sources do not necessarily offer more objective, "factual," or "uncontaminated" accounts than do interview respondents or focus group participants. The fundamental similarity that characterizes all of the material discussed in this chapter is that it has survived – whether for a few hours, or a few centuries. Surviving sources are almost always a finite subset of the universe of sources relevant to any scholarly research, and the properties of that universe are generally unknown and often unknowable.[50] The available sample (particularly with regard to historical sources) is likely not random, and may well be unrepresentative of the broader whole, and/or

---

[48] Interview, DK-6, July 24, 2012.

[49] Example given at manuscript workshop, Indiana University, December 2, 2011. See Trachtenberg (2006, 158–159) for an additional example.

[50] Put differently, "only a part of what was observed in the past was remembered by those who observed it; only a part of what was remembered was recorded; and only a part of what was recorded has survived." The source is Milligan (1979, 185) quoting Gottschalk (1969).

marked by significant bias (Mariampolski and Hughes 1978, 108; Goldthorpe 1991, 213).[51] Many reasons might explain sources' survival, and survival signals neither significance nor objectivity. As political scientist and archival methodologist James Goldgeier has observed, an archival record "is not a truth, it is an artifact."[52]

Different types of pre-existing sources may have different biases.[53] State-generated data, for example, can reflect the agendas and biases of those who created them, and can be oriented and expressed in particular ways for the purposes of communicating with counterparts in other countries, with other state entities, or with society (Chen 2010, 22). Data-gathering agencies may twist or skew statistics – inflate or deflate numbers related to budgets, taxes, personnel, illness, or crime (to give just a few examples), or fail to report certain data – in order to accommodate cultural biases, influence budget allocations, suggest greater state capacity than actually exists (or perhaps lesser capacity, in a bid to attract foreign aid), conceal graft, and for many other reasons. Even if published, statistics must be analyzed and their completeness and reliability evaluated with careful attention to the time periods captured, and consistency in the units of analysis and measurement. "Downstream" sources (containing data that have been processed by the state, e.g., analytical reports or statistical results) may be even more biased than less-processed, raw, "upstream" sources (Chen 2010, 31). Finally, government statistics on phenomena that are more difficult to observe – terrorist networks, the illegal economy, illegal trade, illegal financial transactions, and illegal immigration flows (Sadiq 2005, 182) – are automatically suspect. In short, many factors compromise the availability, validity, and reliability of state-created data.

Other pre-existing sources can have analogous weaknesses. For instance, NGOs' internal documents can be written for funders or other audiences rather than being faithful renditions of organizational priorities or activities. Likewise, even when media offer excellent day-by-day coverage of key events, scholars should be aware of their profiles and ideologies. What implicit or explicit filtering system may be at work sorting stories in and out? Keeping

---

[51] Record-keeping is often haphazard, and government record-keeping "fickle and political" (Curthoys 2005, 364). Further, particular dynamics or phenomena are sometimes simply much better documented in some periods than in others. For instance, according to one scholar we interviewed, much more was written about nationalism in Mexico after the 1910 revolution (interview, DK-2, July 26, 2012).

[52] IQMR at Syracuse University in June 2010.

[53] The subsequent discussion draws on Sadiq (2005) and personal communication with a senior historian, March 14, 2011; see also Chen (2010).

in mind the goals of the researchers who produced the books or articles a scholar is relying on, and considering what biases those researchers may have brought to their projects and the primary data on which they drew, are also important research tasks.[54]

An additional source of bias in pre-existing materials made available by institutions or organizations (including but not limited to archives) are the multiple routes through which and conditions under which materials arrive there (and fail to do so). Bias can be introduced, intentionally or unwittingly, at every step in the construction and operation of such venues in what Hill, drawing on Schutz (1970–1971, Vol. III) describes as a *sedimentary* process. The destruction and discarding of sources by potential donors, their subsequent choices about what to share from what is left, and the choices made by those who ultimately collect, accept, prepare, and organize the materials and put them on offer, can all introduce bias (Hill 1993, 9–19). Further, the stories of the elite and powerful may dominate such venues, particularly when those who operate them believe materials related to well-known people may lend prestige to their institution. Narratives of traditionally marginalized groups, by contrast, may be underemphasized, stored in a way that makes them more difficult to access, or left out completely.[55] Particularly when such venues function as sites of contention or of "negotiating" the past, or if they have been implicitly or explicitly charged with controlling the memory of particular periods, episodes, or actors, they may reflect and emphasize certain social and political perspectives, thereby "manufacturing pertinence" (Fritzsche 2005, 186), while other aspects of history are excluded (Milligan 2005, 160; Robertson 2005, 71).

The multiple and varied types of bias from which pre-existing materials may suffer inevitably provoke epistemological debates about whether and how to interpret them, draw inferences from them,[56] and evaluate their evidentiary value.[57] Those who take an interpretive approach to analysis

---

[54] For an account of various types of biases in historical work, see Thies (2002, 359–362); Lustick (1996) recounts how historians' accounts of the very same events can vary widely due to differences in their personal, methodological, and theoretical commitments, or many other reasons.

[55] The systematic exclusion of certain voices is one rationale for conducting oral history interviews, discussed in Chapter 6.

[56] Goldthorpe (1991) and Dibble (1963) consider the challenges of drawing inferences from pre-existing data, and the former argues that social scientists should not rely exclusively on such data. Shih, Shan, and Liu (2010, 54–57) explore how to create a quantitative dataset from material collected from primary and secondary sources, and Hill (1993, 64–69) also discusses "making sense of" archival data.

[57] For additional useful information on evaluating the evidentiary value of sources and information, see George and Bennett (2004, 97, 99–105, 107–108).

might argue that there is no such thing as objectivity and consequently dismiss efforts to isolate and eliminate bias. More positivist scholars might use various techniques to contextualize their sources and pinpoint the ways in which they are biased, and subsequently seek ways to adjust for any bias identified.

Scholars can begin to assess the objectivity and validity of the information they draw from their sources by carefully scrutinizing them as they gather them, asking what information they might be lacking, and actively seeking to determine what related sources might be missing. They should also investigate the provenance of their sources with an eye to identifying the viewpoints, biases, perspectives, and objectives of their authors or creators. They might ask questions about the founding, history, evolution, reputation, profile, and political orientation of the venue in which they found the sources. To offer a few examples reflecting some of the causes of bias discussed above: was there a particular purpose (commemorative, punitive, esthetic) for constructing the venue? Who gathered or assembled its contents? If the materials were donated, did the donor play a role in the processes or events documented in the archive? What logistical or financial limitations did those who assembled the venue's contents have and how might they have impacted what ended up there? What did the archive compilers expect the uses of the information to be? Is the venue in conflict or cahoots with the government?

An analogous series of questions – generating different types of "external and internal criticism," in historians' parlance (Milligan 1979) – may inform scholars' evaluation of individual sources or groups of sources. When, where, under what conditions, and by whom, was the source produced and/or assembled?[58] What was the producer's or assembler's purpose in generating the source and who was the intended audience? What biases might the producer or assembler have had? Who was present when the source was formulated or discussed, and who approved it? As Charles Tilly has suggested, researchers should seek to "interview" the materials they collect in order to develop theories about the generation of evidence and better understand the structure and sources of bias (Chen 2010, 16).

Scholars may also try to assess how representative the "surviving" sources are of any population of which they might have formed part, and how adequately they reflect the broader range of relevant people, experiences,

---

[58] With regard to a quantitative set of survey data, for instance, scholars might investigate how respondents were sampled and questionnaires administered.

and viewpoints. What other information might be necessary for the researcher to understand the source? How *reliable* is it – how authentic (i.e., not a fake or forgery) and how credible (how likely is it that it accurately transmits the way events occurred, people behaved, etc.)? Was the person who produced the source in a position (geographic, temporal, mental) to know the truth first-hand, and able (socially and physically) and willing to tell it? Is the source consistent or self-contradicting? How well does its meaning accord with other contemporary accounts (Mariampolski and Hughes 1978, 105–110; Goldthorpe 1991, 213; Tosh 2000, 51–62; Thies 2002, 357–359; Trachtenberg 2006, 146–162)?[59] Is the version accessed the only version there is? Was it published?[60]

To be clear, we are not suggesting that materials that do not pass muster on all of these fronts are not useful. On the contrary, their existence, and the particular ways in which they portray, misread, or misrepresent events can be analytically significant. We simply urge scholars to take any biases they encounter into account as they interpret their sources – and to report them in their scholarship so that readers can also take them into consideration.

Collecting ethically

One might think that ethical concerns, which are often closely related to interaction with human subjects, are less likely to come into play when research entails gathering pre-existing materials. This may in fact be the case. However, no matter in what form they gather information, scholars need to treat that information – particularly if it is sensitive or classified, or brings to light dynamics that have significant emotional weight for those involved – with care, remaining ethically *conscious* through the process of gathering and deploying it in their analysis. Through the book, we emphasize that practicing ethical commitment involves more than following an IRB protocol; rather, it also entails considering the potential effects one's actions, interviews, and observations can have on project participants. Analogously, scholars who collect pre-existing research materials should carefully consider the potential ramifications of collecting (and being known to have received) them even when they have no official designation.

[59] Dibble (1963, 204–210) discusses criteria and rules for evaluating testimony (produced by individuals) and "social bookkeeping" (produced by groups or organizations).

[60] Some historians hold that authors can be more candid when they were not writing for posterity or publication (Tosh 2000, 34); personal communication, senior historian, March 14, 2011; but see Hill (1993, 62–63).

Just because a document has been declassified through some official bureaucratic process does not mean that it is not sensitive, for instance. Particularly (but not only) in less-democratic contexts, there can be a considerable gray area between "explicitly marked secret" and "public," and scholars should take care to know where the information they are gathering falls on that continuum. Likewise, they should consider what the information's status implies about how to treat it, about how (and whether) to discuss possessing it, and about what to reveal about how they received it. Read's study of urban state–society relations, for example, drew in part on internally published neighborhood election records from the Beijing city government (2012, 57–77ff.). Records for the year 2000 were happily provided to the author by city officials, but in later years the same records were deemed more sensitive, even though their official status did not seem to have changed, necessitating acquiring them through an indirect and undisclosed source.

In addition, archives and other venues in which scholars collect information often place limitations on the use or redistribution of their holdings. Constraints are often document- or source-specific – for instance, many documents are under copyright. Accessing and using individual oral history transcripts drawn from a broader collection offer an example: some who provided oral histories might allow all materials to be quoted and used, whereas others may maintain copyright, meaning that "fair use" guidelines apply (i.e., only small portions of the transcript can be quoted or incorporated in another scholar's work without securing the copyright holder's permission). Operating ethically means fully adhering to these constraints. At other times, particularly under repressive political regimes, pre-existing materials may have been produced anonymously, with no one claiming ownership. In any of these scenarios, researchers may find themselves navigating political minefields as they seek permission to use, quote, or reprint pre-existing materials in their published work.[61] In short, scholars are just as constrained by ethical standards and considerations when dealing with pre-existing materials as they are when collecting data using other techniques. And even when gathering data involves minimal human *interaction*, their collection can have considerable human *implications* to which scholars should remain attentive.

In sum, understanding as much as possible about their sources and the context in which they were produced, and pairing pre-existing materials with

---

[61] Interview, LM-25, October 21, 2013.

information gathered through more interactive forms of data collection, can enhance the meaningfulness of all sources collected and improve scholars' ability to deploy them effectively. Collecting data in this way instantiates several of the principles underlying good field research, including engagement with context, critical reflection, triangulation, and ethical commitment.

Preparing for and conducting archival field research

While much of the information offered in the previous section is applicable to archival research, a specific set of challenges (and solutions) attend conducting such research in the field. This section considers those issues.[62] Archival research has much to recommend it. The wealth of information archives contain and the level of detail in archival documents can trigger new ways of looking at old issues: archival records can "open a wide window on officialdom," allowing scholars to "see the state 'in action,'" glimpsing behind the "velvet curtain" at the "political backstage" (Diamant 2010, 36, 40, 41, 45, 50).[63] Archival work involves "perpetual surprises, intrigues, and apprehensions" (Hill 1993, 6). Archives can be a site for (and can reflect) political, cultural, and socioeconomic struggles and pressures, however, and scholars must unearth them in order to fully understand archives' contents. Moreover, there are disciplinary biases against archival work (including presentism; see Diamant 2010, 38), and concerns springing from its unpredictable and "necessarily provisional and iterative essence" (Hill 1993, 6).

Of course, archives – and thus archival research – vary significantly. Government archives, university archives, corporate archives, missionary archives, non-governmental or philanthropic organizations' archives, oral history centers, and collections of papers housed privately[64] differ in terms of rules of access, politics, internal practices, and other parameters. Some archives contain only very old documents, while others (such as newspaper archives) receive new documents each week. Some archives reflect public or private investment in preservation and protection, others do not; some are

---

[62] Parts of this section draw on modules taught by James Goldgeier and Elizabeth Saunders at IQMR, and presentations at George Washington University's SICAR.

[63] Diamant (2010) offers an eloquent and compelling discussion of the value of archival work for understanding Chinese politics, and more generally.

[64] In the United States in particular, presidential libraries represent treasure troves of documents and interview transcripts from colleagues, staff, and family of the chief executive. For example, the Kennedy library contains over 1,600 interviews, and the Truman library has more than 500.

well organized while others are in disarray; in some archives, fulfilling requests takes minutes, while in others, it takes months. Generally speaking, in authoritarian regimes (compared with democracies), there may be little presumption that politically relevant information should be available to researchers and more tension surrounding issues of access.

These differences notwithstanding, we believe the strategies discussed here will resonate with and aid most scholars who carry out archival research, no matter what sort of archive they are working in, or how heavily they are relying on the information they find there. We offer two prefatory suggestions. First, as with all data-collection techniques, balance needs to be sought between executing one's pre-determined research strategy on the one hand, and open-mindedness and flexibility – going with what the evidence seems to be indicating, and modifying one's concepts and assumptions as the research unfolds – on the other. Second, scholars should think carefully about what the idiosyncrasies of archival research imply for the rhythm, timing and sequencing of fieldwork. For instance, many scholars who carry out heavily archive-based projects take an initial short "surveying" trip to determine the contents of archives (perhaps developing and deploying a sampling technique) and ultimately revisit archives and reread materials more than once (Hill 1993, 67).

Preparation for archival work

There are several steps researchers can take to prepare for archival work and develop clear goals. Reading the secondary literature on their topic allows scholars to see how debates are structured; scour discussions, footnotes, acknowledgments, and bibliographies for information concerning archives, collections, and documents of potential use; see how archival data can be used to support claims; and begin to envision how they will orient their study vis-à-vis existing work on their topic.[65] Likewise, identifying relevant published collections of interviews and primary documents and examining their introductions and editorial notes to see what archives and sources are mentioned can be very useful. Further, scholars can begin to build their "archive network," contacting the authors of secondary sources, scholars cited therein, and other researchers who have carried out similar studies to ascertain what archives and collections they researched, how they did so,

---

[65] Trachtenberg (2006, 51–58, 199–216) provides useful discussions of how to systematically identify relevant work; Hill (1993, 33–36) offers thoughts on identifying promising archives.

and whether they might be open to communicating about or sharing any of their documents. Once in the field, scholars can expand their networks to include in-country experts (Polillo 2008, 7). To give one example of the value of contacting local academics, the scholar of Mexican nationalism mentioned earlier noted that the idea of looking at notes from textbook commission meetings (to trace the evolution of official nationalist ideas) came to him through talking with historians with years of experience in the education ministry's archive.[66] The same can be done with journalists. Taking these steps can do a great deal to orient scholars and their work. For instance, a researcher working in Europe explained that footnotes from relevant secondary sources, published compilations of archive documents, and conversations with experts at local institutions played an essential role in helping focus his search in actual archives: "Without that I would have been completely overwhelmed."[67]

Researchers should also learn all they can about archival methodology – about systematically searching for relevant sources, and about drawing inferences from documents. They can do so by examining political science scholarship based on archival research, as well as the social science literature focused on archival methods.[68] Engaging with the (admittedly sparse) literature and debates from history and historiography can also help social scientists to develop the tools that they will need to read and interpret different types of sources: a different lens is required to analyze policy memos, advertisements, posters, and lists of donors, to name just a few types of sources.[69] Researchers can also attend institutes and workshops,[70] and possibly audit courses on archival research in the history department at their home university. And they might scan web sites that can introduce them

---

[66] Interview, DK-2, July 26, 2012.   [67] Interview, BR-4, August 9, 2012.

[68] With regard to books, Hill (1993) is an excellent, practical introductory primer; Prior (2003) discusses how to use documents in social science research; Trachtenberg (2006) provides a practical guide to studying international history; and Frisch *et al.* (2012) is likely the most extensive "how-to" source in political science (despite focusing on American politics), helpfully integrating the insights and perspectives of archivists. Mahoney and Villegas (2007) discuss how primary sources (and secondary sources) can be used, and how inferences can be drawn from them.

[69] See, e.g., Tosh (2000). Burton (2005) has assembled a fascinating collection of essays on archival research; in particular, Curthoys (2005) provides a helpful discussion of interpreting historical documents.

[70] SICAR and IQMR were both mentioned previously; other opportunities include the Methods Cafe sponsored by APSA's Interpretive Methodologies and Methods conference group and the short course on archival methodology, both offered during the annual APSA meeting. More specialized workshops also occur; for instance, in November 2010, Stuart Shulman ran a workshop on the US Freedom of Information Act (FOIA), examining electronic content management, e-discovery, redaction, and other topics at the US Department of Agriculture (also available via Webinar).

to archival research: the London School of Economics' "Archives made easy,"[71] H-Net Discussion Networks in general (and H-Diplo Resources in particular, especially "Guides to doing research" under "Organizations"),[72] and the American Historical Association's web site.[73] As they learn more about interpreting sources, scholars may wish to put what they are learning into practice by, for instance, developing draft coding sheets (on which they can get local input once in the field).[74]

As their target archives begin to come into focus, scholars should do what they can to increase their familiarity with them. Beyond learning about their history and evolution, scholars can tap the "archive network" they have begun to create to learn about their target archives' culture, pace, and working environment (e.g., accommodations, clientele, noise, foot-traffic, copier use);[75] their social practices and informal rules (for instance, dress code);[76] and what can be brought into the archive (technology in particular).[77] They can also inquire about how helpful the archivists are and what local customs there might be for working with them (should they bring the archivist a gift of some sort?) and seek to identify other tips for operating in the archives. Scholars might cast a broad net – contacting faculty or graduate students from various disciplines, in the United States or elsewhere – and of course should continue to develop their archive network once in the field. Where better to find people who know an archive inside and out than in and around the archive itself?[78]

Preparation also entails investigating target archives' holdings (determining what exclusions there may be) and internal logic (i.e., the way materials are classified, organized, and ordered), determining the number of items in potentially interesting collections, and identifying what related collections might be useful. Ascertaining what finding aids (brief statements about the scope, structure, and/or contents of a particular collection) are available is also important. To do so, scholars may be able to consult archival inventories

---

[71] www.archivesmadeeasy.org.   [72] www.h-net.org/~diplo/resources.

[73] www.historians.org/info/research.cfm.   [74] Interview, DK-5, July 31, 2012.

[75] Personal communication, January 30, 2011.

[76] In particular, they might check whether the use of ultra-thin gloves to protect the documents is required.

[77] One scholar working in Brazil, for example, was allowed to bring nothing more than paper and pencil into one archive in which she (consequently) spent months in Rio (telephone communication, DK-5, July 31, 2012).

[78] It can even be useful to ask others who work on one's topic or a closely related one – but who do not seem to have used the archive or accessed the documents in which one is interested – why they did not use the archive or collections in question, or whether they know anything about the archive or know anyone who has used it.

and catalogues: some archives publish these on the web or in electronic or print book form. For archives with paper catalogues that can only be accessed from the archive (or with no catalogues at all), researchers might contact scholars or others familiar with the archive, or archive personnel, to seek information about archival holdings. If targeted archives' holdings are in a foreign language, scholars should evaluate their language skills and assess the advisability of using an interpreter.

Another step involved in preparing for archival research (one with implications for fieldwork timing and sequencing) is determining in what *format* (e.g., paper, microfilm, fiche, etc.) the materials of interest are available. Paper can take more time for scholars, archivists, or intermediaries to retrieve; it is also more delicate and may thus take longer to read and process in the archive. As a rule of thumb, the older one's sources, the more fragile (and, likely, less organized) they will be. Microfilm/fiche may be easier to retrieve and handle, but have unique capture challenges: printing from reading machines, if it is possible at all, often requires plunking in coins or using a payment card for each image, which is time consuming. The more familiar scholars become with target archives in advance of beginning work there – perhaps initially during an exploratory trip – the better they can assess how relevant the archives' resources are to their project, how much time research there should take, and which documents to review in what order.[79]

A final aspect of preparation is emotional. While collecting data in the manner under discussion here can be extremely rewarding (and less nerve-wracking than certain types of interviewing or ethnographic work), it can be challenging emotionally – isolating, lonely, and cerebral. Such emotional challenges can, in turn, make it more difficult to deal with the ambiguity fieldwork entails and to summon the patience and persistence required. Both the up-sides and down-sides of archival research need to be planned for in advance.[80] Scholars are encouraged to check log-books to see who else is working in the archive, what topic they are working on, and what documents they are using, and to talk to and befriend others researching there. Beyond the potential for companionship and rich intellectual exchange, such people may have learned some of the archive's tricks and secrets, may have other

---

[79] Hill (1993, 27–39) discusses name-oriented and other archival search strategies.

[80] Concerning archival research's (admittedly minor) physical health risks: scholars may be lifting heavy boxes and sitting for extended periods of time. Those with allergies should consider their exposure to dust in the archives.

relevant information to share, and may be interested in coordinating on requesting and using documents.

Navigating archival access and intra-archival relations

Gaining access to archives and their collections often has both practical and interpersonal aspects. To begin with the practical, scholars should check what restrictions there may be on accessing the archives they wish to visit; verify whether they will be open on the days they plan to visit (keeping national holidays in mind); and confirm their working hours. In addition, they should arrive at their field site with their credentials fully in order. They should determine what paperwork, identification, documentation, permissions (from the country and/or the archive), and/or letters from their home institution are required to gain access to the archive.[81] Investigating whether they need to enter the country on a particular type of visa or register with the archive as a reader is also recommended.

Learning about the terms and process for gaining access to the specific documents they wish to consult is also important; special permission from depositors or a government official, for instance, may be required to view certain collections. Moreover, scholars might be able to arrange in advance for some documents to be ready for their perusal upon their arrival. Indeed, they might need to request them ahead of time; in this case, they will need to know how to place their request (by mail, phone, or internet) and how far in advance to do so. They might also ascertain whether there are any limits on how many items can be requested and examined per day, and whether any access fees are charged.[82]

It can also be advisable to develop good relationships with archivists (and any other intermediaries who retrieve the sources scholars wish to use) for several reasons. Archivists may have the ultimate say on which materials researchers can access. Accordingly, whether archivists look favorably upon a researcher, and whether they are sympathetic to and interested in her project, can make a big difference to her archival experience. For example,

---

[81] Scholars ought to bring several copies of any such letter, with requisite official marks, with them to the field, and perhaps versions translated into the local language.

[82] A further note on requesting materials: when intermediaries are retrieving documents, it can be beneficial to give them broad enough requests such that the scholar is doing the sorting and actual choosing of sources rather than the intermediary. Researchers should also be sure to keep track of what they have requested, rather than relying on archive staff to consistently retrieve (all of) the correct materials – and should not necessarily shy away from requesting closed files or sensitive documents (at least once or twice) in case an archivist or intermediary might be willing to share them.

one interview respondent recounted making a point of learning enough of a local language in Senegal to greet the archivist every day – a strategy that paid off when this scholar was the only visitor allowed to work through lunch and to exceed limits on the distribution of materials.[83] Another suggested that the relationships and trust she built with the clerks at the institution where she was doing research – which she suggested she did by relying heavily on them rather than immediately "going over their heads" to speak with senior staff – resulted in her gaining access to materials other scholars had been unsuccessful in finding.[84] Moreover, archivists who view themselves as the protector of their collections may be reluctant to offer access to scholars they suspect will write something negative based on the materials they wish to access.[85] One of our interview respondents described having just this experience in a German archive: staff members assumed, from a connection the researcher mentioned having with another scholar, that the researcher was not sympathetic to their point of view, and were consequently less forthcoming with materials.[86] Finally, archivists often have intimate knowledge of the collections under their care (including collections whose existence may not be public) and specialized tools to search them (perhaps using finding aids not on the shelves). They may also be willing to introduce researchers who are working on similar topics to each other.

Of course, scholars should not take what archivists say as gospel, nor expect them to know everything about archival collections. Archivists can be powerful political figures in their own right, and may have incentives to portray their institution or its holdings in a certain way, or may have been trained to approach the collections under their care from a particular perspective (e.g., relatively conventional or politically safe). When making recommendations, they may (intentionally or unintentionally) overlook documents in which researchers (with their own perspectives and goals) might be interested, or portray them in a way different from that in which researchers would see them.

These caveats notwithstanding, given the influence archivists can have over one's research experience, identifying connections one might have with archivists (perhaps through one's host institution or an interview respondent), and building relationships and trust with them (perhaps inquiring with

---

[83] Interview, LM-7, September 20, 2012.   [84] Interview, DK-17, August 24, 2012.

[85] Additionally, one never knows when one may need to contact archivists or intermediaries after leaving the field to request missing documents, ask that a particular document be re-photocopied, etc. In this vein, see Hill (1993, 56–57) on "archiving at a distance."

[86] Interview LM-4, August 27, 2012.

others who have worked in the archive about how to do so), can be vital
for facilitating entrée to archives and to specific collections. We offer three
concrete suggestions for gaining archivists' favor and trust.

First, early on in their research, scholars should read archivists' introductory essays in collection inventories. These can reveal a great deal about
archivists, the contents of collections, and what related documents may be
available elsewhere. Second, particularly if their study is politically sensitive,
scholars should seek to present themselves, their topic, and their project in a
neutral or even positive light (for instance, in any "orientation interview"
they have with the archivist: Hill 1993, 41–44). Using uncontroversial language when describing the research, and keeping in mind how archive staff
unfamiliar with the ways of foreign academics might interpret their goals
and behavior, are both good ideas. For example, a scholar studying welfare
largesse with regard to the elderly (and at the expense of other population
segments) in Italy might present the project as one focusing on Italy's
generous support to the aging. Finally, scholars can reassure archivists that
they will use information from the archive responsibly, and perhaps even
agree to keep certain pieces of information confidential (as appropriate for
their study).

Organization and analysis

Given the sea of information in which archival researchers swim, remaining
organized is crucial.[87] Of particular importance, as we discuss elsewhere (see
Chapters 3, 4, and 10), is devising a personally appealing organization system
that is readily searchable, and from which the scholar can easily retrieve
items. Particularly if he anticipates sharing his data or releasing information
for replication, the system should be easily understood by others as well.
A critical facet of a scholar's organizing system should be a log including
every folder extracted from an archive box (whether or not the document in
the folder was collected), perhaps using ATLAS TI (or Excel or Word). Such
logs can be annotated with descriptive information about the documents and
ideas for how they relate to the broader analysis.[88] Further, a system for
highlighting items that look potentially useful (or less useful) and justifying

---

[87] We are grateful to Elizabeth Saunders for the vast majority of the suggestions offered in this subsection,
which she discusses in the presentation on "Archival methods of research" that she gives annually
at IQMR.

[88] Scholars might consider the following naming protocol for documents: Place/Date/ArchivistName/
Series/Subseries/Box/Folder/Document Title.

those judgments could be created. All of these annotations are preliminary steps toward analysis. For those items scholars capture (in hard-copy form or digitally), it is also crucial to keep bibliographic information with the data themselves (see Hill 1993, 69). When photocopying or scanning documents, for example, scholars can copy or scan the title page and/or copyright page and keep it with the other individual pages reproduced; an alternative is to put a slip of paper with the bibliographic information on the copier glass when copying. Analogous processes can be used when taking photos of documents. Alternatively or in addition, scholars can take a picture of the label of the box from which the files that housed the photographed documents were drawn, making sure to capture the folder tab in the picture.

In terms of organizing data (scans of documents, digital pictures, coding sheets, etc.) on their computer, scholars might impose a file/folder structure that mimics the archive's organization, and then organize all of the images they are capturing and other materials they are gathering by folder. Scholars might consider using an image management system such as Picasa to store and display pictures; Picasa adopts the file structure on one's computer and allows the cropping, straightening, rotating, brightening, and whitening of images. Further, scholars can create captions in Picasa (great quotes from particular documents can be added right into the caption field) and tag documents with key words or ideas – and then search document photos by keyword or quote. Ideally, data will also be organized and stored in a way that will be recognizable by computers in the future. However, to reiterate, the most important criterion is that the organization system be intuitive and easy for the researcher to use so his documents remain quickly accessible to him. And as we have also repeatedly emphasized, scholars should back everything up – their framework documents, their logs, their notes concerning sampling, and all their data – by burning them onto a CD, copying them onto a secondary hard drive, or uploading them to a network or cloud storage site. When those options are unavailable, they can email their materials to themselves or a trusted colleague.

Most importantly, scholars should strive to maximize the intellectual value of the organization process by beginning to process and analyze data as they organize them. In doing so, they should consider their broader analytic goals. For instance, if they ultimately hope to conduct discourse or content analysis on the materials they are collecting, that may dictate a particular way of organizing them. They may wish to get all data into one format (perhaps by creating digital pictures of articles for which a hard copy was created in the archive). Fully transcribing documents that contain large amounts of highly salient information for the project,[89] or making a "table of contents" of some documents, noting the page and line number where the most crucial bits of information about particular topics can be found, can be helpful. Scholars should also continue taking notes on, describing, and summarizing their documents and further annotating their log. More broadly, seeking to connect the items they have collected to their data-collection plan and their timeline (if they have created one; see Chapter 3) can be very useful. In sum, developing and deploying a strategy for collecting and analyzing data *in tandem* represents the most efficient route to the research goal. We offer further thoughts on how to do so in Chapter 10.

Conclusion

Gathering pre-existing materials in the field is an important mode of data collection in which practically every scholar who conducts fieldwork engages, even if sporadically. While collecting pre-existing sources is often equated with archival research, this chapter sought to demonstrate that materials that can prove critical to one's research can be of infinite types, and can be found in locations far beyond archives. We strongly encourage scholars not to overlook potential sources of useful knowledge, and to think openly and creatively about the data-collection enterprise. We also compared and contrasted pre-existing materials and the process of collecting them with more interactive forms of gathering data. When working with extant sources, scholars have less influence over what information is potentially available, and thus over what data they can ultimately generate. They are essentially collecting bread crumbs left by earlier actors and scholars who had their own interests and agenda in mind when they produced or collected those sources, and by the archivists who made them available. Despite these differences, a steady commitment to ethical practice is no less important when collecting and analyzing pre-existing sources than it is when engaging in more inter-active forms of data collection. Moreover, because of their differences and the distinct types of data they produce, *combining* less-interactive and more-interactive modes of data collection is an excellent strategy for enhancing inference. For certain kinds of questions and projects, opportunities for triangulation among sources of multiple types abound.

---

[89] Another option, if photos of documents are very clear, is to run them through an Optical Character Recognition (OCR) program to convert them to text.

This chapter also discussed strategies for making theoretically informed and methodologically sound decisions about which pre-existing materials to consult and what information to collect, and for appraising sources' evidentiary value. At the root of many of our suggestions is the importance of engaging with the immediate context in which pre-existing materials were found, learning as much as possible about the more distant context in which they were created, and critically reflecting on how those contexts likely affected the contours, content, tone, and, indeed, resilience of the pre-existing materials a scholar has collected to use in her analysis. We also examined how deploying such materials can help scholars accomplish multiple analytic goals and piece empirical puzzles together.

Throughout, we emphasized the benefits, for the researcher and for readers of her work, of practicing transparency when working with pre-existing materials, another research principle we emphasize. Scholars make myriad choices when collecting pre-existing sources, particularly in an archival context. Documenting those choices as they are made – clearly explaining how and why a certain sampling technique was adopted, or particular archive eschewed – will help scholars remain clear on how the data underlying their conclusions and inferences were compiled. Conveying the details of those choices in their published work will allow readers to develop the same confidence in scholars' conclusions as the scholars themselves have.

Collecting pre-existing materials in the field can be exciting and rewarding – particularly when one happens upon a dataset that had proven elusive, a "smoking gun" document, a bumper sticker with a priceless quote, or a political cartoon that perfectly captures the gist or irony of the political dynamic under study. When considering this form of inquiry, we urge scholars *not* to allow their minds to conjure up stereotypical images of being locked away in the damp, drab depths of a musty archive slowly slogging through heaps of paper by candlelight. As one interviewee put it:

It's possible to trace policy without field research. But connecting the dots in official records reflects countless assumptions about what happened and why ... Digging through archives can test those assumptions, allows you to learn what was in people's minds, what pressures they were under. For me, it's completely exciting.[90]

---

[90] Interview, BR-9, August 16, 2012.

In sum, playing detective – filling out the complex empirical story of a cataclysmic historical event, or a quickly developing international show-down, step-by-step and piece-by-piece from documents written by those who actually sat around the bargaining table, or from daily newspaper accounts – can be exhilarating and profoundly gratifying.

6 | Interviews, oral histories, and focus groups

While not all political scientists consider gathering pre-existing materials to be a core mode of data collection, interviewing has traditionally been an essential technique for gathering data in the field.[1] With the exception of the site-intensive methods discussed in the next chapter, employing other data-collection techniques rarely allows scholars to achieve a level of dynamism or fluidity of interaction with those whose behavior they hope to understand equal to that which can be realized in an interview. Interviews allow us to gather information to generate detailed, holistic descriptions, capture varying perspectives, discuss processes, unearth competing interpretations of events, identify the micro-foundations of macro-patterns, and frame hypotheses (Weiss 1994, 9–11). Moreover, while political actors' formal decision-making processes are more visible and available than ever before in today's information-rich environment, interviews allow us to explore the informal interactions and behaviors that can be equally important to political outcomes (Beckmann and Hall 2013, 297).

Indeed, according to the results of our survey of US political science faculty, interviewing is the most common form of data collection for political scientists who engage in fieldwork. Fully 81 percent of field research projects reported in the survey made significant use of interviews – the highest percentage associated with a data-collection technique about which we asked. Specialists in all subfields use interviews liberally: 92 percent of field research projects undertaken by comparativists involved them, and 84 percent and 71 percent of IR specialists' and Americanists' projects did so, respectively. Even 50 percent of projects reported by political theorists involved interviews. Oral history figured in 31 percent of all projects (and was thus

---

[1] See Dexter (1970, 13), Kvale and Brinkmann (2009, 7–14), and Platt (2012) on the history of interviewing in the social sciences and its emergence as a more important data-collection technique in political science as part of the behavioral revolution and with the greater emphasis on empirical methods of investigation in the mid twentieth century.

employed in a higher percentage of projects than was survey research), and focus groups figured in 13 percent. The frequency with which scholars combine interviews with other data-collection techniques demonstrates that political scientists across the methodological spectrum conduct interviews – even scholars whose main focus is experiments, or who spend most of their days buried deep in a library poring over archival documents.

Despite the significant advantages and prevalence of interviewing, few faculty or graduate students have any formal training in or preparation for conducting interviews in advance of their field research. In fact, graduate students and faculty of all ranks told us, sometimes sheepishly, that they conducted their very first interview only after they had arrived in their field site. As we noted earlier, political science graduate programs tend to focus methodological training on how to *analyze* data rather than on how to *collect* them. Our interview data also suggest that even the qualitative methods or field research methods courses offered in some graduate programs generally dedicate only a couple of hours to the discussion (and sometimes the practice) of interviewing. The assumption seems to be that interviewing requires a skill set that everyone has: if you can talk, you can do an interview.[2] Relatedly, there is relatively little *written* on interviewing in political science; a few recent article symposia (Leech 2002b; Ortbals and Rincker 2009), an intriguing manual penned by political scientist Lewis Anthony Dexter (1970) more than forty years ago, and a recent edited volume (Mosley 2013a) are important exceptions.[3]

Yet while interviewing may look natural or easy to an outside observer, it involves much more than sparking a conversation between a researcher and an interlocutor. Further, scholars differ on what that "much more" entails. More positivist researchers may attempt to remain as neutral as possible while interviewing, hoping that by keeping themselves "out of the data" they will elicit relatively objective approximations of empirical truth that they can use as evidence in their analysis. In contrast, a more interpretive researcher might insist on the subjective nature of the interview itself, understanding it as a vehicle for revealing constructed representations of various potentially competing truth claims. Many field researchers seem to adopt elements from both traditions, as others have also discussed (Soss 2006). No matter how

---

[2] Mosley, in the Introduction to her edited volume on interview research, recalls her advisor's suggestion about interviewing: "Just talk to people" (2013b, 1).

[3] Other political scientists who have written about interviewing include Weiner (1964), Aberbach, Chesney, and Rockman (1975), and Rathbun (2008).

scholars lean epistemologically and think about the production of know-ledge, however, conducting interviews effectively – and feeling comfortable doing so – involves extensive preparation and practice.[4] There is a great deal scholars can and should learn about gaining access to potential respondents, structuring interview protocols, formulating and asking questions, and gaining respondents' trust, to name just a few topics. Lack of preparation in these and other areas can have negative consequences for the quality of the data scholars collect as well as for continued access to respondents.[5]

As with other data-collection techniques discussed in this book, the models and practices of interviewing have been examined in a voluminous literature in anthropology, sociology, and psychology in particular (Adler and Adler 2001; Gubrium and Holstein 2002; Leech 2002b; Kvale 2008; Rubin and Rubin 2004, 104–5). Our aim is not to replace the existing literature – indeed, no book, let alone a single chapter, could. Instead, we hope to build on it by highlighting how the unexpected contingencies of working in the field may influence the conduct of interviews and the data gained from them. Hence, rather than discussing interviewing in its neat, abstract form, we try to reveal the messy reality of interview research in the field, illustrating how field conditions, and the limits and tradeoffs (and opportunities) they create, affect the conduct of interview research. While our discussion concerns face-to-face in-person interviews, some of the advice and lessons we offer are also relevant for telephone, voice-over-internet, or email interviews.

In the chapter's next section, we introduce briefly three types of interview-ing: (1) in-depth interviews with individuals; (2) oral histories exploring a person's memories of the past; and (3) focus groups aimed at uncovering different viewpoints within a group on a set of topics. We highlight their differences in terms of the number of participants, the role of the researcher, and their degree of structure, and consider their strengths and weaknesses. We also discuss combining interviews with other data-collection techniques, showing how triangulating adds analytic value. In the chapter's third section, we draw on scholarship from all subfields of political science to demonstrate

---

[4] Kvale and Brinkmann (2009, 47–60) offer a clear and concise discussion of different epistemological takes on interviewing.

[5] In what he describes as a "small editorial aside" in an article footnote, Goldstein (2002, 672) makes a rather sweeping claim about the deleterious consequences of inadequate preparation for long-term access, writing that: "Our discipline's access to elites in Washington, especially members of Congress, has been hurt by massive amounts of poorly trained students and scholars being unprepared for interviews."

how interviewing provides compelling data that can contribute to every stage of theory building – helping scholars to identify a research question, select cases, refine conceptualization and measurement, generate new hypotheses, and understand causal mechanisms and processes.[6] In the fourth section, we discuss some of the issues that researchers face when interviewing in the field, and share strategies for addressing common challenges. While no single solution will address the array of challenges that scholars interviewing in the field may confront, preparing in advance but remaining flexible in practice, engaging with the cultural and political context of the field site, and critically reflecting on what is being learned – being what Giovanni Sartori referred to long ago as "conscious thinkers" (1970, 1033) – will help guide scholars to effective responses to each unique dilemma. Our suggestions in this final substantive section, then, underline several of the principles that we contend underlie good political science field research.

Types of interviews

We distinguish among and compare three types of interviewing: in-depth interviews with individuals, oral histories, and focus groups.[7] We organize our discussion according to the interview process rather than the status or expertise of the interviewee (elite vs. non-elite). Of course, researchers face divergent challenges and opportunities when they interview respondents from different social classes and who wield different levels of political power, and they may use information gathered through those interviews for different analytic purposes.[8] Nonetheless, with regard to operating in the field, the most important differences among interviews concern the number of individuals involved, the role the researcher plays, and the structure of the interaction (see Table 6.1). Although the boundaries between interview types are fuzzy (one technique can shade into another as researchers employ them in the field), each has characteristic advantages and drawbacks. As we also discuss, they can often be profitably combined – and mixed with other forms of data collection.

---

[6] For a similar discussion focused specifically on in-depth interviewing, see Lynch (2013).

[7] See Morse (2012, 194–197) and Kvale and Brinkmann (2009, 143–160) for finer-grained distinctions and characterizations of interview types.

[8] Scholars have attempted to clarify that in-depth interviews are not exclusively with wealthy or powerful actors, but confusion persists. See Leech (2002b) who draws on Dexter (1970) to discuss what is meant by elite interviewing; see also Dexter's (1970, 3, 18) distinction between "standardized" and "nonstandardized" interviewing.

Table 6.1 Three types of interviewing

		In-depth interviews	Oral history interviews	Focus group interviews
Number of participants		1–2	1	6–10
Role of researchers		Provocateur	Active listener	Facilitator
Interview constitution	**Degree of structure**	Varies from loose to highly structured; less structured than a survey	Low; usually researcher identifies starting point and participant guides narrative flow	Moderate; researcher/facilitator poses questions but order and emphasis shaped by participants
	Question type and ordering	Generally open-ended; questions asked in variable order	Open-ended; narrative proceeds chronologically	Prepared list of open-ended questions; order and emphasis shaped by group
Potential advantages		Can reveal unique perspectives and sensitive, highly charged information	Can reveal unique historical perspective and causal processes	Can reveal tensions and disagreements
Potential disadvantages		Specificity of viewpoints; inefficiency	Particularity; representation as unscientific	Potential for group think

In-depth interviews

When researchers say they "do interviews," they are often referring to in-depth interviews. These can of course vary in formality – our understanding includes a formal appointment with a diplomat arranged months in advance, an informal or even spontaneous meeting with an academic colleague in the field, and everything in between. Such interviews are usually conducted with one individual. On occasion, there will be two interview subjects, often with associated or conjoined sets of expertise, for example, a husband and wife, or two business partners. At other times, the respondent may have a trusted aide he prefers to have present, or an official spokesperson, such as the *okyeame* for Akan chiefs in Ghana (Yankah 1995).[9] Likewise, researchers generally carry out in-depth interviews by themselves, although they may be accompanied by a research assistant or a translator (Fujii 2013). While the researcher may be disinclined to "count" aides and translators as interview participants, every

---

[9] If the number of respondents increases beyond two, the dynamics may shift toward a group interaction more akin to a focus group, described below.

person present, even someone who quietly observes just for a brief moment, can fundamentally shape an interview and the data produced.

The role of the researcher in an in-depth interview may vary depending on how structured an exchange is planned, the nature of the research question, the stage of the project at which he finds himself, his interview objectives, his epistemological perspective, the characteristics of the interviewing context, and the respondent. Nonetheless, in general, the researcher acts as provocateur. He poses stimulating questions, listening actively as he probes and moves the interview forward to cover an array of topics or questions. In-depth interviews are often characterized as conversational, but the interviewee usually spends more time talking than the researcher (a balance referred to as "proportionality").

Greater variation exists with regard to how actively scholars direct the exchange – or redirect it when the respondent goes off in a new direction (an attribute referred to as "directionality"). Some in-depth interviews are highly structured: scholars enter the interview with a precise list of questions prepared in advance to be asked in a particular order.[10] Scholars with these sorts of protocols intervene frequently to guide the conversation, motivate the respondent, and keep the interview focused on their questions. Other interviews are extremely loose, with the order and substance of questions almost entirely guided by the respondent. Interpretive researchers who emphasize the subjectivity of the interview encounter tend to conduct less structured interviews in which topics and themes of importance are identified and constructed through the interaction, and unanticipated detours are the main focus of the analysis. Perhaps most often, in-depth interviews will be somewhere in between. In one form of semi-structured interviewing, for instance, the investigator arrives with a list of "information needed" or "questions to get to," but allows the conversation to unfold in a relatively flexible fashion. Indeed, most researchers seek to keep their minds open to what they can learn when a respondent departs from their agenda – for instance, to illuminate dynamics or questions she thinks are important, or to indicate how she frames debates. Indeed, the tendency toward a lower degree of structure is one of the critical ways in which interviewing differs from survey research. Where the guiding principle of survey interviewing is to

---

[10] Such an approach, which results in interviews being more similar in question content and order, can produce data that are more comparable and allow for hypothesis testing and the quantitative analysis of interview responses (Leech 2002a, 665).

precisely replicate question wording and order across respondents, in-depth interviewing allows for customization to the individual respondent.

With regard to the questions asked in in-depth interviews, no matter how structured the overall exchange, questions are usually open-ended.[11] However, interview questions can vary greatly with regard to how they are formulated and what information they seek. Sometimes scholars ask vague questions, relying heavily upon the interviewee to choose and construct the information conveyed. At other times, researchers formulate queries with the goal of eliciting concrete information about specific events, dynamics, or phenomena, or responses that speak to particular conceptual categories or will help them to measure a particular phenomenon. Of course, given the vagaries of the field context, an interview that was envisioned to be structured may, in the end, become more semi-structured or free flowing.

In-depth interviews can help scholars to gain a sense of social context, to probe how citizens understand the political world, and to derive relevant categories of analysis. They can be particularly well suited for identifying and detailing elite political actors' unique experiences, perspectives, or viewpoints. No other individual will have quite the same perspective as the Minister of Defense for Israel during the conflict with Lebanon in 2006, or the leader of a political party when it made a fundamental change in its platform. In-depth interviews can also be particularly valuable when the topic under study is highly controversial, sensitive, or politically charged, meaning that potential respondents may be reluctant to discuss the matter publicly or in a larger group. Moreover, scholars who carry out interviews can potentially gain more in-depth "meta-data" about their respondents as compared with those who conduct surveys: rather than simply noting that a particular picture or a book was present in the respondent's office or that staff were gathered just before the interview, they can inquire about these things as part of the encounter. What they learn can help scholars to develop additional insight into interviewees' behavior and to draw better inferences and conclusions from their data. Other writings further

---

[11] Closed questions provide pre-determined answers from which respondents choose, limiting their latitude. For excellent discussions of the relative merits of open-ended and closed interview questions, and criteria scholars can use to decide which approach to take, see Aberbach *et al.* (1975, 3–8), Schuman and Presser (1981, 79–112), Aberbach and Rockman (2002, 674), Rivera *et al.* (2002, 686), Beckmann and Hall (2013), and Leech *et al.* (2013). Consider also the use of open-ended questions *together with* a brief questionnaire with closed questions in Rivera *et al.* (2002, 686) and Beckmann and Hall (2013), or in tandem with a lengthy questionnaire as in Stokes *et al.* (2013).

discuss benefits of interviewing compared with survey research (Soss 2006; Leech *et al.* 2013, 209–211).

Interviewing has some identifiable disadvantages, however. Respondents sometimes offer self-serving and distorted accounts. An interview subject might convincingly portray her view to be authoritative and objective, or might suggest that it is uncontested, even when it is biased or controversial. Also, like oral histories, any one interview provides a narrow viewpoint on the phenomenon of interest.[12] And, in the words of one of our own interview respondents – one who advocates conducting interviews in tandem with other data-collection techniques – "done well and reliably," interviews are "expensive in time, money, and thought [and] . . . inefficient."[13]

Oral histories

Oral histories are more often associated with the disciplines of history, and, to a lesser extent, anthropology and sociology (White, Miescher, and Cohen 2001; Charlton, Myers, and Sharpless 2006; Giles-Vernick 2006; Atkinson 2012) than with political science. Nonetheless, even when directed by historians, oral history projects often focus on collecting histories from important political leaders or on important political events.[14] As their name suggests, oral histories are more exclusively focused on the past than are in-depth interviews: they are an oral record of an individual's life experiences (also known as "life histories"), or her memories of an event, or a community's, organization's, or family's history (to give just a few examples). They might be targeted or quite sweeping in scope. The respondent may have been a direct eyewitness to the historical occurrence or time period of interest, or may be conveying knowledge of a past beyond her own lifetime or generation, perhaps recounting memories and stories passed down from older generations.[15] In essence, the personal accounts obtained through oral history research are generally used to crosscheck or supplement incomplete or biased information available in existing written records – that is, to triangulate.

---

[12] Rubin and Rubin (2004, 47–48) and Dexter (1970) offer some criteria to help scholars evaluate the appropriateness of interviewing as a data-collection technique for their project.

[13] Interview, DK-6, July 31, 2012; see also interview, LM-18, September 14, 2012.

[14] For instance, the University of Virginia's Presidential Oral History Program, which includes both political scientists and historians, is working to debrief central political figures in several late-twentieth-century presidential administrations. Dexter (1970, 93–99) offers some additional examples.

[15] We do not make a distinction here, as some historians do, between eyewitness accounts as "oral history" (Perks and Thomson 1998; Thompson 2000) and stories passed down between generations as "oral tradition" (Vansina 1965, 1985).

Oral history, as a research technique, has an important political history itself.[16] In the years following World War II, oral histories frequently focused on the private narratives of political elites, particularly high-level government leaders. Beginning in the 1960s, historians began to popularize oral history as a way to obtain evidence about the past in places where historical events were not recorded in writing, or where the written record systematically excluded the voices of less powerful groups. This movement to study "history from below" paralleled temporally the civil rights and women's rights movements in the United States and the decolonization of much of Africa and Asia.[17] In more recent decades, political scientists and others have begun to use oral histories from above and below. For instance, they have been used to reveal American policymakers' behind-the-scenes perspectives,[18] and to uncover village-level politics and gender dynamics in the process of revolutionary change in China (Seybolt 1996; Hershatter 2011). Unfortunately, political scientists' use of oral history interviewing techniques is seldom acknowledged explicitly in their published work, raising the question of whether scholars could and should engage more directly with the rich literature from the discipline of history on how to conduct this type of interviewing effectively.

Like in-depth interviews, oral histories are usually conducted with one individual at a time. Even when the objective is to learn the history of a particular community or culture, generally scholars conduct a series of individual interviews. When people are speaking in a group, tensions can arise between different narratives and representations of history that can unproductively squelch a particular rendition. Yet the principal idea motivating this technique is that individuals have unique memories and historical understandings of the same dynamics, which merit independent investigation. In view of the strong focus on the individual, it is especially critical for

---

[16] The American historian Allan Nevins founded the first oral history project at Columbia University in the late 1940s. The Columbia Center for Oral History has one of the largest archives of oral history, with over 8,000 audio and video transcripts of interviews. This institution continues to play a leading role in the field, particularly in manuscript management and oral history training. See http://library.columbia.edu/locations/ccoh.html.

[17] The expansion of oral history projects may have been particularly central to the development of African-American studies, gender studies (Bornat and Diamond 2007), and African history (White *et al.* 2001) during this period. Prominent examples of oral history are the work of Theodore Rosengarten (1975), a historian who drew on more than 60 hours of oral history interviews to write about the life of an African-American sharecropper who joined a union and resisted the racial oppression of the South in the 1930s; and Jan Vansina (1965, 1985), who used oral tradition to reveal and legitimize the precolonial history of communities in Central Africa.

[18] For example, on how to respond to Russia after the Cold War (Goldgeier and McFaul 2003).

the researcher to learn in advance all he can about the interviewee and how he or she fits into the historical and political milieu. The researcher can then ask searching questions that will elicit details and nuances of the respondent's perspective and how it contrasts with others'.

Oral histories tend to be less structured, more conversational, and more respondent-driven than in-depth or focus group interviews. The researcher frequently identifies the starting point of an oral history interview by using a known event as an anchor to stimulate the recall of the respondent; he may even present the respondent with relevant documents or photographs for her consideration. As the interview progresses, the researcher may gently probe in an effort to shape the interview or keep the respondent focused on the topics of interest, ask additional open-ended questions, or encourage the interviewee to double back and offer more details on particular subjects. But overall, compared with in-depth and focus group interviews, the interviewer often takes more of a back seat: he provides the time and space for the respondent to tell her story, allows her to drive the chronological narrative, and plays the role of active listener while the respondent guides the flow of the discussion. A researcher who has used oral history interviews to gather information about traumatic events put it this way: "I issue an invitation to hear a narrative, and I speak very little" – while remaining curious, engaged, and respectful.[19] Given the heavily respondent-centric nature of oral histories, the researcher often ends up spending considerable time with each interviewee. Due to the effort and emotional energy respondents often must invest in order to recount a personal narrative from the past, oral histories are frequently conducted during multiple encounters.

Oral history interviews can provide unique historical perspectives on political events for which other sources of information are unavailable – perhaps because the society is closed, due to national security strictures, because written accounts or records were not kept during the time period of interest or have been lost or destroyed, because certain groups' stories and perspectives are excluded from written sources due to discrimination, and so on. For example, MacLean was only able to capture the local Ghanaian experience of the Great Depression using oral histories with elder village residents; the written sources in the British archives were penned exclusively from the viewpoint of British colonial officials in the Gold Coast (2010, 107–108).

---

[19] Interview, DK-19, August 27, 2012.

A potential disadvantage for political scientists of employing this valuable data-collection technique is its alleged "low scientific value" due to the extreme particularity of the data it produces, and its representation by some as more "folklore" than truth.[20] Some scholars may find it hard to imagine that theoretically interesting or generalizable claims could be constructed on the basis of the fine-grained, personalistic information collected through oral history interviewing.[21] Political scientists might meet such objections by shaping their oral history interviews to address targeted theoretical concerns, interviewing multiple subjects, interviewing the same subject multiple times,[22] and perhaps combining oral history with other forms of evidence in a process of triangulation. Carefully describing the conduct of oral histories in one's scholarship and thereby contextualizing the information gained through them – that is, being transparent, a principle of good field research – could also help to enhance the credibility of evidence gathered through this powerful data-collection technique.

Focus groups

In a focus group interview, a set of people are invited to participate in a group discussion on a pre-determined topic or set of issues, and are queried concerning their ideas, views, perceptions, or attitudes. Unlike oral history interviewing in which scholars seek to isolate particular individuals' narratives and representations of history, the goal with a focus group is precisely to generate interaction among participants. While this interviewing technique was initially developed by sociologists in the late 1940s, it is most frequently associated with marketing research and advertising campaigns, which began to use focus groups in the 1950s. Focus groups regained some popularity with social scientists in the late 1970s and into the 1980s, although political

---

[20] One indicator of this viewpoint comes in the form of IRB practices: in 2003, the Oral History Association and the American History Association obtained agreement from the US government to exempt most oral history interviewing from IRB review. Nevertheless, egregious violations of human subjects in other disciplines have provoked increasing vigilance by many campus IRBs, meaning that many projects using oral history are still required to pass some level of local IRB review (Townsend and Belli 2004; Shopes 2007; Schrag 2009). See also www.oralhistory.org/about/do-oral-history/oral-history-and-irb-review.

[21] In a classic essay reflecting on the early maturation of oral history, Grele (1978) responded to critiques that oral histories were at times only collecting unimportant trivia (Tuchman 1996), noting the importance of their being theoretically grounded and methodologically rigorous.

[22] Grele (1998) argues that oral history deepens our understanding of history more than reading the written record does precisely because those who carry out oral histories are interacting with their sources and can return repeatedly to ask them to recount particular events, or explain in more detail.

scientists only began to employ the technique in greater numbers during the 1990s (Copsey 2008). Just as political scientists used focus groups more and more, so too political parties, political campaigns, and incumbent political administrations increasingly employed the technique to uncover attitudes toward particular initiatives, public policies, and campaign strategies (Savigny 2007).

The most obvious distinction between focus groups on the one hand, and in-depth and oral history interviews on the other, is the greater number of participants simultaneously involved in the former. As such, focus groups may seem to augment the efficiency of interviewing, allowing researchers to speak with more individuals. Indeed, this impression may have contributed to the increased use of focus groups over time,[23] given evolving constraints on funding for field research. Yet, the purpose of focus groups is to obtain *group* data, not data associated with particular individuals. Researchers closely monitor how the substance of individuals' comments evolves through the course of intra-group interaction and discussion. Scholars debate the ideal size for a focus group. If the group is too large, individual participants may not have ample opportunity to share their opinions, and may be inclined to withdraw or hold side conversations. Conversely, if a group is too small, it can be difficult for group dynamics and interactions to emerge. While field conditions may recommend a larger or smaller group, typically the most effective focus groups range from six to twelve members (Krueger 1994, 27–28) and last between 1 and 2 hours.

The optimal degree of heterogeneity and familiarity among focus group members is also a source of scholarly disagreement. Ultimately, a researcher's question and hypotheses will drive focus group recruitment strategies (Short 2006, 104). For example, if the researcher wishes to know how political beliefs and political participation vary among generations, she might organize several focus groups of different age cohorts. The field-site context may also affect the extent and type of heterogeneity that is productive for group interaction (see Hennick 2007). In some field sites, women and men would not be combined in one group. In other contexts, mixing individuals of different citizenship statuses or ethnicities within a focus group would hinder the rapport necessary for candid conversation. Researchers also need to consider whether familiarity among focus group participants would increase or decrease their willingness to communicate and divulge information. While

---

[23] Our survey results bolster this point: while only 6 percent of projects reported on that were carried out in the 1960s and 1970s employed focus groups, 15 percent of projects carried out from 2000 on did so.

in some contexts it would be impossible or undesirable to assemble a group of total strangers, in other contexts a group of participants without pre-determined conceptions of each other and with little probability of encountering each other after the focus group would generate better data and enhance the prospects of maintaining collective confidentiality.

Focus groups vary with regard to their degree of structure. Some resemble highly structured group interviews with the researcher's standard set of questions providing the framework for eliciting information (Hertel, Singer, and Van Cott 2009, 307). In others, the researcher poses relatively general or abstract questions about the topic, but the order and time spent on each question are heavily shaped by the participants. In either scenario, the researcher's role is primarily to facilitate the group's interactions (Greenbaum 2000), creating a safe and open environment, without judgment, in which participants feel comfortable sharing their individual opinions and personal experiences. Leading a focus group is as much an art as a science. The researcher must have extensive knowledge of the political and social context in order to anticipate and respond to the verbal and physical cues of trust, obfuscation, withdrawal, reticence, and anger (Wellings, Branigan, and Mitchell 2000) – and to manage conflict, domination,[24] and, importantly, silence. The researcher's goals and contextual conditions also influence whether and how she guides the discussion in and out of controversial terrain. Because of the challenges of facilitating, observing, and recording the conversation, scholars usually conduct focus groups with the assistance of at least one other person. As always, the presence of assistants will affect the data gathered, and researchers should consider the implications of their choice of assistant.

As noted previously, focus group interviewing is uniquely positioned to reveal how individuals interact in a public group setting, exchanging views and influencing each other's perspectives; researchers gain insights both by listening to the conversation and by watching the group encounter. Focus groups can expose the range of ideas, attitudes, norms, or opinions concerning an event, topic, or issue; elucidate the tensions and points of

---

[24] One researcher who frequently uses focus groups prior to developing a survey explained how his study team typically dealt with a domineering focus group participant. One member of the team would approach the person, explain that they noticed that they had "really important things to say," and draw the person away from the group to participate instead in an individual interview (interview, LM-10, September 18, 2012). The literature on focus groups cited earlier provides many additional techniques for dealing with a range of challenging focus group participants. See also www.psfieldresearch.org for a generic handbook that can be adapted for facilitator training.

disagreement among them; and demonstrate how group dynamics shape them. They are particularly useful when an event or issue is contested – when a productive tension can emerge as the focus group proceeds – yet not so charged that individuals are unwilling to speak freely in a larger group. Indeed, while an interviewee's viewpoint may go unquestioned in an in-depth interview or oral history, in a focus group one participant can challenge another or point out inconsistencies. Thus under the right conditions, conducting a focus group allows a researcher to triangulate in real time, gathering multiple perspectives. Focus groups can also be a relatively efficient strategy for collecting information about a community or an organization (e.g., when it was founded, how many members it has, and so on).[25] In all these ways, focus group interviews differ from more particularistic in-depth interviews and oral histories, in which respondents necessarily frame responses in terms of their own characteristics and perspectives (Short 2006, 104–105).

Yet focus groups have some downsides as well. It can take an enormous amount of time to schedule and organize a focus group, as doing so multiplies the access and logistical challenges posed by individual interviewing (discussed later in the chapter). More substantively, participants' opinions can change in the presence of others (Krueger 1994),[26] raising the specter that focus groups may produce "group think," in which dissident opinions are squelched by the tendency to give way to the majority view (Michell 1999).[27] Focus groups may also become dominated by a few strongly opinionated participants (Mosley 2013b, 7). Indeed, social hierarchies may influence respondents' interactions, proliferating positionality issues (Hertel et al. 2009, 307). The focus group setting also increases confidentiality concerns: participants might be unwilling to provide information in the presence of a "group of witnesses" if they believe doing so could come back to haunt them "professionally, politically, or personally" (Dexter 1970, 5). All of these challenges can affect the data that are gathered via focus groups and their evidentiary value. By assembling groups carefully, fostering a welcoming atmosphere, and outlining ground rules, researchers can minimize the possibility of tyrannical consensus, or, at the very least, carefully

---

[25] Interview, LM-10, September 18, 2012.

[26] Of course, these shifts themselves, and the moment at which, way in which, and direction in which they occur, can be important data points.

[27] Copsey (2008) argues that "group think" is less likely for political issues that are salient, and where participants have more firmly held beliefs and opinions, than for preferences about non-political consumer products, for instance.

observe it (Short 2006). And, of course, researchers who notice any of these dynamics should indicate in their notes – and ultimately in their write-up – what occurred, why, and what effects it might have had on the data they collected.

By discussing these different types of interview techniques in turn, we in no way mean to suggest that they are mutually exclusive – quite the opposite. Understanding the differences and complementarities among them, and their advantages and disadvantages, helps researchers choose which one (or more) to use in their projects. For example, focus group interviews can reveal disagreements that might be examined through in-depth interviews, or deep-rooted foundations for a contemporary conflict that could be explored through oral histories. Just as productive can be using interviews in tandem with other types of data collection, to which we turn next.

Combining interviews with other data-collection techniques

Interviewing can be very profitably combined with other kinds of data-collection techniques, and often is. Interviewing may complement site-intensive methods (see Chapter 7), for instance, if ethnographic observations raise critical questions the researcher can then address individually with those whom he is observing. Alternatively, scholars can use written sources and journalistic accounts to contextualize oral history narratives (White 1995; Giles-Vernick 2006, 92–93),[28] to fill in gaps when respondents' memories fail, or to cross-check information conveyed orally. Likewise, information gained through interviewing can help to corroborate or fill gaps in information from written sources or formal accounts, identify different points of view, garner first-hand and behind-the-scenes knowledge, and learn about underlying dynamics. Lynch (2006), for example, combined interviews with archival research in order to plug holes in the archival record and inquire about particular policy actors' motivations. Learning from interviews with Chinese citizens about ongoing changes in state policy helped one of our interview respondents to identify trends and patterns in government statistics on welfare recipients.[29]

Scholars can also conduct interviews and focus groups while designing a survey (Knodel 1997) in order to see whether concepts resonate with respondents, test-drive language, and "get a sense of the opinions, outlooks, or cognitive maps of people who are similar to the research subjects" to

---

[28] Interview LM-7, September 20, 2012.   [29] Interview, DK-18, August 24, 2012.

whom the survey will ultimately be administered. Doing so can inform the themes, question order, language, and pre-specified answers to closed-ended questions included in survey questionnaires (Lynch 2013, 37–38). Rogers (2013) conducted follow-up interviews with survey respondents in an effort to evaluate whether they were understanding questions evoking concepts used in previous survey research on racial group identity and political behavior in the way he intended; when he determined they were not, he conducted more interviews to pinpoint whether the problem related to question clarity or broader conceptual issues. Interviewing can also help scholars establish the universe of cases for a project and develop sampling frames for survey research (Lynch 2013, 34–35). Finally, interviewing can be combined with field experiments. In-depth interviews or focus groups can suggest causal explanations to be tested in experiments; scholars may also interview experiment participants in order to debrief them and to gain information to help them interpret their experimental data.[30]

How interviewing builds theory

Data gained through interviewing can contribute to achieving many analytic goals including (1) formulating research questions, (2) selecting cases, (3) conceptualizing and measuring key variables, (4) generating potential explanations, and (5) illuminating causal processes and mechanisms, and thus help build theory in multiple ways. Of course, researchers operating from different epistemes think about the process and products of interviewing differently, and will thus vary in exactly *how* they use interview data to build theory. We hope our discussion demonstrates that interview data can be analytically useful for scholars regardless of their epistemological commitments.

Formulating and refining research questions

Interviewing can play a critical role in one of the most fundamental stages of any project: the formulation and refinement of the research question. Interviews can be invaluable for double checking that the assumptions that undergird the framing of a research question are correct, and for evaluating whether one's project is original, compelling, and possible to execute.

---

[30] See Chapter 9 for examples.

Accordingly, many researchers carry out informational individual or focus group interviews in which they explore these issues during a preliminary visit, or soon after beginning to conduct fieldwork. Open-ended interviewing can reveal political dynamics or perspectives or illuminate new problems and avenues of inquiry that are not readily apparent in the published literature (and thus, potentially undetectable prior to arriving in the field). For instance, based on interviews she conducted with guerrillas, one of our interviewees expanded her project to examine the role of the media with respect to a broader range of political activism than she had originally anticipated studying.[31]

Case selection

Data sources accessible from a scholar's home institution may not allow her to identify the appropriate universe or relevant sample of cases. Interviews can help scholars to select cases for study that will allow them to test the most promising hypotheses and answer their research question. For example, Baumgartner and his collaborators on the Advocacy and Public Policymaking project, which examines the process of lobbying and policy-making in Washington, DC, sought to identify for analysis the policy issues on which lobbyists were active. They used a database of lobbying reports filed with the US Senate to construct a sampling frame of organizations involved in lobbying, and then drew a weighted random sample of 100 of those organizations. They interviewed a staff member at each organization sampled, asking him to identify the issue he had worked on most recently. The issues those staffers identified became the sample of 98 policy issues (Goldstein 2002, 670; Leech *et al.* 2013).[32]

An interview respondent who was studying how policymakers and members of the scientific community understand and discuss health inequalities sought to perform content analysis on proposed legislation that could affect health inequality. She thus faced the challenge of identifying legislation that had been proposed but never passed. She addressed this challenge through interviews – speaking with epidemiologists and policymakers to identify all legislation proposed (including which ministries might have created draft proposals), in what committees it was developed, where and

---

[31] Interview, DK-5, July 31, 2012.
[32] See also the Advocacy and Public Policymaking project's web site at http://lobby.la.psu.edu.

when it came up, etc. These interviews helped her to create the sampling frame from which she ultimately selected legislation to study.[33]

Conceptualization and measurement

Interviews can also contribute to theory by helping scholars conceptualize and develop strategies to measure key phenomena, and evaluate how cases score on key variables. First, interviewing can aid researchers in exploring emergent concepts, further developing concepts that have not been fully theorized in the literature, or understanding how several concepts are related and linked. It can also help them to identify a concept's contested nature – for example, if interview respondents implicitly or explicitly suggest a range of understandings connected with a particular term (Gallie 1956). Interviews can also reveal the existence of a relatively consensual "on-the-ground" meaning of a particular term that challenges a well-established scholarly conceptualization. For instance, Schaffer (1998) explored everyday understandings of "democracy" in Senegal through "ordinary language" interviews.[34] For his respondents, democracy had little to do with civil liberties and the exercise of political rights through competitive elections; instead, Senegalese spoke of democracy in terms of solidaristic voting, social cohesion, and collective economic security.

Interviews may also help scholars to refine conventional conceptualizations (for instance, by identifying a concept's key subtypes or dimensions), or to challenge standard typologies. For example, through an extensive series of in-depth interviews with current and former leaders of squatter settlements in Lima, Peru, Collier identified several types of settlement formation that had not been examined in the literature on the topic (Collier 1976, 138–139). For another researcher, the information gathered through interviews with former leaders of Brazilian parties that collapsed between 1985 and 1995 and with politicians who had changed parties in the 1980s and 1990s, considered in the context of his knowledge of Chile, Argentina, and Uruguay, led him to realize that "level of institutionalization" was a critical element missing from Sartori's typology of party systems based on the number of parties and polarization of the system.[35]

---

[33] Interview, DK-15, August 21, 2012.
[34] Schaffer's book presents a discussion of the theoretical underpinning and method of "ordinary language interviewing."
[35] Interview, DK-7, August 1, 2012.

Information gained in interviews can also help scholars refine their approach to measurement, no matter whether they are engaging in qualitative or quantitative analysis (Lynch 2013, 34–38). For instance, one of our interview respondents created a new measure of "wheelchair access" using focus groups. He and a co-author asked focus group participants (wheelchair users) to highlight the items that were most important to them on a Department of Justice checklist containing hundreds of requirements for making facilities wheelchair-accessible. Using respondents' input, they devised a measure of "wheelchair accessible" rooted in the wheelchair community, and thus, they believed, more valid.[36] Interviewing can also help scholars to evaluate how well measures of a concept developed in one context work in another.

Relatedly, interviews can be used to acquire data to measure key concepts in a study – to score cases on important variables. Most straightforwardly, interview respondents can identify sources for data scholars can use to measure their central concepts. Yet interviewees can also offer information that directly aids in measurement. Brinks (2008), for instance, aimed to explain variation in the conviction rate for police homicides across Argentina, Brazil, and Uruguay. One aspect of his argument focused on victims' socioeconomic status. However, he met challenges locating the data to score victims on that variable since not all governments published complete police homicide statistics, and because such incidents were not always reported in local newspapers. Hence, Brinks relied heavily on interviewing to determine victims' social class: he asked respondents who had known a victim what kind of job he had held, and how much education he had received, and requested that they place him on a class scale.

Generating hypotheses

Interview respondents' answers to well-crafted questions – and information they provide completely unprompted – can illuminate important causal factors, aiding scholars in generating or developing their arguments. Most basically, researchers may simply ask their interlocutors why a phenomenon occurred as it did, in the hope that their accounts suggest plausible hypotheses.[37] Indeed, sometimes interviewees' responses can be directly converted

---

[36] Interview, DK-14, August 10, 2012.

[37] Of course, respondents' causal interpretations need to be considered with the same rigor and skepticism as any hypotheses the researcher may have developed. See Beckmann and Hall (2013,

into an argument. One of our respondents recounted how an explanation he developed – that open-list proportional representation generates personalistic campaigning – was "direct fed" to him in interviews.[38] Yet interviews can also be used to generate or refine hypotheses in more subtle ways.

For example, interviews can highlight informal exchanges and interactions that have significant implications for important political phenomena. Beckmann (2010) draws on interviews with White House and Senate staffers to uncover informal networks and contacting, and to test the operational tenets of presidential coalition building on Capitol Hill. Lessing (2012) generated hypotheses to explain the interaction between drug trafficking organizations and the state in Mexico, Brazil, and Colombia through interviews with police, army, and government officials, among other strategies. Leebaw's (2011) interviews with various actors involved in the transition from apartheid in South Africa helped her generate and develop her argument that the creation and evolution of the Truth and Reconciliation Commission (TRC) were heavily shaped by a critique of legalism – negative perceptions of the uses and capacity of law rooted in the legalization of violence and human rights abuses under apartheid. Soss explains how long interviews with US welfare recipients helped him to understand how their political action or quiescence resulted, in part, from their understandings of themselves and of their status in relationship to state agencies (2000, 2006).

Illuminating causal processes and mechanisms

Interviewing can also be a crucial strategy for uncovering causal processes and identifying causal mechanisms. For instance, in her study of the high levels of civic engagement by American veterans of World War II, Mettler (2005) used data gained through interviews (as well as a survey) to argue persuasively that both the higher levels of education received by those who took advantage of the GI Bill, *and* their personal experience as participants in the program, led to more active civic participation by the "Greatest Generation." While the nuance might have been missed had the researcher relied

197–198) and Leech *et al.* (2013, 219) for cautions about adopting this line of inquiry in interviews; a scholar interviewed in connection with this project also expressed deep reservations about this type of question (interview, DK-6, July 31, 2012).

[38] Interview, DK-7, August 1, 2012.

solely on the survey data, in interviews veterans frequently described the GI Bill as an inclusive and fair program that treated them like "first-class citizens." In another example, in her study of Chinese workers' propensity to use the legal system to resolve workplace disputes, Gallagher found significant differences between younger and older workers. However, her interviews revealed that the divergence was tightly connected with the major political and economic changes experienced by the older workers through their lifetimes: the causal mechanism at work was not simply demographic, but deeply political (2013).

In sum, interviews can help researchers to accomplish a variety of analytic goals at every stage of inquiry, and ultimately can help them to build theory. Yet interviewing can be challenging in countless ways. The next section explores some obstacles researchers might encounter when interviewing in the field, and offers strategies to overcome them.

Addressing the challenges of interviewing in the field

Throughout this book we strongly advocate, and demonstrate the importance of, carefully preparing for fieldwork. The sociology, anthropology, psychology, and emerging political science literatures on interviewing offer a wealth of practical advice on conducting interviews and analyzing the information they produce, and we strongly urge scholars planning to use this data-collection technique to consult those literatures. In this section we offer strategies to help researchers decide when and whom to interview, construct effective protocols or interview guides, gain access to respondents, carry out and capture interviews, and evaluate the evidentiary value of interview data. We highlight how field conditions can inform research design, interview preparation, and interview conduct – thus shaping what scholars will be able to claim on the basis of their data. Much of the advice we offer is equally applicable to interviews with individuals, oral histories, and focus groups, and throughout the section we seek to highlight issues related to, and strategies that might be particularly useful for, a specific type of interviewing.

At the outset, we want to re-emphasize a point made in Chapter 4: interviewing is not for everyone. It requires a special type of patience, polite persistence, and perseverance, as well as a relatively outgoing personality. One senior scholar suggested that when he was a doctoral student, his advisor had "sent him" to the field on an exploratory trip, an experience that taught him he would *not* be an effective interviewer.[39] Scholars should consciously consider their own needs, as well as those of their project, as they make decisions about which techniques will allow them to collect the data needed to answer their questions.

When and whom to interview

Two linked questions concern how to sequence interviews, and how to choose respondents. Many researchers do some purely informational or exploratory interviews when they arrive at a field site to familiarize themselves with the new context, inquire about available resources, etc. Depending on the amount of time a scholar has available, his question, and the particularities of the field site,[40] it can be advisable to postpone conducting formal interviews with high-profile political actors until he has firmed up his baseline knowledge of the topic through interviewing academics, journalists, and others who *study* the phenomenon, and scouring available written sources.[41] These "softer," often semi-structured, interviews can help researchers to identify which actors to interview, assess data availability, refine interview questions and construct better protocols and interview guides, and acquire basic information that will help them maximize the payoff from later interviews with actors who may only be available once.

Concerning specific respondents,[42] there is no clear metric to identify the "right" interviewees – to ensure that the researcher has not interviewed an "anomalous slice of a larger population, which has distinct central tendencies in its attitudes and behaviors" (Cammett 2013, 142).[43] Whom to interview – and what sampling or selection strategy to employ – will depend heavily on scholars' interviewing objectives, practical considerations, and the field

---

[39] Manuscript review session, Syracuse University, June 2011.

[40] For instance, Boas's (2009) study of electoral campaigning required that he interview and videotape politicians prior to national elections, leaving him less latitude to delay beginning to interview.

[41] Interview, LM-6, August 30, 2012. We emphasize again the need for flexible discipline, however: important political actors can get busy or travel, for instance. Moreover, interviews sometimes materialize out of the blue: a researcher might be interviewing a (very connected) academic, and on a basis of a phone call made by the latter, presto, the former has an interview with the Minister of the Interior in 30 minutes. Taking advantage of such serendipity is often advisable. Balancing comfort, knowledge, and pragmatism is an ongoing challenge when deciding when to conduct interviews (interview, LM-12, September 6, 2012).

[42] We offer additional general thoughts on case selection (at multiple levels) in Chapter 3.

[43] There is likewise no clear metric to help scholars to determine the optimal number of interviews to conduct as the issue is project-dependent. Bleich and Pekkanen (2013, 90–91) suggest a "saturation" model; see also Chapter 10.

context itself. There is a great deal written on sampling and selecting interview respondents (in both the general methodological literature and the literature on interviewing and focus groups), and we strongly urge scholars to consult these resources.[44] Here we offer just a few rules of thumb.

Researchers carry out interviews for different purposes. Among other possibilities, they might be hoping to discover particular pieces of information, obtain certain insights, or understand particular dynamics; they might be using interviews to inform or shape work mainly based on other data; or they might wish to make generalizations from a sample of people interviewed to a larger population of which they form part (Goldstein 2002, 669). In the first and second scenarios, in which scholars are likely using interview data to *develop* causal explanations, they might seek to interview outliers, exemplars, individuals with specialized expertise on a particular topic, actors who can inform them about particular events or outcomes, or those whose voices are missing from accounts gained through other sources (Martin 2013). They will often wish to speak with people connected in multiple ways to, and with varied perspectives on, the issues and questions that are central to their study – in order to avoid becoming convinced by unchallenged narratives or getting labeled as partial to one side of a controversial issue (Dexter 1970, 43).[45] In these cases, some form of non-probability sampling will be optimal to identify interview respondents.

For instance, scholars might engage in quota sampling (in which they set proportions so a sample of interview subjects includes certain segments of the population), purposive sampling (basing selection on characteristics of respondents that are relevant to the analysis), chain-referral or snowball sampling (allowing an initial set of respondents to suggest further respondents, who suggest further contacts, and so on),[46] or even convenience sampling (interviewing those who are available and agree to be interviewed).[47] One less formal way to sample that somewhat combines these techniques is to identify and list, as exhaustively as possible, the scholars

---

[44] For excellent discussions of choosing respondents and of sampling in connection with interviewing, see Weiss (1994, 15–33); Rubin and Rubin (2004, 64–70); Tansey (2007); Beitin (2012, 243–247); Beckmann and Hall (2013, 199–202); Bleich and Pekkanen (2013), and Lynch (2013).

[45] Interview, LM-6, August 30, 2012. Wood (2006), for example, when conducting research on El Salvador's civil war, sought to interview people from organizations connected with the government *and* those aligned with the opposition.

[46] See Bleich and Pekkanen (2013, 87) on the weaknesses of snowball sampling and strategies to mitigate them.

[47] In any of these cases, one might employ a stratified sampling strategy (see, Rivera *et al.* 2002).

writing about and actors involved in the dynamics of interest,[48] and then divide them into categories (government officials, NGO activists, and party leaders, for instance). The categories might be used to organize a series of stratified focus groups. Alternatively, scholars could further divide those categories into types, and then choose a sample of people within each type to interview.[49] Scholars hoping to interview those whose voices are missing or have been systematically excluded naturally face particular respondent-selection challenges. Nonetheless, the more they learn about the research context and the phenomena under study, the easier it will become for those scholars to identify voices they *ought* to be hearing, and are not.

By contrast (and referring back to the third scenario above), the researcher may wish to make claims about a broader group by identifying the opinions, views, or behaviors of a subset of that group through interviews, and then generalizing to the broader group, or may wish to *test* causal explanations. When this is the objective, the ideal technique for choosing interview respondents may be to draw a random sample, as doing so enhances external validity. Drawing a random sample entails obtaining a list of the population of interest (or creating one if existing lists are unavailable, outdated, or systematically biased) in order to create a sampling frame. Given their time-consuming nature, researchers using in-depth interviews, focus groups, and oral histories are less likely to interview a sizable number of people, and thus less likely to need or wish to draw a random sample. As such, we leave discussion of this sampling strategy to Chapter 8, which examines survey techniques.

Each sampling or selection technique has strengths and weaknesses. To mention just a few, as noted above, while random sampling augments external validity, it may not be desirable for scholars who need to find out particular pieces of information that only a handful of actors might have. By the same token, while non-probability sampling does not mean non-careful, non-thoughtful, or non-justified sampling, there is always a risk that scholars who use such sampling techniques will accidentally exclude an important perspective or miss an important narrative strand.[50] If one engages in

---

[48] Scholars might even think of this selection process in terms of the dependent and independent variables in their study, and seek to identify individuals who can offer a range of perspectives on what the value of each variable is; doing so implies the need for strong theory in order to identify those variables (Cammett 2013, 136–137).

[49] Bleich and Pekkanen (2013, 90–91) offer a full description of this respondent-selection strategy.

[50] For instance, a scholar doing research in a remote village in Kenya, rather than accepting a sub-chief's offer to nominate interview respondents, found a list of farms and took a random sample of farmers to interview. The choice proved wise. While the researcher had been assured by the sub-chief that he could find everyone in his jurisdiction, the sub-chief did not know at least two-thirds of the farmers in the researcher's random sample (personal communication, August 23, 2010).

snowball sampling, for instance, the implicit level of trust between the interviewer and the respondent may be raised, but particular categories and types of respondents may lie completely off the snowball's track. Scholars should carefully consider these strengths and weaknesses before making a final decision about how they will select respondents, as their sampling choices have significant implications for the information they gather, and the role interview data can play in analysis and theory building (Lynch 2013, 38–44). Moreover, no matter which technique they adopt, scholars should systematically document each sampling and selection decision they make – describing their choices, highlighting the tradeoffs they faced, and justifying their final decisions.

We recommend that scholars seek to learn as much as they can about their chosen respondents before beginning to interview – for instance, investigating their positions on the phenomenon of interest, and their situation in their immediate milieu and the broader political context. Doing so helps scholars to decide how to contact desired respondents; to recognize the (potentially multiple) ways in which those respondents are connected to their study; and to pinpoint the types of questions that it will be most useful to ask (i.e., on what events, topics, or controversies the subject can shed light). Scholars conducting oral histories often consolidate this information in a biographical background sheet. Learning about the interview participants can also help the researcher to "market" herself and her project appropriately to different respondents (academics vs. policymakers vs. activists, for instance), identifying what to highlight and what to de-emphasize with each.[51] If there is an opportunity, subtly conveying her familiarity with a respondent (and his accomplishments) can demonstrate the researcher's interest and seriousness of purpose.[52] This background knowledge can also enable focus group facilitators to pick up on subtle cues from participants and foresee potential roadblocks to the group's conversation.

Constructing interview protocols

The questions scholars ask and how they ask them influence the quality of their interview data and the way they can be employed in an analysis.[53]

---

[51] See Dexter (1970, 37–38) for an interesting discussion of pitching one's project.

[52] Although see Rivera et al. (2002, 685) on how demonstrating knowledge of respondents may raise questions about anonymity.

[53] Through this subsection, we use the term "interview protocol" for ease of exposition. We neither have specifically in mind, nor mean to suggest that our thoughts only apply to, a highly structured questionnaire; the general principles we offer should be equally applicable to many types of interview guides.

Accordingly, many interviewing manuals offer rules and guidelines about protocol content, wording, tone, and question order (Weiss 1994; Leech 2002a, 667–668; Rubin and Rubin 2004, 146–164, 176–200; Wang and Yan 2012). Below we discuss how factors related to the field context shape protocol construction – for instance, concerning what language is used,[54] what questions are posed and in what order, and how they are phrased.

For more positivist scholars, writing an interview protocol that will generate useful data requires having a clear idea of what information they wish to gain through the interview and how it will be used in the analysis.[55] For these researchers, the research design, field research design, and interview protocol design processes can and should inform each other: the third is a way to translate the first two into action. Writing interview protocols forces a scholar to consider carefully what she will be listening for in interviews, what she thinks she might hear, and how they are linked to her project. Interview questions often connect to some aspect of a study's analytic architecture – they measure a variable, explore the nature of a concept, try to get at a causal process, or aid in case selection, for example. Accordingly, writing them helps researchers clarify their thinking on those aspects of their projects. If a scholar is developing a data-collection plan (discussed in Chapter 3) as he maps out and executes his research, he ought to be able to map each question, and the information he hopes it will generate, back to some aspect of that plan.

We suggest beginning to draft interview protocols well in advance of interviewing, for several reasons. Doing so provides scholars time to revise their protocols thoroughly and solicit local input. Writing and becoming familiar with their interview protocols in advance frees scholars to focus more on their respondents and the information they convey in the interviews themselves. Intense familiarity with the question guide is particularly crucial for focus group moderators, who must pay close attention to the words and body language for up to a dozen people simultaneously. Further, the more familiar a scholar is with his protocol, the more easily and quickly he can

---

[54] If the language or languages spoken in a scholar's field sites is or are not his native tongue, several factors might affect his decision about what language to use in an interview, including his skills in the local language(s), and what effect interviewing in his native tongue will have on the availability of respondents, on the conduct of the interview, and on the quality of the resulting data. The answers to these questions may vary across contexts, social groups, and time. Fujii (2013) discusses interviewing in a language one does not speak and using interpreters.

[55] Of course, we continue to advocate flexible discipline: scholars should not tie any interview to any particular analytic goal in their minds *so* closely that they miss relevant interview insights *not* tied to that goal.

identify essential questions not yet asked should a respondent or focus group member suddenly announce that she only has five more minutes to spend with the researcher.

Writing effective interview questions on the basis of one's research design or data-collection plan is difficult. How can scholars translate their key concepts and variables into concrete indicators, and then work those indicators into questions that respondents can answer in a way that helps scholars accomplish their analytic goals? We offer a few pointers. First, interview questions should be theoretically motivated but expressed in colloquial prose free of jargon so that interviewees can readily understand them. For instance, if the researcher is interested in whether a particular association is involved in broad or dense associational networks, he likely cannot ask an association leader, "Do you consider yourself well integrated in an associational network?" or follow up with, "Would you characterize that network as broad, or dense?" However, he could ask "How many other associations do you work with?"; "What kind of work do you do with them?"; "How often do you work with them?" The researcher can then evaluate the depth and breadth of associational networks based on information garnered through these straightforward and easily intelligible questions.

It is also important to identify colloquial language that is appropriate to the setting and the interlocutor or focus group. For instance, in a country recently transitioned from military rule, a researcher might pose a question about human rights one way when interviewing a human rights activist, and another way when speaking with a military officer. Moreover, scholars should keep in mind that their respondents' frames of reference for particular issues can be very different from their own. For instance, one researcher we interviewed noted that the Peruvian street vendors she had interviewed generally thought of income in three-hour increments (the time they might spend at any one post) rather than in terms of an annual salary.[56] Scholars can offer context-sensitive stimuli without changing the meaning or substance of their questions, and posing questions in terms respondents understand and do not reject will generate better data (see Locke and Thelen 1995).

As scholars develop their interview protocols, it can be useful to pre-test them. Pre-tests may occur in different ways depending upon one's research goals. Scholars with clear hypotheses and highly structured protocols may be able to pre-test them much as one would pre-test a survey questionnaire, using pre-interview trials and/or open-ended discussions. This sort of more

---

[56] Interview, DK-1, July 20, 2012.

structured pre-testing can be particularly important in connection with focus group interviewing, as moderating focus groups requires such intensive preparation and training: pre-testing allows for the evaluation of the perceived meaning and intelligibility of the questions that will guide discussion, *and* provides the moderator opportunities to practice and strengthen her facilitation skills. Ideally, pre-tests are done on a sample of the target population, but they need not be. Many wrinkles, from question wording and order, to phrasing and language, can be ironed out with just a few runs through interview questions with a native speaker of the language in which the protocol is written (particularly if it is not the researcher's native tongue) or someone familiar with the local context.

For others, pre-testing will be understood more loosely, as a way to examine whether questions elicit the kinds of answers a researcher anticipates and avoid provoking negative responses. For instance, one might "float" particular concepts or expressions to see how individuals think about them and to inform how one might ask questions about them. Scholars can often benefit from honing the appropriateness of the language used in their questions by seeking the input of local researchers. Even if these individuals have not done interviewing themselves, they can often evaluate whether the questions a scholar plans to ask are clear and likely to prompt respondents to provide the desired information. If a scholar has contracted research assistants, they may also be able to help.

Of course, most researchers' interview protocols change over the course of their fieldwork as they learn more about the field site, their topic, and their respondents, and apply what they are learning to their original categories or hypotheses. Even with careful pre-testing, scholars often realize that questions need to be added, modified in order to elicit the sought-after information, or abandoned completely because they just "don't work" or are attached to lines of inquiry that have proven to lead nowhere.[57] As we have emphasized previously, researchers should not interpret the iterative nature of fieldwork as a reason to dispense with advance planning, and carefully preparing their interview questions is no exception. Further, as the principle of flexible discipline would suggest, scholars should carefully evaluate the implications of any changes they make to their interview strategies and protocols before they make them – and fully document those choices, their justifications, and their analytic ramifications – so they can be as transparent as possible in their eventual write-ups. And, of course, as

---

[57] Interview, LM-15, September 10, 2012.

scholars develop new hypotheses and de-emphasize others, they should continue to search for evidence, through interviews and other means, that both support and refute their old and new hypotheses, as well as rival ones.

Gaining access to interview respondents

Once interviewees have been chosen, the next challenge is to gain access to them (Goldstein 2002).[58] Encouragingly, respondents are sometimes quite eager to speak with researchers – particularly ones who are interested in what they do and seem understanding, non-judgmental, and trustworthy.[59] Having a connection to a researcher may be useful for some respondents, and others may be very keen to tell their story or their side of a controversy, to unburden themselves, or to expound on their accomplishments or on a topic about which they feel expert (Dexter 1970, 5, 36). Yet most scholars experience some challenges in accessing the people whom they would like to interview in the field. Indeed, for many scholars, gaining access is one of the most frustrating (albeit ultimately rewarding) aspects of field research.

Many factors can complicate accessing potential respondents for interviews.[60] Scholars may be unable to locate those whom they wish to interview. Alternatively, potential respondents may feel uncomfortable being interviewed (or talking about the specific topic at hand), may seek to signal importance by being aloof, or may react negatively to the researcher.[61] Reaching desired interview subjects may be especially difficult in authoritarian and highly controlled or dangerous environments where additional obstacles can arise even once the interview is granted.[62] Not being able to

---

[58] For additional guidance on recruiting respondents, see Dexter (1970, 46–50); Weiss (1994, 33–37); Rubin and Rubin (2004, 93–97); and Beckmann and Hall (2013, 199–202); scholars might also consider recruiting respondents through social networking sites.

[59] Moreover, reluctant respondents can sometimes become enthusiastic ones; one of our interview respondents recounted that simply re-framing her interviews in Chile as *consultas* (more like "questions") rather than *entrevistas* ("interviews") gave the sense that respondents would be teaching, made the encounter sound safer, and encouraged potential respondents to grant interviews (interview, DK-17, August 24, 2012).

[60] Note that many of the access challenges we discuss here are analogous to those considered in Chapter 5.

[61] The *PS* symposium edited by Ortbals and Rincker (2009) offers a range of first-hand accounts of how identity affects access to interview respondents; for additional guidance on such points see Dexter (1970, 46–50); Weiss (1994, 33–37); Rubin and Rubin (2004, 93–97); and Beckmann and Hall (2013, 199–202).

[62] Official "minders" may be assigned to accompany and observe respondents during interviews, or access may be state-regulated. One interview respondent recounted that she had to solicit permission from neighborhood officials in order to interview ordinary people in China (interview, DK-18, August 24, 2012).

reach desired respondents can sometimes have analytic implications. For instance, if a scholar is seeking to develop claims that are generalizable to a larger group on the basis of interviewing a sample of that group, and if many individuals in the sample who are systematically different from the rest of the sample in some way cannot be interviewed (and if they are not systematically replaced), non-response bias can result (see Goldstein 2002, 669–670, for a good discussion).

With regard to strategies for circumventing obstacles, we first suggest that scholars assess precisely how necessary it is to speak with the individuals who have proven difficult to nail down for an interview. How will the study's results be affected if those people cannot be interviewed? Can the data that would be gained from interviewing them be obtained in some other way? How will not reaching them affect the quality and quantity of, and a scholar's confidence in, her evidence? How will it affect her ability to build theoretical arguments? Scholars should also consider what they can learn – with regard to both their project and future contacting efforts – from who turns down their interview requests, and from the way in which and frequency with which they do so (Dexter 1970, 37).

Should scholars decide to pursue elusive respondents, identifying a connection to them – an associate, relative, friend, colleague, or employee, for instance – can prove invaluable for facilitating access.[63] Scholars might also establish an institutional affiliation, or more informally ask for advice or introduction from scholars working on similar topics in the field site (Solinger 2006, 157). Likewise, scholars should remain attentive to opportunities to enter the networks in which target respondents operate (e.g., they might seek to attend the types of events they attend, or get on mailing lists to which they subscribe). Reinhardt (2009, 296), for example, recounting her field research experiences in Brazil, noted that "people who had no interest in returning my phone calls, upon meeting me at a party, would instantly invite me to their office the next day" – perhaps, she surmises, because she passed some sort of "test of . . . sincerity and commitment to the person who had invited me." Connections made using these techniques can very quickly generate a response to an unanswered email or phone call.[64]

---

[63] Interview, LM-5, August 27, 2012.

[64] See also Cammett (2013) on proxy interviewing (e.g., contracting others to do interviewing), especially her discussion of training and managing proxies; scholars considering this option whose research takes place in a country that is not their own should determine whether their research grant precludes paying foreign nationals.

While it may often be easier to arrange interviews with "ordinary people" than with elites, this is far from a universal truth. Indeed, a range of additional challenges may arise when scholars seek to access non-elites for interviews. Ordinary people may be completely consumed with their complicated lives, may have little motivation to convey personal information to researchers, and may be more nervous or suspicious about, and less cognisant of the value of, doing so (Cammett 2013, 128). As such, personal connections can be just as important to facilitate the trust necessary to secure interviews with non-elites. For example, one of our interview respondents needed an insider to "walk him into and around," and introduce him to people in, the several shantytowns in Argentina where he wished to study patron–client relationships. Without that "human imprimatur," he suggested, it would have been unlikely that anyone would have spoken with him (and quite likely he would have been ushered out quickly).[65] Likewise, in Yashar's (2005) work on indigenous politics in the Andes, a small group of indigenous activists in each country she studied invited her to their homes, to conferences, and to workshops, helping to open doors to other indigenous leaders and activists.

In short, the more networking scholars do, the more likely they are to identify valuable connections. While connections sometimes appear out of the blue, often researchers have to work to create, cultivate, and maintain them – and the time they anticipate spending doing so should be factored into their plans.[66] Employing a variety of intermediaries and access points can prevent scholars from becoming trapped in a subset of the larger universe of potential respondents.[67] One of our interviewees realized that she needed to "get off the beaten path" (move beyond the NGO world) to access a more diverse group of resident association leaders in Rio de Janeiro, and did so by "striking up conversation with whomever [she] could" – people in the stores in which she shopped, on the beach, etc. – in order to develop broader networks.[68] Scholars should also keep in mind that the way in which they contact respondents creates an impression and may lead interviewees to draw particular conclusions about the researcher that can affect the information they will offer: like everyone else, scholars are often judged by their associations.[69] One political scientist we interviewed, for instance, was

---

[65] Interview, DK-16, August 21, 2012.

[66] Sometimes respondents in one research project become connections for the next; see Solinger (2006) on the usefulness of maintaining contacts.

[67] Interviews, DK-13, August 8, 2012; DK-19, August 27, 2012.   [68] Interview, DK-13, August 8, 2012.

[69] Interviews, DK-11, August 7, 2012; DK-12, August 8, 2012.

strongly advised *not* to affiliate with any particular research institution as doing so would have pigeonholed her – perhaps opening some doors wider but firmly closing others.[70]

Researchers who are interested in a particular organization, group, or community of people should likewise carefully consider how to "enter" – what cultural etiquette to follow, and whether to enter from the top, the bottom, or via a particular gatekeeper. In some government bureaucracies or communities, for instance, it is critical to start at the top of the hierarchy and obtain official approval to interview respondents at each lower level.[71] In other cases, political hierarchies may be less rigid or less transparent but researchers will nonetheless need a particular person or people to aid them in gaining entrée. And sometimes starting at the "bottom" and proving oneself to those in lower echelons is critical to eventually gaining access to someone at the pinnacle. Moreover, sometimes lower-level bureaucrats, deputies, or staff know more about the workings of an organization – and are more forthcoming – than those at the top. As with many other points we have discussed, the chain of command, and what type of person could most effectively serve as a key facilitator or broker, will differ significantly from context to context. This again highlights the importance of scholars investing the time necessary to understand and engage with their field sites.

Conducting interviews: interviewer effects, rapport, and the ethics of interviewing

The emerging political science literature and the vast sociology, anthropology, and psychology canons on interviewing offer a wealth of useful information about structuring and conducting interviews, addressing topics such as deciding upon location, considering whether to send interview questions in advance, evaluating the need to offer gifts to respondents, introducing oneself and one's work, pacing, re-capturing a wandering interlocutor, probing, asking follow-up questions, wrapping up the interview (or reacting to its early termination by a respondent), requesting additional contacts, thanking respondents, and more.[72] We limit our comments here to three

---

[70] Interview, DK-17, August 24, 2012.   [71] Interview, LM-13, September 7, 2012.

[72] See, e.g., Dexter (1970, 50–54, 58–70), Weiss (1994, 61–119), Aberbach and Rockman (2002), Berry (2002), Leech (2002a), Rivera *et al.* (2002), Rubin and Rubin (2004, 135–146, 164–176), Kvale and Brinkmann (2009, 123–141), Herzog (2012); in political science, see Beckmann and Hall (2013, 288–296) and Leech *et al.* (2013). On oral history interviewing, see Dunaway and Baum (1996), Perks and Thomson (1998), Thompson (2000), Yow (2005) and a host of online resources available through various oral history projects and centers (see The Oral History Association's website,

ways in which the field context influences the conduct and products of interviews: interviewer effects and positionality, rapport, and ethics.[73]

Many scholars believe that a researcher's self-presentation and personality, and a respondent's perception of the interviewer's identity and personal traits (e.g., her gender, ethnicity, marital status, educational level, socio-economic status, and nationality) – in interaction with the research context – shape the interpersonal dynamic of an interview and thus the data collected through it (Dowling 2000; Ortbals and Rincker 2009, 287).[74] Moreover, as discussed in Chapter 4, the effect that particular aspects of a researcher's identity can have on interviewing may be neither predictable nor stable for any one project, let alone between projects (Becker, Bonnzaier, and Owen 2005), and those traits may gain and lose relevance across interviews (Chacko 2004). Several researchers we interviewed remarked how being married, or having children, elevated (and diminished) their status and facilitated (and complicated) mutual respect in their interviews. Others expressed surprise at how they were welcomed or rejected as an "insider" versus an "outsider" in their field site over time. To offer one vivid example of this last dynamic, a scholar of Serbian ethnicity doing research on human rights in the Balkans was harassed and threatened after she criticized Kosovo's declaration of independence during an appearance on CNN. Through a textual analysis of the hate mail and online postings she received, she realized that her correspondents' hostility was rooted in a primordial view of ethnicity that led to her Serbian ethnicity "trumping" other aspects of her identity: "Try as I might to de-ethnify myself, to cloak

---

www.oralhistory.org). On focus group interviewing, see Greenbaum (2000), Krueger and Casey (2009), and Stewart and Shamdasani (2014).

[73] Chapter 4 offers additional information on these topics. See also Dexter (1970, 32–34, 115–128) on a variety of interviewing relationships and a "transactional theory" of interviewing; Mishler (1991, 52–65, 117–135) on the "joint construction of meaning" in interviews and the distribution of power between interviewer and respondent; Woliver (2002) on ethical dilemmas in interviewing; Rubin and Rubin (2004, 79–128) on building "conversational partnerships," "responsive interviewing," ethics, and the stages of interviewing; Warren (2012) on interviewing as a social interaction; Lillrank (2012) on "Managing the interviewer self"; and Cammett (2013, 126–128) on positionality in interview-based research. Kaiser (2012), Marzano (2012), and Miller-Day (2012) offer very good discussions of informed consent, protecting confidentiality, and IRBs, and Kvale and Brinkmann (2009, 61–79) address the central moral and ethical concerns in interviewing.

[74] These issues, captured by some via the term "positionality" and by others via the term "interviewer effects," can be relevant no matter whether the researcher's power is by some measure weaker, on a par with, or greater than that of the respondent. Of course, these effects do not impinge only *during* interviews; a scholar's identity (and her biases) shape the questions she asks and how she asks them, as well as how she perceives and interprets the answers respondents provide (Dexter 1970, 125; Townsend-Bell 2009, 311).

myself in the robes of an academic scholar, ethnicity comes back to define both me and my work" (Subotic 2010).

While there is some consensus among political scientists that these effects occur, positivists and interpretivists differ in their views on how such effects shape the interview exchange and influence the data derived from it, and what can or should be done about it. Scholars engaging in reflexivity explicitly acknowledge the impact identity has on the research experience and weave accounts thereof into their findings and written products.[75] More positivist scholars may also actively seek to identify and estimate how their identity affects data collection – but consider it a source of bias or measurement error (Mosley 2013b, 12–14). One senior scholar described "yearning for" objectivity: "Even though I'm not sure it's possible. I keep working to get rid of everything that is contaminating and all of the biases to get closer to some idea of the truth."[76]

Another aspect of the interaction between the researcher and the respondent that affects interviews and the information gathered from them is whether and how researchers seek to build rapport with and gain the trust of respondents, and how successful they are. After all, negotiating access does not end once a researcher has secured an interview with a desired individual or group. Access to the *information* the scholar is after continues to be negotiated during interviews. The better the researcher understands how respondents see situations (through building rapport), the better he will be able to word or target his questions, and interpret the answers respondents give (Dexter 1970, 119–120). Focus group interviews, for instance, usually begin only after some informal mingling and then a round of introductions so participants can establish rapport with the moderator and each other. Solinger suggests researchers try to establish "mutual authority" in the interview context (2006, 163) – an understanding that both interviewer and interviewee are driving the conversation. A scholar who interviewed actors involved with political transition in South Africa had the palpable feeling that potential respondents needed to understand her feelings before opening up to her – they wanted "some small sign that I 'got them.'"[77]

---

[75] Finlay (2012) offers an enlightening discussion of reflexivity; see also the extensive symposium on fieldwork, identity, and intersectionality edited by Ortbals and Rincker (2009).

[76] Interview, LM-18, September 14, 2012.

[77] Interview, DK-10, August 6, 2012. Leech (2002a, 665–666) suggests several additional strategies for building rapport, and Chakravarty (2012) offers a detailed, and potentially controversial, discussion of building trust.

Of course, researchers should not be so concerned with establishing rapport that they lose objectivity, or the ability to keep interviews on-topic (Rivera *et al.* 2002, 685). One researcher working in China explained, "I try to be empathetic, not sympathetic . . . I try to understand what the world is like through their eyes but try to avoid representing them."[78] Grele describes how the friendly rapport established doing fieldwork can lead to biased questions, answers, and interpretations in oral history interviews:

> On both sides of the microphone, to ease the social situation, to maintain empathy and rapport, we avoid the hard questions and the unsettling answers . . . History without biases and passions is probably impossible and if attainable would be as dull as dishwater. But in doing our fieldwork we must overcome the natural tendencies of social intercourse and remember that we are historians and we are interested in the fullest exposition of the passions of the past, not in gathering material which is acceptable to the present. (1978, 41)

Moreover, particularly when scholars are interviewing people on different sides of an issue (who may nonetheless know each other), carefully balancing empathy and neutrality helps them to avoid poisoning the waters for future interactions.

Perceptions that individuals in the broader field context hold of researchers can also affect interviewing. In some field situations, for instance, being seen with a researcher could endanger interviewees. As Hsueh (2008) writes concerning her fieldwork in China, because she is a foreigner, her being detained by state security when researching sensitive topics would likely lead to no more than a session of detailed and intimidating questioning by a team of "good and bad cops." For those whom she was interviewing, however, the consequences might be far worse. As we have insisted, researchers have an ethical responsibility to protect study participants from harm.[79] Fulfilling that responsibility entails thoroughly investigating the politics of the field context, coming to understand the contingent implications for participants of being involved in the project, and thoughtfully considering whether particular individuals should be excluded from the study, or particular questions left unasked.[80]

In many situations, of course, being associated with a researcher would not be dangerous or stigmatizing for respondents. On the contrary, sometimes

---

[78] Interview, LM-6, August 30, 2012.
[79] For additional discussion of several of the points concerning ethics made here, and others, see Chapter 4.
[80] Interview, LM-8, August 30, 2012.

respondents anticipate that such associations will bring benefits for them or their community, and those expectations must be dealt with ethically. As we discuss in more detail in Chapter 4, it is important to critically reflect on whether and how to give back to participants without aggravating inequalities or inducing envy. For researchers working in relatively impoverished field sites, respondent or community expectations and demands can represent a significant emotional drain.

Carefully adhering to the process dictated by their university IRBs can help researchers to navigate these sorts of ethical challenges.[81] Yet ethical interviewing may entail a more encompassing ethical commitment (MacLean 2013). For instance, before arriving for an interview, researchers should consider whether they will need to gain consent from the respondent alone, or whether other individuals who are superior in an organization – or other groups and communities – may need to provide consent and approval. MacLean found that for a study of American Indian representation in health policy, she needed to obtain nearly fifteen review-board approvals, including from her university IRB, federal and regional IRBs for the Indian Health Service agency of the US government, and formal and informal tribal IRBs for participating tribal nations. To offer another example, for focus groups, researchers often ask all participants to sign a group agreement that she also signs (rather than simply signing an individual consent form as with an individual interview or oral history).

Before an interview begins, it is likewise incumbent upon the researcher to find an appropriate location for it. This is important both because where an interview is conducted (and, accordingly, how comfortable the respondent is) affects the data it generates, but also because finding a private location is often key to assuming the ethical responsibility for ensuring confidentiality if such guarantees were made.[82] Even when a quiet spot is found, curious children, spouses, friends, or colleagues may attempt to drop in, interject, or just quietly listen or observe from afar. Researchers should anticipate these interruptions and develop a culturally appropriate script for turning interlopers away. This can be especially delicate when the subject (or the researcher) is more junior in age, social or political status than the intruder

---

[81] See Brooks (2013) for an illuminating overview of human subjects protection.

[82] To clarify, by "private" we do not necessarily mean "isolated"; a restaurant with few patrons – or indeed a busy restaurant in which no one else could possibly hear the conversation – could be considered "private."

and particularly difficult with a focus group that appears to be an informal, lively discussion among peers.

Further, the process of soliciting informed consent is more than a bureaucratic hurdle to be surmounted by rushing respondents into signing consent forms or offering oral consent. Researchers should strive to make the potential risks *and* benefits of participation as concrete and transparent as possible for potential human subjects. Respondents should know that they can refuse to answer certain questions and may stop the interview at any point. In a focus group, this information is usually conveyed by the moderator at the beginning in a brief discussion of the ground rules; she might also explain that the focus group's objective is to reveal multiple perspectives and not to impose a consensus. Also, the researcher should be aware of, and remain attuned throughout the interview to, cues that suggest discomfort or refusal, even when participants continue to answer questions.[83] This requires particular sensitivity and extra effort in a focus group, where members may feel social pressure to continue participating after agreeing to do so. Moreover, should a researcher believe (or come to believe) that certain information an interviewee conveyed is too sensitive or controversial to be made public or attributed to him or her, it is the researcher's responsibility to protect the respondent, perhaps keeping the information confidential even when the respondent did not request confidentiality.

When guarantees of confidentiality were extended for some or all of the information conveyed in an interview, it is incumbent upon researchers to make the necessary arrangements to maintain those guarantees. Given the richness of data gained through interviewing and the amount of explicit and implicit identifying information found in interview notes, tapes, and transcripts, all of these materials need to be stored in a way that will ensure confidentiality (as required by IRB guidelines). Interview transcripts should include a code rather than the respondent's name, and codebooks with identifying information should be carried and stored safely and separately from the coded interview notes or transcripts. Keeping interview data private and confidential when transporting them across long distances and over borders can be especially important and challenging if data are sensitive – or become sensitive (and sought-after, for instance, by government entities) – due to changing political conditions in the field site.[84]

---

[83] For an eye-opening discussion of the ethical responsibilities entailed in asking interview respondents to relive traumatic experiences, see Wood (2006).

[84] Interview, DK-12, August 8, 2012.

Interviewing in an ethical fashion, in short, means more than simply mouthing one's IRB protocol. Indeed, as we suggest by including "ethical commitment" as one of fieldwork's six guiding principles, we believe ethics are a "way of being" in the field, entailing researchers consistently following the spirit of their pledge to protect those whom they involve in their work. With respect to many of the issues discussed in this and the previous subsection, asking other researchers who have worked in the context or similar contexts about how they faced challenges with ethical implications, and what solutions they devised, can be very helpful.

Capturing information from interviews

In deciding how to capture information from their interviews, researchers face additional important choices: they might audio- or video-record, take notes, do both, or do neither. Several factors may affect choices about capturing interviews (see also Dexter 1970, 54–57; Weiss 1994, 53–57). Sometimes logistical factors dominate capture choices. For instance, scholars may wish to audio- or video-record focus group sessions, as it can be difficult to coordinate the group, employ a coding scheme to track individual participants' contributions, and take notes simultaneously. Moreover, interactions in focus groups can be lively, animated, fast-paced, and nearly impossible to capture with any accuracy without recording.

More often, however, scholars will have a choice about how to capture the content of an interview. When they do, they should consider what information they would like to take away from their interviews, how much information, and in what form. Recording provides a full and faithful record of everything said – a very rich data source that can be used to confirm or clarify points later. By the same token, the amount of data gained can be overwhelming, and can complicate the process of drawing on interviews in later phases of analysis and writing. Anticipating how they will analyze and use information gained from interviews in their study can inform scholars' data-capture choices. If it is important to have long, exact quotes, or if content analysis will be employed to analyze interview data (suggesting the need for a verbatim text), recording may be useful. Of course, even if interviews are recorded, it can be prudent to write down interviewees' responses simultaneously so interview data exist in more than one form. Scholars who take notes while conducting less-structured interviews can also jot down additional questions that occur to them as the interview progresses.

Regardless of how scholars decide to capture respondents' (and their own) spoken words, additional aspects of an interview, and the thoughts and observations that occur to scholars as they conduct it, can also be analytically significant and important to track. For example, information about the context or venue of the interview (and why it took place there); who else was present and for how long; the length of the interview (and why it was as long or short as it was); and researchers' reactions to particular interview responses or to the interviewee's general demeanor, can all be important. Likewise, what was said "off the record," "not for attribution," or "on background" need to be noted.[85] In focus groups, observations about intra-group interactions are critical to record. These "interview metadata" can enrich the value of an interview, serving as a useful memory prompt, contextualizing the information conveyed, and enhancing scholars' ability to interpret it and assess its evidentiary value. Scholars might insert such ideas and reactions right into their interview notes, taking care to distinguish between what the respondent said and what their reactions were (perhaps using a double-entry system), or might create an "interviewer observations sheet" to capture these metadata.[86]

The way in which a scholar decides to capture interview content can affect the data he collects. Some respondents (for instance, those who speak to the media frequently) may feel entirely comfortable being recorded, and may even prefer being recorded. Others may withhold information if a tape recorder is running, or become unnerved by being recorded while interviewers simultaneously write out their responses.[87] While it will not always be possible to determine respondents' preferences, as noted previously, they will often – intentionally or inadvertently – signal their comfort level, perhaps as the researcher offers IRB-mandated statements and inquires about recording and confidentiality. Researchers should be attentive to such cues.

Scholars who take notes during interviews should type them up as soon after the interview as field circumstances permit.[88] Doing so optimizes the quality of the data gathered from the interview. If handwritten notes from an interview cannot be typed up quickly, cleaning them up quickly – filling in

---

[85] See Goldstein (2002, 671) for a discussion of the distinctions among these.

[86] This practice is more commonly associated with survey research than with in-depth interviewing.

[87] While researchers must *always* reveal their intent to record, using pens that are simultaneously audio recorders can deemphasize the presence of the recording device.

[88] Another option is to voice-record details about the interview immediately afterwards; these recordings can be run through a voice recognition program, producing a digital text version of interview notes and impressions. Products such as LiveScribe quickly convert handwritten notes on paper into text on an iPhone or iPad, facilitating organization, tagging, and searching.

unfinished words and half-written sentences – will facilitate typing up the notes later. If interviews are recorded, scholars will need to decide whether to transcribe them.[89] Doing so can be time-consuming or expensive – or both if researchers spend time recruiting[90] and supervising transcribers.[91] A less time-consuming alternative might be to construct a "table of contents" summary of an interview recording by listening to the recording and making a simple notation, every minute or two, concerning the topic of discussion, and adding notes highlighting particularly interesting quotes, or other points they may want to be able to easily identify later. Another option – if good notes were taken during the interview – is to set the recordings aside until the writing stage, when they may prove useful to draw a specific quote or review exactly how a respondent answered a question. Points for which it might be useful to have an exact quote later can be flagged on interview notes.

Assessing and documenting the evidentiary value of interview data

As we suggested in the previous chapter, no source of information can be assumed to provide "the truth." Summarizing the challenges of interviewing, one scholar stated, "You have to accept that people are going to be telling you their version of the truth."[92] Respondents are not obliged to be objective (Berry 2002, 680); indeed, researchers across the epistemological spectrum question whether they can be. Respondents can vary considerably with regard to their knowledge of the events and circumstances researchers query them about, and how clearly they recollect history. Moreover, as the literature on oral history emphasizes, while respondents are being asked to recall the past, they are being interviewed in the present, meaning that the history they recount is unequivocally shaped by their current context and situation. Subjects also differ in terms of how reflective, trustworthy, forthcoming, and given to hyperbole they are. One-on-one with a researcher, people may seek to depict events or dynamics in a certain way, aggrandize their role and downplay that of others (or vice versa), and leave out important information.

---

[89] Kvale and Brinkmann (2009, 177–187) offer a useful primer on transcribing.

[90] Scholars might contract graduate students recommended by faculty contacts, or hire a commercial transcription services provider, either at the field site or after returning to their home institution. Such services can be quite expensive in the United States.

[91] Transcription software is continually developing. Researchers should be sure to investigate the quality of the transcriptions such software produces in the language or languages in which they operate.

[92] Interview, LM-15, September 10, 2012.

Interviewees can lie, more or less blatantly.[93] And, as we noted, respondents are often influenced by their perceptions of the researcher: the same person interviewed about the same topic by two different scholars may offer different information.

These possibilities and limitations are among the strongest criticisms that skeptics level at research based on interview data. If respondents and interviews vary on these parameters – and if there is no clear metric to evaluate whether scholars have interviewed those who can provide the most accurate information concerning their question – what can interview research contribute to a discipline focused on objectivity and generalizability?[94] Interview research raises issues of validity (how effectively the "measuring instrument" – the interview protocol and the interviewer – captures the information it is designed to capture) and reliability (the potential consistency of repeated tests with the measuring instrument, i.e., whether the same answers would be produced if interviews were repeated) (Berry 2002, 679). We suggest four strategies researchers can use to address these potential weaknesses of interviews, and to evaluate the evidentiary value of the data collected.[95]

First, as mentioned above, researchers should seek to interview individuals from as many theoretically relevant categories, with as many differing perspectives or positions on the dynamics of interest, as possible. Doing so will help to attenuate non-response bias. If they are ultimately unable to interview many people, and can establish how those individuals are different from those with whom they spoke (something scholars conducting this sort of research may well be able to do), they might be able to estimate how the absence of those voices affects the data (Goldstein 2002, 672). In the text of their written products or in a methodological appendix (or both), scholars should outline how they sampled and contacted respondents; construct a log of whom they sought to interview, who was interviewed, who was contacted but failed to be interviewed and the reasons why, and how their failure to be interviewed might affect the conclusions that are drawn from the data; and identify the study's response rate.

---

[93] For more on these issues, see Weiss (1994, 147–150); Fujii's (2013) particularly useful, well-illustrated discussion; and Dexter (1970, 100–114).

[94] Several of our interview respondents suggested that such questions about interview research had been posed to them or about their work (e.g., interview, DK-9, August 21, 2012); see Kvale and Brinkmann (2009, 168–171, 293–298) for additional standard criticisms of interview research.

[95] Rubin and Rubin (2004, 71–77) and Kvale and Brinkmann (2009, 241–265, 298–315) discuss similar issues and offer additional advice.

Second, concerning those who *were* interviewed, and in line with our discussion of interview "metadata," actively judging the credibility and reliability of respondents and of the information they provide is critical.[96] To do so, scholars might ask themselves a few sets of questions. Concerning the respondent, what degree of involvement in or exposure to the phenomena of interest did he have? Is he representative of the larger group or community to which he belongs?[97] What goals or ulterior motives might he have had in giving the interview? What biases did he convey?[98] Regarding the interviewing interaction more generally, scholars can think about how the interview context – and the interviewer – might have affected the interviewee and her responses. And concerning those responses, the researcher might consider at what points the respondent was hesitant or evasive (and why she might have been so), and assess how internally consistent, comprehensible, plausible, or self-serving her responses were. This information, perhaps in tandem with a comparative analysis of subjects and the information they provided, can also be included in scholars' write-ups.

While not providing a fail-safe measure of the quality of the information conveyed through an interview, considering these aspects has two benefits. First, if a researcher can identify a respondent's biases during an interview, she can try to counter them as the interview progresses (for instance, by indirectly asking the respondent to "critique his own case") (Berry 2002, 680).[99] Second and more broadly, answering these sorts of questions allows the researcher to make informed judgments about how much distortion respondents might have introduced and in what direction,[100] and thus to evaluate the evidentiary value of the information provided. Doing so may direct the researcher to weigh some interviews, or certain points made in

[96] As Dexter (1970, 108) very aptly states, the key question is not whether respondents are telling the truth, but "What do the informant's statements reveal about his feelings and perceptions and what inferences can be made from them about the actual environment or events he experienced?"

[97] Evaluating the representativeness of respondents who are very eager to be interviewed can be particularly important. Likewise, especially in oral history interviews, a handful of "survivors" (i.e., a small subset of those who experienced a traumatic event) may well be unrepresentative of the broader group (most of whom did *not* survive). For additional basic background on oral history interviewing, see www/historymatters.gmu.edu/mse/oral/how.html.

[98] Much of this could be considered the "latent content" of an interview; see Lynch (2013, 36) on the distinction between overt and latent interview content.

[99] See also Wood (2006, 382) on whether to challenge interview respondents whom the researcher knows are lying.

[100] We can also think of these distortions as "measurement error," or simply as having introduced "error" into the "model of meaning" the researcher is striving to construct (Dexter 1970, 110).

particular interviews, more than others, and allow him to generate estimates of how certain he is of findings based on his interview data.[101]

Third, no matter how central a figure is in a particular event, how authoritative a source seems to be, or how much confidence a scholar may have in her account, a single interview, focus group, or oral history is rarely sufficient to gain the data necessary to understand an event or support an argument. In the vast majority of cases, it is important that scholars acquire additional viewpoints and data through some combination of further interviewing and employing other data-collection techniques.[102] As emphasized throughout this book, engaging in triangulation is the ultimate antidote to doubts about data.

Finally, and to reinforce a point we have made several times, scholars should include as much information about the interviewing process as they can in their write-ups. In addition to the specific points highlighted above, they should offer a general description of how they conducted and captured interviews, document the parameters and resolution of all methodological problems encountered while interviewing (Berry 2002, 679), and perhaps provide the interview protocol. Bleich and Pekkanen (2013) offer a helpful discussion of these issues, and provide templates for creating what they call an "Interview Methods Appendix" and "Interview Methods Tables." Making sure that this information becomes part of the research record – which will be easiest for scholars who begin writing about these issues *while in the field* – ensures transparency,[103] giving readers the tools they need to evaluate interview data, the process through which they were collected, and the conclusions drawn from them.[104]

Conclusion

Conducting interviews enhances any researcher's understanding of the substantive problem he is studying, key concepts, and causal processes. Choices

---

[101] On weighing interview data proportionate to confidence in their validity, see Berry (2002, 680) and Allina-Pisano (2009).

[102] Grele (1978, 30) urges historians to evaluate oral history sources critically and implicitly advocates triangulation when he declares, "it is not the case that all studies of the past done in the past are in error. Nor is it true that oral histories of the dispossessed are ipso facto free of the biases of the larger culture."

[103] Golden (1995) discusses how transparency and confidentiality might conflict and argues that qualitative scholars should aim for replication-enabling transparency nonetheless; Mosley (2013a, 20–26) offers additional cautionary notes.

[104] See also Aberbach *et al.* (1975, 9–12) for ideas about what data about interviews to report and how to report them.

concerning whether, when, and how to engage in interviewing, and which techniques to use, are driven by a combination of factors – the researcher, the nature of the research question, research design, and field circumstances. Because each interview is a unique encounter in a particular time and place, no book can offer infallible solutions to every potential challenge researchers might face when conducting in-depth, oral history, and focus group interviews in the field. Instead, we emphasize the types of issues to consider when addressing these challenges. Scholars will be more successful at landing and conducting interviews in the field if they are clear about their analytic goals; familiar with interviewing methodology; understand the language, history, culture, and economy of the interviewing context; and actively engage with the field site. Preliminary field-site visits can provide knowledge that can help scholars to refine the research question, select cases, and develop the trust necessary to conduct interviews.

We hope we have made clear that the most important task for those conducting interviews in the field is listening. Scholars who become wrapped up in the data chase sometimes lose sight of the fact that their ultimate goals, as field researchers, are to listen, absorb, and learn. Relatedly, it is essential that the subject leave the interview feeling that he or she has been treated with respect. As one scholar eloquently argued over a generation ago, "The respondent is a human being. Whatever value the scholar may attach to the enlightenment he hopes to acquire through ... an interview, he also ought to place value on the dignity, privacy, and courtesy of the person who has granted that interview" (Dexter 1970, 14). We need add no more on this point.

We also wish to highlight that what makes interviews so challenging can also make them enjoyable. In comparison to field experiments or surveys, the human interaction involved in interviewing is often less structured and more open-ended. Both the substantive and interpersonal possibilities are less bounded, and respondents have more power to shape the dynamics and outcomes of interviews. These characteristics can make interviews more unpredictable, demanding that researchers instantaneously devise adequate responses to unanticipated changes in the interview dynamic or setting. Yet interviews also allow researchers and respondents to develop greater rapport – such that a single exchange lasts for hours and reveals tremendous new insights into the research question. Given the great intellectual and personal rewards of conducting interviews, we expect this technique to remain the essential mainstay of the field research repertoire.

7   Site-intensive methods: ethnography and participant observation

Political science has yet to embrace ethnography and participant observation wholeheartedly.[1] The very terms may seem foreign to some in the discipline, resonating with other fields, particularly anthropology, in which they are more centrally employed.[2] Ethnography may even have a certain exoticism, perhaps seeming like an almost mystical practice that some very different kind of scholar might use studying the culture of one small village in a remote corner of the Global South for two or three dogged years.

And yet, many political scientists have employed these methods fruitfully for generations. Fully 34 percent of all field research projects reported in our faculty survey included these techniques (almost always in combination with other techniques). To put this figure in perspective, it is slightly larger than the proportion of projects that employed survey research, and more than two and a half times the proportion of projects that drew on focus groups. According to our survey data, ethnographic techniques are used by political scientists from all subfields, though they are especially prevalent among comparativists. They have also been used in all regions of the world, though somewhat more commonly in Latin America, Africa, the Middle East, and Asia than in the United States, Canada, and Europe.[3] These techniques do, however, display a notable gender gap – the only techniques covered in our faculty survey that do.[4] Our survey data also suggest that the use of

---

[1] Some elements of this chapter have been adapted from Read (2010).

[2] When explaining that she used ethnography in her fieldwork, one scholar described it as "closer to methods used in anthropology" and "not mainstream in political science." Interview, LM-12, September 6, 2012.

[3] Even among field research projects within the United States, 29 percent employed ethnography or participant observation. The corresponding figure for projects including European countries is 27 percent. For Latin America and the Caribbean, Sub-Saharan Africa, the Middle East, and the Asia-Pacific regions, the figures are 46 percent, 53 percent, 47 percent, and 51 percent, respectively.

[4] Site-intensive methods were employed in 44 percent of projects reported by women, as compared to 29 percent of projects reported by men. Pearson Chi-squared tests on the overall sample and on subsamples of United States-only and international projects find this gender difference to be significant at the .02 level or less.

ethnography and participant observation has stayed remarkably constant since the 1960s. Indeed, some of the best-known applications of these methods in political science – such as James C. Scott's work in a Malaysian village and Richard Fenno's study of US House members' behavior in their home districts (discussed in more depth below) – took place long ago. Indeed, as we have noted previously, the type of immersive engagement these techniques entail has been and remains implicit in some of the mainstays of research and funding in the discipline, for example, in the Congressional Fellowship program, Fulbright funding, and so on.

The fact that scholars almost always use ethnography and participant observation in combination with other data-collection techniques suggests that many scholars incorporate insights gained through the employment of these techniques in projects not specifically, or exclusively, designed around them. That is, scholars who use these techniques often do so as part of a process of triangulation, a principle we suggest underlies good field research. Moreover, in conducting interviews for this book, we found that some political scientists hesitated to self-identify as "an ethnographer," even as they asserted the value of in-person observational research. Frequently these scholars expressed uncertainty about the definitions of ethnography and participant observation, and whether their research fitted into those categories. This lack of conceptual clarity and hesitation suggest to us that the figures quoted in the previous paragraph may understate the use of these techniques. Using such techniques to at least *some* degree – even if sporadically – seems almost inevitable when conducting field research. Indeed, doing so is a quite natural aspect of engaging with context, a practice that most field researchers value, and which we also consider a principle of effective field research.

Perhaps in growing recognition of these dynamics, political scientists situated in multiple subfields have of late initiated an important dialogue about how ethnographic research approaches fit within our discipline.[5] These scholarly discussions have been facilitated by the formal institutionalization of a Political Anthropology and Sociology section of the Midwest Political Science Association, as well as the attention given to ethnography in several

---

[5] A recent edited collection by Edward Schatz (2009c) provides an outstanding overview of multiple perspectives on ethnography. Wedeen (2010) deftly surveys both the tensions and the complementarities that arise from the use of ethnography in political science. Other recent discussions include Bayard de Volo and Schatz (2004) and Wood (2007). Older treatments include Fenno's reflections on his method (1986, 1990). In addition, Timothy Pachirat has written a book (forthcoming at the time of this writing) titled *Ethnography and interpretation* (2015).

short courses held at the APSA annual meeting, and at the IQMR, which takes place at Syracuse University each summer.

We believe it is essential to continue and deepen these dialogues. Clearly, debates exist among political scientists about the meaning and value of ethnographic methods. Even ethnographers disagree among themselves. Many scholars highlight the epistemological differences between interpretive and positivist ethnographers (Kubik 2009; Schatz 2009b; Wedeen 2010). Where interpretive ethnographers challenge the possibility of objectivity and seek to maximize their subjective understandings of everyday practices, positivist ethnographers employ ethnography as a method of uncovering a knowable empirical reality, the invisible truth. Additional debates question whether ethnography can or should be used to establish causality or attempt empirical generalization (Schatz 2009a; Wedeen 2010). And political scientists disagree about whether ethnography can be used in combination with other methods, or even other analytic approaches such as formal modeling and statistical analysis (Laitin 2003), or whether a "stand-alone, intrinsic-value political ethnography" model – dedicated to the production of contextualized knowledge – yields more value to our understanding of politics (Schatz 2009a).

In this chapter, we hope to offer some ideas to advance these dialogues. We intentionally include and discuss multiple approaches to ethnography. Our survey and interview research suggests that political scientists do ethnographic research in a variety of ways, and no "pure" template exists. We contend that political science will benefit from a better understanding of how these techniques fit into our discipline, how insights gained from ethnography and participant observation contribute to the study of politics, and what challenges are entailed when engaging in these techniques.

In this chapter, to facilitate exposition as well as to highlight their commonalities, we group ethnography and participant observation together as subcategories of what we call site-intensive methods (SIM, defined below).[6] We begin by clarifying what these techniques mean in practice, and provide a tour of the distinct lineages from which they emerge. We demonstrate that they can take many forms, and contribute to many kinds of research programs, both alone and in conjunction with other methods. In the subsequent section we show that, contrary to the impression some may have, site-intensive methods are well suited for building and testing social science theory, as well as for producing thick, descriptive narrative accounts. The rest

---

[6] Ben Read (2010) introduced this term in earlier work, and it is further developed here.

of the chapter highlights the issues and challenges of preparing for and using site-intensive methods in the field and provides strategies for resolving some of the difficulties researchers encounter when employing these techniques. Throughout, we draw on a wealth of examples from scholars in political science whose research has benefitted from site-intensive work.

What do SIM mean in practice?

This chapter addresses a range of methods that includes various forms of ethnography and participant observation. We believe that, rather than drawing a line between these two traditions, or (as is more common) discussing or working within one with little or no reference to the other, political scientists have much to gain by considering them as parts of a single rubric, which we term "site-intensive methods" (SIM). To begin with, both ethnography and participant observation crucially involve observation. The researcher is not only asking a respondent to talk about an issue, event, or set of behaviors, but is also observing directly the dynamics or behaviors of interest. Despite the conventional distinctions made, we believe that both ethnography and participant observation involve a significant degree of participation by the researcher in the field site.[7] Whether officially and obtrusively, or perhaps without any formal recognition, the researcher participates to varying degrees in the social, economic, and political life of the field context being studied.

Furthermore, despite lively debates in anthropology and sociology that have problematized and essentially overturned the traditional notion of ethnography as a very long stay in one small (often rural and developing-world) community (Gupta and Ferguson 1997a), this stereotype appears to persist in political science.[8] We suggest that both older and newer, narrower and broader conceptions of this general form of research can be thought of as part of a common category of site-intensive methods. The introduction of

---

[7] In seeing the two techniques as substantially overlapping, our position is similar to that of Wedeen, who notes that "the term 'participant observation' is often used as shorthand for the double nature of these [ethnographic] activities, in which a researcher is both an actor and a spectator" (2010, 257). Others take a narrower view of what counts as participation, reserving it for situations in which the researcher joins or takes on the role of the research subjects: for example, becoming a social worker to observe social workers' relationships with their clients, or joining the staff of a political campaign in order to understand campaigns (Brown 1986, 171).

[8] One senior researcher contrasted "pure number-crunching" with "pure ethnography in a village under the baobab tree." Interview, LM-22, October 2, 2012.

this term is not meant to ignite controversy – just the opposite. We hope adopting it will help political scientists to put aside the conceptual baggage associated with ethnography or participant observation, facilitating a conversation about the very important characteristics and practices that unite these methods.

We define site-intensive methods as the collection of evidence from human subjects within their ordinary settings, where the researcher's interaction with the surroundings (as well as his specific questioning) informs the study. We do not conceptualize SIM in black-and-white dichotomous terms, but more as a continuum of the intensity of immersion. Still, at minimum, using SIM implies cultivating a deeper engagement with a locality, context, or set of informants than might occur, for instance, in a project based purely on standard one- to two-hour interviews. At the most basic level, scholars who engage in SIM observe people's everyday practices – they watch them doing what they would be doing even in the absence of the researcher (although, as we emphasize, the researcher's presence must generally be assumed to affect the site and the subjects in some way). SIM encompass forms of field research that are less structured by the researcher than are other techniques, entailing a high degree of contingency or open-endedness. At least to some extent, one waits for information to present itself rather than insisting on immediate answers. As one researcher commented in discussing her site-intensive research techniques: "The key to field research is letting it come to you as opposed to grasping really strongly and tightly at what you think you need to find."[9]

Most field research involves at least a certain degree of immersion in – or engagement with – a locality, broadly construed. Even if a scholar spends her days in the vaults of an archive, she is still likely to be browsing the daily press, catching portions of radio programs, and conversing with local colleagues. If "interviewing" rather than "observation" is a researcher's primary data-collection technique, he still cannot help but take cues from the surroundings: the home, office, or other locale where an interview is held; phone calls a subject takes that interrupt his conversation with the researcher; interactions with other people who happen upon the scene; or documents the subject provides. All of these cues open a window onto the worlds of subjects: they are *data* that help a scholar interpret the information garnered through interactions.

---

[9] Interview, LM-20, September 20, 2012.

Moreover, interviews might lead to follow-up visits, invitations to participate in relevant meetings or events, and so forth, leading to further immersion. For example, at the conclusion of an in-depth interview with a federal official about tribal–state relations, MacLean was invited to stay and participate in a conference call between the federal agency and state government officials on how to implement a new set of bureaucratic rules with tribal authorities. Another researcher recounted how, after the ice was broken during formal interviews with law-enforcement officers, it became possible to observe their work in real time and listen to conversations among them: "I didn't have to ask [permission] after a while. I drove around with them on patrol, doing whatever they were doing. This changed the interviews from semi-structured to a free-flowing format."[10] As interactions multiply and deepen, the attentive researcher naturally slips into a mode of flexible receptivity that goes beyond a simple question-and-answer format. Thus, there need not be a solid line demarcating a boundary where other methods end, and SIM begin.

While our intentionally inclusive conceptualization of SIM might seem to suggest that everyone is using these methods, of course not every political scientist does so. Yet many scholars who conduct field research do. We hope our bringing SIM's prevalence – the use of site-intensive techniques both by those who employ them deliberately and by those who use them casually – into the spotlight will contribute to encouraging a productive dialogue among field researchers of all types on how to engage most effectively in such practices.

Perhaps inevitably, due to the broad use of these methods, site-intensive research can take diverse forms in political science. Projects involving SIM may vary in terms of the length of time spent in any one site, the number of sites studied, and the types of context in which SIM are carried out. Some site-intensive work strives for a high degree of depth in a single locale; other studies pursue shallower immersion in multiple sites.[11] Naturally, this kind of study can proceed in many different types of settings as well, from remote and rural communities to cosmopolitan and urban neighborhoods, from impoverished agrarian villages to astronomically wealthy, post-industrialist enclaves.[12] William Reno (1998) observed warlord politics in rural and urban

---

[10] Interview, BR-10, August 21, 2012.

[11] See Gottlieb (2006) for a useful examination of the tradeoffs between depth and breadth.

[12] Bayard de Volo (2009) candidly discusses her contrasting experiences conducting one ethnographic project in US casinos and another in post-war Nicaragua.

Sierra Leone while Joe Soss (2000) investigated poor peoples' everyday experience of the American welfare system. SIM can even include research where the "site" in question is not a physical location but a more abstract space such as an online community or a transnational network.[13] According to Hardin and Clarke (2012, 3), ethnographic field sites are not restricted to small-scale and localized spaces but include "expansive domains that connect localized and international spheres." Just one example would be political anthropologist Ayça Çubukçu's research on the World Tribunal on Iraq, which consisted of a series of meetings held in several locations over the course of two years (2011).

Despite the fact that SIM may take on many different guises – and even though opportunities for observation or insight often arise seemingly by chance when a scholar is conducting field research – we wish to emphasize that site-intensive methods are not haphazard. Preparing in advance to deploy these methods, consciously considering the many different examples provided by other researchers, and reflecting on one's position in the field site all help improve the use of site-intensive methods. Moreover, SIM can be – and often are – carefully employed in a supplementary role alongside other methods. That is, a researcher may build a project entirely around these techniques, but doing so is a choice, not an imperative. In short, there is no single template for this kind of field research, and political scientists can incorporate SIM into their own projects in a variety of ways.

Throughout this chapter, we discuss in depth two canonical books in political science – James C. Scott's *Weapons of the weak* (1985) and Richard Fenno's *Home style* (1978). We focus on these studies for three reasons. First, these milestone works testify to the multiple forms that ethnography and participant observation can take. The comparison of Scott and Fenno illustrates the striking variety in the length of immersion, number of sites, and types of context involved in site-intensive methods. Second, both books are probably familiar to many readers as archetypes of site-intensive methods. Finally, both authors explicitly detailed the rationale for using these methods and the techniques they employed in order to do so.

First, James C. Scott's *Weapons of the weak* draws on a project that consciously hews close to the classic anthropological model of ethnographic

---

[13] See Gupta and Ferguson (1997a) on the need to revise the "tradition" of ethnography in anthropology in order to study many questions that are global or transnational, where the "site" crosses multiple geographic boundaries. See Staple (2012, vii) on how "evolving global connectivity" blurs the boundaries of field sites and creates new ethnographic social spaces.

field research. Scott describes his book as a "close-to-the-ground, fine-grained account of class relations" in a Malaysian village, population 360, to which he gave the pseudonym "Sedaka" (Scott 1985, 41). He states that he spent at least 14 months in this hamlet, interviewing, observing, and taking part in village life (1985, xviii, 46). Scott provides a forceful explanation for choosing this mode of research: "It goes without saying that I have thought it important to listen carefully to the human agents I was studying, to their experience, to their categories, to their values, to their understanding of the situation" (1985, 42). While framed as an argument specifically for the importance of investigating class consciousness up close rather than deducing it from Marxian theory, his reasoning builds to a more general defense of research that attempts to understand the conflictual and contradictory world of human subjects first-hand and in those subjects' own terms.[14]

The other well-known political study involving in-person immersion looks not at peasants in Southeast Asia, but at elite politicians elected to national-level legislative office in the United States. Richard Fenno's *Home style* was motivated by questions concerning the relationship between politicians and those they claim to represent: "What does an elected representative see when he or she sees a constituency? And, as a natural follow-up: What consequences do these perceptions have for his or her behavior?" (1978, xiii). Fenno's approach to answering these questions was to spend time in the company of members of the US House of Representatives in their home districts. He famously characterizes his research method as "largely one of soaking and poking – or just hanging around," and situates it explicitly within the tradition of participant observation as practiced by sociologists and other political scientists (1978, xiv, 249, 295). (Ethnography is not mentioned.) In the text of the book and its long methodological appendix, Fenno candidly and rather self-deprecatingly explains his modus operandi of accompanying politicians wherever they would let him tag along, building rapport, recording their remarks, and asking questions when possible.

Clearly this was a far "thinner" form of engagement with a research milieu than was Scott's village study. Relative to a single-site project, Fenno traded depth for breadth, studying eighteen different representatives and thus obtaining substantial variation on characteristics such as party affiliation and seniority (1978, 253–254). The total time he spent with each representative ranged from three working days to eleven, averaging six (1978, xiv, 256),

---

[14] On the kind of field research that *Weapons* represents, see also the discussion in Wood (2007, 127–129).

and on some of those days the research subject was available only part of the time. From this comparison, we conclude that site-intensive research can take different forms. That diversity, we posit, results from thoughtful decisions by researchers about how best to answer their particular research questions given what they already know about the context they are studying. The next two sections illuminate how Scott, Fenno, and others have done much more than "just" soaking and poking in the field.

How ethnography and participant observation contribute to theory

Employing SIM can help scholars to accomplish many important analytic tasks. In fact, we would contend that obtaining valid data on some topics in some places may *require* a form of site-intensive research. The following six points highlight the sorts of research tasks, and the kinds of research topics, that SIM are particularly well positioned to address.

Generating new questions and novel hypotheses

One fundamental purpose for ethnography in political science is the inductive generation of new questions and novel hypotheses. For Fenno (1978), the choice to conduct field research by "soaking and poking" was in part driven by his conceptualizing the project as blazing a trail through wholly uncharted territory. He argues that political scientists had previously all but ignored representatives' understandings of their districts and how they behaved there (1978, xiii). Given this theoretical *tabula rasa*, Fenno contends that a "totally open-ended and exploratory" approach was needed:

I tried to observe and inquire into anything and everything these members did. I worried about whatever they worried about. Rather than assume that I already knew what was interesting, I remained prepared to find interesting questions emerging in the course of the experience. (Fenno 1978, xiv)

Throughout the book, Fenno highlights his openness to new questions *and* to new theoretical explanations for the outcomes he observed. Ultimately, this open-ended approach did yield new theories about why politicians and voters act the way they do, even if Fenno soft-pedals them somewhat. The new hypotheses he advances include: House members in the early phases of their careers are most attentive to their districts; members focus most on constituents who are well organized and thus accessible in groups; and constituents care about personal attention, respect, and the assurance of access at least as much as they care about their representative's congruence with their own issue positions (Fenno 1978, 215, 235, 240–242). According to the author, none of these theoretical factors had been highlighted by existing scholarship that had employed other research methods.

Fenno's insights are unquestionably theoretically rich. However, the way in which he discusses his data-collection techniques could unwittingly and unnecessarily diminish the perceived value of site-intensive methods in political science. Fenno's use of the term "soaking and poking" and his heavy emphasis on the unstructured nature of his project suggest that his approach was necessarily speculative and free-form. To be clear, soaking and poking is indeed a productive and sometimes essential way to familiarize oneself with a research site and develop questions; many of our interviewees, including some oriented toward positivist modes of research, talked about its value.[15] But it is equally important to point out that site-intensive methods can and often do depart from this type of research: the unobtrusive observation of the dynamics of a field site is often far more theoretically driven and systematically reflective than what Fenno depicts. Moreover, while site-intensive methods do have enormous value in the beginning phases of a study, they can be usefully employed throughout a field research project. SIM can also be highly useful where theoretical classifications and hypotheses are already well developed and entrenched. In fact, Fenno's own acknowledgments of previous research suggest that he was engaging with a more well-established field than he admits.

Defining and selecting cases

Site-intensive methods can also contribute to theory by allowing scholars to obtain critical information, often lacking from existing datasets, that helps to inform case selection. To give just one example, ethnographic observations may assist scholars in understanding the parameters of the broader population of potential cases. MacLean drew on ethnographic observations to expand the range of individuals who would be counted in the total population of village residents for a survey. On informal walks with neighbors to visit their farms, she realized that a small, but significant, number of people lived in isolated houses close to the fields, but far from the central village.

---

[15] For example, interviews BR-1, June 1, 2012; BR-2, July 30, 2012; BR-5, August 13, 2012; BR-6, August 14, 2012; BR-16, October 31, 2013.

The research team had missed these peripheral housing units in the initial map and census of the village, but local people confirmed that these mostly poor, non-indigenous migrants sent their children to the village school, shopped at the village market, and contributed to village funerals. As such, it was appropriate to consider them as belonging to the village community. Without the use of site-intensive methods, the survey sampling would have been systematically biased.

Another scholar's experiences reveal how site-intensive methods can be combined with other types of data collected during multiple trips to inform case selection.[16] After a pre-dissertation trip, a graduate student, who initially hoped to conduct field research in several districts in two states in India, chose instead to carry out his study in only two neighboring districts in the one state where he had more extensive language ability. During his second visit, a long-haul trip on which he began to collect his dissertation data, he used published government sources to create a census of village communities that had implemented the policy of interest and then randomly selected a subset of villages from that list. The graduate student then visited these randomly selected communities as well as many other neighboring communities, drawing on his interviews, informal conversations, and observations to match each in-sample village with one that was similar in all other aspects except that they had not yet implemented the policy investigated in the student's dissertation. Each of the above examples demonstrates the value of data gained from site-intensive methods for defining and selecting cases for further study, reinforcing an earlier point that SIM are often used in combination with other data-collection techniques.

Developing concepts

Site-intensive research can also help scholars develop conceptualizations of key phenomena. Due to the value placed on parsimony in our discipline, many researchers feel pressure to reduce empirical complexity into stark abstract concepts – as when great heaps of state machinery are categorized dichotomously as either democracies or autocracies.[17] Such constructs may

---

[16] Interview, LM-11, August 31, 2012.
[17] See valuable work by Giovanni Sartori (1970), Robert Adcock and David Collier (2001), Gary Goertz (2006), and David Collier and John Gerring (2009) on the process of concept formation.

seek to capture macro-level phenomena such as regime types, relationships between states, and social classes, as well as micro-level phenomena such as party identification, acts of participation, identities, and interpersonal relationships. Other scholars develop complex conceptual apparatuses in an effort to retain more of the nuances of the underlying world.[18]

Either way, disconnects, incompatibilities, and slippage are bound to occur between concept and reality as the empirical world on which these abstractions are based is intensely elaborate. Cracking open the history of some of the most critical terms we employ reveals a labyrinth of competing definitions, contested measures, and shades of gray. One researcher may find that observed reality falls neatly into the categories that she devised or borrowed from other scholars; another may find such a matching frustratingly elusive and be more eager to analyze how the classification scheme itself was constituted and contested over time (Wedeen 2008, 80–81). Sometimes the gap between accepted concepts and observed reality, always present to a greater or lesser degree, is minimally relevant – what statisticians might refer to as "random noise." Yet on other occasions these gaps can prove critically significant and can spark innovation – a rethinking of what were previously settled conceptual categories.

Site-intensive research provides special opportunities for such innovation. It allows and even forces the investigator to confront the tensions between social science abstractions and the lived world of the people under study in a particularly vivid and immediate way. For example, Frederic Schaffer (1998) spent 14 months in Senegal studying what the concept "democracy" means in that context by examining how people use the word. Repeated visits to the Chinese countryside (along with other sources) gave Kevin O'Brien and Lianjiang Li the material from which they developed their concept of "rightful resistance," referring to forms of collective action that draw on the very norms that power-holders articulate (O'Brien 1996; O'Brien and Li 2006). Prolonged study of a cluster of thirty villages in one region of Senegal gave Dennis Galvan insight into the "institutional syncretism" that resulted from the collision of precolonial society and a bureaucratic state (2004). In sum, this kind of intensive research is particularly valuable for refining, correcting, and even creating the core concepts we use to make sense of the political world.

---

[18] Examples might include Mark E. Warren's associational typologies in *Democracy* and *Association* (2001), and James C. Scott's classic discussion of patron–client ties (1969).

Obtaining hidden data

The data that we need to study many political topics are inaccessible or *hidden* to a greater or lesser extent.[19] Information relating to some topics is intentionally hidden – sensitive, confidential, or even taboo. Powerful people, organizations, or governments may prefer that it not be made known, while less powerful actors may fear the consequences of sharing such information. Unvarnished facts, narratives, and opinions may be purposefully kept behind barriers.[20] For instance, Cyrus Ernesto Zirakzadeh (2009) acknowledged the difficulties he initially faced in finding and talking with Basque nationalist activists in Spain. In another example, it was only by combining statistical analysis with interviewing and participant observation techniques that Soss, Fording, and Schram (2010) could discern how the operations and logics of the "neoliberal paternalist" American social policy governing the poor persistently produced racial inequality and exclusion. Pachirat worked undercover in a Midwest slaughterhouse in order to investigate the hidden politics of violent labor (2011). Indeed, the intentional veiling of information in which political scientists are interested often has political underpinnings: we can imagine, for example, that employers may not want to publicize their everyday practices for requiring citizenship documentation in the United States or Europe, where immigration is a hot-button issue.

Other data may be unintentionally hidden. It is famously difficult, for instance, to operationalize many key concepts such as "democracy" or "representation." Governments in some countries simply do not have the capacity to gather the information necessary to (reliably) produce some of the key indicators that political scientists often use in cross-national research. To give some concrete examples, political scientists have emphasized recently the importance of studying informal institutions, rules that are not formally documented but shape political life in profound ways.[21] For example, Frei-denberg and Levitsky (2006) draw on ethnographic research to reveal the importance of informal party organization in Argentina and Ecuador. They argue that an exclusive focus on the formal statutes of party organization leads to "a flawed understanding" of party politics in much of Latin America

---

[19] Jourde (2009, 20) argues that ethnographic methods enable political scientists to see "political relations and political sites that are generally unseen, or 'unidentified,' by mainstream political science but which are nonetheless meaningful for local political actors." Referring to such things, he borrows Denis-Constant Martin's term "UPO" or "Unidentified Political Object."

[20] Political research on such things – "hidden transcripts," preference falsification, acting "as if," and so forth – is voluminous (Kuran 1989, 1995; Scott 1990; Wedeen 1999).

[21] See Galvan (2004), Helmke and Levitsky (2006), and MacLean (2010).

where extensive informal organizations – from grassroots soccer clubs to clientelist networks – recruit activists and deliver votes without official sanction or recognition by the party (2006, 179). In discussing her approach to analyzing the genocide in Rwanda, Lee Ann Fujii (2009, 12) notes that "the key is finding ways to detect these less visible, but no less important, sets of meaning."

As these examples suggest, and as we discuss in other chapters when examining the challenge of accessing data using other data-collection techniques, the problem of data inaccessibility can plague scholars no matter whether they are researching in authoritarian and repressive environments, or liberal democratic ones. Likewise, it is not a problem that relates more closely to any particular research topic, or to studies of elites as opposed to ordinary citizens. The ubiquity of the challenge makes finding ways to address it critical.

One strategy is simply "cold-calling" – making inquiries about elusive information out of the blue. While this may work under certain circumstances, often it will not, particularly if the information is inaccessible due to its sensitive or controversial nature. Perhaps even worse, such cold-calling might result in a scholar being granted an interview but obtaining answers that are deceptive, simplified, merely the "party line," or the safe response. She might blithely record such information, unaware that it differs from what the informant believes on a more private level. To go beyond such an impasse may require building trust, waiting to observe unguarded moments, or finding other ways of opening access to a broader array of performances and practices by the actors involved in a scholar's area of interest.[22]

In short, one powerful argument for using ethnographic techniques is that in some settings, it may be impossible to obtain valid evidence without using them. Sometimes, building ties of trust and familiarity with one's research subjects and the institutions in which they are embedded is necessary for research to proceed. For more positivist scholars, ethnographic techniques can help "peel the onion" to remove layers of biases in order to arrive at a more reliable approximation of the truth (Allina-Pisano 2009, 54). For more interpretivist scholars, ethnography helps to reveal the contestation over what constitutes the "truth" for different people in different contexts, facilitating the study of how meaning-making operates in everyday practice.[23]

---

[22] Lisa Wedeen (2008, 88–89) discusses the genealogy of the interpretive emphasis on performative practices in her analysis of identity formation in Yemen.

[23] See Kubik (2009) for an excellent comparison of positivist, interpretive, and post-modern approaches to ethnography.

Testing hypotheses

A great strength of site-intensive research techniques is that they offer rich opportunities to collect information on the observable implications[24] of hypotheses that are under scrutiny in a given project. That is, they provide ways to gather data relevant to multiple hypotheses more or less simultaneously from many elements of the research context, and thus to evaluate the extent to which these hypotheses accord with empirical realities. Thus, in a given site on a particular afternoon, one might observe a conversation involving several people, who also periodically respond to knocks on the door, telephone calls, news reports on a television, and so forth. Many fragments of the conversation might provide leverage on hypotheses concerning the various individuals' attitudes and beliefs, or the power relationships among them, or their interactions with others. (Alternatively, an afternoon's observation might be judged to provide little or no valid evidence, if, for instance, a supervisor or other authority figure happened to be present, changing the way subjects would otherwise behave; SIM require constant judgments of this type.) By collecting many forms of information – assertions that are made, grudges that are nursed, imperious or polite expressions used, body language, comments by individual A that later are discussed by individuals B and C after A has left the room, etc. – from many sources, scholars using site-intensive methods thus have particularly rich opportunities to engage in triangulation.

The fine-grained accounts of villagers' narratives, rituals, insults, and struggles in Scott's *Weapons of the weak* can be read as a series of tests of the "false consciousness" hypothesis, i.e., "the assumption that the peasantry (proletariat) actually accepts most of the elite vision of the social order" (1985, 40). The village ne'er-do-well, Razak, provides one such test: "As a beneficiary of local patronage and charity, however reluctantly given, one might expect Razak to entertain a favorable opinion of his 'social betters' in the village. He did not . . . 'They call us to catch their (runaway) water buffalo or to help move their houses, but they don't call us for their feasts . . . the rich are arrogant'" (1985, 12). Others pieces of evidence appear in the poor peasants' perceptions of local misers (1985, 13–22); the celebration that results when a job-displacing combine bogs down in the mud (1985, 163);

---

[24] *Designing social inquiry* called for qualitative researchers to improve hypothesis testing by identifying and evaluating hypotheses' observable implications, of which even a single case may have many (King *et al.* 1994, 28–31). Whether researchers subscribe to or reject other aspects of this book's advice, this point helps to highlight the power of SIM.

and the conflict over the village gate that had protected villagers' paddy-hauling jobs (1985, 212–220).

In *Peripheral visions* (2008), Lisa Wedeen draws on 18 months of field research to reveal the "observable effects" and underlying logics of "performative practices" with regard to nationalism, a particularly complex topic (2008, 15). For example, Wedeen describes the way Yemenis gather routinely in the afternoons to chew "qat" and share intense discussions about politics with friends and even strangers. Drawing on these observations of everyday political participation, she challenges Benedict Anderson's theory of national identity construction by showing how national attachments are constructed in the absence of a strong state in Yemen.

Often, site-intensive research encourages the observation of physical space as well as speech and practices (Yanow 2006). For example, MacLean (2004) observed the implications of different patterns of intra-family reciprocity in the varied architecture of family housing in cross-border regions of Ghana and Côte d'Ivoire. Where the survey data collected on family reciprocity revealed cross-sectional patterns of social support at one particular point in time, the concrete history of building visibly demonstrated the changes over time in how families were organized to support each other. The continued use of older extended family houses in the center of the Ghanaian villages compared to the prevalence of long-established nuclear family villas in the Ivoirian villages supported the hypothesis that differences in reciprocity emerged from longer historical processes of state building, rather than recent changes in the political economy.

Understanding causal processes

Site-intensive methods can also enrich scholars' understanding of causal processes. One way of thinking about how they do so is to suggest that they can help researchers to identify "causal process observations" – "insight[s] or piece[s] of data that provide information about context, process, or mechanism, and that contribute distinctive leverage in causal inference" (Brady and Collier 2004, 277). "Process tracing" is essentially the search for such observations. Some of the most prominent disciplinary discussions about using qualitative methods to identify causal processes have emerged in the context of case-based research using historical sources.[25] Yet ethnography and participant observation can

---

[25] For example, Chapter 10 of George and Bennett (2004) gives an overview of process tracing with an eye toward research based on case studies drawing on historical documents. See also Tarrow (2004).

help scholars to collect data that can be used for the same purpose (even if those using SIM may not think in these terms or use this vocabulary). Indeed, site-intensive methods may be *even better* suited for illuminating causal processes, as they allow for active probing by the researcher rather than relying on the analysis of extant sources.

Fujii (2009) uses site-intensive research – ethnographic observations and purposively selected life history interviews – to understand how peasants could commit mass violence against their own neighbors during the Rwandan genocide in 1994. Fujii resists imposing the assumptions of the "standard approaches" to ethnicity and draws on her understanding of local culture and knowledge to make alternative meanings visible. She refuses to sort actors into fixed categories of "perpetrator" and "victim." Instead, her ethnographic research reveals how actors have varying performances of the "script" for violence. As a result, Fujii views the genocide as having followed a dynamic and contingent causal process.

By contrast, Tsai's (2007) research on public goods provision in rural China provides an outstanding example of how ethnographic observation can be mixed with large-*n* quantitative methods to gain insight into causal processes. In this project, site-intensive observation facilitates the interpretation of a survey of 316 villages in four provinces. Regression models estimated on these data offer evidence that, *ceteris paribus*, villages that possessed certain kinds of social institutions – notably, temple associations and village-wide lineage groups – also tended to provide good roads and schools. In an effort to elucidate the causal link between these social institutions and the outcomes of interest, Tsai carried out a series of focused qualitative comparisons among at least nine villages, visiting each for between 2 and 20 days. She found that in Li Settlement, for example, leaders were able to rally their constituents on the basis of a common lineage and community spirit, facilitating collecting donations to pave a road; in Pan Settlement, by contrast, long-standing conflict among the sublineages impeded similar efforts.

Overall, site-intensive research methods include multiple approaches that make compelling contributions to theory development in the social sciences. In the next two sections, we explore the challenges of preparing for and carrying out site-intensive work in the field.

Preparing to use site-intensive methods in the field

Several prominent political scientists engage in site-intensive research, and the opportunities for dialogue on conducting ethnography in political science are growing. Nonetheless, site-intensive methods are perhaps the least well-known across the discipline. In this section we consider several issues political scientists face when preparing to use these techniques in the field: determining that SIM are worth the effort and time; finding ways to start the process of observational research; balancing depth of immersion against breadth of multiple sites; and managing to be in the right place (to observe) at the right time.

Whether and how to begin

An important question to consider in any project is whether the time and effort involved in site-intensive work are justified, relative to what can be obtained through (for instance) interviews. For some purposes and in some settings, a researcher can ascertain essential pieces of information from those with whom she needs to speak in single sessions. When this is the case, returning to an informant for a second or a tenth encounter may seem like a puzzling waste of time. Moreover, minimizing the time spent with each subject allows one to maximize the number of interviewees. Doing so facilitates triangulation, and may allow a scholar to obtain high degrees of variation on particular variables. If the scholar carries out a sufficiently large number of interviews, she may even be able to reap other benefits of large-n research.

But if SIM are indeed appropriate in a given project, one of the next questions concerns how to begin. How might one initiate a mode of inquiry that goes beyond (for instance) the cut-and-dried format and short duration of an ordinary interview, and instead involves observation that might extend over a protracted period of time? As previously noted, site-intensive research can evolve spontaneously out of other data-collection techniques. The investigator need not have at the outset – much less announce – a clear intention of repeating observational visits over a period of weeks or months. Rather, if people in the research sites accept his presence, he can simply continue to show up and assess, on a rolling basis, what is gained through site-intensive work; this is how Read proceeded in studying para-statal neighborhood organizations in Beijing and Taipei (2012, 287–290). Another approach is to embed oneself in some capacity – taking on a task or function that serves the community under study. For example, a researcher studying community-based organizations in Brazil identified specific ways to assist each organization's mission, for instance leading "train the trainer" English teaching classes and self-esteem workshops for youth. Doing so allowed her to be physically present at each organization for extended periods each day, have casual conversations, and observe phenomena to which other data-collection techniques would not have given her access.[26] Soss conducted participant observation "in a shelter for homeless families, disability support groups, and welfare agencies" in addition to pursuing in-depth interviews (2006, 324).[27]

Immersion: depth vs. breadth

Given that immersion is needed, how deep should that immersion be? We resist the notion that only very long-term immersion can be considered adequate: there is no minimum number of days or months that must be spent in the field in order for one's work to "qualify" as SIM – and no amount of time in the field that *automatically* qualifies one's work as of that type. Instead, we suggest that it is the quality of a scholar's engagement with context while in the field that determines whether he has employed site-intensive methods. This view may conflict with the conceptualization of ethnography as a type of method that requires, indeed is almost synonymous with, lengthy field stays. And we of course agree that, as a general rule, scholars who spend more time actively engaging with a particular context are likely to come to understand it better than scholars who actively engage with that context for less time. Details, nuances, and dynamics of change are more likely to be overlooked by the latter; connections may not be made as deeply, nor relationships solidified as strongly. In some settings and for some purposes, trust between the researcher and her interlocutors may take weeks or months to build. Nonetheless, we believe it is counterproductive to set a bar that effectively excludes researchers who are arguably engaging in site-intensive techniques – hence our more permissive and inclusive understanding of those methods.

No matter how much time they decide to spend in the field in connection with a given project, scholars employing SIM face an inherent tradeoff between depth and breadth: between working more intensively in fewer sites or just one (observing more thoroughly and developing deeper relationships with informants), and carrying out research in more sites but spending less time at each. Many factors will inform scholars' decisions on this front.

---

[26] Interview, DK-13, August 8, 2012.

[27] While we have emphasized the potentially fluid boundaries between SIM and techniques like interviewing, Soss notes that participant observation and interviewing can also be quite distinct enterprises with different strengths and payoffs (2000, 325–328).

The appropriate length of a particular field stay often emerges organically as the dynamics of the stay develop and a scholar learns more. Researchers employing SIM are particularly well placed to build trust when doing so is necessary, to patiently wait and watch for revealing moments or dynamics, and to come to understand the potential and possibilities of a field visit. Logistical concerns may come into play – for instance, the possibility and cost of transportation among sites and the need for multiple sets of accommodations the more sites are included. Likewise, intellectual imperatives will certainly need to be taken into account – for instance, one's language skills, and the similarities, differences, and relationships among the possible field sites.

One specific factor that might play a particularly important role in a scholar's decision about how many sites to study (and thus how long to stay in each) is the number of site-level independent variables she is interested in investigating, and how they vary across contexts. For instance, Scott chose Sedaka due to its apparent typicality, and because previous studies had established a baseline from which to assess change (1985, 90). While he does not explicitly justify his decision to focus on one village, we can surmise that long-term immersion in a single place was required to obtain access to "hidden transcripts," and that variation within the village itself (between elites and poor, and among different informants) was a more important focus than, say, interregional variation between Kedah and Johore. The overall framing of the research also seems to discourage the exploring of different sites: the denizens of Sedaka are intended to speak for peasants everywhere. Fenno adopts a casual tone in *Home style* when discussing how he selected his eighteen congressional representatives for study. He writes that he made "no pretense at having a group that can be called representative, much less a sample" (1978, xiv). But it *is* a sample, of course, and he makes clear that he selected it in such a way as to observe members and districts of different parties, regions, races, ages, levels of seniority, and electoral competitiveness. Thus, he pursued the familiar small-*n* strategy of obtaining variation on a number of potentially important independent variables. The problem of small sample size remained, but Fenno's logic is clear.

There are many reasons one might want to stay in a field site over a longer period of time. We have already mentioned that, in some contexts, trust and familiarity are required to obtain information.[28] As one of our interview

---

[28] The idea that repeat visits to a field site increase respondent trust and rapport was noted by many scholars we interviewed, e.g., interviews, LM-12, September 6, 2012; LM-13, September 7, 2012; LM-16, September 11, 2012.

respondents explained, these benefits do not require a scholar's uninterrupted presence in the field site. Instead, sometimes rapport can be increased by a scholar leaving a field site and returning a few weeks later, thus giving research subjects "time off from you."[29] Further, even the most cooperative and forthcoming of informants may "change their stories" over the course of a single interview and between interviews. Scholars interested in tracing that variation will do well to interact with their subjects on more than one occasion. Just as different question wordings, question orderings, and contexts can lead to quite dissimilar responses in survey research, posing related questions somewhat differently in a series of interviews can result in respondents revealing different and possibly conflicting beliefs and experiences. Moreover, interviewing respondents in the presence of different groups of neighbors or colleagues (if one-on-one conversations are impossible) can lead to interesting response variation if their relationships condition what is revealed. Finally, from the perspective of a more positivist scholar interested in obtaining the "truest" or most objective measure of an individual's perspective, multiple interactions may yield data of higher validity. For more interpretive scholars who emphasize subjectivity, the benefit of multiple sessions may be the inclusion of a greater number of voices and perspectives.

Another factor conditioning the amount of time a researcher will spend at a site, or how many times she will return, concerns the degree to which data collection hinges upon the observation of particular events or dynamics. To the extent that one is essentially waiting around for special circumstances to crop up, the time investment will grow, though the payoff may make it worthwhile. Fenno clearly exercised considerable patience, traveling to each of his eighteen subjects' districts at times when the representative would be present there, then lingering in the background until moments when he became available. He seized upon moments of special insight, when the politician might let slip an unguarded remark or even confide in Fenno something he would ordinarily not reveal to an outsider.

Straus's *The order of genocide* serves as an example of artfully balancing many of the factors we have just discussed. He interviewed approximately 230 Rwandan genocide perpetrators (most of them randomly sampled). He also made trips to five specific locations scattered around the country, speaking to "a cross section of Rwandans, including survivors, perpetrators, current and former officials, and other local leaders" (Straus 2006, 5–6). The information he obtained through the site visits illuminated the specific

---

[29] Interview, LM-20, September 20, 2012.

processes through which catastrophic violence broke out in these communities, processes that turned out to differ from one locale to another.

In sum, multiple factors will condition scholars' decisions about how many field sites to incorporate into their projects, and what to do there. No single model will work for every project. Nonetheless, we hope to have provided some ideas about the considerations that it will be helpful to take into account as scholars chart their course in the field.

Being at the right place to observe at the right time

How can researchers be sure to be in the right place to observe at the right time, particularly if their time and resources are relatively limited? Most researchers' time is constrained by competing professional or personal commitments. Furthermore, funding for field research is not always sufficient to support long-term stays. We raise here a few issues and strategies to consider in order to maximize the time available for observation in the field.

A shorter, preliminary field stay can help scholars to refine the research strategy they will subsequently employ. During such a field stay, a researcher can begin to introduce herself to potential research communities or participants, finalizing the details of her ethnographic visit once she returns to her home institution. Of course, the process of obtaining the access needed to carry out site-intensive work effectively will vary by context. In some places, researchers might need to gain official approval to engage in such work – for instance, from government agencies. In other contexts, such as public meeting places and events, scholars may be able to show up whenever they wish.

One issue scholars may need to consider as they plan site-intensive work is seasonality. Many political topics have a seasonal quality to them. For instance, for a question on political participation, the timing of the electoral cycle might be critical; for an analysis of philanthropy, the proximity to tax collection could be salient; and for an examination of poverty alleviation in Africa, the timing of what are commonly known as the hungry or lean seasons, or the occurrence of major religious holidays, might be important. Holidays and vacations could mean a complete absence of activity in a site such as an office or a legislature, but could provide special opportunities for observation in other settings, such as people's homes. Indeed, scholars should consider how they can "make use" of seasonality, particularly if their project includes more than one site. For instance, they may be able to observe one site when it is "in season," then switch to another site to make it their "off-season" case. Of course, the seasonality of political topics also affects how researchers employ other data-collection techniques. But to take full advantage of direct observation in site-intensive work, researchers must think carefully about how different seasons might affect the presence, salience, or dynamics of the activity under study.

Another factor to consider is how the scholar wishes to position his visit vis-à-vis an "official" event of interest. Many scholars who use ethnography and participant observation have noted that the most revealing interactions can happen immediately after such an event ends. This is similar to the observation made by scholars who conduct in-depth interviews that respondents often gush with candid revelations and acute insights only *after* the recording device is turned off, or the notebook is closed. Researchers can often find good excuses to tarry and observe informal conversations as a group disperses. As always, every effort should be made to record notes on these observations as quickly as possible before one's memory of them fades.

In the preface to *Ambiguities of domination*, a book written on the basis of two-and-a-half years of fieldwork in Syria, Lisa Wedeen writes that, although her research was built around formal interviews, and benefitted from them,

> it was really the events of everyday life, the periods of "hanging" out – of drinking coffee, studying at the university, teaching exercise classes, making olives, baby-sitting, hosting salon-like gatherings in my home, going to films, shopping for groceries, riding the bus with friends to visit relatives in faraway places – that produced the chance encounters and enduring connections that animate this book. (Wedeen 1999, vii)

The leveraging of serendipity and the observation of the everyday, over time, into cumulative insights about the nature of authoritarianism under Hafiz al-Asad epitomizes the long-term payoffs that site-intensive study may yield.

Issues and challenges of using site-intensive methods in the field

In addition to dilemmas about where and for how long to use site-intensive methods, political scientists face additional issues and challenges when employing these techniques in the field. Here we address just a handful: the ethics of observation, the nature of positionality or objectivity, compensation, and interpreting one's experience in the field. While each of these issues may arise when deploying other data-collection techniques, they frequently pose more intense challenges when using SIM.

Ethics of observation

We begin with the ethics of observation and issues around informed consent. Frequently researchers are more attuned to these issues when they are carrying out a survey, in-depth interviews, or an experiment. When using these other data-collection techniques, the researcher and participant can often point to a specific moment when they discussed the study, shared information about the nature of the encounter, and then agreed to proceed. But these questions come into play with SIM as well: what about a participant's ability to refuse to be observed?[30] This is a particularly delicate issue when the scholar has become so immersed that subjects become friends or forget that they are under study.

One of the ways that a researcher can facilitate a more meaningful process of informed consent for ethnographic observation is by ensuring that the project has been introduced publicly to the broader community. Precisely because site-intensive methods require scholars to immerse themselves in observing and understanding the everyday practices of the field sites, the meaning of informed consent frequently goes beyond an individualized contractual exchange and potentially involves the generalized awareness of a wider group of participants. Indeed, in some developing countries, no individual-level interactions can proceed until a village or neighborhood-wide public meeting has been held, where the researcher openly introduces the research team and the study objectives. Even after such a public meeting was followed by the village gong-gong beater passing the news at 5 a.m. in Ghana, MacLean's research team still had to dispel many myths and misunderstandings as they went door-to-door greeting and introducing themselves. Of course, this kind of face-to-face meeting may be neither logistically feasible nor necessary in larger scale communities or advanced industrialized contexts. Nonetheless, many contexts have periodic large, public meetings organized for other purposes, in which a researcher may ask to make a brief introduction. MacLean's work in the United States provides another example. She was invited to deliver formal presentations of her work on Native Americans at large inter-tribal meetings as well as more informal updates at smaller tribal council and committee meetings. These introductions ensured broad awareness of MacLean's role as a participant observer in public meetings, stimulated approval of the study from existing study

---

[30] See Yanow and Schwartz-Shea (2008) on the need to reform IRB policy. The authors emphasize that IRB policy is not designed around ethnography, and that, indeed, ethnography may invert the traditional power relationships where the participants refuse entry to the researcher.

participants, and generated new contacts for additional in-depth interviews. In still other contexts, the researcher may be observing as many different people move in and out of the field sites, without any ready opportunity to introduce herself or to inform the subjects of the study. In these cases, scholars should think carefully about the potential sensitivities of these observations and whether and how to use them in published work without unwittingly harming subjects who were unaware of being observed.

None of the above strategies is useful, however, when the researcher is an unobtrusive or undisclosed participant. Indeed, in this type of project, the scholar has often purposefully chosen to use site-intensive methods in order to understand what is hidden or politically sensitive. As such, the project's success hinges on his ability to observe without subjects being informed fully, or at all, that they are under study. For example, Timothy Pachirat concealed his identity when he applied for a job in an industrial slaughterhouse in Nebraska. Pachirat (2009, 148; 2011) describes how his brown skin, status as a young, male, Southeast Asian immigrant to the United States, and previous manual-labor experience enabled him to be recognized and hired as "typical entry-level slaughterhouse material." For 5½ months, Pachirat worked side-by-side with other employees, sharing stories, eating lunch in the cafeteria, even arranging rides and running errands with one co-worker who became a friend. He never told the workers or management that he was actually a graduate student at Yale University conducting doctoral research.[31] Pachirat recounts his initial paranoia and sense of danger that management might discover his identity.[32]

In these instances, the scholar needs to critically reflect on where he positions himself on the spectrum of ethical behavior presented in Chapter 4, what he feels constitutes an acceptable level of deception, and what the implications of the chosen level are. In the example above, Pachirat was thinking reflexively about the tradeoffs involved with different strategies of access – specifically, how direct access as an undisclosed entry-level worker, as opposed to formal access (with management approval) or proxy access (via interviews outside of the slaughterhouse) would shape what he saw and how he interpreted that information. Pachirat demonstrates the value of

---

[31] Pachirat is explicit that his intention was not to produce an exposé of a particular company, its management, or employees, so he does not report the names of the company or people he met in his published work.

[32] See also Pachirat's interview with James McWilliams, a writer on food politics and animal rights, at www.james-mcwilliams.com/?p=1577, accessed March 12, 2014.

continuing to think reflexively throughout the project, and not just at the initial design stage. He describes how, during the course of his participant observation, the benefits of direct access began to be outweighed by the ethical costs when he was promoted to a quality control position, and thus charged with monitoring and enforcing the slaughterhouse standards. At that point, he decided to quit:

Ultimately, the ethical dilemmas inherent in the work of quality control – both the diversion and redirection required in relating to federal meat inspectors and the surveillance and discipline I imposed on subordinate workers in the plant – became, in my judgment, untenable, and I resigned from my position and left the slaughter-house in December 2004. (Pachirat 2011, 156)

During the rest of Pachirat's field research, he relied on proxy access, observing and conducting interviews as a known researcher with ranchers, slaughterhouse owners and workers, inspectors, and community and union organizers. While the knotty issue of tolerable deception comes up with other data-collection techniques, it may be particularly intense in site-intensive methods and, as we discuss in Chapter 9, in field experiments.

Positionality issues

Researchers using site-intensive methods must also consider how their positionality vis-à-vis study participants influences the data collected. These issues again affect the employment of other data-collection techniques as well, as we note in our broader discussion of positionality in Chapter 4. Nonetheless, the dynamics may become more intense and readily apparent when the researcher is deeply immersed in a particular field context and in consistent contact with study participants. Indeed, both advocates' conception of the primary contribution of site-intensive methods and skeptics' dominant critique thereof center on how the intimate positionality of the researcher in the field site may either facilitate or, alternatively, undermine the validity of the data collected. The implicit (and erroneous) assumption in both of these perspectives is that somehow a scholar using site-intensive methods necessarily becomes an "insider" over time due to their intensive immersion in the field sites.

But using site-intensive methods does not erase positionality or the importance of the scholar's identity and how it is perceived. Drawing on the literature in anthropology and elsewhere (McCorkel and Myers 2003; Schatz 2009b, 6–9), we highlight that a researcher's positionality is constantly shifting and being renegotiated in the multiplicity of contexts discovered in the field. Since any scholar's identity is socially constructed, multivalent, and dynamic, immersion in new cultural and geographic spaces can spur transformations in how the researcher speaks, moves, acts, and is perceived by others in the field sites over the course of a project (Hardin and Clarke 2012). While this is true for any researcher, those using site-intensive methods have a chance to reflect upon and explore the problems posed by their positionality in a deeper way than when using data-collection techniques involving one-shot interactions with subjects. These scholars gain more information through repeated interactions and engagement with context, which can help provide perspective on the dynamics of positionality and how it is shaping the research process.

Indeed, sometimes social differences, or being identified as an outsider, can smooth entrée into a community and enable a scholar to obtain "insider" meanings (Horowitz 1986; Tamale 1996).[33] Fujii (2009, 34–35) found that her status as an obvious outsider in Rwanda allowed her to pose questions that would have made interview respondents anxious or suspicious had they been asked by an insider. In one example, it was only after Fujii's translator reassured a woman that the questions she was being asked were coming from Fujii that the woman calmed down and patiently explained certain events' underlying logics – logics that would have been obvious to most native Rwandans. Power differentials are to some degree inverted in such interactions, as subjects' superior expertise on the research topic is acknowledged. Indeed, this acknowledgment can be extended past the specific domain of the research study to other situations of everyday life. Finally, while a certain amount of cultural competence and knowledge is critical to gain a base level of trust, often an outsider status facilitates open dialogue with multiple groups that may be in persistent conflict with each other. The researcher's outsider status can even be viewed explicitly by historically hostile groups as an opportunity to share information with each other indirectly and thus learn about the other group's views with a hope of improving the relationship.

It is of course impossible to identify the precise effect scholars' position and personal interactions have on the data they collect through SIM. Nonetheless, and regardless of whether scholars perceive their positionality

---

[33] A researcher who worked in a post-apartheid setting in Southern Africa noted that "because I was an outsider, they were more likely to trust me." Interview, LM-12, September 6, 2012.

to be a help or a hindrance, they should do what they can to critically reflect on their role in the field site and its impact on their data. One way scholars can do so is by merging their ethnographic field-note journal with any personal diary they may be keeping, thereby providing a more comprehensive record of the context for the observations. Scholars should also be attentive to opportunities to change their position and somehow level the playing field with the study participants. And even if differences remain, awareness or perhaps even acknowledgment of those differences by the researcher can build trust, potentially bridging or eventually even attenuating disparities.

Compensation and giving back

Given the immersion that site-intensive research entails, researchers who use such techniques may build more extensive personal ties and networks of trust in the communities where they work, and with the study participants who occupy them, relative to those who use other methods. These relationships can facilitate a broader understanding of politics, but may also entail dense webs of obligation. As such, deciding how to "give back" to study participants and communities constitutes a significant challenge in site-intensive research. Indeed, scholars who engage in ethnography and participant observation may be uniquely aware of and affected by any inequalities or friction created between individuals, groups, or communities by the exchange of compensation or gifts.

Given the potential consequences involved, scholars using site-intensive methods often talk to other researchers who have worked previously in the same or similar field sites to find out what kind of compensation might be appropriate in the particular context. Anticipating these issues in advance might be particularly important if the most appropriate and valued gifts must be purchased elsewhere and brought to the field sites. An alternative strategy is to wait until later in the field visit, when the researcher herself has become more immersed and knowledgeable about local practices. Compared to other data-collection techniques such as interviewing or survey research, the quandary of compensation for site-intensive methods is not a one-time transaction with individual respondents, but is navigated over a longer time period simultaneously with individuals and a wider community of participants. This constant negotiation of what is expected and appropriate to give in the field site can be one of the most unexpected and draining aspects of field research. Some scholars describe the weight of the accumulating obligations as "enormous guilt" felt during fieldwork, a feeling that does not diminish with one's departure.[34]

Another way ethnographic researchers can avoid creating inequalities or friction while still giving back is to adopt a collaborative approach to research from the very beginning of a project. Involving participants in project development and implementation may make it more likely that the research will be relevant to, and promote long-term benefits for, the field sites. While we advocate for collaboration more generally in Chapter 4, such an approach may be particularly feasible for researchers using site-intensive methods due to their deeper involvement, often over longer periods of time, with those they involve in their work.

Interpreting and navigating ties to the field

Ethnographic researchers frequently write up their observations of encounters, public events, and activities on a daily basis. As they do so, they often go beyond simply recording discrete facts or events: they interpret, compare, and process their reactions to what they observed. The explicit recognition that scholars using site-intensive methods are continuously reflecting and interpreting is what some scholars have termed an "ethnographic sensibility" (Schatz 2009b, 5) and others "an ethnographic or anthropologic approach to life" (Staple 2012, ix). According to Shehata (2006, 260), ethnographers' reflexive scrutiny and analysis of their interactions with study participants generate more evidence about how those participants think and understand their social world. The scholars' notes often include multiple voices and perspectives on any particular event, and their interpretations often draw on multiple sources. In other words, they triangulate and analyze as they write. Moreover, their deep understanding of the field context strengthens their ability to identify dominant narratives and weed out lies and self-serving patter. Critics of site-intensive methods may question their supposed lack of objectivity, yet scholars using this approach are systematically cross-checking, comparing data gained from different sources, and reading between the lines.

Just as scholars using site-intensive methods are intensely aware of how the field context shapes what they see in, and how they see, the world, they are often very self-conscious in their efforts to reimagine and reconstruct the

---

[34] Interview, LM-5, August 27, 2012.

field site when they continue to interpret and write after they leave the field.[35] Yanow (2009) encourages ethnographic researchers to employ the first-person singular "I" and include in their writing the details of the author's presence – or evidence of "being there" in the field – for example, contextual information about the research setting, time, selection of participants, positionality, and the like. One of the challenges is how to communicate the value of the theoretical knowledge gained to social science audiences without sacrificing too much of the rich complexity and detailed understandings of the various field contexts and insider meanings.[36]

Relatedly, the deep integration experienced by scholars who engage in SIM also necessitates serious reflection about their long-term obligations to communicate and share their interpretation and writing after they have left the field. Communities under study may request follow-up engagement from the investigator because they wish to receive the benefit of the research findings, but they also may wish to remain connected for more personal reasons. One researcher expressed her regret about not maintaining such contacts: "I should have known to keep in touch with people better. I always knew I would return. I wish I could have found time to call every couple of months and say hello. When I returned, a good number of people were annoyed."[37] One caveat is worth noting here, however. Some of the proposed strategies may be particularly challenging to implement for graduate students and young faculty who are at an early stage of their career. But the process of using site-intensive methods in the field can be navigated with ongoing dialogue between the researcher and subject communities about their mutual expectations and responsibilities.

Conclusion

Ethnography and participant observation hardly lie at the core of graduate training in political science today. We have sought to show why these methods deserve much more attention than they have traditionally received

---

[35] See Yanow (2009) on the additional interpretive moments involved in "deskwork" and "textwork" by the ethnographic researcher and reader of an ethnographic text.

[36] Wedeen (2010, 256) highlights the importance of enabling a conversation among political scientists who use different research methods. Hardin and Clarke (2012) highlight the "paroxysm of conscience" that ethnographers experience as they attempt to reconcile the complexity of what they have learned in the field with the demands for knowledge from the academic scientific community.

[37] Interview, LM-5, August 27, 2012.

in our discipline. Much of the political world – motivations, perceptions, preferences – is kept hidden: organizations, politicians, and even ordinary people may wish to present a public face that differs from the inside story. Correspondingly, those who study politics can ill afford to turn their backs on approaches that entail deep engagement with context – one of the principles of good field research – and that are designed to lower the barriers between researchers and reality.

Further, these methods can be adapted to many purposes (hence their cross-disciplinary following). They lend themselves to interpretive modes of research that eschew some of the tenets of positivist social science. But, much more than is commonly appreciated, they can also help scholars with any epistemological approach make significant progress in a host of important analytic tasks, aiding with generating new questions, selecting cases, constructing concepts, establishing and testing hypotheses, understanding causal processes – and, thus, building theory. In addition, no matter what purpose these techniques are used for, employing them almost invariably involves significant critical reflection. Indeed, the field notes that scholars who use SIM typically take are *full* of the type of analytic reflections that we believe are a critical principle of good field research. In addition, given the existence of those very careful notes, scholars who engage in SIM are uniquely positioned to be extremely transparent about their research practices, helping readers to understand their research techniques clearly, and why and how they were employed. This research transparency is yet another principle that we believe underlies effective field research.

The purpose of site-intensive methods is to access information that cannot be obtained using other data-collection techniques. Scholars who use SIM believe that these techniques allow for the collection of highly valid data due to the deep relationships, rapport, and trust that often form between researchers and study participants when these methods are employed. Through prolonged interactions, the researcher aims to get below the surface and past the "party line," and the vague or evasive or unconsidered answer. Watching people in the context of their everyday lives makes available data that could never be captured through a highly structured survey questionnaire or a single interview, useful though those data-collection techniques may be in other ways. Given their particularized and unique strength, scholars often use SIM in tandem with other data-collection techniques, meaning that they are often specifically employed as part of a strategy of triangulation.

Almost by definition, these methods involve an investment of time and effort that is greater than other methods on a per-informant basis. Yet engaging in SIM need not be more "costly" *overall* in time or effort than employing other data-collection techniques discussed in this book. Full-blown immersion for many months at a single site is not the only form that these methods can take. Political scientists may have good reason to split their time among multiple sites, or to use SIM in limited ways to augment other methods.

Finally, we have aimed to articulate an encompassing conception of site-intensive methods as an ensemble of techniques with roots in various parts of the ethnographic and participant-observation traditions. We argue that interpretivists and positivists alike can make good use of these methods. To some political scientists, SIM may seem to lack objectivity and to be impossible to replicate. Though these techniques can be free-form and open-ended – and such research can be highly useful in exploratory studies – it is also possible to apply SIM in systematic ways. Bringing a carefully crafted set of hypotheses to site-intensive work can help the investigator to focus her attention on just those things that pertain. Moreover, as the discipline develops stronger norms around transparency in qualitative as well as quantitative research (as discussed in Chapter 11), ethnographers and participant-observers will be pushed to find ways to make their work more accessible to other scholars.

8 Surveys in the context of field research

Survey research is a thoroughly conventional and seemingly well-honed tool in the political science work-shed. Numerous influential books and articles in the discipline have survey data at their core. It is enshrined in institutions like the University of Michigan's venerable Survey Research Center, together with its longstanding training programs. Doctoral programs commonly require coursework in the kinds of statistical methods used to analyze quantitative survey data, and in many departments it is common for Ph.D. students to base their work on such data.[1] To be sure, it appears that more dissertators and senior scholars conduct secondary analysis on existing aggregate datasets than field their own survey, and this has been the case for some time (Manheim and Rich 1986, 123). Still, original survey research conducted in the field has enjoyed a well-established place in the discipline since its introduction in the social sciences in the 1940s.[2]

A survey was used to collect data in 30 percent of the projects reported in the 2011–2012 FRPS survey – and this figure has stayed quite constant since the 1960s. Further, research within the United States was only slightly more likely to employ a survey than was international work.[3] Scholars in our discipline have conducted surveys in all regions of the world, with a somewhat lower incidence in Western Europe (22 percent of projects involving surveys include locations there) and a somewhat higher one in Sub-Saharan Africa (42 percent), perhaps due to variations in the availability of reliable survey data on political questions. And political scientists from almost all

---

[1] Schwartz-Shea found that 66 percent of a sample of fifty-seven top doctoral programs in political science had a quantitative/statistics methods requirement in the early 2000s (2003, 380).

[2] See Brady (2000) for an overview of the contributions of survey research to the discipline as well as a call for greater support for graduate students and faculty who have both "in-depth area studies knowledge" and training in sophisticated survey methods.

[3] Of projects with field locations only in the United States, 33 percent employed surveys, versus 28 percent of projects that extended to non-US locations.

subfields do survey research in ample numbers, including international relations, public administration and public policy scholars.

In many respects, political science is well equipped to teach researchers how to use this technique. Creating and implementing surveys for academic research requires a number of technical skills, which many standard textbooks, and courses based around them, aim to provide (Rea and Parker 2005; Leeuw, Hox, and Dillman 2008; Fowler 2009; Groves *et al.* 2009; Marsden and Wright 2010). Such texts provide general treatments of key elements of the survey process, from laying the overall design foundations to analyzing the data. In addition to theoretical background on topics such as sampling, they also have much advice to give about multiple kinds of substantive and practical matters that researchers confront in the field, such as minimizing interviewer bias and maintaining ethical standards with human subjects. In short, they constitute an essential starting point.

Vital though these published methodological works are, they convey only part of the wisdom that political scientists who seek to conduct a survey in the field need. Most do not focus specifically on political research, and they cannot do justice to the great variety of surveys that political scientists have devised and carried out. Moreover, they are generally written with applications in the United States (and to a lesser extent Western Europe) in mind. Thus they barely begin to consider the vast range of special circumstances and obstacles that field researchers encounter overseas, or even closer to home. Indeed, some of our interviewees explained ways in which standard prescriptions led them astray or had to be disregarded in the field. These textbooks also are not designed to address all the ways in which survey research might dovetail with other components of a research program.

Published work examining the methodologies of field research, for its part, often centers on modes of data gathering *other* than surveys. One recent overview of fieldwork in the authoritative Oxford Handbook series steered away from specific examples of surveys (Wood 2007). Though this essay placed surveys conducted in the field under the rubric of field research, defining the latter as "research based on personal interaction with research subjects in their own setting" may have shifted the focus away from surveys, which often involve only thin forms of interaction with subjects (Wood 2007, 123). While there are exceptions to this tendency to separate surveys conceptually from more deeply interactive forms of data collection (examples are discussed below, such as Sieber 1973), political scientists sometimes think of fieldwork and survey research as two different things.

In addition to these resources, political scientists who anticipate conducting a survey in the field have at their disposal, and can draw lessons from, the work of those who preceded them. Political scientists, sociologists, economists, anthropologists, and others have confronted the challenges of doing survey work in a wide variety of field settings for many decades (for example: Rudolph and Rudolph 1958; Bulmer and Warwick 1983; Dillman 2002; Converse 2009).[4] The record left by these many creative efforts is long, and implies plenty of practical expertise, sometimes conveyed in methodological appendices or chapter-length reflections on the research process.

However, often this expertise has not been compiled in ways that make it easy for today's researchers to access it. Indeed, even milestone works of political science based on surveys often contain only partial explanations of the fieldwork that underpinned the data collection. For example, *The American voter* included virtually no information regarding how the data upon which it was based were gathered; its preface simply stated that information such as the questionnaires and sample design "may be obtained upon request" from the Survey Research Center at the University of Michigan (Campbell *et al.* 1960, vi). A landmark of post-World War II comparative politics, *The civic culture*, did include the English-language questionnaire and an explanation of the sampling technique used in each of the five countries under study, but otherwise provided only a "very brief outline" of the process that led from the formulation of the original questions to the repatriation of the IBM punch cards containing the data (Almond and Verba 1963, 47). In this work as well, then, some of the central elements of carrying out surveys in the field, and the challenges involved, remain unseen in the background. Moreover, changes in societies and communications technology mean that even when details are shared, yesterday's lessons do not always apply in the present.

The purpose of this chapter is to fill the multiple gaps identified in the above discussion. We examine how the actual practices of survey research are woven into scholars' broader fieldwork endeavors, and stress how scholars' engaging with the survey context can encourage greater survey participation and enhance the quality of survey research more generally. We begin with

---

[4] For early perspectives from the heyday of the modernization school, see also the other articles collected in the Autumn 1958 issue of *The Public Opinion Quarterly*, titled "Special issue on attitude research in modernizing areas." Townsend, Sakunthasathien, and Jordan (2013) recount in detail the story of an ongoing survey project focusing on households and economic activity in Thailand; though rooted in economics, this contains many lessons for political scientists, particularly those working in rural, developing-world settings.

some reflections on the nature of political survey research and the many forms it can take in the field. We also highlight the many opportunities for constructive synergies between survey work and other kinds of data gathering in the field. We discuss multiple ways of using information collected through interviews or archival work, for instance, to inform and improve a survey, and to build upon and enhance findings from surveys through follow-up work. Indeed, as we observe, what could be seen as a boundary or tradeoff between the gathering of thin data on the one hand, and rich, intensive, thick data on the other, can sometimes be transcended. Rather than being mutually exclusive, these different forms of data can feed and inform each other in productive ways.

Next, we dig more deeply into the purposes for which and the conditions under which political scientists might contemplate fielding a survey. As part of this discussion, we address the various ways in which survey research contributes to furthering analytic goals in a project, and to building theory. We anticipate our treatment of this question here by noting that, in our view, surveys are remarkably versatile, with some caveats and limitations. Surveys are generally conducted in order to provide data for use in making descriptive inferences and testing hypotheses. A survey can provide a baseline understanding of the population under study – whatever that population might be – and this can be used to inform further stages of field research, for instance by selecting cases or generating hypotheses to be tested. A survey might even be used to clarify the concepts that are under study in a given project. Still, given the highly structured form that surveys take and their comparatively high cost in terms of time and money, it is more common for a survey to come after such basic elements of a research design as concepts and hypotheses have been largely or entirely settled. As we will again note in connection with experimental research, by the time a scholar takes on the complex process of setting up a survey (often in concert with collaborators), many key analytic choices and tasks will likely already have been made and carried out.

After probing the intersections between surveys and other techniques, and theory and application, the chapter's final two substantive sections consider some of the pragmatic issues that researchers confront as they implement surveys on the ground, such as costs, contracts, and managing survey teams. We explore the kinds of innovations, compromises, and work-arounds that can be necessary where methodologically ideal approaches prove infeasible. In particular, we address some of the complexities and pitfalls entailed in organizing people to make surveys happen. Of course, all of the data-collection techniques discussed in this book can be undertaken either alone or in some form of collaboration. Survey research, however, tends to be particularly collaborative in nature. This may simply mean hiring research assistants to conduct interviews, or may entail more elaborate outsourcing to specialized organizations. Some well-known survey projects – the American National Election Studies and the World Values Survey, for example – involve collaboration on a truly massive scale, pooling the efforts of many investigators, coordinating through steering committees, and receiving multiple waves of funding over time. While many of the points we make could apply to survey research on any scale, our goal is to offer insights and strategies that will be useful for the kinds of projects that one PI or a small group of researchers might initiate.

Surveys' diversity and combining surveys with other data-collection techniques

In survey research, information is gathered using systematic procedures from a population of people or other entities, or from a sample of a larger population.[5] Generally the sample size must be large enough to attain a reasonable degree of representativeness. Beyond these very basic similarities, surveys may be of many types, and may be combined with other data-collection techniques in several ways. This section considers these issues.

Diversity within survey research

Typically the purpose of a survey is to generalize findings based on data gathered from a rigorously sampled subset to the broader population in ways that produce a calculable degree of error.[6] Often survey questions use pre-coded and standardized response categories, to be recorded in quantitative values for later analysis. Yet surveys sometimes do more than produce quantitative data, and the goal need not be generalizing to population characteristics. Surveys often include at least some open-ended questions

---

[5] This definition is adapted from Groves *et al.* (2009, 2). Narrower definitions exclude surveys of subjects other than individual people (Manheim, Rich, and Willnat 2002, 120). But, as discussed below, political scientists and other researchers often use surveys to explore other kinds of populations such as organizations or communities.

[6] For example, it might be calculated that, given sampling error, a survey's point estimate of the average age of a population is 95 percent likely to be within a range from 35.4 to 37.7.

aimed at obtaining information from respondents in a more free-form manner. This material might later be assigned a set of quantitative or categorical codes, or it might remain in a qualitative format. Such qualitative material can serve many purposes. It can function as a check on closed-ended questions, allowing respondents to report things that do not fit into the survey's pre-established answer categories. It might capture information that is sufficiently complex to defy simple multiple-choice formats, such as the process through which a person became committed to a political cause, or the sequence of events in a legal dispute. The purpose might be to obtain an extensive list of items for follow-up study, such as names of influential people in a locality or web sites frequented by participants in a social movement. Nonetheless, most political scientists associate surveys with quantitative data, and producing such data is their comparative strength.

Over the years, political scientists have carried out a huge variety of surveys. With regard to the form of the survey, or its "mode," data may be gathered through traditional face-to-face interviews, or telephone interviews. Surveys may also involve mailed questionnaires, or may be email- or web-based. In all cases, researchers can contract out much of the work involved in a survey to other parties: survey research can thus be done without the PI ever leaving his or her home institution. In this chapter, naturally, we focus on projects that actually take researchers into the field.

In terms of subject matter, political attitudes, voting behavior, and civic engagement have long been core topics in survey research on the United States and other countries. But researchers in our discipline also explore many other topics through surveys, for instance, tolerance, interpersonal networks, and opinions on international relations. Scholars survey the opinions of political elites as well as the public. And far from confining themselves to individual human beings as subjects, they survey groups of people, firms and other formal organizations, and even places. For example, the maintenance of streets and the cleanliness of parks in small Midwestern towns have been surveyed, as one proxy among others for social capital (Rice 2001).

Integrating survey research with other dimensions of a project

As examples mentioned throughout the chapter illustrate, researchers can bring information, familiarity, and social relationships from other phases of the research project and the field research endeavor into the survey process. Here we emphasize ways to integrate survey research with other forms of data collection. Such integration is, in fact, overwhelmingly common in the field research projects reported in the FRPS survey of political scientists. Of the 410 reported field research projects that employed survey research, only 11 (less than 3 percent) involved no other data-collection techniques. Of those 410 projects, 89 percent also used interviews; 55 percent also involved archival research; 42 percent also featured ethnography or participant observation; and 25 percent also drew on focus groups.[7] Projects using surveys also used an average of nearly six (5.7) other techniques. And with regard to analytic techniques, in 85 percent of projects that used surveys to collect data, either qualitative or interpretive approaches or both were among the approaches to analysis that were employed. This highlights the fact that quantitative research often goes hand-in-hand with other forms of inquiry in field-based projects.

More than forty years ago, sociologist Sam D. Sieber published an essay discussing numerous ways in which surveys and fieldwork (as he understood it) could complement and inform one another.[8] Seeking to reconcile "two methodological subcultures" with a history of mutual antagonism, he suggested that each approach could guide the other, with survey results suggesting places for in-depth study, for instance. He also posited that findings generated through one method could be checked, validated, and interpreted by means of the other. Interviews and observation might provide a theoretical structure and hypotheses to be tested with large-n data, which in turn might correct for unconscious biases coloring the qualitative work, such as a tendency to place excessive weight on the views of elites, and the holistic fallacy (the "tendency on the part of field observers to perceive all aspects of a social situation as congruent").[9] Qualitative research, Sieber suggested, could provide case studies to bring statistical relationships to life, while surveys could demonstrate the general applicability of such individual cases (Sieber 1973). His examples centered on sociological studies of schools, unions, and the like, but the arguments apply to a broad set of subjects.

Important epistemological contrasts notwithstanding, political scientists frequently synthesize surveys with more qualitative approaches to data

---

[7] The questionnaire asked respondents to indicate only data-collection techniques that their project made "significant use of."

[8] Sieber defined fieldwork as "participant observation, informant interviewing and use of available records to supplement these techniques in a particular setting" (1973, 1335n2).

[9] As an example of a holistic fallacy corrected by survey results, Sieber discusses a project in which he observed staff members in one large and one small school district. Because staff in the small district treated one another with less formality, he initially inferred that their morale was also higher, which turned out not to be so.

collection. For instance, in a reflective methodological essay about one of her projects in China, Gallagher describes in detail how a set of fifty semi-structured, in-depth interviews with legal aid recipients helped reshape her approach to the large-scale survey that she later conducted, in particular changing the way she thought about key concepts. For example, she realized that the notion of "legal consciousness" contained complexities in the post-socialist context of Shanghai that were not found in the United States context where it had previously been theorized – complexities that could not necessarily be captured in a single linear scale. "The effect on the survey and how I thought about the survey was profound," she writes, further advocating that qualitative interviews be seen as a crucial part of the research design process for survey projects (Gallagher 2013, 185). A scholar interviewed for this book related how an open-ended process of observation and interviewing was used to refine conceptual measures and build survey questionnaires: "I spend several weeks . . . soaking and poking in the communities that I intend to study. That gives me a much better idea of how the variables of interest should be conceptualized, and how the questionnaire should be designed."[10]

On other occasions, multiple elements of an extensive and immersive program of field research can inform the design of a survey questionnaire. For example, during 20 months of research in Japan on siting decisions for "public bads" (airports, nuclear power plants, waste facilities, and incinerators), Daniel Aldrich employed multiple data-collection techniques, including conducting archival research and many in-depth interviews, carrying out extensive content analysis of newspaper articles, and building a database of localities and site choices for noxious facilities. Drawing on what he was learning from these other techniques, he designed a survey inquiring about things like compensation, local politics, and associations. He ultimately distributed the survey to more than 350 individuals in local governments and offices of the national infrastructure ministry. Not just knowing how to phrase the questions, but knowing whom to ask and what to ask about, required knowledge gained through the other activities (Aldrich 2008).

Another common practice is to *follow up* on survey findings by engaging in more in-depth interviewing of survey respondents or others from the target population, seeking to explore key concepts or causal processes, or bolster and explicate survey results. Indeed, the previously cited *Civic culture* employed such a strategy, re-interviewing 539 respondents from the national

[10] Interview, LM-10, September 18, 2012.

cross-section samples (about 10 percent) in order to obtain their "political life history." The authors composed vignettes based around the life stories and world-views expressed in some of these interviews and compiled them in a long chapter illustrating what they depicted as the political cultures of the five countries under study. This approach highlights the rhetorical impact of such personal accounts (Almond and Verba 1963, 46, 402–469).

In another example, Strolovitch commissioned a telephone survey of leaders and staff at 286 advocacy organizations, then followed up through semi-structured interviews with some of the survey respondents, as well as interviewing others. The interviews, she writes, "supplement the survey data by providing a window into the nuances of how, why, and in what context organization officers make the decisions that they do about how to allocate resources" (2007, 240–248, at 247). In Read's work on state-fostered neighborhood organizations in Beijing and Taipei, popular opinion surveys, which found a surprising degree of approval of state-backed groups, helped to frame and guide a series of interviews that explored the perspectives of city residents in more detail (Read 2012). In other instances, analyzing survey data may reveal a particularly puzzling distribution of responses for one question or by one subset of the respondents. This may lead to more focused follow-up interviews with a targeted subset of the survey sample to try to understand such "questionable responses," as one investigator put it.[11]

One recent book exploring the critical role of the early Iowa caucuses in the US presidential nominating process demonstrates how surveys can be integrated with qualitative knowledge. A field survey was administered in January 2008 at the actual caucus sites of each political party in 1,784 Iowa precincts in 99 counties; one participant in each was given a written questionnaire before the beginning of the meeting, resulting in 2,611 completed responses (Redlawsk et al. 2011, 39, 88). The University of Iowa faculty who fielded the survey juxtaposed data it provided with information gathered through a more conventional telephone survey of caucus attenders, and data from other polls. They also integrated their own experience-based knowledge of the caucus process: the first author, for instance, had served five times as chair of his precinct caucus, and also as chair of a county-level party organization in Iowa. Through combining data from multiple sources, the study creates a rich portrait of citizen participation in this important event and builds an argument about the importance of grassroots-based caucuses in the election process.

---

[11] Interview, LM-10, September 18, 2012.

To offer a final possibility, other data-collection techniques can also be used to develop contextual variables that are subsequently linked to individual-level survey data. For example, Melani Cammett used GIS to create a map of the area where she planned to conduct a survey in Lebanon. She located in space the level and types of health care infrastructure in the sampled community. Later, she included in her statistical analysis a variable that indicated the distance to the nearest health center from the respondent's home.[12] In short, as these examples demonstrate, qualitative work can help create better surveys, and survey data can raise questions that can be pursued in greater depth through deeper qualitative follow-up.

Why do a survey? Considerations and contributions to theory

Some field researchers set out from the very beginning of a project with a firm intention to conduct a survey, whether it is a central part of their research design or a peripheral component. Others may arrive in the field uncertain of what the possibilities are for doing a survey, particularly if the setting is an unfamiliar one. We highlight several factors to consider when assessing the pros and cons of including a survey component in a research project. We then discuss the broader issue of what analytic tasks scholars can accomplish with a survey – that is, how surveys contribute to the building of theory in political science.

Factors to consider when contemplating a survey

A primary consideration when scholars are thinking of carrying out a survey, of course, must be the fit with the design and goals of the research. Survey research – alone or in conjunction with other forms of data collection – must show the promise of helping scholars to accomplish key analytic tasks such as descriptive inference or hypothesis testing (as we discuss in the next section), and bringing the overall project a considerable distance toward answering the questions it asks. More broadly, survey work only makes sense if it meshes with the researcher's skills, tastes, and epistemological orientation.

Before proceeding, it is sensible to determine whether existing survey datasets might suffice, making it unnecessary to start from scratch. As a leading survey expert cautions, "Sponsoring a special-purpose survey data

---

[12] Interview, LM-9, August 30, 2012.

collection is a rather expensive solution to an information problem" (Fowler 2009, 3). The search for extant datasets can, in fact, constitute a non-trivial component of fieldwork all of its own. In some settings, academic data repositories will provide an obvious first place to check[13] – and, convenient though they are, the process of sifting through their catalogs and poring over codebooks may take considerable energy. Even if such sources prove fruitless, that does not mean that no one has done the kind of research in question. Individual academics, private research firms and pollsters, and government agencies all may have conducted or commissioned surveys. In many cases, making contacts and asking around are the only ways to find data that are sitting in a drawer or on a computer, possibly available for the asking. It is this type of opacity and uncertainty that sharing data and research transparency – the latter of which we suggest is a principle of good field research – have the potential to mitigate. Yet as a practical matter, some datasets will always be withheld from publicly accessible archives, so there is no substitute for making private inquiries.

Yet even such extensive investigation may not turn up survey data relevant for a scholar's particular research questions, field sites, or time periods. Existing datasets may not focus on the precise questions of interest or operationalize and measure concepts in the way that the researcher finds most compelling. Aggregate datasets are often biased toward more stable countries and regions where survey research firms can operate safely. For example, with the exception of Zimbabwe, the Afrobarometer Data Project has historically included countries that have at least moderate levels of state capacity and are more democratic and economically open. In countries and regions still troubled by war or only recently emerging from conflict, few or no survey data may exist. At other times, the groups a scholar wishes to study may have been neglected in previous survey research. One researcher we interviewed explained how she became one of the very first to conduct a survey with women farmers in a post-conflict setting. Almost no systematic data had been produced in this region and with this population during a long civil war, where many of the roads leading to the location were either

---

[13] Perhaps three of the most well-known archives are those available through the University of Michigan's Interuniversity Consortium for Political and Social Research (ICPSR), the University of Connecticut's Roper Center, and Harvard University's Dataverse. The Council of European Social Science Data Archives (CESSDA) is an umbrella organization that maintains a catalogue of data repositories across Europe. Institutions around the world host data repositories; the University of Amsterdam's Social Science Information System (Sociosite) keeps an extensive list, sorted by country.

destroyed or covered with mines.[14] Conducting one's own survey hence allows scholars maximal freedom to pose exactly the questions they wish to ask to the right people, in the right place, at the right time.

The costs of a survey, in terms of both time and money, bear careful consideration. The factor of time is easily underestimated. Even with what appear to be straightforward and small-scale surveys, the many steps in the process – at minimum, defining the scope of the project, writing questions, designing the questionnaire, hiring and working with any partners involved, pre-testing, sampling, and then collecting, cleaning, processing, and analyzing data – almost always take more time than anticipated. Financial costs vary widely with such factors as the survey's location, mode (for instance, in-person interviews vs. mail or telephone), partners, sample size, degree of methodological rigor, and fit with the established templates of previous projects. Depending on the setting, researchers, even at the graduate student level, should not assume that the monetary cost is beyond reach. For modest surveys, it may be possible for the researcher to do much or all of the work himself to save money. Alternatively, survey organizations can often tailor their work to fit a fixed budget, and may be able to include a small set of questions from one's project on a survey planned for another client. Moreover, a well-designed proposal showing precisely how the data will pay off might be just the thing to attract the favor of a funding organization.

Finally, particular settings may pose their own special challenges to fielding a survey. For example, authoritarian states like China impose administrative constraints on survey research related to social and political issues, and investigators from outside of mainland China are subjected to extensive oversight and special restrictions. The Chinese National Bureau of Statistics and its local counterparts assert jurisdiction over surveys, and often other government agencies request payment as well. Well-connected partner institutions are thus required to carry out survey research in this setting. While noting this imposing regulatory regime, Manion pointed out that still no fewer than thirty-two survey projects in China from 1986 through mid-2008 had resulted in peer-reviewed articles, chapters, and books by political scientists writing in English (2010, 186–187).[15] An overview of research done on public opinion in the Arab world pointed out that, although for decades such studies had been subject to stringent limitations, political change and other factors created an opening for new projects (Tessler and Jamal 2006).

---

[14] Interview, LM-17, September 11, 2012.
[15] This tally included only publications in academic venues outside of China.

In short, political obstacles are among the concerns that must be evaluated in deciding whether or not to pursue a survey, but, like other potential stumbling blocks, they vary in seriousness and can often be overcome. We discuss some related challenges, and strategies for addressing them, in subsequent sections of the chapter.

Surveys' analytical contributions

As we noted in this chapter's introduction, data garnered through survey research may contribute to accomplishing a variety of analytic tasks, in four general ways. They can enrich descriptive inference, for instance, by allowing researchers to examine the distribution of variables across a population or compare subgroups. They can allow for testing hypotheses and, in some circumstances, exploring causal relationships. They can help the investigator refine aspects of the project to be explored in later stages, for instance by revealing which cases deserve special scrutiny or what new hypotheses deserve to be tested. Finally, and less commonly, they can also aid with conceptualization. We consider each in turn below.

Enriching descriptive inference

Surveys offer particular ways of enriching a scholar's descriptive understanding of phenomena under study, sometimes enabling inferences that are impossible or difficult to draw through other data-collection techniques. Surveys may be able to provide information about the political attitudes, behaviors, and experiences of a greater number and variety of respondents than other methods. Most often using a random sampling technique to obtain a representative sample, surveys can help researchers to examine the distribution of key variables in the broader population. This facilitates comparison across subgroups and helps identify patterns, trends, and anomalies. Survey research may capture a greater range of citizen viewpoints than can be obtained from subjects purposefully selected for individual or focus group interviews. In sum, survey research makes several important contributions to descriptive inference, a set of tasks whose value is sometimes discounted by political scientists but that is often an essential part of a field research project.

Testing hypotheses

The second way that surveys may contribute to theory is by enabling the testing of hypotheses. For many researchers, a primary rationale for going to the trouble of conducting a survey is to obtain a dataset allowing for statistical testing of important propositions about an underlying population, such as whether voting turnout rates are higher among voters in a particular age or ethnic category, or whether citizens who are members of a ruling party are more likely than others to receive welfare benefits.

Depending on the exact proposition at issue, and the kinds of assumptions one can make, it can be difficult to assess causal hypotheses using standard cross-sectional surveys. Correlations between observed variables do not necessarily establish whether X caused Y, Y caused X, or both were caused by a third, perhaps unobserved, factor. Experimental designs (discussed in the next chapter) are one response to this problem. One subset of experimental research, survey experiments, involves manipulating the wording or ordering of questions in a survey and assessing the effect on respondents' answers. This approach makes sense where a posited causal factor is amenable to manipulation and random assignment within a survey, such as in a study of how the language in which a policy is described affects support for that policy.[16] Survey researchers take other approaches as well. The use of panel surveys is one approach, such as Baker, Ames, and Renno's study of preference change among voters in Brazil's 2002 presidential election, which successively surveyed the same voters at three points during the campaign (Baker, Ames, and Renno 2006). Brady discusses other approaches, such as quasi-experimental designs (2000, 52–53).

Selecting cases and generating hypotheses

Surveys can also be used as a source of information that shapes the design of later components of a field research project. Though it was not written with survey research in mind, Lieberman's discussion of "nested analysis" suggests logics for selecting cases for in-depth study on the basis of findings from surveys.[17] Large-n analysis might, for example, generate a regression line positing a relationship between two concepts. Follow-up case study work

---

[16] See Mutz (2011) for a detailed treatment of population-based survey experiments. Gaines, Kuklinski, and Quirk (2007) offer a critical overview of the subject.

[17] In Lieberman's article, the units of analysis are specified to be such things as nation-states, provinces, or institutions. He writes that "for most analyses of individual behaviors or attitudes, for which the 'large-N' component of the data is contained in a survey, I would not expect this approach to be feasible, because scholars are unlikely to be able to conduct further in-depth research with the original respondents. Moreover, the prospect of explaining the exceptional nature of a particular individual is unlikely to be of intrinsic interest in the way scholars are likely to be interested in the particularities of larger social units, such as national states" (2005, 436n2). Follow-up with individual survey respondents can certainly be possible, though, and may be valuable for obtaining evidence about what explains observed correlational patterns. Also, surveys are not always of individuals; they sometimes have supra-individual entities (neighborhoods, villages, firms, institutions) as their primary unit of analysis, or individual-level responses may be aggregated into such larger units. Thus, Lieberman's logic can indeed apply to survey work.

could focus on representative cases on the line, for model-testing analysis, or could include off-the-line cases for more preliminary model-building work (Lieberman 2005, 440–446). Another way in which surveys can drive follow-up research is that open-ended survey questions can be used to produce potential explanations that can then be explored as alternative hypotheses. For example, respondents might be asked their opinion of a politician, policy, or law in a closed-ended question with answer categories amenable to quantitative analysis, such as a feeling thermometer. They might then also be asked *why* they indicated a positive or a negative opinion, and these answers could be explored in later in-depth interviews, or else coded and analyzed in quantitative fashion.[18]

Developing concepts

Surveys can also contribute to conceptual development. Survey researchers have to decide, in advance, precisely how they will word each question, structure their instruments, and code respondents' answers. This encourages careful consideration of the underlying concepts. Brady notes that survey researchers spend "extraordinary amounts of energy thinking about how to devise measures of concepts by asking questions," and suggests that controversies concerning measurement in survey question wordings have had the effect of sharpening our grasp of underlying concepts. He cites, as an example, the problem of how to assess a respondent's political tolerance. This has been measured through questions about respondents' willingness to acknowledge the civil liberties of groups they dislike, raising the problem of what kind of group makes an appropriate referent from which to gauge tolerance (Brady 2000, 51). In that example, the concept in question has evolved over the course of decades of study, but a single survey can also offer possibilities for probing the meaning of a concept. For instance, a researcher might include multiple, differing measures of a single concept, or ask respondents to rank answers related to a concept in order of importance or priority.

Preparing for surveys in the field

As with other data-collection techniques, administering a survey in the field frequently involves making fundamental research design decisions after arriving in the field site. While a scholar will likely dedicate extensive thought

---

[18] Interview, BR-3, August 6, 2012.

to designing the survey prior to leaving her home institution, such basics as the structure of the survey instrument, sampling technique, sample size, the mode of the survey, and question selection, ordering, and wording may all be affected if not dictated by the local context. Making decisions about all such matters, and many other details, is part of why preparing to field a survey can and should take substantial amounts of time. One interviewee passionately advocated allowing enough time at the beginning of the project to figure out how things work on the ground and what questions are important, rather than bringing in a preformatted questionnaire, which (as the scholar put it) might reduce our collective knowledge instead of adding to it.[19]

Refining and pre-testing a survey present many opportunities for correcting omissions, catching mistakes, and ensuring that the survey meets the researcher's needs. But surveys may not be open to *as much* ongoing refinement as the other data-collection techniques discussed so far in this book allow. One might do months of ethnography, for example, and in the last week begin probing a new set of questions or issues, with no great harm done. With a survey, the investigator reaches a more definite point of no return. Once the survey is launched or goes "into the field" for primary data collection, changes in overall design or even in tiny details of question wording become extremely costly. Such modifications may mean that data acquired in the second iteration of the survey are incompatible with data gained through the first iteration, and thus of limited or no value.

In short, the iterative process of ongoing research design – which we find to be widespread in field research and whose merits we emphasize – bumps up against some limits in a survey project. Consequently, scholars who contemplate carrying out a survey (or a field experiment, as discussed in the next chapter) need to anticipate their data needs carefully in the early phases of the research process. Indeed, it is in part because of the highly structured – even inflexible – nature of survey research that surveys are typically fielded later in a research project, once many key analytic tasks have already been accomplished, often by employing other data-collection techniques.

The rest of this section discusses several elements of survey planning that scholars will need to carry out in the early stages of their project – although, again, some tasks will need to be completed after arrival in the field. We begin with research partnerships, considering the options of subcontracting a survey firm versus training one's own research team. We then consider designing questionnaires, sampling, and pre-testing in the field.

---

[19] Interview, LM-10, September 18, 2012.

Subcontracting a survey or training a research team

Having opted to pursue a survey, one of the fundamental questions for the researcher is whether to contract out the labor involved to a professional survey organization, to do it herself or with the help of research assistants, or to employ some mixture of these two strategies. The choice may be dictated by local circumstances and the availability of reputable firms and competent assistants, but, in generic terms, each approach entails fairly predictable sets of advantages and disadvantages. Beyond a relatively small sample size, just about any type of survey requires the work of multiple people. Organizations dedicated to this kind of research have staff and equipment on hand, and using their resources can be more efficient than trying to do all the legwork oneself. As well, private firms or academic survey centers have experience in key realms such as the creation of workable sampling frames and the wording of questionnaires, and can provide insight on matters like expected response rates for different approaches.

Conversely, there are also advantages to running the survey on one's own. In some parts of the world, reliable research organizations may simply not exist, or may be prohibitively expensive to contract. Also, the investigator may want the survey to use methods or include features that lie out of the norm for firms whose bread-and-butter work is market research rather than academic inquiry. Finally, self-reliance provides maximum control to the scholar over the integrity of the process – and no one cares about the quality of the data like the PI herself.

In exploring possible collaborations with survey firms and organizations, it is critical to shop around. By eliciting bids from multiple vendors and, when possible, visiting them in person, scholars can get a good sense of how the firms operate. Researchers might also get recommendations from academics who have worked with the firms. Firms with a track record of doing the kind of work that is being planned, whose staff show a substantive interest in the project or the topic of inquiry, and that seem to have a strong commitment to quality might be particularly good partners. Indeed, it is important, even in these early stages, for the PI to set the tone that quality is of paramount importance and that all work relating to the project needs to be done conscientiously. Once scholars begin to negotiate with one or more firms, they should write up the critical project specifications, from sampling to the handling of non-responses to payment, in a scope-of-work document to ensure that everyone understands the expectations for the project.

Investigators with experience working with survey organizations emphasize the importance of taking an assertively hands-on approach to the
partnership throughout the process. If possible, the researcher should be
present at key stages, such as when enumerators are being trained, and
should quickly address anything that deviates from his expectations. One
political scientist recounted an incident in which a firm she had hired
delivered data to her that required many hours of cleaning and fixing: "The
lesson from that was that I wasn't doing enough homework all along;
I needed to be on top of them every step of the way. You should review
what's coming in and not release payments until you are satisfied."[20] (This
scholar decided to train her own team in future projects.)

While PIs need to stay closely involved with their project regardless of the
quality of their partner firm, it is important to highlight that survey research
organizations with proven track records can contribute knowledge and
experience to a project. A researcher who conducted surveys in multiple
countries overseas found staff in reputable survey firms to be "experts in
and of themselves," providing valuable perspective on sampling techniques,
language issues, and how questions on particular topics had fared in previous
polls.[21] It can also be possible to save money and maintain a higher degree
of personal control by contracting a survey outfit for only certain services
and not others. For instance, a researcher could hire a firm's enumerators
to conduct survey interviews, while doing sampling and data entry herself
(or with a team of research assistants). No matter how much or how little of
the work is outsourced, researchers should stay involved and keep on top
of what is being done.

Forgoing survey organizations and training one's own enumerators brings
with it a distinct set of advantages and disadvantages. Doing so can be the
most economical option, and it leaves day-to-day responsibility and oversight in the researcher's own hands, maximizing her ability to ensure that
correct procedures are followed, errors are corrected, and the resulting data
meet the desired quality standards. One political scientist explained how
he had administered a survey in two overseas cities himself, managing a set
of supervisors and building a team of dozens of college students as interviewers. Because the interviewers had no prior experience, they required
considerable training and varied in quality. The intense and protracted work,
and countless details, including resolving squabbles within the team, created

---

[20] Interview, LM-9, August 30, 2012.   [21] Interview, BR-11, August 22, 2012.

headaches: "I was miserable the entire time."[22] The money the scholar saved by not hiring a professional firm, however, allowed him to draw a much larger sample. And, of course, working as part of an international research team can be an enriching experience for students with regard to both methodological knowledge gained, and in-country and international connections made. Another experienced researcher suggested that it is possible to economize by employing local graduate students as enumerators and compensating them by letting them contribute questions designed to advance their own projects.[23]

One comparativist arrived in-country and hastily hired an enumerator in hopes of getting a fast start on a survey. Having been paid half his compensation in advance, the enumerator became frustrated with the challenging work and "ended up running away with my money." Learning from this experience, the researcher vetted assistants more carefully, recruiting them through universities and also through institutions with strong ties to the communities that were the targets of the surveys. Paid on a daily basis and working side-by-side with the PI, later enumerators not only accomplished the primary goal of completing the survey interviews but also provided perspective on their interactions with respondents.[24]

Several of our interviewees were convinced of the merits of organizing and managing the survey process themselves – both with regard to what *they* learned through the process, and in terms of the quality of the result. A scholar of public policy declared resolutely that the "huge investment" in training his own research team was recouped in his confidence in the quality of the data: "Farming this stuff out would have resulted in junk!"[25] A comparativist commented:

In the end, I was glad I didn't work with a survey firm. If I had, I would have outsourced much of what I did to them. I wouldn't have had as much influence over the sampling, wouldn't have been able to have my hands on everything. In the end, I did everything myself, including stapling the questionnaires ... basically I never slept for weeks. I really saw it from the inside. In terms of learning how to do a survey, I think it was incredible training.[26]

Whether one is working through a survey organization or not, the training and management of the staff who will conduct the interviews or otherwise

---

[22] Interview, BR-3, August 6, 2012.   [23] Interview, BR-15, October 25, 2013.
[24] Interview, BR-6, August 14, 2012. Bonilla also emphasized the value of "the interviewing of interviewers" (1964, 149).
[25] Interview, LM-10, September 18, 2012.   [26] Interview, BR-14, October 24, 2013.

stand on the front lines of data collection are paramount. Survey researchers of all stripes agree on this. If interviewers and enumerators shirk or deviate from their responsibilities, or simply fail to put energy into obtaining the cooperation of the subjects of the survey, quality will suffer. (A different problem is putting too much energy into this task, such that interview requests and questions border on the coercive, an experience MacLean had with one of her enumerators early on.) In short, because every project and its emphases, imperatives, and procedures are different, even staff members with previous experience in survey research should receive careful training. Training should be wide-ranging, addressing each step of the survey process including approaching respondents, eliciting informed consent, interacting with respondents as questions are asked, capturing responses and additional information about the interaction, wrapping up the session, potential follow-up, and much more.

Likewise, once the survey is being fielded, a considerable degree of monitoring and oversight is always required in order to ensure that the project is being carried out as the researcher envisions, and to identify and resolve problems. Simultaneously, and just as importantly, scholars should do all they can to help and coach those whose help they have enlisted. Researchers should make themselves available to answer patiently any questions that arise. It can be useful to have periodic meetings with all team members – to address issues and resolve questions, to keep the whole team updated on progress, and to help to build team spirit. Some researchers stress other strategies for reinforcing team members' commitment to the integrity of the research process. Comparativist Lily Tsai personally trained and supervised three teams of ten to twenty students each for her village-level surveys of public goods provision in rural China. She describes traveling with them via bus and train, emphasizing the intellectual and social value of the project in order to increase their commitment, and reinforcing bonds of mutual obligation with them through practices "from advising them on their theses to staying in the same accommodations to hand-washing their laundry when they were busy with survey administration" (Tsai 2010, 258). While not everyone will go to such lengths, most would echo the idea of trying to build a cadre of dedicated research assistants and working with them directly and carefully.

Questionnaire design in the field

Specialized methodological monographs and general textbooks provide critical guidance on the general methodological issues involved in the writing of a survey (Converse and Presser 1986; Fowler 1995, Krosnick and Presser 2010). But crafting questions that address the goals of the research project, that are cast in appropriate terms, that make sense to respondents, and that do not provoke unwanted reactions requires considerable local knowledge as well as proficiency with the general principles of survey research. Indeed, as the examples of combining surveys with other data-collection techniques offered earlier in the chapter illustrated, this is an area that can be significantly informed by data gathered through other aspects of the field research project.

The need to adapt a research design into locally meaningful terms that can be operationalized in a survey questionnaire starts at a high level of generality. What are the underlying concepts that the project aims to assess? How are those concepts manifested in the field environment and in the subjective world of the people who will be enumerating or responding to the survey? Of course, researchers should avoid allowing social science jargon or unfamiliar terms to slip into the questionnaire. Whether in the native tongue or a different language, the words of the survey instrument should probably not be the words used in the project's grant applications or prospectus. Yet even when researchers have successfully accomplished that aspect of "translating" their research design into their questionnaire, they may discover, once they arrive in the field, that the questions they planned to ask – or the particular way they planned to ask them – do not fit the local setting well, and must be rethought. These issues, of course, derive from the fundamental tension in social science between general concepts and the endless particularity and variation of the empirical universe. One example of a controversy of this kind revolving around survey measurement is found in the debate over how "civil society" should be conceptualized and how it should be measured in different contexts.[27]

The practical implication is that researchers need to find appropriate and meaningful ways to connect their theoretical concerns with local realities. The ways to do this are many, of course. Scholars might scour publications based on studies pertaining to the concepts in question and carried out in the setting in which they will field their survey; talk with local colleagues about concepts and how best to express them; and become familiar with settings like the ones in which they will field their survey. For instance, one scholar noted that it was not clear what the concept of social capital was or how it

---

[27] See the symposium on conceptualization and measurement in the *Journal of Civil Society*, vol. 1, no. 3, December 2005. Related controversies are addressed in papers concerning the World Values Survey, www.worldvaluessurvey.org/index_paperseries.

would manifest in a context that differed from Putnam's Italy or Coleman's United States. Nearly three months of intensive qualitative interviews and ethnographic observation were needed to develop an appropriate scale and instrument.[28]

At the level of question wording and (if necessary) the translation of terminology into local languages, complexities abound. Even with seemingly straightforward items of the kind that it might seem could be asked almost anywhere – questions about respondents' dates of birth, marital status, or line of work, for instance – it is important to seek guidance on phrasings in cultures that are not the researcher's own. In Taiwan, to give just one example, it is customary to express years, including birth years, in the numbering system of the Republic of China calendar, counting from the 1911 revolution. Questions about household income are sensitive in many contexts, Western and non-Western, and often require careful wording and the use of approximate ranges. Indeed, one researcher found that poverty was such a stigmatized term that enumerators had to first discuss it "hypothetically" and then circle around to speak of poverty in terms of visible concrete items in the household.[29] Importing question wordings from surveys in other languages almost always presents complications. The task is as complex as any problem of translation, but more acute than most because respondents should not have to strain to make sense of the wording; it must come across as natural to them.

The need for locally appropriate language is even more obvious when it comes to concepts that are specific to the locality: religions, political parties, notions of approval or disapproval and trust or distrust, government agencies, and the like. Professionals and academics with experience polling in the same context can help scholars perfect their questionnaires, and suggest prior surveys that have been fielded in the same context, from which wording can be adopted. Questions can also be tried out on local research assistants, friends, or others in the field.

Although crafting locally suitable questions is of paramount importance, the value of maintaining compatibility with concepts and wordings that are already in wide use in the discipline also deserves emphasis. Many key political variables – party identification, tolerance, political support, etc. – have long track records of operationalization in surveys around the world. Straying from previously accepted wordings can make it more difficult for a researcher to compare her findings with those of other surveys, or to

---

[28] Interview, LM-10, September 18, 2012.   [29] Interview, LM-10, September 18, 2012.

speak to longstanding debates. For this reason, it may be worthwhile to triangulate by including multiple measures of important concepts, for instance one in more "localized" terms and another using phrasing that more closely follows standard international practices.

Sampling

Ideally, sampling entails defining a full population and then randomly selecting a subset for study in such a way that each unit (e.g., individual person or household) within the broader population has an equal chance of being included. Obstacles in the field can complicate sampling, however, necessitating creativity on the part of researchers. A central problem is that for many of the populations that interest political scientists – grassroots NGOs, or informal worker organizations, or citizens who have appeared before local courts – the full population is difficult to define and no list of that population exists. Moreover, even when a list of the target population does exist, it can be inadequate or systematically biased in ways that complicate sampling. For instance, in the United States, sampling from a frame of possible land-line telephone numbers via random digit dialing was once widely considered a good way to survey the general population for many purposes. Since the mid-1990s, however, the practice of individuals having no land-line but only a cell phone has presented an increasing challenge for surveyors and pollsters.[30]

Political scientists have employed a wide range of sampling strategies when conducting surveys in the field, from simple designs to more sophisticated ones employing stratification, clustering, and multiple stages. Interval sampling (such as selecting every seventh individual or unit from an arbitrary starting point) or random-walk sampling (starting at a given point and selecting the individual or unit found after proceeding along a random route) can be effective strategies in cases where no complete population list is available. Sometimes, and for certain purposes, approaches like quota sampling, convenience sampling, anchor sampling, and snowball sampling have to suffice; political scientists and others have also developed methods for improving

---

[30] This is addressed at length in a task force report by the American Association for Public Opinion Research, "New considerations for survey researchers when planning and conducting RDD telephone surveys in the U.S. with respondents reached via cell phone numbers," 2010, accessed February 23, 2014 at www.aapor.org/Cell_Phone_Task_Force_Report.htm. See also Kempf and Remington (2007) and Link *et al.* (2007).

the samples that such non-probability techniques provide.[31] In all types of sampling, the scholar should attempt to discover and document as much as possible about the characteristics of the population as well as subgroups within it. This information can be indispensable at later stages when considering whether and how to weight the data. All sampling strategies entail tradeoffs that researchers must carefully assess, bearing in mind their intellectual aims, local conditions, and the kinds of audiences (e.g., particular journals and their reviewers, dissertation committee members) that will be assessing the choice of sampling technique. We offer some thoughts on these issues in Chapter 3.

Each field setting presents its own kinds of sampling challenges. In most East Asian countries, for example, all households are supposed to be registered in a set of records maintained by the government, which document who lives at what address and include basic demographic information. These records are an attractive resource for survey researchers, as they hold the promise of providing a complete list of the population from which to sample. Indeed, their use is ubiquitous: many pieces of survey research, in China for example, have been based on samples drawn from such household registry records. But these lists pose problems as well. For instance, the Chinese population is divided between those who possess urban household registrations (or *hukou*) and those with only rural documentation. Since the end of the Mao era in the 1970s, rural residents have migrated to cities in immense numbers. Though they sometimes obtain temporary residence permits, they are not included in the regular household records, thus creating a substantial gap between who actually lives in the city and who is present on paper. Even among permanent urban residents, these household lists are only an imperfect guide to who actually lives where, as it is common to move without updating one's paperwork, or to maintain more than one residence. Sampling from these lists can thus introduce systematic bias, leaving out rural migrants and other mobile members of the population.

This problem has given rise to some creative solutions. One approach is for researchers to dispense with the imperfect local system of official household rosters completely, instead making their own list of the residences in a neighborhood. An ambitious way of coping with the problem is the spatial sampling approach developed by Landry and Shen. In this approach,

---

[31] These ideas were raised during a manuscript review session held at Indiana University, December 2011. Alexandra Scacco's paper, "A snowball's chance in Nigeria: finding rioters using respondent-driven sampling," also discusses such techniques. Accessed October 5, 2012 at https://files.nyu.edu/als8/public/research.htm.

"township" is the secondary-level sampling unit, and "household" is the primary-level sampling unit. Once townships have been randomly selected, grid squares defined by lines of latitude and longitude are drawn within them and randomly sampled. Trained surveyors enumerate all the households within those squares, for further random sampling (Landry and Shen 2005; Landry 2010). The resource-intensive nature of this approach means that it is unlikely to supplant simpler methods. What is important to note, however, is that, even given its technical sophistication and potentially (if not practically) universal applicability, this approach was developed and implemented through deep knowledge about specific circumstances in China, from housing densities to the training of enumerators.

A few other innovative sampling methods that political scientists have devised in the absence of an adequate list of the target population bear mentioning. When Berry, Portney, and Thomson began their study of urban citizens' participation in local politics, they sought to assemble a sample of civic leaders and other city elites (among other data sources) in each of five US cities. They included in the sample all city councilors and heads of relevant municipal agencies. In order to ensure the sample also included individuals from the more ephemeral population of grassroots civic activists, they compiled lists of names that had been suggested in responses to a broad mailing to local leaders of many kinds, and by people interviewed in the course of their fieldwork (Berry et al. 1993, 310–311). In research on small-scale, informal-sector businesses and the state in Peru, Roever needed to build a sampling frame of street vendors and microentrepreneurs. Because no list of such people existed, she created one from scratch. Over the course of ten days, her team of fifteen enumerators methodically canvassed a numbered set of city blocks, as well as the rows of stalls inside commercial centers, for each of two business districts in Lima (Roever 2005, 201–206). Scott Straus visited fifteen prisons in which perpetrators of the 1994 Rwandan genocide were held, obtaining and sampling from lists of inmates meeting particular criteria – those who had confessed and been convicted – a striking example of a sampling design that could hardly be conceived without detailed knowledge of the Rwandan justice system gleaned from fieldwork (Straus 2006, 97–103).

Pre-testing in the field

With any form of survey research, carefully pre-testing the survey instrument in advance of formally fielding the survey is *de rigueur*. Inevitably, the initial draft of a questionnaire will need revising to improve question wording, answer categories, comprehensibility, and more. Often many rounds of pre-testing and revision will be necessary, and researchers' schedules must take this into account. For example, even after multiple pre-tests and extensive enumerator training, one scholar sampled three extra villages to implement several complete dry runs of the survey before finalizing the questionnaire.[32] Practicing administration with members of the target population or role-playing proxies from among acquaintances or fellow researchers provides a shakedown of all relevant steps and procedures; the PI can thus identify problems and adjust and revise accordingly, helping him to avoid design-compromising changes further down the line. With regard to the survey instrument itself, pre-testing will show whether, for instance, the human subjects protocol is understandable to the target population, the question-naire is too long or confusing, or additional transitional language is needed between questions. Focus groups or debriefing of respondents after the pre-test can also suggest adjustments to the protocol. Performing basic analysis on the data generated via the pre-test also provides an opportunity to catch important omissions, for instance, of control variables.

Particularly in the field context, the pre-testing phase of a project also provides an opportunity to bolster the training of research assistants or interviewers and, potentially, to strengthen their investment in the project. For instance, PIs can reinforce the importance of subjects' informed consent and the procedures the researcher has established for obtaining it through the pre-test process. That process also allows for discussing and explaining appropriate techniques for probing subjects for answers without leading them in any direction. Researchers can also review questionnaires as they come in to see what administration problems they may suggest (as several of our respondents suggested they should do throughout survey implementa-tion), even if immediate data entry is not possible.[33] If the data from the pilot questionnaires *can* be entered and examined immediately, it may be possible to identify and remedy any remaining problems with the training of enumerators before the survey is formally implemented. Pre-testing also helps research assistants to become better at administering the survey and more confident in their ability to do so, and thus more effective. Further, enumerators who are encouraged to suggest revisions to enhance compre-hension and flow may feel greater ownership of the questionnaire and the

---

[32] Interview, LM-10, September 18, 2012.
[33] Interviews, LM-9, August 30, 2012; LM-13, September 7, 2012.

project as a whole.[34] Finally, a real sense of team spirit can be generated as bonds form and excitement builds through the pre-test process – a camaraderie that can be cultivated through the rest of the project.

Engaging with sites and respondents

Writing in the early 1960s, Bonilla took on the question of how well the model of public opinion surveys prevalent in the United States applied to research in developing areas. He noted that the encounter between survey interviewer and respondent, conventional and straightforward though it may seem, in fact depends on shared assumptions and norms of communication that can be very context-dependent:

A total stranger appears, usually unannounced, and demands admission to the home. He proceeds to extract information about the family relationships of all who occupy the dwelling and then seeks to isolate one specific individual for more extended interrogation. He insists that the ensuing dialogue adhere to a rigid and unfamiliar pattern, frequently giving exact instructions as to the form in which he wants replies and sternly discouraging departures from his prescriptions. Though the subject matter and the phrasing of questions may seem to the respondent argumentative, embarrassing, gratuitously aggressive, or even dangerous, the uninvited visitor proceeds impassively, taking little note of the interviewee's distress or exasperation, all the while refusing to reciprocate by revealing his own sentiments regarding the matters under discussion. (Bonilla 1964, 140)

While modern polling is anything but a novelty in some of the places Bonilla discussed (such as Rio de Janeiro), in many contexts survey interviews with strangers remain a far-fetched or hazardous idea. In developing their strategy to encourage participation in a survey, researchers should carefully consider how respondents might experience their interaction with an enumerator, and how the encounter can be made as smooth and comfortable as possible for them. Taking such steps is the ethical thing to do, and may ultimately allow the survey to generate better data. Developing an effective strategy is far easier, we contend, the better a scholar understands the context in which she is operating.

There are many reasons why members of the target population may be reluctant to agree to take a survey – or to answer particular survey questions. They may simply not wish to spend their time talking to an interviewer or

---

[34] Interview, LM-10, September 18, 2012.

filling out a questionnaire, or may be impatient from too many telephone marketing calls. In some places, fraudsters pose as pollsters, and criminals have been known to use fake surveys to identify vulnerable homes to rob (a reason to exercise restraint, in some contexts, in asking for identifying information). In others, the government or previous colonial rulers may have a history of sending agents to register land or to document revenue and assets for taxation purposes. Overall, the locality may be politically or culturally inhospitable to research. Finally, as the paragraph from Bonilla indicates, surveys from political scientists may include questions on topics that respondents are uncomfortable talking about. They may solicit opinions, or information about affiliations or actions, that respondents would not normally share with strangers, and whose revelation could create awkwardness or conflict with family members, neighbors, or co-workers, or get them into serious trouble.[35]

The problem of how to encourage respondents to answer questions on sensitive topics is one that has generated a substantial methodological literature. Yet any strategy adopted will need to be adapted to the field setting. For instance, a textbook suggests that "embedding one sensitive question (for example, an item on shoplifting) among other more sensitive items (an item on armed robbery) may help make the sensitive item of interest seem less threatening by comparison."[36] About this, one interviewee working in a tense political environment overseas remarked: "Maybe this works in the U.S., but I thought this was terrible advice in my context."[37] Instead, this researcher designed a separate questionnaire for sensitive questions that respondents filled out while the enumerator stood some distance away, and placed in an envelope for added privacy. In another example, Bleck had respondents take a survey on an iPad, allowing the respondent alone to hear sensitive questions. Further, some response codes obscured respondents' actual response (e.g., "fish" stood for "protested often"), and in other instances respondents simply pressed a picture on the iPad to respond rather than answering audibly.

---

[35] The list of topics in political science that people taking surveys might find sensitive is long. To name just a few, respondents might be hesitant to discuss corruption, being offered money in exchange for their votes, participation in protests or opposition activities, or even their true opinions about the ruling party. Work concerning sensitive topics in surveys by political scientists and others includes Silver, Anderson, and Abramson (1986), Berinsky (1999), Tourangeau and Yan (2007), and Ocantos, de Jonge, and Nickerson (2013).

[36] This is found in multiple editions of Groves et al., *Survey methodology* (e.g., 2009, 247–248).

[37] This interviewee (BR-14, October 24, 2013) felt that adding material that was even more sensitive to the survey question would have backfired, thoroughly alienating respondents.

In settings where access to the population under study and sensitivity of research questions pose major problems, some survey researchers employ a strategy of patiently building personal trust and understanding with respondents, akin to that discussed in the chapters on interviewing and site-intensive methods. Jamal's research on associations in Palestine provides an example (2007). This project involved a national survey (carried out by a survey organization), in-depth interviews, and a survey of 425 association members. In a co-authored article, Jamal discussed this latter component of the project, conveying the painstaking approach that she took and the conditions that called for it:

Face-to face interviews were necessary to ensure the participation of respondents. Sometimes, I would have to meet several times with respondents before they agreed to participate. I would often have coffee or tea with them beforehand. I invested a lot of time in casual conversations and in getting to know the potential respondents before we conducted the survey. I discussed my project in detail and explained how their participation was vital to the success of the project. (Tessler and Jamal 2006, 436)

General political tensions in Palestine, skepticism about her credentials and affiliation, and subjects' unfamiliarity with this kind of social science research all necessitated special trust-building efforts:

Further, because most of the population had very little experience in responding to surveys, they wanted to think through their responses very carefully. They often asked for follow-up explanations – which took more time. Furthermore, they sometimes would ask me to answer the question first; they wanted to hear my opinion on certain matters. Most respondents, however, thanked me for their participation in the survey, and a few even felt the survey provided them with the necessary mechanism to vent their complaints. Many felt liberated and important that their opinions mattered. A few respondents, however, were disappointed when I explained that each respondent's observation would "only" be one among hundreds. They felt that their voices were again becoming diluted. Further, due to overall levels of fear, some people became unnecessarily worried when they were randomly selected to participate. Were they under suspicion? (Tessler and Jamal 2006, 436)

In all, she writes, she spent 3 months working 12 hours or more per day to carry out the inquiry. Given the circumstances, it seems fair to conclude that the outcome of the survey project, in terms of response rates and data quality, would have been very different without Jamal's deep engagement with respondents and with the research site more generally – if it were possible to carry out the project at all.

Working in rural China, a different kind of environment but one that also features many obstacles to political inquiry, Tsai strikes a related note in emphasizing the "socially embedded" nature of the survey research endeavor. The investigator depends on ties with local collaborators, government authorities, interviewers, and respondents alike, all of whom may be vulnerable to trouble created by the project itself. Thus, the researcher needs "to invest in building and shaping these social relationships so that they generate trust and mutual obligations." In Tsai's project, this meant giving interviewers time to engage in extensive conversation with officials and others in the villages that fell within the sample, in order to obtain high-quality information and cross-check discrepancies. She contrasts this with traditional approaches to survey research, which have aimed at standardizing and depersonalizing the survey process in an effort to minimize bias and error (Tsai 2010, 255, 258–260).

A researcher working in a different part of the world became dissatisfied with the results of his efforts to train research assistants to his desired levels of competence and responsibility. So he acted as his own enumerator, personally visiting sixty villages and staying half a day or overnight in each. The group discussions he held in these communities produced in-depth, qualitative data and survey data simultaneously. He explains: "I would move back and forth between asking the question on the survey and a more general discussion ... My goal was for them to get lost in the discussion while I was collecting my data." This approach allowed the scholar to ask key questions in a standardized fashion to each group while maintaining an open conversational style that allowed him to probe when necessary: "I would track how people were responding. If I would start to sense someone giving me artificial answers, then I would joke and be friendly and sort of point out that I knew stuff."[38]

These approaches illustrate highly intensive ways of laying groundwork for large-n surveys. In each example, the goal was for scholars to establish their bona fides and build relationships with the population to be sampled in hopes of maximizing the likelihood of obtaining valid data. Other methods include affiliating with local authorities or institutions,[39] or otherwise obtaining the blessing of trusted insiders who can vouch for the researcher. Forming partnerships with local organizations can also encourage respondents to accept a survey and devote time to it. One investigator studying a grassroots

[38] Interview, LM-11, August 31, 2012.
[39] Interviews, LM-5, August 27, 2012; LM-13, September 7, 2012; LM-10, September 18, 2012.

organization distributed survey questionnaires to members of the group through a network of contacts who also were members, and obtained response rates that were "off the charts" compared to similar survey efforts in which requests to participate came directly from the investigator.[40] A researcher working in a conflict setting partnered with an NGO that helped to legitimate her survey. The group, which was compensated for its services, furnished office space, provided one of its staff members as a project manager, and published a newspaper article to help recruit local enumerators. The researcher and the project manager then trained and supervised the enumerators as they carried out sampling and interviews over the course of a month. This arrangement allowed the researcher to access the relevant population while retaining close operational control over the survey process.[41]

These examples all point to the possibility of encouraging survey respondents to share information through a sense of connection with (or an impression of legitimacy of) the researchers, or a desire to help further the project's goals. Yet material incentives sometimes play a role as well. Political scientists vary widely in terms of how much and what type of compensation they offer to respondents, as discussed in more detail in Chapter 4. Respondents might receive cash payments, be enrolled in a lottery, be offered small gifts such as T-shirts – or may be provided no material compensation. Factors such as the length of the questionnaire, the degree of burden it imposes, and local norms shape decisions about what, if anything, should be given to respondents in return for their time and participation.

Conclusion

This chapter has considered some of the opportunities and challenges presented by administering surveys in the field. Whether in the United States or abroad, each context presents its own distinctive possibilities and problems, many of which are not covered in textbooks and may be difficult or impossible to anticipate prior to immersion in the local setting. Political scientists, like researchers in other disciplines, have developed a wide range of strategies to capitalize on these opportunities and address these problems. They have devised methods of overcoming complications and threats to data quality posed by sampling difficulties, sensitive subject matter, inhospitable political climates, wary respondents, and more. The adaptation and perseverance that

[40] Interview, BR-17, November 14, 2013.   [41] Interview, BR-14, October 24, 2013.

doing so requires serve as a vivid manifestation of flexible discipline, a principle underlying good field research. Carrying out a survey in the field means coming up with creative ways to deal with countless details while exercising discipline in various forms – so that researchers and their teams stay on task, and so that the survey obtains valid information and will stand up to methodological critique. Doing so allows researchers to accomplish multiple analytic tasks through their survey: survey research can make multiple contributions to theory.

As noted, sometimes survey research is viewed as not fitting into a classic model of fieldwork. But as this chapter makes clear, survey work should be seen as closely related to, and often pursued in tandem with, other forms of field inquiry. Like other techniques, survey research benefits from close engagement with the local context. Indeed, such engagement is often necessary to design a survey that is feasible and meaningful in a given setting, and to encourage the forthcoming participation of those who populate the setting. Survey research is rarely the sole method of inquiry in a field research project. Rather, it is typical for political scientists pursuing the kinds of data that surveys provide to triangulate, gathering data using other techniques as well (e.g., archival research, interviews, and site-intensive work). Indeed, quantitative data gathering can be integrated with, can be informed by, and can inform a project's qualitative dimensions in many ways. This iterative knowledge-generation, we believe, is one of the hallmarks of field research, and one of the qualities that make it such a powerful form of empirical inquiry.

Yet the point is not just that surveys and other modes of research enrich one another. We also wish to emphasize that, on the ground, in action, the seemingly intuitive distinction between surveys (impersonal, quantitative, involving brief interactions that produce "thin" data) and other field techniques (high-touch, qualitative, involving longer periods of contact that produce "thick" data) often breaks down, partially or entirely. Survey work often requires forms of immersion in field sites. Encouraging respondents to give candid, illuminating answers to certain kinds of questions may require building understanding, identification, and trust in various forms. The information produced through surveys may, when appropriate, be rich and detailed, even if the goal is later to code that information in structured, quantitative forms.

More than any of the other data-collection techniques considered so far (but like field experiments, which are addressed in the next chapter), survey work often necessitates collaboration. This brings out new aspects of the PI's "project manager" role, as discussed in Chapter 4. As the examples above have shown, whether the PI/PM is working with a single assistant, training whole teams of enumerators, or contracting out some of the work to a survey organization, she generally needs to remain as present, engaged, and vigilant as possible. Bringing other people and groups into the project generally means not just training but also motivating collaborators to approach the survey process with appropriate care and with commitment to treating respondents ethically and respectfully.

This chapter has emphasized the ways in which researchers adapt their work to the particularities of a field site. Yet by illustrating such adaptation, we in no way wish to suggest that rigorously preparing for survey research is not critical. Surveys are in no sense a form of research in which "flexibility" should overshadow "discipline" – quite the contrary. What scholars are adapting, we insist, should be a project designed according to general principles of survey research. Projects designed with those principles in mind have firm foundations – and will produce results that make sense to, and are persuasive for, scholarly audiences. Even as a researcher grapples with the challenges of the field, sometimes what she needs most comes from back home. As one experienced investigator said, reflecting on his dissertation research: "The main thing I wish I had going into it was I wish I had done more homework in the academic literature side of things. For example, I wish I'd read a lot more about panel studies, the nuts and bolts about questionnaire design, question wording. I wish I'd been more familiar with debates on partisanship and key concepts. I came back later, and said 'I have decent data but I wish I'd measured it *that* way.' ... People need to read, read, read stuff that's there so they don't have that moment when they kick themselves."[42]

---

[42] Interview, BR-3, August 6, 2012.

9 Experiments in the field

Even as recently as the late 1990s, experiments occupied a small and relatively marginalized niche in political science research. Despite early precursors such as Harold Gosnell's (1926) study of voter turnout in the 1920s and Samuel J. Eldersveld's (1956) study of propaganda and voting behavior in the 1950s, experimental research was traditionally considered to be impractical, if not impossible.[1]

Today, by contrast, experimental methods are both more prevalent and more widely respected than in the past. Druckman *et al.* (2006) found that more articles based on experimental data are being published in top-tier journals, and that they are being cited significantly more frequently than comparison groups of articles. Political scientists have recently published a number of noteworthy books and journal articles on the methodology of experimental research, as discussed below. In addition, more and more graduate programs have added seminars on experimental methodology, and intensive summer training courses have incorporated sessions on the topic.[2] Finally, the creation in 2010 of an APSA Organized Section on Experimental Research, and its introduction of the *Journal of Experimental Political Science* in 2013, provide further evidence that experimental

---

[1] Lawrence Lowell, in his APSA presidential address (1910), advised scholars in the nascent discipline of political science to eschew the model of the natural sciences contending that: "We are limited by the impossibility of experiment. Politics is an observational, not an experimental science." Over sixty years later, Lijphart (1971) described the experimental method as "nearly ideal" but rare due to the "practical and ethical impediments." One overview of the history of experiments in political science emphasizes the ongoing efforts of generations of researchers, holding that this history is "more substantial than most recognize" (Morton and Williams 2010, 3–27, at 9).

[2] For example, the ICPSR includes a week-long session on designing and conducting field experiments. The Empirical Implications of Theoretical Models (EITM) workshop at Washington University has included experimental methods. And the IQMR has sessions dedicated to natural and field experiments. Experiments in Governance and Politics Network (EGAP), a group focusing on experimental work in the political economy of development, holds meetings and maintains a web site (http://egap.org).

methods, and empirical and methodological research based on them, are becoming broadly institutionalized in the discipline.[3]

Findings from the FRPS survey reflect both the relative paucity of field experiments overall since the 1960s, and their recent upswing in usage.[4] Experiments were employed in only 2.8 percent of all reported projects begun from 1955 through 1999. By comparison, focus groups, another relatively uncommon data-collection technique, had more than three times this prevalence in the same time period; surveys were more than eleven times as popular. But experiments have surged. Among projects that our survey respondents began between 2008 and 2011 (the last year covered by the survey), 10.5 percent included experiments. While still only one-third as prevalent as ethnography and participant observation, for instance, experimental research is on the rise. Experiments are about equally common in projects within the United States and those involving international locations, and are used by political scientists of various subfields, including international relations and public administration.

Several developments have likely driven the recent increase in prominence of experiments in political science. The experimental method's ability to provide strong evidence of, and accurately estimate, causal effects, as discussed below, is central to its appeal. Along lines discussed in Chapter 2, influences from other disciplines have also played an important role in encouraging the diffusion of the technique. Laboratory experiments studying political behavior and cognition have been broadly influenced by work in social psychology and behavioral economics. Field experiments by political scientists, meanwhile, received a shot in the arm from the work of developmental economists and institutions associated with them, such as Innovations for Poverty Action (founded 2002) and the Abdul Lateef Jameel Poverty Action Lab at MIT (founded 2003).[5] Indeed, discussions of economists' experimental work have even appeared in magazines and books intended for mass audiences outside of academia.[6] Within political science, experiments have been championed by vocal figures at highly respected

---

[3] The APSA section on Experimental Research counted 409 members in September 2012. As a reference point, the largest APSA section included 1,351 members (Comparative Politics) and the smallest had 183 members (Canadian Politics) in the same time period.

[4] These figures capture projects in which either the use of "field experiments" or the use of "laboratory experiments" was reported, with the latter indicating what we refer to below as "laboratory experiments in the field."

[5] www.poverty-action.org/about/story, accessed December 5, 2013.

[6] See the Parker feature on Esther Duflo and the Poverty Lab (2010) as well as Banerjee and Duflo's book (2011).

institutions. The application of experimentally tested findings in practical politics, for instance in Barack Obama's successful presidential campaigns and through organizations such as The Analyst Institute, have likewise raised their profile.[7] Finally, the growth in experimental research is also driven by a demand for rigorous evaluation of policy interventions by donors, foundations, governments, and non-governmental organizations (Humphreys and Weinstein 2009). All of these theoretical, methodological, and policy innovations have been facilitated by advances in technology, such as the development of computer-assisted telephone interviewing and related software programs (Druckman *et al.* 2006; Sniderman 2011).[8]

As with other research traditions and data-collection techniques considered in this book, the social science literature on field experiments, and on experiments more generally, contains a number of overviews of this technique. Some focus on the technical dimensions of experiments and on analyzing experimental data. We do not here address the fundamentals of experimental design and analysis of experimental data, though we refer readers interested in these topics to appropriate sources.[9]

Instead, and as in the other chapters of this book that focus on data-collection techniques, our main goal is to *contextualize* experimental research in the field. We examine the effect field circumstances have on the deployment of experiments, explore the challenges of using experimental techniques in the field, and offer strategies for addressing them. Throughout, we demonstrate that engagement with context (a core principle of good field research) is at least as important in this research tradition as in others: field experiments are – and must be – grounded in detailed knowledge of the setting and the subject population. Indeed, field experimenters often engage in considerable periods of open-ended study as they conceive and

---

[7] See, for instance, Benedict Carey, "Academic 'dream team' helped Obama's effort," *New York Times*, November 12, 2012, and Issenberg (2012). The Analyst Institute is "a clearinghouse for evidence-based best practices in progressive voter contact," which "assists organizations in building testing into their voter contact efforts." From https://analystinstitute.org/, accessed December 5, 2013.

[8] In addition to the published literature, this paragraph draws on two interviews: BR-17, November 14, 2013 and BR-18, November 18, 2013.

[9] On the specific topic of field experiments, Gerber and Green's text (2012) provides a particularly valuable resource, explaining in detail the process of estimating causal effects while coping with technical complexities in a variety of scenarios. Other important book-length resources on experiments in general are Morton and Williams (2010), Mutz (2011), and Druckman *et al.* (2011a). Gerring (2012, Chapters 9 and 10) provides one explanation of the logic of randomized designs in causal inference. Books with a weaker connection to political science per se that address experimental methods include Cox (1958), Shadish, Cook, and Campbell (2001), and Maxwell and Delaney (2004).

plan their work, and the core ideas behind good experiments often emerge from extended contact with particular locales.

We begin by identifying the key rationales for experimental research, discussing how it differs from observational research, and describing various types of experimental methods. Next, we examine the analytic tasks that can be accomplished by carrying out experiments in the field. In contrast to the chapters focused on observational data-gathering techniques (Chapters 5 through 8), we do not offer an extended discussion of how experiments contribute to theory building by helping scholars achieve multiple analytic goals (e.g., formulating research questions, selecting cases, conceptualizing and measuring key variables, generating potential explanations, and illuminating causal processes and mechanisms). The reason is that experimental methods are generally understood to have a specialized strength and relatively specific application: determining the effect on a given outcome of a particular causal treatment (i.e., determining the causal relationship between a particular "X" and a particular "Y," or identifying "effects of causes").[10] Put in terms of the analytic tasks we discuss in other chapters, we might say experiments are generally and primarily aimed at hypothesis testing. Further, and as we discuss in more detail below, experiments are often conducted at a relatively advanced stage in a given research project. Given this timing – and their elaborate nature and the potentially high cost of carrying them out – scholars generally have laid much of the analytic groundwork for their projects when they reach the point of executing an experiment. We limit our discussion of experiments' analytic contributions, then, to addressing their ability to illuminate specific causal relationships.

As one might expect, given this analytic specialization, experiments are typically combined with the use of other data-collection techniques and analytic methods, and often form one facet of broader research programs that extend through multiple studies. The way in which political scientists draw on interviews, surveys, and ethnography or participant observation – prior to, during, or after carrying out an experiment in the context of any particular study – are the topics of the chapter's subsequent section. Combining multiple methods helps scholars to capitalize on the field context to accomplish a broader range of analytic tasks, *and* helps to mitigate the risk

---

[10] Correspondingly, experiments are less apt for identifying the "causes of effects." As one experimentalist put it, "If you're trying to explain all the variance in a behavior, an experiment is not suitable for that. For example, why do people turn out to vote? There are so many different reasons. That's not best addressed by an experiment. Maybe just a survey." Interview, BR-15, October 25, 2013. Gerring discusses the distinction between effects-of-causes and causes-of-effects analyses (2012, 333–335).

that the experiment will go awry or simply produce uninteresting results. In short, triangulation with other methods – another core principle of good field research – figures prominently in the process of field experimental research.

The final four substantive sections of the chapter address the practical processes of conceiving, developing, and carrying out experiments in the field. While reading published articles based on experimental studies allows one to reverse-engineer, to an extent, the steps the researcher took, such work almost inevitably omits much information about the context and backdrop for the experiment, and many practical details. A handful of reflective and prescriptive essays by practitioners make these steps more explicit and distill general lessons for others to follow.[11] By drawing on this material, and on interviews with other practitioners about their experiences, we provide practical suggestions on how to undertake this form of work efficiently and appropriately. We first consider the benefits of partnering with local organizations such as NGOs or research institutions in the conduct of a field experiment, emphasizing how developing and managing such collaborations require knowledge of the research setting and the strengths and weakness of specific organizations. We then discuss the development, randomization, and application of treatments, as well as dealing with subjects.

Precisely because the experimenter applies a treatment to certain units or subjects, seeking to evaluate the change that is brought about as a result, this form of research raises ethical questions that are absent or less prominent in other modes of research. While most forms of inquiry affect human subjects in some way, field experiments contain one or more elements that call for special ethical scrutiny. These include the deliberate introduction of change in the form of a treatment, the integration of real-world political events and phenomena into the experiment,[12] and (often) the application of treatments on a large scale. Issues are thus raised about obtaining informed consent from those involved in the experiment; the possibility of influencing or

---

[11] Sources of this kind are cited throughout the chapter, and we offer just a few examples here: Gueron (2002), Duflo, Glennerster, and Kremer (2006), Humphreys and Weinstein (2009), Paluck (2009), Humphreys (2011), as well as some of the extended examples in Gerber and Green (2012).

[12] For example, a field experiment conducted by Leonard Wantchekon (2003) was embedded in the context of the 2001 presidential election in Benin. The experiment, conducted in collaboration with campaign managers from major parties, involved exposing residents of certain villages to political appeals based on clientelism, and others to appeals based on policy programs. Wantchekon chose only villages in "safe districts" where certain candidates had such a stronghold that they were very likely to win and thus argued that the experiment could not have changed the result of the election (De La O and Wantchekon 2011).

disturbing important political processes; deceiving participants; and exposing participants to tangible or intangible harms or depriving them of benefits. These matters – all relating to the principle of ethical commitment – are addressed throughout the chapter.

Experimental methods: rationales and types

The theoretical rationale for experimental methods in the social sciences grows out of the goal of understanding causal relationships. In observational studies – those that involve observing or measuring social phenomena as they are found – causal inference can be flawed or questionable, and the direction of causality left uncertain. It can also be difficult to rule out the possibility that unmeasured confounding factors, including selection effects, might bias the estimates of coefficients on explanatory variables.

Experiments, by contrast, hold the promise of offering rigorous tests of specific causal effects. Their advocates note that the challenges to causal inference that haunt observational studies are essentially removed through the design of experimental research, which proceeds as follows. Hypotheses are developed *ex ante*. Variation in the hypothesized causal factor(s) is not left up to "nature," but rather is determined by the researchers themselves, and instantiated in the experiment in the form of different levels or types of treatment. Researchers assign subjects to treatment group(s) and a control group *at random*. A specific manipulation or treatment is applied to the former, and the groups are later compared with respect to outcomes of interest. The randomization makes it possible to assume that the two or more groups are effectively identical in all theoretically relevant aspects except for the applied treatment (and this assumption can be checked by comparing observable measures across the groups). Thus, any statistically significant differences in outcomes are presumed to be attributable to the treatment. Given the above, some consider experiments to be the "gold standard" of empirical work, although others take exception to this characterization.[13]

Experimental field research differs from other types of field study in fundamental ways. Most forms of research considered in this book aim to understand the political world through observational means. Causal

---

[13] See the debate between outspoken advocates such as Duflo *et al.* (2006) and critics such as Deaton (2009). This controversial debate and the notion of a "gold standard" were referred to in the interviews we conducted in connection with this book as well.

processes are studied – perhaps as they are playing out, perhaps after the fact – but they are not created by the investigator herself. Researchers who conduct interviews or surveys do not speak of applying a treatment to those whom they study. Indeed, researchers often strive *not* to affect, manipulate, or disturb their research subjects (as in much site-intensive work) or else are unable to do so (as in archival studies). While interviewers commonly attempt to stimulate or provoke a response through the questions they ask, their goal is generally not to assess the causal effect of the questions themselves. Rather, interviewers hope that the way in which study participants answer the questions they pose will help them to understand and identify the causes of the phenomenon of interest.

The nature of assignment to experimental conditions also differentiates true experiments from what are called natural experiments, or quasi-experiments. In natural experiments, the researcher does not assign the treatment himself, but rather relies on pre-existing processes that have created random or "as-if random" assignment. An example of a natural experiment is Chattopadhyay and Duflo's (2004) study of the effects of the Indian government's quota system for women's political participation on the provision of public goods. The authors exploited the introduction of a 1992 constitutional amendment stipulating that one-third of village council chief positions be reserved for women; in at least two states, villages were chosen to have such a reservation through random assignment. They found that expanding female political representation made access to public goods more equal. In research based on natural experiments, then, the researcher comes upon random or near-random processes, generally after the fact, rather than creating them herself. We thus limit our treatment of natural experiments to a discussion of how field research can help scholars to discover natural experiments.

Gerber and Green suggest that experiments can be thought of as varying in their degree of "fieldness" along four dimensions: contexts, participants, treatments, and outcome measures (2012, 11). On each of these dimensions, a given experiment could be more artificial and removed from populations of interest, or closer to the actual experiences of people in the real world. At one end of the spectrum, a purely non-field experiment exploring voters' responses to political advertisements might take place in a university computer lab, with college students viewing one of two statements from a hypothetical candidate on a computer screen and subsequently registering a response to a question or prompt via a mouse click. In fact, a prominent strain of experimental work in political science (one often used in political psychology)[14] takes place in laboratory settings. In such studies, the researchers have maximal if not complete control over all aspects of the experimental context. They determine whom to recruit as subjects; subjects participate in the experiment in a location chosen by the researchers; the investigators dictate what the subjects see, hear, and experience, including the experimental treatment; they control or prevent interactions with other participants; and they can generally ensure that relatively few subjects will leave in the middle of the experiment rather than completing it. In the middle of the spectrum might be laboratory-in-the-field experiments, discussed below. And at the other end of the spectrum, a purely field-based study might be set in an actual city council election, with real voters receiving in their home mailboxes one of two versions of a campaign message from a real candidate; here the outcome of interest might be subjects' actual vote choice on election day.

Field experiments can be carried out in myriad types of contexts, leading us to consider the multiple roles and meanings of the field. Indeed, conducting an experiment in the field means incorporating into the study some of the complexity, particularity, and richness that characterize actual political settings. To extend the election example, the field study would entail engaging with the politics of an actual city, perhaps buffeted by a budget crisis or a police-brutality scandal in the course of the campaign; it would mean integrating the dynamics of an election cycle, over the course of which citizens' perceptions fluctuate in response to debates, media coverage, and other factors. Field experiments often mean road-testing a particular intervention that is intended by policymakers to be beneficial in some way, as in a program to give voters more information about candidates or to bring women into leadership positions that have historically been closed to them. Such interventions are subjected to real-world stresses and challenges, and their effectiveness rigorously evaluated. To the extent that experimentalists opt for real-world settings, their work suggests that it is not sufficient to study the topics of interest in clinical, laboratory conditions and in ways that are removed from the actual setting of politics.

Field experimentalists inherently aim for a degree of naturalism, in part as an effort to increase the external validity of their study: the ability to generalize the results.[15] In some experiments, participants may not even

---

[14] For instance, see Redlawsk, Civettini, and Emmerson (2010).

[15] Gerber notes that field experiments "aim to reproduce the environment in which the phenomenon of interest naturally occurs and thereby enhance the external validity of the experiment" (2011, 116).

be aware that they are taking part in a study, and thus they may behave as if unobserved, eliminating forms of bias that stem from subjects' awareness that they are under scrutiny. Rarely is this possible when scholars deploy the other data-collection techniques involving human subjects that are discussed in this book, unless researchers engage in some degree of deception. For instance, interviewees are generally fully cognisant that their answers to the questions they are asked are being evaluated and analyzed by their interlocutor. Even in participant observation – a technique scholars may adopt, at least in part, in hopes of blending in to the field context to some extent – researchers' presence can subtly but consistently remind the people with whom they are interacting that they are being studied.

But naturalism also has potential costs, and can increase the number of challenges experimentalists face in conducting their study. Utilizing real-world settings rather than a laboratory, studying actual populations of interest rather than proxies, and extending the study beyond a single sitting or interaction tends to mean sacrificing a degree of control over the experimental milieu and accepting increased complexity and risks to the study's integrity.[16] Humphreys and Weinstein note that, in field as opposed to laboratory experiments, "Features such as the characteristics of subjects, the information available to them, and the precise manner and context in which the treatment is applied are more likely to take on values given by 'nature' rather than being set at the discretion of the investigator" (2009, 369). Participants who are supposed to remain independent may interact with one another instead. Units that are assigned to receive a treatment may end up not receiving it. And subjects may drop out in the middle of an experiment.

As suggested above, a "laboratory-in-the-field" study is a kind of compromise between the pure-laboratory and pure-field extremes. Such studies entail laboratory-like arrangements that are brought to a researcher's field site(s) in order to examine particular populations or naturally occurring situations (Morton and Williams 2010, 296). Such a study involves enhanced verisimilitude on one or more of Gerber and Green's (2012) four "dimensions of fieldness" (contexts, participants, treatments, and outcome measures), but not all of them. For example, some researchers might conduct similar experiments in university classrooms in two or three different

---

[16] For Morton and Williams (2010, 46), in field experiments, "a researcher's intervention takes place in subjects' natural environments and the researcher has only limited control beyond the intervention conducted."

countries, recruiting participants locally in each setting. Even if no other aspect of the experiment has a "field" quality to it, such a project would be substantially different from one conducted in a laboratory at a scholar's home institution, perhaps relying for subjects on the typical American "college sophomore."[17] An example of such a laboratory-in-the-field experiment is found in the work on cooperation between co-ethnics in laboratories in Kampala, Uganda (Habyarimana *et al.* 2007, 2009). The objective of these studies was to disentangle various potential causal mechanisms for co-ethnic cooperation. Other lab-in-the-field studies test theories developed in laboratory environments in the United States in additional contexts. This was the primary objective for experimental work conducted on the dynamics of individual decision-making regarding common-pool resources with local populations in forty-one countries (Ahn, Ostrom, and Walker 2010).

In short, experiments come in various forms, each with characteristic strengths and weaknesses, different levels of control, and diverse sorts of interaction with "the field." This variation notwithstanding, much experimental research has the same goal: rigorously assessing a single causal relationship or a small number of causal effects. The chapter's next section examines this singular analytic focus.

Field experiments' analytic contributions

Previous chapters addressing other data-collection techniques such as interviewing or site-intensive methods have highlighted their versatility, demonstrating how they can be employed throughout the research cycle to aid in accomplishing multiple analytic tasks, including sharpening questions, refining concepts and measures, generating hypotheses, and adjudicating among competing hypotheses. Experiments, by contrast, are typically seen as having a more specific application: assessing a particular cause-and-effect linkage. As such, they are generally carried out after scholars have already refined their questions, and potential explanatory hypotheses. Of the various data-collection techniques we consider, field experiments may be the most narrowly focused, yielding a very specific type of information about politics in

---

[17] While many experimentalists use student subjects in their work (Kam, Wilking, and Zechmeister 2007), scholars debate whether this is a significant problem for external validity. While Sears (1986) raised doubts about the validity of conclusions based on student participants, Druckman and Kam (2011) argue that student subjects do not "intrinsically" undermine a study's external validity.

the field context. For experimentalists, this is balanced by the strength of the evidence that experiments provide for understanding causal relationships.

The causal linkage of interest in a particular experiment may be considered important for several reasons. It may play an important role in a body of theory. It may have practical or policy-related implications, as when researchers determine whether distributing mosquito netting prevents the transmission of malaria, or whether electronic voting machines reduce spoiled ballots. Often the issues at hand are both practical and theoretical, as in research on citizens' decisions whether or not to vote. As Roth (1995) puts it, experiments have three broad types of objectives: "searching for facts," "speaking to theorists," and "whispering in the ears of princes" (that is, aiming to identify policy implications).

Field experiments in political science vary tremendously with regard to topics studied and treatments applied. Voting behavior and voter turnout have been prominent areas for field experiments. In such studies, voters are typically given a treatment in their homes by being contacted by canvassers, phone callers, or mailings, producing findings that have emphasized the role of contact and social pressure in political behavior (Gerber and Green 2000; Michelson 2003; Gerber, Green, and Larimer 2008; Nickerson 2008; García Bedolla and Michelson 2012). Yet experiments examine many other topics, and significant innovation has occurred with regard to approaches to treatments. In research on post-genocide Rwanda, for example, Paluck and Green (2009) studied the question of whether it is possible to change cultural norms of deference to authority. They found that residents of seven communities who listened to a radio program designed to promote independent thinking tended to internalize that message and were more willing to express dissent than were members of a control group.

Advocates maintain that many phenomena that have been studied observationally are amenable to randomized controlled trials. Many field experiments deal with things that individuals do – in other words, micro-level political behavior. Yet with the cooperation of governments, many realms of public policy and larger-scale dynamics and trends – economic growth in small towns, or corruption among government contractors, for example – can potentially be examined through randomized studies. Even so, there are limits to the kinds of questions that can be addressed using experimental techniques. Experiments require a treatment that can be assigned. However, fundamental aspects of individual identity, such as (perhaps) a person's being a New Yorker as opposed to a Minnesotan, or of political structures, such as a country's having a parliamentary or a presidential system of government, can be controlled for but cannot realistically be randomized.[18] There is also the requirement that units in the treatment and control groups remain independent from one another during the study – a criterion that can be difficult to sustain in many kinds of interconnected, communicative populations. Apart from these basic realities, many ethical as well as practical considerations, as discussed below, constrain the options available to scholars who contemplate an experiment.

Given the excitement surrounding field experiments and their rise in popularity, graduate students often clamor to do one. Experimentalists highlight the importance of carefully evaluating the challenges involved before launching such a project, however. For example, in an interview, one scholar cautioned graduate students and junior faculty that field experiments are "inherently very risky" because "a lot of them fall apart."[19] Much of the advice in Chapter 8 concerning the time costs and logistical challenges of surveys also applies to experiments. One interviewee was surprised by the extensive managerial work entailed and concluded that it was "not my strong suit."[20] Thinking through the details of the multiple steps involved in conceptualizing, designing, preparing, and carrying out an experiment, and considering the successes and failures that other researchers have encountered in the field, helps to build a realistic understanding of what it takes to employ this technique effectively.

In sum, experiments are versatile, but subject to limitations, with regard to the topics they can be used to study. Their analytic contributions tend to be comparatively focused. Accordingly, the design of field experiments requires a great deal of analytic precision, and thus they are often most fruitfully employed after critical research design choices have been made. Moreover, carrying out field experiments can be costly, challenging, and risky. For these reasons and several others outlined in the next section, experiments are often combined with other analytic techniques and methods in order to accomplish the objectives of a given research project or agenda.

---

[18] As Humphreys and Weinstein put it: "Many political processes and attributes are likely to remain (and likely ought to remain) unavailable for experimental manipulation: whether governments are authoritarian or democratic, whether regions secede, whether governments launch brutal counterinsurgency campaigns, whether a given individual adopts a given set of preferences, etc." (2009, 374).

[19] Interview, LM-13, September 7, 2012.

[20] "One of the things I didn't quite realize before grad school is that people really vary in their talents that are required for field research. I discovered I'm not that great at the management side. I was more on the data side." Interview, BR-16, October 31, 2013.

Combining experiments with other methods

Field experiments often emerge out of, and form part of, larger research programs involving the use of other data-collection techniques and analytic methods, both before and after an experiment has been conducted. Indeed, the fact that political scientists often employ other kinds of methods in concert with experiments is clearly reflected in the FRPS survey data. Of the 66 field research projects reported in the FRPS survey that employed experiments, only 3 involved no other data-collection techniques. Of projects including experiments, 73 percent also involved the use of surveys; 77 percent involved interviews; and 48 percent involved ethnography or participant observation. Indeed, projects employing experiments also used, on average, nearly 6 non-experimental data-gathering techniques. Almost three-quarters included either qualitative or interpretive approaches to analysis.

In short, while the survey data do not allow us to distinguish the particular role played by experiments versus those played by other methods in the course of a given project, they do make clear that the combination of multiple methods is common among experimentalists. The first part of this section discusses several reasons why this is the case – although the benefits of thorough and multi-method engagement with one's field site form a theme that recurs throughout the chapter. The second explores *how* experiments can be combined with other forms of inquiry.

Why combine methods?

The previous section offered several reasons why field experiments are often carried out in tandem with the use of other research techniques – often *after* those techniques have been used to generate significant knowledge of the experimental context. To reprise briefly, experiments are generally best employed to nail down particular causal relationships, meaning that alternative data-collection techniques and analytic strategies must be used to achieve other core research objectives. Moreover, because experiments can be expensive in terms of time and money, researchers need to be sure they are designed and carried out as effectively as possible. Also, experiments require a high level of analytic clarity. Often, this confidence and clarity only develop later in a project when a scholar has learned a great deal about the field site through analyzing data collected via other methods. One of our interviewees offered the following thought on the issue of sequencing experimental and observational data collection:

I don't think it necessarily has to be that the experiment comes last. But it's hard to imagine the experiment coming out of nowhere. Experiments are usually expensive and time-consuming to run, so people only want to do ones that have a chance of working. That can only happen after either a process of gathering hypotheses that have been established in other literature, or a lot of fieldwork of your own.[21]

Put somewhat differently – like all of the data-collection techniques addressed in this book, experiments (even laboratory studies that are intended to be as generic and generalizable as possible) are employed at a certain time in a certain location, and involve a certain kind of subject pool with particular experiences, cultural standards, norms, ideas, and assumptions. They investigate the effect of a certain kind of mailer or phone call on voter turnout in a certain election in a certain year, for instance, or the influence of a certain kind of technology on women's participation in villages of a certain region of a certain country. The more natural the setting, the more important it is that researchers have a deep understanding of the context in order to design and conduct an appropriate experimental intervention – an understanding of the type that often only comes through previous research on that setting. As Paluck (2009) notes, many essential decisions relating to the conduct of field experiments – some with the potential for life-or-death consequences in zones of high insecurity – emerge from an intimate knowledge of the field context.

In fact, the very idea for a field experiment often emerges out of immersion in a field setting. Identifying worthy topics that are amenable to experimental study – and finding and developing fruitful working relationships with partners – may require long-term engagement with a locale and the questions or problems that it presents. And on a practical level, conducting an experiment – arranging transfers of funds, obtaining approvals, bringing in necessary equipment, timing the roll-out of the study – often requires considerable familiarity with a field site. One example can be found in Olken's experimental studies in Indonesia, examining such topics as the effect of audits and participatory grassroots monitoring on corruption in road-construction projects in 608 villages, as well as the effect of direct democracy and representative democracy on development projects (2007, 2010). Carrying out these studies required deep cooperation with the Indonesian government and one of its development programs. It also required developing a thorough grasp of Indonesia's political history, village conditions in multiple provinces of the country, and the practical workings of both village governance and the

---

[21] Interview, BR-17, November 14, 2013.

financing of construction projects.[22] Paluck (2009) also acknowledges her great appreciation for a primary research team leader from the local area who provided vital feedback throughout the research process.

In addition to helping a researcher learn enough about a context to conduct an experiment there effectively, integrating experiments with other research methods helps to ensure that a research project will pay off. As previously noted, field experiments can fall apart for various reasons, or simply find no support for the hypothesis in question.[23] Several interviewees made the point that pursuing a topic through multiple methods helps to hedge against such occurrences. As one said: "A field experiment should be one component to a research project, but it's most effective when it's embedded in a larger kind of research project with lots of components: qualitative, quantitative, descriptive. So that if it [the experiment] works out logistically and it maps onto interesting theories, that's fantastic, but it doesn't all depend on that."[24]

Finally, it is often pointed out that experiments allow for particularly high internal validity (confidence that the treatment truly has the causal effect it is claimed to have) yet leave external validity (the generalizability of findings) an unanswered question. For experimentalists, a primary solution to the external validity problem is to conduct variations of the same experiment, in the same locale or similar ones, in order to build deeper knowledge of causal relationships. One example of this approach is provided by successive studies of get-out-the-vote (GOTV) techniques in the United States.[25] Researchers can also replicate experiments in other settings in order to test the generalizability of a causal effect, for instance in research on the effects of mandated participation by women in local governance.[26] Yet knowing where and how to carry out follow-on studies that can best advance the research program requires understanding the practically and theoretically relevant characteristics of a given field context – so future experiments can be

---

[22] Olken was affiliated with the World Bank's Jakarta office as a consultant for seven years, and speaks Indonesian. See the cited articles as well as a profile of Olken, "Graft paper," accessed November 17, 2013 at www.american.com/archive/2008/january-february-magazine-contents/graft-paper.

[23] It is often pointed out that negative results, too, can be important contributions to knowledge. Yet, in what is known as "publication bias," journals are less likely to publish such work.

[24] Interview, BR-16, October 31, 2013.

[25] For instance, García Bedolla and Michelson (2012) report findings from experiments that build and expand on earlier GOTV research.

[26] One example is research by Ocantos et al. (2013), replicating the same survey experiment about vote-buying in several Latin American countries. Another is Beath, Christia, and Enikolopov's study of village development councils in Afghanistan that mandate women's participation, building on related work elsewhere (2013).

designed to vary and test these characteristics.[27] In other words, enhancing external validity in experimental research entails significant knowledge of multiple contexts – knowledge that often can only be generated through research in the prospective field sites.

To be clear, this is not to suggest that all field experiments require long-term immersion in the field. As we have sought to suggest, the key fieldwork principle of "engagement with context" is not perfectly correlated with duration of stay. Sometimes an experiment requires relatively little time in the field, though this may be particularly common when the location of the experiment is close to the investigator's home institution and thus already familiar (for example: Han 2009b). Our point is simply that carrying out additional forms of inquiry in tandem with conducting field experiments allows researchers to gather information about the field context that is critical to setting up an effective experiment – whether one is carrying out the initial test of a hypothesis, or seeking to replicate a previous experimental finding. Gathering data using other techniques and employing other methods in combination with experiments also facilitates triangulation and verification – and serves as an insurance policy, ensuring that one's research will be valuable even if the experiment should be derailed.

Ways and means of combining experiments and other techniques

Many experienced field experimentalists attest that learning extensively about subjects through observational methods is often an essential prerequisite for developing meaningful experiments – yet observational methods can also be fruitfully employed in parallel with, or as follow-ups to, experiments. This subsection discusses several ways in which observational and experimental techniques can be combined and sequenced.

Intensive field-based study using observational techniques can lay the groundwork for experimental research. A process of inquiry involving interviews or site-intensive methods, for example, might identify what seems to be a causal relationship that a researcher can then assess through a field experiment. One scholar working in the developing world stressed the importance of inductively generating hypotheses by watching the work of NGOs and having open-ended conversations with members of the communities under study: "If you're going to study this population, you can't generate ideas for effective treatments unless you're actually doing the

---

[27] Interview, BR-16, October 31, 2013.

soaking and poking. It is a high-labor-for-reward situation."[28] According to this researcher, hypotheses derived purely from theoretical expectations in the abstract often fail to find empirical support when they are "parachuted in" for experimental testing. Economists echo such themes. One field experimenter working on agriculture in Kenya noted that interviews and focus groups enabled his team to determine plausible hypotheses explaining their puzzle: why maize farmers used little fertilizer despite the large returns it produces.[29] On the basis of what they learned through this qualitative work, they proceeded to test interventions aimed at lowering barriers to investment in fertilizer.

Yet the ways in which other, generally qualitative, field research techniques augment and facilitate experimental projects go well beyond merely providing a causal hunch. Immersion and qualitative methods also contribute to the core of the experimental design. Dunning explains that, in his co-authored study of fictive kinship or "cousinage" in Mali, extensive interviewing was necessary in order to determine the relationships among multiple ethnic and cousinage groups. These formed a matrix that was used in the random assignment of subjects to treatment categories, a matrix that was tested through initial trials of the experiment and refined in iterative cycles of further interviewing.[30]

Moreover, non-experimental techniques can be sequenced during and after an experiment has been conducted to help researchers to interpret its results. While experiments can provide powerful evidence for or against the existence of the hypothesized causal relationship, other questions often remain to be answered. As one experimentalist put it: "The big natural question is *why*. Field experiments are terrible at telling you why, they just tell you whether or not."[31] That is to say, merely finding a statistically significant average treatment effect does not, in and of itself, explain what brings about that effect. And if no effect is found, there could be many

---

[28] Interview, BR-2, July 30, 2012.

[29] Jonathan Robinson, talk at Center for Global International and Regional Studies, University of California, Santa Cruz, March 5, 2012.

[30] As Dunning writes: "The point is that eliciting a reliable map of cousinage relations from key informants very centrally involved qualitative as well as mixed methods. For instance, to revise our cousinage matrix we conducted qualitative interviews with key informants. We then also employed quantitative analysis of the experimental data from initial trials. To improve the cousinage matrix, we therefore iterated between focused interviews, new versions of the cousinage matrix, and our experimental data to improve the random assignment mechanism in this experiment" (2008, 22). Findings from the study are reported in Dunning and Harrison (2010).

[31] Interview, BR-16, October 31, 2013.

reasons why that is the case – and understanding those reasons is likely to be of great importance for designing a follow-up experiment.[32] While it is possible to build into the experimental design means of addressing "why" or "why not" questions, qualitative and non-experimental quantitative methods can also augment randomized controlled trials, as experimentalists have eloquently described.

For instance, surveys or interviews may be employed in parallel or in sequence to complement the experiment itself, to shed light on the causal relationships in question and the causal mechanisms at work, to interpret its results, and to discover further hypotheses to test (Sherman and Strang 2004; Paluck 2010). Sherman and Strang (2004) advocate the use of ethnography during the course of experimental work, in part as a way of understanding the "why" behind a causal effect. In their example, a randomized controlled trial evaluates a "restorative justice" program in which crime victims meet with the offenders who harmed them in a conference led by a facilitator. The experiment determines whether, for example, victims who participate in such conferences are less likely to experience post-traumatic stress disorder and more likely to hold normal jobs. Ethnographic work proceeds in parallel, with researchers repeatedly visiting program participants over time to gain a deep understanding of their life circumstances and their emotional and psychological responses to the program. The authors maintain that this is useful not only for explaining the mechanisms at work, but also for discovering important but not self-evident hypotheses to test.[33]

While this chapter focuses on true experiments, involving randomized assignment by the investigator to treatment conditions, it is worth noting that field research can also contribute to the discovery of natural experiments. Obtaining data from natural experiments may or may not require extensive on-the-ground investigation. Dunning, however, highlights the importance of fieldwork for locating and identifying random assignments that occur naturally in the world (Dunning 2008, 17–19). Scholars acknowledge that these "natural" occurrences are relatively rare, and that extensive knowledge of the precise circumstances that generated the data is necessary to understand whether the assignment is actually random, and thus whether

---

[32] Interview, BR-17, November 14, 2013.

[33] Ethnographic study could also, they write, explore the emotional reactions of victims who volunteered to participate but were assigned to the control group, perhaps dashing their hopes of confronting the offender and receiving an apology.

the assumptions of experimental research – e.g., that the treatment and control groups are effectively alike in all respects save the treatment itself – are met (Dunning 2012, Sekhon and Titiunik 2012).

In sum, the ways in which other field research techniques augment and facilitate experimental projects, and help scholars to firmly grasp the field context, are many. Regardless of how they are (or are not) combined with other techniques, field experiments entail a series of practical, logistical, and intellectual challenges. The rest of this chapter discusses those challenges, and offers some strategies for addressing them.

Working with partner organizations

Field experiments, like surveys, can be undertaken by lone researchers but often involve larger research teams and intensive collaboration between academics and partner organizations. Because of the rising demand for scientific evidence on which to base decisions about policy and aid resources, many kinds of organizations have become receptive to partnerships with researchers. Field experiments can involve cooperation with partners of several types, notably governments, intergovernmental organizations, foundations and other private funding organizations, political parties, NGOs, academic research groups, private firms, and social movement organizations. This section explores the kinds of collaborations that political scientists have forged and draws out lessons about maintaining such cooperation.

Different kinds of partner organizations have distinct strengths and weaknesses, and the choice of an appropriate partner will depend on the research question and field context. As Duflo *et al.* observe, partnering with government agencies may offer particularly far-reaching support, and allow research on pilot programs and interventions that have a strong chance of eventually becoming policy. These sorts of partnerships, then, have the potential both to benefit the local context, and to facilitate political science research with real-world implications. Yet such cooperation can be elusive, as it may require the approval of high-level officials and extensive coordination within and among bureaucratic agencies. NGOs, by contrast, may be more nimble and adaptable as research partners than state offices are. Further, as donors increasingly seek compelling evidence that funded programs have payoffs, NGOs often embrace cooperation with researchers who can provide solid program evaluations. It may even be possible to work with for-profit firms (Duflo *et al.* 2006, 20–22).

The collaboration necessary to conduct field experiments with a partner organization has advantages and disadvantages. One of the primary advantages is that sharing expenses with a partner organization can reduce the (often significant) cost of carrying out a field experiment.[34] A partner organization may have human resources, such as staff or volunteers, who can make it possible to apply a treatment at the scale that an experiment requires. Further, the input of partner organizations with deep roots in the field site may be necessary for developing treatments that make sense in context. Local organizations or state agencies can help to legitimate an experimental study and to encourage people to participate in it. In conflict-ridden or other hazardous settings, another possible advantage of partnership is an increase in the security provided for the research team.[35] And, to the extent that the treatment is intended to provide some benefit to the locality or to alleviate a problem, local groups can help ensure that the results of the experiment have a lasting payoff: "so the intervention doesn't die when I leave," as one interviewee put it.[36]

Yet partnerships can entail disadvantages and challenges as well. Scholars might have to struggle to balance the policy goals of their partner organization with answering their own theoretical questions (Humphreys and Weinstein 2009; List 2011). In some instances, particularly where partner organizations are not obtaining subjects' consent prior to applying an intervention, conflicting goals and practices may even present the researcher with ethical dilemmas.[37] Also, researchers and non-academic collaborators frequently face different sets of pressures and incentives. For example, political scientists aim to determine impartially what the data say about the effectiveness of a particular program or intervention. Their counterparts, by contrast, may not be as committed to the integrity of the research process or the reporting of its findings; negative results could, in some cases, jeopardize funding or cast leaders in a bad light. One experimentalist even gave examples of members of partner organizations apparently sabotaging an experimental evaluation of their programs, fearing what the results would show.[38]

---

[34] Gerber makes this point (2011, 130).

[35] Paluck (2009) explains how working with an NGO allowed her team to travel in well-maintained SUVs in a large convoy and have access to expanded networks of information regarding outbreaks of violence.

[36] Interview, BR-15, October 25, 2013.

[37] Humphreys explores some of the potential ethical challenges facing researchers doing "embedded" experiments with partner organizations (2011).

[38] Interview, BR-18, November 18, 2013.

Sometimes collaborators may not understand the need to follow the experimental protocol precisely. In other instances, groups may simply lack the capacity to carry out what the researcher needs them to do. One scenario, for instance, is that "the [partner] group thinks that we're going to be able to make this many phone calls, provide this many students, and they grossly overestimate their capacity. If the volunteers don't show up to do it, there's not much you can do about it."[39] People in the partner organization may not be able to administer a treatment in a consistent way to all subjects.[40] For all these reasons, depending on circumstances, it pays to be cautious about delegating crucial elements of the research process – such as random assignment of subjects to treatment groups – to partners, and it is prudent to maintain close, independent oversight of the integrity of the study.[41] Judith Gueron's essay (2002) deals at length with the tensions that can arise between researchers and partner organizations, which, she writes, often commit to a randomized study without fully understanding its implications and challenges.

More generally, partnerships require substantial start-up investments of time to establish contact and build trust. Training collaborators and coordinating their work also can be time-intensive. Our interviewees described building and maintaining relationships with partners as one of the persistent challenges of their experiment projects. As one described it: "Organizations don't like to be treated in very transactional ways: 'You're a source of data, let me come in, let me have your data!' They are kind of mistrustful of me: what's my intention really? Do I really care about the outcome?"[42] Another said that "there's nothing that keeps me up at night more" than concerns about how to communicate with partner groups, without offending them, in ways that reinforce their obligation to keep to the terms of a memorandum of understanding.[43] One experienced researcher stressed the importance of spending time in person with collaborators, "going out to bars," building their commitment to the experiment and encouraging them to air, in advance, any concerns about the project or limitations in their capacity to carry it out.[44] Yet the cautions we discuss elsewhere in connection with forming relationships in the field still stand. For instance, some field experimentalists have found that their political neutrality may be perceived as compromised as they become identified as affiliates of the partner organization.

---

[39] Interview, BR-18, November 18, 2013.   [40] Interview, BR-17, November 14, 2013.
[41] Interview, LM-13, September 7, 2012.   [42] Interview, BR-17, November 14, 2013.
[43] Interview, BR-15, October 25, 2013.   [44] Interview, BR-18, November 18, 2013.

While institutional collaborators may have a lot to offer, it is entirely possible to do field experiments without a partner organization. Researchers working in areas with little NGO activity, and those pursuing theoretical questions that do not happen to dovetail with the agendas of nonprofits or government agencies, all have good reason to go it alone. Political scientists flying solo can apply for grants to support the costs of training their own teams of research assistants to carry out the field experiment. Alternatively, scholars might decide to develop "light-weight" research designs requiring relatively little in terms of institutional support, computer infrastructure, and staff assistance. An example would be an experiment embedded in a survey conducted through face-to-face, in-home interviews, where treatments consist of different question wordings or prompts. One field experimenter explained the choice to refrain from working with an established research institute:

> It's still more financially sound to go on my own, especially as I have these connections [from a previous project]. Someday when I have funds, I can completely delegate it. I also still like to be involved in the process, the sampling process, for instance. I don't know how much I'd want to delegate. It's fun too.[45]

Developing and randomizing the treatment

Developing the experimental intervention, i.e., the treatment, is a crucial step in the process of experimental research. As noted in the previous sections, ideas for treatments sometimes come from prior phases of an investigator's research, or from collaborators. Often – as with research in other fields, such as clinical trials of drugs – treatments are chosen in part because existing evidence of a causal effect is sufficiently plausible, or related research findings sufficiently robust, to justify the work of putting the posited effect to an experimental test. Treatments may also be driven by programs that partners such as donors, NGOs, or government agencies happen to be implementing and wish to evaluate. Naturally, in political science research, the propositions to be tested also generally follow from hypotheses that investigators aim to test, which in turn relate to broader bodies of theory. Thus, as a practical and intellectual matter, there can be multiple sources underlying the choice of treatments.

---

[45] Interview, BR-6, August 14, 2012.

Developing a treatment takes substantial time, and draws upon knowledge of the field milieu. Experimenters often use interviews or focus groups to refine the treatment, and partner organizations play an important role in this process. In part, they do so to ensure that the intervention constitutes a proper and fair test of the causal proposition at hand. Additional goals are to be confident that the treatment will not harm subjects in one way or another, even if in intangible ways, such as making them more cynical about politics, less inclined to vote, more hostile toward rival groups, and so forth. As one interviewee put it: "If there aren't enough other research methods that are applied before the experimental intervention, it can be disastrous, or at least bad. We really owe it to [research subjects] before doing an experimental intervention to check over and over to make sure this isn't going to go awry."[46]

Once the treatment has been developed, the researcher must then randomize the assignment of that treatment. As in other types of research design, randomization can occur at multiple levels. In a field experiment on the effect of solar radios on citizens' perceptions and political views, one scholar identified and matched "twin" villages that were similar in multiple respects, and then randomized which village in each pair received solar radios (the treatment) and which received solar flashlights (the placebo, or control).[47] At the next levels, public lotteries determined which compounds in each village, and which men and women in those compounds, received the items in question.

Yet, particularly in field as opposed to laboratory settings, achieving randomization is not always easy. The following passage, from an essay by Elizabeth Paluck discussing her work in the Democratic Republic of the Congo, nicely illustrates some of the challenges that random assignment may confront in the field:

In an office tucked under palm trees north of Goma, DRC, I squeezed onto a narrow wooden bench with ten researchers and one driver to face the mayor's desk. "*Karibu*, welcome," the mayor smiled at us. I explained that we were evaluating an NGO-produced radio programme about community relations, and I presented him with our *ordres de mission*. He nodded and started to sign and pass them back to us. "'Many people will be grateful that an NGO is showing interest in our situation. You are invited to work in the neighbourhood where I live." I explained that our choice of neighbourhoods and people was random. He smiled a bit regretfully and turned to a faded hand-painted map on the wall. "I should update you on the security situation.

---

[46] Interview, BR-15, October 25, 2013.   [47] Interview, LM-1, April 13, 2012.

You should not go farther than these neighbourhoods here, because outside there has been some fighting." (Paluck 2009, 38–39)

Whether in an effort to protect the research team or direct resources to his home area, the author's host had something quite different from a random draw of neighborhoods and subjects in mind. As Paluck goes on to explain, serious security threats did impinge on the team's work.

Even when the principal actors involved in a study initially agree on the goal of randomization, many other impediments to random assignment can emerge in field settings. Some obstacles include: inadequate training for implementation or capacity to carry it out; social dynamics among team members; a reemergence of previously reconciled competing goals between a researcher and her partner organization – or a reassessment of the partner organization's priorities; and changes on the ground (e.g., a road closure, grant cancellation, NGO organizational failure, or coup). Several scholars highlighted how the procedures for implementing randomization were often very complex, requiring extensive training and supervision of field enumerators with multiple manuals and tables.[48] Others suggested that partner organizations can balk at implementing designs that require giving something of apparent value to members of a treatment group and withholding it from members of a control group, asking "why can't we just give it to them?"[49]

Indeed, even though randomization is a core *methodological* principle of any field experiment, it is important for researchers to consciously deliberate on the ethical issues involved in randomization in their particular field context. Would randomization of an intervention violate central *ethical* principles of justice and beneficence? For example, simple randomization applied to a public health program might mean that the most impoverished and needy communities were last to receive a vital public health solution. The answers from the literature are not straightforward, and depend, to some degree, on whether scholars are focused on the short-term or long-term implications of the experiment, and whether they consider the process or outcome to be more important. Where Deaton (2009) questions the ethics of randomization, Gerber (2011) turns the challenge on its head, pointing to the long-term costs of *not* carrying out randomized trials and thus failing to obtain systematic evidence about whether interventions actually work.[50]

---

[48] Interview, LM-13, September 7, 2012.   [49] Interview, BR-15, October 25, 2013.

[50] List (2011) also makes the argument that the cost of not doing randomized experiments outweighs these concerns.

De La O and Wantchekon (2011) argue that, since resources are limited, random assignment of needed and desirable treatments is actually a more transparent and fair decision procedure.[51] But, since individuals or communities often vary in terms of their level and intensity of need, Humphreys and Weinstein (2009) usefully suggest a strategy of randomizing among those with equal need. Another strategy is to include everyone eventually, but randomly assign the roll-out or timing of when the participants receive the treatment (Blattman *et al.* 2013).

From the perspective of the populations under study, seemingly arbitrary assignment of individuals, communities, or other units to treatment groups can cause offense or at least raise questions. Consequently, scholars emphasized the importance of customizing the randomization process for the specific field site and carrying it out in ways that come across as appropriate. In some cases, scholars advocated the use of public lotteries as locally meaningful. For some others, throwing dice was acceptable. For another who worried that this "might look weird" to community members, enumerators used tables from a book.[52]

Finally, scholars should evaluate whether certain treatments can ethically be randomized at all. One interviewee gave an example of a research team that decided against the randomization of a planned treatment because randomizing would have meant preventing legitimate local political authorities from fulfilling their customary roles in the community.[53] Each of these strategies for dealing with potential ethical concerns has costs and benefits for participants and communities as well as the study that can only be assessed with a deep understanding of the specific dynamics of the field context.

Recruiting and preparing subjects

Experiments can be conducted in ways that involve minimal contact between researchers and subjects, as in non-field-based studies conducted over the web. Commonly, though, a considerable part of the work involved in setting up an experiment lies in recruiting, preparing, and debriefing the people who participate in the study. In some experiments, participants are randomly

---

[51] A similar argument about the greater fairness of randomization was made in several interviews.
[52] Interviews, LM-1, April 13, 2012; LM-13, September 7, 2012.
[53] Interview, LM-13, September 7, 2012.

selected from particular populations, and in others they are recruited through other means. In order to avoid violations of protocol or invalidation of the experiment, all subjects within a given arm of a study must be given the same instructions and guidance, and be kept from influencing one another in the course of the experiment. As one researcher observed, providing just a single example of precautions that must be taken: "You have to explain to them why they can't first watch their friend do the experiment before they do it themselves."[54] In this section, we review a range of considerations involved in recruiting subjects and preparing them to participate in an experiment.

When recruiting participants, the researcher must carefully consider where to do so; how many participants to recruit; and whether and how to compensate subjects for participating in the experiment. Ideally, a scholar's research questions shape the choice of appropriate subject populations. Yet, as we noted previously, in many field experiments researchers collaborate with organizations that may have already identified certain countries, regions, communities, or demographic groups that they wish to target with their intervention.

The question of how many subjects to recruit is related to the issue of how many hypothesized explanatory factors there are to test. While different research questions in different field contexts may necessitate the inclusion of more or fewer, simplicity is usually advised. Proliferating explanatory factors or conditions complicates the analysis of interaction effects, multiplies the number of treatment groups needed, and thus increases the number of subjects who must be recruited in order to obtain the same statistical power.[55] Knowledge of the field context is critical for anticipating whether it is logistically feasible to recruit the desired number of subjects in the available time period.

The ideal number of subjects is also tightly connected to the issue of compensation. Normative standards on subject compensation differ widely by discipline. Psychologists rarely pay subjects on the basis of specific actions they take during an experiment; economists often pay participants contingent on their performance in the experiment; and political scientists seem to be split between these practices (Druckman *et al.* 2011b, 7). If monetary incentives are used in a field experiment, the researcher must devise an appropriate scale of incentives. Morton and Williams (2010) attempt to

---

[54] Personal communication, June 19, 2011.
[55] Statistical power refers to the probability that a test will reject a false null hypothesis.

summarize existing disciplinary norms with an estimate that participants are paid 50 to 100 percent above the minimum wage for the time spent in the lab. Of course, the opportunity cost of time may be more readily estimated when the experiment takes place in a lab, and not the field. Field settings also vary considerably in terms of the normative expectations for immediate financial or in-kind compensation versus a more generalized commitment of long-term reciprocity.[56]

Once participants have been recruited and the appropriate level of compensation established, the next issue to consider is the kind of preparation they will receive. In many field experiments, participants may not know they are involved in an experimental study. Or, they may know that they are engaged in a research project but be unaware to some degree about the central purpose of the investigation. This aspect of field experiments raises the question of how much deception is ethically acceptable. While deception (or incomplete disclosure) may amplify the realism and hence the internal validity of a field experiment, its potential lasting implications for participants and social outcomes raise ethical concerns. For example, some political scientists have studied public officials' responses to contact from citizens in ways that involve deception. In such studies, emails have been sent that appear to be from real voters or constituents, when actually the sender was a fictitious identity created by the researchers, for instance with the purpose of testing differential responses to constituents from varying racial or political backgrounds. Researchers behind such studies have defended them, arguing that deception is necessary to study the phenomenon in question; that the request is routine and the imposition is modest; and that public officials deserve and expect special scrutiny (Butler and Broockman 2011; McClendon 2012).[57] As with compensation, the use of deception varies by discipline so no easy consensus exists. Where psychologists frequently incorporate deception, economists almost never do, and political scientists are fairly divided on the issue (Morton and Williams 2010; Dickson 2011, 65–67; Druckman *et al.* 2011b),[58] often depending on the source of theoretical and methodological inspiration for

---

[56] We offer additional thoughts on compensation in Chapter 4.

[57] Another question, also addressed by McClendon's article, is to what extent such deception might have adverse effects on future research by leaving subjects, or others who learn about the study, with negative feelings.

[58] Druckman *et al.* (2011b, 7) find that 31 percent of laboratory experiments published in the APSR through 2005 used deception. To our knowledge, no similar assessment has been done with field experiments.

the study and involvement in multidisciplinary collaboration. We simply suggest that scholars critically reflect in advance about what seems methodologically necessary *and* ethically appropriate given the political and cultural context of their field sites.

Applying the treatment and following up

Actually conducting the experiment and applying the treatment pose a set of challenges that are often quite specific to experimental research, although principles and strategies for coping with them overlap with those that apply to other methods. Just as with survey research, patient and repeated pretesting is essential. Everyone on the research team should be well-practiced in the procedures for applying the treatment and for handling contingencies. Investigators go to great lengths to try to standardize the experience for all subjects, minimizing or nullifying differences except for those assigned as part of the treatment. For example, enumerators or research assistants who have personal contact with subjects may be randomly assigned to avoid bias stemming from systematic effects of their particular backgrounds. They are also carefully trained in advance regarding how to respond to queries from subjects, requests to withdraw from the experiment, or other special circumstances.

The need to keep subjects in the treatment and control groups independent from one another is vital in experimental research, and this creates a distinctive set of challenges for field investigators. The problem of members of one group being influenced by the experimental conditions to which members of another group are assigned is known as interference (Gerber and Green 2012, 8). One form of interference is spillover. Spillover occurs when "those who are treated in turn alter their behavior in a way that affects other subjects" (Gerber 2011, 130). It presents a problem because control groups experiencing the effects of the treatment in some form or another may bias estimates of the treatment's actual effects.[59] As Gerber states, while laboratory experiments generally are not subject to this problem, it is more likely to crop up in field experiments. An example would be a project in which certain state senators were randomly assigned to a treatment (for instance, being told that details of their campaign finances would be

---

[59] Gerber and Green's book contains a chapter on interference among experimental units (2012, Chapter 8). See also Gerring (2012, 242–246).

publicized to constituents) while others were randomly assigned to a control group. If, during the course of the experiment, senators in the former group changed their behavior in response to the treatment (turning down questionable campaign contributions, for example) and their colleagues in the control group emulated them, this would be a clear case of spillover.

The potential for spillover varies with features of the research design, the treatment, and the research setting. One experimentalist we interviewed struggled with the problem of keeping treatment and control groups separate from one another when the two groups were part of the same organization and had the same leader, and the experiment was to last for weeks. By contrast, maintaining the independence of treatment and control was much easier in studies where subjects were given the treatment individually, whether by email or by knocking on their doors, and outcomes took the form of the subjects' immediate responses. The interviewee observed: "This is kind of an ongoing limitation of field experiments: it's easier to study things where the treatment is really short, but there are a lot of things in the political world where the treatment takes a long time."[60]

Familiarity with the social environment of the field site helps investigators to determine how serious a problem spillover might be and what measures might be taken to prevent it. Evaluating the potential for spillover may require an in-person visit to determine whether households or neighborhoods assigned to treatment are physically proximate to, or are otherwise likely to interact with, those assigned to the control group, for instance.[61] One obvious approach to preventing spillover is to design an experiment in such a way that treatment and control groups are geographically separated. For example, in a study of voter responses to information about candidates' corruption, de Figueiredo, Hidalgo, and Kasahara selected 400 voting precincts in São Paulo through an algorithm that maximized the distance between the treatment and control groups.[62] After lamenting that there were "so many opportunities for spillovers to happen," another scholar advised frequent and open communication with partners and the research team, concluding: "If you are on the ball and can catch them [spillovers] quickly,

---

[60] Interview, BR-17, November 14, 2013.   [61] Interview, BR-2, July 30, 2012.
[62] "When do voters punish corrupt politicians? Experimental evidence from Brazil," unpublished paper, p. 15. The algorithm also incorporated other information that the authors acquired through careful investigation of the city's neighborhoods, obtaining relatively even distributions on income levels, and vote choice in previous elections. As well, the algorithm avoided high-rise neighborhoods in which it would be difficult to ensure that the treatment (flyers with information about candidates) reached the mailboxes of individual households.

then you can save the project."[63] Another approach is to incorporate spill-over into research designs deliberately, measuring it and analyzing its effects. Nickerson, for example, had canvassers in two American cities knock on doors and deliver a get-out-the-vote appeal prior to the 2002 Congressional primary elections. He measured the effect of this exhortation on the propensity to vote of both the person who answered the door and on a second household resident who did not receive the appeal, thus measuring how civic participation is spread from one person to another (Nickerson 2008).

Finally, in some experiments, the last interactive step is debriefing participants afterward to solicit additional information from them, as well as to give them further information about the study in which they took part. Investigators may, for instance, send correspondence to subjects; they may request that they participate in a follow-up survey; they may hold community feedback meetings; or they may sit down with them for open-ended interviews. This is another aspect of experimental research that can be simple in laboratory settings but more difficult in the field. Indeed, in many field experiments, particularly those in which subjects are unaware that they are part of an experiment, no debriefing is conducted.

One purpose of debriefing is to reveal problems that may have occurred in the process of the experiment, such as possible non-compliance on the part of researchers (or their partners) or participants, resulting in a failure to treat. One source of non-compliance is that certain randomly selected individuals and communities might be more difficult to access than others, producing a systematic bias in the treatment group. Another source of non-compliance is individuals' inability or unwillingness to follow instructions. In this instance, the experiment successfully reached the participant, but the person did not actually read, do, or complete what was intended to be the treatment. A second type of problem that debriefing can reveal is that the intended treatment was confounded with something else. In this case, the treatment was designed to create a certain kind of stimulus, X, but instead was perceived as something else, X_2. Following up with participants can also help scholars to interpret the findings from the experiment, for instance by shedding light on the mechanisms through which the treatment exercised its causal effect, or, if no average treatment effect was found, on the reasons why that was so. A further goal can be to determine how enduring any outcomes of the treatment are.

---

[63] Interview, LM-13, September 7, 2012.

The purpose of following up with participants after an experiment is not merely to provide experimenters with further data and to detect problems in the execution of the study, however. Debriefing can also play important roles in conveying information to participants about the research they took part in. At a minimum, IRB guidelines suggest that subjects should be debriefed in projects "involving deception or incomplete disclosure, especially if the research may induce psychological stress, guilt, or embarrassment," allowing the investigators to "explain any deception involved and to help the subjects deal with any distress occasioned by the research."[64] Some experimentalists expressed a belief that investigators have even broader obligations to explain their research to those involved. In part, this is a matter of clearing up puzzlement and suspicion. As one said: "It's kind of ridiculous to not debrief. I've seen lots of cases where the subjects of the field experiment are aware that something totally unnatural and weird happened," and they deserve to have this explained. This interviewee further stated that

disclosure or debriefing is important because I believe that the research should be useful to the people who participated in it, and not just in a trickle-down way, in that it will be useful to them because I find an effect and then convince the World Bank or the government [to act on it], but that this thing that we did is useful in everyday life.[65]

According to this view, follow-up should convey research findings and also engage participants in two-way deliberation about what was learned.

Conclusion

Field experiments, as well as other types of experiments, are becoming more and more prevalent in the study of politics. Clearly, an increasing amount of experimental work is being conducted in the field, or is working its way through the publishing pipeline. Whether or not field experiments revolutionize social policy, as high-profile advocates like Esther Duflo have claimed they will, these methods are being applied to pressing problems around the world and are yielding new insights. Experiments sharply contrast with the other data-collection techniques considered in this book in certain respects.

---

[64] Institutional Review Board Guidebook, Chapter III, accessed December 5, 2013 at www.hhs.gov/ohrp/archive/irb/irb_chapter3.htm.

[65] Interview, BR-19, December 4, 2013.

To conduct an experiment requires a narrowly focused research question and well-defined causal factors and outcome measures. The random assignment of subjects to treatment groups and the deliberate introduction of treatments has no parallel in methods like in-depth interviews and archival research.

And yet a clear theme running throughout this chapter is that effectively conducting field experiments requires deep engagement in a research context and the use of multiple methodologies and skills. The processes and practical challenges of carrying out such research have a great deal of overlap with, and often entail, other forms of fieldwork. This theme resonated in all of our interviews with veteran experimentalists, and of course, it reinforces the core principles articulated in this book. Each stage of experimental research – from conceiving the idea of a treatment to assess, to working with partner organizations, to designing the experimental protocol, to implementing it, to interpreting the results – can benefit from a degree of immersion in the field setting and the use of qualitative techniques such as interviews and site-intensive methods. Still more field research is required as experiment-based research programs are replicated and expanded in new environments and with new types of subject populations, in order to understand how local contexts vary in theoretically relevant ways and to adapt treatments, measures, and protocols appropriately.

As with other data-collection techniques discussed in this book, this chapter also showcases the value of making the methodology of field experiments explicit and transparent in the publication of articles and books, or in standalone essays. Practically every experimental research project that we discussed with our interviewees had an extensive back-story, often with fascinating twists and turns. Such lore is shared informally within the experiment community – yet disseminating it more widely could help a broader population of scholars learn what it takes to conduct a field experiment, thus informing future research. We contend that such transparency, which would shed further light on the strengths and weaknesses of these promising techniques,[66] is particularly important for field experiments, since they are relatively new in political science. Broadening methodological debates around experimental methods could, in turn, stimulate an expansion of the types of research questions experiments address, and of the types of experimental design employed.

Experimentalists sometimes object to the idea that their technique raises special ethical considerations, feeling that they are being singled out unfairly.

---

[66] Interview, LM-9, August 30, 2012.

There is some validity to this. Yet it is also true that most ethical questions stem precisely from those aspects of field experiments that make them distinct and intellectually appealing. Field experiments isolate the effects of a potential causal factor by bringing it into existence in the form of a treatment, and selectively applying it across groups. Intervening in the world in this way helps make field experiments particularly relevant to policy issues and the practice of politics generally – and also necessitates particular forms of scrutiny. The community of experimentalists within political science is in the early stages of addressing some of the ramifications of this research. Merely adhering to the letter of IRB requirements may not always be adequate to avoid harm, let alone to meet higher standards of beneficence. Much thought and consideration are needed as the discipline works out what it means to practice ethical commitment in this mode of research.

10 Analyzing, writing, and retooling in the field

This chapter marks a transition point in the book.[1] Chapters 3 and 4 laid out key aspects of preparing for and organizing field research. Chapters 5 through 9 examined particular data-collection techniques, highlighting some of the challenges researchers face when deploying them in the field, and offering sets of strategies for addressing those challenges. Here, we return to thinking about the research endeavor as a whole.

Gathering information, day-by-day and hour-by-hour, is a critical facet of field research. Yet whether researching in an archive, conducting interviews, or carrying out field experiments, the most effective fieldworkers find a balance between collecting data and handling the related logistical minutiae that all field research involves (which we might characterize as focusing on the "trees") and continually trying to envision the big picture, develop their arguments, and hone their theoretical contributions (that is, keep the "forest" in view). Put differently, throughout their time in the field, good field researchers simultaneously play the role of project manager, deftly devising and executing research routines that lead to the systematic collection of a range of rich data, *and* of principal investigator – head theorist. One way for a scholar to bring the forest into focus, and to bridge the project manager and principal investigator roles, is to begin to analyze the information she is gathering while she is still in the field.

We offer a brief example from one of our interviews to illustrate the intellectual dividends that analyzing information as it is collected can pay. Our respondent initiated fieldwork in Africa with a "beautiful" typology reflecting a "spectrum of violence" on which she hoped to place actors using information conveyed in interviews. Yet, as she began to interview and to analyze what she was being told, she discovered that respondents were not "self-advertising" the characteristics she hoped to use to categorize them. She quickly realized, she recounted, that "nobody is going to hold out a sign

---

[1] Some of the ideas developed in this chapter originated with Julia Lynch (2004).

and say 'I'm a pillager.'" Moreover, through analyzing the data she was gathering, she saw that her pre-determined categories were too static: many respondents fit in more than one category (jumping among them over time), or sat in border areas. While she retained the spectrum as a key piece of her analytic framework, how she thought about it "changed entirely" due to on-the-ground analysis of the data she was bringing together. That modification, she believes, became a strength of the book she ultimately wrote.[2]

To be clear, and as we noted in Chapter 1, we understand "analysis" to comprise a diverse set of tasks and strategies that scholars employ to understand the pieces of the research puzzle individually and in the aggregate, and to fit them into the project as a whole. These tasks vary from less formal "back of the brain" percolating (e.g., reconsidering the interactions observed during a focus group in light of information subsequently gathered from a series of newspaper articles); to organizing, digesting, and processing information; to more formally employing qualitative analytic methods or tests of statistical significance – and everything in between. We think it can be helpful for scholars to engage actively, consciously, and explicitly in all of these forms of analysis while in the field – and to detail how they did so in their written products. As we have sought to demonstrate, the informed iteration between data generation and data analysis that fieldwork entails is what makes it such a powerful mode of inquiry. Correspondingly, the more consciously and systematically scholars engage in these tasks, and the more transparent they are about how they did so, the better their work and the more persuasive its presentation will be.

The central point we wish to underscore in this chapter, then, is that data analysis should not be thought of as a discrete research phase that starts after data gathering has ended: scholars should engage in analysis (in the multiple forms it can take) *throughout their time in the field*.[3] Timely analysis of the information they are collecting allows scholars to move the intellectual ball forward, and to integrate what they are learning and finding back into their projects. That is, analyzing in the field helps them to make sense of what they are absorbing, generate new hypotheses, and identify causal mechanisms. It also allows them to identify problems with their research design or data-collection techniques, and adjust accordingly. The earlier such problems are

---

[2] Interview, LM-20, September 20, 2012.

[3] We understand that our placement of this chapter after the chapters addressing data collection might implicitly suggest that data analysis occurs after data gathering; readers should not interpret the necessarily linear progression of our book as a reflection of how we think – or believe *they* should think – about conducting field research!

diagnosed, the more easily they can be fixed. Likewise, analyzing in the field helps scholars to assess their overall progress, figure out how much work remains, and determine how to use the time they have left in the field most effectively.

This chapter also highlights how helpful it can be to begin to write, and to identify venues in which to present the fruits of one's analytic labors, while in the field. As with analysis, writing in the field can take a range of forms. No matter what format scholars adopt, however, beginning to write in the field pushes them to formulate their ideas clearly and concretely, facilitating analytic progress. If they can create opportunities to present to others (for instance, scholars in their field site) what they are writing, they may be able to get feedback that can inform the data-collection process and the overall research endeavor as well.

We also offer a diagnostic tool to help scholars identify problems with their project, and suggest strategies they can employ to trouble-shoot those problems in the field. Given the iterative nature of field research – and the flexible discipline that underlies it – scholars often make considerable adjustments to their projects while in the field. Nonetheless, we suggest that a researcher's first inclination upon encountering a data-collection or inter-pretive hurdle should not be to tear their project apart or change their research topic. The chapter closes with some concrete strategies scholars can employ to transition smoothly and efficiently from the field back to their home institution. Doing so, we suggest, entails gently rebalancing the intellectual scales toward a fuller focus on analyzing data and writing – a rebalancing that occurs more naturally, easily, and quickly when scholars have gotten a significant head-start on these tasks in the field. Of course, no field researcher will do *all* of what we are suggesting. Rather, we hope they pick and choose among our ideas and adopt (and adapt) those that seem most useful to them.

Analyzing in the field

Just as with our suggestion that scholars "stay organized" in the field, our recommendation that they "start analyzing" while conducting field research may seem so obvious as to not require articulation. Alternatively, scholars in a frenzy to amass more and more data may think it makes no sense to spend any time on tasks that can be carried out later. What benefits, precisely, does gathering and analyzing data simultaneously yield? And what, specifically, do we mean when we suggest that scholars "analyze?" This section addresses those questions. We begin by offering a series of justifications for analyzing in the field. We then describe, in broad brushstrokes, several of the varied set of activities that "analysis" entails that can be carried out in the field. The final sub-section offers a more detailed discussion of coding qualitative data sources.

Most researchers are excited about their question, and thus are automatically evaluating what they can learn from their data as they gather them – that is, analyzing them. Thus much of what we advocate – critically reflecting on the data being collected, making them more intellectually accessible, and writing out initial reactions to and interpretations of them – is likely a natural extension of what many researchers are already doing routinely. That is, for many scholars, our suggestions may amount simply to being more purposive and explicit about (and, as we will suggest, documenting better) what they are already doing. Moreover, our discussion of analytic tasks is merely suggestive and far from exhaustive. Nonetheless, we hope our recommendations offer some inspiration, helping scholars to think more specifically and creatively about the kinds of analytic tasks that they can tackle concurrently with data collection.

Why analyze in the field?

It might seem logical to dedicate one's time in the field to gathering more and more information, postponing the task of analyzing it until returning home. Such thinking has several appeals. It seems to circumscribe the complex set of tasks that need to be carried out in the field and thus to allow the researcher to focus all of her energies on the assignment that can *only* be completed in the field: data collection. Further, it feels efficient: time in the field is often scarce, so best to use it to obtain as much data as possible, leaving most analytical tasks for the post-field stage when (it seems) time will be more abundant. A more bifurcated approach might seem to make particularly good sense for scholars for whom constraints of various types dictate relatively compressed field stays and make return trips unlikely.

We believe that, for most researchers, a better approach is to consider collecting data and analyzing data as processes that move forward simultaneously and in parallel. We offer a series of inter-related reasons. First, collecting and analyzing data in tandem allows researchers to develop a better mental picture of the research context and of their project, and to successively integrate what they are learning about the former into the design of the latter.[4] Fieldwork, as we have insisted, is an iterative process: what the researcher discovers in the field context shapes the way he thinks about the project as a whole, and can help him to refine and strengthen each facet of research design, maximizing the likelihood of effectively answering his question. Indeed, scholars often cycle through the design – data collection – analysis stages several times before they hit on a design that is practically possible and analytically productive. Researchers are advised to take extensive notes as they alter their project architecture, documenting the basis and evidence on which they modified their research design and their field research design. Doing so will help them to avoid practices that can create inferential problems,[5] and to make the research process as transparent as possible.

Second and relatedly, analyzing in the field allows scholars to be more reflective and thus more selective with regard to data collection. That is, carefully considering the information they are collecting allows scholars to assess their data-collection strategy, and to determine whether the information supports their initial hypotheses, refutes pertinent rival explanations, or points to alternative arguments or interpretation. In addition, considering information as it is gathered helps researchers ensure that they are collecting data in ways and forms that make them amenable to analysis using the tools they anticipate using. Doing so also aids in identifying inconsistencies in findings in time to address them, for instance, by conducting follow-up interviews with respondents to ask questions or to discuss preliminary results. Further, taking inventory of, processing, and thinking about the information they are collecting in the field allows scholars to evaluate their progress more effectively – to assess whether they have collected *enough* data and what information they still need to gather.

Third, analyzing and collecting data concurrently can help scholars to hone their data-collection skills. For instance, one scholar we interviewed explained how reviewing her interview transcripts helped her see mistakes

---

[4] Many scholars whom we interviewed emphasized the importance of iteration – for example, interviews LM-6, August 30, 2012; LM-10, September 18, 2012; LM-15, September 10, 2012; LM-17, September 11, 2012; LM-20, September 20, 2012. Of course, how much flexibility one has to make research design choices along the way depends on one's data-collection techniques; scholars doing surveys or experiments, for instance, may need to decide upon and solidify more parameters of the research earlier than scholars engaging in ethnography, for instance.

[5] For instance, it is often suggested that scholars should avoid testing new hypotheses on the same data used to generate them.

she was making while interviewing, and how the way in which she asked questions shaped the answers she received; these self-evaluations helped her to improve her interview guide and become a better interviewer.[6] And finally, even the busiest of field researchers have periods of down time during fieldwork – because interviewees are off on a national holiday or otherwise unavailable, archives are closed, etc. These moments – whether an afternoon or an evening, a weekend or an entire week – can be golden opportunities to chip away at other facets of the research endeavor, such as processing, summarizing – *analyzing* data.

Of course, during a trip of just a few days' or a few weeks' duration throughout which one's schedule stays fully booked, it may seem wholly impractical to analyze the data one is collecting. Particularly if one is working in an archive, it may seem flatly irrational to take the time to read through stacks and stacks of documents rather than simply grabbing everything that seems even tangentially relevant and postponing perusal until later – given that one *can* collect archival documents without reading while one cannot, for instance, conduct interviews without listening. Yet we would posit that, given the heightened importance of spending the available time efficiently on shorter trips, it is even *more* important to assess the value and completeness of the information one is collecting in real time. These assessments can inform decisions about which opportunities (potential interviews, documents) to seize and which to let go – decisions that are even more critical in a short research timeframe.

Rather than cramming their schedules to the extent that they have no breathing room, we suggest scholars on short trips give themselves some time to type up notes, to summarize, even if just briefly – to *think*. One researcher's tale of woe highlights the importance of doing so: with just three weeks to spend in Uganda, she felt she could not take the time to type up most of her interview notes. She regretted that decision when the bag in which she was carrying her handwritten notes – and thus all of her hard-won data – was stolen.[7] Of course, if we think of "data duties" in the field as a continuum with data collection at one end and data analysis at the other, scholars who have very little time to spend in the field will quite reasonably place themselves further toward the data-collection end. We simply suggest that very few scholars will benefit from thinking of their time in the field purely in terms of gathering information.

---

[6] Interview, DK-11, August 7, 2012.   [7] Personal communication, June 3, 2013.

Analysis in the field: forms and functions

As we have noted, analysis comprises a diverse set of activities. In this subsection we consider various general analytic strategies field researchers can adopt based on reading through, thinking through, and taking notes on their sources (for example, field notes, interview notes or transcripts, videos, archival documents, or newspaper articles). For instance, they might create analytic tools; evaluate the reliability of their measures, the validity of their indicators, and the evidentiary value of their data; and trace key parts of their project's analytic architecture. The next subsection addresses more systematic forms of coding.

To begin, scholars can move out from their data sources in many directions to create framework documents and analytic tools (or enhance documents and tools they began to create before leaving for the field as discussed in Chapter 3). For instance, they can draw on their sources to develop lists and tables organizing useful background information. They might construct a glossary of important terms and concepts – particularly if they are not operating in their native language. Kapiszewski (2012) developed elaborate constitutional law lexicons in both Spanish and Portuguese to which she repeatedly turned during (and after) fieldwork for her project on the Argentine and Brazilian high courts. Also, scholars could create lists of important actors or agencies or organizations, annotating them with data about how the individuals and groups relate to the dynamics under study and/or drawing out the social and professional networks within which they operate.[8] Alternatively or in addition, scholars could establish timelines or chronologies of events relevant to their topic, e.g., covering the passage of laws or the evolution of policy in a particular area; tracking chains of events leading to a war or the collapse of a governing coalition; or logging meetings and protests in the course of a social movement or rebellion.[9]

---

[8] Scholars interested in understanding the connections among some set of actors (large or small) might begin to lay the groundwork for quantitative or qualitative network analysis (see, e.g., Diani 2002). Many programs exist to execute the former (see www.gmw.rug.nl/~huisman/sna/software.html). The latter uses data garnered through interviews, archival research, and other forms of close, in-depth data collection on a small number of individual actors/nodes in a network to explore how those actors understand the genesis and nature of the ties that bind them to other actors, and thus resembles a close intellectual or cognitive ethnography. EgoNet.QF is a software tool that helps implement this approach. We thank Matthew C. Ingram for this explanation.

[9] Various kinds of software, much of it web-based, exist for creating timelines, for instance, Timeglider (http://timeglider.com), Timeline*Maker* (www.timelinemaker.com), the SIMILE project's Timeline web widget (www.simile-widgets.org/timeline/), and Google Charts (https://developers.google.com/chart/interactive/docs/gallery/timeline). See Hill (1993, 64–69) on the methodological challenges involved in making timelines.

From the moment they arrive in the field, scholars should also be carefully considering their concepts, and evaluating the reliability of their measures and the validity of their indicators. The validity of their interpretations and inferences will rely on how appropriate and effective these building blocks are. They might ask local experts' help in evaluating the relevance of their concepts and face validity of their measures, or in carefully mapping their measures back to their concepts to see how well the former capture the latter (content validation). Engaging in convergent/discriminant validation of alternative measures (i.e., evaluating the association between the scores produced by alternative indicators) can also help scholars to determine whether they have effectively operationalized their key concepts (see Blalock 1979; Carmines and Zeller 1979; King *et al.* 1994; Adcock and Collier 2001; Goertz 2006). Scholars who engage in triangulation (gathering evidence in different forms from different sources) – a principle of good field research – will need to consider what procedures to use in order to aggregate those different forms of evidence to arrive at measures of key concepts. For instance, given their particular research question, should data garnered via in-depth interviews weigh more than, or less than, or simply differently from data amassed in an archive?

Further, scholars should carefully evaluate the evidentiary value of their data as they are collecting them.[10] By systematically assessing their data's strengths, weaknesses, and biases (and those of the sources from which they were drawn), scholars can generate some estimate of their certainty that the data are valid, thus informing how they use them in their analysis. These assessments – and any change in them over time – should likewise be systematically documented. Engaging in these evaluation and documentation processes helps scholars to convey clear assessment of their data in their written products, thereby increasing transparency and helping them to counter a central critique of scholarship based on fieldwork – that it rests on data that are of questionable utility due to their questionable validity.

Field research plays a critical role in drawing valid descriptive inferences, especially when the empirical terrain is uncharted (i.e., few have studied the phenomenon of interest) or contested. Thus, as scholars collect data, they can also use them to map out key parts of their analytic architecture, again

---

[10] Of course, precisely *how* a scholar evaluates the evidentiary value of her data – what "questions" she asks of them – differs from data type to data type, project to project, and scholar to scholar (depending on their epistemological commitments). We offered some strategies for evaluating data in Chapters 5 through 9.

ideally engaging in triangulation to do so. For instance, they might summarize where a set of interview respondents stands on an essential question. Alternatively, they might compare and combine data gathered from multiple sources (through several interviews, focus groups, or trips to the archive, for instance) to develop a descriptive account of a certain episode or interaction – one element of the broader phenomenon under study. Doing so can lead a scholar to discover that she has obtained very different answers to similar and seemingly objective questions across a few interviews, or that some sources systematically left certain facts or factors out of their accounts; either might signal that the topic at hand is more controversial, more sensitive, or less well understood than she originally believed. This, in turn, might lead to an update of the research design (a change in how the outcome or dependent variable will be evaluated or scored, for instance, or which cases will be compared). Alternatively, a scholar may begin to create a typology of the forms the phenomena under study can take.

Another important analytic strategy is to begin to assess what the data suggest about how different cases – individuals, local units (cities, villages, firms), episodes (strikes or public health crises), and so on – vary in particular aspects. Systematically laying out such information in one or more matrices of cases and variables can reveal gaps and omissions while it is still convenient to make a follow-up inquiry.[11] Presenting the data in such matrices can also facilitate comparison, and help scholars to identify relevant variation. This, again, may potentially lead to adjustments in their research design, perhaps even shifting the unit of analysis.

Consider a project concerning political participation, and in particular urban residents' contact with members of the city council. At the outset, a scholar envisions the unit of analysis to be the individual citizen, and the dependent variable to be the number of contacts a citizen had in the past year with any city council member. In order to identify variation on her dependent variable and a few potential independent variables, the researcher builds a micro-level matrix with a row for each individual in her study, and columns for some of the categories on which information was gathered through interviews: age, sex, partisan affiliation, household income, children's school, civic memberships, and contacting (see Table 10.1). The first four columns show no obvious relationship with the outcome of interest. But sorting the

---

[11] These data matrices can also be quite usefully employed *prior* to embarking on field research to envision key types of variation and develop one's research design. We are indebted to Naomi Levy for the original version of this example.

Table 10.1 Sample micro-level matrix

	Age	Sex	Party ID	Annual household income	Children's school	Civic memberships	Number of contacts with city council members / year
Interviewee 3	42	M	Dem	$37k	Lincoln High School	International Order of Odd Fellows	22
Interviewee 6	32	F	Rep	$76k	N/A (child in day care)	Realtors Council	14
Interviewee 2	41	F	Rep	$69k	St. Mary's Junior High	Downtown Chamber of Commerce	10
Interviewee 5	52	M	None	$33k	Lincoln High School	Church choir	7
Interviewee 4	29	F	Dem	Refused	N/A (no kids)	None	2
Interviewee 7	47	M	None	$101k	East Lake Elementary School	None	1
Interviewee 1	56	F	None	$84k	La Follette Elementary School	Symphony Board of Directors, Book Club	0

table by the dependent variable brings to light possible relationships at levels of analysis higher than the individual. Two of the citizens have children attending the same public high school, and two others are both members of city business associations. This raises the possibility that organizational affiliations, rather than individual-level demographic characteristics, may account for contacting. This discovery suggests a possible shift in the unit of analysis from "individual" to "organization," the construction of meso-level matrices organized around school and associational type, and the gathering of further organization-level information (perhaps examining issues on which the schools or business groups have actively called for city council help, for instance).

Of course, similar types of adjustments might be made in a quantitative analysis. A scholar studying presidential politics in Central and Eastern Europe since the transition to democracy, for instance, might begin her inquiry expecting the unit of analysis to be a president (or presidential administration). Discovering significant heterogeneity with respect to dynamics during a single presidential administration, however, would recommend a shift in the unit of analysis from "president" to "president-year." Drawing on all of the strategies suggested in this sub-section, we hope our main point is clear: there are many ways in which scholars can get in dialogue with their data, and begin to learn from them, while they are in the field collecting them.

Coding qualitative data sources

Coding qualitative sources essentially entails reducing many words to fewer words, or converting words to numbers, with the goal of identifying patterns and trends. The more informal types of coding mentioned in the previous subsection – digesting, processing, and making qualitative data more accessible – might be most useful earlier in a scholar's time in the field while she is still nailing down the contours of the project, confirming she is on track, and beginning to identify trends. The more formal or systematic coding that we discuss here, and computer-assisted coding in particular, is more profitably carried out once scholars have their analytic framework relatively well developed, since a great deal of thinking and analyzing must happen *before* such programs can be effectively employed. As such, using such programs maximally – to help with coding – while in the field may be inadvisable for scholars doing just a few weeks or a month of fieldwork. Nonetheless, even for those scholars, such programs can be useful more minimally for data management purposes. While we also briefly touch on techniques for processing quantitative data, given the wealth of literature in political science that examines coding, assembling, and cleaning quantitative datasets, we focus on how scholars can process their qualitative data sources while in the field.

Scholars hailing from different epistemological traditions may think differently about coding qualitative data sources, and follow different procedures. Scholars in the interpretive tradition, for instance, may question whether evidence is embedded in text in an objectively identifiable way, and may believe that any interpretation of a text is just one of many possible interpretations (Wesley 2014, 3–4). Likewise, they may prefer a more holistic approach to processing qualitative data. Rather than simply parsing, categorizing, or sorting, they may focus on *how* categories are constructed, excavating divergences in meanings and considering how concepts are constituted differently by different people at different times, thereby complicating the notions of categorization and calling into question the possibility of neat counting. More positivist scholars may hold that words and concepts can be identified and counted, and that such quantification is a meaningful representation of the (relatively straightforward and comprehensible) content of the qualitative data source at hand. We hope all kinds of scholars will find the suggestions we offer here directly applicable to their research, or will be able to think of possible analogues in their own work.

As noted previously, scholars from any epistemological tradition can begin to analyze their qualitative sources from the day they begin to collect them – by reading through them (or listening to them, or viewing them), and taking notes. They may make note of the new information, important ideas, useful examples, or revealing quotations the sources contain; code for key words and concepts, noting how words are being used and what ideas or dynamics are repeated or, conversely, missing altogether; quantify qualitative information; or register their reactions to particular pieces of data (why is it relevant? how does it fit?) and to each source as a whole (Gibbs 2007, 35–57; Emerson, Fretz, and Shaw 2011). As scholars learn more about the field context, the types of ideas they trace and codes they assign will likely change – and they should reflect on what those changes suggest for their analysis and argument.

Taking these steps while gathering material in the field is more efficient (and less daunting) than poring through pages and pages of interview transcripts, or hours of video, months later. It can also spark sharp insights and expose connections between sources and among pieces of information, facilitating intellectual progress. As they carry out these tasks, scholars may also develop additional analytic strategies and tools to identify patterns or trends in the data and sources. For instance, they might develop a framework for processing and systematizing ethnographic observations into a series of analytic portraits, or create a preliminary index or concordance of particular words, concepts, or events and begin to identify patterns in the codes (Gibbs 2007, 73–89).

We offer a few examples. Using paper and pencil (as per the rules of the archive in which she was working), a researcher studying the effect of the media on political activism in Latin America systematically coded every tenth issue of a major national newspaper in each country under study for any information concerning activism, repression (or a relenting thereof), and nine categories of "taboo content."[12] Another scholar studying presidential campaign strategies in Latin America through television advertisements began to code the 59 hours of tape he collected in the field on various parameters including the objective, form, style, and temporal focus of each advertisement.[13] Both scholars conducted inter-coder reliability checks and kept detailed notes regarding their coding decisions.[14]

When appropriate and desired, scholars may code qualitative sources using quantitative or qualitative content analysis.[15] Quantitative content analysis, which has a longer tradition (see, e.g., Holsti 1969), is "a systematic, replicable technique for compressing many words of text into fewer content categories based on explicit rules of coding," or, more briefly, "a research technique for the objective, systematic and quantitative description of the manifest content of communication" (Berelson 1952, 74). Scholars can use quantitative content analysis to analyze both what is said and how it is said in a particular source, at the level of word, theme, or "item of communication" (i.e., article, speech, etc.). At its most basic, quantitative content analysis groups words and phrases into semantic categories and counts word frequencies, semantic frequencies, and the frequency of coding categories.[16] Qualitative content analysis identifies ideas or themes by analyzing manifest and latent content, and other formal aspects and features of text (Mayring 2000, 4). Techniques for systematic

---

[12] Interview, DK-5, July 31, 2012.   [13] Interview, DK-3, July 27, 2012.

[14] For a useful discussion of using inter-reliability checks to validate conclusions based on interview transcripts, see Kurasaki (2000).

[15] See the article symposium organized by Herrera and Braumoeller (2004) for an enlightening comparison of content analysis and discourse analysis.

[16] Note that the technique has evolved considerably, and can now do much more than quantify (see, e.g., Neuendorf 2001; Krippendorff 2003; Franzosi 2008). Stockmann (2010) offers a useful discussion of using content analysis to analyze media content.

qualitative content analysis of texts (or qualitative document analysis, QDA) have been developed since the early 1980s (Mayring 2000, 1).

Over time, multiple types of computer software have been created that can assist with quantitative or qualitative content analysis – that is, that can help scholars to organize and manage, and systematically code and analyze textual data. Given that quantitative content analysis is the older tradition, many more software programs are available to assist with it (see, e.g., Skalski 2002, 225–226, for a discussion and list). Since the late 1980s, various computer-assisted qualitative data analysis software (CAQDAS) packages have also been developed to support textual interpretation, for instance Atlas.TI, HyperRESEARCH, MAXqda, NVivo, NUD*IST, QDA Miner, and win-MAX.[17] Such programs have moved far beyond their "code and retrieve" origins to allow for the operationalization of complex procedures and approaches.[18] A growing literature on their use, and an increasing number of web-based resources[19] and web-based training sessions,[20] are becoming available.[21]

Field researchers considering content analysis should evaluate the potential benefits and limitations of the available techniques and software far in advance of fieldwork. It may only be possible to procure their preferred software in advance of leaving for the field, and learning to use it may be time-consuming. The literature on CAQDAS considers a range of issues related to using automated content analysis, and the costs and benefits of employing computer-assisted coding (see, e.g., Barry 1998; Fielding and Lee 1998; Bourdon 2002; Gibbs *et al.* 2002; Lu and Shulman 2008); the strengths and weaknesses of different CAQDAS programs and how to choose among them (see, e.g., Barry 1998; Bong 2002; Thompson 2002; Gibbs 2007; Lewins

---

[17] Beyond these off-the-shelf programs, open-source web-based suites of tools are also being developed, such as the Coding Analysis Toolkit (CAT), a free service of the Qualitative Data Analysis Program (QDAP) hosted by the University of Pittsburgh's University Center for Social and Urban Research and the University of Massachusetts, Amherst's College of Social and Behavioral Sciences (www.umass.edu/qdap/). The Public Comment Analysis Toolkit (PCAT, http://pcat.qdap.net/about.aspx), a cloud computing platform, facilitates web-based collaborative text analysis and is particularly good at analyzing and categorizing small pieces of text (such as electronic comments); more generally, see the eRulemaking Research Group at the University of Massachusetts, Amherst (http://people.umass.edu/stu/eRulemaking/index.html).

[18] Fielding and Lee (1998, 199, 202) and Gibbs, Friese, and Mangabeira (2002) discuss the evolution of these programs. See also Mangabeira, Lee, and Fielding (2004).

[19] See, e.g., http://onlineqda.hud.ac.uk/Step_by_step_software/index.php.

[20] See, e.g., http://www.qsrinternational.com/training-and-events.aspx.

[21] In addition, the National Science Foundation has sponsored workshops to introduce political scientists to text analysis (see, e.g., Tools for Text – http://toolsfortext.wordpress.com/ – at the University of Washington).

and Silver 2007); guidelines for use (e.g., Kelle 1995; Mayring 2000; Seale 2002; Lewins and Silver 2007; Hermann 2008); the relative merits of quantitative vs. qualitative content analysis (e.g., Mayring 2000); whether data produced via such analysis meets assumptions for statistical analysis of data; and how to pair CAQDAS software with other tools, such as geographical information systems (GIS) (Fielding and Cisneros-Puebla 2009).

Once they are in the field, scholars can begin to think more specifically about ways to use the software. The potential of qualitative data analysis software programs – in particular whether CAQDAS software programs are really only suited for data management or can also help scholars to interpret texts, examine relationships among concepts in a text,[22] and produce qualitative analysis (Gibbs 2007) – continues to be debated. For some scholars, reading the excerpts produced as output by such programs (bits of interview transcript or full archival documents) can be unsettling. Furthermore, if the requested themes or codes overlap, certain points, passages, or paragraphs may be repeated in the output, amplifying their apparent importance inappropriately. Moreover, even the strongest proponents of such programs hold that they ultimately support rather than replace scholars' direct interaction with text (Mayring 2000, 18), and should be understood as analytic resources or tools to be selected and employed once scholars have identified their approach to and procedures for analysis (Fielding and Lee 2002, 197). As such, for scholars who do use these programs, those who are in the field for shorter periods of time may be more likely to use them more minimally to help organize the material they are amassing and creating (e.g., memos and notes),[23] while those on longer field stays may be more likely to use them more extensively to conduct content analysis (or textual analysis) and manipulate, search, and report on coded text (Gibbs *et al.* 2002, 11–12).

For scholars with more positivist leanings, a key to successful content analysis is that it be transparently rule-guided, with clearly defined coding categories and carefully established coding criteria. Evaluating the reliability of coding is also important – both its *stability* (the extent to which they can consistently re-code the same data in the same way over time) and its

---

[22] Thompson (2002) argues strongly against the idea that the software can be used for this purpose.

[23] Chapter 3 discusses other organizational techniques. Examples of workflow applications include database programs (e.g., Access); bibliographic software (e.g., EndNote, Zotero, and Sente [Mac only]); and programs that manage digital files and facilitate the writing process (e.g., Scrivener and DEVONthink [Mac only]). Programs such as DMP Tool help researchers generate data management plans such as those increasingly required by funding agencies like the National Science Foundation and the National Institutes of Health. See also Healy's useful discussion (www.kieranhealy.org/files/misc/workflow-apps.pdf), and Long (2008) on organizing workflow around quantitative analysis.

reproducibility (the degree to which different people employing the same coding scheme code particular pieces of text in the same category) – given that the generalizability of the conclusions drawn from content analysis depends in great part on its reliability. Researchers should also try to assess the *accuracy* of their coding – the extent to which the classification of a text corresponds to a standard or norm statistically.[24] More interpretive scholars may see things quite differently. For them, the notion of coding being "accurate" makes little sense, as the ideas that emerge as information is collected in the field are by definition constituted, contested, and multi-valent. For all scholars, the reflective evaluation of data that they carry out as collection proceeds should be carefully documented, as the specifics will likely fade from their memories long before they return to their home institutions.

Scholars collecting quantitative data will also want to take steps to increase their accessibility and to understand them better. For instance, survey researchers may enter responses into a database as the questionnaires come in and, ultimately, use tools such as the online Survey Documentation and Analysis (SDA) system, the online data analysis system created by Dataverse, R, Stata, or SPSS to identify substantive trends in the data. Cleaning, reformatting, and standardizing survey data in the field can help scholars to identify problems with survey administration, and allow them to run potentially illuminating descriptive statistics and start to see what important variables look like. Time permitting, scholars may even begin to explore the relationships among critical variables through frequency tables, histograms, cross-tabulations, bivariate scatterplots and the like, or may run some preliminary analyses on a random subset of the data. What the scholar sees and learns can have implications for how they carry out the rest of the data-collection process.

Creating a dialogue with one's fieldwork and data in these ways is undoubtedly thought- and time-consuming. For more than one scholar we interviewed, however, doing so became an enjoyable – even exciting – activity.[25] No matter what process researchers choose to employ in order to dig into their data, doing so in the field gives them an opportunity to further investigate ideas or dynamics they realize they do not understand, make helpful revisions to their research design, and begin to think about their

---

[24] www.colostate.edu/Depts/WritingCenter/references/research/content/page2.htm, accessed July 8, 2012.

[25] Interviews, DK-13, August 8, 2012; DK-14, August 10, 2012.

data in a more integrated, holistic manner. That is, as scholars organize, examine, code, and compare their data, and consider the recurrent or aberrant observations, categories, or themes they observe (and what is absent), they can begin to reflect on what questions the evidence raises that might complicate their analytical framework, which data seem most applicable to each component of the analysis, and how well their initial findings or insights relate to the middle-range questions posed in the study, as well as the broader questions that motivate it. Writing in the field can help them to do all of these things even more efficiently and effectively.

Writing and presenting work-in-progress

During short field research trips, coding, processing, and evaluating data may be all that time allows. But, particularly on longer field-stays, researchers may have the opportunity for more advanced analysis. Beginning to think synthetically across the project, bringing together different strands of evidence, and generating or developing their arguments while in the field context can help scholars to motivate, organize, and discipline their work. For instance, they might ask themselves some of these partially overlapping questions: How well do the data fit with – or how thoroughly do they contradict – hypotheses or arguments developed before entering the field (or since arrival)? What rival arguments do they refute – or support? Have the causal mechanisms underlying long-standing or emerging hypotheses and arguments been identified, and do observed causal processes line up with the hypotheses? Have the observable implications of hypotheses and causal mechanisms been assessed? If scholars are using process tracing, what are process tracing tests revealing about the arguments (see, e.g., Falleti and Lynch 2009; Bennett 2010; Collier, Brady, and Seawright 2010, 184–196; Gerring 2010)? Stepping back from the field helps scholars to select the appropriate analytic tools and begin to employ them to develop broader themes and arguments.

Further, and particularly if scholars can engage in the type of analysis just mentioned, it can be extremely beneficial to put pen to paper, or fingers to keyboard, and begin to write.[26] The idea of writing in the field may sound exciting to some – a way to mark progress. For others it may inspire trepidation. For all parties, we hasten to emphasize that writing can take

---

[26] Indeed, funders sometimes require some accounting of the research process or narrative report.

many forms, not all of which are meant for wide circulation. For example, researchers may find it useful to compose memos, even just to themselves, that link together some of their observations, or develop parts of the emerging story (or stories). They might summarize one or more cases (no matter what "case" means for them) or compose short narratives analyzing particularly telling episodes or anecdotes the research has unearthed.

Beginning to write in the field – starting to integrate the information scholars are gathering into their evolving analytic framework – forces them to think through how to draw descriptive and causal inferences. Of the many examples they have of a particular phenomenon, which one or two are the most illustrative, meriting discussion in detail? How can different forms of evidence be brought to bear simultaneously as they seek to make particular points? Precisely how (by what logic) do elements of their data – passages from interviews, constitutional clauses, experimental results, and the like – support their arguments, contradict them, or support rival accounts? And how can those connections be clearly expressed in writing?[27] Taking early stabs at drawing such analytic maps in the field will give scholars a leg up when it comes time to fully develop and formalize their descriptions and explanations.

As we have noted, in addition to beginning to write out their analysis, scholars should also compose detailed summaries of their research procedures, and make some initial attempts to articulate how their fieldwork led them to the descriptive and causal inferences they have drawn and to their analysis as a whole. Clearly and completely documenting – and justifying – the context in which data were collected, the choices made while collecting them (for instance, concerning case selection, sampling of interview respondents, data-capture strategies, etc.), and the procedures used to do so are critical elements of research transparency. Scholars can also begin to write out clear descriptions of the contributions field research made during each phase of the research cycle – for instance, documenting the procedures they used to measure variables, determine the validity of measures, and develop and test hypotheses. Such documentation is most easily and effectively produced in the field rather than months later when the details of such choices have become cloudy. That is, the benefits of field research are more present – and more easily identified and described – when scholars are in

---

[27] Scholars whose ability to make these connections clearly is constrained by word limits dictated by the venues in which they wish to publish (as is often the case for qualitative scholars) might consider adopting active citation; see Moravcsik (2010, 2013) and Elman and Kapiszewski (2013).

the field than at any other moment. Being transparent in these ways, we submit, is an important principle of good field research.

Engaging in the kind of higher-order, synthetic and critical reflection necessary to write about these issues is intellectually challenging and can also be nerve-wracking (although it can be equally nerve-wracking to avoid doing so). Hovering above the detailed information being collected and the knowledge being built – gaining sufficient perspective on the project to think and write coherently about the big picture (what we have referred to as "the forest") – is hard. Doing so likely requires scholars to set aside time in their calendar and grant themselves permission to take a break from the regular business of data gathering. Initial gear-grinding notwithstanding, delving into this process early in field research and returning to it regularly can result in it becoming a familiar and helpful task, rather than a chore that gets put off until it is too late for it to shape day-to-day decisions about data collection.

Researchers often share their work-in-progress with others, and even formally present it, while in the field. There are many different ways to share one's research, and each can provide critical motivation as well as feedback. For instance, scholars can engage in informal discussions with the individuals and communities who participated in the study, and investigate ways to present their analysis and writing (even in preliminary and imperfect form) to them. Providing study participants (interview subjects, local research assistants) with an opportunity to interpret and react to one's analysis before it is written up and published can be intimidating, as they may resist or challenge one's interpretations. It is important to bear in mind that such disagreement does not necessarily mean that the scholar misunderstood or is wrong. Scholars should also guard against such preliminary discussions leading to their "cooptation" or discouraging them from making critical statements. As Schram and Caterino (2004, 20) note, scholars can and should maintain "a powerful critical connectedness," continuing to think analytically while being fully engaged. Yet researchers certainly learn from such dialogues. Including these other voices in their final research products (using attributive tags or describing the types of people or communities who presented these views), candidly acknowledging how their and their subjects' interpretations of the same dynamics or phenomena were in tension or conflict, can be very enlightening for readers.

Graduate students may share their evolving ideas about their analysis with their dissertation advisors, perhaps sending periodic "missives from the field" (a few paragraphs or several pages in length) describing how the research is progressing and highlighting questions and concerns. More advanced researchers may present preliminary versions of their ideas and findings to academics based at local institutions, or other scholars who have worked on the same kinds of topics or materials. The researcher's host institution (if she has one), or other local universities, think-tanks, or discussion groups, can also provide fora in which to make presentations and bounce ideas off fellow researchers and others who are in a good position to provide reactions and insights. Finally, a scholar might write up versions of her work to present at workshops or conferences, or to submit to a research institute as a working paper or to a journal as a research note. All of this has the great benefit of pushing the researcher to spell out – in concrete terms and complete sentences – the ideas that are taking shape in her head. Moreover, signaling to advisors or colleagues that progress is being made may deepen their interest in and support for the project. Most importantly, feedback received in response is timely: the researcher is still in a position to make good use of it in adjusting the direction of her field research as necessary.

Trouble-shooting and retooling

A field research project in which everything runs according to plan, without unexpected twists, turns, and moments of agonizing self-doubt, is a rare occurrence. Rather, it is common for things to go awry in ways small and large. While plenty can go wrong logistically and operationally when one is living and working in an unfamiliar environment, we focus here on some common intellectual and analytic forms of trouble that can crop up in one's research. Practically every researcher adjusts some aspect of her project in the field: very few researchers execute to a "T" the project they described in their dissertation prospectus or mapped out in a grant application prior to leaving their home institution. Scholars making minor adjustments yet still operating within the main framework of the original research design should discuss such changes with colleagues, carefully consider their implications for other aspects of the project and for the claims they ultimately hope to make, fully document the contours and justification for each change, and seek to keep their data-collection plan in line with their evolving design choices.

While the utility of modifying some aspect of their project dawns on some researchers gradually, for others the need for minor changes jumps right out. Consider a project one of our interview respondents described, concerning education in post-conflict Bosnia and Croatia. In Bosnia, the researcher studied schools in six towns that varied with regard to type of school curricula and population demographics (two towns were mono-ethnic, two were evenly divided between ethnicities, and two were dominated by one ethnicity but had a sizable population of the other). When the scholar arrived in Croatia, however, she realized that towns with parallel population demographics did not exist: Croatia was mostly Croat with pockets of Serbs. Consequently, she needed to build her sampling frame differently in Croatia in order to develop a similar comparison. She oversampled towns with many Serbs (so they would not be missed in the sample), and chose one with a large population of Italians that had both a Croat-language school and an Italian-language school (in order to compare the experiences, across the two contexts, of Croats attending schools in which the language of instruction was not their own).[28]

Sometimes researchers experience disruptions that seem more threatening to their project and daunting to resolve, however. They may have the sensation, as they begin to collect data in the field, that things are quite different from what they expected, and that their prior assumptions are wrong. They may encounter major obstacles to collecting data they believed would be readily obtainable. Knowledgeable interviewees might laugh at the ideas they have developed and come to cherish about the politics of the locality. In other words, scholars might feel as if their project is "broken." As notes of disillusionment start to creep into their thinking, alternative research topics may begin to look more appealing than the one they had in mind when they set out.

Most often these or other forms of dissonance and self-questioning do not signal a research crisis. What appear to be big problems can actually be big opportunities to rethink particular aspects of a project or even the theoretical framework. While on rare occasions field researchers have abandoned their project *in toto*, mid-stream, and continued with an entirely new question and theoretical framework, more commonly relatively small adjustments suffice to get a project that seems derailed back on track. Things often work themselves out as researchers learn more, speak with a broader assortment of people, identify different routes to the kind of data they need, and become more comfortable in and knowledgeable of the field setting. Of course, scholars should not cling intransigently to an unworkable plan. As we have emphasized, fieldwork often entails a good deal of iteration, and flexible discipline is a key principle of good field research. Significant changes

---

[28] Interviews, DK-6, August 1 and 30, 2012.

sometimes do need to be made. Nonetheless, engaging in incremental modifications to one's project first, setting (and sticking to) reasonable deadlines for resolving difficulties before contemplating large-scale alterations, and extensively considering all aspects of such changes before making them, are good rules of thumb.

As scholars consider what to do, staying on an even keel and remaining patient (but avoiding paralysis) are important. They should seek to carefully diagnose the problem and what is causing it, and do their best to ensure that the "fix" under consideration addresses the problem instead of making things worse. We cannot overestimate the importance of *talking with others* – trusted peers, advisors, local scholars, or whoever else could help – while seeking to identify the source of the problem and the optimal fix. No matter what challenge one is facing, many other researchers have faced comparable problems and experienced similar kinds of uneasiness and self-doubt, and most have found ways to amend their projects productively. Clearly articulating the problem and discussing it with other academics can often lead researchers to hit upon a solution themselves.

The kinds of problems that political scientists generally encounter in field research often fall into particular categories. We identify a critical set in Table 10.2. The first type of problem is as fundamental a challenge as one is likely to face: the researcher cannot answer her question. On the one hand, the root cause of the problem may be practical, involving problems obtaining needed data. Perhaps the library containing an essential collection just closed for a year of renovations. Or the newspaper back-files she planned to scour are only spottily available. Or she has trouble meeting the kinds of people she planned to interview. Or the government ministry in which she hoped to conduct extensive inquiries brusquely rejected her overtures.

If access to data is the problem, a patient strategy of building the kinds of networks and trust that can open the right doors, as discussed in previous chapters, may be the fix. If the sources being sought are truly beyond reach, or at least not available within a workable time-frame, the scholar should carefully investigate the kinds of information that *are* available, and determine what sorts of substitutions will work. For example, if the initial plan was to obtain finely detailed original reports from local officials, perhaps less detailed provincial-level summaries or yearbooks would suffice.[29]

---

[29] Changes in data-collection technique can also occur because scholars realize that something they did not expect to be able to access *is* available. A scholar studying presidential campaign strategies in Latin

Table 10.2 Trouble-shooting and retooling

Problem	Possible causes	Possible fixes	Should I change my topic?
I can't answer the question	1 Inability to obtain necessary data/information	Explore alternative approaches to gathering the data, or alternative types of data	Only if all approaches would produce wholly inadequate data
	2 Unanswerable or poorly specified question	Recast, tighten, or sharpen the research question	Only if no re-specification of the question works
I'm surprised by the answer, or my hypotheses seem wrong	1 Researcher is not getting the full story	Employ strategies to deepen and broaden information gathering	Only if no adequate avenue to gather information opens
	2 Initial hypotheses *were* wrong	Develop / return to alternative hypotheses and/or work with the new direction in which findings are pointing	Only if nothing of value can be gained from pursuing the question in its current framing
	3 Theories in which the project is framed are poorly suited to the subject	Seek to reframe the topic within a different theoretical approach	Only if every effort to reframe topic is unsuccessful
I'm losing interest in my project	1 Root problem is one of the above conditions	(See above)	
	2 Project is fine but researcher is bored or burned out	Take a break, streamline the work flow, and/or re-motivate	No
	3 Research question is out of step with empirical realities	Return to original impetus behind the project; reformulate research question	Only if recasting project is unsuccessful

Source: adapted from a table presented by Julia F. Lynch in the modules on field research at the IQMR.

Researchers may also replace data-collection techniques that have proven suboptimal. One strategy is to move away from interviewing toward the use of more site-intensive methods. For instance, one of our respondents who was studying informal workers in Latin America began data collection by interviewing leaders of street vending organizations with a formal protocol of questions derived from the literature on the informal economy. Recognizing that the terms she was using did not apply to street vendors' reality, meaning that continuing with those interviews would produce superficial and likely misleading data, she instead initiated more free-wheeling conversations with vendors, ultimately engaging in something more closely resembling participant observation.[30]

On the other hand, it is possible that the reason why a scholar cannot answer his research question is because the question itself is poorly specified. Perhaps the question has not been asked in a way that it can be answered. Or perhaps the variables inherent in the question have not been operationalized in a way that provides a workable roadmap for collecting the kind of data that are needed to answer the question. If so, then on the basis of the researcher's growing familiarity with the field site, and in consultation with peers and advisors, she may be able to recast, tighten, or sharpen the research question.

Another form of problem arises when the researcher has begun to develop an answer to his question, but that answer brings challenges of its own – surprising him, or suggesting that his original hypotheses were wrong. This outcome could result from a few conditions. The researcher may not yet have dug deep enough – interviewed sufficient numbers of people, found the right documents – to get the full story. If he believes this may be the cause of the problem, persisting and drilling through the surface will help him to accurately assess the plausibility of his original hypotheses. Alternatively, the researcher may not have been looking at or thinking about the topic in the most intellectually productive way – or may simply not have known enough about it – preventing him from developing the optimal research design. While this may feel like a setback, it is critical that the scholar not turn a blind eye to evidence that suggests that his hypotheses are wrong. The goal, after all, is to develop a valid answer to the research question.

America was unexpectedly able to access full sets of videos of candidate advertisements from multiple past elections, allowing him to extend the temporal scope of his project (interview, DK-3, July 27, 2012).

[30] Interview, DK-1, July 20, 2012.

Discovering information that falsifies initial hypotheses and suggests different explanatory leads to pursue constitutes an exciting step toward that end. A final possibility is that not just a researcher's hypotheses, but the theories around which he designed his study, have turned out to fit poorly. If he decides this is the crux of the problem, he may need to engage in a farther-reaching overhaul of the project, reframing the topic within a different theoretical approach.

A final type of challenge, which may be more likely to occur during longer field trips, arises when scholars lose interest in or become detached from their project. Again, this challenge can have multiple causes. It may stem from one of the obstacles discussed above (and may thus be solvable through the steps we just outlined). Or it could be that the project is fine but the researcher is burned out. What may help in this situation is for the researcher to take a break from the project and allow herself to come back refreshed and remotivated. Most seriously, this challenge could spring from a deep-rooted dissatisfaction with the research question, or the researcher discovering that the way in which he has been looking at things is out of step with the empirical realities he is finding.

Under these conditions, a searching, top-to-bottom reconsideration of the project – though not necessarily a radical change of topic – may be called for. The scholar might start by returning to the original impetus behind the project and seeking to reformulate the research question in a way that still draws on that original motivation but fits better with the reality he has found in the field. For example, Bleck initially focused her dissertation research on evaluating the effect faith-based versus secular education had on voting behavior. However, she soon realized that the ways in which people thought about political participation were quite different from how she had theorized the outcome: a good deal of political mobilization was occurring outside of voting. As a result, she broadened her research question and ultimately included questions about non-electoral forms of political behavior in her survey and interviews.[31]

In sum, when faced with what seems like a research crisis in the field, we suggest scholars take the following steps: identify the type of problem that has arisen, pinpoint its root causes, and then cope with it in a way that is direct, reflective, and constructive. Of course, the trouble that any

---

[31] Recounted by Jaimie Bleck in a presentation entitled "Education, citizenship and democracy in Mali" at Indiana University on October 3, 2013.

given researcher (or his or her students) encounters in the field may not precisely match one of the three categories we have outlined. Nonetheless, trouble-shooting problems that arise in the field *while still in the field* offers scholars an opportunity to work through important conceptual, inferential, or theoretical issues while they can still modify data collection to support their revised project.

Just as stasis or rigidity are rarely the solution when significant problems are encountered, throwing the project out and starting over from scratch are likely called for in only a very limited set of circumstances: as readers will have noted, the answer to the question posed in the final column of Table 10.2 – "Should I change my topic?" – is *never* a simple "yes." Generally one is best off pursuing a re-worked or considerably adjusted version of the planned project – as the multiple ideas in the "possible fixes" column attending each problem suggest. We hasten to emphasize that the fact that almost all scholars' projects change *does not mean* that planning should be abandoned! In fact, having a detailed plan can help scholars to diagnose precisely what has gone wrong where, which facet or facets of the project need to be modified to address the problem, and what other parts of the project that "fix" might affect.[32]

Assessing progress: when is enough enough?

No matter whether they are on a fieldwork trip of a week's duration, or one that extends into many months, scholars can lose perspective on the project as a whole, and lapse into a state of single-minded focus on gathering information and resolving the challenges that attend that quest. We might term this kind of tunnel vision "field goggles." For instance, field researchers might continue to gather more and more information of the same kind – conducting more interviews, grabbing more archival documents, or scanning more newspaper articles – even if the information thereby gained is redundant or only marginally concerns the topic or concepts on which the project focuses. Or they might track down an infinite series of leads and contacts, whether or not they contribute tangibly to the project, and regardless of whether they will have time to interact with them. Alternatively, they may become fixated on the micro-level problems, hassles, and challenges of the

---

[32] Interview, DK-13, August 8, 2012.

data-accumulation process, disregarding larger questions – for instance, concerning the uses to which the laboriously collected data will be put.

Such behavior can go hand-in-hand with other problems: a sense of burnout or ennui; feeling adrift and disconnected from one's advisor, colleagues, or collaborators; and an aversion to thinking about where the project as a whole stands and what will happen after returning from the field. Such issues can be exacerbated by other complicating factors, such as trouble with housing or funding, or disruption in one's family or personal relationships. While it is natural (and beneficial) to become immersed in fieldwork and engaged with the context, slipping into less-than-fully focused research for long periods poses real dangers. Getting into a data-collection rut can mean squandered opportunities and wasted time, and may spell trouble later if the heaps of data the researcher is tirelessly collecting ultimately do not help him to answer his question or adjudicate among rival arguments.

Of course, there is no way to avoid getting absorbed at points in what we have called "the trees" – the minutiae of data collection and digestion. Resolving lingering data-access problems, and making micro-level analytic progress (e.g., by working through a long list of newspaper articles that one has sampled, or trying to piece together every minute detail of a particular event from a series of sources) are important. Indeed, well-reasoned decisions and small victories on this level are the stuff of "good days" during field research. But researchers need to keep these tasks in perspective. The activities one carries out in the field are, after all, a means to an end, not an end in themselves. The execution of such tasks needs to remain connected with "the forest" – the overall project and the broader goal of answering the core questions under investigation. Researchers should continually seek to assess how close they are to clearly envisaging, and to having the necessary support for, the answers to their questions and the claims they wish to make.

But how can such assessments be made? How can scholars know when they can confidently answer "Yes!" to the perennial question, "Have I collected enough data?"[33] The best way to keep tabs on headway is to evaluate progress periodically at *both* the micro and macro levels. For instance, continuing to develop and update their initial data-collection plan (discussed in Chapter 3) as fieldwork progresses – consistently seeking to

---

[33] Of course, not all field research is infinitely open-ended. For many scholars, circumstances – the fact that they can only be away from family for so long, or grant or visa limitations – will dictate when they are finished. These scholars face a somewhat different problem: developing and writing up their project based on the data they were able to gather during what may have been a circumscribed period of time in the field.

affirm the connections, big and small, between data collection and analysis on the one hand, and the core elements of the project on the other – can help scholars assess progress and keep research on track. By periodically tallying up what information has been collected and comparing it with the current list of "items to get," researchers can determine whether enough data have been gathered, from sufficiently different sources, on all relevant variables, causal mechanisms, and causal processes, so that each can be reliably and validly measured or evaluated across cases.

Assessments concerning whether the researcher has collected sufficient appropriate data to meet his analytic needs must be made in relation to the specifics of a given project.[34] Nonetheless, we suggest a few pointers. First, it can be useful for a scholar to carefully distinguish between data he absolutely must collect in order to answer his question effectively, and data it would be beneficial to have but that, in a pinch, he could do without – because they are not critical to measuring or assessing his key variables, concepts, ideas, or main hypotheses, or substantiating his central argument. Second, of those critical data, scholars should determine which are only available in the field site and which might be found elsewhere (on the web, in reference libraries that are accessible from their home institution, etc.). As we have noted elsewhere, as more and more material is placed online, the boundaries of what information can only be obtained through field research are shifting.

Scholars should also keep in mind that they have several options if they discover that they are missing crucial data after they return to their home institution. They can dig and re-dig through the materials they collected to see whether some data or data sources, looked at in a slightly different way from how they had envisioned, could fill in any lacunae that they identify. They can also double check whether access to the missing data is possible from home. They might also ask their former research assistants or other local contacts for help. For example, after Kapiszewski returned to the United States from dissertation research, she realized that she needed statistics on the Brazilian Supreme Court's case load that she had neglected to collect while in the field. A Supreme Court clerk with whom she had spoken various times found all the data for her and sent them to her electronically. Read asked an undergraduate from his home institution, who happened to

---

[34] Indeed, for some projects it is quite obvious when data collection is complete; the scholar seeking to collect all of the videos showing presidential candidates' advertisements in previous elections, for instance, had a list of all the advertisements, making it patently obvious when he had collected the final video (interview, DK-3, July 27, 2012).

be living in Taipei for language study, to spend a morning in the National Taiwan Library imaging pages of figures that he had come to realize he needed. Further, the possibility of going back into the field should not be dismissed. Taking a quick, targeted trip (perhaps as a junior faculty member converting a dissertation project into a book) some time after one's main forays can be extremely productive. One scholar we interviewed, for instance, was unable to complete his research on presidential elections because the final contest in one of his country-cases went into an unanticipated second round; he did follow-up research, however, when he attended an international conference in that country a year after returning from his main research trip.[35] If all else fails, scholars may be able to work around missing information, perhaps acknowledging the gap in their write-up but demonstrating that they are nonetheless able to make their points or advance their argument.

If checking data-collection progress against their data-collection plan can help scholars assess where they stand with respect to the trees, additional steps are needed to determine where they stand with respect to the forest. Engaging in the kinds of analysis and writing discussed above – digesting and analyzing data as they come in, *thinking* about them, and placing them within the project's analytic architecture – can help scholars to evaluate their progress on the more macro level. They may ask themselves, do I have the data to evaluate my initial hypotheses, any new hypotheses I developed, and alternative or competing hypotheses? Have I developed a clear, succinct, and well-supported argument? If I were to start writing now, what would be the organization of my book or dissertation, or the subheadings of my article or chapter? Do I have sufficient information to flesh out those chapters or sections? Critically reflecting on – and perhaps writing out – the answers to these kinds of questions can help researchers to calculate what else needs to be done in order to wrap up field research.

Depending on the kind of project, other forms of self-assessment may be appropriate. For exploratory modes of field research in which the purpose is to lay the groundwork for a future project rather than to answer a specific research question, for instance, a scholar might ask herself whether the topic or issue that will frame the proposal or prospectus has been clarified? Is the dependent variable, or the outcome to be explained, clear? Have I uncovered something surprising so the research question can be posed as a puzzle? How feasible will it be to collect the information needed to answer the question?

---

[35] Interview, DK-3, July 27, 2012.

Have cases to explore been selected? Trying their hand at developing a plausible data-collection plan can help scholars engaging in exploratory research to see how far they have come in their formulation of the project; that is, constructing such a plan might help scholars to gauge the endpoint, rather than serving as the starting point, of exploratory field research.

We close with two points. First, significant benefits can accrue from reaching out to others when trying to assess progress. Scholars familiar with the field context can help with assessing the likelihood of collecting (or may have ideas about how to collect) "still-to-get" data, for instance. And advisors or colleagues far-removed from one's project can often infuse the evaluation process with some bigger-picture perspective. Second, researchers typically do not end up needing as much information as they feel compelled to collect when they are knee-deep in the field. Indeed, it is very common for researchers who have returned from long months of fieldwork to lament the amount of material they collected that sits unanalyzed in cardboard boxes or on their hard drives. Scholars would do well to keep this in mind as they balance the utility of potential data sources against the days or weeks it may take to collect them.

Wrapping up and transitioning back to the home institution

As we have sought to emphasize throughout this book, field research is an iterative, non-linear process composed of overlapping stages without hard boundaries. Scholars can and should continue to design field research while they execute it; analyze data while they gather them; and write up their observations and insights as they learn. We continue in this vein here, highlighting the link between critically assessing progress and winding things down in the field on the one hand, and (re-)initiating operations in the home institution on the other. And we offer strategies for handling this critical transition smoothly while maintaining research productivity.

The final weeks or days in the field can easily become a harried tangle as the researcher tries to gather last bits of information, schedule final interviews, say farewells, and handle the logistics associated with packing up and leaving. Nonetheless, there are ways to impose order on the pre-departure rush, and to facilitate departure itself. For instance, at this point in field research the temptation might be particularly strong to switch into full-throttle data-gathering mode, postponing routine organizational tasks such as transcribing interviews, penning and sending final thank-you emails, fleshing out field notes, and labeling digital images of important documents.

Yet such tasks are harder to do effectively as time passes, and the days or weeks after scholars return to their home institution will be no less hectic than their last moments in the field. As such, it is important to carry out such key clean-up duties prior to departure. Just as crucial are efforts to get re-attuned to the rhythms and deadlines of the home institution, and pre-arrange things that will be needed upon return: office space, syllabi, textbook orders, and the like.

Even if scholars are able to employ these management strategies, particularly with research trips that have lasted several months or more, transitioning away from the field setting and back to the home institution is disruptive, involving uprooting and replanting processes that consume time, attention, and energy.[36] Relocating entails most of the usual hassles involved with moving, but also gives rise to less tangible trials. On the level of daily routines and social relationships, returning to one's home institution means stepping out of one world and into another, which almost invariably occasions emotional and psychological dislocation, and cultural and financial jolts. For graduate students, the transition usually means moving back *down* the totem pole from the lofty heights of being solo PI to being a student receiving feedback from, and required to report to, faculty advisors.[37] For faculty, returning from the field entails facing the demands and pressures of their home institution: teaching obligations, expense reports, and perhaps colleagues who feel returnees owe committee service after having been away. Finally, it means reorienting to a new phase of the research project.

From the perspective of project management (and intellectual continuity), a key goal is to recommence the analysis and writing processes as soon as possible. Doing so allows scholars to build on the creative energy and vivid images still lingering from the field,[38] and helps to prevent the transition from field to home institution from generating a long productivity gap. While this point in the project is a natural time for a break, it is important to keep up momentum lest a well-deserved period of rest evolve into extended wheel-spinning. Doctoral students in particular often consume months and months after returning from the field "organizing" the

---

[36] While many of the points in this section will be most applicable to scholars for whom the field setting and home institution are located in distinct locales, many may also apply to scholars who are transitioning from more of a focus on data collection to more of a focus on data analysis without changing locations.

[37] Personal communication from a graduate student who had just returned from field research, October 6, 2013.

[38] Trachtenberg (2006, 183–197) offers some ideas about writing up historical projects based on primary data that are also applicable to scholars writing up more contemporary studies.

information they have collected before getting down to the task of writing dissertation chapters. Scholars working with wrenching questions on topics such as conflict or violence or poverty may find it particularly difficult to re-experience as they read back through their sources, digest their data, and analyze what they have learned.

Yet the root cause of delays and stalling is often scholars feeling over-whelmed by the analytic and intellectual tasks that lie before them. Doing fieldwork was one thing, they may think, but now they have to "say some-thing smart."[39] Indeed, to some degree it may be true that the skills that allow scholars to excel at fieldwork differ from those involved in drawing all of the information gathered together to make a theoretical contribution to the relevant literature. Moreover, while those engaging in purely quantitative analysis have something more of a template to follow – their variables and data to some degree suggest what model and method to use – qualitative or multi-method analysis is less formulaic.[40] In short, uncertainty about their ability to "say something smart" – and about *how* to do so – can be paralyzing for some scholars.

Initiating analysis in the field, we have suggested, can lay the groundwork and serve as a template for continuing forward, helping scholars to get going and gain momentum in this new phase of the project. Yet there are other things researchers can do to carry on and stay motivated. To begin, it can be a good idea to plan out (and write out) a timeline for completing the written product they hope to generate on the basis of their fieldwork, including some milestones to hit within a week, two weeks, a few months, and six months of returning from the field. These milestones might be administrative, organiza-tional, social, analytical, or compositional, among others. Based on that schedule, scholars can assign themselves discrete tasks to do each day or each week in order to achieve those goals.[41] The idea is to have a concrete way to document continued progress (or highlight a lack thereof) toward organizing and ordering information, thinking through data and drawing conclusions, developing an argument within the relevant theoretical frame-works, and creating a research product.

One set of initial goals might relate to dispatching any residual adminis-trative tasks that were not completed in the field. A related set of goals might

---

[39] Interview, DK-15, August 21, 2012.   [40] Interview, DK-7, August 1, 2012.

[41] As a general guideline, scholars might budget one or two months per dissertation or book chapter – and at least a year to complete a dissertation or book manuscript (once they are spending most of their time writing).

concern making sure that electronic and hard-copy data are organized in an intuitive way so that sources can be easily inventoried and accessed. Scholars might set themselves clear deadlines for assessing how confident they are in their initial coding schemes and considering whether a switch to (or away from) coding software might be warranted; for obtaining, learning, and starting to use any data analysis software they elect to employ; and for transcribing, coding, entering, or cleaning particular tranches of data. It can also be extremely useful for researchers to nail down – and write down – all relevant methodological details, assembling the notes created as choices were made in the field into one clear, coherent document.

With regard to professional relations, graduate students should seek to reconnect, and start sharing thoughts and ideas, with advisors promptly – even if (perhaps especially if) they remain uncertain about how the multiple pieces of their project fit together. It is self-defeating to lie low in the belief that they will make a better impression once they have it all figured out. Likewise, more advanced scholars might reach out to colleagues to debrief. Graduate students might also create, or join, a writing group consisting of students from their own subfield or various subfields. Such groups can provide useful feedback, reveal what is interesting to others and how they respond to evolving ideas, and establish deadlines to hit. In a similar vein, faculty might arrange an ongoing "draft exchange" with other faculty. More generally, graduate students and faculty alike should hasten to reintegrate into their broader scholarly networks – through attending conferences, re-subscribing to listservs from which they unsubscribed in the field, starting to read blogs they had been neglecting, etc. All of these people and groups can serve as sounding boards as scholars strive to "get their head out of the field" and continue to formulate and seek to test their ideas about what they have learned.

Finally, with regard to writing, a useful first step is thinking strategically about *what* to write.[42] Generating an annotated table of contents can help a scholar to get a holistic handle on the project, develop ideas about how to structure the final product, and think through how the data collected map to that structure. One political scientist we interviewed suggested that, to complement her table of contents, she wrote a one-page summary of what the argument for each chapter would be *and* what evidence she had to make that argument. Doing so forced her to sort through all of the data she had collected to identify those connected to the real core of what she wanted to say.

---

[42] Numerous excellent publications offer strategies for making writing progress, for example, Sternberg (1981), Becker (1986), and Booth *et al.* (1995).

She talked this document through with an expert in her field to solidify it before beginning to write any part of her dissertation.[43] Yet starting big – by trying to develop the main argument of the piece one hopes to write based on data collected in the field, for instance – may ultimately backfire: if the argument does not come together easily (because the scholar has not completed sufficient analysis to develop it), she may put off writing altogether.

It can be better, both psychologically and intellectually, to begin with low-hanging fruit; after all, the sections of one's article or chapters of one's book or dissertation need not be written in order. Scholars might write (or continue writing) an evolving series of memos to themselves, for instance. They could start by writing up some manageable portion of the project as a freestanding paper. This might be an aspect they are particularly inspired to set to paper; or a facet they are certain will end up in their article, dissertation, or book; or a piece with which they are sure they can make a contribution to the relevant literature. Scholars who take this route might set themselves a deadline by proposing the paper for presentation at a disciplinary conference or similar venue. Alternatively or in addition, scholars may write pieces for non-academic audiences – for instance, the policy community or an NGO. One way or the other, they might aim to write a little bit each day, measuring progress in number of hours, number of pages, or some other way. By putting one foot in front of the other, even if ever so slowly, everyone can make steady progress toward their writing goals.

A final re-entry issue concerns the challenges of remaining connected to the field context. We can think of these challenges in several ways. Some scholars have a difficult time *fully extricating* themselves from the field site. They may have seen or heard or sensed or felt things that continue to reverberate in their mind and heart. Or they may have ongoing obligations that can be helpful and productive, or draining. Fairly and efficiently dealing with these ties – while trying to make analytic progress – can be difficult, and scholars struggling to devise strategies to do so should consult others who have experienced similar challenges. By contrast, some scholars may find the sudden severing from the field context disorienting, and may yearn for ways to stay in touch. Doing so can sometimes be simple and straightforward. Staying abreast of ongoing events in the field site can help them remain connected. Further, we mentioned previously how local contacts, collaborators, and informants can fill in data gaps that may emerge once one has

---

[43] Interview, DK-13, August 8, 2012; see also "Design: the key to writing (and advising) a one-draft Ph.D. dissertation" (www-users.cs.umn.edu/~carlis/one-draft.pdf, accessed September 1, 2012).

returned home. Digital communications technologies and online social networks can be particularly helpful in these regards.

A related question concerns how researchers can "give back" to a community or project participants *after* returning to their home institution. Researchers have often been criticized for taking their data and running: they may get promoted for publishing information they "extracted" from a community in what that community may view as an arcane and unreadable format, while the community gets nothing (Mihesuah 1993). Even in remote parts of rural Africa, some communities resent the lack of follow-through from previous generations of scholars. Beyond the current power inequalities this highlights, the downstream result can be the inaccessibility of particular communities for future researchers. One way to ameliorate this situation and to practice ethical commitment is for researchers to write up their results in a simple and concise format and make that product available for project participants and people from the communities they studied. Indeed, sometimes those individuals can suggest accessible and appropriate outlets, for instance web sites where findings may be posted or email lists through which material can be distributed to interested subscribers.

Remaining connected to the field context in some way often helps scholars to make the most of, and even enhance, what they discovered and developed during fieldwork. Bringing themselves "back to the field," if only virtually or mentally, may help them to interpret and reinterpret data. Data are not objective pieces of information: they were created at a particular moment and place and gain meaning because of that context. Planning for the possibility of reconnecting with elements of that milieu, whether by retaining multiple means of contacting respondents or research assistants, or by taking detailed notes on the atmosphere, visitors, and contents of archives or libraries, *in addition to* those taken on the specific records or books they perused, can help scholars to continue to access the field site and its many complexities and dynamics even once they have left.

Conclusion

This chapter emphasized the importance of analyzing one's data *as one is collecting them*. Based on a broad understanding of the notion of "analysis," the chapter outlined multiple ways in which analyzing data in the field helps scholars to make good intellectual progress, arrive at meaningful interpretations, and draw strong descriptive and causal inferences. Concomitantly, it addressed how particular aspects of research design – and sometimes even the basic architecture and aims of one's project – can and perhaps must be renegotiated as fieldwork progresses. It also offered a trouble-shooting guide to help researchers map a path from analytic problems to appropriate solutions. And the chapter demonstrated how scholarly imperatives such as building an argument, linking data and evidence to claims and conclusions, and connecting one's work to broader theoretical frameworks can fruitfully inform one's thinking, analyzing, *and writing* in the field. The chapter also offered some strategies for assessing progress, and transitioning from the field site back to the home institution.

Our biggest take-home message is that, to the degree possible, scholars should avoid the scenario of returning home with crates of papers or thousands of computer files and only *then* starting to try to make sense of them. Instead, consistently giving themselves the time and mental space to actively engage with their data *throughout* their time in the field – imposing order on the material that they are gathering, and identifying, carefully considering, and resolving practical and intellectual complications early on – can pay great analytic dividends.

Throughout, we have highlighted the fundamentally iterative nature of field research, and the non-linear nature of the broader research process of which it forms part. We have emphasized the importance, to all sorts of crucial analytic tasks, of the scholar critically reflecting on what she is learning about the field site and her topic as she engages with her research context or contexts. And we have continued to underscore the merits of flexible discipline: giving oneself the latitude to make well-reasoned, incremental changes to one's research design as one learns and analyzes in the field is a quintessential example of this critical principle of good research. And we have shown that documenting the analytic tasks carried out in the field – carefully describing how concepts were measured, data and hypotheses evaluated, and information aggregated to support an argument, and explaining why those tasks were carried as out as they were, when they were – can help scholars to produce scholarship that is more transparent, in which they can more easily and clearly demonstrate the rigor and power of their research.

11 The future of field research in political science

We began this book by making the case for critical reflection and active discussion within the discipline of political science on the nature of field research and its role in the production of knowledge. With a few recent exceptions that we surveyed in Chapter 1 and throughout this book, most writing on field research methods comes from outside political science. Since the beginning of the twentieth century, anthropologists and sociologists have initiated and indeed dominated many of the scholarly debates on how to conduct field research. Yet, for decades, large numbers of political scientists from all subfields have engaged in diverse types of field research around the world. Accordingly, it is well past time for our discipline to become more vigorously involved in the dialogue about the practices and principles of field research. While this book draws on insights and ideas from other disciplinary debates, our main goal is to contribute to and accelerate discussion of field research within political science.

Whether, why, and how political scientists value field research depends in part on their epistemological priors. While many members of the discipline consider field research a sound basis for understanding the world and for building theory, some have their doubts. To be clear, this is not a simple dichotomy between scholars who recognize, and those who question, the value of field research. Even those who value fieldwork have different views on its contributions – views that reflect fundamentally divergent perspectives on how we know what we know about politics and the world, and hence how we learn about them. Discussions about field research inevitably connect to, and also enliven, disciplinary debates over the value of descriptive inference, the merit of case studies, and whether and how we should seek to generalize, explain causal processes, and interpret meanings.

Accordingly, we have sought to create a book that addresses this broad audience, offering a comprehensive account of what field research is in our discipline, how it is done, and why it is conducted. Rather than write this book narrowly for any one subgroup within the discipline, we have aimed to start an inclusive conversation. In order to problematize the concept and practices of field research from multiple perspectives, we collected extensive original data on the fieldwork experiences of a wide range of scholars – reviewing published empirical scholarship based on data gathered from fieldwork, fielding an original survey of US political science faculty, and conducting sixty-two in-depth interviews with political science faculty and graduate students.

This chapter's next section summarizes the book's main arguments about the dynamics and conduct of field research in political science, which are buttressed by the findings of our multi-faceted empirical inquiry. The chapter then proceeds to examine how broader trends and changes in politics, technology, the discipline, and academia more generally might influence field research practices in the coming years. We close with a clarion call to the discipline, exhorting political scientists to "spread out," to collaborate more around field research, to think and write more about field research practices and products, to re-envision graduate methods training, and to give greater institutional acknowledgment to quality field research. Each step would help to advance our overall objective: encouraging recognition of the tremendous and multi-faceted value of field research to the discipline of political science.

The nature, practices, and principles of field research in political science

Throughout this book, we have developed three main arguments about the nature, practices, and principles – and thus the role – of field research in political science. Here we recap more briefly our first two arguments concerning the commonalities that exist across diverse types of fieldwork, and how scholars' iteration among the many data-collection and data-analysis tasks they carry out in the field helps make fieldwork a powerful form of inquiry. Thereafter, drawing on the first two arguments, we elaborate more fully on our third, showing the ways in which a shared set of principles underpins good fieldwork across the discipline. Each of these arguments bolsters an overarching theme of the book: that field research adds significant value to political science scholarship, and to our understanding of politics around the world. The volume's chapters provide multiple examples of the many ways in which fieldwork creates such value. And, we note, confidence in this view was also expressed again and again in our interviews.[1] Repeatedly,

---

[1] It bears noting that, while we sought to interview scholars who had engaged in fieldwork *and* those who had not, the vast majority of our respondents had carried out some field research. That said, our

when the question arose of whether or not respondents would have been able to carry out their research projects without conducting field research, the response was a resounding "no!"[2] Our three primary arguments, then, are in part an effort to unpack and make clear the full range of reasons why, and the processes through which, the research activities that scholars carry out in the field add value to their scholarship.

Commonality within diversity

Our first set of arguments holds that, despite great variety in the contours, content, and conduct of political science field research, fieldwork in the discipline has a common center. To be sure, our research clearly demonstrates – and points made throughout the book illustrate – that no single, ideal-typical form of fieldwork dominates the discipline today. For instance, field research projects carried out in different settings tend to have divergent characteristics. Chapter 2 showed how projects conducted entirely in the United States and those including international locations tended to have somewhat different profiles; field research also can look different in democratic and authoritarian contexts, in rich and poor places, in urban and rural settings, and so forth. Projects vary in part with regard to the structure of the research: the number of trips across which the fieldwork is spread; the number of distinct locations or field sites visited; and the amount of time spent there. Some fieldwork is done on a shoestring, while some is financed by six-figure grants. And field research varies in terms of how collaborative it is – with regard to hiring research assistants (RAs) and working with colleagues and partner organizations, for example.

It is also the case that field research has changed over time. Compared with previous cohorts, political scientists today spend less time in the field and use less funding to support their research. Further, they tend to pair information collected in the field with more data acquired from other sources. Some field techniques have proven to be hardy perennials, including interviews, surveys, and what we call site-intensive methods (ethnography and participant observation), while newly emergent techniques such as field experiments are building a following. In short, no single template or stereotype adequately

interviewees did include scholars whose projects relied less heavily on data they collected themselves and more heavily on existing sources (e.g., LM-4, August 27, 2012; LM-7, September 2, 2012; LM-12, September 6, 2012; LM-14, September 7, 2012; LM-22, October 2, 2012; LM-23, November 8, 2012).
[2] For instance, interviews, DK-11, August 7, 2012; LM-5, August 27, 2012; LM-16, September 11, 2012.

captures field research in political science, and several of fieldwork's integral parameters are in motion.

This variation across types of scholars and over time has multiple sources. Perhaps most fundamentally, political scientists hold a broad range of epistemological positions: some are committed positivists and others are dedicated interpretivists (although, as we discuss below, the great majority lie somewhere in between). The diverse range of phenomena political scientists study calls for different modes of inquiry as well. One would not likely use the same techniques to study, say, the political beliefs of pre-World War II anti-colonialist leaders in India or Vietnam, and state-by-state trends in the effects of voter registration laws on turnout in the United States. The growing availability of digital data over time has likely affected the degree to which scholars ground their research in data they gathered in the field versus data that were available online. Differential access to funding may also matter to fieldwork styles: our survey data reveal that, on average, Ph.D. students at programs ranked among the discipline's top 20 obtain substantially more resources for international fieldwork than students in other programs.

Furthermore, political scientists' field research practices change over their careers and lifetimes. Many of our interview respondents related how the addition of a partner, spouse, or children in their lives (as well as health needs or challenges associated with growing older) changed the cost–benefit calculation of doing lengthy field research in faraway places, particularly in very remote and/or dangerous contexts.[3] Similarly, faculty face competing pressures at different junctures to fulfill teaching and service obligations. More seasoned scholars returning to places where they have previously conducted research often operate very differently from how they did on their first forays due to the knowledge and connections previous trips helped them to develop;[4] likewise, senior scholars may delegate more aspects of field research to RAs.[5]

On what basis, then, do we find a common center? To start with, field research of all types involves an array of recurring practical, emotional, ethical, and analytic challenges. Regardless of their epistemological leaning,

---

[3] E.g., interviews DK-7, August 1, 2012; LM-2, April 14, 2012. In the life-history interviews conducted by Munck and Snyder, senior scholars of comparative politics disagreed on whether field research becomes more difficult to do as one's career progresses. On the one hand, Juan Linz contended that "established" senior scholars "can and should do fieldwork later in [their] career"; on the other hand, Philippe Schmitter explicitly cited his age as a challenge to continuing to conduct field research because of the tremendous amount of energy it requires; James Scott agreed that while it would be more difficult to do fieldwork in his mid-60s, he could do it (Munck and Snyder 2007, 187, 337, 368).

[4] Interviews DK-17, August 24, 2012; LM-8, August 30, 2012; LM-9, August 30, 2012.

[5] Interviews LM-2, April 14, 2012; LM-9, August 30, 2012.

subfield, substantive interest, or rank, political scientists inevitably confront at least some of these hurdles in the field. Put differently, *all* field research is difficult to do well, and effectively employing each data-collection technique discussed in this book requires significant preparation, practice, and skill.

Moreover, our empirical analysis reveals that, in coping with these challenges, field researchers in political science have shared instincts and tendencies, and draw on a common stock of wisdom that cuts across the discipline's presumed cleavages. With regard to epistemology, many (if not most) field researchers occupy a middle position on the positivist–interpretivist spectrum, eclectically taking cues from both ends and refusing to acknowledge what are sometimes conceived as absolute choices and irreconcilable differences between competing camps. Relatedly, field researchers often employ both qualitative and quantitative logics, sometimes infused with interpretivist approaches, whether in explicit or in unannounced ways. Qualitative work forms a part of the great majority of field research projects, but contrary to some impressions, field research is not an exclusively qualitative enterprise. Projects that include the gathering of quantitative data, through surveys, experiments, or other means, have their own particular characteristics and challenges but also share much in common with other types of field research endeavor. Finally, it is an atypical scholar who *just* conducts focus groups, or *only* does field experiments. Instead, political scientists tend to employ multiple data-collection techniques within the same project. This is, in fact, a well-established practice, not the result of a recent "mixed-method" fad in the discipline.

In sum, we find that most field researchers operate in a zone of overlapping common tendencies, in which positivists and interpretivists, quantitative and qualitative scholars, and political scientists of every subfield share a great deal. The commonality of our experiences and practices, despite the tremendously diverse nature of our field research experiences, has several important implications. First, it suggests that we ought to be able to – *and should* – sustain a discussion about fieldwork in the discipline. As an eclectic enterprise with a surprisingly common core, field research capitalizes on, facilitates, and potentially advances this dialogue across significant disciplinary divides. Indeed, in our interviews and in the open-ended questions in our survey of US faculty, respondents seemed eager to reflect upon, analyze, and talk at length about the field research they had conducted.[6] Second, it

---

[6] Although we were prepared to conduct the interviews in approximately 30 minutes, almost all interviews lasted over an hour and respondents noted that numerous topics remained untouched.

suggests that we ought to be able to – *and should* – work together across subfields and substantive areas much more than we do to develop and strengthen fieldwork practices, to devise strategies to capitalize on fieldwork's unique value-added in our scholarship, and to develop a language that allows us to articulate more clearly what fieldwork contributes to the discipline.[7] As we have emphasized and firmly believe, fieldwork is a common disciplinary good. Finally, the commonalities among diverse forms of fieldwork suggest that we ought to be able to – *and should* – identify shared principles that underlie and guide good fieldwork. We have taken a first step toward doing so.

Shared practices: data collection, data analysis, iteration, and layered learning

A deeper look at the commonalities shared by field researchers takes us to the second primary argument that this book has developed. Field research entails much more than simply collecting data. Rather, a scholar's fieldwork tends to advance multiple analytical dimensions of a research project. Far from merely filling in empty spreadsheet cells, literally or figuratively, the data scholars collect in the field and the insights they derive from them feed back into core intellectual dimensions of a research project, often changing the way a scholar thinks about and designs her work. We thus advocate a reconceptualization of the meaning of field research as an inherently iterative process, in which scholars continually update key elements of their projects – including the question, concepts, research design, and theories – based on an ongoing analysis of information acquired in the field.

While conceiving of research as a linear succession of specific phases with fieldwork sandwiched between "research design" and "analysis" may be useful as a heuristic, this understanding of the research process does not reflect the dynamic complexity of fieldwork in the real world. Most of our interviewees noted that fieldwork has had far-reaching effects on their thinking, and on their analysis, during multiple stages in the research process. As one commented, "when you carry out field research, your brain makes connections in ways that it can't from just reading ... you absorb information in a more critical way because you're using all of your senses."[8]

---

[7] Various interviewees lamented the lack of such a language, e.g., interviews DK-2, July 26, 2012; DK-4, July 30, 2012.

[8] Interview, DK-7, August 1, 2012.

Another interviewee suggested that, while scholars might understand the words a subject or political actor says or writes, "without context and background [gained through field research], you have no idea of the *meaning* of what they are saying."[9] Fieldwork can also lead researchers to identify causal processes or enrich their understanding of complex causal pathways. One interviewee insisted that in the absence of field research, "you misinterpret data – you won't understand the inter-connections and causal patterns," in other words, you will not understand *why* your findings are statistically significant.[10]

Furthermore, scholars with whom we spoke described an extensive set of feedback loops. A scholar's initial research question drives many basic research design choices, such as major concepts to employ, hypotheses to investigate, sites to visit, and information sources with which to start. But once fieldwork begins, what is learned in the field feeds back into and sharpens both research design *and* field research design. To give just a few examples, carefully considering the data they are collecting can suggest to scholars the need to clarify the initial question, consider an alternative hypothesis, include an additional field site or different cases, add a previously neglected data-collection technique, or make contact with members of a previously unknown group of stakeholders in the political process. New concepts can emerge (or a scholar can refine those with which he began his study), and researchers can discover or devise new strategies for measurement, through their experiences on the ground. Through such constructive iteration, fieldworkers respond directly to what they are learning and to changes in research conditions in ways that tend to correct misconceptions or ill-conceived design decisions. While these feedback cycles can feel rather jerky and uncomfortable to the researcher him- or herself, they allow field research projects to be well designed, grounded in relevant data, and primed to produce strong theory about politics.

There are at least two things our conceptualization of field research as iterative does *not* imply. First, it does not imply that fieldwork cannot be (or is not) planned. There are tradeoffs associated with most changes scholars make to their projects based on discoveries in the field, and their costs and inferential implications need to be carefully considered. Scholars can only think critically about these changes if they have carefully designed their field

---

[9] Interview, DK-17, August 24, 2012; see also LM-4, August 27, 2012.

[10] Interview DK-18, August 24, 2012; see also LM-17, September 11, 2012.

research to begin with: only if the project *has* a plan is the notion of a "change" to the project meaningful, and can its implications be assessed. Second, fieldwork's eclecticism and its iterative nature do *not* imply a lack of rigor. They do not mean that fieldwork is haphazard and unsystematic. Rather, scholars who carry out field research carefully track their projects' many moving intellectual parts. For instance, they take careful notes about the data they are collecting and the processes used to collect them, and seek to assess their initial hypotheses systematically while continuing to look for evidence to refute (or support) alternative explanations.

Drawing together these points, we submit that scholars who study parts of the world with which they are not familiar (whether they be near or far) *without* doing fieldwork there – without engaging with those contexts – can misunderstand and misinterpret empirical reality. This can have grave consequences for inference and analysis, leading researchers to (for instance) set up experiments incorrectly, or to ask unintelligible, misleading, or simply irrelevant questions in interviews or surveys. It is simply difficult to use most data-collection techniques effectively without sophisticated knowledge of the context in which they are being deployed. Moreover, scholars who use existing datasets without knowledge of the context in which they were produced may be unable to assess the data-generation process, the validity of the data, or the validity and reliability of the measures used to evaluate the phenomena being studied. Without understanding the context in which data were collected, scholars can have a much harder time building well-specified models and interpreting their findings; indeed, they may completely misidentify or misinterpret them.[11]

All of the practices discussed in this subsection allow scholars who conduct field research to engage in what we might call "layered learning," which helps them to avoid these sorts of pitfalls. That is, as scholars collect, consider, and analyze data in the field, they gain new layers of knowledge. And as they think through the fundamentals of their research project in light of that knowledge, their projects are strengthened and enhanced, leading to yet more learning. All of this has positive implications for their intellectual progress and products. Indeed, it is in great part this layered learning that occurs in the field that allows scholarship based on field research to deliver such a powerful intellectual punch.

---

[11] In fact, as one interview respondent put it, if one doesn't "know the field context . . . you don't even know what variables to put in your model" (interview, LM-8, August 30, 2012).

Principles of field research in political science

As we posited in the book's introduction and have discussed throughout, six principles underpin and animate effective field research practices in political science: engagement with context, flexible discipline, triangulation, critical reflection, ethical commitment, and transparency. Before advocating for the utility of these principles, we quickly emphasize two framing points made when we first introduced them. First, we did not cut these principles from whole cloth with the intent of imposing them on our unsuspecting colleagues in the discipline. We identified them through an analysis of publications based on field research, the incipient writing on field research in the discipline, and our in-depth interviews with and survey of a diverse group of US-based faculty. We do not (merely) propose that they *should* underlie good field research, we suggest that they already *do*, if often only implicitly. As such, we are describing as much as we are prescribing.

Second, we do not offer these principles as a standard template to be rigidly followed. How they are prioritized, combined, and applied is contingent: it will differ from scholar to scholar, project to project, and context to context. Nonetheless, we do believe that there is sufficient commonality in the fundamentals of fieldwork for the spirit of these principles to be usefully followed by all political scientists who do field research. And we posit that political scientists who conduct fieldwork in a way that closely hews to these *process*-related principles will be better positioned to produce outstanding scholarship based on field research.

Engagement with context

First, we argue that engagement with the field research context is a critical principle of good fieldwork. We start with this principle because it gets at the essence of what field research is and the doors it opens. Field research requires "being there." Personal proximity to the political phenomena, people, or information sources under study matters in large part because it enables – virtually forces – the investigator to see and learn from the surrounding context rather than merely acquiring disconnected fragments of data.

What engaging with a context means and how fieldworkers do so, of course, vary: researchers' strategies will differ, and different projects and field sites will require distinct techniques. Engaging with context can mean looking for opportunities to linger with one's interviewees, perhaps staying for an extended conversation over a dinner that includes the subject's friends or family. It can mean flipping through the books on a library shelf, or record boxes in an archive, that surround the one originally sought. It can mean realizing that the content of an informant's phone conversation with a colleague, overheard during an interview, contradicts what the informant had just said to the researcher. It can mean learning that local historians have published a compilation of documents that directly address one's research question.[12] It can mean seeing the bewildered look on the face of a survey pre-tester when asked a question one had thought was perfectly clear. As one of our interviewees noted, engagement might mean a thoroughness that leads to knowing one's cases "really, really well."[13] Becoming engaged might include partaking in discussions and collaborating with local scholars, as well as incorporating local literature and sources.[14] It might involve affiliating with a host institution or forming an important link with an NGO.[15] Or it might entail knowing the language, history, and culture of one's field sites, or being familiar with nuanced variation within cases.[16]

In dozens of different ways, our interview respondents conveyed to us that engagement with context and the resulting case knowledge are indispensable for field research to be effective and to provide value. For instance, some scholars suggested that engaging with context augmented their ability to identify "bullshit,"[17] and avoid "superficial" analysis.[18] Another suggested that close engagement allows one to understand things in an *interactive* way, and absorb information in a more critical way, because one is using all one's senses and registering things holistically; fieldwork, he suggested, "shoves questions at you."[19] More specifically, scholars suggested that the long-term relationships developed in the field helped them to "navigate the system" and gain access to people,[20] untangle power relations,[21] and understand the meaning of interview responses.[22] One scholar articulated the idea directly:

to be stopped by a well-armed soldier in the middle of nowhere is an experience you have to go through to understand things . . . fieldwork remains a huge reality check on the basic dynamics of society, of economy, on how people interact; a lot of those really basic insights you can only get by going to the country.[23]

---

[12] Interview, BR-4, August 9, 2012.

[13] Interview, LM-8, August 30, 2012. Also interviews, LM-4, August 27, 2012; LM-9, August 30, 2012; DK-6, July 31, 2012.

[14] Interview, LM-5, August 27, 2012. Also interviews, LM-4, August 27, 2012; LM-8, August 30, 2012.

[15] Interview, LM-16, September 11, 2012.   [16] Interview, LM-9, August 30, 2012.

[17] Interviews, LM-2, April 14, 2012; DK-17, August 24, 2012.   [18] Interview, LM-8, August 30, 2012.

[19] Interview, DK-7, August 1, 2012; DK-4, July 30, 2012, said something similar.

[20] Interview, DK-17, August 24, 2012.   [21] Interview, LM-8, August 30, 2012.

[22] Interview, DK-18, August 24, 2012.   [23] Interview, LM-22, October 2, 2012.

We hasten to clarify three points. First, while they may often be closely connected, engagement with a particular context is not necessarily directly proportional to the amount of time spent there. How much time a scholar needs to spend in a context in order to engage with it can vary considerably. The most important source of that variation may be *knowledge* of context,[24] which can be garnered in several ways. As our respondents emphasized, carefully preparing – developing appropriate language skills and relevant knowledge of the history, culture, economics, and politics of one's field sites (Perecman and Curran 2006), perhaps by taking area studies courses, watching local television broadcasts, reading local newspapers, meeting expatriates – and employing other strategies for becoming familiar with a place can set scholars up to engage more quickly and effectively upon arrival. This can help offset the time restraints sometimes imposed by funding limitations, or a scholar's life circumstances. As well, scholars who have visited a location many times have built up a reservoir of knowledge about the place and how to accomplish research there that may dramatically reduce the amount of time they need on any one trip.[25] In sum, engagement with a particular place has more to do with a scholar's connection to it and how she uses her time there than the absolute quantity of time spent on any one visit.

Second, we are not suggesting that all researchers must actively engage with their field sites throughout their time there. How much engagement is necessary and optimal depends (again) on a scholar's familiarity with the context and the analytic goals of the particular field stay. For those who *already understand* a context prior to a certain field research foray, intense engagement with it may be less crucial. Likewise, if one seeks simply to give an exploratory test to a particular idea or carry out a delimited shadow case study, extensive engagement with a context may be less critical for analytic success.

Finally, we would be remiss to neglect what are sometimes perceived as potential downsides of deep engagement in the field. At least some of our interview respondents cautioned that all-consuming immersion in a field site can bring a risk of losing objectivity.[26] Yet others suggested that the benefits of fieldwork outweighed that potential cost. As one scholar noted, "I think

---

[24] Interviews, LM-5, August 27, 2012; LM-6, August 30, 2012; LM-9, August 30, 2012.

[25] One interview respondent made this point quite directly, suggesting that, while a returned Peace Corps volunteer might be able to do very successful field research in a summer, it might take a 23-year-old who had never been out of his home country a year to conduct effective fieldwork (interview, LM-22, October 2, 2012).

[26] E.g., interview, DK-17, August 24, 2012.

the objection that you lose your objectivity actually underestimates the human capacity for creativity [and] the ability of the researcher to be very conscious of what he or she is doing ... Getting friendly and getting very comfortable with people allows you to dig deeper into their subjectivities."[27] Field research, we would concur, enables just this type of creativity.

Flexible discipline

Field researchers, who are often under resource constraints of various types, need to ensure that each step they take and decision they make advances their overall analytic objectives. Yet they should not be *so* focused that they miss opportunities for soaking and poking, or for productive serendipity, and not *so* rigid that they refuse to amend aspects of their project that their evolving understanding has shown to be untenable. We capture this tradeoff in the notion of "flexible discipline." Acting according to this principle means working to stay on task – by keeping the overarching goals of one's project in mind, planning, organizing, anticipating research challenges, and carefully logging one's progress – while at the same time giving oneself the latitude to accommodate and adapt to unforeseen challenges and opportunities. To give an example, we suggested in Chapter 3 that scholars create (even before they enter the field), and operate based on, a detailed and well-organized data-collection plan – yet we emphasized that this plan does not lock them into a fixed list of chores. Rather, it helps them move back and forth between their project's key abstract concepts and the range of possible sources of evidence on the ground. It serves as a guideline to help them to identify which field activities to prioritize but also demands ongoing creativity as it is continually updated and revised.

Two interviewees expressed the "flexible" part of this principle quite clearly: sometimes, said one, you need to "get a little 'lost'" and allow yourself to "stumble across things" in the field.[28] Another admonished, "And for God's sake, don't ... think that you have a precise task and can just do that."[29] Without putting a name to it, scholars gave us countless examples of how this principle underlay their research process, and the ways their research was enhanced by it. One scholar explained that her pre-field preparation had been essential, but that she nonetheless had to adapt and carefully refine her study in an iterative fashion as she gathered new information. She offered a telling example of how initial interviews prompted a substantial reframing of

---

[27] Interview, LM-11, August 31, 2012.   [28] Interview, LM-4, August 27, 2012.
[29] Interview, LM-10, September 18, 2012.

the research question, from when and why a particular foreign policy decision had been made to how policies emerge without any precise decision being made at an identifiable point in time.[30] Another scholar who had planned to engage in formal interviewing of presidential candidates in Latin America retooled to carry out participant observation instead as he was invited on campaign trips; the same scholar found himself suddenly needing to develop strategies to collect videos he did not anticipate being able to secure (and then find ways to deal with old Betamax tapes).[31] When the government of the country in which another researcher was conducting fieldwork expelled refugees from a neighboring country, the new political reality led her project to become more policy-focused, and meant reallocating the amount of time spent in different field locations.[32]

Of course, emphases will differ by scholar and by project: while some researchers feel more comfortable prioritizing flexibility, others emphasize discipline. To offer just one example tilted toward the latter, Beckmann and Hall (2013) present a highly positivist, "just the facts" perspective on how they interviewed Washington elites, recounting how they asked their core questions; collected the relevant data; and sought to minimize the degree to which respondents went off on tangents, drove the conversation, or regaled them with stories. Overall, however, given the challenges *and* opportunities that fieldwork contexts often present, we believe most scholars will be best served by finding a balance between being flexible and being disciplined in the execution of their research.

Triangulation

We use the term "triangulation" to refer to gathering data from multiple sources in an effort, for instance, to measure a certain concept or assess a particular hypothesis. More loosely, we also refer to collecting different perspectives and views – whether that is accomplished through consulting a "number of different archival sources"[33] or being sure to "talk to people on different sides of an issue"[34] – as triangulation. The core objective is to collect information that clearly and fully reflects the empirical reality under study, and that allows the scholar to cross check data and sources.[35] Triangulation can be

---

[30] Interview, LM-15, September 10, 2012.   [31] Interview, DK-3, July 27, 2012.
[32] Interview, LM-16, September 11, 2012.   [33] Interview, LM-4, August 27, 2012.
[34] Interview, LM-6, August 30, 2012.
[35] Interviews, LM-12, September 6, 2012; LM-18, September 14, 2012.

important in research of all kinds, but the opportunities for triangulation that field research offers are an essential aspect of its power as a form of inquiry.

Some scholars triangulate while using a single data-collection technique. For instance, they may independently interview a variety of subjects about a single political event, or compare the accounts of multiple informants at a given site in which they are engaging in participant observation. Others triangulate with data gathered using more than one technique. Field experiments offer a way of testing a causal relationship for which other techniques have uncovered evidence, for example. Indeed, the fact that political scientists tend to employ multiple data-collection techniques in a single project suggests that field researchers habitually triangulate. Still other scholars may use different techniques to address different aspects of a project rather than to triangulate on one, strictly speaking. Furthermore, some investigators explicitly build triangulation into their research design, while for others it is a matter of noticing things that reinforce or challenge other observations. One way or the other, triangulating offers countless opportunities to find information that contradicts or supports one's initial hypotheses, thus facilitating the development of well-reasoned and persuasive political accounts.

In myriad ways, scholars we interviewed emphasized that there is no better antidote to doubts about data, and no better way to increase our confidence about their evidentiary value, than triangulation. For instance, going to campaign rallies helped one scholar who studied presidential candidates to see how much trust he could put in the rendition of campaign messages mentioned in other data sources, and how much of a candidate's message he was measuring by just analyzing television advertisements; likewise, watching the television ads informed his interviews.[36] Two scholars noted how on-the-ground knowledge gained through observation and participant observation helped them to interpret statistics and data gained through other collection techniques.[37] Another who had done archival work in Europe noted the repeated interplay between the questions she asked and what she learned from oral interviews and information extracted from documents garnered in the archives.[38]

While triangulation is often elective, sometimes it is a necessity, if little or only incomplete data can be obtained using any one technique. For instance, lamenting that "President [X] was not a guy who wrote stuff down," one scholar described how it was necessary to research far beyond the president's

---

[36] Interview, DK-3, July 27, 2012.   [37] Interviews, DK-18, August 24, 2012; DK-19, August 27, 2012.
[38] Interview, LM-7, September 20, 2012.

personal papers and diaries in order to answer questions about what drove military intervention.[39] No matter what their motives for triangulation, scholars need to be selective about how they carry it out. Even when multiple sources suggest the same thing, researchers must be cautious about drawing conclusions, as the subjective perspectives of interested parties cannot be taken as the gospel truth. Further, researchers can become stretched too thin in their quest to find multiple types of data to measure each important concept, support each hypothesis, and help to determine how each causal mechanism works. Knowing when to stop can be difficult. Nonetheless, our respondents seemed to agree that thoughtful, considered triangulation benefitted their work and augmented their confidence in their conclusions.

Critical reflection

By critical reflection, we mean actively thinking about the choices faced at every point of the research process,[40] the practices employed, the data collected, and what is being learned in the field. One scholar described what she terms "self-reflexivity" as "constantly thinking about what did I do wrong, and how could I have done it better."[41] Most of our interviewees agreed that thinking critically is an omnipresent aspect of field research,[42] and emphasized the importance of continually allowing ideas and conclusions based on initial analysis carried out in the field to filter back into and inform the many decisions field research entails. Indeed, this principle lies at the heart of the iterative nature of field research, and is central to the assessment processes discussed in the last chapter, which facilitate the detection of problems in one's project early on.

One scholar explained that, from the first interviews she carried out, she continually considered how she could encourage her respondents to talk about, and feel as comfortable as they could reliving, the traumatic events that were the subject of the interviews. She came up with the idea of creating settings in which her respondents felt like they were controlling the interview.[43] Relatedly, a number of scholars mentioned reflecting critically on how they presented themselves, and on how they were perceived, by those

---

[39] Interview, LM-19, September 18, 2012.   [40] Interview, LM-14, September 7, 2012.
[41] Interview, LM-13, September 7, 2012.
[42] Indeed, one scholar went as far as suggesting that scholars should consciously *set aside time* to think while in the field – planning the time in as part of their research schedule (interview, DK-14, August 10, 2012).
[43] Interview, DK-19, August 2, 2012; many other scholars mentioned critical reflection in connection with gaining access, e.g., DK-11, August 7, 2012; DK-12, August 8, 2012; DK-17, August 24, 2012; and LM-7, September 20, 2012.

with whom they interacted.[44] One researcher noted how she had quickly realized that her respondents were drawing conclusions about what she "represented," motivating them to react to her in a particular way and convey only certain information.[45]

Other scholars highlighted their continual self-questioning about whether their research question was genuinely interesting, or ripe for investigation.[46] For example, one wondered whether her project was a construction of what Westerners think is important in the countries she studied, rather than reflecting what local citizens perceived as being important.[47] Through speaking at length with the subjects of a field experiment, another researcher learned that they were more concerned with problems like hunger than they were with the topics under investigation, and gave thought to the implications of this for the research project.[48] Still others reflected on the *content* of interviews. One realized that her respondents were answering questions in the context of the moment and contemporary political events and hence sought a strategy to create some distance between her conversation and the immediate political context.[49]

All these examples illustrate the importance of reflecting on what one is doing in the field while doing it. Outstanding researchers engage in this sort of mental processing in parallel with their daily work, allowing them to identify problems before they grow unmanageable, and capitalize on opportunities to improve their projects. While it may seem self-evident that fieldworkers should engage in such self-scrutiny, they can easily fall into unreflective routines as they "fight fires," addressing the seemingly endless logistical and practical challenges that gathering data entails. This can result in important leads – potentially significant hypotheses – going unpursued, and data being irretrievably biased. Effective field research requires critical reflection and the cognitive habits it implies – an ongoing drumbeat of questions such as: Why am I doing what I am doing? What am I doing right? What am I doing wrong? And what could I or should I be doing differently?

---

[44] Beyond the examples in this paragraph, other interviewees said similar things, such as DK-12, August 8, 2012; DK-18, August 24, 2012; LM-5, August 27, 2012; LM-6, August 28, 2012; and LM-11, August 31, 2012.

[45] Interviews DK-10, August 6, 2012; LM-15, September 10, 2012; and LM-10, September 18, 2012, also highlighted that both interviewers and interviewees have biases that affect their interaction and the data it produces.

[46] E.g., interview, DK-19, August 27, 2012.   [47] Interview, LM-5, August 27, 2012.

[48] Interview, BR-2, July 30, 2012.   [49] Interview, DK-11, August 7, 2012.

Ethical commitment

Ethical commitment to the individuals whom researchers have involved in their projects, and to people in their field sites more broadly, is another key principle of good fieldwork. Of course, scholars think about ethics differently and make distinct choices, depending on their analytic proclivities, the nature and sensitivity of their topic, and the context in which they are working. As we have suggested previously, we might think of a spectrum of ethical commitment with a minimalist "do no harm" conception of ethics,[50] or the goal of reducing to a minimum risks to study participants (and field-site inhabitants more generally) at one end,[51] and a more ambitious notion of beneficence,[52] or a self-imposed obligation for one's research to have some positive impact, at the other.[53] Certainly, considering the discipline as a whole, there are scholars at all points along this spectrum. Nonetheless, our research revealed that, for most, acting ethically in the field means something more than submitting their projects to relevant IRBs and following their rules and guidelines.[54] Moreover, this principle is tightly intertwined with the other five. For instance, as one scholar mentioned, deep knowledge of context allows one to be more ethical over time as one develops sensitivities and better understands nuances.[55]

Regarding specific ethical issues our respondents discussed, some worried about "extracting" information from people without giving back. To recipro-cate, one trained a respondent on email and basic computing techniques,[56] and another chose as RAs a group of students who would truly benefit from and appreciate the opportunity, and would be able to use the training to obtain access to greater professional opportunities.[57] Another respondent expressed concern about issues that can arise after researchers leave the field, should information they collected become critical or sensitive in the future.[58] Others worried about how much scholars should disguise their research in order to facilitate interaction with others. Still others considered whether it is

---

[50] E.g., interview, DK-17, August 24, 2012.

[51] Interview, LM-15, September 10, 2012. In fact, the spectrum even extends beyond a minimalist perspective. We were frankly surprised by the number of scholars who reported that they did not even go through their home institution's IRB process. For example, interviews, DK-5, July 23, 2012; LM-18, September 14, 2012.

[52] Interview, DK-19, August 27, 2012.

[53] Interviews, LM-13, September 7, 2012; LM-16, September 11, 2012.

[54] See also Scheyvens and Storey (2003, 233–237).   [55] Interview, LM-7, September 20, 2012.

[56] Interview, DK-1, July 20, 2012.

[57] Interview, LM-1, April 13, 2012; LM-13, September 7, 2012, mentioned something similar.

[58] Interview, DK-12, August 8, 2012.

possible to "compensate" for costs imposed on subjects or "resolve" ethical dilemmas, and pondered the wisdom and utility of sending copies of one's work back to the field site.[59] And still others wondered whether, by conducting their work in an ethically sound fashion, they could avoid creating problems for future researchers.

On this issue, then, our respondents seemed to have more questions than answers, although their careful consideration of the questions reveals sensitivity to the issues at hand. It is also the case that, given the number of lives that one typically touches while in the field – for a moment, or for an extended period – one could clearly become paralyzed worrying about ethical issues. Moreover, as one scholar cautioned, while IRBs typically assume that researchers are all-powerful and respondents all-vulnerable, this is hardly the case in all circumstances.[60] We can offer no precise answers to the many troubling ethical dilemmas that field researchers inevitably face in their field sites. Rather, we simply underline the notion that thoughtful consideration of one's position on the ethical spectrum just mentioned, and self-conscious and active commitment to that position, are elements of all good field research.

Transparency

Engaging in research in a transparent fashion entails keeping track of, documenting, and justifying how one collected and analyzed data in the field, and the choices one made while doing so. Closely related to critical reflection and ethical commitment, being transparent in these ways helps scholars to operate more systematically and produce more persuasive studies,[61] and makes it easier for others to learn from – and to evaluate and replicate – their work.

As noted previously, we are introducing this principle on a more prescriptive than descriptive basis. Most scholars' fieldwork practices remain largely opaque, and even our interview respondents rarely discussed the ways in which their work was transparent. This situation hinders analytic progress. Colleagues who have packed suitcases and headed out into the intellectual unknown have accumulated an immense amount of collective knowledge – experience produces practical wisdom – and it is in our interest to learn from one another. Yet capitalizing on this stock of *savoir-faire* is not easy. Books

---

[59] Interview, LM-22, October 2, 2012.   [60] Interview, LM-17, September 11, 2012.
[61] Interview, DK-15, August 21, 2012.

and articles that draw on fieldwork rarely contain summaries of their authors' fieldwork practices that are sufficiently thorough to serve as guidance or inspiration. Authors rarely delve into the details and problems of data collection, let alone discuss how they analyzed and interpreted their data, or how they iteratively updated their original research designs.

Of course, there are important exceptions, as noted in previous chapters. Some scholars do give extended discussions of their field research practices in their written products (e.g., Fenno 1978; Scott 1985; Wedeen 1999; Wood 2003). And others offer separate accounts or reflections on what they did in the field (e.g., Tessler and Jamal 2006; Wood 2006; Paluck 2009). Yet because this wisdom is scattered in many different places and not (generally) studied, it is more difficult to access and digest.

Despite current practice, many of our interviewees acknowledged the importance of – or even argued persuasively for – transparent research practices when we brought it up. As one scholar explained, "The burden is on the person who does fieldwork to show how it was done; what is credible about that approach."[62] Another scholar invoked "science" when she explained the special burden of transparency that qualitative field researchers carry: "The thing we always hear about science is that we should be transparent. That's really important for fieldwork too to be transparent about what we do. Especially when you are soaking and poking and doing qualitative interviews."[63] Even when publication space is restricted, transparency contributes to an improved understanding of – and evaluation of – the data and insights derived from the field.[64]

Transparency has reasonable limits. It need not mean spending as much time documenting one's research as doing it. Carefully documenting one's research practices takes time, after all – time that some might feel would be better spent collecting more data or analyzing it. Further, to the degree that one's *data* are confidential, for example, one's data-collection practices may need to be kept confidential as well. Nonetheless, given the payoff – in terms of our ability to evaluate qualitative research effectively, and our ability to learn from it – we believe transparency can and should be a goal for scholars who collect their own data through fieldwork.

---

[62] Interview, LM-17, September 11, 2012.

[63] Interview, LM-13, September 7, 2012; also, LM-11, August 31, 2012.

[64] As one scholar summarized, "Transparency is good – we need to know how scholars developed their ideas. And it's important for future generations to learn about building knowledge." Interview, DK-11, July 30, 2012. See also Punch (1986, 15).

The six principles: application and implications

These six principles animate field research from the time a project is being conceived through the time it is being written up, and the best research rests on a careful consideration of each one. This does not necessarily mean, however, that each principle is equally salient at every moment. Indeed, they may sometimes be in tension or outright conflict with one another. A strong commitment to confidentiality, for instance, could complicate offering a detailed account of data-collection practices (Brooks 2013, 87). Likewise, engagement with the field context and flexible discipline might clash momentarily – as a scholar yearns to find out more about a tantalizing phenomenon related but not central to the project he is pursuing in the field. At such moments, scholars will need to evaluate whether to prioritize engagement or discipline.

These potential conflicts notwithstanding, we believe that the six principles of fieldwork most often reinforce one another, producing a stable and identifiable foundation for excellent field research. We offer just a few examples of the synergies among them, some of which were intimated previously. Engagement with context and critical reflection, for instance, help scholars put into practice their commitment to ethics. Unless a scholar develops a nuanced understanding of the context in which she is working – and is *thinking* about what she is learning – it will be difficult for her to discern what constitutes "ethical behavior" in that context. Engagement with context also facilitates triangulation, helping scholars to identify the various voices and perspectives that must be brought into their inquiry. Likewise, critical reflection facilitates flexible discipline and transparency: scholars need to be thinking critically about what they are doing in order to identify moments when flexibility should override discipline, and to be able to clearly articulate the processes through which they generated and analyzed data, and how those processes affected their evidence, inferences, and conclusions.

What are the implications of articulating and following these six principles of good field research? We suggest four. First, we believe scholars who follow these principles simply do better fieldwork. Discussing and developing them can help improve the teaching of fieldwork practices and give new practitioners general guidelines to follow as they build experience. Second, we believe articulating these principles – bringing to the fore the tacit consensus that has begun to form around them – helps to illustrate how difficult and time-consuming it can be to carry out field research. We do not wish to enter into debate about whether field research is more or less difficult than other forms of inquiry. Rather, we simply highlight that these principles demonstrate the time- and resource-intensity of field research – realities that we think deserve institutional recognition, as discussed below.

Third, we believe – and hope – that articulating these principles facilitates the disciplinary evaluation of field research, offering a basis for assessment not specific to any mode or type of fieldwork or any data-collection technique. Finally, we hold that these principles could serve as a basis for developing a common language for talking about field research. Developing and using a set of clear terms to discuss fieldwork practices – a vocabulary that captures and reflects these mutually agreed-upon principles – will help scholars to describe their field research and illustrate its effectiveness more easily, helping both proponents and skeptics see its value more clearly.

To close this section, we briefly highlight how the three arguments the book advances overlap and intersect. First, each of the three arguments explicates aspects of how field researchers in political science constitute a coherent if diverse community, with widely shared strategies, practices, and norms, and how this community contributes in extraordinary ways to the generation of new knowledge in political science. Second, it is because of the commonalities that underlie field research in the discipline that there *can be* a set of principles for good fieldwork. And finally, due to the value that field research adds, it is worth articulating these principles rather than leaving them implicit. We expand on these points further in the chapter's conclusion.

The future of field research

Having examined the history of field research in political science and explored scholars' experiences and practices of recent decades and the present day, we now shift our thinking toward the future, discussing how a series of dynamics will shape the need for and nature of field research in the years to come. The first two issues that we discuss – changing ethical norms and evolving disciplinary standards for transparency – link tightly to the last two principles of field research just mentioned, underscoring the centrality of some of the most critical debates in political science today for the future of field research. Subsequently, we consider the effect that changes in world politics, technology, and the availability of funding will have on fieldwork in the discipline.

Evolving ethical norms

Recent contestation and changes in the norms governing the ethical conduct of research are sure to affect field research in the future. Over the past several years, political scientists have joined other scholars in the social sciences to voice complaints about the increasing stringency of campus-level IRBs in the United States (Yanow and Schwartz-Shea 2008). One commonly espoused viewpoint was that since the requirements to protect human subjects had originated in an effort to regulate biomedical research, they were frequently inappropriate when applied to the social sciences. Some scholars also worried that the increasing decentralization of IRB enforcement meant that the local application of federal rules was inconsistent, leaving more room for good intentions to lead to bad outcomes.

In response to some of these concerns from social scientists, as well as others from the natural and health sciences, in late July 2011 the federal government proposed a sweeping reform of the set of human subject rules known as "The Common Rule."[65] Many of these reforms aimed to expand the federal government's power to regulate human subject research, and extend protections to more people.[66] For example, institutions receiving *any* federal funding would be required to apply the federal rules to *all* projects, even those that were not funded by the federal government.[67] With regard to the social sciences in particular, research involving surveys and interviews posing minimal risk to respondents would be exempted from IRB review; the reforms also sought to encourage clarification and standardization of consent forms. Government officials rationalized these and other changes as working to modernize the existing system and clarify federal expectations in order to streamline the entire IRB process.

The spirit of these federal guidelines – the protection of people whom scholars involve in their research – remains the same. However, the revised rules, if approved as originally conceived, could have both positive and negative *practical* effects for political science field research. On the one hand, more types of research would likely be considered "exempt" from full IRB review, simplifying and expediting the approval process for many scholars

---

[65] The Common Rule outlines *one* series of criteria for ethical supervision, informed consent, and the protection of human subjects at fifteen federal entities. See David Brown, "U.S. proposes rule changes for human subjects research." *Washington Post*, July 23, 2011. To our knowledge, as of March 2014, the rule changes proposed in 2011 had still not been implemented.

[66] See "Regulatory changes to ANPRM" at www.hhs.gov/ohrp/humansubjects/anprmchangetable.html.

[67] Many universities had already implemented this policy in the prior era of growing stringency in order to ensure proper and consistent compliance for all projects.

using survey and interview research. On the other hand, the increase in standardization of informed consent forms could make it more difficult for researchers to customize their forms for politically sensitive or foreign cultural contexts. This, in turn, could potentially compromise their ability to help their human subjects understand the risks they might face and benefits they might enjoy as a result of participating in research projects. This outcome would of course be at odds with the overall goals of protecting human subjects and ensuring *informed* consent.[68]

While federal human subject rules are being rewritten from the top-down, other ethical norms are changing from the bottom-up. Academics appear to be discussing and writing about these issues more frequently (Schrag 2010; Brooks 2013). In recent literature on field research, for example, scholars highlight the need for constant vigilance about ethical challenges and reflect critically on how best to respond before, during, and after data collection in the field (Punch 1986, 13; Scheyvens and Storey 2003, 233–37; Osaghae and Robinson 2005; Wood 2007).[69] As noted in Chapter 9, field experiments raise new kinds of ethical considerations on which the discipline should thought-fully reflect. In addition, there is growing concern on the part of some scholars that academic research should somehow benefit the people whom scholars involve in their studies, reflecting a shift from the historical focus on protection from harm to a new emphasis on beneficence.[70] For many scholars, this objective has translated concretely into sharing research results with field-site communities and study participants, particularly prior to publication in academic outlets.[71] Furthermore, in certain cases, "human subjects" themselves are initiating discussions and proposing new sets of rules and practices (Mihesuah 1993; American Indian Law Center 1999; Caldwell and Davis 2005).

New technologies have both helped and hindered scholars' efforts to fulfill their ethical obligations. For instance, the computers on which researchers

---

[68] In late August 2011, the APSA encouraged its members to voice their reactions individually and also solicited comments for discussion and resolution by the APSA Council at the national conference in Seattle in September 2011. APSA also contributed a response as a member of the Consortium of Social Science Associations (COSSA). The Social and Behavioral Science White Paper from COSSA responding to the proposed rule changes is available at: www.cossa.org/advocacy/2011/SBS-White-Paper-ANPRM-10-26-11.pdf.

[69] In addition, several books on field research either have "ethical challenges" in the title or have separate chapters dedicated to ethical dilemmas, e.g., Wilson (2005), Mertus (2009), Paluck (2009), and Thomson, Ansoms, and Murison (2012).

[70] The *idea* itself is not new; beneficence is one of the three core principles outlined in the Belmont Report in 1979. The other two are respect and justice.

[71] Schnabel (2005, 31) goes further to argue that study participants "should be considered the true owners of the data, which is held in trust (but not owned) by the researcher."

now routinely store enormous quantities of data in electronic form can be password-protected; further, electronic files can be encrypted and data can be uploaded and stored securely on a remote server or in "the cloud" (Romano 2006). Radsch (2009) highlights how important it was for her respondents in Egypt and Lebanon to be aware of her extensive efforts to maintain the security of their data. Nevertheless, electronic data can be challenging to organize and protect from accidental loss; moreover, they may be open to theft or hacking by a much broader range of people than materials research-ers store away in their closets in locked suitcases. New technologies have also made it much easier for scholars to share preliminary descriptions of research activities and research results with their field-site communities via personal blogs and organizational web sites. Of course, researchers who do so must be as vigilant about anonymizing the data and text as they are when publishing an article or book in order to protect project participants effect-ively (Sriram *et al.* 2009).[72]

In sum, the continuing evolution of top-down mandates concerning human subjects rules, the emergence of bottom-up initiatives, and the lack of clarity about how they will interact suggest a changing landscape with regard to the protection of human subjects. Given that ethical commitment is a key principle of good field research, scholars should closely monitor these debates and discussions, and continue to think critically about how best to protect the people they involve in their research.

Changing disciplinary standards about transparency

Over the past several years, political scientists have organized initiatives and developed proposals to facilitate data sharing, and to encourage greater transparency with regard to data collection, analysis, and interpretation.[73] These initiatives have begun to generate a discipline-wide conversation about the merits of providing access to the qualitative and quantitative data that support empirical claims in published work. As part of the discussion, the question has also been raised of whether, and how, scholars must explain the processes through which those data were collected and through which analytic conclusions were drawn from them.

---

[72] Sriram makes a similar point about the necessity to anonymize preliminary drafts that are circulated via email. Students and faculty often share early drafts that may still contain identifying information with other colleagues, who may then unwittingly forward them or even post them online.

[73] These advances are based on many years of discussion; see, e.g., the symposium on verification and replication in *PS: Political Science and Politics* in September 1995.

For instance, in 2010, an APSA Working Group on Data Access and Research Transparency (DA-RT) was formed and tasked with reformulating APSA's policies on the sharing of data and transparency in research practices. By October 2012, the DA-RT Working Group's recommendations had been adopted as APSA policy and approved for inclusion in the association's authoritative statement of ethical principles (the *APSA Guide to Professional Ethics, Rights and Freedoms*). In addition, two sub-committees had formed to develop clear, consensual, tradition-specific guidelines for implementing DA-RT principles.[74] APSA will likely build on these ongoing initiatives, for example by encouraging the adoption of incentives such as journal, publisher, and funder mandates to promote the sharing of data and greater transparency in research practices.[75]

An associated but separate effort focused on helping scholars who do qualitative work to instantiate DA-RT principles – the creation of an "active citation" standard – has been advanced by Andrew Moravcsik (2010). Active citation entails digitally enhancing citations in publications based on qualitative research by hyperlinking them to a Transparency Appendix (TRAX). The TRAX enriches traditional citation formats with excerpts from the underlying sources, and annotations indicating how those sources support the contentions in the text. The TRAX, in turn, can also be hyperlinked to the actual sources when they can be legally and ethically shared. Some academic journals, particularly in the field of law, are also requiring verification and retention of authors' original interview transcripts as a prerequisite for publishing research that uses those interviews as evidence (Sriram 2009, 61–64).

A related initiative is the launching of the Qualitative Data Repository (QDR) at Syracuse University.[76] Complementing existing institutional venues for storing and sharing data (e.g., ICPSR and Dataverse), QDR represents an important part of the infrastructure underlying the data-sharing initiatives mentioned above. Specifically, it offers scholars who gather data as part of qualitative and multi-method research a venue in which to

---

[74] Drafts of these guidelines were published as an appendix to the introduction to a symposium on data access and research transparency in the January 2014 issue of *PS: Political Science & Politics* (Lupia and Elman 2014).

[75] APSA's move in this direction is consistent with, and may have been encouraged by, the National Science Foundation's (NSF) earlier step to require that scholars whose research they fund share the data they collected or generated in the course of their work (see the NSF's *Proposal and award policies and procedures guide, part ii: award and administration guide*).

[76] See Elman, Kapiszewski, and Vinuela (2010). QDR, available at https://qdr.syr.edu, is funded by the National Science Foundation.

store and share them. Scholars can establish different levels of access to their data, helping to address potential human subjects and copyright concerns.

As we alluded to in our previous discussion of transparency, the arguments for sharing data are that doing so facilitates replication, permits secondary data analysis and spurs new research, and fosters greater collaboration among political scientists. Supporters have also emphasized how increased visibility into scholars' data, data-collection practices, and data-analysis techniques can facilitate the evaluation of all political science research, and serve important pedagogical purposes, allowing students to practice analytic techniques on downloaded data, and learn from scholars' discussions of how they carried out their research. In short, supporters believe these initiatives will improve the quality of political science research.

Critics hold that strengthening disciplinary norms for data sharing would carry unacceptable risks of identification for interview participants, highlighting that some subjects will simply be unable or unwilling to have their identity revealed and/or information they provide made available to other scholars. Others have noted the thorny intellectual property issues entailed by greater transparency.[77] Some interpretive scholars have also raised concerns about the epistemological basis of the sharing initiatives, especially the motivating view that replicability is desirable and achievable. Given their belief that knowledge is socially constructed, they question the premise that "raw data" exist, and consider it unlikely that any two scholars could interpret or understand data in exactly the same way.

Regardless of researchers' individual positions on these issues, norms are being debated and are likely to change to encourage a greater degree of transparency. Those changes will have a range of implications for political scientists who conduct field research. IRB protocols will need to be carefully (re)crafted, and scholars will have to develop ways to ensure that the individuals with whom they interact understand the implications of sharing their information with a very large audience, and are willing to provide their consent for researchers to do so. This type of *informed* consent could be difficult to secure from populations with less exposure to technology. Indeed, in some instances, protecting human subjects will imply sharing data only in partial form, or only after a resource-intensive process of contextualization.

With regard to another potentially worrying implication, the disciplinary encouragement of data sharing could place increasing value on collecting

---

[77] To date, these criticisms have been voiced informally in roundtable discussions but have not yet been published.

"shareable" data, which might influence what research questions scholars ask, and where and how they go about gathering the data to answer them. This could place field researchers under cross-pressures – intellectual pressure to ask innovative questions about evolving dynamics in newly open or contentious areas, for instance, and disciplinary pressures to ask safer questions about less-conflictual dynamics in more stable contexts. Finally, the time and expense involved in preparing data for sharing may be more difficult for most graduate students and some junior faculty to accommodate than for senior faculty. Changes in these norms, then, have the potential to augment existing disciplinary inequalities. More optimistically, evolving norms of data sharing will encourage those collecting piles of data during field research to treat those data even more carefully and to organize them systematically from the very beginning so that sharing down the line will be smoother and easier.

While these changes are important and impending, field researchers need not worry excessively. These initiatives are being constructed and advanced carefully and gradually in ways that involve open and inclusive intra-disciplinary (and, indeed, inter-disciplinary) dialogue. To give just two examples, all of the proposed changes to APSA's *Ethics Guide* were circulated to the Association's membership and posted on the APSA web site, and public debate and comment solicited. In addition, two roundtables addressing transparency issues were held at the APSA annual meeting in 2013, and another was held at the 2014 conference. Political scientists who engage in field research should remain attentive to – and indeed contribute to – these conversations, as evolving norms of transparency have the potential to impinge in multiple ways on how they conduct research in the field.

Geopolitical change and field research

Major shifts in world politics have shaped scholarly interest in and approaches to field research in political science in fundamental ways, as Chapter 2 discussed. For example, decolonization in Asia and Africa after World War II stimulated scholars to pay more attention to the politics of newly independent nations. The beginning of the Cold War then spurred the development of area studies centers in the United States, which provided extensive financial and institutional support for field research in particular regions. While the geopolitical implications of the major transformations the international political system has undergone during the last few decades have not yet come fully into focus, it seems clear that these dynamics will also have important implications for the future of field research in the discipline. The fall of the Soviet Union and the transitions to democracy in Eastern Europe obviously helped drive the spike in field research in this region in the 1990s. Similarly, the economic development of East Asia and the rising prominence of China have drawn successive waves of scholars to those areas.

Some of these geopolitical dynamics have complicated field research as well as energized it. For instance, the attacks of September 11, 2001, and the multiple wars and popular uprisings in the Middle East and North Africa in the 2000s have changed the political terrain in this region, both attracting new research attention and making on-the-ground study more difficult. The same could be said of the recent trend toward "democratic rollback" and authoritarian resilience, and of ongoing patterns of widespread civil unrest and violence (Themnér and Wallensteen 2011; Møller and Skaaning 2013). Moreover, in some instances these changes have generated attempts at increased control by funding agencies and university administrators. One scholar we interviewed expressed concern about the chilling effect that legislation passed in the wake of 9/11 (such as the Patriot Act), and evolving attitudes on the part of some universities about where students should study or what faculty travel should be funded with university monies, could have on research and the stream of students into Ph.D. programs.[78]

All of these events and phenomena in world politics have created new arenas for cutting-edge research, influencing the types of questions political scientists pose and where and how they conduct field research to answer them. Political changes and our desire to understand them have brought new urgency to research on issues such as political identity, religion, citizenship and nationalism, state failure and state-building, and inequalities with regard to class, ethnicity, and gender. Topics such as global governance, resource extraction, health, migration, environmental degradation, civil war, and corruption have risen in salience. Moreover, the growing importance of non-state actors – from terrorist groups to multinational corporations to transnational social movements – in many regions of the world have also influenced the form and focus of fieldwork.

Of course, even major world events do not necessarily have an *immediate* effect on field research. American political scientists do not flock to hot spots around the world in the same way that news correspondents or International Crisis Group researchers do. Very few of our survey respondents reported having done research in places like Sudan, Iraq, and Afghanistan. More

---

[78] Interview, DK-12, August 8, 2012.

generally, as we noted, only a minority within our discipline has a taste for working in particularly unsettled or even dangerous settings such as conflict zones. Yet, for decades, a persistent subset of political scientists has summoned the nerve to pursue research on pressing but sensitive topics in unstable political environments – areas of authoritarian rule, violence, or post-conflict reconstruction – and this will surely continue to be the case. These colleagues will face challenges of all kinds, including elevated levels of personal danger, and will need to use innovative data-collection techniques to obtain empirical evidence that may be intentionally hidden. They could also face significant temporal cross-pressures: while they may feel compelled to do their work as quickly as possible given unstable dynamics, it may actually take them a comparatively *longer* time to unravel and understand complex and quickly evolving phenomena in contexts that are in flux.

Scholars working in such contexts will also face more acute ethical challenges, requiring them to engage in careful and continuous critical reflection. For instance, gaining entrée and working in areas of conflict often require scholars to collaborate with multiple local partners and other individuals on the ground. Their responsibilities to their subjects are hence multi-layered and complex, often involving organizations, colleagues, and family members, rather than simply individual informants (Sriram *et al.* 2009). In extreme cases, the consequences of identification for some participants in certain scholars' research projects could be truly life-and-death. And scholars may need to anticipate and continually reevaluate the appropriate degree of transparency versus concealment as they carry out research and write up their findings.[79] In short, working on sensitive topics in conflictual areas raises the stakes of informed consent, anonymity, and confidentiality, and complicates already knotty ethical issues around analysis and write-up.

Whether in an area of high conflict or not, American researchers, and researchers affiliated with American institutions, may need to delicately negotiate their entry into some field sites because of the contentious role the United States plays in global politics and the possibility of anti-American sentiment (Katzenstein and Keohane 2007). In an unsettled world of new geopolitical friends and enemies, researchers may find it particularly tricky to develop and express their own position and stance in the field. Evolving geopolitics, then, will present both opportunities and risks for scholars engaging in field research in the future.

---

[79] See discussions by Gallaher (2009, 138) and Pachirat (2009).

Technological advancement and field research

Since the mid-1990s, the world has witnessed an unprecedented expansion of information and communication technologies with far-reaching consequences for field research. Technological change has made much more information publicly available and readily accessible online, expanding access to both old and new data sources. For example, while statements from the leaders of a rebel group might only have been available through in-person interviews in the past, since the early 1990s groups such as the Zapatistas in Mexico have actively provided updates on their mission and recent activities on their web site.[80]

More broadly, technological changes have opened up new virtual spaces for political action, interaction, and inquiry, generating novel questions ripe for study. For example, scholars today are keen to understand the role of social media such as Facebook and Twitter in organizing and publicizing massive social protests in the Middle East (Radsch 2009), and when, how, and why the Chinese government censors social media posts (King *et al.* 2013). Advances in technology have also facilitated the development of new data-collection techniques. For example, new communication technologies permit researchers to conduct in-depth interviews or survey interviews without going to the field, via email, text, telephone, or Skype.[81] Further, scholars now write scripts to "scrape" enormous amounts of information from the web. Such changes further blur the hazy boundaries between field research and other modes of data collection. For example, in the aftermath of the Boston Marathon bombings, one scholar began a project by doing "traditional" oral history interviews and using site-intensive methods in and around the blast sites and then expanded the project using social media to crowd-source oral histories from people who recount how they experienced or learned about the incident wherever they were, near and far.[82]

Given these changes and other technological advancement that will likely occur, will field research become less and less necessary in the future? Our analysis suggests that, while the technological revolution has influenced and

---

[80] See http://enlacezapatista.ezln.org.mx. See Russell (2005) for an example of an analysis based on Zapatista web sites and email lists.

[81] In the fall of 2011, Survey Monkey boasted of having over 8 million customers, including 100 percent of the Fortune 100 companies. See www.surveymonkey.com. Competition for online survey work among YouGov, Knowledge Networks, Zoomerang, Qualtrics, and others indicates the growing popularity of these applications in business and academic research.

[82] See the press release describing the project at www.fitchburgstate.edu/news/professor-launches-oral-history-project-about-marathon-bombing.

will likely continue to influence *how* and *how much* field research is conducted and *where* it is carried out, the practice itself will remain critical for developing deep knowledge about politics around the world. For instance, if archival documents can be downloaded electronically, or if mass public opinion datasets include the precise questions scholars wish to pose, they may be freed up to focus on in-depth interviews or ethnographic observation. Indeed, technological innovation opens up many new avenues for triangulation. Moreover, particularly given political scientists' interest in understanding volatile political dynamics, many scholars will be asking questions in places and situations in which electronic data have not become publicly available. Field research, and the opportunities for engagement and exploration it provides, will continue to be essential for understanding these contexts.

Furthermore, technology is not unbiased. Electronic data may reflect the views, behaviors, and priorities of elites – and may be directed (and thus biased) toward users of computers and mass media. As such, sources and materials available online may not reflect the perspectives of all actors, especially the less elite, wealthy, urban, or literate. Indeed, even in settings where digital information of one kind or another is available in ample quantities, fieldwork is often required to ask new questions and blaze new trails. As one of our interviewees put it, "there are zillions of kinds of data that you can't get online."[83] Finally, even if every imaginable piece of data were available electronically, and electronic sources could represent all of the perspectives important to a particular study, immersion in the political context where those pieces of evidence were created would still be critical to interpret them effectively. A virtual connection is simply not equivalent to "being there."

Happily, getting there is easier than ever before. While the technology for travel has not changed as dramatically as have other forms of technology in the recent past, in many contexts the cost and time associated with travel have shrunk. This change, combined with disciplinary pressure to generalize, may place growing demands on field researchers (or may help them fulfill their existing desire) to increase the number of field sites they visit, and/or to consider expanding their comparisons to include more geographically distant field sites.

It also bears noting that technologically advanced approaches and solutions are not by definition superior. Indeed, for many data-collection techniques involving human interaction, any interference between the subject and the

---

[83] Interview, DK-7, August 1, 2012.

researcher – even a simple audio-recording device on the table – might distract, diminish rapport, and degrade data quality. In some instances, the old-fashioned, low-tech approach – note-taking on a tablet of paper – may in fact be better. Still, there can be no question that technological change, in particular the increasing accessibility of the internet, and the growing power and versatility of web-enabled mobile computers (e.g., phones and tablets) will continue to shape fieldwork practices. Researchers will surely come home with fewer *things* (business cards, photocopies of documents, paper questionnaires, hard copies of books and reports) and more digitized information. Anyone who has stayed in touch with far-away research contacts and collaborators via video-chat or social networking platforms surely feels a shrinking of the distance between "field" and "home," a trend that will continue.

Advances in communications and travel have changed and will also continue to change the human experience of the researcher. Fieldwork is no longer as isolating as it was for many in the past. Even when working in remote, rural areas, scholars are often able to call, email, or video-chat with their family, friends, colleagues, and advisors.[84] In some cases, technology may allow a scholar's partner to accompany him or her to the field while continuing to carry out his or her own work duties remotely. Of course, while being able to connect with family more cheaply and frequently can certainly provide needed emotional support, it can also place weighty emotional demands on field researchers who may feel they are required to do "double duty" – both dealing with the multi-faceted challenges entailed by field research *and* resolving the day-to-day problems that arise with their family at home. It may also subtly change the ways in which researchers interact with the field setting, perhaps encouraging them to spend more of their spare time in front of a computer screen and less of it immersing themselves in local tea houses and theaters, thus diminishing peripheral forms of engagement with context. Nonetheless, having more social support in the field will doubtless be welcomed by many.

Technology is not an unalloyed good, of course, and its multiple implications for the conduct of field research need to be carefully considered.[85]

---

[84] Even for scholars who work in areas without cell-phone service or electric power, in most contexts communication centers are far easier to reach than they were several decades ago.

[85] We have mentioned just a small subset of these implications; the subsections on ethics and transparency highlighted others. To offer one additional downstream example, the internet increases the likelihood that some project participants will see what scholars write about them, thus potentially affecting their views of that scholar, and how (and whether) they choose to interact with him in the future.

Nonetheless, the technological revolution will not retreat. Instead, advancing technological change will continue to shift the boundary between information that can only be obtained via fieldwork and information that can be attained through other means, slowly but surely changing the methods, nature, function, and goals of field research.[86] As those changes proceed, political scientists should think creatively about how technology can facilitate, and indeed enhance, field-based inquiry.

Funding for field research

The sources from which scholars acquire funding to support field research, and the amount of funding they are able to secure, have critical ramifications for the questions they ask and the type of research in which they engage. Our survey and others' research suggest that, overall, the amount of funding available to support field research in political science may have decreased in recent years. As we saw in Chapter 2, nominal funding levels have risen over time, but, in real terms, projects started between 2000 and 2011 generally involved somewhat less money relative to projects of the previous two decades. Of course, projects vary widely in funding amounts, and some continue to be handsomely financed.[87] Moreover, given that the amount of time scholars spend in field sites has also been declining, average project funding on a per-day basis has been flat.[88] Thus the funding picture is mixed, but certainly sobering. The discipline can hardly expect a golden age of funding abundance in the near future, meaning that many faculty and graduate students will continue to face financial constraints on their field research. These challenges have their roots on both the demand side (grant applicants) and the supply side (funders).

On the demand side, at least with regard to funding for dissertation research, Agarwala and Teitelbaum observe that graduate students in political science (and sociology) seem to win fewer Fulbright–Hays Doctoral Dissertation Research Abroad (DDRA) fellowships, Social Science Research Council International Dissertation Research Fellowships (IDRF), and National Science

---

[86] Scheyvens and Storey (2003, 233–237) conclude that technology will change field research strategies less than we argue here.

[87] More technically, using the US consumer price index to adjust for inflation, as we did in our calculations in Chapter 2, oversimplifies the complex landscape represented by the actual purchasing power of dollars spent in various times and places around the world.

[88] Of course, the decreased time in the field may in fact be a *result* of scholars' inability to secure sufficient funding for longer stays.

Foundation awards, relative to competitors in the humanities, history, geography, archaeology, and anthropology. They suggest that, in part, this results from methodological trends. As political science and sociology departments have beefed up requirements for training in quantitative methods, students are left with little time for "contextual work that would include courses in language, history, culture, and area studies" and thus "their applications often fail to provide convincing evidence of their capacity and need to conduct fieldwork" (Agarwala and Teitelbaum 2010, 284). On the supply side, after the boom years of the 1990s, the endowments of US colleges and universities posted modest returns in the ten years from mid-2003 to mid-2013, and were rocked by the global economic downturn after 2008.[89] Further, many public universities have been hard hit by draconian cuts in state budgets for higher education.[90] And funding for federal agencies that support research grants – for instance the Fulbright–Hays fellowship program,[91] the National Science Foundation,[92] Title VI,[93] and others – has been dramatically reduced or significantly threatened.

It is vital to contemplate how continued restraints on certain types of funding may affect political science field research in the future. Undoubtedly,

[89] Reports from the National Association of College and University Business Officers attest to this. See, for instance, "Average annual one-, three, five, and ten-year total returns for U.S. higher education endowments and affiliated foundations for periods ending June 30, 2013," accessed on February 22, 2014, at www.nacubo.org/Documents/Endowment%20Files/ 2013NCSEPublicTablesOneThreeFiveandTenYearReturnsRevised.pdf, and "Average and median annual investment rates of return for U.S. college and university endowments and affiliated foundations, fiscal years ending June 30, 2013–2004," accessed on February 22, 2014, at www.nacubo. org/Documents/Endowment%20Files/2013NCSEPublicTablesAnnualRatesofReturn.pdf.

[90] Since 2008, at least forty-three states have made cuts in higher education. In many states, the 2011 fiscal year cuts were even deeper than those carried out between 2008 and 2010 (Johnson, Oliff, and Williams 2011).

[91] In late May 2011, the federal government officially announced that the Fulbright-Hays fellowship program for doctoral dissertation research abroad would be cancelled for 2011–2012 – the first complete suspension of the program since 1964. In the 2012 fiscal year the program funded 84 projects in 23 disciplines, far below its previous average of 108 projects annually (5,338 fellowships were awarded from 1964–2012). Figures are from "FY 2012 summary – Fulbright–Hays Doctoral Dissertation Research Abroad Program," accessed on February 22, 2014, at http://www2.ed.gov/ programs/iegpsddrap/awards.html.

[92] In 2013, legislation funding the National Science Foundation barred research on political science unless it promoted the "national security or the economic interests of the United States." In response, the NSF cancelled its summer 2013 grant cycle. A funding bill signed into law in January 2014 removed the restrictions on political science. See, for instance, "U.S. political scientists relieved that Coburn language is gone," accessed on February 22, 2014, at http://news.sciencemag.org/funding/2014/01/u.s.-political-scientists-relieved-coburn-language-gone.

[93] See Anna Grzymala-Busse, "Area-studies centers are vital but vulnerable," September 30, 2013, accessed on February 22, 2014, at https://chronicle.com/article/Area-Studies-Centers-Are-Vital/ 141939.

those who wish to conduct fieldwork will need to expand the scope of their funding search, looking far beyond the traditional sources while remaining attentive to potential conflicts of interest when conducting fieldwork funded by donors, corporations, or NGOs.[94] A related option might be to seek out opportunities to collaborate with researchers or institutions in the places they wish to study – a trend that is already evident in projects based around field experiments.[95] Yet even if these routes are pursued, funding constraints and the tendency toward shorter-duration field research that they may induce will affect the questions political scientists can answer, and thus the questions they ask. For instance, scholars might be less willing to tackle very complex (but substantively important) issues that necessitate longer periods of field-work, and may emphasize more policy-relevant questions.[96] Likewise, funding limitations may make it more difficult for political scientists to work in remote and difficult-to-access places, conflict settings (where field research can take considerably longer to complete)[97] or contexts known to be particularly expensive. Most broadly, if funding becomes harder to come by, it may simply be that fewer political scientists carry out field research.

Finally, it seems important to consider the ways in which funding constraints may exacerbate inequalities. As we noted earlier, students at higher-ranked institutions are able to secure more funding for international dissertation research than their counterparts at less-elite schools. While this may simply reflect meritocratic processes through which students are selected into graduate programs and proposals are selected for funding, it behooves the discipline to ensure that students from many backgrounds have a shot at obtaining resources for fieldwork. Only a subset of those graduate students and faculty who are unable to acquire private or public funding will be able to self-finance their field research.[98] While we can do little more than speculate on two other potential trends, it is worthwhile to think about whether funding constraints could result in fewer graduate students conducting field research (as what little money there is will be granted to more advanced scholars who are a better bet for funders), and

---

[94] The increased availability of funding from sources such as the Department of Defense would also have critical implications for field research.

[95] Interview, LM-8, August 30, 2012.   [96] Interview, LM-9, August 30, 2012.

[97] Romano (2006, 441) estimates that field research in contexts of conflict takes three to four times longer than elsewhere. Our data provide little evidence that political scientists working in conflict settings spend more time in the field than those working elsewhere, but data collection may be less efficient.

[98] Another probable effect will be longer doctoral program completion times. Many graduate students will likely attempt a second round of grant applications before making the final decision not to conduct field research.

whether field research will increasingly be carried out by scholars with greater independent financial means.[99]

In sum, important and ongoing changes in several areas – ethical norms, disciplinary standards for transparency, world politics, technology, and funding – will shape field research in political science in significant ways in the future. These trends will create new challenges *and* new opportunities for political scientists who engage in fieldwork. Scholars' willingness and ability to address the former and embrace the latter will lead to continued changes in the role and nature of field research in the discipline.

Conclusion: a clarion call to the discipline

Throughout this final chapter and the book as a whole, we have advanced three arguments, each illuminating how it is that field research in political science makes tremendous contributions to our knowledge about politics, and to theory building in the discipline. First, we have demonstrated the heterogeneity of political science field research and shown its unifying commonalities, arguing that this "bounded eclecticism" helps make field research a formidable technique for generating rich data and analytic insights. Second and relatedly, we have highlighted the ways in which fieldwork advances multiple analytical dimensions of a research project: as scholars collect and consider their data, they engage in layered learning that inspires informed iteration among data collection, data analysis, and key elements of research design. And finally, we have argued that six simple but crucial principles underlie good political science field research. In this concluding section, we draw on those arguments to issue a clarion call to the discipline, challenging political scientists of all epistemological leanings and all subfields to *spread out* and give more attention to under-studied parts of the world, to *collaborate* more in connection with field research, to *think and write* more about field research, to *re-envision graduate methods education*, and to *recognize* the contributions of field research in more tangible ways.

Spreading out

As was noted in Chapter 2, US-based political scientists have concentrated their field research on certain parts of the world and neglected others.

---

[99] The data we collected through our survey do not show an increase in self-funded fieldwork.

Locations within the United States have been the focus of much field study, but looking just at international destinations, we see substantial imbalances. Europe, particularly Western Europe, has attracted the lion's share of research visits, though its predominance is declining. In the rest of the world, certain places are studied fairly intensively, such as the capitals and other major cities of Latin America and East Asia, while other locations such as much of Africa, Central Asia, and Southeast Asia are conspicuously under-studied. Political scientists are far more likely to study rich countries than poor countries.

It is not difficult to speculate about the reasons, which we may consider more or less valid, for this bunching-up. Many political scientists seek to study how those in power wield authority and influence, and certain forms of power are geographically concentrated. A researcher pursuing a project on international financial regulation is more likely to do interviews in London than in Yogyakarta. Furthermore, scholars may feel pressure to study larger countries that seem more "significant," and from which findings may be generalizable to other significant locales. We may also tend to study places (and parts of places) where English is more likely to be spoken. And disciplinary currents that flag certain topics and places as trendy and mar-ketable for grant-writing, job-landing, and book-publishing purposes can be difficult to fight.

Still, we pay a price for our relative neglect of certain areas, and there are significant gains to be made by spreading out. Our understanding of key concepts may be biased if they are developed based on special reference to particular cases and not to others. And there is a danger of reproducing within the academy the biases and inequalities that exist in the actual political world. Put more positively, as we have emphasized, field research advances knowledge by bringing existing ideas and concepts into contact with new phenomena and empirical realities. A broader geographical base of field research is certain to help drive innovation. Some relatively little-studied places have clear intrinsic importance, whether we think of Tunisia, Somalia, Iran, Afghanistan, Burma, Vietnam, or Indonesia. Perhaps less intuitively, learning more about poorly understood locales can lead to the development of significant new insights about what is different and significant about the places we thought we already "got," and about how the international system works more generally. Moreover, precisely because we do not know where the next global "hot spot" or crisis zone will be, developing expertise on areas around the world through on-the-ground experience will help build a more well-rounded discipline that can address the political problems of tomorrow, whatever they might be. Thus, political science should work toward directing more resources – human, financial, and intellectual – toward under-studied parts of the world.

Collaborating

Our second call is for enhanced collaboration and coordination around field research. This call has several components. First, we strongly encourage scholars to consider different ways they might make their own field research into a more collaborative enterprise. In 2006, an APSA Working Group on Collaboration noted that collaborative work was expanding significantly in political science, particularly among faculty and students who were asymmetric by rank. We believe it would be hugely beneficial to transfer that spirit to field research in various ways. Collaboration between and among US scholars with complementary strengths and skills is of course fundamental. For instance, collaboration between a scholar better-versed in quantitative methods and another with stronger qualitative skills would encourage a widening of the data-collection net, and expand the types of analysis that could be performed on data gathered in the field. But fieldworkers might also coordinate more closely, for instance, with researchers or others in the contexts that they study – for instance, with those who have language skills that they lack, or who have mastered the deployment of certain data-collection techniques in those contexts. Developing ethical, productive, and mutually beneficial partnerships of these types – and maintaining objectivity while doing so – are continuing challenges for field research, and should be topics of significant debate.

Another way in which political scientists who conduct field research can act in a collaborative manner is by sharing their data, as well as information and ideas about field research. Data sharing is a key tenet of research transparency, one of the principles underlying good field research. Yet collaboration can and should go beyond sharing data. Ideas about and strategies for conducting fieldwork are often shared informally among small subsets of students, between students and mentors who have conducted field research, or among pairs of faculty who have done so. Even for those who are part of such networks, the information relayed is usually partial in at least two related ways. First, these conversations cannot thoroughly cover all of the topics relevant and critical to field research. Second, and more generally, the individual perspectives and particular experiences of a few students or faculty cannot possibly reflect the richness and heterogeneity of fieldwork in the discipline.

This imperfect situation should be addressed, in part, through the development of online field research information resources. For instance, the Methods Coordination Project (MCP), an online bibliography curated by coordinators with expertise in different methodological areas, provides lists of readings concerning a variety of data-collection techniques, as well as writing about field research more generally.[100] Future iterations of MCP will allow users to interact with one another, and to share information on particular topics or geographical locations. Moreover, in close association with this book project, we are developing an independent web site that will allow scholars to share their field research experiences and the fieldwork practices and strategies they have developed.[101] The site will offer resources such as templates for organizing materials, and for letters requesting affiliation, introducing oneself and one's project, or inviting participation in a study. Ultimately, we hope that interactive fora will develop in which researchers leaving for, working in, or returning from field sites around the globe can exchange basic logistical information, contacts, and ideas. Our hope is that field researchers from the United States and around the world will find new ways to communicate about past experiences and future plans, helping each other and everyone to do better field research.

Thinking and writing about field research

We hope this book advances, and lends energy and impetus to, emerging conversations about whether, when, where, how, and why political scientists should conduct field research. Our call on this front is a simple one: we encourage scholars to join the conversation. Just as ours are not the first words on any of the many complex issues raised in this book, they hardly can be the last. We challenge scholars to strongly disagree with us, to draw, build and improve on what we have offered here, and to innovate in many other directions. By thinking and working together, we can construct a strong intellectual infrastructure guiding the conduct of field research.

If the attitudes of the colleagues whom we had the pleasure of interviewing in the course of our research for this book are any indication, political scientists have much to contribute to this dialogue. As we noted before, more

---

[100] The MCP is available online at https://qdr.syr.edu/mcp; its URL may change.
[101] The web site can be found at www.psfieldresearch.com.

often than not, these interviews extended far beyond an hour as faculty and graduate students carefully related the challenges they faced and the solutions they devised in the field, forthrightly divulged their mistakes to us, proudly shared their successes, and clearly articulated what they learned from it all. At many points during these conversations, respondents also expressed the wish to know how others had handled similar dilemmas in the field. We were left with the enduring impression that there is an unmet need for careful consideration of fieldwork in political science.

We very much hope our book can accelerate ongoing conversations, spark a wide range of new debates, and inspire scholars to *write about* and publish on their fieldwork experiences. They might do so by penning stand-alone methodological pieces. But just as important are more explicit and detailed narratives, in substantive work based on field research, of political scientists' research strategies, the methodological and ethical dilemmas they faced in the field, the criteria they used to adjudicate among solutions, the choices they made, and the outcomes they engendered. To the degree possible, these narratives can be integrated into the body of books and articles; when space limitations impinge, they could be included as web appendices, for instance. Heeding this call, which is of course in line with initiatives for greater research transparency, would advance the disciplinary dialogue concerning the practices and value of field research, *and* facilitate the teaching of field research methodologies, discussed below.

Re-envisioning graduate methods training

Across the United States, graduate programs in political science uniformly emphasize methods courses that teach students techniques for data *analysis*. The importance of learning how to deploy tools of data *collection* effectively is immensely underappreciated. Gaining the skills to collect data carefully and systematically, particularly in the context of field research, is at least as crucial for doing good research as learning how to analyze data. Without precision with regard to data collection, scholars' analyses may lose meaning: garbage in, garbage out.

Given this reality, we call on graduate programs to reconsider the structure of their methods requirements. As it stands, students are often required to take three, four, or even five methods courses, while the pressure to complete graduate studies in a timely manner has not abated. These courses are critical for students to gain data-analysis skills. Yet this requirement often prevents students from taking courses that would provide them with the tools they need to be effective at data collection, such as language courses,[102] courses on ethnography or interviewing techniques, or courses focusing on particular geographical regions in the United States or around the world. We urge graduate programs to afford students who wish to engage in field research the time to take these sorts of courses, *and to award them credit for doing so*. Taking these courses would make students far more effective at fieldwork; moreover, as Agarwala and Teitelbaum's (2010) alarming study makes clear, the knowledge gained from such courses can be immensely important for securing funding for field research. To be clear, those who engage in fieldwork should also be required to take a range of courses on data analysis, and become conversant in multiple analytic techniques. Our simple proposal is that students *also* have the opportunity to take, and receive the appropriate credit for taking, the courses that will help them to carry out their inquiries most effectively.

We also strongly recommend that graduate programs develop, and consistently offer, stand-alone courses on field research.[103] To be clear, we refer here not to qualitative methods courses that have a week or two on interviewing or archival research, but to full quarter- or semester-long courses focused completely on preparing for and carrying out field research, and engaging in the multiple data-collection techniques discussed in this book. The significant commonalities that mark field research in the discipline make it possible to include such instruction in graduate education, and the intrinsic difficulty of carrying out field research effectively makes it critical to do so. The goal of such courses would not be to standardize field research practices, but rather to more systematically share lessons about how to design, prepare, and manage fieldwork.[104]

Offering such courses would provide multiple benefits. Ideally, they would incorporate readings on and discussions of how field research methods and practices relate to the range of topics covered in qualitative and quantitative methods courses, clarifying the sometimes tenuous connections

---

[102] As one expert respondent put it, rather bluntly, "you're going to do something terribly incompetent, or you're going to know the language" (interview, LM-18, September 14, 2012).

[103] As one interview respondent put it, in many graduate programs, the current attitude toward such courses is one of "benign neglect" (interview, BR-9, August 16, 2012).

[104] There are of course existing opportunities to learn about field research. Short courses on field research are already taught at APSA, and at the summer Institute on Qualitative and Multi-Method Research. These courses have significant value and are a critical foundation for many students in graduate programs that do not offer field methods courses. However, these courses are extremely compressed; as a result, heated discussions must be cut short, nuanced points simplified, and practicing techniques shortchanged.

between data collection and data analysis. Indeed, as we have noted, field research is relevant for research design, concept formation, gaining causal leverage, and many other crucial analytic tasks. Likewise, the ways in which scholars design their projects and plan to deploy qualitative or quantitative analytic methods have a range of implications for field research design and execution. Further, advanced reading, reflection, and preparation for field research will help scholars design stronger research projects (and write more specific dissertation prospectuses), and will reduce uncertainty heading into the field. They will also enable researchers to make better snap decisions, develop more effective contingency plans, and revise their field research strategies in appropriate ways when they encounter obstacles in the field.

Such courses would also expose students to a range of experiences and practices and provide them with space and time to digest and discuss what they are learning. First, such classes would call on them to critically reflect on the relative value of various approaches and strategies to fieldwork. Since much of the published literature on fieldwork methodologies is written from the perspective of other social science disciplines, such courses could also help students to translate the insights from those literatures into the context of political science. Further, students would benefit from having a forum for engaged discussion about the texts, rather than having to process the debates on their own. Finally, such courses would give students the opportunity to practice techniques they might use in their own projects, and develop the skills to evaluate other scholars' field research. Graduate students have gotten the signal from the discipline that mixed method research is valued, but they are infrequently given the tools to do it well.

These proposals for re-envisioning graduate methods training will doubt-less be controversial. Students always face tradeoffs in balancing required field and method seminars during their short period of active coursework. Department chairs, graduate directors, and faculty are under increasing pressures to ensure graduate students make "normal progress" and finish their degrees in a timely manner. Yet the undeniable truth is that preparation is critical for effective field research. We should not encourage graduate students to parachute into an unknown place and commence research without the benefit of instruction in techniques and approaches that have proven effective for generations of political scientists. The methodologies of field research, and the ancillary skills needed to do it effectively, can be taught and should be an important component of graduate education in political science.

Recognizing the contributions of field research

Most political science departments assess a scholar's productivity during graduate school, recruitment, promotion, and merit reviews in terms of the quantity and quality of articles and books published (in addition to evaluating their teaching effectiveness and service contributions), and the time it took the scholar to produce them. Thus, field research is rewarded insofar as it results in dissertations and publications in what the discipline considers a reasonable timeframe. This is not fundamentally wrong; after all, the primary purpose of field research is to create new knowledge. It is thus reasonable to assess the value of fieldwork, in part, by evaluating the knowledge it generates – the publications a scholar is able to produce on its basis.

Still, this arguably creates inequities and disincentives for field research. As our interviewees and survey data have attested, fieldwork has many costs. Preparing to carry it out, securing funding, and actually conducting field research are extremely time-consuming, for instance, and the second of these introduces a great deal of uncertainty into one's academic trajectory. As our survey results show, many scholars spend significant amounts of time in the field – and these numbers do not reflect the time intense preparation for fieldwork takes. Of course, subjecting oneself to these costs, and finding ways to overcome the significant challenges and hardships that fieldwork itself can entail, is a choice; no one is *forced* to do field research. Nonetheless, as we have sought to demonstrate throughout this book, for some of the questions that political scientists wish to ask and answer, there is no other way to gather the necessary information, no other way to identify the relevant dynamics – no other way to create the public good that knowledge represents – than through "being there." And "being there" has costs.

Moreover, publications alone do not fully reflect the value that field research creates. Fieldwork, particularly when guided by the principles we have identified, enables scholars to deepen the discipline's general understanding of politics throughout the United States and the world. It brings – and brings alive – knowledge about critical places that the vast majority of us will never visit, and allows it to accumulate. It allows us to knit important international connections and build rich epistemic communities. It allows scholars who have done fieldwork in a particular location to better evaluate the research of others who study that location. It allows faculty to guide and train graduate students on crucial forms of inquiry. And it helps political scientists to contribute much more – and much more authoritatively – to public debate, and, in some circumstances, to key foreign policy decisions. In other words, we all benefit handsomely, in multiple ways, from the fieldwork a subset of us does.

Given the time fieldwork takes to execute, and the enduring value of the contributions it enables scholars to make, we believe that departments, universities, and professional associations should reward fieldwork with greater institutional recognition. First, departments should acknowledge the time required for fieldwork when evaluating the progress of graduate students and the productivity of job candidates and of faculty coming up for tenure and promotion. They should take into account the fact that amassing original data and accumulating understanding through layered learning in the field requires time – time that scholars who can take advantage of ready-made data sources are able to spend writing. Second, while the value that good fieldwork adds *beyond* that which is reflected in the publications scholars write based on field research is difficult to assess, it unarguably exists, and should be rewarded – perhaps through the establishment of additional prizes or awards for outstanding fieldwork along the lines of that already created by APSA's Comparative Democratization section, and certainly in political science departments' periodic evaluations of faculty. The discipline, in other words, should establish standards of productivity that fairly reflect the special kinds of work and effort that field research requires, and the unique and multi-faceted contributions it makes to political knowledge.

To conclude: we hope this book helps to propel an open and fruitful disciplinary debate that moves us toward accomplishing the five goals just outlined. Doing so, we are convinced, will encourage members of the profession to do more field research and help them to do it *well*. In this way, political scientists will continue to produce cutting-edge, standard-setting scholarship that provides compelling answers to significant political questions.

Appendix: Methodology for survey and in-depth interviews

The Field Research in Political Science survey

Why *survey* our political scientist brethren about their field research? This may seem a surprising component of a work of methodology, a genre that contains more prescription than description. Though our book does, among other things, put forward suggestions for how to conduct field research as efficiently as possible (best practices), obtaining a baseline of what people do in the field (existing practices) was also important. Such a survey of the profession as a whole has never been done before. Without a broad empirical picture of what colleagues do and have done, those who write about field research and its history run the risk of mischaracterizing the actual state of things. In dispensing advice on any area of human affairs (marriage, business leadership, waging war), there is a serious danger of over-generalizing from one's own experiences. In addition to providing essential context for the book's prescriptive arguments, and its explication of the ways in which field research contributes to knowledge, we also believe that the survey results will be of use to many people. That includes, for instance, political scientists who do or are considering fieldwork, or who advise students and plan curricula. Colleagues in other fields, administrators, and funding organizations may also benefit from the findings.

The Field Research in Political Science web-based survey of faculty went into the field beginning on November 20, 2011, and the last responses were received in the summer of 2012. The instrument was developed over the course of half a year and three rounds of pilot testing, in consultation with survey methodologists at the University of California at Berkeley, Northwestern University, and Indiana University. In the survey we defined conducting *field research* as "leaving your home institution to collect data or information that significantly informs your research." As the instructions to respondents indicated, this definition includes trips of any duration, to field sites near or far, to collect information in any form. Archival research, interviews, field experiments, surveys, participant observation, ethnography, and more can all be part of fieldwork.[1] In the course of writing this book we opted to expand our definition of field research slightly, to "leaving one's home institution in order to acquire data, information, or insights that significantly inform one's research." The addition of "insights" highlights, for the reader's benefit, our theme that field research is about more than just the accumulation of data, but we are confident that the survey would not have been meaningfully different had we included this word in the definition there.[2]

It would be possible to ask political scientists questions about their field research practices *in toto* or in general, but (particularly for experienced scholars) that would mean inquiring about diverse activities spanning long periods of time, the answers to which could only be vague. Instead, the survey was structured around the individual *field research project*. This was defined as an academic research project, of which field research was one component, aimed at producing scholarly work such as a conference paper, an article or set of articles, a dissertation, or a book.[3] Respondents were asked a set of questions about their preparation for field research, and (at the end) other questions about their backgrounds and several open-ended questions about lessons learned in the field. The core of the survey consisted of batteries of questions focusing on specific field research projects. Respondents were given one such battery concerning their *first* field research project, then another about their *most recent* project (if any other projects had been undertaken and completed, or nearly completed, since the first project).

---

[1] To help clarify the meaning of "field research," so that all respondents might think about it in the same ways, the survey included the following information: "One's own personal presence at the field site(s) is an integral part of our definition. If you sent a graduate student to a field site to do research on your behalf, then the student did field research, but you did not. If you spent a month in the field training RAs who continued working for two months after you left, then you did a month of field research. Traveling to other institutions to have conversations with colleagues there is considered field research, if what is learned from those conversations constitutes information that significantly informs your research. Conducting interviews by telephone from your home institution, however, is not considered field research. Checking out books from the library at a nearby university is not field research, but taking notes on an archive collection at that university is. Accessing data in remote locations via the internet would not be considered field research, but traveling in person to obtain access to existing datasets would."

[2] It is hard to imagine a scholar setting out on a field research project seeking only "insights" and not either "data" or "information" of any kind.

[3] The following clarifying information was included: "We are interested in projects on which you were either the primary researcher or one of a group of primary researchers. A single field research project may involve one or many field research trips (close together or far apart in time), to one or multiple locations."

Those with extensive experience were given the option of completing a third battery about the project that they felt was *most representative* of their field research as a whole.

We aimed to survey the entire profession in a highly inclusive fashion, though to make the project tractable we confined ourselves to colleagues working at US institutions. APSA provided its list of all United States-based political science faculty; thus, our respondents were not limited merely to APSA members. After some cleaning and verification, this provided an initial sampling frame of 10,558 political scientists. In all, invitation emails were sent to a randomly selected sample of 5,188 members of this set. The number of invitations delivered to actual political scientists was 4,962.[4] Of these, 1,142 people took the survey, yielding a response rate of about 23 percent. The subset of political scientists who agreed to take the survey corresponds closely to the full sampling frame in many observable respects, diverging slightly in others.[5] It is almost certain, however, that the survey shows a response bias toward those who had conducted field research – despite our hope, stated in the invitation emails, that political scientists of all backgrounds would participate. Only 16.5 percent of respondents had no field research experience and no plans to undertake field research. It seems reasonable to think of the survey as representative of political science faculty who have done field research, though not necessarily of the profession's faculty as a whole. Respondents' average age was forty-seven and average Ph.D. year was 1997.

The faculty survey generated two sets of data: one in which the observations are respondents ($n = 1,142$), and one in which the observations are field research projects reported by those respondents ($n = 1,468$). Chapter 2 presents many results from the survey, and other findings are reported elsewhere in the book. In later articles we will present more detailed analysis of particular topics such as funding, languages, and locations.

---

[4] Those whose email accounts produced delivery-failure responses (and for whom no new contact information could be found), those who had left the profession, and those who replied to say they were not political scientists were dropped from the sample.

[5] Women constituted 37 percent of survey respondents but only 30 percent of the sampling frame. Proportions of political scientists identifying with each of eight major subfields among the respondents are within 3 percentage points of the proportions in the sampling frame, except that comparativists are over-represented by 6 percentage points and theorists are under-represented by 4 percentage points. In terms of rank, adjuncts, assistant professors, associate professors, and full professors constituted 11, 34, 26, and 29 percent of respondents, respectively, and 12, 27, 26, and 34 percent of the sampling frame. Faculty from Ph.D.-granting departments are somewhat overrepresented, at 43 percent of respondents and 38 percent of the sampling frame.

In-depth interviews of political science faculty and graduate students

In addition to the survey, we also conducted in-depth interviews with a diverse group of faculty and a few graduate students from April 2012 through December 2013: 62 scholars in total. These interviews allowed us to probe in more detail how scholars thought about and carried out field research. As noted in the book's chapters, the interviews were designed to last 30 minutes but often spanned over an hour as researchers recounted stories and reflected on their experiences.

We used a purposeful selection strategy to choose the respondents. Our intention was to draw on the expertise of scholars who had conducted and published scholarship based on extensive fieldwork in a variety of places and using different data-collection techniques. The collective experience of the researchers we interviewed covers every continent; both the advanced industrialized and developing world; democratic and authoritarian regimes; and rural and urban settings. For each of the data-collection techniques covered in the book, we have interviewed at least 11 and up to 22 scholars who have employed it previously in the field.

We also aimed for our sample of interviews to capture gender, rank, and subfield diversity in the discipline. We have interviewed 30 men and 32 women. In terms of rank, our respondents include: 3 non-academics, 2 graduate students, 22 assistant professors, 18 associate professors, and 17 full professors. Our sample is heavy on comparativists (42) but also reflects the views of Americanists (7), theorists (2), IR scholars (6), policy specialists (2), and others (3). While political science faculty and graduate students were the target respondents, we also interviewed a handful of faculty in other disciplines where appropriate, including history, sociology, law, and economics.

Each of the co-authors conducted interviews either in-person, by telephone, or via voice-over-internet software. All respondents were guaranteed full anonymity, as we wished to solicit their candid insights on past and current successes and failures. The co-authors each tailored a longer interview guide for individual participants. Our styles varied in terms of how structured the conversations remained during the course of the interview.

References

Aberbach, Joel D., James D. Chesney, and Bert A. Rockman. 1975. "Exploring elite political attitudes: some methodological lessons." *Political Methodology* 2 (1):1–27.

Aberbach, Joel D., and Bert A. Rockman. 2002. "Conducting and coding elite interviews." *PS: Political Science and Politics* 35 (4):673–676.

Abramson, Scott, and Graeme Blair. 2011. "Borders as a natural experiment: assessing the causal effects of British colonialism in Sub-Saharan Africa." Paper presented at the Midwest Political Science Association annual meeting. Chicago, IL, March 31 – April 1.

Adcock, Robert, and David Collier. 2001. "Measurement validity: a shared standard for qualitative and quantitative research." *American Political Science Review* 95 (3):529–546.

Adida, Claire L. 2014. *Immigrant exclusion and insecurity in Africa: coethnic strangers.* Cambridge University Press.

Adler, Patricia, and Peter Adler. 2001. "The reluctant respondent." In *Handbook of interview research: context and method*, ed. Jaber F. Gubrium and James A. Holstein. Thousand Oaks, CA: Sage Publications.

Agarwala, Rina, and Emmanuel Teitelbaum. 2010. "Trends in funding for dissertation field research: why do political science and sociology students win so few awards?" *PS: Political Science and Politics* 43 (2):283–293.

Agger, Robert E., Daniel Goldrich, and Bert E. Swanson. 1964. *The rulers and the ruled: political power and impotence in American communities.* New York: Wiley.

Ahn, T. K., Elinor Ostrom, and James Walker. 2010. "A common-pool resource experiment with postgraduate subjects from 41 countries." *Ecological Economics* 69 (12):2624–2633.

Aldrich, Daniel P. 2008. *Site fights: divisive facilities and civil society in Japan and the West.* Ithaca, NY: Cornell University Press.

Alger, Chadwick F. 1963. "United Nations participation as a learning experience." *The Public Opinion Quarterly* 27 (3):411–426.

1966. "Interaction and negotiation in a committee of the United Nations General Assembly." *Peace Research Society (International) Papers* 5:141–159.

1970. "Research on research: a decade of quantitative and field research on international organizations." *International Organization* 24 (3):414–450.

Allard, Scott W. 2009. *Out of reach: place, poverty, and the new American welfare state.* New Haven, CT: Yale University Press.

Allina-Pisano, Jessica. 2009. "How to tell an axe murderer: an essay on ethnography, truth and lies." In *Political ethnography: what immersion contributes to the study of power*, ed. Edward Schatz, 53–73. University of Chicago Press.

Almond, Gabriel A. 1946. "Politics, science, and ethics." *American Political Science Review* 40 (2):283–293.

Almond, Gabriel A., and Sidney Verba. 1963. *The civic culture: political attitudes and democracy in five nations.* Princeton University Press.

American Indian Law Center. 1999. *Model tribal research code: with materials for tribal regulation for research and checklist for Indian Health Boards.* 3rd edition. Albuquerque, NM: American Indian Law Center.

Ames, Barry. 2001. *The deadlock of democracy in Brazil.* Ann Arbor: The University of Michigan Press.

Amit, Verid. 2000. "Introduction: constructing the field." In *Constructing the field: ethnographic fieldwork in the contemporary world,* ed. Verid Amit, 1–18. London: Routledge.

Anderson, Benedict. 1991. *Imagined communities: reflections on the origin and spread of nationalism.* London: Verso.

Apostolidis, Paul. 2010. *Breaks in the chain: what immigrant workers can teach America about democracy.* Minneapolis: University of Minnesota Press.

Atkinson, Robert. 2012. "The life story interview as mutually equitable relationship." In *The Sage handbook of interview research: the complexity of the craft,* ed. Jaber F. Gubrium, James A. Holstein, Amir B. Marvasti, and Karyn D. McKinney, 115–128. Thousand Oaks, CA: Sage Publications.

Autesserre, Séverine. 2010. *The trouble with the Congo: local violence and the failure of international peacebuilding.* Cambridge University Press.

Bailey, Carol. 2006. *A guide to qualitative research.* Thousand Oaks, CA: Sage Publications.

Bajpai, Rochana. 2011. *Debating difference: group rights and liberal democracy in India.* New Delhi: Oxford University Press.

Baker, Andy. 2009. *The market and the masses in Latin America: policy reform and consumption in liberalizing economies.* Cambridge University Press.

Baker, Andy, Barry Ames, and Lucio R. Ren. 2006. "Social context and campaign volatility in new democracies: networks and neighborhoods in Brazil's 2002 elections." *American Journal of Political Science* 50 (2):382–399.

Baldez, Lisa. 2002. *Why women protest: women's movements in Chile.* Cambridge University Press.

Baldwin, Kate. 2013. "Why vote with the chief? Political connections and public goods provision in Zambia." *American Journal of Political Science* 57 (4):794–809.

Banerjee, Abhijit, and Esther Duflo. 2011. *Poor economics: a radical rethinking of the way to fight global poverty.* New York: PublicAffairs.

Banfield, Edward C. 1958. *The moral basis of a backward society.* Glencoe, IL: The Free Press.

Barber, James David. 1965. *The lawmakers: recruitment and adaptation to legislative life.* New Haven, CT: Yale University Press.

Barnes, Jeb, and Nicholas Weller. 2012. "Finding pathways: case selection for studying causal mechanisms in mixed-methods research (September 21)." Available at SSRN: http://ssrn.com/abstract=2150372 or http://dx.doi.org/10.2139/ssrn.2150372.

Barnett, Michael N. 1997. "The UN Security Council, indifference, and genocide in Rwanda." *Cultural Anthropology* 12 (4):551–578.

 2002. *Eyewitness to a genocide: the United Nations and Rwanda.* Ithaca, NY: Cornell University Press.

Barrett, Christopher, and Jeffrey Cason. 2010. *Overseas research: a practical guide*. Baltimore, MD: Johns Hopkins University Press.

Barry, Christine. 1998. "Choosing qualitative data analysis software: Atlas/ti and Nudist compared." *Sociological Research Online* 3 (3):1–17.

Bass, Gary Jonathan. 2000. *Stay the hand of vengeance: the politics of war crimes tribunals*. Princeton University Press.

Bauer, Raymond Augustine, Ithiel de Sola Pool, and Lewis Anthony Dexter. 1963. *American business and public policy: the politics of foreign trade*. New York: Atherton Press.

Baumgartner, Frank R., Jeffrey M. Berry, Marie Hojnacki, David C. Kimball, and Beth L. Leech. 2009. *Lobbying and policy change: who wins, who loses, and why*. University of Chicago Press.

Bayard de Volo, Lorraine. 2009. "Participant observation, politics and power relations: Nicaraguan mothers and U.S. casino waitresses." In *Political ethnography: what immersion contributes to the study of power*, ed. Edward Schatz, 217–236. University of Chicago Press.

Bayard de Volo, Lorraine, and Edward Schatz. 2004. "From the inside out: ethnographic methods in political research." *PS: Political Science and Politics* 37 (2):417–422.

Beath, Andrew, Fotini Christia, and Ruben Enikolopov. 2013. "Empowering women through development aid: Evidence from a field experiment in Afghanistan." *American Political Science Review* 107 (3):540–557.

Becker, Heike, Emile Bonnzaier, and Joy Owen. 2005. "Fieldwork in shared spaces: positionality, power and ethics of citizen anthropologists in Southern Africa." *Anthropology Southern Africa* 28 (3&4):123–132.

Becker, Howard S. 1970. *Sociological work: method and substance*. Chicago, IL: Aldine.

   1986. *Writing for social scientists: how to start and finish your thesis, book, or article*. University of Chicago Press.

Beckmann, Matthew N. 2010. *Pushing the agenda: presidential leadership in U.S. lawmaking, 1953–2004*. New York: Cambridge University Press.

Beckmann, Matthew N., and Richard Hall. 2013. "Elite interviewing in Washington, D.C." In *Interview research in political science*, ed. Layna Mosley, 196–208. Ithaca, NY: Cornell University Press.

Beitin, Ben K. 2012. "Interview and sampling: how many and whom." In *The Sage handbook of interview research: the complexity of the craft*, ed. Jaber F. Gubrium, James A. Holstein, Amir B. Marvasti, and Karyn McKinney, 243–254. Thousand Oaks, CA: Sage Publications.

Bennett, Andrew. 2010. "Process tracing and causal inference." In *Rethinking social inquiry: diverse tools, shared standards*, ed. Henry E. Brady and David Collier, 207–220. Lanham, MD: Rowman & Littlefield.

Bennett, Andrew, and Colin Elman. 2006. "Complex causal relations and case study methods: the example of path dependence." *Political Analysis* 14 (3):250–267.

Berelson, Bernard. 1952. *Content analysis in communications research*. New York: The Free Press.

Berinsky, Adam J. 1999. "The two faces of public opinion." *American Journal of Political Science* 43 (4):1209–1230.

Bernard, Russell. 2006. *Research methods in anthropology: qualitative and quantitative approches*. 4th edn. New York: AltaMira Press.

Berry, Jeffrey. 2002. "Validity and reliability issues in elite interviewing." *PS: Political Science and Politics* 35 (4):679–682.

Berry, Jeffrey M., Kent E. Portney, and Ken Thomson. 1993. *The rebirth of urban democracy.* Washington, DC: The Brookings Institution.

Biggs, Jeffrey R. 2003. *A congress of fellows: fifty years of the American Political Science Association Congressional Fellowship Program.* Washington, DC: APSA.

Blalock, H. M. 1979. "Measurement and conceptualization problems: the major obstacle to integrating theory and practice." *American Sociological Review* 44 (6):881–894.

Blattman, Christopher, Eric Green, Jeannie Annan, and Julian Jamison. 2013. *Building women's economic and social empowerment through enterprise: an experimental assessment of the Women's Income Generating Support (WINGS) program in Uganda.* Washington, DC: World Bank.

Blee, Kathleen M. 2002. *Inside organized racism: women in the hate movement.* Berkeley: University of California Press.

Bleich, Erik, and Robert Pekkanen. 2013. "How to report interview data." In *Interview research in political science*, ed. Layna Mosley, 84–105. Ithaca, NY: Cornell University Press.

Boas, Taylor. 2009. Varieties of electioneering: presidential campaigns in Latin America. Unpublished Ph.D. diss., Department of Political Science, University of California, Berkeley.

Bong, Sharon. 2002. "Debunking myths in qualitative research." *Forum: Qualitative Social Research* 3 (2):1–44.

Bonilla, Frank. 1964. "Survey techniques." In *Studying politics abroad: field research in the developing areas*, ed. Robert Edward Ward, 134–152. Boston: Little, Brown.

Bonura, Carlo. 2008. "Indeterminate geographies of political violence in southern Thailand." *Alternatives* 33 (4):383–412.

Boone, Catherine. 1992. *Merchant capital and the roots of state power in Senegal, 1930–1985.* Cambridge University Press.

Booth, Wayne, Gregory Colomb, and Joseph Williams. 1995. *The craft of research.* University of Chicago Press.

2003. *The craft of research.* 2nd edn. University of Chicago Press.

Bornat, Joanna, and Hannah Diamond. 2007. "Women's history and oral history: developments and debates." *Women's History Review* 16 (1):19–39.

Borneman, John, and Abdellah Hammoudi, eds. 2009. *Being there: the fieldwork encounter and the making of truth.* Berkeley: University of California Press.

Bourdon, Sylvain. 2002. "The integration of qualitative data analysis software in research strategies: resistances and possibilities." *Forum: Qualitative Social Research* 3 (2): 1–30.

Box-Steffensmeier, Janet, Henry Brady, and David Collier, eds. 2008. *The Oxford handbook on methodology.* New York: Oxford University Press.

Brady, Henry E. 2000. "Contributions of survey research to political science." *PS: Political Science and Politics* 33 (1):47–57.

2010. "Data-set observations versus causal-process observations: the 2000 US presidential election." In *Rethinking social inquiry: diverse tools, shared standards*, ed. Henry E. Brady and David Collier, 237–242. Lanham, MD: Rowman & Littlefield.

Brady, Henry E., and David Collier, eds. 2004. *Rethinking social inquiry: diverse tools, shared standards.* Lanham, MD: Rowman & Littlefield.

2010. *Rethinking social inquiry: diverse tools, shared standards.* 2nd edn. Lanham, MD: Rowman & Littlefield.

Brass, Paul R. 2003. *The production of Hindu–Muslim violence in contemporary India.* Seattle: University of Washington Press.

Brinks, Daniel M. 2008. *The judicial response to police killings in Latin America.* Cambridge, New York: Cambridge University Press.

Brooks, Sarah M. 2013. "The ethical treatment of human subjects and the Institutional Review Board process." In *Interview research in political science*, ed. Layna Mosley, 45–66. Ithaca, NY: Cornell University Press.

Brown, Michael K. 1981. *Working the street: police discretion and the dilemmas of reform.* New York: Russell Sage Foundation.

1986. "Direct observation: research in a natural setting." In *Empirical political analysis: research methods in political science*, ed. Jarol B. Manheim and Richard C. Rich, 164–185. New York: Longman.

Brown, Stephen. 2009. "Dilemmas of self-representation and conduct in the field." In *Surviving field research: working in violent and difficult situations*, ed. Chandra Lekha Sriram, John C. King, Julie A. Mertus, Olga Martin-Ortega, and Johanna Herman, 213–226. New York: Routledge.

Brysk, Alison. 2013. *Speaking rights to power: constructing political will.* Oxford University Press.

Bulmer, Martin. 1984. *The Chicago school of sociology: institutionalization, diversity, and the rise of sociological research.* University of Chicago Press.

Bulmer, Martin, and Donald P. Warwick. 1983. *Social research in developing countries: surveys and censuses in the Third World.* Chichester and New York: Wiley.

Burgess, Robert G. 1982. "Approaches to field research." In *Field research: a sourcebook and field manual*, ed. Robert G. Burgess, 1–11. London and Boston: G. Allen & Unwin.

1994. *Field research: a sourcebook and field manual.* London: George Allen & Unwin.

1995. *In the field: an introduction to field research.* New York: Routledge.

Burton, Antoinette, ed. 2005. *Archive stories: facts, fictions, and the writing of history.* Durham, NC: Duke University Press.

Butler, Daniel M., and David E. Broockman. 2011. "Do politicians racially discriminate against constituents? A field experiment on state legislators." *American Journal of Political Science* 55 (3):463–477.

Caldwell, Joyce Y., and Jamie D. Davis. 2005. "Culturally competent research with American Indians and Alaska Natives: findings and recommendations of the First Symposium of the Work Group on American Indian Research and Program Evaluation Methodology." *American Indian and Alaska Native Mental Health Research* 12 (1):1–21.

Cammett, Melani. 2013. "Using proxy interviewing to address sensitive topics." In *Interview research in political science*, ed. Layna Mosley, 125–143. Ithaca, NY: Cornell University Press.

Cammett, Melani, and S. Issar. 2010. "Bricks and mortar clientelism: sectarianism and the logics of welfare allocation in Lebanon." *World Politics* 62 (3):381–421.

Campbell, Andrea Louise. 2003. *How policies make citizens: senior political activism and the American welfare state.* Princeton University Press.

Campbell, Angus, Philip E. Converse, Warren E. Miller, and Donald E. Stokes. 1960. *The American voter.* New York: Wiley.

Carapico, Sheila, Janine Clark, Amaney Jamal, David Romano, Jilian Schwedler, and Mark Tessler. 2006. "The methodologies of field research in the Middle East." *PS: Political Science and Politics* 39 (3): 417–441.

Cardona, Christopher. 2008. Politicians, soldiers, and cops: Colombia's *La Violencia* in comparative perspective. Unpublished Ph.D. diss., Department of Political Science, University of California, Berkeley.

Carlson, Allen. 2005. *Unifying China, integrating with the world: securing Chinese sovereignty in the reform era.* Stanford University Press.

Carlson, Allen, Mary E. Gallagher, Kenneth Lieberthal, and Melanie Manion. 2010. *Contemporary Chinese politics: new sources, methods, and field strategies.* Cambridge University Press.

Carmines, Edward, and Richard Zeller. 1979. *Reliability and validity assessment.* Thousand Oaks, CA: Sage Publications.

Carpenter, Daniel P. 2001. *The forging of bureaucratic autonomy: reputations, networks, and policy innovation in executive agencies, 1862–1928.* Princeton University Press.

2010. *Reputation and power: organizational image and pharmaceutical regulation at the FDA.* Princeton University Press.

Chacko, Elizabeth. 2004. "Positionality and praxis: fieldwork experiences in rural India." *Singapore Journal of Tropical Geography* 25 (1):51–63.

Chakravarty, Anuradha. 2012. "'Partially trusting' field relationships: opportunities and constraints of fieldwork in Rwanda's postconflict setting." *Field Methods* 24 (3):251–271.

Chandra, Kanchan. 2004. *Why ethnic parties succeed: patronage and ethnic head counts in India.* Cambridge, New York: Cambridge University Press.

Charlton, Thomas L., Lois E. Myers, and Rebecca Sharpless, eds. 2006. *Handbook of oral history.* Lanham, MD: AltaMira Press.

Chattopadhyay, Raghabendra, and Esther Duflo. 2004. "Women as policymakers: evidence from a randomized policy experiment in India." *Econometrica* 72 (5):1409–1443.

Cheah, Pheng. 1999. "Grounds of comparison." *Diacritics* 29 (4):2–18.

Chen, Xi. 2010. "State-generated data and contentious politics in China." In *Contemporary Chinese politics: new sources, methods, and field strategies*, ed. Allen Carlson, Mary Gallagher, Kenneth Lieberthal and Melanie Manion, 15-32. Cambridge University Press.

Christensen, Thomas. 1996. *Useful adversaries: grand strategy, domestic mobilization, and Sino-American conflict, 1947–1958.* Princeton University Press.

Ciccariello-Maher, George. 2013. *We created Chávez: a people's history of the Venezuelan Revolution.* Durham, NC: Duke University Press.

Cohen, Cathy J. 1999. *The boundaries of blackness: AIDS and the breakdown of Black politics.* University of Chicago Press.

Collier, David. 1976. *Squatters and oligarchs: authoritarian rule and policy change in Peru.* Baltimore, MD: Johns Hopkins University Press.

1993. "The comparative method." In *Political science: the state of the discipline II*, ed. Ada Finifter, 105–119. Washington, DC: The American Political Science Association.

1995. "Translating quantitative methods for qualitative researchers: the case of selection bias." *American Political Science Review* 89 (2):461–466.

Collier, David, and Robert Adcock. 1999. "Democracy and dichotomies: a pragmatic approach to choices about concepts." *Annual Review of Political Science* 2 (1):537–566.

Collier, David, Henry E. Brady, and Jason Seawright. 2010. "Sources of leverage in causal inference: toward an alternative view of methodology." In *Rethinking social inquiry: diverse tools, shared standards*, ed. Henry E. Brady and David Collier. Lanham, MD: Rowman & Littlefield.

Collier, David, and John Gerring. 2009. *Concepts and method in social science: the tradition of Giovanni Sartori*. New York: Routledge.

Collier, David, and James Mahoney. 1993. "Conceptual 'stretching' revisited: alternative views of categories in comparative analysis." *American Political Science Review* 87 (4):845–855.

　 1996. "Research note: insights and pitfalls – selection bias in qualitative research." *World Politics* 49 (1):56–91.

Collier, David, Jason Seawright, and Gerardo L. Munck. 2010. "The quest for standards: King, Keohane, and Verba's *Designing social inquiry*." In *Rethinking social inquiry: diverse tools, shared standards*, ed. Henry E. Brady and David Collier, 33–64. Lanham, MD: Rowman & Littlefield.

Converse, Jean M. 2009. *Survey research in the United States: roots and emergence 1890–1960*. New Brunswick, NJ: Transaction Publishers.

Converse, Jean M., and Stanley Presser. 1986. *Survey questions: handcrafting the standardized questionnaire*. Beverly Hills, CA: Sage Publications.

Copsey, Nathaniel. 2008. *Focus groups and the political scientist*. European Research Institute Working Paper Series. University of Birmingham.

Cox, David R. 1958. *Planning of experiments*. New York: Wiley.

Cross, Mai'a K. Davis. 2011. *Security integration in Europe: how knowledge-based networks are transforming the European Union*. Ann Arbor: University of Michigan Press.

Çubukçu, Ayça. 2011. "On cosmopolitan occupations." *Interventions: International Journal of Postcolonial Studies* 13 (3):422–442.

Curthoys, Ann. 2005. "The history of killing and the killing of history." In *Archive stories: facts, fictions, and the writing of history*, ed. Antoinette Burton. Durham, NC: Duke University Press.

Dahl, Robert Alan. 1961. *Who governs? Democracy and power in an American city*. New Haven, CT: Yale University Press.

Dallmayr, Fred. 1997. "Introduction: toward a comparative political theory." *Review of Politics* 59 (3):421–427.

　 2004. "Beyond monologue: for a comparative political theory." *Perspectives on Politics* 2 (2):249–257.

De La O, Ana L., and Leonard Wantchekon. 2011. "Experimental research on democracy and development." In *Cambridge handbook of experimental political science*, ed. James N. Druckman, Donald P. Green, James H. Kuklinski, and Arthur Lupia, 384–396. Cambridge University Press.

Deaton, Angus. 2009. *Instruments of development: randomization in the tropics, and the search for the elusive keys to economic development*. National Bureau of Economic Research (NBER) Working Paper 14690. Cambridge, MA: NBER.

Dexter, Lewis A. 1946. "Political processes and judgments of value." *American Political Science Review* 40 (2):294–301.

　 1970. *Elite and specialized interviewing*. Evanston, IL: Northwestern University Press.

Diamant, Neil J. 2010. "Why archives?" In *Contemporary Chinese politics: new sources, methods, and field strategies*, ed. Allen Carlson, Mary E. Gallagher, Kenneth Lieberthal and Melanie Manion, 33–50. Cambridge University Press.

Diani, Mario. 2002. "Network analysis." In *Methods of social movement research*, ed. Bert Klandermans and Suzanne Staggernborg, 173–200. Minneapolis: University of Minnesota Press.

Dibble, Vernon. 1963. "Four types of inference from documents to events." *History and Theory* 3 (2):203–221.

Dickson, Eric S. 2011. "Economics versus psychology experiments: stylization, incentives, and deception." In *Cambridge handbook of experimental political science*, ed. James N. Druckman, Donald P. Green, James H. Kuklinski, and Arthur Lupia, 58–69. New York: Cambridge University Press.

Dillman, Don A. 2002. "Navigating the rapids of change: some observations on survey methodology in the early twenty-first century." *The Public Opinion Quarterly* 66 (3):473–494.

Domhoff, G. William. 1978. *Who really rules? New Haven and community power reexamined*. New Brunswick, NJ: Transaction Books.

Dowling, Robyn. 2000. "Power, subjectivity and ethics in qualitative research." In *Qualitative research methods in human geography*, ed. I. Hay, 23–49. Melbourne: Oxford University Press.

Druckman, James N., Donald P. Green, James H. Kuklinski, and Arthur Lupia. 2006. "The growth and development of experimental research in political science." *American Political Science Review* 100 (4):627–636.

2011a. *Cambridge handbook of experimental political science*. Cambridge University Press.

2011b. "Experimentation in Political Science." In *Cambridge handbook of experimental political science*, ed. James N. Druckman, Donald P. Green, James H. Kuklinski, and Arthur Lupia, 3–14. Cambridge University Press.

Druckman, James N., and Cindy D. Kam. 2011. "Students as experimental participants: a defense of the 'narrow data base.'" In *Cambridge handbook of experimental political science*, ed. James N. Druckman, Donald P. Green, James H. Kuklinski, and Arthur Lupia, 41–57. Cambridge University Press.

Duflo, Esther, Rachel Glennerster, and Michael Kremer. 2006. *Using randomization in development economics research: a toolkit*. Massachusetts Institute of Technology Department of Economics Working Paper Series. Cambridge, MA: MIT Press.

Dunaway, David, and Willa K. Baum, eds. 1996. *Oral history: an interdisciplinary anthology*. 2nd edn. Lanham, MD: AltaMira Press.

Dunning, Thad. 2008. "Natural and field experiments: the role of qualitative methods." *Qualitative and Multi-Method Research* 6 (2):17–23.

2012. *Natural experiments in the social sciences: a design-based approach*. Cambridge University Press.

Dunning, Thad, and Lauren Harrison. 2010. "Cross-cutting cleavages and ethnic voting: an experimental study of cousinage in Mali." *American Political Science Review* 104 (1):21–39.

Eldersveld, Samuel J. 1956. "Experimental propaganda techniques and voting behavior." *American Political Science Review* 50 (1):154–65.

Ellermann, Antje. 2009. *States against migrants: deportation in Germany and the United States*. Cambridge University Press.

Elman, Colin, and Diana Kapiszewski. 2013. "Data access and research transparency in the qualitative tradition." *PS: Political Science and Politics* 47 (1):43–47.

Elman, Colin, Diana Kapiszewski, and Lorena Vinuela. 2010. "Qualitative data archiving: rewards and challenges." *PS: Political Science and Politics* 43 (1):23–27.

Emerson, Robert M. 1983. *Contemporary field research: a collection of readings*. Boston: Little, Brown.

    2001a. *Contemporary field research: perspectives and formulations*. 2nd edn. Prospect Heights, IL: Waveland Press.

    2001b. "Introduction: the development of ethnographic field research." In *Contemporary field research: perspectives and formulations*, ed. Robert M. Emerson, 1–26. Prospect Heights, IL: Waveland Press.

Emerson, Robert M., Rachel I. Fretz, and Linda L. Shaw. 2011. *Writing ethnographic fieldnotes*. 2nd edn. University of Chicago Press.

Falleti, Tulia, and Julia Lynch. 2009. "Context and causal mechanisms in political research." *Comparative Political Studies* 42 (9):1143–1166.

Fearon, James D. 1991. "Counterfactuals and hypothesis testing in political science." *World Politics* 43 (2):169–195.

Fearon, James, and David Laitin. 2008. "Integrating qualitative and quantitative methods." In *The Oxford handbook of political methodology*, ed. Janet Box-Steffensmeier, Henry E. Brady, and David Collier, 756–776. Oxford University Press.

Featherman, David L. 2006. "Foreword." In *A handbook for social science field research: essays and bibliographic sources on research design and methods*, ed. Ellen Perecman and Sara R. Curran, xvii–xx. Thousand Oaks, CA: Sage Publications.

Feldman, Martha S., Jeannine Bell, and Michele Tracy Berger. 2003. *Gaining access: a practical and theoretical guide for qualitative researchers*. Walnut Creek, CA: AltaMira Press.

Fenno, Richard F., Jr. 1978. *Home style: house members in their districts*. Boston: Little, Brown.

    1986. "Observation, context, and sequence in the study of politics." *American Political Science Review* 80 (1):3–15.

    1990. *Watching politicians: essays on participant observation*. Berkeley, CA: Institute of Governmental Studies.

Fielding, Nigel, and Cesar Cisneros-Puebla. 2009. "CAZDAS–GIS convergence: toward a new integrated mixed method research practice?" *Journal of Mixed Methods Research* 3 (4):349–370.

Fielding, Nigel, and Raymond Lee. 1998. *Computer analysis and qualitative research*. London: Sage Publications.

    2002. "New patterns in the adoption and use of qualitative software." *Field Methods* 14 (2):197–216.

Fine, Gary Alan. 1995. *A second Chicago school? The development of a postwar American sociology*. University of Chicago Press.

Finlay, Linda. 2012. "Five lenses for the reflexive interviewer." In *The Sage handbook of interview research: the complexity of the craft*, ed. Jaber F. Gubrium, James A. Holstein, Amir B. Marvasti, and Karyn D. McKinney, 317–332. Thousand Oaks, CA: Sage Publications.

Finnemore, Martha, and Kathryn Sikkink. 2001. "Taking stock: the constructivist research program in international relations and comparative politics." *Annual Review of Political Science* 4:391–416.

Flikschuh, Katrin. 2014. "The idea of philosophical fieldwork: global justice, moral ignorance, and intellectual attitudes." *The Journal of Political Philosophy* 22 (1):1–26.

Fowler, Floyd J. 1995. *Improving survey questions: design and evaluation*. Thousand Oaks, CA: Sage Publications.

2009. *Survey research methods*. 4th edn. Thousand Oaks, CA: Sage Publications.

Fox, Jonathan. 2007. *Accountability politics: power and voice in rural Mexico*. Oxford, New York: Oxford University Press.

Franzosi, Roberto. 2008. "Content analysis: objective, systematic, and quantitative description of content." In *Content analysis*, Vol. I, ed. Roberto Franzosi, xxi–l. Thousand Oaks, CA: Sage Publications.

Freidenberg, Flavia, and Steven Levitsky. 2006. "Informal institutions and party organization in Latin America." In *Informal institutions and democracy: lessons from Latin America*, ed. Gretchen Helmke and Steven Levitsky, 178–200. Baltimore, MD: Johns Hopkins University Press.

Frisch, Scott, Douglas Harris, Sean Kelly, and David Parker. 2012. *Doing archival research in political science*. Amherst, NY: Cambria Press.

Fritzsche, Peter. 2005. "The archive and the case of the German nation." In *Archive stories: facts, fictions, and the writing of history*, ed. Antoinette Burton, 184–208. Durham, NC: Duke University Press.

Frymer, Paul. 2008. *Black and blue: African Americans, the labor movement, and the decline of the Democratic party*. Princeton University Press.

Fujii, Lee Ann. 2009. *Killing neighbors: webs of violence in Rwanda*. Ithaca, NY: Cornell University Press.

2013. "Working with interpreters." In *Interview research in political science*, ed. Layna Mosley, 144–158. Ithaca, NY: Cornell University Press.

Gaines, Brian J., James H. Kuklinski, and Paul J. Quirk. 2007. "The logic of the survey experiment reexamined." *Political Analysis* 15 (1):1–20.

Gallagher, Mary. 2013. "Capturing meaning and confronting measurement." In *Interview research in political science*, ed. Layna Mosley, 181–195. Ithaca, NY: Cornell University Press.

Gallaher, Carolyn. 2009. "Researching repellent groups: some methodological considerations on how to represent militants, radicals, and other belligerents." In *Surviving field research: working in violent and difficult situations*, ed. Chandra Lekha Sriram, John C. King, Julie A. Mertus, Olga Martin-Ortega, and Johanna Herman, 127–146. New York: Routledge.

Gallie, W. B. 1956. "Essentially contested concepts." *Proceedings of the Aristotelian Society* 56:167–198.

Galvan, Dennis. 2004. *The state must be our master of fire: how peasants craft culturally sustainable development in Senegal*. Berkeley: University of California Press.

García Bedolla, Lisa, and Melissa R. Michelson. 2012. *Mobilizing inclusion: transforming the electorate through get-out-the-vote campaigns*. New Haven, CT: Yale University Press.

Garcia Ponce, Omar, and Leonard Wantchekon. 2011. Echoes of colonial repression: the long-term effects of the 1947 revolt upon political attitudes in Madagascar. Paper presented at the APSA annual meeting. Seattle, September 1–4. Available at SSRN: http://ssrn.com/abstract=1903315.

Gaventa, John. 1980. *Power and powerlessness: quiescence and rebellion in an Appalachian valley*. Urbana: University of Illinois Press.

Geddes, Barbara. 2002. "The great transformation in the study of politics in developing countries." In *The state of the discipline*, ed. Ira Katznelson and Helen V. Milner, 342–370. New York: W. W. Norton & Co.

2003. *Paradigms and sand castles: theory building and research design in comparative politics*. Ann Arbor: University of Michigan Press.

Gendron, Richard, and G. William Domhoff. 2009. *The leftmost city: power and progressive politics in Santa Cruz*. Boulder, CO: Westview Press.

George, Alexander L., and Andrew Bennett. 2004. *Case studies and theory development in the social sciences*. Cambridge, MA: MIT Press.

Gerber, Alan S. 2011. "Field experiments in political science." In *Cambridge handbook of experimental political science*, ed. James N. Druckman, Donald P. Green, James H. Kuklinski, and Arthur Lupia, 115–138. Cambridge University Press.

Gerber, Alan S., and Donald P. Green. 2000. "The effects of canvassing, direct mail, and telephone contact on voter turnout: a field experiment." *American Political Science Review* 94 (3):653–663.

2012. *Field experiments: design, analysis, and interpretation*. New York: W. W. Norton.

Gerber, Alan S., Donald P. Green, and Christopher W. Larimer. 2008. "Social pressure and voter turnout: evidence from a large-scale field experiment." *American Political Science Review* 102 (1):33–48.

Gerring, John. 2007. *Case study research: principles and practices*. New York: Cambridge University Press.

2010. "Causal mechanisms: yes, but." *Comparative Political Studies* 43 (11):1499–1526.

2012. *Social science research: a unified methodology*. Cambridge University Press.

Gibbs, Graham. 2007. *Analyzing qualitative data*. London: Sage Publications.

Gibbs, Graham, Susanne Friese, and Wilma Mangabeira. 2002. "The use of new technology in qualitative research. Introduction to issue 3(2) of FQs." *Forum: Qualitative Social Research* 3 (2):1–35.

Giles-Vernick, Tamara. 2006. "Oral histories: oral histories as methods and sources." In *A handbook for social science field research: essays and bibliographic sources on research design and methods*, ed. Ellen Perecman and Sara R. Curran, 85–95. Thousand Oaks, CA: Sage Publications.

Godrej, Farah. 2009. "Response to 'What is comparative political theory?'" *Review of Politics* 71 (4):567–582.

Goertz, Gary. 2006. *Social science concepts: a user's guide*. Princeton University Press.

Goertz, Gary, and James Mahoney. 2012. *A tale of two cultures: qualitative and quantitative research in the social sciences*. Princeton University Press.

Golden, Miriam. 1995. "Replication and non-quantitative research." *PS: Political Science and Politics* 28 (3):481–483.

Goldgeier, James, and Michael McFaul. 2003. *Power and purpose: U.S. policy toward Russia after the Cold War*. Washington, DC: Brookings Institution Press.

Goldstein, Kenneth. 2002. "Getting in the door: sampling and completing elite interviews." *PS: Political Science and Politics* 35 (4):669–672.

Goldthorpe, John. 1991. "The uses of history in sociology: reflections on some recent tendencies." *British Journal of Sociology* 42 (2):211–230.

Goodman, Sara Wallace. 2014. *Immigration and membership politics in Western Europe.* Cambridge University Press.

Gosnell, Harold F. 1926. "An experiment in the stimulation of voting." *American Political Science Review* 20 (4):869–74.

Gottlieb, Alma. 2006. "Ethnography: theory and methods." In *A handbook for social science field research: essays and bibliographic sources on research design and methods*, ed. Ellen Perecman and Sara R. Curran, 47–68. Thousand Oaks, CA: Sage Publications.

Gottschalk, Louis Reichenthal. 1969. *Understanding history: a primer of historical method.* 2nd edn. New York: A. A. Knopf.

Greenbaum, Thomas L. 2000. *Moderating focus groups: a practical guide for group facilitation.* Thousand Oaks, CA: Sage Publications.

Grele, Ronald. 1978. "Can anyone over thirty be trusted? A friendly critique of oral history." *The Oral History Review* 6:36–44.

1998. "Movement without aim: methodological and theoretical problems in oral history." In *The oral history reader*, ed. Robert Perks and Alistair Thomson, 38–52. London: Routledge.

Grofman, Bernard, ed. 2001. *Political science as puzzle solving: interests, identities, and institutions in comparative politics.* Ann Arbor: University of Michigan Press.

Groves, Robert M., Floyd J. Fowler, Jr., Mick P. Couper, James M. Lepkowski, Eleanor Singer, and Roger Tourangeau. 2009. *Survey methodology.* 2nd edn. Hoboken, NJ: Wiley.

Grzymala-Busse, Anna M. 2002. *Redeeming the communist past: the regeneration of communist parties in East Central Europe.* Cambridge University Press.

Gubrium, Jaber F., and James A. Holstein. 2002. *The handbook of interview research: context and method.* Thousand Oaks, CA: Sage Publications.

Gueron, Judith M. 2002. "The politics of random assignment: implementing studies and impacting policy." In *Evidence matters: randomized trials in education research*, ed. Frederick Mosteller and Robert F. Boruch, 15–49. Washington, DC: Brookings Institution Press.

Gupta, Akhil, and James Ferguson, eds. 1997a. *Anthropological locations: boundaries and grounds of a field science.* Berkeley: University of California Press.

1997b. "Discipline and practice: 'The field' as site, method, and location in anthropology." In *Anthropological locations: boundaries and grounds of a field science*, ed. Akhil Gupta and James Ferguson, 1–46. Berkeley: University of California Press.

Haas, Ernst B. 1964. *Beyond the nation-state: functionalism and international organization.* Stanford University Press.

Habyarimana, James, Macartan Humphreys, Daniel N. Posner, and Jeremy M. Weinstein. 2007. "Why does ethnic diversity undermine public goods provision? An experimental approach." *American Political Science Review* 101 (4):709–725.

2009. *Coethnicity: diversity and the dilemmas of collective action.* New York: Russell Sage Foundation.

Haddad, Mary Alice. 2007. *Politics and volunteering in Japan: a global perspective.* Cambridge University Press.

Hallowell, John H. 1944. "Politics and ethics." *American Political Science Review* 38 (4):639–655.

1946. "Politics and ethics: a rejoinder to William F. Whyte." *American Political Science Review* 40 (2):307–312.

Han, Hahrie C. 2009a. *Moved to action: motivation, participation, and inequality in American politics.* Stanford University Press.

2009b. "Does the content of political appeals matter in motivating participation? A field experiment on self-disclosure in political appeals." *Political Behavior* 31 (1):103–116.

Hardin, Rebecca, and Kamari Maxine Clarke. 2012. "Introduction." In *Transforming ethnographic knowledge*, ed. Rebecca Hardin and Kamari Maxine Clarke, 3–34. Madison: University of Wisconsin Press.

Häusermann, Silja. 2010. *The politics of welfare state reform in continental Europe: modernization in hard times.* Cambridge University Press.

Heaney, Michael T., and John Mark Hansen. 2006. "Building the Chicago school." *American Political Science Review* 100 (4):589–596.

Heimer, Maria, and Stig Thøgersen. 2006. *Doing fieldwork in China.* Honolulu: University of Hawaii Press.

Helmke, Gretchen, and Steven Levitsky, eds. 2006. *Informal institutions and democracy: lessons from Latin America.* Baltimore, MD: Johns Hopkins University Press.

Hennick, Monique M. 2007. *International focus group research: a handbook for the health and social sciences.* New York: Cambridge University Press.

Hermann, Margaret. 2008. "Content analysis." In *Qualitative methods in international relations*, ed. Audie Klotz and Deepa Prakash, 151–167. Chippenham and Eastbourne: Palgrave Macmillan.

Herrera, Yoshiko, and Bear Braumoeller. 2004. "Symposium: discourse/content analysis." *Qualitative Methods Newsletter* 2 (1):15–39.

Hershatter, Gail. 2011. *The gender of memory: rural women and China's collective past.* Berkeley: University of California Press.

Hertel, Shareen, Matthew Singer, and Donna Lee Van Cott. 2009. "Field research in developing countries: hitting the road running." *PS: Political Science and Politics* 42 (2):305–309.

Herzog, Hanna. 2012. "Interview location and its social meaning." In *The Sage handbook of interview research: the complexity of the craft*, ed. Jaber F. Gubrium, James A. Holstein, Amir B. Marvasti, and Karyn D. McKinney. Thousand Oaks, CA: Sage Publications.

Hill, Michael. 1993. *Archival strategies and techniques.* Thousand Oaks, CA: Sage Publications.

Hochschild, Jennifer L. 1986. *What's fair: American beliefs about distributive justice.* Cambridge, MA: Harvard University Press.

Holsti, Ole. 1969. *Content analysis for the social sciences and humanities.* Reading, MA: Addison-Wesley.

Horowitz, Ruth. 1986. "Remaining an outsider: membership as a threat to research rapport." *Journal of Contemporary Ethnography* 14 (4):409–430.

Howard, Lise Morjé. 2008. *UN peacekeeping in civil wars.* Cambridge University Press.

Howard, Marc Morjé. 2004. "Obtaining and recording data." *Qualitative Methods* 2 (1):7–10.

Howard, Philip, Aiden Duffy, Deen Freelon, Muzammil Hussain, Will Mari, and Marwa Mazaid. 2011. The project on information technology and political Islam. Research Memo. Seattle, University of Washington.

Hsueh, Roselyn. 2008. "Crossing the river by feeling for stones: conducting research in varying contexts in China." Paper presented at the APSA annual meeting. Boston, MA, August 28-31.

Huckfeldt, R. Robert, and John D. Sprague. 1995. *Citizens, politics, and social communication: information and influence in an election campaign*. Cambridge University Press.

Humphreys, Macartan. 2011. "Ethical challenges of embedded experimentation." *Comparative Democratization (APSA-CD)* 9 (3):10, 23–29.

Humphreys, Macartan, and Jeremy Weinstein. 2009. "Field experiments and the political economy of development." *Annual Review of Political Science* 12:367–378.

Hunter, Floyd. 1953. *Community power structure: a study of decision makers*. Chapel Hill: University of North Carolina Press.

Hymans, Jacques E. C. 2006. *The psychology of nuclear proliferation: identity, emotions, and foreign policy*. Cambridge University Press.

Immergut, Ellen M. 1992. *Health politics: interests and institutions in Western Europe*. Cambridge University Press.

Isacoff, Jonathan. 2005. "Writing the Arab–Israeli conflict: historical bias and the use of history in political science." *Perspectives on Politics* 3 (1):71–88.

Issenberg, Sasha. 2012. *The victory lab: the secret science of winning campaigns*. New York: Crown.

Jacobs, Alan M. 2011. *Governing for the long term: democracy and the politics of investment*. Cambridge University Press.

Jamal, Amaney A. 2007. *Barriers to democracy: the other side of social capital in Palestine and the Arab world*. Princeton University Press.

Jenco, Leigh Kathryn. 2007. "'What does heaven ever say?' A methods-centered approach to cross-cultural engagement." *American Political Science Review* 101 (4):741–755.

   2010. *Making the political: founding and action in the political theory of Zhang Shizhao*. Cambridge University Press.

Johnson, Nicholas, Phil Oliff, and Erica Williams. 2011. "An update on state budget cuts: at least 46 states have imposed cuts that hurt vulnerable residents and cause job loss." Washington DC: Center on Budget and Policy Priorities. Available at www.cbpp.org/files/3-13-08sfp.pdf.

Jourde, Cedric. 2009. "The ethnographic sensibility: overlooked authoritarian dynamics and Islamic ambivalences in West Africa." In *Political ethnography: what immersion contributes to the study of power*, ed. Edward Schatz, 201–216. University of Chicago Press.

Jung, Courtney. 2008. *The moral force of indigenous politics: critical liberalism and the Zapatistas*. Cambridge University Press.

Kaiser, Karen. 2012. "Protecting confidentiality." In *The Sage handbook of interview research: the complexity of the craft*, ed. Jaber F. Gubrium, James A. Holstein, Amir B. Marvasti, and Karyn D. McKinney, 457–464. Thousand Oaks, CA: Sage Publications.

Kam, Cindy, Jennifer R. Wilking, and Elizabeth J. Zechmeister. 2007. "Beyond the 'narrow data base': another convenience sample for experimental research." *Political Behavior* 29 (4):415–440.

Kapiszewski, Diana. 2012. *High courts and economic governance in Argentina and Brazil*. New York: Cambridge University Press.

Katzenstein, Peter J., and Robert O. Keohane, eds. 2007. *Anti-Americanisms in world politics*. Ithaca, NY: Cornell University Press.

Katznelson, Ira. 1982. *City trenches: urban politics and the patterning of class in the United States*. University of Chicago Press.

Kayuni, Happy, and Adel Saleh Mohmed. 2013. "Field research for hire: the politics of consultancies." *Symposium: Field Research in Africa: New Challenges and Strategies in the 21st Century* 9 (1): 12–13.

Keating, Christine. 2011. *Decolonizing democracy: transforming the social contract in India*. University Park: Pennsylvania State University Press.

Kelle, Udo, ed. 1995. *Computer-aided qualitative data analysis: theory, methods and practice*. Thousand Oaks, CA: Sage Publications.

Kempf, Angela M., and Patrick L. Remington. 2007. "New challenges for telephone survey research in the twenty-first century." *Annual Review of Public Health* 28:113–126.

Key, V. O. 1949. *Southern politics in state and nation*. New York: A. A. Knopf.

Kim, Claire Jean. 2000. *Bitter fruit: the politics of Black-Korean conflict in New York City*. New Haven, CT: Yale University Press.

Khagram, Sanjeev. 2004. *Dams and development: transnational struggles for water and power*. Ithaca, NY: Cornell University Press.

Khan, Shahnaz. 2005. "Reconfiguring the native informant: positionality in the global age." *Journal of Women in Culture and Society* 30 (4):2017–2035.

King, Gary, Robert O. Keohane, and Sidney Verba. 1994. *Designing social inquiry: scientific inference in qualitative research*. Princeton University Press.

King, Gary, Jennifer Pan, and Margaret E. Roberts. 2013. "How censorship in China allows government criticism but silences collective expression." *American Political Science Review* 107 (2):1–18.

Kingdon, John W. 1984. *Agendas, alternatives, and public policies*. Boston: Little, Brown.

Kitschelt, Herbert. 1989. *The logics of party formation: ecological politics in Belgium and West Germany*. Ithaca, NY: Cornell University Press.

Knodel, John. 1997. "A case for nonanthropological qualitative methods for demographers." *Population and Development Review* 23 (4):847–853.

Kocher, Matthew, and David Laitin. 2006. "On Tarrow's space." *APSA-CP Newsletter* 16 (2):8–18.

Kohli, Atul. 1987. *The state and poverty in India: the politics of reform*. New York: Cambridge University Press.

Kohn, Margaret. 2003. *Radical space: building the house of the people*. Ithaca, NY: Cornell University Press.

Kollman, Ken. 1998. *Outside lobbying: public opinion and interest group strategies*. Princeton University Press.

Krasner, Stephen D. 2009. *Power, the state, and sovereignty: essays on international relations*. London: Routledge.

Krippendorff, Klaus. 2003. *Content analysis: an introduction to its methodology*. Thousand Oaks, CA: Sage Publications.

Krosnick, Jon A., and Stanley Presser. 2010. "Question and questionnaire design." In *Handbook of survey research*, ed. Peter V. Marsden and James D. Wright, 263–314. Bingley: Emerald Group.

Krueger, Richard A. 1994. *Focus groups: a practical guide for applied research*. 2nd edn. Newbury Park: Sage Publications.

Krueger, Richard, and Mary Anne Casey. 2009. *Focus groups: a practical guide for applied research*. 4th edn. Thousand Oaks, CA: Sage Publications.

Kubik, Jan. 2009. "Ethnography of politics: foundations, applications, prospects." In *Political ethnography: what immersion contributes to the study of power*, ed. Edward Schatz, 25–52. University of Chicago Press.

Kuran, Timur. 1989. "Sparks and prairie fires: a theory of unanticipated political revolution." *Public Choice* 61 (1):41–74.

1995. *Private truths, public lies: the social consequences of preference falsification*. Cambridge, MA: Harvard University Press.

Kurasaki, Karen. 2000. "Intercoder reliability for validating conclusions drawn from open-ended interview data." *Field Methods* 12 (3):179–194.

Kvale, Steinar. 2008. *Doing interviews*. Thousand Oaks, CA: Sage Publications.

Kvale, Steinar, and Svend Brinkmann. 2009. *Interviews: learning the craft of qualitative research interviewing*. Thousand Oaks, CA: Sage Publications.

Laitin, David D. 2003. "The perestroikan challenge to social science." *Politics & Society* 31 (1):163–184.

Landry, Pierre F. 2010. "Using clustered spatial data to study diffusion: the case of legal institutions in China." In *Contemporary Chinese politics: new sources, methods, and field strategies*, ed. Allen Carlson, Mary Gallagher, Kenneth Lieberthal, and Melanie Manion, 219–235. Cambridge University Press.

Landry, Pierre F., and Mingming Shen. 2005. "Reaching migrants in survey research: the use of the global positioning system to reduce coverage bias in China." *Political Analysis* 13 (1):1–22.

Lane, Robert Edwards. 1962. *Political ideology: why the American common man believes what he does*. New York: Free Press of Glencoe.

Lee-Treweek, Geraldine, and Stephanie Linkogle, eds. 2000. *Danger in the field: risk and ethics in social research*. London: Routledge.

Leebaw, Bronwyn Anne. 2011. *Judging state-sponsored violence, imagining political change*. Cambridge University Press.

Leech, Beth, L. 2002a. "Asking questions: techniques for semistructured interviews." *PS: Political Science and Politics* 35 (4):665–668.

2002b. "Symposium: interview methods in political science." *PS: Political Science and Politics* 35 (4):663–688.

Leech, Beth L., Frank R. Baumgartner, Jeffrey M. Berry, Marie Hojnackie, and David C. Kimball. 2013. "Lessons from the 'Lobbying and policy change' project." In *Interview research in political science*, ed. Layna Mosley, 209–224. Ithaca, NY: Cornell University Press.

Leeuw, Edith Desirée de, J. J. Hox, and Don A. Dillman. 2008. *International handbook of survey methodology*. New York, London: Lawrence Erlbaum Associates.

Lerman, Amy E. 2013. *The modern prison paradox: politics, punishment, and social community*. Cambridge University Press.

Lessing, Benjamin. 2012. "The logic of violence in criminal war: cartel–state conflict in Mexico, Colombia, and Brazil." Unpublished Ph.D. diss., Department of Political Science, University of California, Berkeley.

Lewins, Ann, and Christina Silver. 2007. *Using software in qualitative research: a step-by-step guide*. Thousand Oaks, CA: Sage Publications.

Liddle, R. William. 1996. *Leadership and culture in Indonesian politics*. Sydney: Allen & Unwin.

Lieberman, Evan. 2001. "Causal inference in historical institutional analysis: a specification of periodization strategies." *Comparative Political Studies* 34 (9):1011–1035.

2004. "Preparing for field research." *Qualitative Methods* 2 (1):3–7.

2005. "Nested analysis as a mixed method strategy for comparative research." *American Political Science Review* 99 (3):435–452.

Lieberman, Evan, Marc Howard, and Julia Lynch. 2004. "Symposium: field research." *Qualitative Methods* 2 (1):2–15.

Light, Paul Charles. 1995. *Still artful work: the continuing politics of social security reform*. 2nd edn. New York: McGraw-Hill.

Lijphart, Arend. 1971. "Comparative politics and the comparative method." *American Political Science Review* 65 (3):682–693.

Lillrank, Annika. 2012. "Managing the interviewer self." In *The Sage handbook of interview research: the complexity of the craft*, ed. Jaber F. Gubrium, James A. Holstein, Amir B. Marvasti, and Karyn D. McKinney, 281–294. Thousand Oaks, CA: Sage Publications.

Lin, Ann Chih. 2000. *Reform in the making: the implementation of social policy in prison*. Princeton University Press.

Link, Michael W., Michael P. Battaglia, Martin R. Frankel, Larry Osborn, and Ali H. Mokdad. 2007. "Reaching the U.S. cell phone generation: comparison of cell phone survey results with an ongoing landline telephone survey." *Public Opinion Quarterly* 71 (5):814–839.

Lischer, Sarah Kenyon. 2005. *Dangerous sanctuaries: refugee camps, civil war, and the dilemmas of humanitarian aid*. Ithaca, NY: Cornell University Press.

2011. "Civil war, genocide, and political order in Rwanda: security implications of refugee return." *Conflict, Security & Development* 11 (3):261–284.

List, John A. 2011. "Why economists should conduct field experiments and 14 tips for pulling one off." *Journal of Economic Perspectives* 25 (3):3–16.

Loaeza, Soledad, Randy Stevenson, and Devra Moehler. 2005. "Symposium: should everyone do fieldwork?" *APSA-CP Newsletter* 16 (2):8–18.

Locke, Richard, and Kathleen Thelen. 1995. "Apples and oranges revisited: contextualized comparisons and the study of labor politics." *Politics and Society* 23 (3):337–367.

Loewenberg, Gerhard. 2006. "The influence of European émigré scholars on comparative politics, 1925–1965." *American Political Science Review* 100 (4):597–604.

Lofland, John, David Snow, Leon Anderson, and Lyn Lofland. 2006. *Analyzing social settings: a guide to qualitative observation and analysis*. 4th edn. Belmont, CA: Wadsworth.

Long, J. Scott. 2008. *The workflow of data analysis using Stata*. College Station, TX: Stata Press.

Lowell, Lawrence. 1910. "The physiology of politics." *American Political Science Review* 4 (1):1–15.

Lu, Chi-Jung, and Stuart W. Shulman. 2008. "Rigor and flexibility in computer-based qualitative research: introducing the coding analysis toolkit." *International Journal of Multiple Research Approaches* 2 (1):105–117.

Lupia, Arthur, and Colin Elman. 2014. "Openness in political science: data access and research transparency – introduction." *PS: Political Science and Politics* 47 (1):19–42.

Lustick, Ian S. 1996. "History, historiography, and political science: multiple historical records and the problem of selection bias." *American Political Science Review* 90 (3):605–618.

Lyall, Jason. 2009. "Does indiscriminate violence incite insurgent attacks? Evidence from Chechnya." *Journal of Conflict Resolution* 53 (3):331–362.

Lynch, Cecelia. 1999. *Beyond appeasement: interpreting interwar peace movements in world politics*. Ithaca, NY: Cornell University Press.

Lynch, Julia. 2004. "Tracking progress while in the field." *Qualitative Methods* 2 (1):10–15.

  2005. "Can one country be better than two for comparative politics?" *Italian Politics and Society* 60:8–10.

  2006. *Age in the welfare state: the origins of social spending on pensioners, workers, and children*. New York: Cambridge University Press.

  2013. "Aligning sampling strategies with analytic goals." In *Interview research in political science*, ed. Layna Mosley, 31–44. Ithaca, NY: Cornell University Press.

MacLean, Lauren M. 2004. "Empire of the young: the legacies of state agricultural policy on local capitalism and social support networks in Ghana and Côte d'Ivoire." *Comparative Studies in Society and History* 46 (3):469–496.

  2010. *Informal institutions and citizenship in rural Africa: risk and reciprocity in Ghana and Côte d'Ivoire*. New York: Cambridge University Press.

  2013. "The power of the interviewer." In *Interview research in political science*, ed. Layna Mosley, 67–83. Ithaca, NY: Cornell University Press.

Mahoney, James. 2000. "Path dependence in historical sociology." *Theory and Society* 29 (4):507–548.

  2001. *The legacies of liberalism: path dependence and political regimes in Central America*. Baltimore, MD: Johns Hopkins University Press.

  2003. "Strategies of causal assessment in comparative historical analysis." In *Comparative historical analysis in the social sciences*, ed. James Mahoney and Dietrich Rueschemeyer, 337–372. New York: Cambridge University Press.

  2010. "After KKV: the new methodology of qualitative research." *World Politics* 62 (1):120–147.

Mahoney, James, and Gary Goertz. 2004. "The possibility principle: choosing negative cases in comparative research." *American Political Science Review* 98 (4):653–669.

  2006. "A tale of two cultures: contrasting qualitative and quantitative research." *Political Analysis* 14 (3):227–249.

Mahoney, James, and Celso Villegas. 2007. "Historical enquiry and comparative politics." In *Oxford handbook of comparative politics*, ed. Carles Boix and Susan Stokes, 73–89. Oxford University Press.

Malinowski, Bronislaw. 1961. *Argonauts of the Western Pacific: an account of native enterprise and adventure in the archipelagoes of Melanesian New Guinea*. New York: E. P. Dutton. Original edition, 1922.

Mangabeira, Wilma C., Raymond M. Lee, and Nigel G. Fielding. 2004. "Computers and qualitative research: adoption, use and representation." *Social Science Computer Review* 22 (2):167–178.

Manheim, Jarol B., and Richard C. Rich. 1986. *Empirical political analysis: research methods in political science*. 2nd edn. New York: Longman.

Manheim, Jarol B., Richard C. Rich, and Lars Willnat. 2002. *Empirical political analysis: research methods in political science*. 5th edn. New York: Longman.

Manion, Melanie. 2010. "A survey of survey research on Chinese politics: what have we learned?" In *Contemporary Chinese politics: new sources, methods, and field strategies*, ed. Allen Carlson, Mary Gallagher, Kenneth Lieberthal, and Melanie Manion, 181–199. Cambridge University Press.

Mariampolski, Hyman, and Dana Hughes. 1978. "The use of personal documents in historical sociology." *The American Sociologist* 13 (2):104–113.

Marsden, Peter V., and James D. Wright. 2010. *Handbook of survey research*. 2nd edn. Bingley: Emerald Group.

Martin, Cathie Jo. 2013. "Crafting interviews to capture cause and effect." In *Interview research in political science*, ed. Layna Mosley, 109–124. Ithaca, NY: Cornell University Press.

Marzano, Marco. 2012. "Informed consent." In *The Sage handbook of interview research: the complexity of the craft*, ed. Jaber F. Gubrium, James A. Holstein, Amir B. Marvasti, and Karyn D. McKinney, 443–456. Thousand Oaks, CA: Sage Publications.

Maxwell, Scott E., and Harold D. Delaney. 2004. *Designing experiments and analyzing data: a model comparison perspective*. New York: Psychology Press.

Mayring, Phillip. 2000. "Qualitative content analysis." *Forum: Qualitative Social Research* 2 (1):1–28.

Mazzuca, Sebastian, and James Robinson. 2009. "Political conflict and power sharing in the origins of modern Colombia." *Hispanic American Historical Review* 89 (12):285–321.

McClendon, Gwyneth H. 2012. "Ethics of using public officials as field experiment subjects." *The Experimental Political Scientist* 3 (1):13–20.

McCorkel, Jill, and Kristen Myers. 2003. "What difference does difference make? Position and privilege in the field." *Qualitative Sociology* 26:199–231.

McNabb, David E. 2010. *Research methods for political science: quantitative and qualitative approaches*. 2nd edn. Armonk, NY: M. E. Sharpe.

Mertus, Julie. 2009. "Maintenance of personal security: ethical and operational issues." In *Surviving field research: working in violent and difficult situations*, ed. Chandra Lekha Sriram, John C. King, Julie A. Mertus, Olga Martin-Ortega, and Johanna Herman, 165–176. New York: Routledge.

Mettler, Suzanne. 2005. *Soldiers to citizens: the G.I. bill and the making of the greatest generation*. Oxford University Press.

Michell, Lynn. 1999. "Combining focus groups and interviews: telling how it is; telling how it feels." In *Developing focus group research: politics, theory and practice*, ed. Rosaline S. Barbour and Jenny Kitzinger, 36–46. London: Sage Publications.

Michelson, Melissa R. 2003. "Getting out the Latino vote: how door-to-door canvassing influences voter turnout in rural central California." *Political Behavior* 25 (3):247–263.

Mihesuah, Devon. 1993. "Suggested guidelines for institutions with scholars who conduct research on American Indians." *American Indian Culture and Research Journal* 17 (3): 131–139.

Miler, Kristina C. 2010. *Constituency representation in Congress: the view from Capitol Hill*. Cambridge University Press.

Miles, Edward. 1970. "The logistics of interviewing in international organizations." *International Organization* 24 (2):361–370.

Miller, Lisa Lynn. 2008. *The perils of federalism: race, poverty, and the politics of crime control.* Oxford University Press.

Miller-Day, Michelle. 2012. "Toward conciliation: institutional review board practices and qualitative interview research." In *The Sage handbook of interview research: the complexity of the craft,* ed. Jaber F. Gubrium, James A. Holstein, Amir B. Marvasti, and Karyn D. McKinney, 499–508. Thousand Oaks, CA: Sage Publications.

Milligan, Jennifer. 2005. "What is an archive? In the history of modern France." In *Archive stories: facts, fictions, and the writings of history,* ed. Antoinette Burton, 159–183. Durham: NC: Duke University Press.

Milligan, John. 1979. "The treatment of an historical source." *History and Theory* 18 (2):177–196.

Mills, C. Wright. 1956. *The power elite.* New York: Oxford University Press.

Mishler, Elliot. 1991. *Research interviewing: context and narrative.* Cambridge, MA: Harvard University Press.

Møller, Jørgen, and Svend-Erik Skaaning. 2013. "The Third Wave: inside the numbers." *Journal of Democracy* 24 (4):97–109.

Monroe, Kristen R. 1996. *The heart of altruism: perceptions of a common humanity.* Princeton University Press.

Moravcsik, Andrew. 2010. "Active citation: a precondition for replicable qualitative research." *PS: Political Science and Politics* 43 (1):29–35.

    2013. "Transparency: the revolution in qualitative research." *PS: Political Science and Politics* 47 (1):48–53.

Morse, Janice. 2012. "The implications of interview type and structure in mixed-method designs." In *The Sage handbook of interview research: the complexity of the craft,* ed. Jaber F. Gubrium, James A. Holstein, Amir B. Marvasti, and Karyn D. McKinney, 193–204. Thousand Oaks, CA: Sage Publications.

Morton, Rebecca B., and Kenneth C. Williams. 2010. *Experimental political science and the study of causality: from nature to the lab.* Cambridge, New York: Cambridge University Press.

Mosley, Layna. 2003. *Global capital and national governments.* New York: Cambridge University Press.

    ed. 2013a. *Interview research in political science.* Ithaca, NY: Cornell University Press.

    2013b. "'Just talk to people?' Interviews in contemporary political science." In *Interview research in political science,* ed. Layna Mosley, 1–28. Ithaca, NY: Cornell University Press.

Munck, Gerardo L. 2004. "Tools for qualitative research." In *Rethinking social inquiry: diverse tools, shared standards,* ed. Henry E. Brady and David Collier, 105–121. Lanham, MD: Rowman & Littlefield.

    2007. "The past and present of comparative politics." In *Passion, craft, and method in comparative politics,* ed. Gerardo L. Munck and Richard Snyder, 32–59. Baltimore, MD: Johns Hopkins University Press.

Munck, Gerardo L., and Richard Snyder. 2007. *Passion, craft, and method in comparative politics.* Baltimore, MD: Johns Hopkins University Press.

Mutz, Diana Carole. 2011. *Population-based survey experiments*. Princeton University Press.

Nagar, Richa, Farah Ali, and Sangatin Women's Collective. 2003. "Collaboration across borders: moving beyond positionality." *Singapore Journal of Tropical Geography* 24 (3):356–372.

Neuendorf, Kimberly. 2001. *The content analysis guidebook*. Thousand Oaks, CA: Sage Publications.

Newman, Abraham. 2008. *Protectors of privacy: regulating personal data in the global economy*. Ithaca, NY: Cornell University Press.

Nickerson, David W. 2008. "Is voting contagious? Evidence from two field experiments." *American Political Science Review* 102 (1):49–57.

Norton, Anne. 2004. *95 theses on politics, culture and method*. New Haven, CT: Yale University Press.

O'Brien, Kevin J. 1996. "Rightful resistance." *World Politics* 49 (1):31–55.

O'Brien, Kevin J., and Lianjiang Li. 2006. *Rightful resistance in rural China*. Cambridge University Press.

Ocantos, Ezequiel Gonzalez, Chad Kiewiet de Jonge, and David W. Nickerson. 2013. "The conditionality of vote-buying norms: experimental evidence from Latin America." *American Journal of Political Science* 58 (1):197–211.

Olken, Benjamin A. 2007. "Monitoring corruption: evidence from a field experiment in Indonesia." *Journal of Political Economy* 115 (2):200–249.

2010. "Direct democracy and local public goods: evidence from a field experiment in Indonesia." *American Political Science Review* 104 (2):243–267.

Ortbals, Candice, and Meg Rincker. 2009. "Symposium: fieldwork, identities and intersectionality – negotiating gender, race, class, religion, nationality, and age in the research field abroad." *PS: Political Science and Politics* 42 (2):287–328.

Osaghae, Eghosa, and Gillian Robinson. 2005. "Introduction." In *Researching conflict in Africa: insights and experiences*, ed. Elisabeth Porter, Gillian Robinson, Marie Smyth, Albrecht Schnabel, and Eghosa Osaghae, 1–6. New York: United Nations University Press.

Ostrom, Elinor. 2010. "A long polycentric journey." *Annual Review of Political Science* 13:1–23.

Pachirat, Timothy. 2009. "The political in political ethnography: dispatches from the kill floor." In *Political ethnography: what immersion contributes to the study of power*, ed. Edward Schatz, 143–162. University of Chicago Press.

2011. *Every twelve seconds: industrialized slaughter and the politics of sight*. New Haven, CT: Yale University Press.

2015. *Ethnography and interpretation*. New York: Routledge.

Paller, Jeff. 2013. "Ethnography as empirical strategy: process, networks, and spontaneity." Paper presented at the APSA annual meeting. Chicago, IL, August 29 – September 1.

Paluck, Elizabeth Levy. 2009. "Methods and ethics with research teams and NGOs: comparing experiences across the border of Rwanda and Democratic Republic of Congo." In *Surviving field research: working in violent and difficult situations*, ed. Chandra Lekha Sriram, John C. King, Julie A. Mertus, Olga Martin-Ortega, and Johanna Herman, 38–56. London: Routledge.

2010. "The promising integration of qualitative methods and field experiments." *The Annals of the American Academy of Political and Social Science* 628:59–71.

Paluck, Elizabeth Levy, and Donald P. Green. 2009. "Deference, dissent, and dispute resolution: an experimental intervention using mass media to change norms and behavior in Rwanda." *American Political Science Review* 103 (4):622–644.

Parker, Ian. 2010. "The poverty lab." *The New Yorker* (May 17): 78–89.

Perecman, Ellen, and Sara R. Curran, eds. 2006. *A handbook for social science field research: essays and bibliographic sources on research design and methods*. Thousand Oaks, CA: Sage Publications.

Perks, Robert, and Alistair Thomson, eds. 1998. *The oral history reader*. London: Routledge.

Perry, Elizabeth J., and Xun Li. 1996. *Proletarian power: Shanghai in the Cultural Revolution*. Boulder: Westview Press.

Peskin, Victor. 2008. *International justice in Rwanda and the Balkans: virtual trials and the struggle for state cooperation*. Cambridge University Press.

Pierson, Paul. 1995. *Dismantling the welfare state? Reagan, Thatcher and the politics of retrenchment*. Cambridge University Press.

  2000. "Increasing returns, path dependence, and the study of politics." *American Political Science Review* 94 (2):251–267.

Platt, Jennifer. 1996. *A history of sociological research methods in America: 1920–1960*. Cambridge University Press.

  2012. "The history of the interview." In *The Sage handbook of interview research: the complexity of the craft*, ed. Jaber F. Gubrium, James A. Holstein, Amir B. Marvasti, and Karyn D. McKinney, 9–26. Thousand Oaks, CA: Sage Publications.

Pohlandt-McCormick, Helena. 2005. "In good hands: researching the 1976 Soweto uprising in the state archives of South Africa." In *Archive stories: facts, fictions, and the writing of history*, ed. Antoinette Burton, 299–324. Durham, NC: Duke University Press.

Polillo, Simone. 2008. "Archives as fields? A personal narrative on comparative-historical research." *Trajectories: Newsletter of the ASA Comparative and Historical Sociology section* 19 (2):7–9.

Polsby, Nelson W. 1980. *Community power and political theory: a further look at problems of evidence and inference*. 2nd edn. New Haven, CT: Yale University Press.

Pressman, Jeremy. 2008. *Warring friends: alliance restraint in international politics*. Ithaca, NY: Cornell University Press.

Prior, Lindsay. 2003. *Using documents in social research*. Thousand Oaks, CA: Sage Publications.

Przeworski, Adam, and Henry Teune. 1970. *The logic of comparative social inquiry*. New York: Wiley-Interscience.

Przeworski, Adam, and Frank Salomon. 1988, rev. 1995. *On the art of writing proposals: some candid suggestions for applicants to Social Science Research Council competitions*. New York: Social Science Research Council. Available at www.ssrc.org/publications/view/the-art-of-writing-proposals.

Punch, Maurice. 1986. *The politics and ethics of fieldwork*. Qualitative Research Methods Series 3. Beverly Hills, CA: Sage Publications.

Putnam, Robert D. 1993. *Making democracy work: civic traditions in modern Italy*. Princeton University Press.

Pye, Lucian W. 1964. "The developing areas: problems for research." In *Studying politics abroad: field research in the developing areas*, ed. Robert E. Ward, 5–25. Boston: Little, Brown.

Radsch, Courtney. 2009. "From cell phones to coffee: issues of access in Egypt and Lebanon." In *Surviving field research: working in violent and difficult situations*, ed. Chandra Lekha Sriram, John C. King, Julie A. Mertus, Olga Martin-Ortega, and Johanna Herman, 91–107. New York: Routledge Publications.

Ragin, Charles. 1987. *The comparative method: moving beyond qualitative and quantitative strategies*. Berkeley: University of California Press.

2000. *Fuzzy-set social science*. University of Chicago Press.

2004. "Turning the tables: how case-oriented research challenges variable-oriented research." In *Rethinking social inquiry: diverse tools, shared standards*, ed. Henry E. Brady and David Collier, 123–138. Lanham, MD: Rowman & Littlefield.

Rathbun, Brian. 2008. "Interviewing and qualitative field methods: pragmatism and practicalities." In *The Oxford handbook of political methodology*, ed. Janet M. Box-Steffensmeier, Henry E. Brady, and David Collier, 685–701. Oxford, New York: Oxford University Press.

Rea, Louis M., and Richard A. Parker. 2005. *Designing and conducting survey research: a comprehensive guide*. 3rd edn. San Francisco: Jossey-Bass.

Read, Benjamin L. 2010. "More than an interview, less than Sedaka: studying subtle and hidden politics with site-intensive methods." In *Contemporary Chinese politics: new sources, methods, and field strategies*, ed. Allen Carlson, Mary E. Gallagher, Kenneth Lieberthal, and Melanie Manion, 145–161. Cambridge University Press.

2012. *Roots of the state: neighborhood organization and social networks in Beijing and Taipei*. Stanford University Press.

Read, Benjamin L., Lauren Morris MacLean, and Melani Cammett. 2006. "Symposium, field research: How rich? How thick? How participatory?" *Qualitative Methods* 4 (2):9–18.

Redlawsk, David P., Andrew J. W. Civettini, and Karen M. Emmerson. 2010. "The affective tipping point: do motivated reasoners ever 'get it'?" *Political Psychology* 31 (4):563–593.

Redlawsk, David P., Caroline J. Tolbert, and Todd Donovan. 2011. *Why Iowa? How caucuses and sequential elections improve the presidential nominating process*. University of Chicago Press.

Reinhardt, Gina. 2009. "I don't know Monica Lewinsky and I'm not in the CIA. Now how about that interview?" *PS: Political Science and Politics* 42 (2):295–298.

Reno, William. 1998. *Warlord politics and African states*. Boulder, CO: Lynne Rienner Publishers.

2013. "The problem of extraterritorial legality." In *Interview research in political science*, ed. Layna Mosley, 159–178. Ithaca, NY: Cornell University Press.

Rice, Tom W. 2001. "Social capital and government performance in Iowa communities." *Journal of Urban Affairs* 23 (3–4):375–389.

Rich, Andrew. 2004. *Think tanks, public policy, and the politics of expertise*. Cambridge University Press.

Rivera, Sharon, Polina Kozyreva, and Eduard Saravskii. 2002. "Interviewing political elites: lessons from Russia." *PS: Political Science and Politics* 35 (4):683–688.

Robertson, Craig. 2005. "Mechanisms of exclusion: historicizing the archive and the passport." In *Archive stories: facts, fictions, and the writing of history*, ed. Antoinette Burton, 68–86. Durham, NC: Duke University Press.

Robson, Colin. 2002. *Real world research: a resource for social scientists and practitioner-researchers.* Madden, MA: Blackwell.

Roever, Sally. 2005. "Negotiating formality: informal sector, market, and state in Peru." Unpublished Ph.D. diss., Department of Political Science, University of California, Berkeley.

Rogers, Reuel R. 2013. "Using interviews to understand racial group identity and political behavior." In *Interview research in political science,* ed. Layna Mosley, 225–243. Ithaca, NY: Cornell University Press.

Romano, David. 2006. "Conducting research in the Middle East's conflict zones." *PS: Political Science and Politics* 39 (3):439–441.

Rosengarten, Theodore. 1975. *All God's dangers: the life of Nate Shaw.* New York: Alfred A. Knopf.

Roth, Alvin E. 1995. "Introduction to experimental economics." In *The handbook of experimental economics,* ed. John H. Kagel and Alvin E. Roth, 1–110. Princeton University Press.

Rubin, Herbert J., and Irene S. Rubin. 2004. *Qualitative interviewing: the art of hearing data.* 2nd edn. Thousand Oaks, CA: Sage Publications.

Rubinstein, Jonathan. 1973. *City police.* New York: Farrar.

Rudolph, Lloyd, and Susanne H. Rudolph. 1958. "Surveys in India: field experience in Madras State." *The Public Opinion Quarterly* 22 (3):235–244.

Russell, Adrienne. 2005. "Myth and the Zapatista movement: exploring a network identity." *New Media & Society* 7 (4):559–577.

Sadiq, Kamal. 2005. "Lost in translation: the challenges of state-generated data in developing countries." In *Perestroika! The raucous rebellion in political science,* ed. Kristen Monroe, 181–199. New Haven, CT: Yale University Press.

Sartori, Giovanni. 1970. "Concept misformation in political science." *The American Political Science Review* 64 (4):1033–1053.

Saunders, Elizabeth N. 2011. *Leaders at war: how presidents shape military interventions.* Ithaca, NY: Cornell University Press.

Savigny, Heather. 2007. "Focus groups and political marketing: science and democracy as axiomatic?" *British Journal of Politics and International Relations* 9 (1):122–137.

Schaffer, Frederic Charles. 1998. *Democracy in translation: understanding politics in an unfamiliar culture.* Ithaca, NY: Cornell University Press.

Schatz, Edward. 2004. *Modern clan politics: the power of "blood" in Kazakhstan and beyond.* Seattle: University of Washington Press.

　　2009a. "Conclusion: what kind(s) of ethnography does political science need?" In *Political ethnography: what immersion contributes to the study of power,* ed. Edward Schatz, 303–318. University of Chicago Press.

　　2009b. "Ethnographic immersion and the study of politics." In *Political ethnography: what immersion contributes to the study of power,* ed. Edward Schatz, 1–22. University of Chicago Press.

　　ed. 2009c. *Political ethnography: what immersion contributes to the study of power.* University of Chicago Press.

Scheyvens, Regina, and Donovan Storey, eds. 2003. *Development fieldwork: a practical guide.* Thousand Oaks, CA: Sage Publications.

Schnabel, Albrecht. 2005. "Preventing and managing conflict: the role of the researcher." In *Researching conflict in Africa: insights and experiences*, ed. Elisabeth Porter and Gillian Robinson, 24–44. New York: United Nations University Press.

Schrag, Zachary. 2009. "How talking became human subjects research: the federal regulation of the social sciences, 1965–1991." *The Journal of Policy History* 21 (1):1–35.

2010. *Ethical imperialism: institutional review boards and the social sciences, 1965–2009*. Baltimore, MD: Johns Hopkins University Press.

Schram, Sanford F., and Brian Cateri. 2004. *Making political science matter: debating knowledge, research, and method*. New York University Press.

Schuman, Howard, and Stanley Presser. 1981. *Questions and answers in attitude surveys: experiments on question form, wording, and context*. Thousand Oaks, CA: Sage Publications.

Schutt, Russell. 2009. *Investigating the social world: the process and practice of research*. Thousand Oaks, CA: Pine Forge Press.

Schutz, Alfred. 1970–1971. *Collected papers*. 3rd edn. 3 vols. The Hague: Martinus Nijhoff.

Schwartz-Shea, Peregrine. 2003. "Is this the curriculum we want? Doctoral requirements and offerings in methods and methodology." *PS: Political Science and Politics* 36 (3):379–386.

2006. "Judging quality: evaluative criteria and epistemic communities." In *Interpretation and method: empirical research methods and the interpretive turn*, ed. Dvora Yanow and Peregrine Schwartz-Shea, 89–113. Armonk, NY: M. E. Sharpe, Inc.

Schwartz-Shea, Peregrine, and Dvora Yanow. 2012. *Interpretive research design: concepts and processes*. New York, London: Routledge.

Scott, James C. 1969. "Corruption, machine politics, and political change." *American Political Science Review* 63 (4):1142–1158.

1985. *Weapons of the weak: everyday forms of peasant resistance*. New Haven, CT: Yale University Press.

1990. *Domination and the arts of resistance: hidden transcripts*. New Haven, CT: Yale University Press.

Seale, Clive F. 2002. "Computer-assisted analysis of qualitative interview data." In *Handbook of interview research: context and method*, ed. Jaber F. Gubrium and James A. Holstein, 651–670. Thousand Oaks, CA: Sage Publications.

Sears, David O. 1986. "College sophomores in the laboratory: influence of a narrow data base on social psychology's view of human nature." *Journal of Personality and Social Psychology* 51:515–530.

Segal, Jeffrey Allan, and Harold J. Spaeth. 1993. *The Supreme Court and the attitudinal model*. Cambridge University Press.

Sekhon, Jasjeet S., and Rocio Titiunik. 2012. "When natural experiments are neither natural nor experiments." *American Political Science Review* 106 (1):35–57.

Sentilles, Renee. 2005. "Toiling in the archives of cyberspace." In *Archive stories: facts, fictions, and the writing of history*, ed. Antoinette Burton, 136–155. Durham, NC: Duke University Press.

Seth, Vanita. 2010. *Europe's Indians: producing racial difference, 1500–1900*. Durham, NC: Duke University Press.

Seybolt, Peter J. 1996. *Throwing the emperor from his horse: portrait of a village leader in China, 1923–1995*. Boulder, CO: Westview Press.

Shadish, William R., Thomas D. Cook, and Donald T. Campbell. 2001. *Experimental and quasi-experimental designs for generalized causal inference*. Boston: Houghton Mifflin.

Shaffir, William, and Robert A. Stebbins. 1991. *Experiencing fieldwork: an inside view of qualitative research*. Newbury Park: Sage Publications.

Shapiro, Ian. 2004. "Problems, methods, and theories in the study of politics, or: what's wrong with political science and what to do about it." In *Problems and methods in the study of politics*, ed. Ian Shapiro, Rogers Smith, and Tarek Masoud, 19–41. New York: Cambridge University Press.

2007. *The flight from reality in the social sciences*. Princeton University Press.

Shehata, Samer. 2006. "Ethnography, identity and the production of knowledge." In *Interpretation and method: empirical research methods and the interpretive turn*, ed. Dvora Yanow and Peregrine Schwartz-Shea, 244–263. Armonk: M. E. Sharpe, Inc.

Sherman, Lawrence, and Heather Strang. 2004. "Experimental ethnography: The marriage of qualitative and quantitative research." *The Annals of the American Academy of Political and Social Science* 595:204–222.

Shih, Victor, Wei Shan, and Mingxing Liu. 2010. "The central committee, past and present: a method of quantifying elite biographies." In *Contemporary Chinese politics: new sources, methods, and field strategies*, ed. Allen Carlson, Mary Gallagher, Kenneth Lieberthal, and Melanie Manion, 51–68. Cambridge University Press.

Shopes, Linda. 2007. "Negotiating Institutional Review Boards." *AHA Perspectives Online* 45 (3).

Short, Susan E. 2006. "Focus group interviews." In *A handbook for social science field research: essays and bibliographic sources on research design and methods*, ed. Ellen Perecman and Sara R. Curran, 103–115. Thousand Oaks, CA: Sage Publications.

Sieber, Sam D. 1973. "The integration of fieldwork and survey methods." *American Journal of Sociology* 78 (6):1335–1359.

Sikkink, Kathryn. 2011. *The justice cascade: how human rights prosecutions are changing world politics*. New York: W. W. Norton & Co.

Silver, Brian D., Barbara A. Anderson, and Paul R. Abramson. 1986. "Who overreports voting?" *American Political Science Review* 80 (2):613–624.

Sinton, Diana Stuart, and Jennifer Lund. 2007. "What is GIS? A very brief description for the newly curious." In *Understanding place: GIS and mapping across the curriculum*, ed. Diana Stuart Sinton and Jennifer Lund, xiii–xviii. Redlands, CA: ESRI Press.

Skalski, Paul. 2002. "Computer content analysis software." In *The content analysis guidebook*, ed. Kimberly Neundorf. Thousand Oaks, CA: Sage Publications.

Skocpol, Theda. 2003. *Diminished democracy: from membership to management in American civic life*. Norman: University of Oklahoma Press.

Skocpol, Theda, Marshall Ganz, and Ziad Munson. 2000. "A nation of organizers: the institutional origins of civic voluntarism in the United States." *American Political Science Review* 94 (3):527–546.

Skocpol, Theda, and Vanessa Williamson. 2012. *The Tea Party and the remaking of Republican conservatism*. Oxford University Press.

Slater, Dan. 2010. *Ordering power: contentious politics and authoritarian leviathans in Southeast Asia*. Cambridge University Press.

Sniderman, Paul M. 2011. "The logic and design of the survey experiment: an autobiography of a methodological innovation." In *Cambridge handbook of experimental political science*, ed. James N. Druckman, Donald P. Green, James H. Kuklinski, and Arthur Lupia, 102–114. New York: Cambridge University Press.

Soifer, Hillel. 2006. "Authority over distance: explaining variation in state infrastructural power in Latin America." Unpublished Ph.D. diss., Department of Government, Harvard University, Cambridge, MA.

Solinger, Dorothy. 2006. "Interviewing Chinese people: from high-level officials to the unemployed." In *Doing fieldwork in China*, ed. Maria Heimer and Stig Thøgersen, 153–167. Honolulu: University of Hawaii Press.

Soss, Joe. 2000. *Unwanted claims: the politics of participation in the U.S. welfare system*. Ann Arbor: University of Michigan Press.

2006. "Talking our way to meaningful explanations: a practice-centered view of interviewing for interpretive research." In *Interpretation and method: empirical research methods and the interpretive turn*, ed. Dvora Yanow and Peregrine Schwartz-Shea, 127–149. Armonk, NY: M. E. Sharpe.

Soss, Joe, Richard C. Fording, and Sanford F. Schram. 2010. *Disciplining the poor: neoliberal paternalism and the persistent power of race*. University of Chicago Press.

Sriram, Chandra Lekha. 2009. "Maintenance of standards of protection during writeup and publication." In *Surviving field research: working in violent and difficult situations*, ed. Chandra Lekha Sriram, John C. King, Julie A. Mertus, Olga Martin-Ortega, and Johanna Herman, 57–68. New York: Routledge.

Sriram, Chandra Lekha, John C. King, Julie A. Mertus, Olga Martin-Ortega, and Johanna Herman, eds. 2009. *Surviving field research: working in violent and difficult situations*. New York: Routledge.

Staple, Jennifer. 2012. "Foreword." In *Transforming ethnographic knowledge*, ed. Rebecca Hardin and Kamari Maxine Clarke, vii–x. Madison: University of Wisconsin Press.

Steinmetz, George. 2005. "Positivism and its others in the social sciences." In *The politics of method in the human sciences*, ed. George Steinmetz, 1–56. Durham, NC: Duke University Press.

Sternberg, David. 1981. *How to complete and survive a doctoral dissertation*. New York: St. Martin's Griffin.

Stevenson, Randy. 2005. "Making a contribution: the role of fieldwork in scientific research programs." *APSA–CP Newsletter* 16 (2):12–16.

Stewart, David, and Prem N. Shamdasani. 2014. *Focus groups: theory and practice*. 3rd edn. London: Sage Publications.

Stockmann, Daniela. 2010. "Information overload? Collecting, managing, and analyzing Chinese media content." In *Contemporary Chinese politics: new sources, methods, and field strategies*, ed. Allen Carlson, Mary Gallagher, Kenneth Lieberthal, and Melanie Manion, 107–128. Cambridge University Press.

Stokes, Susan Carol. 1995. *Cultures in conflict: social movements and the state in Peru*. Berkeley: University of California Press.

Stokes, Susan, Thad Dunning, Marcelo Nazareno, and Valeria Brusco. 2013. *Brokers, voters, and clientelism: the puzzle of distributive politics*. New York: Cambridge University Press.

Stone, Clarence N. 1988. "Preemptive power: Floyd Hunter's 'community power structure' reconsidered." *American Journal of Political Science* 32 (1):82–104.

1993. "Urban regimes and the capacity to govern: a political economy approach." *Journal of Urban Affairs* 15 (1):1–28.

Straus, Scott. 2006. *The order of genocide: race, power, and war in Rwanda*. Ithaca, NY: Cornell University Press.

Strolovitch, Dara Z. 2007. *Affirmative advocacy: race, class, and gender in interest group politics*. University of Chicago Press.

Subotic, Yelena. 2010. "No escape from ethnicity? Confessions of an accidental CNN pundit." *PS: Political Science and Politics* 43 (1):115–120.

Swain, Carol M. 1993. *Black faces, black interests: the representation of African Americans in Congress*. Cambridge, MA: Harvard University Press.

Tamale, Sylvia R. 1996. "The outsider looks in: constructing knowledge about American collegiate racism." *Qualitative Sociology* 19 (4):471–495.

Tansey, Oisin. 2007. "Process tracing and elite interviewing: a case for non-probability sampling." *PS: Political Science and Politics* 40 (3):765–772.

Tarrow, Sidney. 2004. "Bridging the quantitative–qualitative divide." In *Rethinking social inquiry: diverse tools, shared standards*, ed. Henry E. Brady and David Collier, 171–179. Lanham, MD: Rowman & Littlefield.

2006. "Space and comparative politics." *APSA–CP Newsletter* 17 (1):1–4.

Tashakkori, Abbas, and Charles Teddlie, eds. 2003. *Handbook of mixed methods in social and behavioral research*. London: Routledge.

Teles, Steven Michael. 2008. *The rise of the conservative legal movement: the battle for control of the law*. Princeton University Press.

Tessler, Mark A. 2011. *Public opinion in the Middle East: survey research and the political orientations of ordinary citizens*. Bloomington: Indiana University Press.

Tessler, Mark, and Amaney Jamal. 2006. "Political attitude research in the Arab world: emerging opportunities." *PS: Political Science and Politics* 39 (3):433–437.

Thelen, Kathleen Ann. 1991. *Union of parts: labor politics in postwar Germany*. Ithaca, NY: Cornell University Press.

Themnér, Lotta, and Peter Wallensteen. 2011. "Armed conflict, 1946–2010." *Journal of Peace Research* 48 (4):525–536.

Thies, Cameron. 2002. "A pragmatic guide to qualitative historical analysis in the study of international relations." *International Studies Perspectives* 3 (4):351–372.

Thomas, Megan C. 2012. *Orientalists, propagandists, and ilustrados: Filipino scholarship and the end of Spanish colonialism*. Minneapolis: University of Minnesota Press.

Thompson, Paul. 2000. *The voice of the past: oral history*. 3rd edn. New York: Oxford University Press.

Thompson, Robert. 2002. "Reporting the results of computer-assisted analysis of qualitative research data." *Forum: Qualitative Social Research* 3 (2):1–42.

Thomson, Susan, An Ansoms, and Jude Murison, eds. 2012. *Emotional and ethical challenges for field research in Africa: the story behind the findings*. London: Palgrave Macmillan.

Thun, Eric. 2006. *Changing lanes in China: foreign direct investment, local governments, and auto sector development*. Cambridge University Press.

Tilly, Charles. 1997. "Means and ends of comparison in macrosociology." *Comparative Social Research* 16:43–53.

Tolman, Deborah L., and Mary Brydon-Miller. 2001. *From subjects to subjectivities: a handbook of interpretive and participatory methods.* New York University Press.

Tosh, John. 2000. *The pursuit of history: aims, methods, and new directions in the study of modern history.* Harlow: Longman.

Tourangeau, Roger, and Ting Yan. 2007. "Sensitive questions in surveys." *Psychological Bulletin* 133 (5):859–883.

Townsend, Robert B., and Mériam Belli. 2004. "Oral history and IRBs: caution urged as rule interpretations vary widely." *Perspectives on History: The Newsmagazine of the American Historical Association* 42 (9):11–12.

Townsend, Robert M., Sakunthasathien Sombat, and Rob Jordan. 2013. *Chronicles from the field: the Townsend Thai project.* Cambridge, MA: MIT Press.

Townsend-Bell, Erica. 2009. "Being true and being you: race, gender, class, and the fieldwork experience." *PS: Political Science and Politics* 42 (2):311–314.

Trachtenberg, Marc. 2006. *The craft of international history: a guide to method.* Princeton University Press.

Tripp, Aili Mari. 2002. "Combining intercontinental parenting and research: dilemmas and strategies." *Signs: A Journal of Women in Culture and Society* 27 (3):794–811.

Tsai, Lily L. 2007. *Accountability without democracy: how solidary groups provide public goods in rural China.* Cambridge University Press.

　　2010. "Quantitative research and issues of political sensitivity in China." In *Contemporary Chinese politics: new sources, methods, and field strategies*, ed. Allen Carlson, Mary Gallagher, Kenneth Lieberthal, and Melanie Manion, 246–265. Cambridge University Press.

Tuchman, Barbara. 1996. "Distinguishing the significant from the insignificant." In *Oral history: an interdisciplinary anthology.* 2nd edn., ed. David Dunaway and Willa K. Baum, 94–98. Lanham, MD: AltaMira Press.

Van Evera, Stephen. 1997. *Guide to methods for students of political science.* Ithaca, NY: Cornell University Press.

Vansina, Jan. 1965. *Oral tradition: a study in historical methodology.* London: Routledge & Kegan Paul.

　　1985. *Oral tradition as history.* Madison: University of Wisconsin Press.

Vigneswaran, Darshan, and Joel Quirk. 2013. "Quantitative methodological dilemmas in urban refugee research: a case study of Johannesburg." *Journal of Refugee Studies* 26 (1):110–116.

Vu, Tuong. 2010. *Paths to development in Asia: South Korea, Vietnam, China, and Indonesia.* New York: Cambridge University Press.

Walsh, Katherine Cramer. 2004. *Talking about politics: informal groups and social identity in American life.* University of Chicago Press.

Wang, Jinjun, and Ying Yan. 2012. "The interview question." In *The Sage handbook of interview research: the complexity of the craft*, ed. Jaber F. Gubrium, James A. Holstein, Amir B. Marvasti, and Karyn D. McKinney. Thousand Oaks, CA: Sage Publications.

Wantchekon, Leonard. 2003. "Clientelism and voting behavior: evidence from a field experiment in Benin." *World Politics* 55 (3):399–422.

Ward, Robert E. 1964a. "Common problems in field research." In *Studying politics abroad: field research in the developing areas*, ed. Robert E. Ward, 49–78. Boston: Little, Brown.

　　1964b. *Studying politics abroad: field research in the developing areas.* Boston: Little, Brown.

Warren, Carol. 2012. "Interviewing as social interaction." In *The Sage handbook of interview research: the complexity of the craft*, ed. Jaber F. Gubrium, James A. Holstein, Amir B. Marvasti, and Karyn D. McKinney. Thousand Oaks, CA: Sage Publications.

Warren, Mark E. 2001. *Democracy and association*. Princeton University Press.

Wedeen, Lisa. 1999. *Ambiguities of domination: Politics, rhetoric, and symbols in contemporary Syria*. University of Chicago Press.

  2008. *Peripheral visions: publics, power, and performance in Yemen*. University of Chicago Press.

  2009. "Ethnography as interpretive enterprise." In *Political ethnography: what immersion contributes to the study of power*, ed. Edward Schatz, 75–94. University of Chicago Press.

  2010. "Reflections on ethnographic work in political science." *Annual Review of Political Science* 13:255–272.

Weiner, Myron. 1964. "Political interviewing." In *Studying politics abroad: field research in the developing areas*, ed. Robert Edward Ward, 103–133. Boston: Little, Brown.

Weinstein, Jeremy M. 2007. *Inside rebellion: the politics of insurgent violence*. Cambridge, New York: Cambridge University Press.

Weiss, R. S. 1994. *Learning from strangers: the art and method of qualitative interview studies*. New York: The Free Press.

Weldes, Jutta. 2006. "High politics and low data: globalization discourses and popular culture." In *Interpretation and method: empirical research methods and the interpretive turn*, ed. Dvora Yanow and Peregrine Schwartz-Shea, 176–186. Armonk, NY: M. E. Sharpe, Inc.

Wellings, Kaye, Patrick Branigan, and Kristi Mitchell. 2000. "Discomfort, discord, and discontinuity as data: using focus groups to research sensitive topics." *Culture, Health and Sexuality* 2 (3):255–267.

Wesley, Jared. 2014. "The qualitative analysis of political documents." In *From text to political positions: text analysis across disciplines*, ed. Bertie Kaal, Isa Maks, and Annemarie van Elfrinkhof, 135–160. Amsterdam: John Benjamins.

White, Luise. 1995. "They could make their victims dull: gender and genres, fantasies and cures in colonial Southern Uganda." *American Historical Review* 100 (5):1379–1402.

White, Luise, Stephan Miescher, and David William Cohen, eds. 2001. *African words, African voices: critical practices in oral history*. Bloomington: Indiana University Press.

Whyte, William Foote. 1943. "A challenge to political scientists." *American Political Science Review* 37 (4):692–697.

  1994. *Participant observer: an autobiography*. Ithaca, NY: ILR Press.

Wight, Daniel. 2008. "Most of our social scientists are not institution based . . . they are there for hire – research consultancies and social science capacity for health research in East Africa." *Social Science & Medicine* 66 (1):110–116.

Wilson, J. Zoë. 2005. "Certainty, subjectivity, and truth: reflections on the ethics of wartime research in Angola." In *Researching conflict in Africa: insights and experiences*, ed. Elisabeth Porter, Gillian Robinson, Marie Smyth, Albrecht Schnabel, and Eghosa Osaghae, 124–139. New York: United Nations University Press.

Wolcott, Harry. 2005. *The art of fieldwork*. Walnut Creek, CA: AltaMira Press.

Wolfinger, Raymond E. 1971. "Nondecisions and the study of local politics." *American Political Science Review* 65 (4):1063–1080.

  1973. *The politics of progress*. Englewood Cliffs, NJ: Prentice-Hall.

Woliver, Laura. 2002. "Ethical dilemmas in personal interviewing." *PS: Political Science and Politics* 35 (4):677–678.

Wong, Janelle. 2006. *Democracy's promise: immigrants and American civic institutions*. Ann Arbor: University of Michigan Press.

Wood, Elisabeth Jean. 2003. *Insurgent collective action and civil war in El Salvador*. New York: Cambridge University Press.

2006. "The ethical challenges of field research in conflict zones." *Qualitative Sociology* 29 (3):373–386.

2007. "Field research." In *The Oxford handbook of comparative politics*, ed. Carles Boix and Susan Carol Stokes, 123–146. Oxford, New York: Oxford University Press.

Worcester, Kenton W. 2001. *Social Science Research Council: 1923–1998*. New York: Social Science Research Council.

Yankah, Kwesi. 1995. *Speaking for the chief: "Okyeame" and the politics of Akan royal oratory*. Bloomington: Indiana University Press.

Yanow, Dvora. 2006. "How built spaces mean: a semiotics of space." In *Interpretation and method: empirical research methods and the interpretive turn*, ed. Dvora Yanow and Peregrine Schwartz-Shea, 368–386. Armonk, NY: M. E. Sharpe, Inc.

2009. "Dear author, Dear reader: the third hermeneutic in writing and reviewing ethnography." In *Political ethnography: what immersion contributes to the study of power*, ed. Edward Schatz, 275–302. University of Chicago Press.

Yanow, Dvora, and Peregrine Schwartz-Shea. 2008. "Reforming Institutional Review Board policy: issues in implementation and field research." *PS: Political Science and Politics* 41 (3):483–494.

Yashar, Deborah J. 2005. *Contesting citizenship in Latin America: the rise of indigenous movements and the postliberal challenge*. Cambridge, New York: Cambridge University Press.

Yow, Valerie Raleigh. 2005. *Recording oral history: a guide for the humanities and the social sciences*. 2nd edn. Lanham, MD: AltaMira Press.

Zirakzadeh, Cyrus Ernesto. 2009. "When nationalists are not separatists: discarding and recovering academic theories while doing fieldwork in the Basque region of Spain." In *Political ethnography: what immersion contributes to the study of power*, ed. Edward Schatz, 97–118. University of Chicago Press.

Zuern, Elke. 2011. *The politics of necessity: community organizing and democracy in South Africa*. Madison: University of Wisconsin Press.

Index